Wine
Report
2007

Tom Stevenson

LONDON NEW YORK MUNICH
MELBOURNE DELHI

FOR DORLING KINDERSLEY
Senior Editor Simon Tuite
Senior Art Editor Helen Spencer
US Editor Christine Heilman
Executive Managing Editor Adèle Hayward
Managing Art Editor Nick Harris
DTP Designer Traci Salter
Production Assistant Clare McLean

PRODUCED FOR DORLING KINDERSLEY BY
Sands Publishing Solutions
4 Jenner Way, Eccles, Aylesford, Kent ME20 7SQ
Project Editors David & Sylvia Tombesi-Walton
Project Art Editor Simon Murrell

FOR TOM STEVENSON
Editor Pat Carroll
Tasting Logistics Jeff Porter, Evenlode Press

Revised American Edition, 2006
Published in the United States by
DK Publishing
375 Hudson Street
New York, NY 10014

06 07 08 09 10   10 9 8 7 6 5 4 3 2 1

A Cataloging-in-Publication record for this book
is available from the Library of Congress.

ISBN 13: 978-0-7566-2257-2
ISBN 10: 0-7566-2257-3

WD126

DK books are available at special discounts for bulk
purchases for sales promotions, premiums, fund-
raising, or educational use. For details, contact:
DK Publishing Special Markets, 375 Hudson Street,
New York, NY 10014 or SpecialSales@dk.com

Printed and bound in China by Leo Paper Group

Discover more at

www.dk.com

CONTENTS

Introduction
Win a case of vintage champagne

The world of wine moves so fast and is expanding so quickly that *Wine Report* has become addictive for anyone who is seriously interested in wine.

You have to be bitten by the wine bug to appreciate its contents, but once bitten, it becomes clear just how indispensable *Wine Report* is. Alistair, the manager of my local wine bar (Summertown Wine Café—try it out), even reads it in the bathroom; movers and shakers in the wine trade would not be seen dead without a copy; MWs swear by it; and sommeliers just love it. Brian Julyan, the chief executive of the Court of Master Sommeliers Worldwide, recommends *Wine Report* as essential reading for those taking their MS examination, and the book is waved in the air at Master of Wine seminars, where students are told that it is "required reading."

We've also had some great reviews, on top of which, the first edition was voted Best Wine Guide in the World, while the second edition was voted Best Wine Book in the World—consecutive bests in world being a unique achievement in the history of the Gourmand International Awards.

It's nice to have such critical accomplishments, and it's reassuring to know that readers cannot wait for the next edition. However, I am still amazed by how many people I meet, inside the trade and out, who are obviously besotted by wine, yet have not—until that moment—even heard about the book! How on earth can we get through to these potential readers? With your help, hopefully. Wherever you are in the world, seek out like-minded friends and colleagues who have not seen *Wine Report* and show them the book. If they buy a copy, ask for the receipt, and if you think you have been particularly successful in spreading the word, mail your receipts to DK Publicity Department (WR07), 80 Strand, London WC2R 0RL, England, and I'll send a case of vintage champagne to the reader with the most. (Details of the winning entry will be published in the next edition.)

Tom Stevenson

About This Guide

This is not so much a "How to Use" section as an explanation of the brief that I gave to contributors, and the parameters they applied (or did not!).

Contributors

Every contributor to *Wine Report* was my personal choice. For the most part, they are the expert's experts in their various specialist areas. For some regions there are no experts, and I had to twist the arm of the most strategically placed professionals to tackle such reports. There have been small changes in contributors since the first edition, and I imagine there will be more in the future. *Wine Report* has very specific needs, so if some contributors come and go, the going has nothing to do with their expertise on the subject and everything to do with how I expect it to be applied. Ideally, I would like to see no more than one report per contributor, since this would project the desired specialist ambience, but it will take time to achieve.

Opinions expressed by contributors

These are, of course, their own. I am not referring specifically to the Opinion section of each report (which is dealt with separately below), but rather the more general way in which they report a story. For example, the way that François Lefort (Grape Varieties) writes about GMOs could not be further from the way that Monty Waldin (Organic & Biodynamic Wines) covers the subject. I respect both of these contributors' opinions, although I do not completely agree with either of them. (Anyone interested in my view should look at www.wine-pages.com/guests/tom/gm.htm.)

Reader's knowledge level

Unlike most other wine books, *Wine Report* assumes a certain level of knowledge. Therefore, there are rarely any explanations for technical terms or even references to historical incidents. Readers are expected to know what these terms mean and what the references refer to, or at least have the intelligence and curiosity to look them up.

News and Grapevine items

Regional reports include news affecting the region and its producers, wines, and consumers. This may incorporate gossip and rumor but not marketing or sales stories unless they are of an exceptional or very hot nature. Non-regional reports have their own structure. It should be noted that, for Wine & Health, Beverley Blanning has been specifically commissioned to report the bad news as well as the good and, if anything, to err on the side of the former rather than the latter. I want to give readers as much good health news as possible, but *Wine Report* is for wine enthusiasts and cannot afford to be vulnerable to accusations of selective reporting of this sensitive issue.

Opinion

Contributors have quite a free hand to spout off about anything they feel strongly about, but there are certain categories of opinion that are obligatory. These are, essentially, anything that is currently practiced, legally or not, that the contributor believes should not be, and anything that the contributor believes should be happening, but is not. Contributors should always attempt to balance their criticisms with practical solutions. Readers should expect to see the same opinions repeated or refined in each edition, unless the situation changes, which would be news in itself.

Vintage Reports

Each regional contributor provides an advance report on the very latest harvest (the year before date of publication for the Northern Hemisphere, the actual year of publication for the Southern Hemisphere), plus brief updates on the previous five vintages. In the first edition, it was difficult enough to get some contributors to rate vintages on a 100-point scale, but most toed the line. However, everyone was using a different yardstick, so, from the second edition, all vintage ratings conform to the following definitions.

100	No vintage can be accurately described as perfect, but those achieving a maximum score must be truly great vintages.
90–99	Excellent to superb.
80–89	Good to very good.
70–79	Average to good.
60–69	Disappointing.
40–59	Very bad.
0–39	Disastrous.

Vintage ratings should merely be seen as "betting odds." They express the likelihood of what might be reasonably expected from a wine of a given year. The higher the rating, the fewer the exceptions; quality and consistency do, to some extent, go hand in hand.

Top 10s

If percentile ratings for vintages did not set the cat among the pigeons, then these Top 10s of producers and wines certainly did. Very few contributors were worried about listing the 10 best of anything, but several were extremely reluctant to put that list in order of preference. Eventually most agreed to do this, but readers might come across the odd list that looks suspiciously as if it is in alphabetical order....

There was no requirement for each Top 10 to be fully utilized. If a contributor truly believes that, for example, only five or six producers or wines deserve a place in a particular Top 10, then that is perfectly acceptable. Furthermore, it was permitted to place the same producer or wine in more than one list. Such coexistence could even apply to the Greatest and Best-Value Producers or Best Bargain Top 10s.

Prices

All prices in this guide are average retail prices, including tax, per bottle, expressed in the local currency of the country of origin. This is not a buyer's guide; the wines listed are supposed to be the greatest, best-bargain or most exciting or unusual, without restricting the choice to those that happen to be available on any specific market.

Greatest Wine Producers

My guidelines to the contributors made it clear that their choice should be "regardless of status." In other words, even if there is some sort of acknowledged hierarchy, such as Bordeaux's *cru classé* system, the contributor should not feel restrained by it. On the other hand, if a contributor agrees entirely with a perceived hierarchy, there was nothing preventing him or her from following it slavishly. Some contributors set themselves their own criteria. Dan Berger, for example, told me that for his greatest producers, he had decided: (a) the winery had to be in business for at least 10 years, and production over that period had to have remained substantially the same; (b) the winery had to use substantially the same fruit sources, mainly from owned or leased vineyards, for the last 10 years, and not deviate from a house style; (c) the ownership and winemaking had to be consistent over the last 10 years; and (d) the winery must make at least two wines that have achieved the highest levels of quality without ever deviating from that level, even in a mediocre vintage.

Dan's criteria represent a very professional way of ascertaining greatness, but they are not ones that I would impose on all contributors. Furthermore, the term "greatest" is relative: it does not necessarily mean that the producer is intrinsically great. The best producer in California should be intrinsically great, but although the greatest producer in Belgium must, by definition, be its greatest, in practice it will be no more than "interesting." Readers should expect the Greatest Producers list to change the least of all the Top 10s from year to year.

Fastest-Improving Producers

Whether good or bad, reputations tend to stick well beyond their shelf life, which is why this particular Top 10 is probably the most useful. While the rest of the market lags behind, you can benefit from the insider knowledge of *Wine Report*, buying up top-performing wines long before others cotton on and prices increase.

New Up-and-Coming Producers

While Fastest-Improving Producers will probably be well-established wineries that have perked up, this Top 10 focuses on the newer producers that are the ones to watch. In some of the more conservative traditional areas, "new" will be relative and should perhaps be taken to mean newer, or a producer whose wines used to be sold only from the cellar door but have recently become more widely available.

Best-Value Producers

This is self-explanatory.

Greatest-Quality Wines

Each contributor has his or her own method for determining their greatest wines. I am sure that many do as I tend to do, and that is to list the greatest I have tasted within the last 12 months, rather than the greatest wines *per se*. True experts in classic areas will probably have notes on thousands of wines tasted in the last 12 months, and of these there could be 50-some wines that would justifiably achieve a top score. Most contributors could probably fill their Top 10 Greatest Wines several times over. (Most years I could fill the Top 10 Greatest Alsace Wines twice over with just Zind Humbrecht's wines.) Thus, realistically, this should be viewed as merely "10 of the greatest." Then, of course, we have to put them in order of preference, which can be a real pain. How, for example, is it possible to say whether the greatest red bordeaux is better than the greatest Sauternes, or the greatest Alsace Gewurztraminer better than the greatest Alsace Pinot Gris? If David Peppercorn and I find this difficult, what about Nick Belfrage and Franco Ziliani? The range of wines in Italy is far more complex. So, what most contributors end up with is "10 of the greatest in a less-than-logical order of preference." This would worry me in any other book, but readers of *Wine Report* are supposed to be sophisticated enough to understand that this is fascinating enough in its own right.

Best Bargains

Although most will be relatively inexpensive, bargains do not necessarily have to be cheap. It is easier to find bargains at lower prices, just as it is easier to find great wines at higher prices, but it is possible to find relative bargains at any price point. In theory, the greatest, most expensive bordeaux could be the number-one Best Bargain.

Most Exciting or Unusual Finds

This could be an unusually fine wine from what is normally a below-standard region, winery, or grape. It might be an atypical wine, or the first of a certain variety or style. Each wine listed will carry a brief explanation of why it is so exciting and/or unusual.

The 100 Most Exciting Wine Finds

Each contributor was asked to submit four wines for consideration for this section of the book, which meant approximately 160 wines. Only contributors for the emerging or more obscure wine regions were allowed to proffer wines from their Greatest Wines. The rest had to select wines from either their Best Bargains or Most Exciting or Unusual Finds, otherwise this section would be stacked with Pétrus, Krug, Romanée-Conti, the quality of which most readers will be aware of, but few can afford. I then tasted the wines blind, grouped by variety or style, culling almost 40 percent (which is why I limited myself to just two wines from Champagne and two wines from Alsace). Contributors also provided a tasting note, which is followed by my own comment.

Bordeaux

David Peppercorn MW

In 2004, many vineyards were caught in a pincer movement. The vines were intent on compensating for the previous year's half-crop, while INAO was reducing the permitted *rendement*.

DAVID PEPPERCORN MW

The cutting of the *rendement* was one of the moves intended to cut the surpluses that now threaten the economic equilibrium of the region.

While, of course, the main target for lower and properly enforced yields is principally to reduce the vast lake of Bordeaux Rouge, it would be a mistake to imagine that more favored properties were not also affected by the new lower ceilings on yields.

The fashionable view now prevailing in Bordeaux is that the main tool of vineyard management when it comes to levels of production is green-harvesting, which means reducing the number of bunches per vine. During the 2004 growing season, many estates went through their vineyards twice, instead of the customary once, and even then often found it difficult to get down to the new lower levels.

Why not prune the vines more severely to start with, you may say. The reason habitually given is that the fluctuating conditions of each season can make this risky. The main factors are frost (in fact, very rare except as

DAVID PEPPERCORN MW When David Peppercorn went to Bordeaux as a Cambridge undergraduate in September 1953, it was the beginning of a lifelong love affair. He became a Master of Wine in 1962 and was chairman of the Institute of Masters of Wine from 1968 to 1970. It was while David was a buyer for IDV (International Distillers & Vintners) in the 1970s that he started writing about wine, making his debut as an author with the award-winning *Bordeaux* (Faber & Faber, 1982). His *Wines of Bordeaux* (Mitchell Beazley) has been updated every other year since 1986 (2004 being the latest edition). David now spends his time traveling, writing, and lecturing. He is married to Serena Sutcliffe MW.

a small, localized phenomenon) and flowering irregularities, leading to losses by *coulure* or *millerandage* (much more common) and hail (fortunately very rare except in Sauternes). In other words, growers like to keep their options open.

But there is a downside to green-harvesting. It stimulates the vine to further growth, in exactly the same way as a naturally small harvest encourages the following year to produce a larger one—2004 compensating for 2003, 1992 compensating for 1991, *et al*. Is there a way out of this vicious circle?

There are owners who have waited and watched who now say yes, there is an answer: do nothing! It was a test year for this traditionalist view in 2004, so I was delighted to discover that at two Médoc estates that have always set their faces against crop-thinning—the Barton estates Léoville and Langoa in St-Julien, and Sociando-Mallet, the Haut-Médoc's most distinguished unclassified *cru*—normal yields in the low 50s of hl/ha were reported. Jean Gautreau at Sociando-Mallet told me that he prefers to see what arrives in the vats before regulating his yields by bleeding the vats. His wines never look overconcentrated, incidentally. The Bartons thinned only some young vines that do not go into the *grand vin*. All three properties made superb wines. These vineyards seem to have achieved a natural equilibrium.

One should also point out that crop-thinning is not the end of the matter. If you go down that route, the remaining grapes compensate by swelling more, increasing the ratio of juice to skins, which in turn must be corrected by "bleeding" the vats to restore the situation. Some of Bordeaux's most unbalanced, overconcentrated wines are the result of excessive vat-bleeding. One sometimes has the impression, now, that such is the burden of political correctness that many producers feel they have to crop-thin, and cannot see a way out.

Grapevine

• In *Wine Report 2006*, I reported that André Lurton had installed a Tribaies (machine for sorting mechanically harvested grapes) in his new *chai* at Rochemorin. When tasting the resulting wine, I found the quality of the 2004 spectacular, especially when compared with La Louvière and Cruzeau. Now he is installing another machine at La Louvière.

• How did the Tribaies deal with 2005? I visited Philippe Boudet, who has been developing the machine over the last five years, in December 2005 and was fascinated to learn the difference in the raw materials in the vineyard between 2004 and 2005. In 2004 the Tribaies had eliminated between 25 and 30 percent of the Merlots. In 2005 the comparable figure was 5–10 percent.

Cru Bourgeois: appellants fight on

The appeal against the new Cru Bourgeois classification rumbles on. As reported last year, the court said that the growers have a case and referred it back to the Ministry of Agriculture. The ministry has appointed the same committee but has removed members who were also proprietors of properties in the new classification, thus addressing one of the 76 appellants' complaints. However, it seems that so far no visits to properties have been carried out; another crucial demand.

Now another bone of contention has surfaced. The reconstituted committee has asked for samples of the same vintages as were requested in 2001, namely 1994 to 1999. Now, with 2000–03 in bottle, the appellants would like these to be taken into consideration. As if this were not enough, seven of the 76 have launched a claim, based on a passage in the court's judgment, that the committee was not competent to make the classification in the first place, so the whole 2003 classification should be declared null and void and the whole process should start again.

1855 classification—then and now

In *The World of Fine Wine* magazine, Jim Budd celebrated the 150th anniversary of the famous classification by seeing what would happen today if one classified the Médocs by price, as in 1855. The results are interesting. The average prices of the Firsts are double those of the next highest, Léoville-Las-Cases. Of the top 60 wines, 11 were not classified in 1855: Sociando-Mallet, Haut Marbuzet, Siran, Labégorce-Zédé, Chasse-Spleen, Gloria, Meyney, Angludet, Phélan-Ségur, Poujeaux, and de Pez. On the other hand, 12 *crus* on the 1855 list dropped off the 2005 list: Belgrave, Dauzac, Durfort-Vivens, Lynch-Moussas, Pouget, Ferrière, La-Tour-Carnet, Croizet-Bages, Desmirail, Camensac, Pedesclaux, and Marquis d'Alesme-Becker.

Grapevine

• **Bordeaux Oxygène** is a new association of sons and daughters of Bordeaux proprietors, great and small, banding together to promote their wines. There is a wide range of appellations, from Bordeaux red and white to Crus Classés Haut-Médoc, Pessac-Léognan (La Lagune, Malartic-Lagravière, and Smith-Haut-Lafitte), and several top St-Emilions, with plenty of variety in between. Their aim: to be a breath of fresh air and to bring a more youthful image to their wines.

• **Caroline Frey** had no sooner finished her studies than her father propelled her to the twin responsibilities of manager and winemaker at the family's Troisième Cru Classé (Haut-Médoc) Château La Lagune, just prior to Vinexpo. Her credentials are impressive: a star pupil of Denis Dubourdieu at Bordeaux's Faculty of Oenology, she won a scholarship in 2002 to work at his Clos Floridène property in Graves.

Opinion:
Overproduction in Bordeaux

Last year it was announced that a decision had been made to pull up 10,000 ha of Bordeaux vineyards to address overproduction at the level of Bordeaux generics. So what progress is being made? I recently had the opportunity to discuss progress with someone from the Ministry of Agriculture agency charged with implementing this policy. What came out was this: the timescale set out by the ministry is three years. Anyone who accepts pulling up his or her vines also loses all planting rights for the future. During the first year, very few vines have, in fact, been pulled up. There is no "targeting" of vineyards to be eliminated—such as those planted on unsuitable land in the last 20 years—only certain appellations that qualify, such as Bordeaux generic, Bordeaux Côtes, and Médoc. One problem facing growers is what else can be done with the land. If a vineyard is near a conurbation, it can be turned into a housing site, which is clearly very profitable. Otherwise, most alternative agricultural uses are equally fraught with problems. The *fonctionnaire* from the ministry was in gloomy mood!

Grapevine

• **Château L'Arrosée** has always been rather a secret wine. It never belonged to any of the tasting groups in the region, so a special visit was required to taste the wines. At their best (1982, 1989, 1990), they were among the best *crus classés* in St-Emilion, but had become less consistent during the 1990s. Then, two years ago, François Rodhain, the long-time owner, decided to sell and retire. The new owner, Roger Caille, wanted to take some time to sort out the *chais* before showing his wines for the first time at Vinexpo 2005 on Bill Blatch's stand. The first vintage he was happy with was 2004, and it looked very promising. No doubt he will be even more pleased with 2005.

• **Château Faugères has been sold.** Everyone who has watched what Corinne Guisez has achieved here and at the adjoining Castillon vineyard of Cap de Faugères since her husband's untimely death will have been sad to hear that she was selling. It seems that none of her children wanted to take over. But the good news is that the new owner, Silvio Denz, originally from Switzerland, is as enthused as Corinne Guisez was—and he began well by inviting all his neighbors in St-Emilion and Castillon to a party! Faugères is being tipped as a candidate for promotion to *cru classé* status when the revision of the classification is unveiled in 2006.

Vintage Report

Advance report on the latest harvest
2005

If 2003 was the year of tropical heat, 2005 was the year of drought. In fact, the driest growing season ever was recorded. But, as so often in Bordeaux's maritime climate, there were refreshing showers at crucial moments and the vines dug deep to find reserves of water, although the water table is now at a dangerously low level. The vintage began early in Pomerol and was virtually finished by the time of the Ban des Vendanges in St-Emilion on September 18. Most of St-Emilion was harvested in the last two weeks of September, while the Médoc started in the last week of September and finished in good conditions in early October. Throughout the region, growers are in a state of euphoria. The quality is being compared to 2000 and yields, while well down on 2004, are only slightly below those of an average year. The red wines are characterized by their profound color and aromatic intensity combined with the balance and succulence of the fruit and tannins. The dry white wines are aromatic with good freshness, while Sauternes has made a large crop of wine characterized by the exceptional purity of botrytis and wonderful freshness—a great year here!

Updates on the previous five vintages
2004

Vintage rating: *Left Bank—Red: 95, White: 90, Sweet: 90; Right Bank—Red: 95*

After the very small crop of 2003, the vines were raring to go in 2004 and, with much stricter limits on yields now being imposed by the INAO, most vineyards had to work hard to keep their production within the prescribed limits. Damp August conditions tested growers' nerves, but then the hoped-for high-pressure system kicked in on August 31 and stayed in control until October 10, with most picking concentrated between September 27 and October 14. This is a year of consistent quality across the region, with wines showing lovely harmony with beautiful fruit flavors and rich, ripe, well-integrated tannins with a freshness that enhances the flavors and is developing real complexity. The Sauternes have a lovely freshness that balances the fruity richness of wines that have real character and are classic after the exceptional sugar levels of 2003. This is a vintage that, overall, will give much pleasure.

2003

Vintage rating: *Left Bank—Red: 93, White: 80, Sweet: 98; Right Bank—Red: 82*

The extreme heat of June, July, and August caused growers many problems, not least when to pick. Those who delayed until September were rewarded by more moderate conditions. The more vulnerable Merlots on the Right Bank suffered most and results there are very uneven. But great wines with a markedly exotic character were made in St-Estèphe especially, and also in Pauillac and St-Julien. Margaux, surprisingly, produced some wines of great breed and typicity. Pessac-Léognan is less good. The crop was half the normal size, or less. Sauternes had an exceptional year with quantity and even richer wines than 2001.

2002

Vintage rating: *Left Bank—Red: 92, White: 90, Sweet: 88; Right Bank—Red: 86*

The year that was very nearly a disaster was saved by a classic high-pressure system in September. The Left Bank Cabernets were able to take full advantage of this and very fine wines resulted in Pauillac, St-Julien, and St-Estèphe. The first tastings in bottle also showed Margaux doing better than expected, while the general level in the Médoc appellations was uniformly high. Excellent botrytis in Sauternes also means another fine vintage there. But *coulure* had already accounted for much of the old-vine Merlot on the Right Bank and the weather change was just too late to help the Merlots produce top quality. Those with good levels of Cabernet Franc benefited. The dry whites have an attractive fresh fruitiness.

2001

Vintage rating: *Left Bank—Red: 90, White: 90, Sweet: 98; Right Bank—Red: 90*

These wines continue to develop well. They are not 2000s (the exceptions prove the rule), but they do have balance, length, elegance, and breed—even lovely succulent fruit flavors in the best *crus*. They are variable but clearly superior to the 1999s. The dry whites are very fruity and elegant. Sauternes are outstanding, probably the best year since 1990.

2000

Vintage rating: *Left Bank—Red: 98, White: 92, Sweet: 85; Right Bank—Red: 98*

Nature managed to provide what the market had prayed for, with an exceptional spell of weather from July 29 until October 10. Temperatures were well above average and there was very little rain, hence the thick skins that gave very powerful, deep-colored wines. Features of the year include consistency across the region and the outstanding character and typicity of the wines. Each tasting at whatever level continues to confirm the quality of these wines. The exceptionally high standard of so many of the wines is greater than in 1990 or 1989. Perhaps the potential of the vintage has been better realized than ever before. Unfortunately, Sauternes missed out, yielding about one-third of its normal crop and a quality that is good but not special.

GREATEST WINE PRODUCERS

1. Château Lafite
2. Château d'Yquem
3. Château Ausone
4. Château Pétrus
5. Château Margaux
6. Château Léoville-Las-Cases
7. Château Lafleur
8. Château Latour
9. Château Haut-Brion/La Mission Haut-Brion
10. Château Pichon-Longueville-Lalande

Grapevine

• **Domaine Clarence Dillon** announced in May 2005 that it was creating a subsidiary, Clarence Dillon Wines, to launch a new premium Bordeaux under the brand name Clarendelle, which consists of a classic Merlot/Cabernet Sauvignon/Cabernet Franc red blend and a Semillon/Sauvignon Blanc white blend.

FASTEST-IMPROVING PRODUCERS

1. Château Lafite *Very good from 1982 to 1990 but has moved into another gear as of 1996.*
2. Château Ausone *Some of the greatest wines in Bordeaux since 1998; more sensual and just more of everything—look for 2002!*
3. Château Pavie-Macquin *Since Nicolas Thienpont and Stéphane Derenoncourt took charge in 1995, the progress has been continuous and consistent. There are not many better 1997s for current drinking, and watch for 2000 and 2004.*
4. Château Calon-Ségur *A new generation of wine lovers has forgotten that this used to be one of the most sought-after crus in the Médoc. The climb-back was at first steady (1995, 1996) and is now spectacular (2000, 2002, 2003, 2004).*
5. Château Brane-Cantenac *This classic Margaux was criticized for being weak, but Henri Lurton is quietly rebuilding its reputation. Take a look at the underrated 1999.*
6. Château Pontet-Canet *Outstanding since 1996.*

7 Château du Tertre *The real potential is now being realized, especially since the marvelous 2000.*

8 Château Dauzac *André Lurton's team has been building an entirely new reputation here since 1996. The 1998 shone through in a Decanter blind tasting in 2005.*

9 Château Malartic-Lagravière *The investment and commitment of the new owners here are now paying off. The 2002 is outstanding.*

10 Château Berliquet *Since Patrick Valette began his consulting here, the true class of this well-balanced cru has started to shine through.*

NEW UP-AND-COMING PRODUCERS

1 Château Messile Aubert (Montagne-St-Emilion)
2 Château Trianon (St-Emilion)
3 Château Joanin-Bécot (Côtes de Castillon)
4 Château Brillette (Moulis)
5 Château Marseau (Côtes de Franc)
6 Château La Sergue (Lalande-de-Pomerol)
7 Château Belle Vue (Haut-Médoc)
8 Clos Puy Arnaud (Côtes de Castillon)
9 Château Haut-Carles (Fronsac)
10 Château Preuillac (Médoc)

BEST-VALUE PRODUCERS

1 Château Langoa-Barton (St-Julien)
2 Château du Tertre (Margaux)
3 Château Haut-Chaigneau (Lalande-de-Pomerol)
4 Château Sociando-Mallet (Haut-Médoc)
5 Château Pavie-Macquin (St-Emilion)
6 Château Dauzac (Margaux)
7 Château Haut-Batailley (Pauillac)
8 Château Beauregard (Pomerol)
9 Château Durfort-Vivens (Margaux)
10 Château Tour Haut-Caussan (Médoc)

GREATEST-QUALITY WINES

1 **Château Pichon-Longueville-Lalande 1982** (€285)
2 **Château Montrose 1990** (€237)
3 **Château Palmer 1990** (€100)
4 **Château Lafite 1990** (€236)
5 **Château Latour 1985** (€167)
6 **Château Léoville-Barton 1990** (€87)
7 **Château d'Yquem 1990** (€223)
8 **Château Gruaud-Larose 1982** (€140)
9 **Château Sociando-Mallet 1996** (€33.50)
10 **Domaine de Chevalier Blanc 1988** (€58)

BEST BARGAINS

1 **Château Messile-Aubert Montagne-St-Emilion 2003** (€13)
2 **Kressmann Monopole Bordeaux Blanc 2004** (€5.90)
3 **Château Patâche d'Aux Médoc 2000** (€14)
4 **Château Sociando-Mallet Haut-Médoc 1998** (€17.50)
5 **Château Brillette Moulis 2001** (€15)
6 **Château Malartic-Lagravière Rouge Pessac-Léognan 2001** (€30)
7 **Château de Malle Sauternes 1999** (€19)
8 **Château Tour Haut-Caussan Médoc 2003** (€13)
9 **Château Fourcas-Dupré Listrac 2000** (€13)
10 **Château Thieuley Bordeaux Blanc 2004** (€6)

MOST EXCITING OR UNUSUAL FINDS

① **Château Lezongars L'Enclos Premières Côtes de Bordeaux 2001** (€10) *The wine really performs well above its station— a tribute to the English family that has resurrected this cru and to the underrated terroir of the Premières Côtes.*

② **Château Ducla Expérience XII Bordeaux Blanc 2004** (€12) *This very special wine owes its character to its unusual selection within a large property of 52 percent Sauvignon Gris with 48 percent Sauvignon Blanc and fermentation in cask with lees stirring, which gives a full-flavored, creamy, spicy impression and an extra lift at the finish.*

③ **Château Brassac Bordeaux Supérieur 2003** (€7.50) *This is the Kressmann portion of a joint enterprise in the Entre-Deux-Mers region with Dourthe. This wine performed especially well for 2003, with plenty of luscious fruit as well as sturdy tannins.*

④ **Relais de Durfort-Vivens Margaux 2003** (€18) *Lovely perfume and very pure fruit flavor—outstanding for a second wine in 2003.*

⑤ **Château Peybonhomme Les Tours Premières Côtes de Blaye 2003** (€7) *One of the relatively few biodynamic Bordeaux châteaux, this is a wine of character with fresh, scented, expansive fruit that fills the mouth. An excellent wine for the year.*

⑥ **Clos Floridène Graves Blanc 2004** (€12) *Once more, Professor Denis Dubourdieu shows how to produce a wine to challenge the much more expensive ones from Pessac-Léognan. Wonderful fruit aromas on nose and palate.*

⑦ **Château Lacombe-Noaillac Médoc 2002** (€10) *Jean-Michel Lapalu's flagship property Patâche d'Aux has an established pedigree of quality, but it has taken time to bring this vineyard to its potential. This is a classic example, with structure and some richness, that shows the potential here.*

⑧ **Château Picoron Côtes de Castillon 2003** (€5.50) *Very fresh fruit and balance for 2003 from an important and innovative producer. What value!*

Grapevine

• **Douglas Morton** has been appointed UK consultant for the Conseil Interprofessionnel du Vin de Bordeaux (CIVB). He is very well known in the British wine trade as a former managing director of Baron Philippe de Rothschild UK and in California as a former managing director of Opus One. CIVB says that it has made the appointment to improve its understanding of the complex and competitive British market.

• **A post-mortem** on the 2004 *primeur* campaign gives further evidence of the polarization of the market. Overall, average prices were 4 percent higher than for 2002 and 18 percent lower than for 2003. However, in the over €50 bracket (6 percent of the market), prices were plus 20 percent on 2002 and minus 27.5 percent on 2003. First rumors about the 2005 market suggest the 2003 prices could be a benchmark.

Burgundy

Clive Coates MW

Ever wondered why a well-noted wine did not come up to the mark when you drank it?

CLIVE COATES MW

Did the wine critic, who wrote fulsomely about the wine in cask, overrate it? Were you or the wine having a bad day? Laurent Ponsot of Morey-St-Denis's Domaine Ponsot has come up with an answer. If the wine has suffered excessive heat between him and you, those in the know will be able to verify it by a characteristic of a specially adapted label. So you will have total justification in rejecting it before you have to pay for it. During a trip to the United States, Ponsot discovered his wines upright on a shelf in full sun in a so-called fine-wine store!

I've had the same experience. At a Clos de la Roche/Clos St-Denis vertical/horizontal in New Haven a decade or so ago, most of the Ponsot wines were disappointing. But when I subsequently compared my notes with what I had tasted *chez* Ponsot (and *chez* Coates with wines bought directly from the domaine), I found my conclusions were different. Ponsot's Clos de la Roche Vieilles Vignes is one of the great wines of Burgundy. He makes his wine with a very minimum of sulfur. There is no new oak. This makes his wines more vulnerable to bad handling than most. The American wines had been "temperature abused"!

But now he has discovered a solution. He has found a label producer nearby: Pierre Personne, Société DEPP, Gevrey-Chambertin. Personne's wine labels include a small white circle, ⅓ in (8 mm) in diameter. When

CLIVE COATES MW is the author of *Côte d'Or* (Weidenfeld & Nicolson, 1997), which has won various awards, including Le Prix des Arts et des Lettres from the Confrérie de Tastevin, "the first time that a book on wine and a non-Burgundian have been so honored for 30 years." He is now working on a second edition. From 1985 to 2005 he was author-publisher of the award-winning monthly fine-wine magazine *The Vine*. His latest books are *The Wines of Bordeaux* (Weidenfeld & Nicolson, 2004) and *The Great Wines of France* (Mitchell Beazley, 2005).

bottles are subjected to excessive heat, the white becomes gray, and never reverts to white. The price is some 10 cents (€0.10) per label. The wine is made in temperature-controlled conditions *chez* Ponsot at 54°F (12°C) and is normally shipped in refrigerated containers. If wholesalers and retailers subject the bottles to unsuitable temperatures, their customers will find out. Currently these labels change color at temperatures in excess of 108°F (42°C), which one sincerely hopes rarely happens to bottles of wine.

Ponsot is now working with his label manufacturer on producing a label that will indicate whether the temperature has exceeded 68°F (20°C). Wholesalers, transporters, restaurateurs, and retailers—watch out! Why should Ponsot and others work their socks off to produce fine, natural wine, only for it to be ruined by bad handling?

Grapevine

- **Slowly but surely,** the Hospices de Beaune is adjusting to the 21st century. Yes, the wine is still produced by three different entities: the vines looked after by a neighboring *vigneron*; the wine made in the Hospices cellar; the *élevage* entrusted to a Beaune *négociant*. But reform has begun. Wine auctioneers from Christie's now conduct the auction. A range of older wines was sold off in November 2005, and outsiders were free to bid for a symbolic first cask of each lot (though the *négoce* will still mature it). It's a discreet acknowledgment that the existing situation is farcical. The next step is for the Hospices to assume control of everything from wine to bottle, as do all the other domaines.

- **More scandal in Beaujolais.** Hardly had *l'affaire du vin de merde* (see *Wine Report 2004*) died down when further eruptions hit the Beaujolais. This time it concerned allegations of malpractice at one of the vinification centers in the huge Georges Duboeuf empire. An employee, since fired, had blended together Beaujolais of different origins and appellations. Whether this was an inadvertent error or a deliberate attempt to besmirch the Duboeuf reputation, we do not know. The mistake was soon discovered and the wine never even bottled, let alone sold. Technically, no offense occurred. It is not illegal to blend wine; only to pass it off as something it isn't. Moreover, Georges Duboeuf, for all the size of his kingdom (he sells 15 percent of all Beaujolais), is the last person in Beaujolais one could conceive of getting involved in anything infamous.

- **The long-established and well-reputed firm** of Roland Remoissenet Père & Fils has been sold to a consortium of American businessmen led by Edward and Howard Milstein. Remoissenet produced fine wines in the 1940s, 1950s, and 1960s but fell on harder times more recently, as its traditional sources increasingly bottled and marketed their wines themselves. It is believed that one of the attractions for the purchasers is the very large stock of old wines. The existing contract with Domaine Thénard of Givry for part of the latter's annual production of Le Montrachet, Corton Clos du Roi, Grands Echezeaux, etc continues.

Opinion:
Why is Chablis often disappointing?

When Chablis is good, it is one of the outstanding values in the wine world. Its price is half that of an equivalent Côte d'Or *premier* or *grand cru*. The largely non-oaked wines are crisp in acidity and so are very food-friendly. The minerally flavors are subtle and delicious. If you want confirmation, try a 2002 from a top source such as Raveneau, Vincent Dauvissat, William Fèvre, Louis Michel, or Domaine des Malandes.

Yet sadly this is the tip of an iceberg, the bulk of which is weak, evanescent, lacking fruit, and devoid of interest even in the best of vintages. When very young, it at least possesses the attraction of youth, but these pleasures soon turn hollow. Why, we ask, why?

• The *vignoble* is young. Between 1984 and 2004 the area under vine expanded from under 2,000 ha to 4,669 ha. So most of the vines are young.

• Chablis overproduces. The average harvest over the past five years in the white-wine sectors of the Côte de Beaune yielded 45 hl/ha. Chablis, Chablis *premier cru*, and Chablis *grand cru* (I leave out Petit Chablis to be fair) produced 55 hl/ha.

• Eighty-five percent plus of Chablis is collected by machine. Machines can't sort out the good from the bad. So: not the optimum selection method for producing fine wine.

• The Chablis climate is marginal. Here we are, exposed to the prevailing westerly wind, picking as much in October as in September. The weather often changes for the worse after the equinox, compromising the quality of the fruit.

Is there a solution? There is a simple one: insist on only the best; be prepared to pay a bit more. But only if the quality warrants it.

Grapevine

• **Jacky Truchot-Martin** of Morey-St-Denis retired in 2005 and sold his 7-ha estate to Parisian François Feuillet, PDG of Trigano. Feuillet already possesses a small domaine, based in Nuits-St-Georges, that is leased on a share-cropping basis to David Duband of Chevannes.

The two will now be able to add Charmes-Chambertin and Clos de la Roche to their portfolios.

Vintage Report

2005

The winter of 2004/05 was not especially cold, though there were plenty of days of frost; but spring was late in arriving, causing a delayed budbreak. Precipitation was low, however, and this was to become the essential background to the 2005 growing season. Neither was the summer particularly hot, though there was a heat wave in May, which led to a normal and efficient flowering. There were some hailstorms early in the season, mainly affecting the Côte de Nuits, and a more serious outburst in Santenay and Chassagne on the Sunday evening after July 14, but after that hardly a drop of rain was experienced in the Côte d'Or until September. At this stage, one could see a small potential harvest of healthy but thick-skinned, concentrated berries. All looked very promising, provided the tannins arrived at maturity at the same time as the sugar/acid ratio was at its optimum. You could see the effect of the hydric stress more in the top vineyards on the slope than in the generics on the plain. The leaves around the fruit, at the base of the canopy, were already dried out. It did, admittedly, aid those growers who strip these leaves in the run-up to the harvest. Yet, despite the drought, August had been only intermittently warm and sunny, and as September progressed, growers were beginning to get anxious about the lack of water. Happily, this arrived on Tuesday, September 6—one whole morning of solid, but thankfully not violent, precipitation. Thereafter the skies cleared, and September became increasingly sunny and warm. The Côte d'Or harvest was all but complete by the weekend of October 1.

The Domaine de la Romanée-Conti started picking early, on Thursday, September 15, while most domaines, even in the Côte de Beaune, were not planning to harvest until Monday the 19th and in the Côte de Nuits on Thursday the 22nd. By this time, it had begun to get quite cold during the night, and even on sunny days the temperature rarely exceeded 77°F (25°C).

First reports are very enthusiastic: a medium-sized harvest of very healthy, ripe, concentrated fruit in both colors, on a par with—or very nearly as good as—1999 and 2002. The red wines of the Côte de Nuits are particularly good. As for the whites, there being little malic acid, they will probably resemble more the lush 1999s than the crisp and minerally 2002s.

As a result, word already having escaped before the 2004s were put on the market, this former vintage has been released at very reasonable prices, in some cases lower than those of 2003. At the Hospices de Beaune auction of the 2005s, prices for the red wines climbed 14 percent, the whites 9 percent. We can certainly anticipate increases of at least this order, perhaps even more, when the domaine 2005 wines are released in December 2006.

In Chablis, in the Côte Chalonnaise, in the Mâconnais, and in the Beaujolais, the 2005 vintage seems to have been similarly successful. In all, this is one of the best Burgundy vintages in recent years.

Updates on the previous five vintages
2004

Vintage rating: *Red: 82, White: 85*

Bottled from vintage time in 2005 through to the early summer of 2006, the 2004s have progressed positively since they were first available for tasting in cask.

The summer of 2004 was inauspicious, causing problems of oidium (downy mildew) to be added to concerns about preventing vines from compensating for having produced only half a normal crop in 2003. The latter was resolved by an even more Draconian approach to debudding and deflowering than usual (plus green-harvesting for those too lazy to attack the vines at the outset). The former was to have its effect on the cleanliness of the lees of the resulting wine, so compromising the *élevage*.

The quality of the vintage was mightily improved by fine weather in September, which resulted in very fragrant wines of medium body, with high acidities but delicious perfumes. In October 2005, growers were happy to acknowledge successful, virile, medium-bodied whites, but were still undecided about the reds: they had the fruit; would they have the texture?

The 2004s took a long time to evolve. Malos were late, and there was a great deal of malic acidity. It was September 2005 before they could be safely judged. The whites are fragrant, forward, and not a bit too lean, if certainly brisk and fresh. The reds will continue to fatten out to their advantage. Like the whites, they are pure and elegant: again, for the medium term.

This is a very good year in Chablis and the Côte Chalonnaise, though not up to 2002 or 2005. It is a good if not inspired vintage in the Mâconnais and the Beaujolais.

It will be a vintage for drinking in the short term while we wait for the 2002s and 2005s to develop.

2003

Vintage rating: *Red: 80, White: 60*

Now in bottle, the 2003s are in many respects rather more civilized than they appeared to be in cask. Yet this is neither a very classic nor a very sophisticated vintage. After a torrid summer, the fruit was picked unprecedentedly early, before the tannins were fully ripe or the flavors had reached full maturity, despite sugars being high (and acidities low). Those red-wine producers who dared to hang on found themselves with wines that are more elegant and have greater dimension than those who panicked. But in general the whites are lush, somewhat tarty, and without the essential minerality of true burgundy (this applies to the Côte Chalonnaise and Chablis as well as the Côte d'Or), while the reds have flavors that suggest California or Côte Rôtie rather than the purity of the Côte d'Or. They have good color, soft tannins (for growers, sensibly, did not overmacerate or overoak), and low acidities. There is a parallel with 1997: juicy wines, without great finesse, for early drinking. The Beaujolais, however, are excellent.

2002

Vintage rating: *Red: 88, White: 90*

The more the 2002s evolve, the more I like them. Now that they are safely in bottle, one can see whites that are yet better than 2000, 1999, and 1995, the standouts of the decade, and reds that, if not quite having the flair of 1999, are a close second.

The vintage was of a reasonable size (less than 2004, more than 2003) and conditioned by excellent September weather, sun and wind, which had the effects of concentrating sugars and flavor, plus the acidities at the same time. The whites are excellent all the way from Chablis to the Côte Chalonnaise, though just a tad too rich in the Mâconnais; and the reds are equally successful, for once, in the Côte de Nuits, the Côte de Beaune, and the Côte Chalonnaise. The Beaujolais are good, but eclipsed by 2003.

2001

Vintage rating: *Red: 80, White: 70*

My four-year-on comprehensive tasting (July 2005) demonstrated clearly that, like 2000, this is a divided vintage, though at a higher level. There was, simply, more rain in the Côte de Beaune than in the Côte de Nuits in September, and the weather improved toward the end of the month, enabling the Côte de Nuits, which normally harvests a week later than the

Côte de Beaune, to enjoy better harvesting conditions. There are even some in Burgundy who prefer the slightly more austere 2001s in the Côte de Nuits to their equivalents in 2002. I personally find them less succulent, and so less appealing, but I do not deny their balance, depth, or *terroir* definition. There are some fine Côte de Nuits reds, which should not be missed. The whites, across the board from Chablis to the Mâconnais, are good but not as fine as 2000 or 2002. Drink them soon. The Beaujolais, now tiring, are indifferent.

2000

Vintage rating: *Red: 70, White: 80*

Given essentially the same weather pattern—i.e., rain in September—a surprisingly rather better result for the whites of the Côte de Beaune than the reds. There are plump, juicy, if for the most part quite forward, white wines, but, as my four-year-on tasting in July 2004 confirmed, the Côte de Beaune reds are rather dull. There is an absence of fruit. The Côte de Nuits are very much better: medium in weight, succulent, clean, and full of fruit. Wines for the short term, but worthy of note. It was very good, though not quite as good as it could have been (buy the top estates only), in Chablis; mediocre in the Côte Chalonnaise, especially in red; decent in white Rully and Montagny and Mâconnais; ordinary, and now past its best, in Beaujolais.

GREATEST WINE PRODUCERS

1. Domaine Jean Grivot
2. Domaine Anne Gros
3. Maison/Domaine Louis Jadot
4. Domaine Leflaive
5. Domaine Leroy
6. Domaine de la Romanée-Conti
7. Domaine Georges Roumier
8. Domaine des Comtes Lafon
9. Domaine Armand Rousseau
10. Domaine Comte Georges de Vogüé

FASTEST-IMPROVING PRODUCERS

1. Maison Bichot (Beaune)
2. Maison Chanson (Beaune)
3. Maison Camille Giroud (Beaune)
4. Drouhin-Larose (Gevrey-Chambertin)
5. Humbert Frères (Gevrey-Chambertin)
6. Lamarche (Vosne-Romanée)
7. Jean-Marc Millot (Nuits-St-Georges)
8. Domaine Nudant (Ladoix)
9. Louis Remy (Morey-St-Denis)
10. Rossignol-Jeanniard (Volnay)

NEW UP-AND-COMING PRODUCERS

1. Jean-Marie Burgaud (Morgon)
2. Raphaël Coche (Domaine JF Coche-Dury, Meursault)
3. David Croix (Maison Camille Giroud, Domaine Duchet, Beaune)
4. Olivier Lamy (St-Aubin)
5. Benjamin Leroux (Comte Armand, Pommard)
6. Louis-Michel Liger-Belair (Vosne-Romanée)
7. Virgile Lignier-Michelot (Morey-St-Denis)

8 Hughes Pavelot (Domaine Jean-Marc Pavelot, Savigny-Lès-Beaune)

9 Sylvain Pataille (Marsannay)

10 Carl Voorhuis (Domaine D'Arduy, Corgoloin)

BEST-VALUE PRODUCERS

Go for 2002 for now, or 1999 if you can still find it (for red wines); 2005 for the future.

1 Domaine Stéphane Aladame (Montagne)

2 Domaine Anita & Jean-Pierre Colinot (Irancy)

3 Domaine Christophe & Fils (Fyé) (for Chablis)

4 Domaine Ghislaine & Jean-Hughes Goisot (St-Bris-Le-Vineux)

5 Domaine Christophe Grangemoulin (Rully)

6 Domaine Henri & Paul Jacqueson (Rully)

7 Domaine Gilles Jourdan (Comblanchien) (for Côte de Nuits Villages)

8 Domaine Bruno Lorenzon (Mercurey)

9 Domaine Lucien Muzard & Fils (Santenay)

10 Domaine Jean-Marc Pavelot (Savigny-Lès-Beaune)

GREATEST-QUALITY WINES

1 **Corton-Charlemagne 2002** Domaine Roland Rapet (€80) *2008–20.*

2 **Charmes-Chambertin 1995** Domaine Denis Bachelet (€100) *Now–2035.*

3 **Le Chambertin 1995** Domaine Louis Jadot (€300) *Now–2035.*

4 **Chambolle-Musigny Les Amoureuses 1995** Domaine Robert Groffier (€120) *Now–2030.*

5 **Le Musigny 1993** Domaine Leroy (€800) *2008–38.*

6 **La Tâche 1993** Domaine de la Romanée-Conti (€600) *2008–38.*

7 **Bonnes-Mares 1990** Domaine Georges Roumier (€200) *Now–2030.*

8 **Le Musigny 1989** Maison Joseph Drouhin (€200) *Now–2020.*

9 **Le Chambertin 1985** Domaine Armand Rousseau (€150) *Now–2012.*

10 **Clos de Vougeot 1937** Domaine Camuzet (€250) *Still splendidly vigorous.*

Grapevine

• **Takeover at Domaine Duchet, Beaune.** Early in 2005, an intense battle between rival suitors was resolved in favor of American businessman Roger Forbes, who has taken charge of this 4-ha estate. The domaine includes, *inter alia*, 0.25 ha of Corton-Charlemagne. The winemaking has been entrusted to David Croix, who will take on Duchet in addition to his responsibilities at Maison Camille Giroud.

• **Following the untimely death** of Philippe Engel, at just 49 years of age, his 2005 crop was sold as fruit to Maison Albert Bichot, resulting in no Domaine René Engel wine for this very promising vintage.

• **We will also miss Denis Mortet,** who died suddenly in January 2006, also at age 49. Since 1991, when he split the family estate with his brother Thierry, he had built up his 11-ha Gevrey-Chambertin domaine to one of Burgundy's very finest.

• **Further sad news,** as two elder statesmen of the Burgundian wine fraternity pass away: Bernard Clair, owner of the section of Bonnes-Mares that overlaps from Chambolle-Musigny into Morey-St-Denis, and Michel Gouges, father and uncle, respectively, of Christian and Pierre, today in charge of Domaine Henri Gouges, the best and longest-established estate in Nuits-St-Georges.

BEST BARGAINS

1 **Bourgogne Côte d'Auxerre Chardonnay 2004** Domaine Ghislaine & Jean-Hughes Goisot (€5.80) *Stunning generic wines are made by this charming couple in St-Bris-Le-Vineux near Chablis. Try their Sauvignon St-Bris, too.*

2 **Irancy 2003** Domaine Anita & Jean-Pierre Colinot (€12) *A few miles from St-Bris, Irancy produces the only village wine Pinot Noirs in this part of Burgundy (the rest are generic). The Colinots in fact offer six different examples. The year 2003, though very hot, is a splendid vintage here. Not commercially imported, but it should be.*

3 **Chablis Vieilles Vignes 2004** Domaine Christophe & Fils (€7) *A rising Chablis star is Sébastien Christophe, who lives in a farm surrounded by corn above the grands crus outside Fyé. This is very pure and really quite concentrated.*

4 **Bourgogne Rouge 2002** Domaine Ghislaine Barthod (€13) *The land on the "wrong" side of the road opposite the vineyards of Chambolle produces very stylish, similar wine. Ghislaine Barthod's example is delicious, and ready now.*

5 **Marsannay Rosé 2004** Domaine Bruno Clair (€8.50) *Pinot Noir makes delicious rosé. Clair's is one of the best. Drink this while it is young and fresh and move on to the 2005 as soon as it is on the market (mid-summer, probably).*

6 **Rully Les Pucelles 2004** Domaine Henri & Paul Jacqueson (€10) *My favorite Côte Chalonnaise white wine. Consistently full of fruit, harmonious, fresh, and elegant.*

7 **Côte de Nuits Villages 2002** Domaine Denis Bachelet (€15) *Not as well known as Côte de Beaune Villages but well worth investigating, especially from a master such as Bachelet. Potentially sumptuous.*

8 **Givry Clos Jus 2002** Domaine François Lumpp (€14) *Perhaps the best Côte Chalonnaise red I have tasted from this vintage. Pure, intense, and long on the palate.*

9 **St-Aubin Clos de la Chatenière 2002** Domaine Hubert Lamy & Fils (€22.50) *Half the price of Puligny-Montrachet, yet better than all but the top offerings of a handful of the senior Puligny growers; 2002 is a splendid white-wine vintage.*

10 **Savigny-Lès-Beaune La Dominode 2002** Domaine Jean-Marc Pavelot (€15.50) *The best grower in Savigny's best wine in a fine red-wine vintage. Will still keep. Save room for the 2005.*

Grapevine

• **Bouchard Père & Fils** built a new state-of-the-art winery on an industrial estate between Savigny-Lès-Beaune and the highway, just in time for the 2005 vintage.

• **The agrément system,** the procedure by which wines obtain *appellation contrôlée* approval, is being reformed, as predicted in *Wine Report 2006.* Henceforth, the wines will be assessed after bottling, not when they have barely finished fermenting. This new arrangement will come into force for Volnay, Chassagne-Montrachet, Santenay, and Viré-Clessé with the 2005 vintage, but will not cover all of Burgundy until after 2007.

MOST EXCITING OR UNUSUAL FINDS

❶ Marsannay Cuvée Ancestrale 2002 Domaine Sylvain Pataille (€18) *Expensive for a Marsannay, but you would think it was a Gevrey-Chambertin premier cru. Very old vines, of course.*

❷ Nuits-St-Georges Les Perrières Blanc 2004 Domaine Henri Gouges (€35.90) *A rare wine from Pinot Noir vines that have mutated to produce white fruit. Individual and delicious.*

❸ Gevrey-Chambertin Clos St-Jacques 2002 Domaine Armand Rousseau (€70) *In the view of all five owners in this* climat, *Clos St-Jacques produces wine third only to Chambertin and Chambertin Clos de Bèze in the commune:* grand cru *quality at* premier cru *prices.*

❹ Bourgogne Blanc Cuvée Oligocène 2002 Domaine Patrick Javillier (€8) *Generic wine from soil very similar to Meursault: tastes like it, too.*

❺ Maranges Clos de la Boutière Cuvée Vieilles Vignes 2002 Domaine Edmond Monnot (€9.10) *An intensely flavored wine from a neglected commune at the very bottom of the Côte d'Or.*

❻ Bourgogne Rouge 2002 Domaine Ghislaine Barthod (€7.50) *From soils similar to those of Chambolle-Musigny but on the "wrong" side of the road.*

❼ Morgon Côte de Py 2003 Domaine Louis-Claude Desvignes (€8) *Proper Beaujolais (not the wishy-washy Nouveau stuff) from the best grower in the most distinctive cru in the region. A stunning vintage, too.*

❽ Morey-St-Denis Blanc Les Monts-Luisants 2002 Domaine Ponsot (€30) *Largely from very old Aligoté: no malolactic. Unique.*

❾ Bourgogne Aligoté de Bouzeron 2005 Aubert & Pamela de Villaine (€8.50) *When Aligoté is as good as this is—and this is the best—you wonder why it is not more widely planted (but only until you sample a standard version).*

❿ La Romanée 2002 Comte Liger-Belair (€250) *The first vintage of this wine was vinified and bottled by Louis-Michel Liger-Belair on behalf of his family (previously the vineyard was leased out). Quite outstanding. The wine of the vintage.*

Grapevine

• **Domaine Charles Thomas** has been sold. Following family dissension, Domaine Charles Thomas, the estate part of merchants Thomas Moillard, has been sold. The purchasers, with the help of outside investors, are Jeremy Seysses of Domaine Dujac in Morey-St-Denis and Etienne de Montille of the eponymous property in Volnay. The 18-ha estate—which extends from Chambertin, Clos de Bèze, to Pommard, and includes Corton Clos du Roi, Corton-Charlemagne, Clos de Vougeot, Romanée-St-Vivant, and Bonnes-Mares, as well as a large slice of Vosne-Romanée, Les Malconsorts (part of which is enclaved into La Tâche)—has been underperforming in recent times. These two talented winemakers have divided the spoils between them.

• **Domaine de la Vougeraie,** the 32-ha estate based in Prémeaux, has lost its talented manager, the French-Canadian Pascal Marchand, who, until 1999, was the guru behind Pommard's Clos des Epeneaux. Marchand left in March 2006 and set up as a merchant.

Champagne

Tom Stevenson

BCC became the second-largest group in Champagne on March 22, 2006, when Bruno Paillard finalized the deal to purchase Lanson International, firmly pushing Vranken-Pommery Monopole down into third place.

TOM STEVENSON

The purchase price for Lanson was €122.7 million ($150.3 million). The fact that BCC inherited €400 million in debts had some commentators shaking their heads, but although this effectively increased the price to €522.7 million ($646.3 million), it should be realized that Lanson International also includes the entire former Marne et Champagne business, plus Besserat de Bellefon. On its own, Lanson is potentially worth half a billion euros, if properly run and financed, but the inclusion of Marne et Champagne, Besserat de Bellefon, and four châteaux in Bordeaux made it the deal of the century, and no one was better qualified to recognize this than BCC's two founders: Bruno Paillard and the new PDG at Lanson, Philippe Baijot. When I first met this dynamic duo in 1980, Baijot was the sales manager for Marne et Champagne, and Paillard was the company's export consultant. They know full well that Lanson is the primary

TOM STEVENSON has specialized in Champagne for more than 25 years. *Champagne* (Sotheby's Publications, 1986) was the first wine book to win four awards, and it quickly established Tom's credentials as a leading expert in this field. In 1998, his *Christie's World Encyclopedia of Champagne & Sparkling Wine* (Absolute Press, revised 2003) made history by being the only wine book ever to warrant a leader in any national newspaper (*The Guardian*), when it published a 17th-century document proving beyond doubt that the English used a second fermentation to convert still champagne into sparkling wine at least six years before Dom Pérignon even set foot in the Abbey of Hautvillers. Tom has judged in France, Germany, Greece, the United States, and Australia, and he is chairman of the champagne panel at the *Decanter* World Wine Awards. His annual Champagne Masterclass for Christie's is always a sellout.

profit-maker, but if any of those initially interested in bidding for Lanson International understood how much of an additional asset Marne et Champagne could be, it had to be Baijot and Paillard. It's odds-on that they will increase Marne et Champagne's market value and annual profitability. Unlike the Mora family, who inherited this low-profile, cash-rich business then sought the limelight of a *grande marque* but purchased it at the very top of an overpriced market, ending up relative paupers in the process.

The €122.7 million ($150.3 million) was split between the Mora family, which owned 55 percent of Lanson International, and the French investment bank Caisse d'Epargne, which owned the balance of 45 percent. The rumor is that the price was shared slightly differently than the percentage ownership would normally dictate, but exactly why and what the precise

Grapevine

• **History ends for Berry Bros.** when, after shipping Champagne Binet nonstop since 1887, they switched to Mailly Grand Cru for their prestigious own-label. Buyer Simon Field MW obviously has his finger on Champagne's pulse because he could not have picked a better time to move to this cooperative. With exclusively *grand cru* vineyards from one village only, this cooperative has always had the potential to produce something special, and since the harvests of 1995 and 1996, that is exactly what they have been doing.

• **Only an idiot** would declare a lousy year like 2001 a vintage, but in setting up a forthcoming vertical of preview vintages, I discovered that Charles Philipponnat will be releasing a 2001 Clos des Goisses in the distant future. So, is Charles an idiot? I think not. Clos des Goisses is a special vineyard, especially its steep, so-called "south-south" facing slope, where grapes can burn in hot years and ripen in even the worst years when all around fail to do so. I have very fond memories of Clos des Goisses from another terrible vintage, the 1951, so I will approach the 2001 Clos des Goisses with an open mind. In the meantime, this is how Charles Philipponnat explained the decision

to release another "lousy" vintage exactly 50 years later: "Yes, we dared do it, and no, we are not completely crazy. We harvested before the rain at 10.5 percent potential alcohol [when the average in the rest of Champagne was 8.5 per cent—TS] and produced only 5,000 bottles out of a potential of 50,000, and the average bottling for Clos des Goisses is 15,000–20,000. We think that with only a small *dosage* it is fine. Even good. You will find out!" Others declaring the best-forgotten 2001 vintage include Duval-Leroy (Authentis Cumières), Moutard (Cuvée 6 Cépages), and Oudinot (Marks & Spencer).

• **Be on the lookout** for Mumm's forthcoming new prestige *cuvée*, as yet unamed. A sneak preview of the inaugural 1998 vintage, due to be launched in 2007, and the followup 2002 vintage, revealed a champagne of true class. Plots of mature vines in 12 *lieux-dits* spread over eight *grands crus* have been put aside for this new wine, but only four or five plots will make it to the final blend in any one year. Unlike the non-vintage Mumm Grand Cru, this Champagne exudes finesse and gets my thumbs-up.

• **Dominique Demarville left Mumm** in August 2006 to join Veuve Clicquot.

split is are uncertain because the only ones who know are not telling. However, the division of the money received cannot be far off the actual percentages of ownership, thus the Moras got around €67.5 million ($83.15 million), and we know that they immediately paid off a €16-million loan from Crédit Lyonnais, leaving them with barely more than €50 million ($61.6 million). This not only demonstrates the folly of buying at the top of a market, but also illustrates perfectly how much of uncle Gaston's money they blew away. They had inherited a business widely reported at the time to be worth FF3–4 billion ($580–711 million); and had they sold up, instead of buying Lanson, and placed the money in a safe-as-houses bank account with an average interest of just 3 percent per annum, the Mora family would be worth well over €1 billion now, instead of just 50-odd million.

Grapevine

• **The dole for one of Champagne's best winemakers!** Hervé Jestin, who has done so much to lift the quality of Duval-Leroy, has had his marching orders "for reasons of difference in opinion" according to Carol Duval. Since Jestin was made to sign a non-disclosure agreement, it remains a bit of a mystery, although both parties agree that nothing untoward went on. The rumor is that Jestin would not share the recipes for his blends! Suffice to say that I think Duval-Leroy has lost more than Jestin, who could, as far as I'm concerned, walk into any *grande marque* house and do the job well. He is succeeded at Duval-Leroy by Sandrine Logette, an oenologist who has worked at this house since 1991. I wish her well, but she has big shoes to fill.

• **Two fine additions** to the Champagne library were published in 2005. *Caves de Champagne* by Michel Jolyot (Atelier Jolyot, October 2005) is a pictorial journey through the cellars of Champagne as captured by the photographer who snapped a famous shot of John Lennon in the streets of New York. *Les Clés de Vins de Champagne* (CIVC, 2005) breaks the mold of promotional literature. This is not simply a thick pamphlet, but a legitimate book of substantial size (12 × 8½ in [30 × 22 cm], 295 pages), which is chock-full of historical, climatical, geological, and technical facts, figures, tables, and maps—a treasure trove of information for all champagne aficionados, available from the CIVC in person for €15 or €20 if ordered by mail. An English-language edition should be available in the first quarter of 2007, although the title and price were unknown at the time of going to press.

• **Champagne has joined up** with port, sherry, Napa Valley, Oregon, and Washington State to launch the Center for Wine Origins. When launching this initiative, Bruno Paillard, representing CIVC, stated, "Regardless of what side of the Atlantic you come from, we all agree that great wine is made in unique places all over the world and that these unique place names must be protected." But which side of the Atlantic *does* matter, since the Center for Wine Origins is located in Washington, DC, and is funded by the EU. It's all about educating US consumers and US policy-makers *vis-à-vis* the importance of location and accurate labeling. The associated website can be found at www.wineorigins.com.

TAITTINGER SOLD AGAIN

In September 2005, controlling interest in Groupe Taittinger was sold to Starwood Capital, the American investment and hotel group, for €2.6 billion ($3.2 billion). Groupe Taittinger was built on the profits of the family's champagne business and comprises Bouvet-Ladubay, Domaine Carneros (jointly with Kobrand), Baccarat crystalware, and, most significantly, Société du Louvre. The latter is the majority shareholder in the Hotel Lutetia and the Hotel de Crillon in Paris, the Hotel Martinez in Cannes, and the 900-strong budget-hotel group Envergure. Although Taittinger was a publicly owned company, the family still controlled 35 percent of the shares. That was split across a large, diverse family, 30-some members of which held positions throughout the group. However, many of them could barely bring themselves to talk to one another. In 2003, the Belgian billionaire Baron Albert Frère increased his holding from 16 to 25 percent, exacerbating the rift in the family, into which Starwood stepped in 2005. Starwood's sights were firmly fixed on the Société du Louvre, and its strategy had always been to sell on Champagne Taittinger. Of the eight bids in all, perhaps the strongest opposition the family faced was from the Indian-owned United Breweries. Luckily for them, this bid was opposed by the CIVC, which expressed concern about Indian ownership because India does not recognize the Champagne appellation. Where this moral high ground was when an American firm purchased Taittinger the year before is anybody's guess! In June 2006, it was announced that the winning bid of €660 million ($850 million) came from Claude and Pierre-Emmanuel Taittinger backed by Crédit Agricole du Nord-Est. The sale includes all three wine domaines, but the level of indebtedness is believed to be very high.

Grapevine

• **Jean-Claude Rouzaud** has stepped down in favor of his son, Frédéric, who is now responsible for the entire Louis Roederer group, including Deutz (although it remains under the day-to-day control of Fabrice Rosset), Château de Pez, and Château Haut-Beauséjour in Bordeaux, Domaines Ott in Provence, Roederer Estate and Scharffenberger in California, and the port house of Ramos-Pinto. Some observers cannot believe that Jean-Claude Rouzaud won't be able to resist poking his nose in, but that is precisely why he has moved to Paris. He wants to be far enough away to avoid the temptation to keep popping in, but near enough to be on hand if Frédéric seeks his advice.

Besides which, those observers have obviously not noticed how much he is enjoying life with his second wife!

• **Young Benoît Marguet-Bonnerave** reports that his mother suddenly stopped production of Champagne Marguet-Bonnerave exactly 100 years after two Bonnerave brothers made the family's first champagne. He claims she sold off the entire 2005 crop as grapes without telling him. Forced to strike out on his own, Benoît has purchased Taittinger's old cellars in Ambonnay, where he now makes champagne under his own brand, Champagne Marguet, with grapes from his wife's vineyard on the Côte des Blancs, and Pinot Noir purchased from a friend in the Montagne de Reims.

Opinion:
Champagne's suicidally high yields

With the right climatic conditions, the Champagne region can ripen a bumper crop of grapes and produce truly beautiful wines: 1982 is a perfect example. Sparkling wines can tolerate higher yields than still white wines, which in turn can tolerate higher yields than red wines, so it does not surprise me that I tasted many excellent *vins clairs* from 2004, despite that year averaging 23,000 kg/ha. Indeed, the quality of 2004 is generally superior to 2005, even though the yield that year was less ("only" 18,000 kg/ha). Furthermore, given Champagne's marginal climate, in which spring frosts can be devastating, it is expedient for growers to prune for higher rather than lower yields. However, everything is relative. History demonstrates that it is likely to rain in Champagne during the harvest. It did in 2005. Just a bit. Less than normal, in fact, but temperatures were higher than average, and gray rot on the Pinots Noir and Meunier reduced the quality. In 2001, when the grapes were so massive, they were close to bursting before it rained; and when it rained, it bucketed down. So the *Champenois* are caught between a rock (frost)

Grapevine

• **Chanoine has purchased** the Champagne F Bonnet brand from Rémy Cointreau. Philippe Baijot, PDG at Chanoine at the time (see lead story on Lanson), told me: "It makes sense to bring the two Bonnets together. When we advertised Alexandre Bonnet, we were never sure how much benefit Rémy Cointreau received, since one Bonnet is the same as another to many consumers. No doubt they had similar worries. But now we have both, it doesn't matter."

• **A new "top-tier" range** called Diamant has been launched under the Vranken brand. The first four *cuvées* are a Brut NV, two vintage champagnes (starting with a Brut 1999 and a Rosé 1998), and a prestige *cuvée*. Whether this will upgrade the Vranken name is open to question, but the decision to spin off a clear

glass version of Heidsieck & Co Monopole's old Diamant Bleu bottle will further dilute the reputation of a former *grande marque* that has been demoted to a "fighting brand" under the Belgian's regime. In May 2006, Vranken-Pommery bought 21 ha of vineyards for €20 million. The purchase of vineyards by houses is rare, since SAFER usually steps in at the last moment to award the sale to one or more growers.

• **Perrier Jouët has released** a new glass alongside its 1998 vintage of Belle Epoque. Designed by Serena Sutcliffe MW, with the Belle Epoque flowers discreetly etched on the upper surface of the base of the glass, it makes previous enameled glasses look kitsch by comparison. Furthermore, unlike those enameled glasses, this is high-quality stemware that drinks beautifully.

and a hard place (rain). It is not simply a matter of aiming for high yields to offset any reduction from frost damage, but also a question of not allowing the crop to become so large that typical harvest conditions will at best lower the quality, while at worst fairly common downpours will result in disasters like 2001. This can be achieved by pruning generously to hedge against frost, but pruning long and rubbing off buds to spread out the load and increase ventilation; then, when necessary, fine-tuning by green pruning. Recent average yields, however, illustrate that the majority of growers are not just hedging against the prospect of frost but are aiming for dangerously high yields. Not just dangerous from a quality perspective, but also dangerous in terms of attracting a rebuke from the EU, which will view an average of 146.5 hl/ha (as in 2004) for a fine wine with the sort of reputation champagne has in a much less accommodating light than either INAO or the French Ministry of Agriculture has done so far. Will Champagne get its own house in order first? The CIVC hopes to raise the maximum permitted yield including PLC to 15,000 kg/ha (95.5 hl/ha), which in itself is fine, but if the *Champenois* can average 23,000 kg/ha when the maximum permitted yield is 13,000 kg/ha, one must wonder what on earth they will average when that is bumped up to 15,000 kg/ha.

Grapevine

• **If trade observers were curious why,** after more than a decade of brilliantly raising standards at Deutz, Odilon de Varenne should suddenly up sticks and move to Henriot, then his decision to leave Henriot after barely two years must be even more of a conundrum, especially since Gosset already has a *chef de cave*. Were there plans afoot to edge out Jean-Pierre Mareignier after 25 years of service? Rumors have been rife, so here's the truth. Mareignier is staying, and that comes directly from Béatrice Cointreau, who told me that he had actually requested help. This makes sense when you take into account that since Cointreau took over Gosset 13 years ago, production has increased from a static 500,000 to rising 1.2 million bottles. The *chef de cave*'s job had literally doubled, and with exports having tripled over the same

period, Cointreau needed someone who would relish the idea of traveling, and Mareignier did not. Odilon de Varenne was a good choice for many reasons, not least because he and Mareignier are old school chums. Varenne has three specific primary duties at Gosset: (1) he takes over the entire production after the wines are disgorged; (2) he is responsible for raising levels of traceability; and (3) he will assist the sales team at tastings around the world.

• **Veuve Clicquot's** first-ever non-vintage *rosé* has been launched. It is a Pinot Noir-dominated *cuvée* with 12 percent red wine, and reserve wines of up to nine years of age comprise one-third of the blend. Veuve Clicquot produced the first-ever vintaged champagne *rosé* in 1777.

Vintage Report

Advance report on the latest harvest
2005

A perfect flowering in June, with dry, sunny weather, followed by a hot and wet July—conditions that allowed the vines to access Champagne's high levels of organic matter in the soil (often higher than 3 percent, and sometimes more than 4 percent), causing exceptional cellular growth of the berries prior to *véraison*. A fresh August, followed by a warm and humid September, resulted in about 14 percent gray rot in the black varieties, particularly Meunier. This variability mitigated against 2005 being a true vintage. Definitely not in the class of 2002; probably on par or just below 2004, although some producers may make better 2005s. This is a winemaker's year. Jean-Baptiste Lecaillon, the *chef de cave* at Roederer, told me: "If you are a good blender, one plus one can often equal three, but in 2005 one plus one equals four!" From tasting the *vins clairs*, I found Chardonnay overwhelmingly the best variety, with Le Mesnil-sur-Oger its most successful *cru*. Pinot Noir has the edge over Meunier, with Verzy and Verzenay standing out.

Updates on the previous five vintages
2004
Vintage rating: *85–88*

The *vins clairs* are classic, with the best acids I have tasted in years (thanks to the diurnal difference). When I stated last year that this is a vintage on steroids, I meant that it was huge and boosted by an injection of exceptional sunshine. The quality is good to very good, with excellent acids and purity.

2003
Vintage rating: *50–90*

The *vins clairs* of Jacquesson best reflected 2003's sumptuous richness, while Krug and Roederer displayed exceptional acidity for the year. (One of those rarely mentioned facts is that acidification has always been permissible in Champagne, while it remains illegal farther south, except for this sweltering hot year, when a unique dispensation was given.) Considering the small size of the crop and proportionately greater scarcity of Chardonnay, a number of houses might not release a standard vintage, but any producer who has not done his or her best to make a small volume of pure 2003, even if only for in-house use, will live to regret it as global warming continues and they have no library bottles to learn from.

2002

Vintage rating: *85–90*

This is without doubt a vintage year, and a very special one, too, marked by the *passerillage* that reduced the crop in some vineyards by up to 40 percent and endowed the wines with the highest natural alcohol level since 1990 (which itself was the highest since 1959). It is definitely a Pinot Noir year, with Aÿ-Champagne the most successful village. There are some fine Chardonnays, but in general they are less impressively structured and lack acidity. Not that the Pinot Noirs are overblessed with acidity. Low acidity is a key feature of this vintage, with *vins clairs* tasting much softer than their analyses would have us believe.

2001

Vintage rating: *35*

Dilute, insipid, and unripe. Anyone who declares this needs their head tested.

2000

Vintage rating: *80*

Virtually vintage-quality ripeness, but more of a good non-vintage year, although there are a lot of *Champenois* who believe that 2000 is a magical number, so we can expect more declarations from this year than it really deserves. However, good, even great, champagne can be made in almost any year if the selection is strict enough, and with so many 2000s likely to be marketed, there should be plenty of good bottles to pick from. Generally soft, forward, and easy-drinking in style, while some really special wines—such as Philipponnat's Clos des Goisses, Jacquesson Dizy 1er Cru Corne Bautray, and Pierre Gimonnet's Fleuron *en magnum*—will be great.

Grapevine

• **Laurent Fresnet takes over** from Odillon de Varenne at Henriot. He comes from the Coopérative Vigneronne at Vertus, which he has managed since 2001. Before that, he was in charge of production at Champagne Cazals. An oenologist, Fresnet has winemaking experience in New Zealand, South Africa, Portugal, and Provence.

GREATEST WINE PRODUCERS

1. Krug
2. Pol Roger
3. Billecart-Salmon
4. Louis Roederer
5. Bollinger
6. Deutz
7. Jacquesson
8. Gosset
9. Pierre Gimonnet
10. Vilmart

FASTEST-IMPROVING PRODUCERS

1. Vilmart
2. Mumm
3. Pommery
4. Mailly Grand Cru
5. Bruno Paillard
6. Philipponnat
7. Duval-Leroy
8. Pannier
9. Moët & Chandon
10. Vve Devaux

NEW UP-AND-COMING PRODUCERS

1. Serge Mathieu
2. Henri Mandois
3. Fluteau
4. Bruno Paillard
5. Chanoine's Tsarine range
6. Henri Giraud
7. Audoin de Dampierre

BEST-VALUE PRODUCERS

1. Charles Heidsieck
2. Serge Mathieu
3. Henri Mandois
4. Duval-Leroy
5. Alfred Gratien
6. Bruno Paillard
7. Lanson
8. Louis Roederer
9. Drappier
10. Piper-Heidsieck

GREATEST-QUALITY WINES

1. = **Vintage 1995** Krug (€209)
1. = **Dom Pérignon 1998** Moët & Chandon (€99)
3. **Cuvée Sir Winston Churchill 1996** Pol Roger (€115)
4. **Grande Cuvée NV** Krug (€120)
5. **Cuvée William Deutz 1998** Deutz (€90)
6. **Brut Millésimé 1999** Louis Roederer (€40)
7. **Amour de Deutz 1999** Deutz (€102)
8. **Grand Millésime 1999** Gosset (€41)
9. **Belle Epoque Rosé 1999** Perrier Jouët (€120)
10. **Cuvée Royale Brut 1998** Joseph Perrier (€32)

BEST BARGAINS

1. **Club de Viticulteur Brut 1999** Henri Goutorbe (€18)
2. **Brut Rosé Millésimé 2000** Deutz (€34.90)
3. **Brut Millésimé 1999** Louis Roederer (€40)
4. **Brut Cuvée Victor Mandois 2000** Henri Mandois (€30)
5. **Brut Millésimé 1998** Mumm (€35)
6. **Nostalgie 1998** Beaumont des Crayères (€23.65)
7. **Cuvée Royale Brut 1998** Joseph Perrier (€32)
8. **Cuvée Royale Blanc de Blancs NV** Joseph Perrier (€28)
9. **Réserve Brut Blanc de Noirs NV** Michel Loriot (€13.90)
10. **Chouilly Grand Cru Cuvée des Crayères Brut 1999** Simart-Moreau (€13.55)

MOST EXCITING OR UNUSUAL FINDS

1 **Le Clos 2000** Henri Mandois (€45) *This brand-new, single-vineyard, pure Meunier demonstrates that Champagne's supposedly inferior grape variety can be a class act.*

2 **Mumm de Cramant NV** Mumm (€45) *Now reminiscent of the best cuvées of Crémant de Mumm in the old days.*

3 **Les Aventures Grand Cru Blanc de Blancs NV** AR Lenoble (€49) *A single-vineyard champagne from Les Aventures, a lieu-dit at the foot of Château de Saran, blended from three truly exceptional vintages (1990, 1995, and 1996). Just 940 cases produced.*

4 **Brut Millésimé 1998** Mumm (€35) *The best Mumm vintage of the 1990s. Excellent. Has finesse and complexity. Will age beautifully.*

5 **Coeur de Cuvée 1993** Vilmart (€72 per magnum) *If I'm going to have oak in my champagne, with fruit closer to burgundy, then this recently released magnum is my choice.*

6 **Cuvée Royale Blanc de Blancs NV** Joseph Perrier (€28) *Lovely biscuity fruit and excellent acidity are the key to this cuvée's consistent quality and impressive potential longevity. One of Champagne's best-kept secrets.*

7 **Clos du Moulin Premier Cru NV** Cattier (€50) *This fresh, elegant single-vineyard blend of 1995, 1996, and 1998 will achieve great complexity.*

8 **Egérie Brut 1998** Pannier (€42) *You might be confused by the "Brut" on the label, yet "Extra Brut" on the neck booklet (see Grapevine below), but there is no doubting the intense, knife-edge fruit, which is clearly capable of slow and graceful maturation as layers of complexity unfold.*

9 **Cumières Rouge Coteaux Champenois 1999** René Geoffroy (€22.22) *The first vin tranquil to make any Top 10 in my Champagne report, this is the best Coteaux Champenois Rouge I have tasted in years. Lovely Pinot Noir fruit, with nicely developed bottle aromas. Although approaching its peak, it shows no sign of decline.*

10 **"O.R. 1735" 1997** J De Telmont (€35) *The cork and cap on this creamy-complex champagne are secured by a string ficelle, as in the 18th century.*

Grapevine

• **Confused by the samples** of Pannier's Egérie 1998 submitted to my annual champagne tasting at Château de Boursault, my tasting coordinator wondered if it should be logged on to the computer as a Brut, as per the label, or an Extra Brut, which is how it is described in the booklet hanging from the bottle's neck. We checked with Terry Kenny, Pannier's export manager, who had been fearing this moment. "When we ordered the label, we thought that it would be a Brut," he said, "but at our in-house tastings it was decided that 3.5 g of residual sugar would make the ideal *dosage*, so we put Extra Brut on the neck label." Technically an Extra Brut (0–6 g) is also a Brut (0–15 g), so there was nothing illegal, but it would be helpful for the consumer to know if the champagne has a very low *dosage*.

Alsace

Tom Stevenson

After more than 30 years, the saga of Kaefferkopf's *grand cru* classification finally came to a head, as it became this region's 51st *grand cru*.

TOM STEVENSON

In 1975, the first list of 94 proposed *grands crus* was submitted to INAO for consideration; 25 of these were classified in 1983, a further 23 were awarded *grand cru* status in 1985, and another two in 1988. In *The Wines of Alsace* (Faber & Faber, 1993), I included Kaefferkopf as one of the 51 Alsace *grands crus* profiled, even though there happened to be only 50 at the time. I did this because, unlike many Alsace *grands crus*, Kaefferkopf was authentic, famous, and deserving, having been the very first named vineyard in Alsace to have its boundaries delimited (in 1932 by a Colmar tribunal) and the only named site to be defined in the original AOC Alsace of 1962.

So, why was Kaefferkopf not classified as a *grand cru* until 2006? For the very reason that made it famous in the first place: its traditional practice of blending two or more grape varieties, which was contrary to the pure varietal concept of Alsace Grand Cru. The authorities would not allow this exception to the rule and, quite rightly, a significant number of growers refused to be bullied by the bureaucrats. Even some who had never produced blends

TOM STEVENSON specializes in champagne, but he is equally passionate about Alsace. In 1987 he was elected a *confrérie oenophile* of the Confrérie Saint-Etienne, when he was the sole person to identify a 50-year-old wine made from Sylvaner. In 1994, his 600-page tome *The Wines of Alsace* (Faber & Faber, 1993) won the Veuve Clicquot Book of the Year award in the US and attracted the mother of all reviews in the UK from Malcolm Gluck, who declared: "It is not simply the best book about Alsace wines ever written, or the most penetrating book about a French wine region ever written; it is the greatest wine book ever written, period." A revision is in the pipeline but more than a few years away. Tom is chairman of the Alsace panel at the *Decanter* World Wine Awards.

(Kaefferkopf is also known for its pure varietal Gewurztraminer and Riesling wines) objected to its demise. After all, the producers of Kaefferkopf were for decades the sole standard bearers of high-quality blends. Edelzwicker had long become synonymous with Zwicker and thus cheap *vin ordinaire*.

If the *Champenois* could get INAO to accept that champagne *rosé* may be produced by blending a little red wine with white for no other reason than most *rosé*-style champagnes had always been made that way, then INAO should have accepted the traditional practice of blending Kaefferkopf from different varieties. Especially since the blending of different varieties to make a white wine is a classic technique, whereas blending red with white to make pink is illegal anywhere else in the EU!

Another excuse why the authorities refused to classify Kaefferkopf was because of the geological diversity of its topsoil. However, although geological uniformity is often spouted by those supporting the expansion of an authentically sized *lieu-dit* into an overblown *grand cru*, geology can only be true to the subsoil, not the topsoil, and all of the Kaefferkopf classified by the tribunal is situated on pure granite.

So here we are, 31 years after the first *grands crus* were proposed and 16 years after the bureaucracy belatedly recognized, but did not classify, Kaefferkopf. This famous vineyard has at last achieved its true position in the Alsace hierarchy. Approximately 70 ha have been classified, compared to the 67.81 ha delimited by the Colmar tribunal in 1932, and although some previously classified Kaefferkopf vineyards have been excluded, their owners have the right to use the Kaefferkopf name for the next 25 years! The authorized grape varieties are Gewurztraminer, Riesling, and Pinot Gris (each as a single variety or blended) plus Muscat (part of a blend only). Currently the vineyards are planted with approximately 59 percent Gewurztraminer, 35 percent Riesling, 5 percent Pinot Gris, and 1 percent Muscat.

Alsace should be screwed

Alsace wines are ideal for the latest screwcap technology, but few Alsace producers have taken advantage of this. The biggest stumbling block is that, apart from the so-called *grands maisons*, relatively few Alsace producers are seriously involved in export markets where the benefits of these closures are widely accepted by large and increasing numbers of fine-wine consumers, but not the French. Even Domaine Paul Blanck, the most screwcap-minded of all Alsace exporters (started in 2001 and now bottles *grands crus* under screwcap), does not dare to use these closures for its wines on the home market. Although Trimbach is one of Alsace's most widely exported brands, it won't invest in the technology until it is accepted in the US, its most important export market (although there is hope with Parker's prediction back in 2004 that screwcaps "will become the standard for the majority of the world's wines"). Meanwhile, Willm has supplied the Swedish Monopoly with 16,000 bottles of its recently launched 2004 Pinot Gris/Riesling (not tasted). Other producers using screwcaps include Jean-Pierre Frick (Pfaffenheim) and Gustave Lorentz (Bergheim), but generally the takeup is very poor considering how well youthful aromatic white wines respond to this technology. If Alsace producers wait for French consumers to catch on without doing anything proactive, I fear they will wait forever. They need to follow the example of Blanck and sell *grands crus* under screwcap but not restrict this to export countries. They should take this initiative to the home market and make a bold statement in the process, such as selling exactly the same wine in both cork and screwcap, but charging 10 percent extra on the screwcap bottles. Only then will the average French consumer of Alsace wine stop and think. Perhaps it might also be instructive to sell a mixed case of cork and screwcap wines to lay down for a few years for comparative purposes?

Grapevine

• **Tokay disappears as of 2006,** when the varietal designations Tokay d'Alsace and Tokay Pinot Gris must be replaced by Pinot Gris, plain and simple. The reaction to this should clarify any doubts as to whether they are French or German in Alsace, since over 11 percent of the Pinot Gris submitted to my annual tasting at CIVA carried the Tokay designation, and that is the highest percentage I have encountered in five years!

• **Black Tie®** is a new, upmarket blended white wine produced by the Pfaffenheim cooperative. Intended to retail at €10, Black Tie consists of 60 percent Pinot Gris and 40 percent Riesling. If we are to believe the label, this is a selection of the best Pinot Gris and Riesling grown in the cooperative's not inconsiderable 235 ha of vineyards. The label is tastefully understated on a bottle that is tissue-wrapped and presented in a textured black gift box. While naturally suspicious of any wine that puts presentation and name first, I welcome such obvious marketing ploys in any instance that involves raising the standard of generic blends. Following the demise (in quality) of Edelzwicker, any attempt to raise standards can only be for the good.

• **At the 2005 *Decanter* World Wine Awards,** the Regional Trophy for the Best Alsace Riesling went to Pierre Sparr 2001 Riesling Grand Cru Schoenenbourg, and the Best Alsace Sweet Wine went to Schoenheitz 1998 Riesling Holder Vendanges Tardives Cuvée Adrien.

• **The 9th World Riesling Competition** was held in Strasbourg on March 8, 2005. There were exactly the same number of wines entered as last year (569), but from 16 rather than 11 countries. Of these entries, 61 received gold medals and just six were awarded trophies, three of which were from Alsace (Riesling Schiefferberg 2004 Willy Gisselbrecht, Riesling 2004 Joseph Moellinger, and Riesling Vendanges Tardives Vallée Noble 2002 Seppi Landmann).

Opinion:
Alsace lets its wines do the talking

My rant against the false god of "physiological ripeness" in *Wine Report 2006* attracted a lot of sympathetic correspondence from like-minded producers (not just in Alsace). The general consensus was that as long as enough dry wines are produced in Alsace, they (me included) have no argument with those who produce sweeter styles. However, concerns were expressed that if sweet wines are not confined to VT and SGN (or any other, specifically sweet-wine category), the traditional reputation of Alsace as a dry-wine region will become lost; and once it is lost, the Alsace wine industry will struggle on a sweet-wine image, since the market for such wines is so limited. Famous producers will still be able to sell sweet wines at high prices, but others will suffer.

Some correspondents complained about the "arrogance" of one very famous proponent of "physiological ripeness." As lesser-known growers without any export reputation, they felt powerless when slapped down by this particular producer, who made them feel ignorant of such basics as when to pick a grape. They thanked me for using Trimbach's world-class dry Riesling, Clos Ste-Hune, and Cuvée Frédéric Emile to demonstrate the fallacy of his words. No one can slap down Trimbach, whose example has encouraged many to remain true to their own ideals and not be seduced by the sweet-toothed god of "physiological ripeness." If others are seduced, they should at least be honest with themselves, come out of the candy closet, and declare themselves sweet-wine producers.

Some of these very same correspondents had noted my heading "Luxembourg: The New Alsace?" in the latest revision of *The Sotheby's Wine Encyclopedia* (DK, 2005) and online at wine-pages.com, but they wanted to let their dry wines do their own talking. At the time, it did not occur to me that this would result in any significant increase in the number of wines submitted to my annual tasting at CIVA. There are usually around 350 wines waiting for me, but in 2006 the number jumped to 432, mostly due to those growers who took the time to write to me, submitting their wines for the first time. I always find plenty of excellent Alsace wines to recommend, but the extra numbers pushed the standard up, especially for Pinot Noir. I wish I could tell you about the fabulous wines, both dry and sweet (and very sweet!) that failed to make the cut for this year's Top 10s, but you'll have to go to wine-pages.com for that!

Vintage Report

Advance report on the latest harvest

2005

A typically cold winter with hard frosts in December and January. A lack of rain between November and March reduced water reserves, potentially restricting yields. A wet and mild April encouraged an excellent budburst, followed by a perfect flowering in high temperatures at the end of May. Warm weather from mid-June until late July encouraged the vines to develop well. The first half of August was fine, and although the second half of the month was cold and varied, this helped preserve acidity levels. Fine, sunny weather from the end of August enabled the grapes to ripen in clean and healthy conditions, with humid conditions towards the end of the harvest promoting good botrytis. Overall, 2005 is better than 2004, with brighter fruit flavors. This vintage possibly vies with 2001 and 2002, but the wines need time to confirm precise qualities. As far as the grapes were concerned, Gewurztraminer was the best all-around performer, while Riesling was the most variable (however, some Rieslings were as good as the best Gewurztraminers). Pinot Gris was excellent. All other varieties good to very good. Ideal conditions for botrytis suggest excellent botrytized (as opposed to *passerillé*) VT and SGN.

Updates on the previous five vintages

2004

Vintage rating: *Red: 86, White: 87*

After the exhausting task of tasting more than 350 acid-deficient wines from 2003, it was a delight and a pleasure to taste over 430 wines from 2004, which is definitely a more classic vintage, with good fruit and excellent acidity levels. Not in the same class as 2002 or 2001, but it has a distinct edge over 2000 and is certainly fresher, fruitier, and more classic than 2003.

2003

Vintage rating: *Red: 93, White: 65*

There is no doubt that the oppressively hot year of 2003 provided an exceptional and extraordinary growing season, but apart from—potentially—Pinot Noir and a handful of anomalies, the quality is neither exceptional nor extraordinary. Ploughing through 350 wines from this vintage in March

2005 was one of the hardest, most unenjoyable, but academically most instructive tasting experiences of my life. Acidification was allowed by special dispensation, but not everyone took advantage and, of those who did, very few got it right, whereas many of those who did not acidify failed to produce wines of any elegance. Most are ugly with a deadness of fruit. Pinot Noir should be the star, but I have not yet tasted a glut of great Pinot Noir, although the optimist in me hopes that I will have more exciting news to report in the next edition of *Wine Report*. Putting to one side Pinot Noir, the most expressive 2003 grapes were Pinot Gris, which in fact looked as black as Pinot Noir on the vine and were made with a natural *vin gris* color.

2002

Vintage rating: *Red: 85, White: 89*

Although there is some variability in quality, the best 2002s have the weight of the 2000s, but with far more focus and finesse. Riesling definitely fared best and will benefit from several years' bottle-age, but Gewurztraminer and Muscat also performed well. The Gewurztraminers are very aromatic, with broad spice notes, whereas the Muscats are exceptionally fresh and floral. Pinot Gris was less successful. Some extraordinary SGNs have been produced.

2001

Vintage rating: *Red: 88, White: 90*

Most growers rate 2000 over 2001, but size is not everything, and this vintage has the finesse and freshness of fruit that is missing from most of the 2000 bruisers. The hallmark of the 2001 vintage is a spontaneous malolactic that endowed so many of the wines with a special balance. You hardly notice the malolactic in the wines. It's just a creaminess on the finish, more textural than taste, and certainly nothing that can be picked up on the nose. Although I'm an avid fan of non-malolactic Alsace wine, this particular phenomenon left the fruit crystal clear, with nice, crisp acidity.

2000

Vintage rating: *Red: 90, White: 80*

A generally overrated, oversized vintage, but with a few stunning nuggets. Lesser varieties such as Sylvaner and Pinot Blanc made delicious drinking in their first flush of life but have since tired. The classic varieties lack finesse, although some exceptional VTs were made. Excellent reds should have been made, but many were either overextracted or heavily oaked.

GREATEST WINE PRODUCERS

1. Domaine Zind Humbrecht
2. Domaine Weinbach
3. Trimbach (Réserve and above)
4. JosMeyer
5. Marcel Deiss (intensely sweet *complantage* wines only)
6. René Muré
7. Hugel (Jubilée and above)
8. Ostertag
9. André Kientzler
10. Léon Beyer (Réserve and above)

FASTEST-IMPROVING PRODUCERS

1. JosMeyer
2. Jean Becker
3. Hugel
4. Robert Faller
5. Lucien Albrecht
6. Paul Blanck
7. Albert Boxler
8. André Rieffel
9. Antoine Stoffel
10. Dirler-Cadé

NEW UP-AND-COMING PRODUCERS

1. Laurent Barth
2. André Kleinknecht
3. Leipp-Leininger
4. Gruss
5. Yves Amberg
6. Domaine Stirn
7. Jean et Daniel Klack
8. Clément Klur
9. Fernand Engel
10. Baumann-Zirgel

BEST-VALUE PRODUCERS

1. JosMeyer
2. Jean Becker
3. Lucien Albrecht
4. René Muré
5. Rolly Gassmann
6. Schoffit
7. Laurent Barth
8. Meyer-Fonné
9. Jean-Luc Mader
10. Paul Blanck

GREATEST-QUALITY WINES

1. ***Riesling Grand Cru Schlossberg 2004** Domaine Weinbach (€22)
2. **Riesling Grand Cru Geisberg 1995** Robert Faller (€24.50)
3. ****Riesling Grand Cru Brand Samain 1991** JosMeyer (€32)
4. ***Gewurztraminer Grand Cru Hengst 2004** Zind Humbrecht (€40.40)
5. ***Riesling Grand Cru Brand 2004** JosMeyer (€24.90)
6. ***Riesling Cuvée Frédéric Emile 2004** Trimbach (€30 – not yet released)
7. ****Pinot Gris Grand Cru Rangen 2004** Zind Humbrecht (€43.20)
8. ***Muscat Herrenweg 2004** Zind Humbrecht (€21.70)
9. ***Pinot Noir Elevé en Barrique 2002** André Kleinknecht (€10)
10. ***Pinot Noir M 2004** Laurent Barth (€12)

Grapevine

• **Laurent Barth** steams into number one in the New Up-and-Coming Producers with his first vintage, 2004, from 3.5 ha of organically farmed vineyards in Bennwihr. His Pinot Noir is the best 2004 tasted, while his 2004 Gewurztraminer Grand Cru Marckrain is another stunner. Its complex, fresh, spicy-peachy fruit makes it a great wine now, but it will be even greater in five years. An exciting new name making some excellent wines sold at sensible prices.

BEST BARGAINS

1. **Riesling Grand Cru Wineck-Schlossberg 2004** Clément Klur (€12)
2. ***Riesling Vieilles Vignes 2004** Gruss (€6.10)
3. ***Riesling Westerweingarten 2004** Anstotz (€6.20)
4. ***Riesling Grand Cru Schlossberg 2004** Domaine Weinbach (€22)
5. **Riesling Grand Cru Geisberg 1995** Robert Faller (€24.50)
6. ***Pinot Noir 2002** Yves Amberg (€6.30)
7. **Pinot Gris Grand Cru Marckrain 2002** Domaine Stirn (€9.80)
8. ***Muscat Domaine de la Tour Blanche 2004** Jean et Daniel Klack (€5.60)
9. **Gewurztraminer 2004** Leipp-Leininger (€9.50)
10. **Alsace E de Engel NV** Fernand Engel (€4.50)

MOST EXCITING OR UNUSUAL FINDS

1. ***Riesling Vieilles Vignes 2004** Gruss (€6.10) *High-quality, truly dry Riesling at an unbelievably low price.*
2. ****Riesling Grand Cru Brand Samain 1991** JosMeyer (€32) *This beautiful, petroly, off-dry, late-picked (but not vendange tardive) Riesling is a classic from the master of finesse in mature Riesling. JosMeyer's use of "Samain" indicates that the grapes were picked on November 11, St. Martin's Day.*
3. ***Gewurztraminer Grand Cru Hengst 2004** Zind Humbrecht (€40.40) *Truly dry Gewurztraminer was rare even before the pagan god of "physiological ripeness" was conceived, but at just 3.9 g of residual sugar, this 2004 is a* textbook example for New World devotees trying to achieve intense varietal character of this grape in a dry-wine format.
4. ***Riesling Grand Cru Schlossberg 2004** Domaine Weinbach (€22) *This truly dry Riesling has great purity, intensity, and finesse, demonstrating that Weinbach's "magic" exists beyond the veil of sweetness found in some of its other cuvées.*
5. ***Riesling Grand Cru Brand 2004** JosMeyer (€24.90) *Fascinating comparison with JosMeyer's 1991 Brand Samain, this wine is from the same vines— but not late-picked—13 years later.*
6. ***Pinot Noir Elevé en Barrique 2002** André Kleinknecht (€10) *One of the two best Alsace Pinot Noirs tasted this year—not from a high-profile name, and €3.50 cheaper than the lowest-priced Alsace Pinot Noir to grace this report in previous years. Needs to be cellared for two years.*
7. ***Pinot Noir M 2004** Laurent Barth (€12) *Even less well known, this is Laurent's first harvest! Equal in quality to above, and will improve but can be drunk now. Presumably "M" stands for Marckrain, a grand cru, thus not allowed on the label of a Pinot Noir.*
8. ***Pinot Gris Fondation 2004** JosMeyer (€21.60) *The best truly dry Pinot Gris tasted this year.*
9. ***Muscat Grand Cru Spiegel 2004** Dirler-Cadé (€11.60) *Not the quality of Zind Humbrecht's Herrenweg Muscat, but only two points adrift and 53 per0cent of its price.*
10. ***Crémant d'Alsace NV** Paul Zinck (€7) *The best Crémant d'Alsace tasted this year.*

*Notes: * Dry, ** Off-dry*

oire Valley

Charles Sydney

The current crisis in France's vineyards is creating a fascinating battleground for a face-off between market-conscious producers and an administration increasingly trying to protect itself by hiding in the past.

CHARLES SYDNEY

Essentially a fight for balance, this struggle is evident all along the Loire.

In Muscadet, the better growers increasingly use debudding, deleafing, and crop-thinning to ensure healthier, riper grapes. They now regularly pick at over 12 degrees natural potential alcohol and 4 g/l or so of acidity, completely changing the face of Muscadet to make wines that easily hold their own against the Loire's popular Sauvignons.

Less good producers are finding it ever more difficult to sell their wines, and the growers' *syndicat* calculated that supply is 10 percent greater than current demand. In the face of a relatively unsuccessful attempt to pay less profitable producers to rip up vineyards, the *syndicat* decided to reduce permitted yields by 10 percent for *sur lie* wines from an already serious 55 hl/ha.

In itself, the idea isn't bad, but doing it the week before harvest, a whole growing season after yields had effectively been determined through pruning, is mind-bogglingly stupid and will have absolutely no effect on the quality of the (excellent) 2005 vintage. What it will do is

CHARLES SYDNEY has spent more than 15 years in Chinon as a *courtier en vins*— a wine broker—specializing in the Loire Valley. Based at the heart of the region, he works exclusively on the export market, creating a partnership between the leading producers and the more forward-looking importers. He has an almost evangelical desire to encourage growers to make wines that appeal to the public, at the same time leaning on the specialized press to understand the sometimes dramatic changes happening in one of the richest and most diverse wine regions of the world.

prevent successful growers from selling 10 percent of their crop, condemning them to penury, since that 10 percent corresponds to their commercial margin—otherwise known as their salary. It might have been better to let markets force the incompetent to change jobs!

Modernists v. traditionalists

In Anjou-Saumur, the more committed *vignerons* are progressing in their bid to make world-class dry Chenins, with 2005 seeing them pick perfectly ripe, "golden" grapes, which are then fermented and matured in new oak, giving deeply complex and satisfying whites light-years ahead of the Anjou Blancs of the past.

Perversely, the INAO hasn't seen fit to grant them a new appellation and has refused them the right to use the name "Loire Renaissance." At the same time, it is working on the creation of two new village appellations in Saumur: Brezé for the whites and Le Puy Notre Dame for the reds. Because these villages are highly reputed for the *typicité* of their wines, the move would be laudable if not for the fact that the village name will be used for wines from any one of the 51 communes within the "generic" appellation of Saumur!

Farther upstream, massive strides have been taken to rid Loire reds of their "green, tannic, and herbaceous" tag by searching for genuine phenological ripeness. In a move first seen in Saumur-Champigny, growers in Chinon, Bourgueil, and St Nicolas have really started to push to make softer, less acidic, and more patently gulpable wines.

No longer happy to follow the *ban de vendanges* or potential alcohol to decide when to pick, these *vignerons* are increasingly using the ripeness of tannins in the seeds and skins as an indicator of the state of the harvest. With the lovely 2005s, you're going to see the tendency of ever-suppler wines go a step further even than in 2003 and 2004. And, for once, the *syndicats* are with them, with Chinon president Jean-Max Manceau and Fred Filliatreau in Saumur-Champigny helping lead the way forward.

Grapevine

• **You can't say** wine growers aren't constructive. After several years' work restoring a fine 15th-century house in the middle of the town, the *vignerons* of Sancerre have just opened the Maison des Vins de Sancerre—part tourist office, part museum, and part lesson in local geology. Their next step is a *jardin aux arômes* for the kids. Although they received some government money, the growers came up with 70 percent of the cash themselves.

THE BATTLE OVER
TERROIR

Not content with having micro-appellations like Touraine Noble Joué (that work), others like Amboise, Azay-le-Rideau, and Mesland (that don't), and the odd one like Cour-Cheverny and Orléans-Cléry (that frankly shouldn't exist), the move in the Touraine is to create even more village appellations.

So now there are plans afoot to create appellations for Chambord, Oisly, Seuilly, and Chenonceaux, less than a year after the famous Château de Chenonceau itself had to give up making wine, closing down its winery for lack of demand.

It's true that, in a market where both whites and reds sell for less than they cost to produce, something needs to be done, but the answer could be simple: emulate those growers who are creating markets by using good vineyard-management and winemaking techniques to make increasingly intense, aromatic, and complex Sauvignons.

Upstream in Sancerre and Pouilly Fumé, things are better. To reinforce their reputation, growers and *négociants* have signed a *charte de qualité* based on yield control, ripeness, and the quality of the harvest.

But the classic example of French bureaucracy is found at the eastern end of the Loire in tiny St-Pourçain. Here, as in Muscadet, the INAO reduced the permitted yield by 10 percent to 62 hl/ha, though it was less of a problem here, since Jacques Vigier, the cooperative director, had already reduced the average yield to below 50 hl/ha through enforced spring debudding and summer thinning.

Less amusing is this VDQS appellation's move to achieve full AOC status. To protect the "authenticity of the *terroir*," the INAO obliges producers to use the same percentage of varieties used prior to promotion. This year, the Cave produced a Pinot Noir with an intensity and fruit often lacking in "Big Brother" Sancerre—a result that owes much to a yield of just 44 hl/ha. But Jacques has a problem: he has to spoil everything by blending it with Gamay.

As if to rub it in, the growers were visited by the INAO chief for a pep talk on the benefits of the AOC. Perhaps a good idea, but telling these peasant farmers that, once they have full AOC status, they'll have no choice but to raise prices as whole new markets automatically open up ("There are a billion Chinese who'll want your wine simply because it's an *appellation contrôlée*") has to be one of the dumbest lines ever.

Welcome to France!

Grapevine

• **Gérard Depardieu**—the man foreigners must think is France's only actor—is rumored to be selling Château de Tigné in the Anjou after nearly 20 years. Maybe Mick Jagger could be interested? He already owns the (haunted!) Château de Fourchette up near Amboise.

Opinion:
A change for the better

It's time the wine trade learned to taste with their palate and nose and not with preconceptions. Recent massive improvements in the vineyard and winery have changed the Loire's Chenins and Cabernet Francs beyond recognition. So much so that we consider the "beeswax and quince" Chenins and "green-bean and lean" Cabernets to be made from unripe grapes—not just a thing of the past but actually faulty. So you can imagine how galling it is to hear press and buyers alike trot out the same old tasting notes.

But it's worse in Muscadet. In the past, growers thought they needed acidity (usually 6 g/l or more) to keep their wines fresh. Some people were picking so unripe that they couldn't pick by machine because the grapes were too hard to come off the vines. But the guys have grown up and they are picking riper and riper grapes, keeping all that freshness in by not taking the spritz out of the wine when they bottle *sur lie*. So it hurts to see tasting notes like "a great balance of fruit to acidity" for an unchaptalized Muscadet with just 3.5 g/l acidity. Come on, guys and gals—it's time to see just how good these wines can be!

Grapevine

- **Clear evidence** of the changes in France: the *vignerons* of Muscadet have just elected Pierre Chainier as president of the local CIVN *interprofession*. Pierre is not just a *négociant*, but a Touraine *négociant*. Worse still for anyone familiar with the old Clochemerle-esque partisanship of rural France, he's already president of the Touraine-Anjou-Saumur Interloire *interprofession*. Will wedding bells be ringing in the near future?

- **Pays Nantais producers** are proposing to rip up 2,500 ha of Muscadet and 1,000 ha of Gros Plant (out of some 13,000 and 3,000 ha, respectively) in an effort to balance supply and demand. Despite

compensation of more than €2,000 per hectare, so far only around 500 ha have been pulled up, with promises of 400 ha to come. But rather than paying people not to make wine, wouldn't the money be better used helping growers achieve the full potential of their wines by investing in an oenological advisory group like the SICAVAC in Sancerre?

- **Touraine growers** have sent more than 22,500 hl of excess production to be distilled, which makes some 3 million bottles of pretty well unsaleable 2004 wines we won't have to drink and makes space in their cellars for the excellent 2005 vintage

Vintage Report

Advance report on the latest harvest
2005

Right across the Loire, things were looking pretty good all year, with a hot, sunny spring and a summer spoiled only by the odd hailstorm in July hitting Vouvray and some villages of Sancerre.

Red—Since weather conditions were perfect, the vast majority of growers in Chinon, Bourgueil, and Saumur-Champigny waited to pick. A hint of rain in early October helped unblock the vegetation where it had suffered from drought. The result is a plethora of really soft, deep reds with wonderfully ripe natural *sucrosité* and appetizing freshness.

Muscadet—The good guys picked at high natural ripeness, with low yields and nicely balanced acidities, which keeps all the natural freshness of the CO_2 from the *sur lie* bottlings. There is a nice hint of yellow gold in the wines (a reflection of maturity) and loads of lovely fruit and natural *gras*.

Sauvignon Blanc—Growers in Sancerre, Pouilly, and the Touraine worked hard to control yields through spring debudding and an increased use of grassed-through vineyards. Most made a conscious effort not to let the grapes overripen, and the result is wines with great concentration, freshness, and real Sauvignon *typicité*. A few growers had problems with the end of fermentations.

Chenins—The grapes ripened beautifully, and in the Anjou in particular there are some wonderfully concentrated, intense, and pure dry Chenins made the "new" way with hand-picking, oak fermentation, and long *sur lie* maturation.

Sweet wines—In Vouvray and Montlouis there are some lovely *demi-secs* and more than enough *moelleux* to please, though few growers pushed ripeness much above 20 or 21 degrees at harvest, because they still have stocks of the great 2003.

Coteaux du Layon—After watching the crop ripen through *passerillage*, a weekend of rain at the end of October set off a concentration through botrytis that left growers harvesting virtually the entire crop by November 10, with perfectly balanced, fruit-filled *cuvées* coming in between 20 and 23 degrees and the occasional sticky at over 25 degrees.

Updates on the previous five vintages

2004

Vintage rating: *Red: 85, Muscadet: 95, Sauvignon: 80, Dry Chenin: 80, Moelleux Chenin: 80*

Unusually uneven. In the west, the Muscadets have great concentration and freshness, and the Chenins of the Anjou are delightful. The reds are balanced and fresh, on the lines of 2002. Farther east, things were more difficult. With the Sauvignons from the Touraine through to Sancerre and Pouilly, those growers who used newer techniques of vineyard management to keep yields low made attractive, *typé* wines from healthy grapes. The others had to sift through excessive quantities of unripe, rotten garbage. Stick to the good growers.

2003

Vintage rating: *Red: 95, Muscadet: 95, Sauvignon: 85, Dry Chenin: 90, Moelleux Chenin: 95*

One of the greatest-ever Loire vintages. Despite worries from outside the region that wines may be lacking in acidity, the Muscadets, dry and sweet Chenins, and the reds have concentration, fruit, and balance that surpass 1990 and 1997. The Sauvignons may have lacked aroma, but the top *cuvées* are lovely. Prices are still more than reasonable.

2002

Vintage rating: *Red: 85, Muscadet: 95, Sauvignon: 90, Dry Chenin: 90, Moelleux Chenin: 85*

Sauvignons are quite ripe, the Muscadets are of rare exception, and there are great Chenins: this is a superb year for dry whites—better than 1996. These are excellent wines for aging. The reds, which are healthy, solid, and lively, are equal to the 1996s or slightly lower in quality. Their limiting factor is, sometimes, reduced potential longevity, yet they are better than the average quality of the reds produced farther south in France.

2001

Vintage rating: *Red: 75, Muscadet: 80, Sauvignon: 85, Dry Chenin: 85, Moelleux Chenin: 75*

The dry whites, Chenin and Sauvignon, are better than in 2000, but not as exceptional as the 2002s, and they should be drunk up. The Pinot Noirs of Sancerre *et al* are extremely average, as indeed are the Cabernet Francs, most of which should be consumed between now and 2009. Generally, Bourgueil and Chinon will outlive Saumur-Champigny and St Nicolas de Bourgueil. Although it was, at the time, the best year for sweet wines since 1997, you should still stick to better producers for *moelleux* Chenins and look among the top *crus* of the Layon rather than Vouvray for finely balanced and intense stickies.

2000

Vintage rating: *Red: 80, Muscadet: 80, Sauvignon: 80, Dry Chenin: 80, Moelleux Chenin: 70*

Both the Cabernet Franc and Pinot Noir reds are ready to drink, in a soft style with gentle blackberry fruit. They look like the 1997s, but with more freshness of fruit. The whites are more heterogeneous, with Savennières (for Chenin) and Sancerre (for Sauvignon) the greatest successes.

GREATEST WINE PRODUCERS

1. *Jacky Blot, Domaine de la Taille aux Loups (Montlouis, Vouvray) and Domaine de la Butte (Bourgueil)
2. *Claude Papin, Château Pierre Bise (Anjou, Savennières, Coteaux du Layon)
3. *Didier Dagueneau (Pouilly Fumé)
4. *Jo Pithon (Anjou, Savennières, Coteaux du Layon)
5. *Vincent Pinard (Sancerre)
6. *Philippe Vatan, Château du Hureau (Saumur-Champigny)
7. Alphonse Mellot (Sancerre)
8. *Domaine Charles Joguet (Chinon)
9. Thierry Germain, Domaine des Roches Neuves (Saumur-Champigny)
10. Domaine Vacheron (Sancerre)

FASTEST-IMPROVING PRODUCERS

1. Château de Passavant (Anjou)
2. Philippe Pichard (Chinon)
3. Gérald Vallée, Domaine de la Cotelleraie (St Nicolas de Bourgueil)
4. *Domaine de la Paleine (Saumur)
5. *Denis Goizil, Domaine du Petit Val (Coteaux du Layon)
6. *Domaine Henri Bourgeois (Sancerre)
7. *Pascal & Nicolas Reverdy (Sancerre)
8. *Jean Douillard (Muscadet Sèvre & Maine)
9. Joël Ménard, Domaine des Sablonettes (Anjou, Coteaux du Layon)
10. Les Frères Couillaud (Muscadet Sèvre & Maine)

NEW UP-AND-COMING PRODUCERS

1 *Katia Mauroy, Domaine de Bel Air (Pouilly Fumé)
2 Antoine Souzay (Saumur-Champigny)
3 Clément Quintin (Coteaux du Giennois)
4 Arnaud Hérivault, Domaine d'Orfeuilles (Vouvray)
5 *Florian Mollet (Sancerre, Pouilly Fumé)
6 *François Crochet (Sancerre)
7 Vincent Ricard (Touraine)
8 *Stéphane Brancherau, Domaine des Forges (Anjou, Savennières, Coteaux du Layon)
9 Stéphane Sérol (Côtes Roannaises)
10 Stéphane Cossais (Montlouis)

BEST-VALUE PRODUCERS

1 *Rémi & Jean-Jacques Bonnet, Château la Tarcière (Muscadet Sèvre & Maine)
2 *Luc & Jérôme Choblet, Domaine des Herbauges (Muscadet Côtes de Grandlieu)
3 Les Frères Couillaud, Château la Morinière (Muscadet Sèvre & Maine)
4 Quintin Frères (Coteaux du Giennois)
5 *Cave du Haut-Poitou (Haut-Poitou)
6 Château Marie du Fou (Fiefs Vendéens)
7 Château de Passavant (Anjou)
8 *Jacky Marteau, Domaine de la Bergerie, Domaine Jacky Marteau (Touraine)
9 Cave des Vignerons de Saumur (Saumur)
10 *Claude Papin, Château Pierre Bise (Anjou, Savennières, Coteaux du Layon)

GREATEST-QUALITY WINES

1 **Coteaux du Layon Rablay Le Vilain Canard 2003** Domaine des Sablonettes (€25.60 per 50-cl bottle)
2 ***Sancerre Le Chêne St Etienne 2000** Domaine Henri Bourgeois (€50)
3 ***Pouilly Fumé Silex 2004** Didier Dagueneau (€50)
4 ***Vouvray Sec Clos de la Bretonnière 2004** Jacky Blot Domaine de la Taille aux Loups (Loire Valley, €10)
5 ***Coteaux du Layon Beaulieu Les Rouannières 2003** Château Pierre Bise (€15 per 50-cl bottle)
6 ***Saumur-Champigny Lisagathe 2003** Philippe Vatan Château du Hureau (€15)
7 **Saumur-Champigny Marginale 2003** Thierry Germain (€17)
8 **St Nicolas de Bourgueil L'Envol 2004** Domaine de la Cotelleraie (€11)
9 **Vin de Pays de la Vienne Ampelidae Le K 2003** Frédéric Brochet (€15)
10 ***Chinon Clos de la Dioterie 2003** Domaine Charles Joguet (€17)

BEST BARGAINS

1 ***Vouvray Sec Clos de la Bretonnière 2004** Jacky Blot Domaine de la Taille aux Loups (€10)
2 ***Savennières 2004** Château Pierre-Bise (€8.50)
3 ***Muscadet Sèvre & Maine Sur Lie La Levraudière 2005** Château la Tarcière (€3.10)
4 ***Muscadet Côtes de Grandlieu Sur Lie Le Fief Guérin 2005** Domaine des Herbauges (€4.20)
5 **Muscadet Sèvre & Maine Sur Lie 2004** Château la Morinière (€4.20)

⑥ ***Haut-Poitou VDQS Sauvignon 2005** Cave du Haut-Poitou (€3.52)

⑦ **Cabernet d'Anjou 2005** Château de Passavant (€4.50)

⑧ **Saumur Rouge Les Villaises 2003** Cave des Vignerons de Saumur (€5.70)

⑨ **Fiefs Vendéens-Mareuil VDQS Rosé 2005** Château Marie du Fou (€5.15)

⑩ **Coteaux du Giennois VDQS Sauvignon 2005** Quintin Frères (€5)

MOST EXCITING OR UNUSUAL FINDS

① ***Menetou-Salon Honorine 2004** La Tour St Martin (€13) *Remarkable quality for the difficult 2004 vintage. The wine is fermented and matured on its lees with bâtonnage in new oak. Using that much oak and succeeding with a balance of concentration, fruit, and freshness make this quite a treat.*

② ***Saumur Blanc Les Fresnettes 2004** Château de Targé (€11.50) *Good dry white Saumur is still pretty rare, but wines like this are starting to show a style distinct from the less defined Vouvrays and the heavier Anjou Chenins from schist. This was picked by hand, hyper-ripe (no botrytis) and fermented in oak. Edouard Pisani-Ferry is so excited by this style that he's been swapping parcels of Saumur-Champigny to get his neighbors' plots of Chenin.*

③ ***Saumur-Champigny Cuvée X 2004** Château de Targé (€15) *This Cabernet Franc was picked by hand with real phenological ripeness at around 14 percent. After a five-day maceration in stainless steel, Ed decanted it into 400-liter oak double barriques to ferment before leaving it to mature for a year in cask.*

④ **Fiefs Vendéens-Mareuil VDQS Rosé 2005** Château Marie du Fou (€5.15) *The Fiefs Vendéens is one of those regions I'd just about given up on until this wine turned up. Made from a mix of Pinot Noir, Gamay, and Cabernet Sauvignon (making it pretty well unique in the Loire), it looks good, it tastes good, and it's inexpensive.*

⑤ **Coteaux du Layon Rablay Le Vilain Canard 2003** Domaine des Sablonettes (€25.60 per 50-cl bottle) *Made by a mildly mad Joël Ménard, this is full of those lovely mandarin-confit flavors that come with perfectly ripened Chenin Blanc … but the vineyard isn't considered good enough for the AOC—hey, there's a bump of gravel on the schist—so it has been marked for declassification. Buy it while it lasts!*

⑥ ***Touraine Gamay Cuvée d'Eos 2003** Domaine Jacky Marteau (€9) *From one of the stars of the appellation, who just works at getting ripe, healthy grapes and then vinifying them properly. Made with 100 percent Gamay, this was just left to ripen and ripen and ripen, finally being picked by hand at 15 percent alcohol with an average of just 35 hl/ha. As well as being big, fat, and full, it keeps that essential Loire fraîcheur.*

⑦ **Vin de Pays de la Vienne Rosé Ampelidae Le χ 2004** Frédéric Brochet (€15) *χ as in Greek letter chi … and much better than anyone has the right to expect from "mere" Vin de Pays de la Vienne—which Frédéric Brochet is almost alone in using. Pink Pinot Noir, fermented in barriques and all very bio, with no chemicals in the vineyards. The only additive was a few milligrams of sulfur.*

❽ Touraine L'Effontée 2004
Vincent Ricard (€19 per 50-cl
bottle) *Hats off to Vincent for
succeeding in a difficult vintage for
Sauvignon Blanc. This one, picked
by hand, came in at 21.9 degrees
potential alcohol! Fermented and
matured in oak, it's lovely and
clean (no easy feat in 2004) and
fresh, despite having some 150 g
of residual sugar per liter.*

**❾ *Sancerre Les Monts Damnés
2004** Didier Dagueneau (€100)
*I've been waiting to see what
Didier would do in Sancerre since
watching him plant part of this
plot in the prime Monts Damnés
vineyard of Chavignol. Picked
by hand, the wine has all the
elegance and intensity I associate
with Didier's wines, with perhaps*

*an extra layer of fat coming from
that Kimmeridgean marl. To get
your hands on this wine, you'll just
have to go there and grovel!*

❿ Quincy Silice 2002 Jacques Sallé
(€17) *Jacques runs his 5.5-ha
vineyard according to biodynamic
rules, making hugely ripe
Sauvignon with a concentration
that is exceptional for Quincy's
sandy soils—a reflection of tiny
20-hl/ha yields and the age of the
vines, some of which go back to
1926. It is this concentration
that lets Jacques get away with
fermenting the wine in oak, which
merely adds yet another layer of
gras to the wine.*

* An asterisk indicates a producer with
whom Charles Sydney works as a courtier.

Grapevine

• Celebrations are off in top Coteaux
du Layon *cru* Chaume, which in 2003
was awarded *premier cru* status—the
first in the Loire. Two growers in
next-door Quarts de Chaume have
complained that the *premier cru* bit
could confuse the consumer and also
that they can no longer declassify their
wine "down" to Chaume (something
that no one has ever actually done).
Unfortunately, the Conseil d'Etat has
agreed with them. Most upsetting for
the Chaume growers is that those
who also have vines in the Quarts de
Chaume invariably put a lot of effort
into making this their top *cuvée*—
effectively working to justify the
Quarts de Chaume's claim to *grand
cru* status. Worse still, it seems that one
of the plaintiffs uses cryo-extraction
to be sure to make a *moelleux*.

• **The average size** of independent
estates is increasing as smaller, less
successful, and perhaps less efficient
growers call it a day—a repeat of the
consolidation and investment of the
mid-90s. But it's happening to big fish,

too. Having swallowed Muscadet-
based Vinival last year, giant Grands
Chais de France has bought Saumur
négociant and grower Lacheteau,
reputed locally for its sparkling
wines and internationally for its
provocatively named Kiwi Sauvignon.

• **Interloire hired a New Zealander,**
ex-Marks & Spencer buyer,
Languedoc winemaker, and consultant
Sam Harrop, to help growers of
Cabernet Franc to avoid making
"green-bean and lean" wines. Working
with a dozen producers in the region,
he made suggestions on harvest date,
cold maceration, use of yeasts, etc.
The ideas were fine, the methods
great—unfortunately, Interloire may
have chosen the wrong growers.
Domaine Lavigne in Saumur-
Champigny and Couly-Dutheil in
Chinon are both well aware of the
need to pick ripe: at both estates the
2005s came in at 13.9–15+ percent
alcohol. The wines are scrummy—
loads of red fruit and blackberries,
and not a bean to be seen.

Rhône Valley

Olivier Poels

Jaboulet has a new boss. The famous Jaboulet house, founded in 1834 and one of the most renowned names in the Rhône Valley, has been sold to Jean-Jacques Frey.

OLIVIER POELS

Frey, the Swiss businessman who owns Château La Lagune and has a 45 percent interest in Billecart-Salmon, continues to make acquisitions in the wine sector. The final price, which has not been revealed, was substantial enough to beat off a significant offer from the Guigal family, who were also interested in obtaining the domaine. The new owner has said he intends to maintain the existing team in place, notably the young generation represented by Laurent Jaboulet, who has been in charge of winemaking for several years now. The Jaboulet domaine is a superb vineyard, with a surface of around 100 ha, situated in the well-known appellations of the Rhône Valley, including the famous Hermitage. The La Chapelle *cuvée*, named after the Saint-Christophe chapel that overlooks the vineyard, is its flagship wine. Vintages such as 1961, 1978, and 1990 are among the most collectible bottles of the 20th century. A recent extensive and detailed tasting, however, showed weaknesses in some of the vintages of the 1990s. The situation improved in 2001, when a second label was introduced: La Petite Chapelle. The 2003 vintage has a very high profile and confirms that La Chapelle is back in the wine elite. Jaboulet's other *cuvées* include an excellent Côtes du Rhône, Parallèle 45, and a remarkable Crozes-Hermitage, Domaine de Thalabert, which delivers consistent high quality and is similar to Hermitage.

OLIVIER POELS is a journalist at *La Revue du Vin de France* and a member of the Comité de Dégustation. He also produces wine programs for French TV channel LCI and is coauthor of the *Guide Malesan des Vins de France* and *Classement des Meilleurs Vins de France*.

Irrigation: the crisis deepens

After several years of severe drought in the southern Rhône Valley, growers have again demanded a reexamination of the irrigation ban. Some areas in Lirac and Châteauneuf-du-Pape had no rainfall at all in the summers of 2003, 2004, and 2005. The dehydrated vines produced very low yields, and the grapes found it hard to reach maturity because of hydric stress. Growers fear the situation could get worse and claim that controlled irrigation in specific *terroirs* would not only provide more abundant harvests but would also increase quality.

Grapevine

• **Côte Rôtie producers** are not prepared to compromise when it comes to the proposed bypass around Lyon. The extension plans could affect a significant part of the appellation vineyards. They have decided to fight the controversial project and have already found hundreds of supporters from other wine regions in France, where petitions are circulating.

• **Domaine de la Mordorée** will release a new *cuvée* to pay tribute to the very high quality of the 2005 vintage. Following La Plume du Peintre, which celebrated the 2003 vintage in Châteauneuf-du-Pape, this special selection will be made from the vineyards located in Lirac. The expected volume of the *cuvée* is 3,000 bottles.

• **Jean-Pierre Perrin** of Château de Beaucastel was elected chairman of the Académie du Vin de France in 2005. In the present crisis, the association has a serious challenge ahead to defend growers' interests.

• **Hermitagé wine** is being revived by Michel Chapoutier. During the 18th and 19th centuries, Hermitage from the Rhône Valley was often added to barrels of bordeaux to give the wine more color and body—a technique that is now forbidden under AOC rules. Michel Chapoutier, in collaboration with Michel Rolland, the famous Pomerol winemaker, produced two barrels of *hermitagé* wine in 2005. The wine is top-quality Hermitage from Chapoutier blended with Pomerol from Château Le Bon Pasteur. This exceptional wine, which celebrates an old winemaking tradition, has been bottled in magnums and jeroboams, and will be sold on the Web in aid of the Chapoutier Foundation.

• **Two new *cuvées*** for the British market: Ted the Mule is a Côtes du Rhône from the winery Ogier; and Bizz is a good, inexpensive Grenache/Shiraz blend produced by the Cave de Cairanne for restaurants and bars.

• **Delas has invested €2 million** in a new winery and sales outlet at Saint-Jean de Muzols. Since 1977 this famous house has belonged to Champagne Deutz, which has itself taken over by Champagne Louis Roederer in 1993, since when there has been a marked improvement in quality, especially in recent years.

• **Philippe Jaboulet,** the 52-year-old general manager of Domaine Jaboulet Aîné until the business was sold to JJ Frey, is going to create his own domaine in Crozes-Hermitage. He has acquired 11 ha of Domaine de Thalabert's 45 ha and intends to buy more land in the appellation.

Opinion:
New *crus* on board

Announced unofficially in *Wine Report 2006* and now confirmed, Beaumes de Venise and Vinsobres have been promoted to *cru* status. At the same time, four villages—Puymeras, Plan de Dieu, Massif d'Uchaux, and Plateau de Sinargues—were admitted to the Côtes du Rhône Villages appellation. While this is good news for those who have waited for the recognition of typicity and *terroir*, it could be argued that creating more *crus* doesn't help the average consumer to comprehend the already complicated appellations in this region. There is at least one benefit of *cru* status: the positive impact it has on the quality of the wine produced, due to stricter regulations such as lower yields. However, is it worth spending time, money, and energy to obtain recognition for a village that no one can locate on a map, even in its own neighborhood? This cuts to the heart of the AOC debate, because although the system was originally very good, the burgeoning of new appellations is confusing to consumers and may ultimately have a negative effect on French vineyards. The world wants labels that are easy to understand, but some French producers still haven't gotten the message. As we say in France, *le mieux est l'ennemi du bien* (leave well enough alone).

Gallo not chicken

Gallo has signed an agreement with the Taillan Group, whereby Gallo will have exclusive distribution of Taillan's Côtes du Rhône (called Pont d'Avignon in the United States). The wine will sell at around €15 a bottle for a target volume of 6 million bottles. Again, the American firm has demonstrated its ability to win contracts—this time in competition with French wine traders—highlighting the French inability to address foreign markets and to compete with branded wines. Perhaps they spend too much energy in defending the interests of small villages (*see above*) and don't have enough stamina left for worldwide competition. So Gallo will promote Côtes du Rhône in the United States. There is little chance that the American consumer has ever heard of, or ever will hear of, Plan de Dieu or Massif d'Uchaux.

Vintage Report

Advance report on the latest harvest

2005

A rainy spring, a dry summer, and a bright, sunny September gave a winning ticket to the Rhône Valley in 2005. With a maturity that came early, this vintage has produced rich, though extremely balanced, wines. In the north (Hermitage, Côte Rôtie), the 2005s could match the excellent 1990s. In the south, the same conditions produced the same results: the Grenache is stunning, with a remarkable balance between alcohol, fruit, and acidity. Yields were generous, so wines will be widely available.

Updates on the previous five vintages

2004

Vintage rating: *Red: 91 (North: 82–90, South: 90–98),*
White: 88 (North: 80–90, South: 89–95)
After the 2002 rains and the heat wave of 2003, 2004 marked a return to a classic vintage in the Rhône Valley. Very favorable weather conditions during September produced very healthy, ripe grapes. The harvest schedule was normal: between September 6 and mid-October. Concentration is remarkable and alcohol levels are quite high, but the consequences of 2003 are still visible: yields are 20 percent lower than normal. In the south, the 2004s seem better balanced than the 2003s.

2003

Vintage rating: *Red: 95 (North: 90–97, South: 88–93),*
White: 89 (North: 83–90, South: 85–90)
The north had one of its earliest vintages. The south needed more patience, since drought delayed ripening. The grapes were perfectly healthy and quality was exceptional, despite a slight lack of acidity. The wines have high alcohol levels and very rich, mature tannins: the 2003s will keep for a very long time.

2002

Vintage rating: *Red: 70 (North: 70–75, South: 55–60),*
White: 73 (North: 70–75, South: 60–65)
Dramatic rainfall destroyed a large part of the harvest, especially in the Vaucluse region. An average vintage in the north.

2001

Vintage rating: *Red: 90 (North: 88–92, South: 85–90), White: 90 (North: 88–92, South: 88–90)*

A solid vintage in the north. Some wines are too acid and coarse, but the best are powerful and long. Some problems of dilution and tartness in the south.

2000

Vintage rating: *Red: 91 (North: 90–93, South: 90–93), White: 90 (North: 88–92, South: 87–91)*

Good but supple wines, with a lot of fruitiness in both parts of the valley. Most of the wines will not age very long.

GREATEST WINE PRODUCERS

1. Jean-Louis Chave (Hermitage)
2. Château d'Ampuis (Côte Rôtie)
3. M Chapoutier (Hermitage, Châteauneuf-du-Pape)
4. Château de Beaucastel (Châteauneuf-du-Pape)
5. Henri Bonneau (Châteauneuf-du-Pape)
6. Tardieu-Laurent (Cuvées Vieilles Vignes)
7. Clos des Papes (Châteauneuf-du-Pape)
8. Domaine de la Janasse (Châteauneuf-du-Pape)
9. Domaine Jamet (Côte Rôtie)
10. Domaine du Vieux Télégraphe (Châteauneuf-du-Pape)

FASTEST-IMPROVING PRODUCERS

1. Domaine de la Mordorée (Châteauneuf-du-Pape)
2. Domaine Clos du Caillou (Châteauneuf-du-Pape)
3. Yves Cuilleron (northern Rhône)
4. Domaine du Colombier (northern Rhône)
5. Domaine Yann Chave (red wines)
6. Domaine de la Présidente (Châteauneuf-du-Pape)
7. Ferraton Père & Fils (Hermitage)
8. Domaine de la Citadelle (Côtes du Lubéron)
9. Pierre Coursodon (St-Joseph)
10. Domaine du Tunnel (St-Péray)

NEW UP-AND-COMING PRODUCERS

1. Domaine Renouard (Costières de Nîmes)
2. Domaine Les Bruyères (Crozes-Hermitage)
3. Domaine Montirius (Vacqueyras)
4. Domaine des Martinelles (Crozes-Hermitage)
5. Domaine Saint Roch (Lirac)
6. Domaine de Piaugier (Côtes du Rhône-Villages)
7. Domaine du Trapadis (Côtes du Rhône-Villages)
8. Cros de la Mûre (Châteauneuf-du-Pape)
9. Domaine Longue Toque (Gigondas)
10. Château de Rozier (Costières de Nîmes)

BEST-VALUE PRODUCERS

1. Domaine de la Citadelle (Côtes du Lubéron)
2. Domaine la Réméjeanne (Côtes du Rhône)
3. Domaine des Amadieu (Côtes du Rhône-Villages)

④ Perrin & Fils (Côtes du Rhône)

⑤ Cave des Vignerons d'Estézargues (Côtes du Rhône)

⑥ Marcel Richaud (Côtes du Rhône-Villages)

⑦ Château des Nages (Costières de Nîmes)

⑧ Domaine Les Gouberts (Gigondas)

⑨ Château Val Joanis (Côtes du Lubéron)

⑩ Château Mourgues du Grès (Costières de Nîmes)

GREATEST-QUALITY WINES

① **Ermitage L'Ermite 2003** M Chapoutier (€180)

② **Châteauneuf-du-Pape Cuvée Spéciale 2003** Tardieu-Laurent (€60)

③ **Côte Rôtie La Mouline 2001** E Guigal (€300)

④ **Hermitage La Chapelle 2003** P Jaboulet (€50)

⑤ **Châteauneuf-du-Pape 2003** Château de Beaucastel (€40)

⑥ **Côtes du Rhône-Villages Rasteau 2003** Gourt de Mautens (€32)

⑦ **Condrieu Côte de Vernon 2003** Georges Vernay (€45)

⑧ **Châteauneuf-du-Pape 2003** Domaine du Vieux Télégraphe (€30)

⑨ **Châteauneuf-du-Pape 2003** Clos des Papes (€30)

⑩ **Châteauneuf-du-Pape Vieilles Vignes 2003** Domaine de la Janasse (€50)

BEST BARGAINS

① **Côtes du Rhône Terre d'Aigues 2004** Marcel Richaud (€4.50)

② **Côtes du Lubéron 2003** Domaine de la Citadelle (€8.40)

③ **Côtes du Rhône 2004** Domaine de la Mordorée (€6.10)

④ **Coteaux du Tricastin 2003** Château La Décelle (€8)

⑤ **Crozes-Hermitage Les Croix 2003** Domaine Les Bruyères (€10)

⑥ **Côtes du Rhône Villages Kayyâm 2004** Mas de Libian (€7)

⑦ **Vin de Pays de la Principauté d'Orange 2004** Domaine de la Janasse (€8)

⑧ **Crozes-Hermitage Vieilles Vignes 2003** Domaine du Murinais (€10)

⑨ **Vacqueyras Réserve des 2 Monardes 2004** Domaine La Monardière (€9.50)

⑩ **Crozes-Hermitage Château de Curson 2004** Etienne Pochon (€13.50)

MOST EXCITING OR UNUSUAL FINDS

① **Costières de Nîmes Scamandre 2003** Domaine Renouard (€14) *An incredible Costières de Nîmes, very deep and full-bodied.*

② **Ermitage L'Ermite 2003** M Chapoutier (€180) *A minerally and complex wine produced from tiny yields.*

③ **Châteauneuf-du-Pape Cuvée Spéciale 2003** Tardieu-Laurent (€60) *No new oak for this special cuvée, but very old Grenache (over 100 years). It pays homage to the great CDPs of the past.*

④ **Vacqueyras 2003** Domaine Montirius (€11.50) *In its brand-new winery, Domaine Montirius is now at the top, as this richly fruity and expressive wine shows.*

⑤ **Condrieu Côte de Vernon 2003** Georges Vernay (€45) *An incredible Viognier—simply the best expression of the appellation.*

⑥ **Côtes du Rhône Villages Kayyâm 2004** Mas de Libian (€7) *An excellent Côtes du Rhône, which gives pure fruit pleasure.*

⑦ **Côtes du Rhône Terre d'Aigues 2004** Marcel Richaud (€4.50) *Marcel Richaud is the star of Cairanne. All his wines are renowned and sought after by connoisseurs.*

Jura & Savoie

Wink Lorch

For the tiny wine regions of Jura and Savoie, developing links with tourism, particularly with local restaurants, is deemed the most important defense against the growing crisis in the French wine industry.

WINK LORCH

The Jura is revamping its Route du Vin for an official relaunch in 2007. A new brochure listing hotels, restaurants, and tourist sites, as well as producers in the area, was produced for summer 2006. Growing in popularity is the biennial Fête de Ploussard in Pupillin (2006), which alternates with the Fête de Trousseau in Montigny les Arsures (2007) over the third weekend in August. In 2005, the Fête de Trousseau included a gastronomic lunch prepared by top local chefs to match a series of Trousseau wines—it was sold out on both days. A new tourist initiative is a "picnic with the *vigneron*" event, held for the first time in June 2006. The participating *vignerons* will supply picnicking facilities and, of course, samples of their wine. Jazz bands and other entertainments are promised, too.

In Savoie, there is a less cohesive initiative, but the importance of tourism is recognized as crucial. They, too, have a Route du Vin for the main vineyard areas, but the Comité Interprofessionnel recognizes a need to forge closer links with restaurants and hotels, of which few are actually in the vineyard areas. One noble exception is the Auberge les Morainières, a small restaurant in the heart of the Jongieux region on the slope of the

WINK LORCH is a wine writer and educator with a passion for the mountains and a chalet in the Haut-Savoie. She is a past chairman of the Association of Wine Educators and has contributed to several books, including Time-Life's *The Wine Guide*, *The Global Wine Encyclopedia*, and Le Cordon Bleu's *Wine Essentials*. Wink particularly enjoys enthusing about wines from vineyards in sight of snowcapped mountains, whether the Andes, the Alps, or the Jura. She divides her time between London and the French Alps.

Marestel *cru*. A tastefully restored building, it is an ideal place to enjoy a range of good Savoie wines, including Marestel, by the glass.

In both Jura and Savoie, the emphasis that local restaurants place on their regional wines is a matter for concern. With the exception of the top restaurants, where chefs pride themselves on matching local produce with wines from the area, many more modest restaurants offer a simple list of appellations and/or grape varieties with no indication of producer or vintage. Often these come from one *négociant*, because it makes life easier for the restaurateur. Markups on the local wines may be excessive. Louis Magnin of Savoie spotted one of his top wines, which sells at the cellar door for €15, listed at €65 in a restaurant in Megève. On the other hand, Christophe Menozzi, a top sommelier in the Jura, commented that *vignerons* do not make enough effort to communicate with the local sommelier groups, and despite initiatives from the sommeliers inviting *vignerons* to tastings, few make time to attend.

Local grapes: new studies

Fall 2005 saw the very basic laboratory at the Syndicat des Vins de Savoie in Chambéry housing no fewer than 60 demijohns bubbling away, the first micro-vinification exercise of this size from clonal trials of Mondeuse, Altesse, and Jacquère. Roussanne (known as Bergeron in Savoie) and the unusual black Persan grape were also micro-vinified, but there was insufficient crop to keep the clones separate. Savoie suffers from a lack of clonal diversity, which is why the trial was set up. In particular, it is hoped to establish the best new clones of Mondeuse and Altesse, since these are most often chosen for new plantings. Growers are planting less of the rather bland Jacquère grape (the most planted variety) and the ubiquitous Gamay and Pinot Noir, as demand for the more interesting Mondeuse and Altesse wines increases.

In the Jura, a report published in February 2006 specified the best *terroirs* for growing the Trousseau grape (thought to be identical to Portugal's Bastardo), following a detailed survey by retired geology professor Michel Campy, together with Christian Barnéoud of the Chambre d'Agriculture de Franche-Comté. Traditionally, Trousseau has been considered best when grown in the clay-rich gravel outcrops in the northern part of the Arbois appellation around Montigny Les Arsures. A late ripener, it needs a light-textured soil. With increased demand for the variety, and only around 100 ha planted, the study aimed to test its suitability elsewhere in the region.

Fifteen plots growing mature Trousseau, situated from the far north to the far south of the Jura, were examined geologically, and a blind tasting of

2004 wines from each plot confirmed that the fullest styles of Trousseau are produced around Montigny. There is plenty of potential for lighter wines in other areas, however, because these are enjoyed by local consumers. The report should serve as a blueprint for *vignerons* across the region who want to expand their holdings or even plant this local variety for the first time.

Château-Chalon site classified

The AOC Château-Chalon vineyard area was formally recognized in January 2006 by the French ministry for ecology and sustainable development as a "classified site." A charter known as the *chartre de Fontrevaud* was signed by local representatives agreeing to protect the landscape and the wine of Château-Chalon. This step is a precursor to being recognized by UNESCO. Château-Chalon now belongs to the exclusive club of classified historic vineyards, in company that includes St-Emilion, the Douro, and Tokaj.

Dumping spat

Dumping of *vin jaune* by Jura *négociants* has caused fury among Jura producers. In March 2005, two local supermarket chains were selling *vin jaune* for just €11.20 per clavelin (62-cl bottle), compared to a normal price of €20–30. Vine growers protested to the supermarkets, explaining that production costs could not be covered at this price and demanding that the price be raised to a more realistic level of at least €15. Growers marched into the offending supermarkets, intending to take the bottles from the shelves, but the supermarket had already removed them. Later they reappeared at a higher price. In the fall 2005 wine-fair season, *vins jaunes* were once again on sale at below €12.

Grapevine

• **Ovarius,** a new decanter designed by Jura physicist Michel Patois and Jura sommelier Christophe Menozzi of restaurant Le Comtois in Doucier, was launched in 2005. Made from hand-blown glass and shaped like a wide-based teapot with an erect spout, it is ideal for young wine and *vin jaune*, which need plenty of aeration in a very short time. A few minutes in the decanter is all it takes, since the shape acts as a particle accelerator. Stamped on the decanter is the equation $Ec = \frac{1}{2}mv^2$.

• **Crémant du Jura** sold in 2005/06 has been granted a special derogation by the INAO to spend only nine months (instead of 12) *sur lattes*. This follows the very small 2003 vintage and is the second time this derogation has been granted in the past five years. Crémant is one of the most successful AOCs in the region, but apparently this leeway won't be allowed again.

Opinion:
Jura needs a cohesive approach

The Jura is undoubtedly the most complicated wine region in the world in terms of its plethora of wine styles. Crémant du Jura and *vin jaune* are the only styles where one knows what to expect; the reds, whites, and *vins de paille* are hugely varied, depending on grape variety and vinification styles. Reading the label or looking at a wine list rarely gives any indication of style.

Most Jura producers hand-sell a significant proportion of their wines at the cellar door or at tasting *salons*. But how is anyone supposed to choose a Jura wine off the shelf, or from a wine list? I have put this question repeatedly to Alain Baud, president of the Jura Société de Viticulteurs. It seems that the Jura *vignerons* cannot agree on the terms to use on their labels, and back-label explanations remain purely voluntary. Baud sees no prospect of change here. He also points out that INAO policy forbids naming grape varieties on the label. Many Jura producers have been flouting this for years, and Baud hopes for official authorization to use varietal labeling.

Each year I taste more and more Jura wines that I believe would excite international palates: Chardonnays to rival burgundy; fresh Savagnins that tingle with lemony acidity and match a range of foods wonderfully; Trousseau and Pinot Noir reds with depth of fruit yet refreshingly lightweight; luscious *vin de paille* or sweet wines sold under other designations. But what chance is there of anyone outside the region discovering these wines if they are not described properly? They will remain confined to the cellars of certain restaurants and a select group of curious consumers unless the growers (and the INAO) agree to give more descriptive labels.

Savoie has to raise its game

Savoie, too, has wines that are improving, but once again few people get to know about these for two main reasons. First, the average quality of certain wines, in particular from the largest *crus*, Apremont and Abymes, and from some of the *négociants*, is too low. These are the wines most often drunk by visitors to the French Alps, and one bad experience is likely to put them off Savoie wines forever. The growers have been encouraged to reduce yields, but this has still not gone far enough. Too many wines are weak and insipid, whereas the best growers demonstrate that very decent wines can be made. Second, there is a lack of regional promotion, especially toward avid wine consumers. Growers in the Combe de Savoie area have formally complained to the Syndicat des Vins that the Comité des Vins de Savoie (CIVS) is not doing enough to promote the region's wines. The CIVS works with French journalists to promote the region, but it does not do enough with the public. For the future of the region, promotion must be improved to justify growers' charging the higher prices they need to sustain lower yields and greater work.

Cerdon authenticity under threat

Misuse of the term *méthode ancestrale* remains a problem for Bugey. Bugey Cerdon VDQS is the only quality *rosé* sparkling wine to be made by the *méthode ancestrale*, and the region is asking the INAO to restrict the term *méthode ancestrale* to quality (AOC and VDQS) wines. This would outlaw wines such as the Boisset-owned Pellin Rosé Vin Mousseux Demi-Sec, labeled "Méthode Ancestrale" and made from bought-in Gamay.

Grapevine

● **Jean Rijckaert,** the *négociant* and grower based in the Mâconnais, can sleep soundly at night now that he has proved his commitment to the Jura region by hiring a full-time assistant based near Arbois to oversee both vineyards and vinification in the Jura.

● **The Fruitière Vinicole d'Arbois,** the largest wine cooperative in the Jura and one of the first in France, celebrated its 100th anniversary in 2006. Formed by 31 *vignerons* following the phylloxera crisis, it has 111 members farming about 25 percent of AOC Arbois. It has also announced that it will join forces with the much smaller Fruitière (cooperative) in Poligny. To celebrate the occasion, 100 bottles of Arbois wines were locked up for 100 years in the walls of Château Béthanie, the co-op headquarters.

● **From 2007,** *vin jaune* from AOCs Arbois, Côtes du Jura, and Etoile is likely to undergo *agrément* tasting and analytical tests before bottling after its six years of maturation. This is one of the measures of the rewritten AOCs for the region likely to have been approved by mid-2006. It follows similar measures taken in 2004 for AOC Château-Chalon (a *vin jaune* by definition).

● **Vendange Tardive** is a designation sought by the Syndicat des Vins de Savoie in their rewritten AOCs. Increasing numbers of Savoie *vignerons* make a late-harvest wine from Jacquère, Altesse, or Bergeron (Roussanne) but are not allowed to use the term on labels.

● **Vins du Bugey** have a good chance of being promoted from their current VDQS status to AOC for the 2006 vintage. At the time of writing, the official rubber stamp is being eagerly awaited, after more than 10 years of battling. The proposals have already been approved by the regional INAO, and growers are likely to be highly demotivated if promotion is not granted by the Paris-based INAO.

Vintage Report

Advance report on the latest harvest
2005

Jura—Following two contrasting and extreme vintages, growers were relieved to have a normal and healthy growing season, albeit fairly dry and hot compared to the average. It was quite an early harvest and weather remained good throughout the picking period, extended by some of the best growers to the latter half of October. Crucially, unlike 2003, acidity was maintained, and this, combined with good concentration and modest yields, promises extremely well for all varieties and styles of wines.

Savoie—Unusually, growers had little to complain about in this vintage. True, August was rather cool and wet at times, giving a few disease problems for the usual culprits, Gamay and Pinot Noir, but September and October provided glorious, dry, warm, and sunny weather. Perfect picking conditions allowed patient growers to wait as long as possible to pick the late-ripening Mondeuse grapes. This has ensured better physiological ripeness than usual, even if (as ever) this variety needs quite hefty chaptalization. Most whites from Bergeron (Roussanne) and Altesse grapes did not need any chaptalization. The wines of all varieties promise well, with good balance of fruit and structure.

Updates on the previous five vintages
Ratings for vin jaune *and* vin de paille *are included in the scores for white wines.*
2004

Vintage rating: *Jura—Red: 80, White: 82; Savoie—Red: 74, White: 78*

Jura—After a wet summer, September was dry and warm. Crop levels were high and selection was crucial to have any chance of making good wines. Much Chardonnay was picked for Crémant, and the grapes were also sufficiently healthy for drying for *vin de paille*. Savagnins were picked at good sugar and acidity levels, crucial for *vin jaune*. Green-harvesting was practiced by many growers with black varieties, and the resulting Trousseau wines show particularly well from good producers; other black varieties were less successful.

Savoie—Extremely dry until the second week of August, but then rain arrived in abundance, and by early September, growers were under pressure from disease. But the harvest was saved later in the month with constant fine, sunny weather that dried out the rot. Excess quantity was a problem, but the grapes were generally healthy and sugar levels were extremely reasonable. Late varieties Altesse, Jacquère, and Mondeuse did best, and those growers who were selective have produced reasonably concentrated wines. However, overall, this is not an exciting vintage.

2003

Vintage rating: *Jura—Red: 86, White: 76; Savoie—Red: 83, White: 81*

Jura—The harvest was around five weeks earlier than normal, and quantities were down 30 percent. Dealing with low acidity was a big challenge, especially for Savagnin wines destined for *vin jaune*, which need to withstand nearly seven years of aging. Other 2003 whites were ready early, though some producers were still loath to bottle early: this is a very atypical vintage with some overripe fruit flavors sometimes taking away any *jurassien* character. However, reds, for once, are actually red in color and taste of ripe fruit!

Savoie—The hot, dry conditions led to an early harvest of supremely healthy grapes that required extremely careful cellar handling, especially of low acidity levels. Low quantities of Chignin Bergeron and Altesse (for Roussette de Savoie) mean that few wines are still available. However, the best producers made deliciously fruity whites, which still retain some alpine freshness. Mondeuse can be overtannic despite the high level of fruit.

2002

Vintage rating: *Jura—Red: 86, White: 90; Savoie—Red: 79, White: 77*

Jura—A period of fine weather in fall gave overall good quality. Nearly all varieties showed both good natural ripeness and high acidity levels. This bodes well for *vin jaune* in the future. Chardonnays are proving excellent, with good weight and balance. Trousseau reds are good, too.

Savoie—Good late September weather saved the harvest, following a difficult August. Mondeuse did well in places, with some good results. Altesse is varied, though some interesting late-harvest versions have been made.

2001

Vintage rating: *Jura—Red: 65, White: 73; Savoie—Red: 60, White: 68*

Jura—A difficult, fairly small, and variable vintage. AOC Château-Chalon was declassified, but some decent *vin jaune* should be produced. Other wines show variation, but some elegant and balanced Chardonnays and Savagnins were made.

Savoie—Medium-quality vintage, especially difficult for reds, but some reasonable whites made.

2000

Vintage rating: *Jura—Red: 79, White: 83; Savoie—Red: 79, White: 85*

Jura—A good-quality vintage overall, with attractive fruit characteristics and reasonable structure but some lack of concentration, often due to high yields. Whites continue to age well.

Savoie—A good year overall, with concentrated Bergeron and Altesse. All but the finest Mondeuse wines need drinking now.

GREATEST WINE PRODUCERS

Jura
1. Domaine André & Mireille Tissot
2. Domaine Labet Père & Fils
3. Jacques Puffeney
4. Jean Rijckaert
5. Domaine Jacques Tissot
6. Domaine Berthet-Bondet
7. Domaine Ganevat

Savoie
1. Domaine Prieuré Saint-Christophe
2. Domaine Dupasquier
3. André & Michel Quenard

FASTEST-IMPROVING PRODUCERS

Jura
1. Domaine Pignier
2. Domaine Ligier Père & Fils
3. Domaine de la Renardière

4. Frédéric Lornet
5. Domaine de la Tournelle

Savoie
1. Jean-Pierre & Philippe Grisard
2. Denis & Didier Berthollier
3. Jean-Pierre & Jean-François Quenard
4. D&P Belluard
5. Domaine Jean Perrier & Fils (Haute Sélection Gilbert Perrier range)

NEW UP-AND-COMING PRODUCERS

Jura
1. Domaine de la Borde
2. Rémi Treuvey
3. Jean-Marc Brignot

Savoie
1. Gilles Berlioz
2. Domaine Saint-Germain
3. Domaine Genoux

BEST-VALUE PRODUCERS

Jura
1. Daniel Dugois
2. Domaine Rolet
3. Domaine Baud Père & Fils
4. Château Béthanie, Fruitière Vinicole d'Arbois

Savoie
1. Domaine de l'Idylle
2. Edmond Jacquin & Fils
3. Domaine Jean Vullien & Fils
4. Cave du Prieuré
5. Pascal & Annick Quenard
6. Cave de Chautagne

GREATEST-QUALITY WINES

Jura: *The 1998 vin jaune and Château-Chalon still need at least five years' aging. The other whites are of burgundian (non-oxidative) style to drink from now.*

1. **Château-Chalon 1998** François Mossu (€28 per 62-cl bottle)
2. **Arbois Vin Jaune 1998** Domaine Jacques Tissot (€28 per 62-cl bottle)
3. **Château-Chalon 1998** Domaine Berthet-Bondet (€28 per 62-cl bottle)
4. **Côtes du Jura Savagnin Cuvée Privilège 2003** Domaine Ganevat (€13)
5. **Arbois Chardonnay Les Bruyères 2003** Domaine André & Mireille Tissot (€13.80)
6. **Côtes du Jura Chardonnay Les Varrons 2002** Domaine Labet Père & Fils (€11)

Savoie
1. **Vin de Savoie Mondeuse Tradition 2003** Domaine Prieuré Saint-Christophe (€15)
2. **Chignin Bergeron Saint Anthelme 2004** Denis & Didier Berthollier (€9)
3. **Roussette de Savoie Cuvée Prestige et Tradition Elevé en Fûts 2004** Jean-Pierre & Philippe Grisard (€7)
4. **Roussette de Savoie Marestel 2003** Domaine Dupasquier (€7)

BEST BARGAINS

Jura
1. **Côtes du Jura Chardonnay 2002** Domaine Rolet (€7.50)
2. **Arbois Pupillin Savagnin Ouillé des Plantées 2004** Domaine de la Borde (€7.50)
3. **Côtes du Jura Fleur de Savagnin 2002** Domaine Labet Père & Fils (€9)

Savoie
1. **Vin de Savoie Pinot Noir 2003** Domaine Dupasquier (€5.30)
2. **Chignin Mondeuse Vieilles Vignes 2004** André & Michel Quenard (€6.10)
3. **Vin de Savoie Mondeuse Les Taillis 2004** Domaine Saint-Germain (€5.50)
4. **Roussette de Savoie Marestel 2004** Cave du Prieuré (€7.20)
5. **Vin de Savoie Mondeuse La Saxicole Prestige 2003** Domaine de l'Idylle (€8.50)
6. **Roussette de Savoie Château de Monterminod 2004** Domaine Jean Perrier & Fils (€7.50)
7. **Roussette de Savoie Marestel 2004** Edmond Jacquin & Fils (€8)

Grapevine

- **Residual sugar levels** of chaptalized Savoie whites will be limited to 6 g/l for Vins de Savoie and 8 g/l for Roussette de Savoie if new AOC proposals are passed.

- **La Percée du Vin Jaune 2007**, the annual weekend festival in Jura, will take place on February 3–4, 2007 in the historic town of Salins les Bains. A record 50,000+ visitors attended the event in Lons le Saunier in February 2006.

MOST EXCITING OR UNUSUAL FINDS

Jura

① **Mélodie Arbois 2004** Domaine André & Mireille Tissot (€40 per half-bottle) *An icewine made from Savagnin grapes picked between 4 and 7 am at an unusually low 14°F (−10°C) on December 22. At 11 percent alcohol it is incredibly delicate; sweet but with wonderful acidity and apricot/lemon flavors.*

② **Côtes du Jura Chardonnay A la Percenette 2004** Domaine Pignier (€9) *Pignier's first foray into "Burgundian-style" Chardonnay. The fruit has great purity, perhaps because the domaine is in conversion to biodynamic methods, and this works well with light use of fairly new oak barrels.*

③ **Arbois Pinot Noir 2003** Jacques Puffeney (€11) *From this extraordinary early vintage, 60-year-old Pinot vines produced a very low yield. Fermented and aged in foudres for one year and then transferred to second- and third-fill barrels. A resounding success, giving a delicious Pinot.*

④ **Arbois Trousseau Singulier 2004** Domaine André & Mireille Tissot (€12) *Quite simply one of the most intense Trousseaux I've ever tasted. Stéphane Tissot vinified this special parcel from low-yielding vines separately to produce a singular wine, fermented in conical wooden casks and aged in demimuids (600-liter barrels).*

⑤ **Côtes du Jura Les Goulesses 2003** Sylvie & Luc Boilley (€13) *This supremely balanced and flavorsome red is from an old parcel of Trousseau, complanted with a little Poulsard. The vintage gave wonderful concentrated fruit, yet there is a lively character to the wine, too.*

⑥ **Arbois Grain de Folie 1997** Domaine de la Pinte (€30) *La Pinte owns relatively large proportions of Savagnin and makes several styles. Its folie was to keep this wine in barrel for seven years (the length of time for vin jaune) but keeping the barrels topped off, giving an interesting, intensely flavored result.*

Savoie

① **Vin de Savoie Ayze Gringet 2004** D&P Belluard (€7.50) *The tiny cru between Geneva and Chamonix specializes in sparkling wines from the Gringet grape (related to Traminer). This, however, is the best still wine from Ayze, made from vineyards partly in conversion to biodynamic methods.*

② **Vin de Savoie Arbin Mondeuse Harmonie 2004** Les Fils de Charles Trosset (€8) *Trosset is often cited in lists of the best Mondeuse wines. The domaine never returns my calls, so I've never visited. But, for the first time, one of their purchased wines did very well in my blind tastings.*

③ **Vin de Savoie Trilogie 2004** René & Béatrice Bernard (€6.50) *This serious Apremont producer had some Marsanne in its vineyard, which has been hidden away in their wines for years. Before the Marsanne was uprooted, a special wine was produced, blending it with Chardonnay and Jacquère. Lovely yellow fruit flavors.*

④ **Vin de Savoie Chignin Bergeron Le Bergeron d'Elisa 2004** Jean-Pierre & Jean-François Quenard (€14 per half-bottle) *Increasing numbers of Chignin producers leave some grapes to make a late-harvest Roussanne (Bergeron) wine. Some noble rot has given a delicately honeyed wine. Not sweet enough to match dessert; delicious on its own.*

Southwest France

Paul Strang

Bomb scares are hardly everyday events in the southwest, but a meeting of 300 Cahors growers in the sleepy town of Luzech was delayed for an hour while the venue was searched for explosives.

PAUL STRANG

Jacques Bex, president of the local Chamber of Agriculture, was given the hot seat as umpire at this get-together, to which every Cahors grower had been invited in the expectation of a vote on the future of the structure of the appellation. Bex had hoped to put a plan to them all, but the opposing *syndicats*, one representing the independent growers and the other the *coopérateurs*, had not been able to agree on the plan among themselves, let alone recommend it to their members. One group, called Expression des Terroirs, was at daggers drawn with another, called The Committee for the Rebirth, in which the ubiquitous Vigouroux clan are big players. The disputes all seem linked to byzantine local politics in which the aims of those concerned are impossible to discern.

Meanwhile Cahors is in crisis, with nobody apparently willing to address the real problem, which seems remote from the arguments about structures: what to do about the price of the wine, which often has to be sold by the growers at a loss. The Council of the Lot has voted a once-and-for-all sum to help the situation, but it will be forthcoming only if the growers can get their act together, which seems a forlorn hope; furthermore, it will be linked to promotion rather than relieving hardship.

PAUL STRANG is recognized as one of the leading experts on the wines of southern France, where he has had a home for more than 40 years. He is the author of *Wines of Southwest France* (Kyle Cathie, 1994), which was shortlisted for the Drink Book of the Year by the Glenfiddich awards. Another book, *Take 5000 Eggs* (Kyle Cathie, 1994) deals with the markets, fêtes, and fairs of southern France and was also short-listed for Glenfiddich in 1997.

Cahors' problems go back a long way. Some say that the appellation rules admitted land that was not capable of yielding quality wine, and that the rules should be altered to eliminate inferior *terroirs*. That idea goes over like a lead balloon, of course, and was the immediate cause of Perrin (Château Lagrézette) retiring hurt from the fray. Others say that the one cooperative at Parnac let them down through lack of imaginative management at a crucial time. Others blame the big local *négociants* for abusing their position by becoming important growers themselves with an accent on marketing, which conflicted with their position as representatives of other growers. Yet others blamed invaders from outside, restaurateurs, jewelers, and other businessmen with no experience of winemaking themselves but who saw the possibility of making money out of an appellation that had boomed during the 1970s. All these groups have caused confusion by producing different styles of wine, the market as a result having little idea of what Cahors is supposed to be, except that the false tag of "black wine" still lingers. It is all the more surprising that a handful of good growers, many of whom are from families that go back to pre-phylloxera days, still fly the flag in the hope that one day someone will sort out the problems of what should be the most successful area in the southwest.

Elsewhere in the region, appellations where growers manage to work with, rather than against, each other go from strength to strength. Jurançon, for example, is finding a place in the world market that distinguishes its wines from other stickies by promoting the good acidity of its grape varieties, Gros and Petit Manseng. Rivalry is friendly, with producers holding joint tastings and meetings to discuss each other's wines and compare technical notes on work in the vineyard and *chais*.

Grapevine

• **Jean-Baptiste Monpezat,** brother to the prince consort of the Queen of Denmark, may be quitting his Château Léret-Monpezat in Cahors and moving to the UK with his English wife. A few years back, Monpezat was obliged to seek the help of Georges Vigouroux in trying to restore the fortunes of his vineyard, and Vigouroux took a controlling interest in the wine operation. Monpezat retained his château with a modicum of surrounding land, but he will presumably be seeking a buyer, and Vigouroux can be expected to gain complete control in the vineyard. Léret-Monpezat is one of the dwindling number of the so-called Seigneurs Cahors, a grouping that is already substantially under Vigouroux control.

ONE HAIL OF A DAY

Friday the 13th was bitterly unlucky in May 2005 for many growers in Bergerac, where more than 400 ha of vines, mainly in the southern part of the appellation, were all but destroyed. The villages of Eymet, Sadillac, Singleyrac, and Ribagnac were so badly hit by hailstones the size of cherries that any chance of a harvest was destroyed at a stroke. As many as 100 growers were affected: Luc de Conti, Richard Doughty, and the Girardets at La Maurigne suffered serious damage. Storms also destroyed the crop of François Avallon at Entraygues and Peraldi at Domaine des Thermes in the Côtes du Brulhois. A reminder that in a year generally thought to be first class, some growers can so easily lose out.

ALL CHANGE AT PECHARMANT

Daniel Hecquet, in what he calls "a moment of folly," has bought La Métairie, and Château Theulet in Monbazillac has bought Les Bertranoux. Ten years ago both these estates were high fliers, but their owners have died. Madame Pécou, formerly associated with Bertranoux, has set up on her own as Château d'Elle with a small vineyard of but 2 ha. Over at Château de Tiregand, the long-established Saint-Exupéry family is restructuring its vineyard with much denser plantation and is taking the opportunity of introducing more Malbec into the *encépagement*. Daniel Costes, Bergerac's answer to Michel Rolland, is consultant here.

BRUMONT BOUNCES BACK

Alain Brumont, whom many had written off on account of his business troubles, has typically bounced back. Despite a brush with the courts, an injection of capital from Crédit Agricole should keep the Brumont ship afloat for at least seven years. He is slimming down his range of wines to the *entrée-de-gamme* Torus (very good it is, too), Montus Prestige, Bouscassé Vieilles Vignes, and the flagship Le Tyre. No more basic Montus or Bouscassé, though Brumont will continue to develop a range of wines that bridge the AOC/*vin de pays* gulf, using local grape varieties.

Grapevine

- **The craziness** of the strict application of appellation rules cannot be better demonstrated than by the case of Thierry Casse of Domaine Barbazan in Madiran. The statute requires that a grower is restricted to a maximum of 60 percent Tannat in the parcels of vine qualifying for AOC, even though many growers pride themselves on making a pure Tannat wine as their *tête de cuvée*. Thierry has other grapes, but they are not yet mature so cannot be counted as part of the total. He has, however, produced an excellent 100 percent Tannat wine but is not allowed to call it Madiran and is obliged to label it as a *vin de pays*.

Opinion:
Varietal labeling arrives

Better late than never: the wine bureaucrats have at last conceded the right—in some areas, at least—of growers to put the name of the grape variety (or varieties) they have used on the label.

This may add to the confusion in the public conception of the southwest, where many of the grapes have names unknown to the great world outside: Mansois in Marcillac, Duras and Len del'El in Gaillac, Négrette in Fronton, and so on. But food-labeling regulations require manufacturers to list all the ingredients in their products, even if most people could not tell you what ascorbic acid is. It may not be good marketing for front labels to be weighed down with factual information to the detriment of pretty design, but surely back labels, instead of containing a lot of flowery poetry (which seems to be a French specialty), could at least indicate the *encépagement* of the wine.

What kind of oak?

The phrase *élevé en fûts de chêne* does not mean much on its own (except that the wine will cost extra); the buyer is surely entitled to know whether the barrels are new, old, or a mixture of the two, and for how long the wine has been aged in them. He or she might then have a fairer idea of the kind of wine to expect.

BIB catches on

Bag-in-box is all the rage in the southwest; even distinguished growers are offering a range of wines in this format. True, the quality of the wine is what matters, and most growers will not bag up their best *cuvées*. True, too, that there is some difference of opinion about how long the wine will last in the bag, even before it is broached. All the same, the idea has caught on, especially in the 5-liter size, which is ideal for the refrigerator.

Grapevine

• **Fabien Olaiz,** the energetic young Basque in charge of export marketing at Producteurs Plaimont, tells me that the *cave* is anxious to forge links between its member-growers and its English customers. Thirty of the growers are therefore seriously studying English, which is quite extraordinary in view of the general reluctance on the part of growers in the Midi to speak anything other than French or Occitan. It is intended that many of the growers will welcome Anglophones to their vineyards and *chais*—a truly unique initiative by a cooperative.

Vintage Report

Advance report on the latest harvest

2005

After a wet winter, the rain stopped at Easter and many parts of the region had no more until the first week of September, when suddenly 6 in (150 mm) fell in 24 hours, causing widespread flooding. The buds had broken on time and flowering was punctual, but the continued drought had gradually caused a blockage in the flow of juice from the roots to the fruit. What looked like an early harvest took place on time and, for the most part, in excellent conditions. A Bergerac grower writes, "2005 seems for the moment to have all the characteristics to be found in a great vintage; exceptional concentration as much in color as in acidity, with high sugar levels. In short, there is plenty of everything. What is a bit disturbing is the heavy pressure such a vintage brings on the winemaker, and it would be easy to fall into caricature. I have therefore chosen the path of moderate extraction to show off the weight of the vintage without it becoming too overwhelming. We will see in a few months' time." Reds and whites seem to have profited equally from the conditions, save where hail and storms wrought their strictly local damage. In Jurançon and Madiran, the usual Indian summer was punctuated with showers, but these may have enhanced the quality of the wines rather than the reverse.

Updates on the previous five vintages

2004

Vintage rating: *Reds: 88, Whites: 85, Sweet: 86 (90 in Jurançon)*

The earlier part of the growing cycle had been warm and dry, ensuring regular development of the fruit without too much interference. The rains in August were welcome at first; but damp, humid weather persisted beyond the point where spraying was possible. The crop remained surprisingly healthy and the harvest was abundant, too much so perhaps. The dry whites show more acidity than usual, though with sometimes less fruit; the reds could well develop much better than expected. Very late sunshine saved the day for the sweet wines. A year that could bring surprises in due course.

2003

Vintage rating: *Reds and Whites east: 68, further west: 85, Sweet: 92*

This was the notorious heat-wave year, in which the southwest suffered worse than any other region. Drought was compounded by extraordinarily hot sun, which grilled the fruit on the vines. Early-picking reds were disappointing, lacking acidity and phenolic development, but rich in ripe fruit, which will call for early drinking; some growers voluntarily declassified their wines. Later pickers, particularly in the hills of the east of the region and in Madiran and Irouléguy, did much better, profiting from mid-September rain. A splendid fall yielded magnificent sweet wines throughout, although the acidity indispensable in Jurançon was often lacking.

2002

Vintage rating: *Reds and Whites Cahors and westward: 85, eastward: 75, Sweet: 89*

The farther west, the better the wines—a sudden burst of late sunshine in September producing a rise in sugar levels west of the A20, sometimes causing almost welcome problems. Fronton, Gaillac, and Marcillac never really recovered from a cool midsummer, though all areas made above-average sweet wines.

2001

Vintage rating: *Red: 90, White: 85, Sweet: 88*

An excellent year, now proving even better than expected, especially where growers were able to guard against low acidity and high sugar levels. The wines seem to be keeping better than at first thought, too. Still at their peak, though the sweet whites will continue to improve.

2000

Vintage rating: *Red: 88, White: 85, Sweet: 92*

A very good year all around, the sweet whites being exceptional. The reds are mostly well balanced with enough tannins to ensure continued improvement.

Grapevine

• **Didier Dagueneau** has at last introduced his Jurançon to the market. He withheld his 2003 while he launched a lawsuit against his cork supplier, but the 2004, fully up to the hype, has just been released in tiny and expensive quantities (see "Most exciting or unusual finds" list).

GREATEST WINE PRODUCERS

1. Clos de Gamot (Cahors)
2. La Tour des Gendres (Bergerac)
3. Domaine Elian Da Ros (Marmandais)
4. Domaine Tirecul-la-Gravière (Monbazillac)
5. Domaine Arretzia (Irouléguy)
6. Domaine Cauhapé (Jurançon)
7. Domaine de la Ramaye (Gaillac)
8. Clos Triguedina (Cahors)
9. Domaine Cosse-Maisonneuve (Cahors)
10. Domaine Capmartin (Madiran)

FASTEST-IMPROVING PRODUCERS

1. Domaine Mouthes-les-Bihan (Côtes de Duras)
2. Clos de Verdot (Bergerac)
3. Domaine de l'Ancienne Cure (Monbazillac)
4. Domaine Causse-Marines (Gaillac)
5. Clos d'Yvigne (Saussignac)
6. Château Terre Vieille (Pécharmant)
7. Château de Tiregand (Pécharmant)
8. Château de Bloy (Montravel)
9. Domaine Ameztia (Irouléguy)
10. Château Masburel (Montravel)

NEW UP-AND-COMING PRODUCERS

1. Didier Dagueneau (Jurançon)
2. Château Masmontet (Montravel)
3. Château Condom-Perceval (Côtes de Duras)
4. Domaine de l'Homs (Cahors)
5. Château d'Elle (Pécharmant)
6. Domaine de Mioula (Marcillac)
7. Domaine des Coteaux d'Engravies (Vignerons Ariégeois)
8. Domaine Lancement (Vin de Pays de Thézac-Perricard)
9. Domaine Lou Gaillot (Vin de Pays de l'Agenais)
10. Domaine du Bois Simon (Coteaux du Brulhois)

BEST-VALUE PRODUCERS

1. Producteurs Plaimont (Côtes de St Mont)
2. Château Jonc Blanc (Montravel)
3. Château Barréjat (Madiran)
4. Château Palvié (Gaillac)
5. Château Plaisance (Fronton)
6. Château les Ifs (Cahors)
7. Château Miaudoux (Saussignac)
8. Domaine de Gouyat (Montravel)
9. Château Latuc (Cahors)
10. Château Meyragues (Gaillac)

GREATEST-QUALITY WINES

1. **Gaillac Vin d'Autan 1989** Vignobles Robert Plageoles et Fils (€30)
2. **Cahors Clos St Jean 2001** Gamot (€20)
3. **Bergerac La Gloire de mon Père 2000** Luc de Conti (€25)
4. **Gaillac Le Combe d'Avès 2000** Domaine de la Ramaye (€13)
5. **Monbazillac Cuvée des Monstres 1998** Thierry Desprès (€40)
6. **Cahors Prince Probus 1998** Clos Triguedina (€15)
7. **Marmandais Clos Baqueys 2001** Domaine Elian Da Ros (€15)
8. **Madiran Cuvée du Couvent 2000** Domaine Capmartin (€10)
9. **Cahors Les Lacqueys 2001** Domaine Cosse-Maisonneuve (€15)
10. **Madiran Cuvée Charles de Batz 2001** Domaine Berthoumieu (€10)

BEST BARGAINS

1 **Entraygues Blanc Sec 2003**
Domaine de Méjanassère (€4.50)

2 **Marcillac Lo Sang del Païs
2004** Domaine du Cros (€4.50)

3 **Cahors Tradition 2002**
Domaine de Paillas (€8)

4 **Pécharmant Tradition 2001**
Clos les Côtes (€5)

5 **Fronton Cuvée Don Quichotte
2002** Domaine le Roc (€9)

6 **Côtes de Duras Sauvignon
2004** Domaine de Laulan (€5)

7 **Fronton Cuvée Prestige Rouge
2002** Domaine Baudare (€6)

8 **Bergerac Rouge Tradition 2003**
Domaine de Libarde (€3)

9 **Côtes de Gascogne Blanc
Moelleux 2003**
Domaine le Bouscas (€5)

10 **Madiran Cuvée Joris 2003**
Château Laffitte-Teston (€5)

MOST EXCITING OR UNUSUAL FINDS

1 **Jurançon Les Jardins de
Babylone 2004** Didier Dagueneau
(€40 per 50-cl bottle) *More
than well worth waiting for,
Dagueneau's first vintage in
Jurançon, a mere 8,000 bottles
or so, shows all his skill as a
master winemaker. He manages
to bring to the deep south a
touch of his native Loire.*

2 **Buzet La Badinerie du Pech
2002** Domaine du Pech (€10)
*Since Magali Tissot took over from
her father in 1997, she and her
partner Ludovic Bonnelle, bio
producers to the nth degree, have
made this the outstanding
property in the appellation.*

3 **Côtes du Brulhois Cuvée Dothi
2004** Domaine des Thermes (€6)
*There is a buzz about this
appellation, where the use of
Tannat and Fer Servadou serves*
*to distinguish the wines from the
Bordeaux satellites adjoining.*

4 **Madiran 100 percent Tannat NV**
Domaine Barbazan (€6) *A talented
newcomer waiting for AOC status
(see Grapevine), producing an
elegant and relatively easy Madiran
next door to Domaine Pichard.*

5 **Madiran 2003** Château de Viella
Ricaut (€8) *A single-domaine
(4 ha only) wine from Plaimont, in
which the aim of vinification is to
accentuate the fruit and minimize
the tannins, while preserving the
Madiran character. Should be
ready in 2007.*

6 **Saussignac Cuvée Coup de
Coeur 2000** Richard Doughty
(€15) *Exciting to rediscover this
pioneer in Saussignac who is not
allowing himself to be crowded out
by less worthy newcomers.*

7 **Pécharmant Cuvée Veuve
Roches 2001** Domaine du Haut-
Pécharmant (€9) *A powerful wine
with a deal of Cabernet Franc
and a very firm structure. The
wine needs 10 years in all to
show its best.*

8 **Côtes de Duras Sauvignon
2005** Domaine de Petit-Malromé
(€4) *A splendid interpretation of
this well-worn grape, the wine
aged on its lees and having
wonderful bite. Another bio grower.*

9 **Marmandais Le Vin est une
Fête/Vignoble d'Elian Entrée
du Gamme 2003/4** Domaine
Elian Da Ros (€7) *The name of
the wine changes each year, so
does its style, depending on Elian's
caprice, hence it is always
surprising and exciting.*

10 **Rosette 2004** Domaine de
Coutancie (€4) *This diminutive
subappellation of Bergerac is having
a comeback, and here is one of its
best. All that a moelleux should be,
and a perfect summer apéritif.*

Languedoc-Roussillon

Paul Strang

"Low alcohol, we're French," pleads consultant oenologist Michael Paetzold in a surprising move to induce growers to produce lower- rather than higher-alcohol wines.

PAUL STRANG

According to Paetzold, the French, at a time of public health considerations and more Draconian drunk-driving laws, are turning to "lighter" wines to win back the taste of a certain sector of the public. Growers in the south are still, after 20 years, producing wines of ever-increasing alcoholic power (16 degrees being not uncommon in the 2003 vintage). They may, however, be out of step with French consumer fashion. The reduction in yield resulting from overmaturity of the grapes has certainly allowed a general improvement in quality, but at the same time it has encouraged greater concentration of sugar, and thus of potential alcohol. The use of energetic yeasts in the vinification has not exactly compensated.

Following experiments to see whether various grape varieties could express their distinctive and expressive aromatic qualities at lower strength, Paetzold has become the prophet of dealcoholization, bringing levels down from 14.5 degrees to 11. He describes the process as a kind of osmosis, akin to that used to desalinate salt water. First, the wine is submitted to high pressure in a fine membrane, which enables the alcohol to be separated from the juice; the separated alcohol and juice are then put into different containers. The volume of the alcohol is adjusted by

PAUL STRANG is recognized as one of the leading experts on the wines of southern France, where he has had a home for more than 40 years. He is the author of *Wines of Southwest France* (Kyle Cathie, 1994), which was shortlisted for the Drink Book of the Year by the Glenfiddich awards. Another book, *Take 5000 Eggs* (Kyle Cathie, 1994) deals with the markets, fêtes, and fairs of southern France and was also shortlisted for Glenfiddich in 1997.

adding back as much as may be necessary to bring it to the required level. According to Paetzold, the molecules of the wine are not affected; it would require a pressure of more than 3,000 bars to change their makeup, he says.

Such a process is not, strictly speaking, permitted in France, but this has not stopped rebel Vincent Pugibet from giving it a shot. He says that the limited amount of irrigation he is allowed to give his grapes (all grown in non-AOC vineyards) has not reduced alcohol levels by as much as he would have liked, so he has adopted the new osmosis idea experimentally. He has started making a fantastically aromatic pure Chardonnay that measures a mere 9 degrees of alcohol in bottle. There may be some loss of complexity and power, but there are signs that French opinion considers there are more gains to be made on the everyday swings than on the more sophisticated roundabouts.

New techniques call for investment and some growers are pressing the French government to legislate to legalize the process. David Boissier, marketing director at rebranded Listel, says that the new style is very popular with women and young people. Pugibet claims it is so thirst-quenching that it could help relaunch wine consumption in France and solve the problems of overproduction. "Anyway, a low-alcohol wine does not get in the way of anyone who wants to produce *vins de gastronomie*," he says. It remains to be seen how the market responds.

Down in Roussillon, Gauby has his doubts about tinkering with wines in this way. He says he manages to make wines that have all the hallmarks of his *terroir* without making them rise much above 12 degrees. Others persist in the mistaken idea that the more alcohol the better, but perhaps their days are numbered?

Grapevine

• **More and more growers** are turning to organic production in the Midi. Gold medals have recently been won at international bio competitions by Domaine Jolliette for its white Côtes Catalanes Vin de Pays 2002, Domaine de la Rourède for both its Rivesaltes Ambré Blanc 2002 and its Muscat de Rivesaltes 2004, Vignobles Montfreux de Fages AOC Coteaux du Languedoc for its Cuvée des Pères Rouge 2001, and by Château des Auzines Corbières Hautes Terres Rouge 2003.

• **Côtes du Roussillon Les Aspres AOC** has been on sale since January 2005. The wines must be domaine-bottled and aged in bottle for at least a year before being marketed. Their logo is a large white pebble with "A" on it. As with Côtes du Roussillon Villages, at least three grape varieties must go into the blend, and Cinsault cannot be one of them.

WINE TO DYE FOR

Hard on the heels of the Carignan revival, Alicante Bouschet is the next once-despised *cépage* of the Languedoc to claim the attention of adventurous growers. Traditionally it was regarded merely as a vulgar *teinturier*—one of those few black grapes that produces red juice. In 1829, at the beginning of the great 19th-century boom in Languedoc, a *teinturier* from the north was crossed with Aramon to obtain a hybrid called Petit Bouschet. It gave color to the then weak wines of Languedoc but not alcohol, so the next step was to cross the new hybrid with Grenache. The result was Alicante Bouschet (Alicante being a synonym for Grenache), a *teinturier* grape that resists heat and drought, is early-maturing, and is easy to grow. Its yields, however, must be strictly controlled if the Alicante Bouschet is to produce a wine of any quality.

Arnaud Warnery of Domaine de l'Ocelle at Saint-Christol has started to prune his Alicante Bouschet so hard that the yields are brought back to 35 hl/ha, but he claims that the real secret with this grape is to allow the fruit to wither on the vine and to dry out before harvesting. He says that the wine develops more aromas and finesse and that the tannins, sometimes quite fierce in this variety, soften nicely. The wine has fashionable minerality and will keep well.

Many others believe in late harvesting. Bousquet at Pech-Redon, best known for his lovely La Clape wines, today vinifies his Alicante Bouschet by *macération carbonique* and leaves it on its lees for four months. The result is a wine of silky *gourmandise*. Philippe Rustan at Mas d'Aimé is another, but he vinifies his like a white wine with direct pressing and barrel-fermenting. Michel Guiraud at Roquebrun also picks late. He calls his wine Le Sirop.

A more conventional style is the latest line at Château Ollieux Romanis, with its 110-year-old vines yielding a mere 25 hl/ha of peppery wine with a flavor of black cherries. According to Olivier Jullien, "There are no bad grape varieties, just people who don't know how to grow them."

Grapevine

• **If you were concerned** that Olivier Jullien had abandoned making white wine (his were some of the best white Languedocs), you may be comforted by the news that he has bought a new vineyard of 80-year-old white Carignan. Olivier has always been keen on swapping vineyards with his neighbors, so the latest move should come as no surprise. Carignan Blanc is on its way to becoming the cult white grape, being the foundation of the white wines at Conte de Floris, for example. Other evangelists of this *cépage* include Robert and Kim Cripps at Domaine de Poujol, Julien Zemott at Le Pas de l'Escalette, and Steve and Martine Colombe, newcomers at Domaine Pic Aubeil down in Roussillon.

FIRST *CRU* FOR CORBIERES

Corbières-Boutenac is the first *cru* of Corbières to be given official recognition. The name may be used for hand-harvested wines produced in the communes of Boutenac, Montseret, Saint-Laurent de la Cabrerisse, Fabrezan, Ferrols, Ornaisons, and Luc sur Orbieu, all in the north-central part of the appellation. Boutenac includes such well-known names as Grand-Crès, Canos, Roque-Sestières, Aiguilloux, Fontsainte, Grand Moulin, and La Voulte-Gasparets. It also houses the main Syndicat de Producteurs as well as a busy cooperative.

Corbières-Boutenac is restricted to red wine only, and grape varieties permitted reduced to just Carignan, Grenache Noir, Syrah, and Mourvèdre, which might be expected, but the percentages of Carignan and Syrah are interesting and perhaps prophetic. Carignan must account for between 30 and 50 percent of a grower's black grapes, and Syrah is subject to a maximum of 30 percent of a vineyard. The wine must be a blend of at least two varieties, of which one must be Carignan, a variety particularly suited to the Boutenac *terroir* because of its warm, if very windy, climate. Following the example of Boutenac, Sigean and Lagrasse look likely to be the next *crus* of Corbières to gain recognition.

Grapevine

• **Recent invaders of the region** include (again) Bernard Magrez, who has bought the 22-ha domaine La Magnanerie at St-Chinian, where he has asked the famous Alain-Dominique Perrin, controversial winemaker from Cahors, to help him (Perrin already buys in wines from Languedoc for which he acts as *négociant*); Vincent Sauvestre of Maison Béjot at Meursault, who has bought Château Boutignane at Lagrasse in the Corbières, a 70-ha domaine with a *cave* said to have been designed by students of Eiffel; and Ortwin Kandler, former director of Airbus Industries, who has bought Château Tourril in the Minervois.

• **A new kind of 340-liter barrel** called Muid d'Oc has recently been launched by Séguin-Moreau. It is thought to be the ideal size for the aging of the finest wines of the south. It was tested by 15 or so growers, among them Cyril Chamontain at Château de Négly in La Clape, on their 2002 and 2003 vintages before being launched on the market. Many growers of Grenache and Carignan have found that there is a loss of fruit as well as a risk of excessive oxidization in conventional 225-liter barrels. Hence, there is a demand for larger containers with thicker staves, where the effect of oxygen is slower and the character of the fruit is better preserved. The rather smaller ratio of wood to volume also helps prevent an intrusive taste of oak. The size also makes the cask easier to handle than the more conventional, though larger, *demi-muid*.

Opinion:
Respect the *terroir*

The "crisis" in Languedoc has attracted so much attention from the media, where Francophobia is shamefully rife, that it is easy to cast the wine producers in the role of head-in-the-sand idiots.

The real problem lies with French consumers and their government. In the first few years of this millennium, the percentage of French men and women who never drink wine has risen by a third—from 30 percent to 40 percent of the adult population. Fewer people give up wine when they have become accustomed to drinking it than those who never take it up in the first place; the problem lies largely with the drop in new recruits.

There is a mistaken perception that France is losing out in world trade, but French wine exports have largely held up in terms of volume, though market share has fallen. This fall in market share is not surprising, since no country could dominate the vastly enlarged international wine market the way French wine did 30 years ago. The real problem for French growers is that they need to fill the gap caused by the collapse of their internal market.

One way of achieving this might be to address the tastes of younger drinkers. In addition to lower-alcohol wines, a new market is being exploited by the production of *vins de soif* with sexy labels and packaging. There is already a vogue for what has been termed "Les Petits Rouges." These need not necessarily be low-alcohol wines; Michel Escandes, son of one of Minervois's stars, says these do not correspond with his philosophy. He produces a pinkish red (at 13 degrees) *saigné* from ultra-ripe Mourvèdre—fruity with gentle tannins and meant to be drunk cool, and packaged in a clear glass bottle with a capsule closure. Others following suit include distinguished domaines such as Virgile Joly (Joly Rouge—geddit?).

The problem for Languedoc growers is that French drinkers have not been persuaded that the Midi can produce wines of real quality, which is why cooperatives in 2005 had still not sold half of their previous year's production. Many producers have started copying the New World in an attempt to expand exports overseas. But French consumers, even in the Midi, are none too keen on New World styles, so growers have the problem of trying to serve two masters at once—something that is technically and logistically difficult both in vineyard and *chai*. Hence the multiplicity of *cuvées* that growers in the south tend to produce.

Lovers of good wine will hope that the better independent growers, who seem to be managing the crisis better than most, will stick to the basis of their success—a loyalty to their *terroir* and producing what suits it best, without trying to distort nature. New arrivals from other winemaking areas, French or otherwise, should study local conditions and traditions before trying to make wines in their own non-Languedoc image. They don't often work.

Those who cannot sell their wines to their fellow Frenchmen will have to learn from colleagues such as Pierre Clavel, who manages to export 80 percent of his production. Producers are beginning to realize that the best markets (the Netherlands, Germany, the UK, and Switzerland) are reacting against the blockbuster styles with which Midi growers were bombarding them 10 years ago, and that such wines are a betrayal of *terroir* rather than the best interpretation of it. This is why the INAO and ONIVINS, instead of laying down hard and fast rules about which grapes should go into which AOCs and in what proportions, should recognize that growers want to grow those varieties that best suit their *terroir*. Furthermore, not all the rules are equally relevant within the entirety of any given appellation.

Grapevine

• **The decrees** for the new appellations St-Chinian Blanc and the two communal appellations St-Chinian Berlou and St-Chinian Roquebrun all became effective from the 2004 vintage, but the reds could not be sold under their new names until January 2006. For the white St-Chinian, a minimum of 30 percent Grenache Blanc is required, the other permitted varieties being Marsanne, Roussanne, and Vermentino (a.k.a. Rolle). No single variety may exceed 70 percent. Reflecting their contrasting *terroirs*, the rules for Berlou and Roquebrun are very different: a minimum of 30 percent Carignan is required at Berlou, while at Roquebrun the trio of Syrah/Grenache/Mourvèdre must be at least 30 percent.

• **The first AOC examples** of white Faugères reached the market in 2006. The wines are fruity and exotic whites based on Roussanne, Marsanne, Grenache Blanc, and Vermentino.

• **The rules for white** Costières de Nîmes have been changed. The permitted grape varieties are Clairette, Grenache Blanc, Bourboulenc, Ugni Blanc, Roussanne, Vermentino, Macabeu, Marsanne, and Viognier. Ugni Blanc must not exceed 30 percent and will be phased out after 2010. Viognier is limited to 10 percent. The wine must be a blend of at least two different grape varieties. The maximum yield is 60 hl/ha.

Vintage Report

Advance report on the latest harvest

2005

Hopes are high everywhere, even if no one predicts the vintage of the century. A moderately wet winter was followed by a later spring than 2004, but the summer was good, without excessive heat, and the sunshine was punctuated by convenient storms. The vintage was on time but immediately preceded by violent rain, which may have spoiled some of the early-maturing varieties. The later picking season was, however, perfect, with only a short cold spell in the first few days of October. Growers forecast a year of ripe but not over-sugary fruit, good phenolic development, and overall good balance. The relatively small production of white wines seems as promising as that of the reds. Quantities are well down on 2004.

Updates on the previous five vintages

2004

Vintage rating: *Red: 90, White: 88*

This year marked a return to more normal conditions after the torrid heat of 2003. The long, cool summer was redeemed by late sunshine, which has given the wines splendid balance, ripe but not too ripe fruit, good phenolic development, just the right touch of acidity, and soft tannins. The later-harvested Grenache and Mourvèdre were particularly successful. Some growers, however, had difficulty with rot following rain just before the harvest, because the drying Tramontane wind failed to materialize. This is the only question mark over the best year since 2001. Production levels were noticeably up.

2003

Vintage rating: *Red: 78, White: 80*

The notorious hot year lives up to previous forecasts of wines rich in fruit and the best ready for early drinking. Some grapes were burned (particularly in La Clape), and there were blockages in maturity; sometimes the grapes at the back of the bunches were riper than those exposed to the sun.

Thick skins and pulp lacking in moisture made for intense colors and easily extractable juice. Acidity is weak except in some late-picked wines, especially the older Carignan, and the tannins are sometimes stemmy and green, otherwise flabby. This was a year that showed off the benefits of *assemblage* rather than varietals. High alcohol levels everywhere, sometimes too high, as in the Minervois. Very much a year for experienced growers, some of whom outshine the standard for the year with ease. The whites were more successful than the reds, though Pic-St-Loup and Terrasses du Larzac did well because of the cooler nights on the higher ground. Production was well down compared to 2002.

2002

Vintage rating: *Red: 83, White: 80 (60 for both in the flooded areas of eastern Languedoc)*
Much better than first expected. The style is generally more delicate than either surrounding year, with some finesse and elegance even from producers noted for their macho tendencies. The best wines are from areas benefiting from the late Indian summer: all Roussillon, Aniane, and Montpeyroux. Quantities are down.

2001

Vintage rating: *Red: 92, White: 92*
This has emerged in general as superior to 2000. A heat-wave summer produced very ripe fruit, good sugar levels, and plenty of natural concentration. The quantity was down on 2000. The best year since the legendary 1998. Most whites will need drinking, but the reds will still keep.

2000

Vintage rating: *Red: 90, White: 90*
An excellent and abundant year. There was some disparity in harvesting times, reflected in varying sugar levels. The wines are sometimes maturing later than the flattering 2001s. Notable successes included Roussillon, Fitou, St-Chinian, Faugères, and Pic-St-Loup. Only the very best whites need keeping any longer.

GREATEST WINE PRODUCERS

1. Domaine Gauby (Calce, Roussillon)
2. Roc d'Anglade (Vin de Pays du Gard)
3. René Rostang (Anglade, Coteaux du Languedoc)
4. Domaine Peyre-Rose (Pézenas)
5. Domaine Font Caude (Montpeyroux)
6. Domaine Ferrer-Ribière (Terrats, Roussillon)
7. Domain d'Aupilhac (Montpeyroux)
8. Clot de l'Oum (Roussillon)
9. Domaine Bertrand-Bergé (Fitou)
10. Le Conte des Floris (Pézenas)

FASTEST-IMPROVING PRODUCERS

1. Clos de Gravillas (St-Jean de Minervois)
2. Domaine Matassa (Calce, Roussillon)
3. Domaine Olivier Pithon (Calce, Roussillon)
4. Mas de Martin (Grès de Montpellier)
5. Château de Valflaunès (Pic-St-Loup)
6. Mas Cal Demoura (Montpeyroux)
7. Domaine Maria Fita (Fitou)
8. Mas d'Auzières (Grès de Montpellier)
9. Domaine des Grécaux (Montpeyroux)
10. Domaine Virgile Joly (Terrasses de Larzac)

NEW UP-AND-COMING PRODUCERS

1. Domaine Vacquer (Roussillon)
2. Domaine d'Anglas (Montpeyroux)
3. Domaine Malys-Anne (Minervois)
4. Domaine de Fraïsse (Faugères)
5. Domaine Boisantin (Montpeyroux)
6. Domaine des Carmes (St-Chinian)
7. Château d'Or et de Gueules (Costières de Nîmes)
8. Domaine Ellul-Ferrières (Grès de Montpellier)
9. Château Montel (Grès de Montpellier)
10. Mas des Dames (Pézenas)

BEST-VALUE PRODUCERS

1. Mas de Bressades (Costières de Nîmes)
2. Château de l'Euzière (Pic-St-Loup)
3. Mas de la Seranne (Aniane, Terrasses de Larzac)
4. Cave Coopérative de Cascastel (Fitou)
5. Domaine de Barroubio (St-Jean de Minervois)
6. Château Lauriga (Roussillon)
7. Mas Brunet (Terrasses de Larzac)
8. Domaine Coston (Terrasses de Larzac)
9. Domaine Jean-Baptiste Sénat (Minervois)
10. Domaine Roque-Sestière (Corbières)

GREATEST-QUALITY WINES

1. **Côtes du Roussillon Villages Muntada 2002** Domaine Gauby (€50)
2. **Vin de Pays des Côtes Catalanes Le Soula Blanc 2003/Vin de Pays des Fenouillèdes Le Soula Rouge 2002** Domaine Gauby (€28)
3. **Vin de Pays du Gard Roc d'Anglade 2002** Rémy Pédréno (€20)
4. **Coteaux du Languedoc Terre de Sommières Les Combes 2002** René Rostang (€12)
5. **Vin de Pays de l'Hérault Rouge 1998** La Grange des Pères (€20)
6. **Côtes du Roussillon Ciel Liquide 2003** Domaine Padié (€20)
7. **Minervois Les Aspres 2003** Domaine Cros (€18)

⑧ **Vin de Pays de l'Hérault Carignan 1999** Mas d'Aimé (€10)

⑨ **St-Jean de Minervois Cuvée Nicolas 2003** Domaine de Barroubio (€32 per 50-cl bottle)

⑩ **St-Chinian Les Schistes 2002** Domaine Borie-la-Vitarlèle (€12)

BEST BARGAINS

① **St-Chinian Lo Tabataïre 2002** Domaine du Tabatau (€9)

② **Faugères 2003** Domaine du Météore (€4)

③ **Vin de Pays des Côtes Catalanes Le Ciste 2003** Domaine Eric Laguerre (€8)

④ **Pic-St-Loup Tradition 2003** Domaine Lavabre (€5)

⑤ **La Clape Tradition 2003** Château des Marmorières (€6)

⑥ **Limoux 2003** Domaine La Batteuse (€8)

⑦ **Côtes du Roussillon Villages Tradition 2002** Domaine des Schistes (€7)

⑧ **St-Chinian Tradition 2003** Domaine de Landeyran (€7)

⑨ **Corbières Marquise de Puivert 2002** Château de Cabriac (€7)

⑩ **Corbières Cuvée Le Prieuré 2002** Château de Vaugelas (€6)

MOST EXCITING OR UNUSUAL FINDS

① **Côtes du Roussillon Ciel Liquide 2003** Domaine Padié (€20) *More than an exciting young grower, a "school of Gauby" vigneron heading for the top. An object lesson in* élevage.

② **Minervois Les Aspres 2002** Domaine Cros (€18) *The* tête de cuvée *from a mover and shaker in the Minervois, who is experimenting—for example, with Pinot Noir and Nebbiolo— while retaining his Aramon, Alicante, and Picpoul Noir.*

③ **Coteaux du Languedoc La Clape Cuvée Blanc 2003** Mas du Soleilla (€14) *A basically rather delicate wine, with a good percentage of Bourboulenc (a La Clape specialty grape), is given a ritzy* élevage.

④ **Coteaux du Languedoc Rouge 2002** Domaine de Montcalmès (€8) *An unexpectedly limpid and elegant red from Syrah, Grenache, and Mourvèdre. The contrast with near neighbors Daumas Gassac illustrates the meaning of* terroir.

⑤ **Vin de Pays de Lodève Cuvée Blanc 2003** Domaine Pas de l'Escalette (€15) *A revelatory white from unfashionable Carignan Blanc and Terret, with Grenache Blanc to add respectability.*

⑥ **Vin de Pays du Mont Baudile Cinsault 2002** Domaine La Terrasse d'Elise (€12) *Surprising because of its light, perfumed fruit, gently heightened with sensitive oak aging. Cinsault fights back.*

⑦ **Vin de Pays des Côtes Catalanes La Vendemmiaire 2003** Domaine La Balmière (€10) *A rare Vendanges Tardives Grenache Rouge, aged in one-year-old barrels.*

⑧ **Vin de Pays du Mont Baudile Le Carignan de Familongue 2003** Domaine de Familongue (€6) *Sixty-year-old vines with a yield of only 28 hl/ha ensure a perfect expression of Carignan, here raised in barrel.*

⑨ **Vin de Pays d'Oc Alicante 2003** Domaine Christin (€6) *A remarkable expression of this much-despised grape; dark, fruity, and surprisingly approachable.*

⑩ **Muscat de Rivesaltes Ambré 2003** Domaine des Chênes (€10) *A return to form from this pioneering property; lovely fruits confits and already a hint of rancio.*

Vins de Pays
& Vins de Table

Rosemary George MW

That old chestnut, an all-embracing *vin de pays* for the whole of France, has reared its head again.

ROSEMARY GEORGE MW

This time it does seem that there is a sense of urgency, with the optimists hoping that it may provide a solution to the problems besetting the French wine industry. Rather than the ill-fated Vin de Pays des Cépages de la France, the proposed name is Vin de Pays Vignobles de France, and the declared intention is to have something in place for the 2006 vintage. The wine, which will be labeled by grape variety, will have to come from vineyards registered as *vin de pays* for more than three years, and chaptalization is forbidden, as it is for all *vins de pays*.

If this *vin de pays* does become reality, it marks a significant shift in the French attitude to its wine industry. By allowing the creation of brands that cover the whole of the country, it represents a sharp move away from regionality. Hitherto France's wines have always been based on provenance and, in the case of appellations, on *terroir*. You are expected to know that Chablis comes from Chardonnay or that Côte Rôtie is made from Syrah. Alsace is almost unique as an appellation with a grape variety on the label. Consequently, the Vins de Pays d'Oc were considered quite innovative in allowing varietal labeling, while also retaining an indication of provenance. In contrast, a Vin de Pays Vignobles de France will be able

ROSEMARY GEORGE MW was lured into the wine trade by a glass of the Wine Society's champagne at a job interview. Realizing that secretarial work was not for her, she took the wine-trade exams, becoming one of the first women to qualify as a Master of Wine in 1979. She has been a freelance wine writer since 1981 and is the author of nine books, including *Chablis* (Sotheby Publications, 1984), *French Country Wines* (Faber & Faber, 1990), *The Wines of New Zealand* (Faber & Faber, 1996), and *The Wines of the South of France* (Faber & Faber, 2001). Her most recent book, *Walking Through the Vineyards of Tuscany* (Bantam Press), was published in 2004.

to come from anywhere in France, allowing a blend of wines from more than one region—except, of course, those regions without any *vins de pays*, such as Champagne, the Côte d'Or, and Alsace.

The objective behind the new *vin de pays* is to confront the huge competition coming in the form of the varietal wines of the New World, notably from Australia, where it is possible to blend wines produced hundreds of miles apart. The big players in the market would like the same flexibility for France. In the new markets, such as Korea or China, the cachet comes from buying a French wine. Wine drinkers have no idea whether it comes from Bordeaux or Burgundy; they don't understand the difference. France is the key to the wine's quality. So Vignobles de France will allow the really big producers, such as Les Grands Chais de France, UCCOAR (Union des Caves Co-opératives de l'Ouest Audois et du Razès), and Castel, to put across a simple message: this wine is French.

What remains to be seen is whether the key movers in the Vin de Pays d'Oc will actually accept this new *vin de pays* readily. They consider themselves to be in a powerful position, currently accounting for 96 percent of all varietal French wine, thus providing the only effective competition to the New World. For the moment they say that they are neither for nor against, but they do have reservations that there will be less guarantee of quality than with their own quite strictly controlled Vin de Pays d'Oc. However, you can't help feeling that political clout and vested interests also play their part here.

Progress in Bordeaux and Beaujolais

This time last year, Bordeaux was considering the creation of a *vin de pays* to cover the wines of the Gironde. Things have not moved speedily, and there is now talk of a larger *vin de pays* that would cover not only Bordeaux, but also the vineyards of southwest France, in the departments of the Dordogne, Lot-et-Garonne, Landes, and Pyrenées-Atlantique, as well as both *départements* of the Charente, thus stretching from the Loire to the Pyrenees. The large and successful Vin de Pays des Côtes de Gascogne would be firmly excluded. The name still has to be finalized, but Vin de Pays de l'Atlantique is the suggestion. Another obstacle is the need to set up an administrative framework for *vins de pays* in the Gironde, where previously there was none. It also means that subscriptions hitherto paid to the INAO for appellation wines will go to ONIVINS for *vins de pays*.

The hope is to have the new *vin de pays* in place for the 2006 vintage, and thus give the Bordelais the opportunity of making something other than Bordeaux Rouge. The main beneficiaries would doubtless be the Bordeaux *négociants*, who would be able to create regional brands with varietal labels. How much it will help the myriad small growers in the Gironde remains to be seen. However, the authorities are adamant that this is not intended to be a dumping ground for substandard claret.

Things are moving slowly in Beaujolais, too. Yet again there is hope that something will be in place for the 2006 vintage. The name of the proposed new *vin de pays* is still top secret. The delimited area is likely to include villages that are not part of Beaujolais—it will extend as far as the Coteaux Lyonnais on the eastern outskirts of Lyon and will include grape varieties that have nothing to do with Beaujolais: not only Gamay and Chardonnay, but also Syrah, Merlot, Sauvignon, and Viognier, as in the nearby Vin de Pays de l'Ardèche, and not only varietal wines, but also *bis-cépages*, such as Gamay/Syrah. This could provide an opportunity for the creation of new styles of wine with more appeal to the modern palate. Once in existence, the new *vin de pays* would come under the umbrella of Vin de Pays des Comtés Rhodaniens.

Grapevine

• **Some of the more geographically defined** *vins de pays* aspire to appellation status. One that is more likely than most to succeed is the Vin de Pays de la Haute Vallée de l'Orb. These are some of the more northerly vineyards of the Midi, and also some of the coolest. North of Faugères, the nights are cooler, the altitude is higher, and chestnut trees grow well. The Haute Vallée de l'Orb covers some 12 villages, making it one of the largest *vin de pays de zone*, but for the moment only about 1,400 ha are in production, with 12 cellars and four cooperatives. There is no doubt that the cooler climate suits Chardonnay and Pinot Noir, and undoubtedly produces some of the best examples of these varieties in the Midi.

Sancerre producer Alphonse Mellot Père et Fils has acquired 9 ha of vineyards in the Coteaux Charitois, upstream from Sancerre and based on the same grape varieties (Sauvignon and Pinot Noir), as well as Chardonnay. The plan is to produce two wines, La Galère, based on Sauvignon, and La Guigne, from Pinot Noir.

• **Jean-Marc Brocard,** one of the largest Chablis producers, both as grower and *négociant*, has extended his activity across the departmental boundary to include the Coteaux de Tannay, a little-known *vin de pays* in the Nièvre. The result is a delicate Chardonnay with a hint of minerality.

• **The commune of Marseillan** is now allowed in Vin de Pays d'Oc wines. Previous examples of Marseillan were Vin de Pays de l'Hérault. Cinsault, which was previously restricted to *rosé*, can now also be used as a red varietal.

OLD VARIETIES GAIN SPICE FOR NEW LIFE

Carignan was the established grape variety of the Midi for a long time and, as such, produced generous quantities of pretty nondescript wine, thus necessitating the extensive planting of the so-called *cépages améliorateurs*, namely Syrah and Mourvèdre. However, over the past few years Carignan has gradually been enjoying something of a revival. Certainly in the heart of the Languedoc there is a realization that, with low yields and old vines, there is quality to be found in Carignan, with a growing number of growers putting considerable effort into extracting the very best from the variety. Among the leaders of this movement are Nicole and John Bojanowski at Clos du Gravillas, on the edge of the Minervois, and Sylvain Fadat at Domaine Aupilhac in Montpeyroux. Other wines worth seeking out are Le Carignator from Domaine Rimbert and Vieilles Vignes Carignan from Domaine de Nizas.

Attention is also being paid to other long-neglected grape varieties of the Midi. Oeillade, a close relation to Cinsault, is produced by Thierry Navarre in Roquebrun as a *vin de table*. Navarre is also cherishing another threatened grape variety, Ribeyrenc. The red-juiced Alicante Bouschet, once even more scorned than Carignan, is another variety enjoying a revival in its reputation, such as at Domaine des Crès-Ricards and at Domaine Ollieux Romanis. Again, low yields seem to be the key to quality.

LOWERING ALCOHOL LEVELS

In the quest for fully ripe grapes, with an emphasis on phenolic ripeness, alcohol levels of 14 degrees and more are becoming commonplace. The Pugibet family at Domaine la Colombette, outside Béziers, decided to address the problem, launching a red, white, and *rosé* at a mere 9 degrees of alcohol, under the name of Plume de Colombette.

The red is a Syrah/Grenache blend, the white a Chardonnay, and the *rosé* a pure Grenache. The wines are labelled *vin de table partiellement déalcolisé*. The original alcohol in the wine is removed by a form of reverse osmosis, and then a suitable amount is replaced; the process sounds quite unnatural, but the wine actually tastes remarkably good. Needless to say, such creative thinking has fallen foul of the French authorities. Father and son were required to explain themselves to the Répression des Fraudes, but they now have permission to produce Plume de Colombette on an experimental basis alongside their full-strength *vins de pays*.

Opinion:
Many reasons behind *vin de pays*

The charm and attraction of the *vins de pays* lie in their infinite and often-unexpected variety. *Vins de pays* appeal to those growers who have a somewhat cavalier attitude to appellation regulations—indeed, some prefer to remain *vin de table*, which entails even less administrative hassle. The downside, however, is the impossibility of putting any regional indication on the label other than a postal code; nor is a vintage permitted for a *vin de table*, but there are usually imaginative ways around that problem, a lot number being an obvious solution.

Such *vins de pays* and *vins de table* comprise the *crème de la crème*. There is a great mass of *vin de pays* produced all over southern France in particular that have no merit whatsoever. These are wines that will be sent off for distillation before the arrival of the next harvest to make room in the vats, or sold for less than cost price merely to help the cash flow of the floundering cooperative. Eighty percent of the wines of the Languedoc are sold *en vrac* (in bulk); with the enormous drop in French wine consumption, resulting partly from the negative attitude of the government, there is an urgent need to adapt to changing market circumstances. Anonymous *vins de pays* are not what the market needs.

What is needed is more of the wonderful wines that are the product of a talented wine producer's creativity, and there is no limit to the imaginative reasons that growers have for not conforming to their appellations. If you grow a grape variety that is not allowed in your area, say Riesling in the Languedoc, there is no way that you can put Riesling on the label, so you label it purely by the vineyard name. If you make a wine that is too high in alcohol for your appellation, it has to be declassified into *vin de pays*. That is the reason Gérard Gauby's delicious white wines are *vin de pays*, while his red wines are Côtes du Roussillon. Oliver de Moor in the Chablis village of Courgis also grows Sauvignon in the adjoining appellation of St-Bris, but in 2003 his wine was refused its *agrément* because it had reached 15 degrees. It tasted beautifully in balance, with rich flavors, but was declassified into a mere *vin de table*. If you usually make an appellation, you have to say before you pick your grapes that you are going to make a *vin de pays*, otherwise your wine is declassified into *vin de table*, as happened in this instance. René Rostaing in the northern Rhône labels his Les Lézardes Viognier *vin de table* simply "to be different," because it allows him the flexibility he sees the New

World enjoying. And his reputation as a grower is more than sufficient for the wine to sell on that basis.

There is a feeling in some quarters that appellations are no longer relevant. David O'Brien at Château Vignelaure Coteaux d'Aix-en-Provence has moved steadily away from the appellation. Vignelaure is too cool to ripen Grenache Noir properly, but the grape is obligatory for the appellation. O'Brien feels that varietal labeling is more important to the consumer these days: most people do not know what to expect from a Coteaux d'Aix-en-Provence wine. He considers that losing the right to use "château" on the label is a small price to pay for the flexibility gained by producing *vin de pays*. It should be left to the producer to concentrate on quality.

Perhaps the last word should go to Louis-Marie Tesserenc at Domaine de l'Arjolle. He enthuses, "The advantage of the *vins de pays* is that we can have fun and enjoy ourselves making all these different wines." Therein lies the diversity of the *vins de pays*. You never quite know what you will encounter next, and it is certainly worthwhile trying out an unknown *vin de pays* on a restaurant wine list. You might be disappointed, but you are much more likely to be delightfully surprised by a new discovery.

Contentious *copeaux*

It looks as though the issue of oak chips is finally about to be resolved. They were accepted by the European Union at the end of 2005 and therefore should be authorized in France during 2006—a move that will be welcomed by large *vin de pays* producers.

Grapevine

• **Blending white and red grape varieties,** currently forbidden in Vins de Pays d'Oc, may soon be permitted. This is a long-established practice in Côte Rôtie, and it should soon be possible to find *bis-cépages* based on Syrah and Viognier.

• **At Domaine de l'Arjolle** in the Côtes de Thongue, where Zinfandel has been in production since 2000 as Z de l'Arjolle, Vin de Table de France, Louis-Marie Tesserenc has turned his attention to South America and, inspired by Chilean examples, is planting Carmenère. He hopes to

have it in production by 2009. Since its historical home of Bordeaux is really too cold for Carmenère, Tesserenc believes it will do better in the Côtes de Thongue.

• **Gerard Départdieu,** in conjunction with Bernard Magrez, has produced his first wine from the Midi, a Vin de Pays d'Oc called Ma Référence. It is a Merlot/Cabernet Sauvignon blend, with 18 months in oak, and it comes from vineyards near Belvès du Razès, on the Massif de la Malepère, southeast of Carcassonne.

everal of the estates in these lists also have a reputation for their appellation wines.

GREATEST WINE PRODUCERS

1. Domaine de Trévallon (Bouches du Rhône)
2. Domaine de Clovallon (Oc/Haute Vallée de l'Orb)
3. Domaine Gauby (Côtes Catalanes)
4. Mas de Daumas Gassac (Hérault)
5. Domaine la Grange des Pères (Hérault)
6. Domaine Vaquer (Côtes Catalanes)
7. Producteurs Plaimont (Côtes de Gascogne)
8. Domaine la Croix Belle (Côtes de Thongue)
9. Domaine de l'Arjolle (Côtes de Thongue)
10. Domaine Cazes (Côtes Catalanes)

FASTEST-IMPROVING PRODUCERS

1. Jean-Louis Denois (Oc)
2. Domaine Magellan (Côtes de Thongue)
3. Ampelidae (Vienne)
4. Domaine de Cazeneuve (Côtes Catalanes)
5. Domaine Matassa (Côtes Catalanes)
6. Domaine Pertuisane (Côtes Catalanes)
7. Domaine de Ravanès (Coteaux de Murviel)
8. Domaine de la Marfée (Hérault)
9. Vignelaure (Coteaux du Verdon)
10. Vignoble Guillaume (Franche-Comté)

NEW UP-AND-COMING PRODUCERS

1. Domaine de la Croix Ronde (Haute Vallée de l'Orb)
2. Domaine de Montplézy (Côtes de Thongue)
3. Clos du Gravillas (Côtes de Brian)
4. Domaine Ste-Hilaire (Oc)
5. Domaine Ste-Rose (Oc)
6. Domaine Levin (Jardin de la France)
7. Puechamp (Cévennes)

8. Le Chemin des Rêves (Hérault)
9. Domaine des Crès Ricards (Côtes de Céressou)
10. Domaine St-Jean du Noviciat (Oc/Coteaux de Bessilles)

BEST-VALUE PRODUCERS

1. Domaine Condamine l'Evêque (Oc)
2. Producteurs Plaimont (Côtes de Gascogne)
3. Domaine Condamine Bertrand (Oc)
4. Mas Montel (Oc/Gard)
5. Domaine Camp Galhan (Oc/Duché d'Uzès)
6. Domaine de St-Lannes (Côtes de Gascogne)
7. Domaine Granoupiac (Oc)
8. Domaine de Perdiguier (Coteaux d'Ensérune)
9. Domaine Cazes (Côtes Catalanes)
10. Domaines Paul Mas (Oc)

GREATEST-QUALITY WINES

1. **Vin de Pays des Bouches du Rhône Rouge 2003** Domaine de Trévallon (€50)
2. **Vin de Pays des Côtes Catalanes Blanc Vieilles Vignes 2002** Domaine Gauby (€27)
3. **Vin de Pays de la Haute Vallée de l'Orb Les Aires Viognier 2004** Domaine de Clovallon (€10.80)
4. **Vin de Pays de l'Hérault Grenache Blanc 2002** Domaine Virgile Joly (€24)
5. **Vin de Table de France Les Lézardes Viognier 2004** Domaine René Rostaing (€20)
6. **Vin de Pays de l'Hérault Blanc 2004** Mas de Daumas Gassac (€30)
7. **Vin de Pays des Cévennes Puechamp 2003** Antarès (€11.50)
8. **Vin de Pays des Côtes Catalanes Le Credo 1996** Domaine Cazes (€36.80 magnum)

⑨ Vin de Pays des Côtes de Thongue Cascaïllou 2003 Domaine la Croix Belle (€14.50)

⑩ Vin de Table Muscat Passerillé 2001 Domaine Lacoste (€22.60)

BEST BARGAINS

① Vin de Pays de la Haute Vallée de l'Orb Cuvée Jade Chardonnay 2004 Domaine de la Croix Ronde (€6)

② Vin de Pays des Côtes de Thongue Rosé Cuvée Georges Sutra 2004 Domaine de Montplézy (€4.80)

③ Vin de Pays d'Oc Vermentino 2004 Domaine Ste-Hilaire (€5.50)

④ Vin de Pays d'Oc Sauvignon 2004 Domaine de la Baume (€5.45)

⑤ Vin de Pays de la Haute Vallée de l'Aude Chardonnay 2004 Domaine Rives Blanques (€3.80)

⑥ Vin de Pays du Jardin de la France Sauvignon 2004 Domaine Levin (€6.50)

⑦ Vin de Pays du Jardin de la France Cabernet Franc 2004 Domaine de la Haronnière (€4.80)

⑧ Vin de Pays des Côtes de Brian La Part des Anges 2003 Clos Centeilles (€7.40)

⑨ Vin de Pays d'Oc Cabernet Sauvignon/Grenache Noir 2004 Les Mazets (€3.80)

⑩ Vin de Pays des Terroirs Landais Sables Fauves Moelleux 2004 Domaine de Cavaillon (€4)

MOST EXCITING OR UNUSUAL FINDS

① Vin de Pays des Coteaux de Tannay Chardonnay 2001 Les Caves Tannaysiennes (€4.90) *You could almost mistake this for a Chablis, but it comes from just across the departmental boundary.*

② Vin de Pays de la Haute Vallée de l'Orb Cuvée Jade Chardonnay 2004 Domaine de la Croix Ronde (€6) *A beautiful cooler-climate Midi wine, showing the benefits of microclimate.*

③ Vin de Pays des Côtes de Céressou Cousin Cousine Alicante Bouschet 2004 Domaine Crès-Ricards (€7) *Shows just how good this variety can be with low yields and careful winemaking.*

④ Vin de Pays des Côtes de Brian Rendez-Vous du Soleil 2002 Domaine de Gravillas (€12) *A pure Carignan from a firm believer in that grape variety. A wine that conveys a true sense of place.*

⑤ Vin de Table de France Vin d'Oeillades [2004] Domaine Navarre (€4.50) *An appealing example of a forgotten grape variety. Young, fresh, and spicy.*

⑥ Vin de Pays des Côtes de Thongue Delphine de Morgan Dernière Cueillette Chardonnay 2001 Domaine de l'Arjolle (€20) *Intriguingly dry flavors, almost like France's answer to sherry, with a note of oxidation.*

⑦ Vin de Pays des Coteaux Charitois Le Montaillant Pinot Noir 2003 Domaine des Hauts de Seyr (€6) *An appealingly fresh northern Pinot Noir from a very much off-the-beaten-track vineyard.*

⑧ Vin Mousseux de Qualité Castapiane Méthode Traditionnelle 2002 St Jean du Noviciat (€8.50) *From Alicante Bouschet, Cinsault, and Carignan— an alternative to sparkling Shiraz.*

⑨ Vin de Table de France Sauvignon [2003] Domaine de Moor, Courgis (€10) *This is declassified St-Bris, since, at 15 degrees, the alcohol level is too high. Beautifully balanced.*

⑩ Vin de Pays des Côtes de Gascogne Prestige d'Hiver Sélection 2004 Domaine de St Lannes (€8) *From passerillé Gros Manseng; rich and peachy.*

Germany

Michael Schmidt

Cooperatives: dynamic or static? German wine growers suffered a series of economic crises in the mid-19th century—phylloxera, peronospera, oidium, and a collapse in grape prices.

MICHAEL SCHMIDT

As a consequence of these crises, laws were passed in 1866/67 that allowed the establishment of cooperatives, many of which are still active today.

More recently, increasing competition—first through the creation of the European Union, followed by a flood of cheap imports from the New World—has resulted in a consolidation of the German wine cooperative structure, and in 2005 there were 231 growers' associations, 137 of them with their own winemaking facilities. With over 30,000 ha, 58,000 members own approximately one-third of the country's vineyard area and account for one-third of production. In regions like Baden and Württemberg, this share rises to over 70 percent. The Badischer Winzerkeller in Breisach is Germany's largest cooperative, supplied by 75 associate cooperatives with an annual average output of 250,000 hl from 6,000 growers. These figures illustrate that the cooperatives wield a substantial amount of muscle in the German wine industry, which has attracted mutterings of discontent. To investigate claims that cooperatives are often more interested in storage

MICHAEL SCHMIDT has been involved with the wines of Germany for more than three decades, and he visits estates and producers in his native country several times a year. Back in Britain he runs his own wine school (www.wineschmidt.co.uk) in Surrey and Hampshire. He is a judge at the International Wine and Spirit Competition and has worked as a consultant on a number of publications, including advising on the selection of recommended wines for the German chapter of *Sotheby's Wine Encyclopedia* (Dorling Kindersley, 1988–2005).

volume, bottling capacities, and the latest in filtration and centrifuge technology than the quality of the end product, I invited 50 or so of the more highly rated cooperatives to send a selection from their range.

The majority decided to make it easy on my palate by ignoring my request, leaving two possible conclusions: either they lacked the confidence to have their wines scrutinized by a taster familiar with international competition, or they were simply not interested in representation on the international stage. However, the wines that did arrive substantiated the cooperatives' claim of being able to select the best material from a wide choice of sites and growers for their premium wines. Many have also started to reward applied vineyard management, healthy grapes, and yield restriction rather than bulk and sugar content. Another strength of the German system is members' obligation to deliver all the harvest to their cooperative, whereas in other countries growers can hold back the cream of the crop for their own bottlings.

If one were to pick one name only to represent the best in German cooperatives, it would probably be the Pfalz outfit Vier Jahreszeiten of Bad Dürkheim for its consistency of quality over a long period. However, acknowledgment must also go to Winzergenossenschaft Mayschoss-Altenahr of the Ahr region and Württemberg's Weinmanufaktur Untertürkheim, which have propelled themselves into the elite of German producers in a very short time. While the former can boast some real Riesling and Spätburgunder treasures, the latter does particularly well with the local specialty Lemberger and some red and white *cuvées*.

In cooperative county Baden, the lead is firmly in the hands of the Pfaffenweiler Weinhaus, but their colleagues in Oberbergen have made a bit of a specialty of the Weiss- and Grauburgunder varieties. Other domaines that deliver good value for money are the co-ops of Oberrotweil and Affental in Baden, Brackenheim and Remstal in Württemberg, the Bergsträsser Winzer of the Hessische Bergstrasse, Ruppertsberg and Wachtenburg in the Pfalz, and Thüngersheim in Franken. However, nothing excites wine lovers more than a new find, and I do not mind admitting that, after having tasted the wines submitted by the Franconian Winzerverein Sommerach, I felt compelled to visit their cellars in search of Silvaner, Grauer Burgunder, Traminer, and Scheurebe.

Finally, one yardstick I would not use to pick wines from cooperatives is the display of medals awarded by the Deutsche Landwirtschaftsgesellschaft (German Agricultural Society) or its equivalent regional boards. According to the DLG's 2005 presentation booklet, out of 4,747 entries in the categories of still and sparkling wines, more than 3,900 were given medals! With this pass rate, winning something is almost guaranteed!

Three Bs back on track

In 2005, local business magnate Joachim Niederberger added the highly revered Deidesheim estate of von Buhl to his 2002 acquisition of the equally prestigious house of Bassermann-Jordan in the same village. If the rapid improvements at the latter domaine over the last four years are anything to go by, von Buhl will soon be restored to its former glory. Before financial and leadership crises in the 1980s and 1990s led to a decline in standards, both estates belonged to the Pfalz region's legendary triumvirate of Riesling producers often respectfully referred to as the "Three Bs." Third member Bürklin-Wolf also suffered a period of instability, but was back on track as long ago as the 1993 vintage, when the enthusiasm and vision of Christian von Guradze began to bear fruit.

1990 Spätburgunder 15 years later

In a year when Parker's *Wine Advocate* finally acknowledged the existence of serious German Pinot Noir, *Wine Report*'s man on the scene had already moved on to investigate the aging potential of these wines in a comprehensive tasting of perhaps the first great Spätburgunder vintage of 1990, painstakingly put together by Baden wine impresario Sigbert Hiss. A small but highly qualified team, including Germany's leading online wine magazine's chief taster Markus Hofschuster and Jürgen von der Mark, one of only three German Masters of Wine, dissected and discussed 25 wines in a marathon tasting.

Most of the wines came from Baden, but Franken, Rheinhessen, the Pfalz, and the Rheingau were also represented. Initial apprehension soon gave way to excitement as the tasters discovered that the number of still-enjoyable bottles by far outweighed those that were over the hill. Even some wines from lesser-known stables showed surprisingly well, with Soder's Kirchberg *Auslese* exhibiting classic compost and vegetal notes, while Dörflinger's Müllheimer Pfaffenstück *Auslese* was taking its time to unfold aromas of undergrowth, pepper, and even curry. Typical characteristics of mature Spätburgunder were also featured by three *Spätlesen Trockens* from Endingen's Reinhold and Cornelia Schneider, Müller's Ihringer Winklerberg, and a Waldulmer Pfarrberg from the relatively unknown Benz estate. Heated discussions greeted Bernhard Huber's "R" and the *Auslese* from Rheinhessen producer Kühling-Gillot. Both were unusually deep in color and showed absolutely no signs of age, but I found the pronounced cassis aromas of one and the strong inky notes of the other somewhat atypical. There was no controversy, however, about the two wines from the Frankenmeister Paul Fürst! Nobody minded that we had been slipped a "ringer" Frühburgunder with hints of chocolate and biscuits, quite juicy, still firm, and very long. My top mark went to his Spätburgunder, with its velvety texture and cherry fruit excellently supported by some gamey and minerally notes.

Verdict: since 1990, top Spätburgunder producers have perfected their art and you can happily trust their premium wines from the better years not only to last but also to improve over 10 years or so.

Germany's best Spätburgunder grown in France?

After international boundary realignments following World War II, several growers in Schweigen, the southernmost village of the Pfalz region, found that some of their vineyards had "moved" to Alsace. Generous in victory, the French allowed them to keep their property and cross the border to tend their vines. This rare triumph over officialdom was further compounded by an agreement to award the harvest from these sites German rather than French status.

An interesting twist has been added to this geographical oxymoron by the fact that Schweigen grower Friedrich Becker produces some of Germany's greatest Pinot Noirs from these very vineyards. In the eyes of leading wine critics, the 2003 vintage of the Spätburgunder Res from the St Paul site appellation and the *Großes Gewächs* from the Kammerberg are a breakthrough to world-class Pinot Noir. The family of Becker's closest local rival Bernhart has owned vineyards in the Wissembourg district of Alsace since 1900. All their Pinot Noir grapes come from that side of the border, and in 1999 for once they managed to steal a march on their competitor with a Spätburgunder Auslese Trocken Selektion R from the Rädling site, scoring an impressive 93 points in Germany's leading wine guide. Perhaps the older Alsace generation may regret their generosity: "Alsace Pinot Noir rivals Burgundy *grands crus*" would have made a headline to be proud of!

Grapevine

• **Riesling and the petrol mystery.** When at the London stage of the Riesling World Tour 2005 an English Master of Wine put the unique fumy aroma shown by some mature Riesling wines down to the use of unripe grapes, I had to reassure myself it wasn't 1 April! Theories explaining the petrol aromas from Riesling have included anything from the influence of slate to the effects of extreme exposure to sun. German research scientists have found that the petrol tone is caused by the compound 1,1,6-trimethyl-1,2-dihydronaphtalene (TDN for short) from the chemical group of hydrocarbons created during bottle-aging by the decomposition of carotenoids, a collection of color pigments also known as a precursor to vitamin A.

Opinion:

Great Growth: second-class?

In *Wine Report 2006*, I discussed some of the teething troubles of the new classification introduced by the German premium wine growers' association, Verband deutscher Prädikatsweingüter (VdP), with particular consideration of some of the critical issues relating to their jewel in the crown—the *Großes Gewächs* (Great Growth) category. I have no reason to doubt the assurances given to me by the president and various members of the VdP that they are working on these problem areas, and I hope that some of the nitpicking that follows may be used as food for thought.

In my mind there can be no doubt that wine drinkers who take an interest in rankings and classifications of fine wines expect the terms *grand cru* or *Großes Gewächs* to describe the very best a particular region has to offer. In Germany, critics unanimously agree that the most outstanding dry white wine for the past couple of vintages has been the G-Max Riesling from the Rheinhessen estate of Klaus Keller. Not designated a *grand cru* and without a vineyard appellation, the wine belongs to the category of *Orts- und Gutswein*, the third and lowest tier of estate and village wines meeting no more than the general requirements set out by the rules of the classification. Keller has some outstanding *Große Gewächse*, too, but, at less than half the price of G-Max, they appear to be rated as second-class.

Dream scores similar to those of the G-Max were also achieved by Tafelwein Pinot Noir Trocken from Pfalz producer Friedrich Becker, who managed to underline this success with an almost equally impressive Spätburgunder Tafelwein Res Trocken. Becker's one *Großes Gewächs*, Schweigener Kammerberg, at a third of the price of the Res, also appears to rate as third-class in his own estimation. Will other members follow suit and place their own *Tafelwein* equivalent of Super-Tuscans on top

Grapevine

- **A straight swap of a bottle** of Romanée-Conti for a bottle of Pinot Noir from Württemberg shows how far German red wine has come over the past 20 years. Having heard of the astonishing success of Hans-Peter Wöhrwag's 2003 Untertürkheimer Herzogenberg (made from Dijon clone 77) in an international tasting that included some top-class burgundies, a wealthy Swiss businessman was so desperate to get his hands on a rare but, at €22.50, relatively inexpensive bottle that he offered the world's most expensive and sought-after red burgundy in return. An offer that could not be refused!

of what was intended to be the top? Or can they be toppled by the executive of the VdP to put the *groß* back into *Großes Gewächs*?

A variation on the theme of Great Growth rule-bending appears to be the release of two *Große Gewächse* from the same vineyard by Pfalz top man Hansjörg Rebholz, with his Gold edition representing a selection from one particular parcel within the Sonnenschein site. I get the idea of a special selection within a vineyard, as also practiced, among others, by red-wine maestro Hehle from the Ahr estate Deutzerhof with his Melchior and Apollo renditions, but it gives the award of the Great Growth status to a vineyard's remaining wine the whiff of a consolation prize. One name I'm not prepared to mention is that of a Spätburgunder grower who heats the juice during fermentation of his Great Growth. To me the jammy character of this wine stood out like a sore thumb in a comprehensive tasting of 2003 red *Große Gewächse* and made a mockery of any *terroir* aspirations.

Finally, as a general observation, not all wines shown at the annual Great Growth previews hit the high notes. Despite some misgivings by the VdP, I still think the consultation of a limited number of independent experts in the pre-selection process would help. They need not be involved in the final decision-making but, in the case of consistent criticism of particular wines, the VdP judges may consider a thorough reexamination.

Grapevine

• **A fungus** to do battle with phylloxera is being researched by the Geisenheim viticultural institute. Contrary to common belief, the vine-root-gnawing aphid is alive and well in German vineyards and gradually mutating into a more powerful louse thought capable of threatening even American rootstock. The scientists' secret weapon is *Metarhizium anisopliae*, a soil fungus. The intended biological warfare is designed to replace chemical agents whose long-term effects are considered harmful to the environment in general and groundwater in particular.

• **A recently released wine** probably makes 2003 the longest German harvest in history. It began August 25, 2003, when the first Bacchus grapes were picked in the Pfalz village of Edesheim, and ended more than six months later on February 25, 2004,

when Franken grower Hubert Göbel from Randersacker finally gave up waiting for *Eiswein* temperatures and picked what was left of his Rieslaner grapes. He was rewarded with a splendid *Trockenbeerenauslese*.

• **"Riesling Unplugged, Elbling plugged"** is the result of a legal wrangle between Nahe grower Martin Tesch and the Mosel estate of Matthias Hild. As reported in *Wine Report 2006*, Tesch and his Ahr colleague Kreuzberg registered the term "Unplugged" for a special edition of Riesling and Spätburgunder wines made without the interference of man or machine. An attempt by Hild from the Upper Mosel village of Winchingen to market a back-to-basics Elbling from 50-year-old vines using the same name attracted an injunction ordering the plug back into the Elbling bottle.

Vintage Report

Advance report on the latest harvest

2005

If growers are to be believed, 2005 could become another vintage of the century, combining the fruit of 2004 with the body and power of 2003, and comparable to the great 1959 and 1947. Warm weeks in the spring facilitated a problem-free flowering period. Despite ample rainfall in the summer, almost uninterrupted sunshine in September and October led to an early ripening of the grapes, with many areas concluding their harvest two weeks ahead of the long-term annual average. All 13 regions were unanimous in reporting excellent physiological ripeness of the grapes with an optimum ratio of sugar and acids. These results were not achieved without difficulty, since some areas had to cope with rot caused by the humid conditions. Continuous reduction of foliage and the removal of affected bunches paid off with a healthy crop, albeit down 10 percent on 2004, with an estimated total of 9 million hl.

Updates on the previous five vintages

2004

Vintage rating: *White: 91, Red: 85-88*
(provisionally, best still in cask)

Despite the adverse effects of inclement weather conditions experienced by some regions in the spring, the eventual harvest total of 10–11 million hl proved slightly above average for the last 10 years. Summer showers provided ample water supplies, avoiding a repeat of the 2003 stress syndrome. Phenological data showed that developments followed the pattern for an average year. The final ripening period began toward the end of August with grapes in a very healthy state and very little sign of any disease. A much more drawn-out ripening period in the fall than 2003 proved a bonus to growers looking for more fruit and less alcohol. Stable pH values, sound acidity levels, and an almost simultaneous occurrence of physiological and sugar ripeness resulted in lively, refreshing wines, filling a gap left by the blockbuster 2003. Another vintage proving the importance of fall above all other seasons.

2003

Vintage rating: *Dry white: 85, Red: 94, Sweet white: 96*

A record-breaking vintage with the driest and warmest growing conditions in Germany since 1540! The starting gun for the harvest was fired in early August, 102 degrees *Oechsle* for a *Spätlese* reported by the middle of that month, the first *Trockenbeerenauslese* grapes gathered at the end of September, and the earliest frozen berries for *Eiswein* picked on October 24. Several growers reported must weights of over 300 degrees *Oechsle* for their TBAs with Mosel estate Markus Molitor bringing in some grapes at a new all-time high of 331. Harvest conditions were ideal and most grapes achieved at least *Spätlese* level. Mainly due to the lack of precipitation, quantity was down by 20 percent, with an estimated 8 million hl total. Expectations of a vintage of a century did not materialize, as many growers struggled to find the right balance between alcohol, fruit, and acidity. Quite a number of inharmonious dry white wines were the result, many with borderline residual sugars. For red-wine producers skillful enough to control the alcohol, perfection was possible. Also a year for great noble whites despite a lack of botrytis.

2002

Vintage rating: *Red: 81, White: 92*

Germany generally enjoyed an even growing season with an almost-perfect balance of sunny days and rainfall until the end of September. The ripeness level of grapes was 10–12 days ahead of normal when the fall deluge arrived, though most of the grapes for QbAs and *Kabinetts* had already been picked. Growers going for premium-quality wines faced nail-biting times, but lessons learned from the difficult 2000 vintage paid off. A green harvest at most estates had reduced the number of bunches by some 20 percent, giving rot very little opportunity to spread, and this preventive measure was helped by the generally cool fall temperatures. In November and December, patient growers were rewarded with grapes of *Auslese*, *Eiswein*, and *Trockenbeerenauslese* quality.

2001

Vintage rating: *Red: 92, White: 90*

Favorable weather conditions until the end of August led to well-advanced degrees of ripeness, but hopes for an outstanding vintage were somewhat dampened by September rains. However, a sun-blessed October dispelled fears of rot, and the continuation of fine weather right into November rewarded patient growers with *Auslese* grape material. The majority of the harvest total weighed in at *Kabinett* level. Red-wine producers in the Ahr, Pfalz, Baden, and Württemberg reported an almost-perfect balance of phenolic and sugar ripeness. The Rheingau was less fortunate, with severe hailstorms devastating some of the crop in October. One of the earliest harvests ever of frozen grapes for *Eiswein* took place at a few sites in the Nahe on November 11, though almost all other regions were more than adequately compensated by a big, five-day freeze in mid-December, producing must concentrations of up to and above 200 degrees *Oechsle*.

2000

Vintage rating: *Red: 68, White: 72*

It may have been a miracle vintage in Bordeaux, but no such luck in Germany. Any expectations after an optimal cycle up to July were dashed by rainfall throughout the summer. Subsequent swelling and bursting of the grapes led to an early onset of rot in September, accelerating at a rate that defied the efforts of all but the most meticulous growers to salvage any healthy material. Only continuous removal of rotten bunches and severely selective hand-picking at the final stage produced a small number of fine wines, while the less fussy mechanical harvesters stood every chance of devouring grapes already affected by acetic bacteria. An average of more than 100 hl/ha for the country's vineyards will not have advanced the cause of German wine.

Listings are for white wines unless stated otherwise.

GREATEST WINE PRODUCERS

1. Keller (Rheinhessen)
2. Egon Müller (Saar)
3. Emrich-Schönleber (Nahe)
4. Fritz Haag (Mosel)
5. Rebholz (red and white, Pfalz)
6. Fürst (red and white, Franken)
7. Dönnhoff (Nahe)
8. Weil (Rheingau)
9. Leitz (Rheingau)
10. Wittmann (Rheinhessen)

FASTEST-IMPROVING PRODUCERS

1. Reinhold & Cornelia Schneider (red and white, Baden)
2. Fritz Becker (red and white, Pfalz)
3. Stodden (red, Ahr)
4. Schäfer-Fröhlich (Nahe)
5. Heymann-Löwenstein (Mosel)
6. St Urbans-Hof (Mosel)
7. Weingart (Mittelrhein)
8. Spreitzer (Rheingau)
9. Fürst Löwenstein (Franken/Rheingau)
10. Mosbacher (Pfalz)

NEW UP-AND-COMING PRODUCERS

1. Ziereisen (red and white, Baden)
2. Wachtstetter (red, Württemberg)
3. Brennfleck (Franken)
4. Groebe (Rheinhessen)
5. Beurer (Württemberg)
6. Tesch (Nahe)
7. Schloss Proschwitz (Sachsen)
8. Weinmanufaktur Untertürkheim (red and white, Württemberg)
9. Markus Schneider (red and white, Pfalz)
10. Winzerverein Sommerhausen (Franken)

BEST-VALUE PRODUCERS

1. Didinger (Mittelrhein)
2. Matthias Müller (Mittelrhein)
3. Manz (Rheinhessen)
4. Merkelbach (Mosel)
5. Weingart (Mittelrhein)
6. Vier Jahreszeiten Winzer (Pfalz)
7. Friedrich Becker (Pfalz)
8. Knab (Baden)
9. Sermann-Kreuzberg (Ahr)
10. Horst Sauer (Franken)

GREATEST-QUALITY WINES

1. **Brauneberger Juffer Riesling Trockenbeerenauslese 2003** Fritz Haag, Dusemonder Hof, Mosel (€2,900 per bottle)
2. **Scharzhofberger Riesling Auslese Goldkapsel 2004** Egon Müller, Saar (€154 per half-bottle)
3. **Monzinger Halenberg Lay Riesling Trocken Großes Gewächs 2004** Emrich-Schönleber, Nahe (€40.60)
4. **Schweigener Kammerberg Spätburgunder Trocken Großes Gewächs 2003** Friedrich Becker, Pfalz (€28)
5. **Leiwener Laurentiuslay Riesling Spätlese Feinherb Erste Lage 2004** Sankt-Urbanshof, Mosel (€15)

6. **Weißer Burgunder Auslese Trocken *** 2004** Reinhold & Cornelia Schneider, Baden (€18)
7. **Malterdinger Bienenberg Grauer Burgunder Spätlese Trocken Großes Gewächs 2004** Bernhard Huber, Baden (€18)
8. **Cuvée X (Merlot/Cabernet Sauvignon) Trocken 2003** Wöhrwag, Württemberg (€21)
9. **Escherndorfer Lump Silvaner Trocken Großes Gewächs 2004** Horst Sauer, Franken (€16)
10. **Lemberger Junges Schwaben 2003** Wachtstetter, Württemberg (€20)

BEST BARGAINS

1. **Weißer Burgunder Trocken 2004** Gehring, Rheinhessen (€3.90 per litre bottle)
2. **Thüngersheimer Ravensburg Silvaner Trocken 2004** Winzergenossenschaft Thüngersheim, Franken (€3.15)
3. **Trollinger Trocken Alte Reben 2003** Kistenmacher-Hengerer, Württemberg (€5.40)
4. **Riesling Spätlese 2004** Göttelmann, Nahe (€5.50)
5. **Spätburgunder Trocken 2003** Friedrich Becker, Pfalz (€6.30)
6. **Dürkheimer Schenkenböhl Gewürztraminer Auslese 2004** Vier Jahreszeiten Winzer, Pfalz (€6.50)
7. **Hambacher Schlossberg Riesling Sekt Trocken 2003** Hambacher Schloss eG, Pfalz (€6.55)
8. **Bopparder Hamm Riesling Auslese 2004** Didinger, Mittelrhein (€7.50)
9. **Spätburgunder 'C' *** 2003** Reinhold & Cornelia Schneider, Baden (€18)
10. **Weinolsheimer Kehr Riesling Eiswein Pauline 2004** Manz, Rheinhessen (€15 per half-bottle)

MOST EXCITING OR UNUSUAL FINDS

① **Lemberger Junges Schwaben 2003** Wachtstetter, Württemberg (€20) *Almost exclusive to Württemberg, this red variety (known as Blaufränkisch in Austria) does have the potential to excite. I liked it so much, I bought, well, not quite the company, but a case!*

② **Syrah 2004** Ziereisen, Baden (€28) *An avid admirer of Côte Rôtie and Hermitage, Hanspeter Ziereisen managed to rock me with his perfect doppelgänger of a fine northern Rhône Syrah. Pepper and spice in abundance! And more complex than the big and bold 2003.*

③ **Homburger Kallmuth Spätlese Tradition Trocken 2004** Fürst Löwenstein, Franken (€13.50) *An exciting blend of Riesling and Silvaner with a herbal and mineral character clearly reflecting terroir. Viognier-like scents of peach and apricot add a tantalizing twist.*

④ **Traminer Concept No. 1 Trocken 2004** Winzerverein Sommerhausen, Franken (€8) *Franconia is not a natural home for this variety. But as an addict of all that has Traminer in its name, for sheer drinkability I prefer the subtle aromas and leaner structure of this wine to some of the sugar, scent, and alcohol explosions from more southerly origins.*

⑤ **Urban 2004** Graf Adelmann, Württemberg (€9.80) *Graf Adelmann is a savior of revered species threatened by extinction. The Urban may not share the distinction of his Muskattrollinger, but nevertheless it makes a nifty little red that I'd be happy to quaff in preference to many a jammy Trollinger—or Gamay, for that matter.*

⑥ **Dürkheimer Schenkenböhl Gewürztraminer Auslese 2004** Vier Jahreszeiten Winzer, Pfalz (€6.70) *A hint of pétillance and moderate alcohol of 11 percent give this zesty sweetie the kiss of life. Aromas of ginger, hazelnuts, and apricots provide added value not reflected in the price.*

⑦ **CasaNova Cabernet Sauvignon Trocken 2003** Kreuzberg, Ahr (€22) *First time around, Kreuzberg Senior was condemned to tear out his secret stash of Cabernet Sauvignon planted without official blessing, but now enthusiasts travel from abroad to get their hands on the legitimate successor.*

⑧ **Viognier Trocken 2004** Philipp Kuhn, Pfalz (€6.90 per 50-cl bottle) *A marked acidity sets the tone for Viognier's debut in Germany. More of an alternative to than competition for the conventional style.*

⑨ **Grüner Veltliner Trocken 2004** Koegler, Rheingau (€8.50) *One of only three German estates to experiment with Austria's bread-and-butter variety. Koegler's maiden vintage exhibits plenty of the peppery character associated with typical "Gru-Vee."*

⑩ **Acolon Trocken 2004** Remstalkellerei, Württemberg (€4.06) *I lack enthusiasm for the new wave of German red crosses, but this Dornfelder x Lemberger combination is fruity, velvety, and good value.*

Italy overview

Nicolas Belfrage MW & Franco Ziliani

Gianni Zonin, one of Italy's principal wine producers, with 1,800 ha of vineyard spread over 11 estates, has given a stark warning to the Italian wine industry.

"The world of Italian wine is in trouble. If we don't come out of this crisis in a hurry, I see thousands of jobs being lost in vineyards, in cellars, in distribution, and in the media." Zonin urges producers, government, and consumer groups to get together to work out a social pact that would bring about a reduction in taxes on wine, a reduction in selling prices, a rethink of established methods of distribution, and a relaunch of the image of wine. "There is talk of a modest recovery in wine consumption," Zonin continues, "but the reality is that the price of grapes is in strong decline, that in four years the wine sector has contracted by 11 percent, that millions of hectoliters are due for distillation, that exports are falling even to countries where wine consumption is rising. And who knows how long we are going to be able to fend off the wines of other producer nations in the internal market?"

Zonin argues that Italy cannot afford a collapse in the wine industry—it is too important for the national economy, constituting, as it does, the largest part of the agro-alimentary sector. But "the crisis is not just economic. Defending wine means defending our identity," he maintains.

Zonin declares himself convinced that many small wineries will disappear and that there will be concentration in all areas of wine production and distribution. There are positive aspects of this, he says, since the Italian wine industry currently suffers from chronic fragmentation and will have to fight in the future against the international colossi. Being aware of realities—something Zonin apparently believes is not currently the case—will at least allow for a response to what the future is likely to bring.

Piero Antinori, too, has pronounced on the crisis facing Italian wines at present: "The basic problem is that we have entered a cycle characterized by worldwide overproduction of 'premium wines.' The inevitable consequence is ever more aggressive competition, pressure on prices, as well as on the need to raise average quality. We need to take cognizance of this new situation, which is destined to continue long enough for things to return to balance—probably five to seven years." Antinori concluded by emphasizing the importance of maintaining quality.

Emilio Pedron, president of the giant GIV (Gruppo Italiano Vini), has also voiced concern. He says that a major shakeup of the much-fractioned and inefficient Italian viticultural-oenological scene is needed to get rid of a lot of the dead wood. Wits are predicting that the major vineyard owner in Tuscany in a few years will be Monte de' Paschi di Siena, the bank that funded a large part of the massive investment of recent times.

According to Riccardo Cotarella, one of Italy's most acclaimed oenologists, very much of the "modernist" (read Cab-Merlotist) persuasion, "the world of Italian wine has gotten its PR message all wrong. We have dwelt too much on varieties of ancient cultivation, forgetting that we are in fact a recent arrival among producers of quality wine. The defense of old traditions, being quite out of phase with market trends, has not proved a winning strategy. The debate over so-called autochthonous [indigenous] grape varieties is also mistaken, since what gives character to wines is mainly *terroir*. In this regard, the French example is illuminating." Is he referring to the current crisis in French quality wine, we wonder?

DOCG sticking with cork

Italy's Ministry of Agriculture has turned down the request of Unavini (the national union of wine-producing organizations) to allow synthetic corks or screwcaps for DOCG wines. This category, despite including such anomalies as basic Chianti and some pretty ordinary Soave, will therefore remain as a guaranteed sanctuary for wine lovers demanding the bark of the cork oak, leaving unchanged law number 164 of 1992, according to the spirit of which, closures other than cork would undermine the image of the nation's loftiest vinous creations.

Illva looks east

Illva, the large Italian producer famous for Amaretto di Saronno, has made a further leap in the world of wine. After having taken over Corvo (Duca di Salaparuta) and Florio (Marsala), it has now spread its tentacles into China. Following protracted negotiations with Yantai Changyu Pioneer Wine, Illva has beaten rivals such as Rémy Cointreau for control of the massive Chinese company with an investment of some €44.5 million. The directors of Changyu, based in the eastern province of Shandong, will retain 45 percent of the shares. "China is the future," commented Augusto Reina, CEO of Illva. "The consumption of wine in China stands today at 0.3 liters per capita, but it is growing rapidly, expected to more than double between now and 2010. Our entry into Changyu should open doors in the future not only for us but also for Italian wines generally."

Off to the still

Parts of Italy, notably Sicily (much trumpeted as the Old World's California), are once again, as in the bad old days of the European "wine lake," pursuing an aggressive policy of state-funded distillation of unwanted table wines. The Ministry of Agriculture applied not long ago to the EU Agriculture Commissioner for the right to distill several million hectoliters at a well-nigh derisory price (though presumably higher than the Sicilians, who put in for a hefty share, thought they could get for their overproduced plonk elsewhere). Paradoxically, after so many years—nay, decades—as a major bulk-wine exporter, Italy has never previously imported as much wine as it does currently (up 8.5 percent year on year), with more than 1.5 million hl purchased, mainly from Spain but also from France, Portugal, and (you guessed it) the United States.

Counterfeit wine rife in US

Wine piracy in the United States remains widespread. According to Coldiretti, the Italian farmers' organization, exports to the US, currently 30 percent of the total by value, could perhaps be doubled if counterfeit versions of Chianti, Barolo, and Marsala, as well as varietal labels such as Sangiovese, Refosco, Barbera, and Moscato—all purporting to be made in Italy—could be stopped. Life is not made any easier by the EU's capitulation to pressure from the US and elsewhere to allow the use of nongeographic (stylistic or fantasy) names like Amarone, Ripasso, Brunello, and Vino Nobile under certain conditions by non-Italian producers.

Grapevine

• **Italy is the number one** wine exporter to the United States, according to recent figures released by VeronaFiere, organizers of Verona's annual Vinitaly wine fair. They claim that the US is due to become the world's biggest wine-consuming nation by 2008. Over a recent eight-month period, Italy sold 1.283 million hl of wine to the US for a value of €629 million—10 percent up in volume and 16 percent up in value over the previous comparable period. VeronaFiere, in an effort to take full advantage of the trend, is organizing tours, tastings, and seminars in major US cities.

Northern Italy

Nicolas Belfrage MW & Franco Ziliani

The situation for Italy's most famous fizz Asti (formerly Asti Spumante) is, it seems, less than sparkling.

NICOLAS BELFRAGE MW   FRANCO ZILIANI

The Asti consortium recently released figures revealing that sales year on year over a six-month period were just under 20 million bottles—a fall of 3.2 percent. A major drop was felt on the home market, where sales fell from 3.1 million to 2.4 million—a fall of 22.8 percent. Consortium president Paolo Ricagno announced a major promotional effort, the McKinsey project, to win back customers over a four-year period. The prime target would be Italy, with a major push to boost sales over Easter 2006. "We have to get the bottles on restaurant and wine-bar tables at the aperitif hour, and as the ideal accompaniment to our traditional sweets," he said.

NICOLAS BELFRAGE MW was born in Los Angeles and raised in New York and England. He studied in Paris, Siena, and London, earning a degree at University College London in French and Italian. Nick has been specializing in Italian wines since the 1970s and became a Master of Wine in 1980, the first American citizen to do so. He is the author of the double-award-winning *Life Beyond Lambrusco* (Sidgwick & Jackson, 1985), *Barolo to Valpolicella* (Mitchell Beazley, 1999), and *Brunello to Zibibbo* (Mitchell Beazley, 2001). Nick is a regular contributor to *Harpers Wine and Spirit Weekly* and *The World of Fine Wine*.

FRANCO ZILIANI is a freelance writer who has specialized in Italian wines since 1985. He is a regular contributor to the English periodicals *Harpers Wine and Spirit Weekly*, *Decanter*, and *The World of Fine Wine* (where he is also a member of the editorial board), the California magazine *Wine Business Monthly*, the French magazine *La Revue du Vin de France*, the Italian periodicals *AIS Lombardia News*, *Spirito di Vino*, *LaVINIum*, and *VQ*, and the Italian weekly magazine *Il Corriere Vinicolo* (the official organ of Unione Italiana Vini). Franco publishes a weekly wine newsletter, *Bvino*, which is mailed to 28,000 wine enthusiasts, and a wine blog, *Vino al vino* (www.vinoalvino.org).

Another important target is Germany, which, despite the current crisis, remains the number-one export market, holding fairly steady while sales in the United States have dipped by nearly 20 percent and in Britain by 14 percent. The good news, however, is from emerging markets such as Russia, where sales are up just over 100 percent, with Japan, Central America, and Oceania all on upward trends.

Pinot *Fraudolento*

The Pinot-Grigio-that-isn't saga continues. Italy's most popular and most tampered-with white wine has once again found itself at the center of a scandal, as is presumably inevitable when demand for a product so far outstrips supply. Seven producers of the Veneto region are under investigation by Padua's Nucleo Anti Sofisticazione (NAS; fraud squad) for buying cheap *vino da tavola* at €10,000 per 300-liter tank (100 tanks over the past two years) and selling it off as Pinot Grigio and other IGT or DOC wines to major producers. Sale price? €60,000—a nice 500 percent markup! The producers reported to be implicated are Grappolo Trading of Bigarello (Mantua), Eurovini of Portogruaro (Venice), Italvini of Arcole (Verona), Azienda Agricola Fattori Gianfranco of San Bonifacio (Veneto; no relation to any other producer called Fattori), Eredi Bartolini of Basigliano (Udine), EuroComm of Vicenza, and Cantine Poli of Gambellara, whose head, Silvano Poli, was previously sentenced to four years in prison for diverse frauds.

Grapevine

• **Bartolo Mascarello,** one of the great traditionalists of Barolo, died in March 2005 following a long illness. Bartolo began his vinous career in the early 1960s, taking over from his father a business built on sales of wine in demijohn, which he gradually transformed into sales by the bottle. He was one of the last, in this age of the *cru*, to believe that Barolo is best when it derives from a blend of Nebbiolo grapes of different provenances; and of course he had no time for *barriques*.

Opinion:
Contradictory information

That Italy is a land of contradictions is accepted by all, yet recently the Italian wine scene seems to be outdoing itself in producing non sequiturs.

The first one is that sales to certain markets, the United States in particular, where Italy is number one, are doing well, and sales to Russia and other new markets are increasing, while in the once-key markets of Germany and the UK sales remain weak. Indeed, in the UK, Italy has slipped to a humiliating fifth place after the US, with its weak dollar and low prices.

The second contradiction is that certain wines that were going great guns a few short years ago are in a state of near-total collapse: super-Tuscans, those highfalutin, high-priced fantasy jobs with an IGT denomination and plenty of *Wine Spectator*–style concentration and oak, led the way in the disaster stakes, but other wines that had become overpriced in the boom times, such as Barolo or Barbaresco or even Chianti Classico, are suffering too. However, there are (as there should be in a good contradiction) signs that some of the upper DOC(G)s, having realigned themselves pricewise in relation to the world market, are making a comeback.

Grapevine

At last, the long journey of Picolit through the bureaucratic jungle leading to DOCG has concluded. Differences between Picolit DOCG and the old DOC will be a reduction in the maximum crop allowed, down to 50 quintals per hectare, and lengthening of the prescribed drying period, which will facilitate a reduction to 42 percent in the yield pressed from the grapes, resulting in a maximum yield of 21 hl/ha.

• The enormous Cantina di Soave in the town of Soave has merged with the cooperative of Illasi in eastern Valpolicella. Between them, they will have 1,700 members with 4,100 ha of vineyard and five wineries, accounting for 34 percent of DOC Soave and 47 percent of DOC Valpolicella.

Vintage Report

Advance report on the latest harvest

2005

In quantity terms the north was down on the previous year: Piemonte by 10 percent, Lombardy by 15 percent, Trentino-Alto Adige, Friuli, and Emilia by 20 percent, Veneto by 25 percent. In Piemonte the grapes most favored were the early ripeners, such as Chardonnay and Pinot Nero (for sparkling wines), which had good acidity and healthy levels of tartaric as distinct from malic acid. Middle ripeners such as Moscato and Brachetto bombed, suffering widespread rot and lack of balance. In the red department, Dolcetto did reasonably well, Barbera much less so. Those Nebbiolo producers who pruned rigorously and held on till the rains had passed and the sun reappeared at the end of the first week of October, and who didn't get clobbered by hail, did all right. It won't be a famous Barolo/Barbaresco vintage, but there will be some good to very good wines, favoring aroma over power. Market-wise, prices are holding steady or falling—no one is talking of increases even with rising costs.

In Lombardy's Oltrepò Pavese and Franciacorta, the picture was similar: early-ripening Chardonnays and Pinots for sparkling wines came in healthy and balanced; Barberas and Bonardas picked in September were compromised. Exceptionally, the late-picked Nebbiolos of the Valtelline turned in some excellent wines.

In Trentino-Alto Adige, early predictions of abundant yields were dashed by September rains, which hit the important white grapes especially hard. This area being a major source of all-conquering Pinot Grigio, already far better represented on labels than on the ground, one can only anticipate trouble, with yet another scandal waiting to happen. Qualitatively the verdict would be pretty good for base wine for sparklers, fairly good for whites, not brilliant for reds, especially where vineyards are not carefully tended.

In Veneto it was a difficult year, with various fungal diseases and some fairly destructive hailstorms. The worst was reserved for September, however, with harvest rains causing widespread rot in Valpolicella, Soave, and Bardolino. In western Veneto, production was way down and quality was indifferent, though eastern growers fared better. Not a bad year for Prosecco.

Friuli-Venezia Giulia produced some good—light but aromatic—white grapes in 2005, though reds, always vulnerable to underripeness in these parts, suffered from a lack of sunshine from mid-August on. Late-harvest grapes fared the best.

Updates on the previous five vintages

2004

Vintage rating: *Red: 92, White: 90*

This vintage has largely lived up to its promise as (with 2001) one of the best of the century, not that that's saying too much (yet). Following two difficult years, 2004—a year of measured heat and rainfall, with the added bonus of fine weather at harvest time—came up trumps for both quantity and quality, whites as well as reds. The whites of Friuli, Alto Adige, Trentino, Veneto, Lombardy, and Piemonte show great finesse and brightness, with rich, intense fragrances and aromas. Reds are marked by solid structure, good varietal characteristics, balance, and excellent aging potential. Piemontese reds Nebbiolo, Dolcetto, and Barbera showed a significant increase in sugar levels, and acid levels were ideal, the wines combining the best of traditional structure with modern roundness, fruit, and balance.

2003

Vintage rating: *Red: 88, White: 82*

One of the shortest harvests in the past 50 years, following the absolute shortest, 2002. The year was marked by high temperatures and drought, the good news being that grapes remained universally healthy; the bad being that many were raisined, baked, or overconcentrated. A very early harvest, whites being picked in many cases in the first half of August, reds not much later. Those who go in for mega-wines will like the 2003s, but balance was not easy to come by and was achieved, when it was achieved, in well-tended, deep-rooted vineyards. Barolo and Barbaresco attracted some raves, as did Valpolicella and other reds, but it was a year, when all is said and done, for careful selection.

2002

Vintage rating: *Red: 70, White: 80*

In retrospect, from certain points of view, not as bad as we thought at the time, nor certainly as bad as the international pundits have painted it. In Piemonte, it's true, many Barolos/Barbarescos were produced in tiny quantities or not at all, due to hail damage or general lack of ripeness, but Nebbiolos of lesser denominations, as well as Barberas and Dolcettos, often benefited from the addition of grapes from great vineyards normally reserved for the *crus*. A similar comment could be made in Valpolicella— wines not as big as usual but drinking nicely now. As for whites, some growers in Soave were declaring 2002 to be the best year for a decade, and indeed there was plenty of freshness and nerve, if less alcohol, in whites of other northern zones: Gavi, Alto Adige, and Friuli.

2001

Vintage rating: *Red: 94, White: 90*

The first year of the new millennium had points of excellence to rival those of the previous six. There were predictions of Barolos and Barbarescos at the highest quality levels, possibly capping the achievements of the previous six years. Other Piemontese wines were excellent too, with Barberas and Dolcettos of great concentration and structure. Nebbiolo (Chiavennasca) in Valtellina was also splendid. A very good year, too, for the whites of Friuli and for the Soaves of Veneto, as well as for the reds of Valpolicella.

2000

Vintage rating: *Red: 90, White: 86*

A very hot year more or less everywhere, giving rise to wines of great concentration and power, albeit lacking a bit in subtlety. An excellent year for the Pinot Neros of Alto Adige, but also very good for the aromatic varieties Sauvignon and Gewurztraminer throughout the northeast. In Alba Barolo, Barbaresco, and Barbera recorded the sixth excellent vintage in a row, the previous historical record being a mere three (1988, 1989, and 1990). The Amarones of Valpolicella enjoyed ideal conditions in the post-harvest drying period, so there are some superb wines.

Lists compiled by Franco Ziliani.

GREATEST WINE PRODUCERS

1. Bruno Giacosa (Barolo & Barbaresco)
2. Giacomo Conterno (Barolo)
3. Giuseppe Mascarello (Barolo)
4. Triacca (Valtellina)
5. Cantina Produttori Terlano (South Tyrol)
6. Ca' del Bosco (Franciacorta)
7. Borgo del Tiglio (Friuli)
8. Romano Dal Forno (Valpolicella)
9. Elio Grasso (Barolo)
10. Pieropan (Soave, Veneto)

FASTEST-IMPROVING PRODUCERS

1. Mario Gagliasso (Langhe)
2. Vietti (Langhe)
3. Schiavenza (Langhe)
4. Bartolo Mascarello (Langhe)
5. La Ferghettina (Franciacorta)
6. Fondazione Fojanini (Valtellina)
7. Paolo Scavino (Langhe)
8. Unterortl Castel Juval (South Tyrol)
9. Ettore Germano (Langhe)
10. Borgogno (Langhe)

NEW UP-AND-COMING PRODUCERS

1. Luigi Drocco (Langhe)
2. Cascina Corte (Langhe)
3. Brunnerhof Mazzon Kurt Rottensteiner (Alto Adige)
4. Le Strie (Valtellina)
5. Bossi Fedrigotti (Trentino)
6. Rosset (Valle d'Aosta)
7. Lo Triolet (Valle d'Aosta)
8. Garlider (South Tyrol)
9. Pacherhof Huber (South Tyrol)
10. Edoardo Sobrino (Langhe)

BEST-VALUE PRODUCERS

1. La Crotta di Vegneron (Valle d'Aosta)
2. Brezza (Langhe)
3. Cascina Minella (Langhe)
4. Oddero Fratelli (Langhe)
5. Comm GB Burlotto (Langhe)
6. Aurelio Settimo (Langhe)
7. Le Ragose (Valpolicella)
8. Brovia (Langhe)
9. Livia Fontana (Langhe)
10. Bricco del Cucù (Langhe)

GREATEST-QUALITY WINES

1. **Barolo Monprivato Riserva Cà d'Morissio 1997** Giuseppe Mascarello, Langhe (€125)
2. **Barolo Sarmassa 2001** Brezza, Langhe (€40)
3. **Barolo Rocche 2001** Vietti, Langhe (€50)
4. **Barolo Bricco Boschis Vigna San Giuseppe Riserva 1999** Cavallotto, Langhe (€35)
5. **Barolo Ginestra Vigna Casa Maté 2001** Elio Grasso (€40)
6. **Barolo Bricco delle Viole 2001** Vajra, Langhe (€40)
7. **Barolo Rocche dei Brovia 2001** Brovia, Langhe (€45)
8. **Amarone della Valpolicella Classico Marta Galli 1999** Le Ragose, Valpolicella (€40)
9. **Amarone di Marchetto 2001** Trabucchi, Verona (€30)
10. **Barbera d'Alba Falletto 2003** Bruno Giacosa, Langhe (€30)

BEST BARGAINS

1. **Dolcetto di Dogliani 2004** Cascina Minella, Langhe (€5.50)
2. **Rosso di Valtellina 2003** Arpepe, Valtellina (€7)
3. **Arneis del Roero Bricco delle Ciliegie 2004** Giovanni Almondo, Roero (€6.50)
4. **Teres Rosato 2004** Comm GB Burlotto, Langhe (€7)
5. **Südtiroler Vernatsch Haselhof 2004** Brigl, Alto Adige (€5.50)
6. **Nebbiolo d'Alba 2001** Luigi Drocco, Langhe (€7)
7. **Bardolino Le Fraghe 2004** Matilde Poggi, Verona (€5)
8. **Langhe Freisa 2004** Mario Cozzo, Langhe (€6)
9. **Dolcetto d'Alba Vughera 2004** Schiavenza, Langhe (€6.50)
10. **Dolcetto di Dogliani 2004** Bricco del Cucù, Langhe (€6)

MOST EXCITING OR UNUSUAL FINDS

1. **Barolo Monprivato Riserva Cà d'Morissio 1997** Giuseppe Mascarello, Langhe (€125) *From one of the famous crus of Barolo, Monprivato at Castiglione Falletto, this Riserva, matured for 48 months in large Slavonian oak barrels, is surely one of the greatest Barolos ever produced by Mauro Mascarello. It somehow combines immediate drinkability with an ability to age well over an extended period of time.*
2. **Barolo Torriglione 2001** Mario Gagliasso, Langhe (€25) *Gagliasso is the only grower at La Morra to vinify this excellent cru in purezza since 1999, refining it in both*

barriques (with low toast) and large Slavonian barrels. The result is a wine of great character with velvety tannins balanced by well-judged acidity. A wine of limited availability (4,500 bottles), this is already very agreeable but destined for a long and positive evolution in bottle.

❸ Barbaresco 2002 Cigliuti, Langhe (€20) Though 2002 was a difficult year in the Langhe, this top-flight grower of Neive, a traditionalist open to new ideas and one of the points of reference for the denomination, has nonetheless succeeded in producing this highly valid straight Barbaresco in place of the two crus—Serraboella and Vigne Erta—that he usually makes. For drinking young, though it could develop well with a couple of years in bottle.

❹ Amarone di Marchetto 2001 Trabucchi, Verona (€30) The interest of this wine is not just that it's a wonderful Amarone of an excellent year, but that it comes not from the Classico zone of Valpolicella but from the somewhat maligned hills east of Verona. Aromatic and complex, it combines an array of perfumes (herb, fruit, licorice, garrigue, minerality) with a crisp, lively acidity that cuts out any stickiness.

❺ Fumin Chambave 2003 La Crotta di Vegneron, Valle d'Aosta (€10) Fumin is a red grape native to the Valle d'Aosta, making a wine, in the hands of this excellent cooperative, of spicy aroma and a palate of wild berries and tar—quite tannic. This is a wine that is well capable of standing up to the red-meat and cheese-based dishes of the region.

❻ Langhe Freisa 2004 Comm GB Burlotto, Langhe (€8) Freisa may be the mamma of Nebbiolo. It comes in various styles: still and fizzy, sweet and dry. This one is youthful and unoaked, purple of hue and aggressive of perfume, structured like Nebbiolo but nervous and almost sharp like Barbera, with an interesting range of aromas. Above all, it is highly drinkable.

❼ Rosso di Valtellina 2003 Arpepe, Valtellina (€7) From one of the few traditionalist producers remaining in Valtellina, this Nebbiolo-based red is vinified in stainless steel, then aged for three months in 50-hl barrels. Good example of a "mountain" Nebbiolo, with pointy acidity but plenty of flavor and aroma to back it up.

❽ Dolcetto di Dogliani 2004 Cascina Minella, Langhe (€5.50) An excellent year for Dolcetto, and this is Dolcetto as it ought to be, made by an intelligent modernist with his eye on preservation and exaltation of fruit. The color is intense and vivid, and the nose and palate are strikingly fresh.

❾ Barbera d'Alba Cannubi Muscatel 2003 Brezza, Langhe (€8.50) A great year for Barbera. The hot summer brought the grapes to full ripeness at relatively low acid levels. Brezza is a traditionalist producer who ages in large Slavonian oak and has made a classic Barbera.

❿ Alto Adige Riesling 2004 Falkenstein, Alto Adige (€12.50) Riesling is obviously not a grape generally associated with Italy, but there are those who would dispute that Alto Adige is part of Italy. This wine achieves the aromatic fragrance associated with the grape and promises an interesting development for the future.

Central & Southern Italy

Nicolas Belfrage MW & Franco Ziliani

After 18 years of separation, the two consortia of Chianti Classico have agreed (according to some; constrained, according to others) to merge.

NICOLAS BELFRAGE MW   FRANCO ZILIANI

In 1987, after numerous major producers (such as Antinori) had expressed their unwillingness to continue supporting its promotional activities, the Consortium had divided into the Consorzio Vino Chianti Classico, responsible for technical, viticultural, and legal matters, and the Consorzio Gallo Nero, dispenser of the famous black-rooster insignia and responsible for press and publicity. With this decision, it is back to being just one big happy family again, with all producers of Chianti Classico having to sport the black rooster on their bottle neck as part of the DOCG sticker. The fact

NICOLAS BELFRAGE MW was born in Los Angeles and raised in New York and England. He studied in Paris, Siena, and London, earning a degree at University College London in French and Italian. Nick has been specializing in Italian wines since the 1970s and became a Master of Wine in 1980, the first American citizen to do so. He is the author of the double-award-winning *Life Beyond Lambrusco* (Sidgwick & Jackson, 1985), *Barolo to Valpolicella* (Mitchell Beazley, 1999), and *Brunello to Zibibbo* (Mitchell Beazley, 2001). Nick is a regular contributor to *Harpers Wine and Spirit Weekly* and *The World of Fine Wine*.

FRANCO ZILIANI is a freelance writer who has specialized in Italian wines since 1985. He is a regular contributor to the English periodicals *Harpers Wine and Spirit Weekly*, *Decanter*, and *The World of Fine Wine* (where he is also a member of the editorial board), the California magazine *Wine Business Monthly*, the French magazine *La Revue du Vin de France*, the Italian periodicals *AIS Lombardia News*, *Spirito di Vino*, *LaVINIum*, and *VQ*, and the Italian weekly magazine *Il Corriere Vinicolo* (the official organ of Unione Italiana Vini). Franco publishes a weekly wine newsletter, *Bvino*, which is mailed to 28,000 wine enthusiasts, and a wine blog, *Vino al vino* (www.vinoalvino.org).

that the law had recently changed to make the consortium the state's sole representative in the dispensing of the DOCG qualification had of course no bearing on the decision by the many go-it-aloners to rejoin the fold.

The Chianti Classico Consortium now consists of 600 associates with a combined production of 260,000 hl of wine annually and a turnover of half a billion euros.

Fraudulent Chianti: arrest made

One of the functions of the new Chianti Classico Consortium is to investigate scams such as the one reported in a recent Gallo Nero bulletin. The communiqué reports that Piero Conticelli "is accused of defrauding Chianti Classico producers by selling them wine purporting to be Chianti Classico, but produced outside the DOCG denomination. Conticelli, who is currently under arrest for fraud, owns 200 ha of Chianti Classico vines spread over two Chianti Classico estates, and also owns vineyards outside the Chianti Classico area. The equivalent of over 9 million bottles of (so-called) Chianti Classico has been seized by Italian authorities from top Tuscan estates, including Ruffino. Authorities immediately called in the Consorzio Vino Chianti Classico to … thoroughly check all aspects of production on selected Chianti Classico estates—this includes tallying what is planted in the vineyards with what is produced."

This is not the only case of scandal touching major Tuscan producers in 2005: an earlier one involved Frescobaldi, after a raid by the Guardia di Finanza, Italy's fiscal police, on the Frescobaldi cellars at Pontassieve, as well as on their Fattoria Castiglioni in Val di Pesa. The alleged violation of regulations concerns the provenance of grapes used in wine production, in terms both of varieties employed and zones of origin.

"Of course we source wines from outside," commented Vittorio Frescobaldi, president of Marchesi de' Frescobaldi, "but only for bottling as *vino da tavola* or to be sold at our farms in bulk." The investigation has since disappeared somewhere under the carpet.

But back to Signor Conticelli. The authorities have allowed the wine currently in distribution—in Ruffino's case, under the Aziano 2002 and Riserva Ducale 2002 labels (both Chianti Classico)—to remain on sale because it might be genuine. Ruffino is nonetheless stuck with 60,000 cases of wine in its cellars that will have to be sold as *vino da tavola*. There is no suggestion, it should be emphasized, that Ruffino or any of the other companies are in any way complicit in the fraud.

All in all, though, it makes you wonder where some of the stuff under these famous brands (we could name others more famous and certainly more costly still) comes from.

TERUZZI & PUTHOD IS JUST AN APERITIF

The Campari Group has bought 100 percent of the Teruzzi & Puthod winery of San Gimignano for €12 million. Teruzzi & Puthod, formerly the property of Enrico Teruzzi and Carmen Puthod, is the largest in the San Gimignano area with 194 ha, 90 of which are planted to vines. Their principal wines are Terre di Tufi and Vernaccia di San Gimignano. Annual turnover is over €4 million, 80 percent of which comes from exports. The Campari portfolio already includes Sella & Mosca of Sardinia and Enrico Serafini of Piemonte. The rumor is that the purchase is the first move in a campaign of acquisitions on the part of Campari.

THREE CENTURIES NOT OUT

Chianti producer Melini celebrated 300 years in the wine business in 2005. The Melini family of 1705 were prosperous entrepreneurs from the Sieve Valley, producing the Tuscan wine of the time, Vermiglio, at their premises in Pontassieve. In 1860 Laborel Melini starting "bottling" his wines in wicker flasks, which were easier to distribute. The last scion of the family was Luigi Melini, who died in World War I. Subsequent owners were Buitoni of Perugia, Martini & Rossi, and, currently, Gruppo Italiano Vini (GIV), one of Italy's two biggest producers (with Caviro of Romagna) in terms of volume and value (total turnover in 2004 was €236 million).

Grapevine

• **Arezzo province in Tuscany** has regaled the bewildered international consumer of Italian wines with yet another obscure DOC: Pietraviva. The green light was given by the National Wine Committee after a process initiated in 1999. Wines of the new denomination went on sale from fall 2005. White grapes figuring in the makeup of Pietraviva are Malvasia Bianca and Chardonnay, while reds include Sangiovese, Canaiolo, Ciliegiolo, and the inevitable Merlot and Cabernet.

• **Tenuta di Sasso,** the estate recently created by brothers Piero and Lodovico Antinori, will have a brand-new winery designed by architect Gae Aulenti by the 2007 vintage. By 2006, Campo di Sasso's vineyards at Bibbona in the northern Maremma will consist of 70 ha planted to Cabernet Franc, Petit Verdot, and Merlot. The 75,000-sq-ft (7,000-sq-m) winery will be almost entirely underground to minimize environmental impact, and will, in the words of its creator, be "a sculpture in the countryside." Production capacity will be around 3,500 hl, and the winery will make around 50,000 bottles a year. The first wine of the new *azienda* is already out, the 2003 Insoglio del Cinghiale, which will stand at the base of the quality pyramid. The second wine, Il Pino di Biserno, will come on stream in 2006, with the top *cru*, Il Biserno, following later.

• **Marchesi de' Frescobaldi,** which had already reacquired the 50 percent of Luce della Vite that Constellation Brands had bought from Mondavi, has now purchased from Constellation the 50 percent stake in Ornellaia that also belonged to Mondavi. Frescobaldi now owns 100 percent of the prestigious 91-ha Bolgheri property, founded in 1981, ironically by Lodovico Antinori of the family of their greatest rivals, Marchesi Antinori.

Opinion:
Chianti with a Sicilian twist?

Among the instigators of the remarriage of the Chianti Classico consortia is undoubtedly Ser Lapo Mazzei, the grand old man of Chianti Classico, who has worked for years to this end. "The rules [governing Chianti Classico production] will have to change now, with the inclusion of other vines capable of more rapid maturation, in particular certain Sicilian varieties, as well as an experimental grape that has done very well in the Maremma."

The fact that Ser Lapo's estate, Fonterutoli, has a large subsidiary in the Scansano zone of the Maremma may have something to do with his enthusiasm for the latter, though to qualify, the vine in question would have to be planted in the Chianti Classico region, where it might not fare so well. Agronomists were left scratching their heads, however, about the mystery Sicilian grape or grapes being referred to, since it is unlikely that anything that ripens in good time so far south would do so very frequently farther north. Suggestions that inclusion of Sicilian grape varieties in Chianti Classico might be in the form of wine rather than of Chianti-grown grapes have been dismissed as preposterous.

Ser Lapo does, however, remind us that "until the birth of the DOCG, Chianti Classico used to be blended with 15 percent of grape must from Puglia." Such a thing, which will probably be detectable by DNA testing before long, would today be quite illegal and therefore perfectly unthinkable.

Pure Brunello

Despite a recent vote by the consortium of Brunello di Montalcino confirming growers' determination to keep Brunello as a 100 percent Sangiovese wine, the debate continues to rage over whether certain producers are slipping something "ameliorative" into the blend. A noted wine journalist (name on application) was recently approached on the subject by a couple of officials of NAS (fraud squad), who referred to wines having being seized by the authorities in Denmark as well as to a growing number of articles on the part of foreign journalists hinting at the unauthorized "improvement" of Brunello. The journalist in question was particularly miffed over rumors that he, among other hacks, was in some way responsible for the illicit carryings-on, rather than the producers who may or may not be perpetrating them; or at least that he was in some way culpable for having written about it. "Is this not," he asked, "a method rather of the mafia than of a civilized democratic state?"

Vintage Report

Advance report on the latest harvest

2005

Volume-wise, compared with 2004, central Italy suffered a bit less than the north, while the south more or less broke even. Tuscany was the main loser, down 20 percent, with the Marche and Lazio down 10 percent, Abruzzo and Campania down 5 percent. Puglia, Sicily, and Sardinia were all up 5 percent.

Tuscany, already a highly variegated region in terms of climatic conditions and altitude, was more leopard-skinned than ever in 2005. Rainfall was in excess of the norm in some parts, like Chianti Classico and Montalcino, while in the areas just west of Florence—Montalcino, Montespertoli, and Empoli—there was less than usual. Some places, like parts of Rufina, experienced savage hailstorms, while many other areas got away scot-free. Harvesting in the classic zones began around the last week of September, and what fruit was picked before the end of that week was quite healthy. But the first week of October saw persistent rain, which caused considerable rot. Timing was everything this year, and luck played its part, too. The same was largely true for Umbria and Lazio.

The picture was similar along the east coast, though quality was said to be quite high for grapes picked before the rains of early October. Verdicchio and Montepulciano, respectively champions of the Marche and Abruzzo, fared well from earlier pickings but found it hard going after the washout of early October. A knowledgeable oenologist in Abruzzo estimated that perhaps 30 percent of the wine was of good or very good quality, 70 percent questionable to poor.

Reports from southern regions like Campania and Puglia are more sanguine, noting that, while September rains did cause some disturbance at vintage time, results were largely satisfactory and in many cases superior to those of 2004. This holds especially for the very late-picked Aglianico of Campania, Basilicata, and northern Puglia. On the other hand, grape prices at source are taking a hammering even compared with last year, having fallen by up to 30 percent in some places.

It is wise to separate the islands of Sicily and Sardinia from the mainland in 2005. Conditions here were nothing like as difficult as in the rest of the country, and there are reports of (largely) healthy, well-balanced grapes and wines on the level of good to excellent.

Updates on the previous five vintages

2004

Vintage rating: *Red: 95, White: 90*

In central Italy and most of the south, all the factors for exceptional wine were in place: growth stages all normal, slow and gradual sugar accumulation, good balance of components in the fruit, appropriate yield ratio between grapes and wine. There were no hot spells during the summer months, no frosts in the spring or later, and humidity levels stayed normal. What was needed, however, in particular for late-maturing varieties, was an exemplary September, bestowing sunny days, a touch of rain, and good diurnal temperature differences. Which was precisely what central viticultural areas west of the Apennines, and some southern areas, received. In Tuscany, Brunello di Montalcino was given the first maximum rating of five stars since 1997, and it was a similar story in Chianti Classico and Montepulciano. In Tuscany, Romagna, the Marche, Lazio, Campania, and Sardinia, the judgment was "exceptional." Only along the eastern coast, toward the south—in Abruzzo, Molise, and especially Puglia—was quality compromised to some extent by vintage-time rain.

2003

Vintage rating: *Red: 88, White: 80*

A year of drought and very high temperatures, with little relief in the evenings. Vineyards worst affected were toward the center, these conditions being more normal in the south—for example, Puglia's principal reds, Negroamaro and Primitivo, especially those planted to *alberello*, thrived in the conditions. But it was too much for most whites, which tended to emerge flabby and overweight, and many reds, especially those lacking deep roots or planted in well-drained soil. Sugar ripening was very advanced in many places, but it was not necessarily accompanied by polyphenolic ripeness, which made for too many unbalanced wines. As in the north, the classic wines will need careful selecting.

2002

Vintage rating: *Red: 67, White: 79*

The shortest vintage in quantity for 50 years, qualitatively 2002 has proved not as bad as predicted. White wines like Verdicchio are fresh and fragrant, with plenty of nerve. Sangiovese in Tuscany had a poor time of it, but there is so much Merlot and Cabernet these days that they can compensate. Lower-than-average temperatures, plenty of rain, and freak weather conditions made a mess of things along the east coast, but modern techniques saved a lot that would have gone down the pan in 1992.

2001

Vintage rating: *Red: 93, White: 93*

A good year virtually everywhere. Marginally better, perhaps, than 1997, although that vintage received much more hype. Perhaps 2001 was less anomalous than 1997, with wines more in the mainstream but at a higher-than-normal level, whereas 1997s in retrospect seem almost too ripe, too much of a good thing. In Chianti Classico, the level was very good from the start, and the emerging wines confirm that it is a year of excellent aroma, concentration, and balance. In the south, Puglia and Sicily enjoyed ideal conditions. All in all, a very satisfactory outcome for both whites and reds.

2000

Vintage rating: *Red: 88, White: 82*

A very hot year, with a dry summer, giving rise to wines that are concentrated and potent, but lacking in elegance, with a slightly baked character—especially in central Tuscany. In some places the vegetation was temporarily arrested by the heat, yielding alcoholic wines with unripe tannins. On the east coast and in the south, where the varieties are more used to coping with such conditions, everything went swimmingly. As a rule, though, better for reds than whites.

Lists compiled by Franco Ziliani.

GREATEST WINE PRODUCERS

1. Case Basse Soldera (Montalcino)
2. Fattoria di Felsina (Chianti Classico)
3. Fontodi (Chianti Classico)
4. Lisini (Montalcino)
5. Isole e Olena (Chianti Classico)
6. Poggio di Sotto (Montalcino)
7. Montevertine (Chianti Classico)
8. Castello della Sala (Umbria)
9. Mastroberardino (Campania)
10. Palari (Sicily)

FASTEST-IMPROVING PRODUCERS

1. Camigliano (Montalcino)
2. Gianni Brunelli (Montalcino)
3. Valdicava (Montalcino)
4. Gorelli Le Potazzine (Montalcino)
5. Querciabella (Chianti Classico)
6. Rocca di Montegrossi (Chianti Classico)
7. Le Bonce Giovanna Morganti (Chianti Classico)
8. Marramiero (Abruzzo)
9. Marisa Cuomo Gran Furor Divina Costiera (Campania)
10. Benanti (Sicily)

NEW UP-AND-COMING PRODUCERS

1. Velenosi (Marche)
2. Podere Guado al Melo (Tuscany)
3. Cantine del Notaio (Basilicata)
4. Tenuta Zicari (Puglia)
5. Feudi della Medusa (Sardinia)
6. Di Marzo (Campania)
7. Le Querce (Basilicata)
8. Enrico Ceci (Marche)
9. Cantine Carrozzo (Puglia)
10. Cantine Petrelli (Puglia)

BEST-VALUE PRODUCERS

1. Caprili (Montalcino)
2. Farnese (Abruzzo)
3. Mocali (Montalcino)
4. Michele Satta (Bolgheri)
5. Tenuta Il Poggione (Montalcino)
6. Bosco (Abruzzo)
7. Ciavolich (Abruzzo)
8. Agricole Vallone (Puglia)
9. Candido (Puglia)
10. Librandi (Calabria)

GREATEST-QUALITY WINES

1. **Marsala Vergine Riserva 1962** Carlo Pellegrino, Sicily (€45)
2. **Brunello di Montalcino 2000** Gorelli Le Potazzine, Montalcino (€30)
3. **Brunello di Montalcino Riserva 1999** Case Basse Soldera, Montalcino (€100)
4. **Rosso di Montalcino 2002** Poggio di Sotto, Montalcino (€60)
5. **I Sodi di San Niccolò 1999** Castellare di Castellina, Chianti Classico (€35)
6. **Brunello di Montalcino Ugolaia 1999** Lisini, Montalcino (€40)
7. **Flaccianello della Pieve 1990** Fontodi, Chianti Classico (€40)
8. **Fontalloro 1990** Felsina, Chianti Classico (€40)
9. **Val di Neto Rosso Magno Megonio 2003** Librandi, Calabria (€25)
10. **Faro Palari 2003** Palari, Sicily (€35)

BEST BARGAINS

1. **Canaiolo 2004** Montenidoli, Tuscany (€9)
2. **Rosso di Montalcino 2003** Argiano, Montalcino (€8)
3. **Montepulciano d'Abruzzo Vigna Corvino 2003** Pasetti, Abruzzo (€6)
4. **Castel del Monte Rosé 2004** Rivera, Puglia (€4.50)
5. **Vivaio Salento Rosato 2004** Vigneti Reale, Puglia (€4.50)
6. **Vino Nobile di Montepulciano 2003** Contucci, Montepulciano (€12)
7. **Savuto Rosso 2003** Odoardi, Calabria (€6.50)
8. **Falanghina di Bonea 2003** Masseria Frattasi, Campania (€5)
9. **Campi Flegrei Falanghina 2004** Cantine Farro, Campania (€5)
10. **Carignano del Sulcis Grotta Rossa** Cantina Santadi, Sardinia (€7)

MOST EXCITING OR UNUSUAL FINDS

1. **Marsala Vergine Riserva 1962** Carlo Pellegrino, Sicily (€45) *This outstanding Marsala, recently made commercially available, has spent an amazing 43 years in cask. Made from Grillo and Catarratto grapes, it has evolved into an ethereal, otherworldly beverage of astonishing nuance and complexity.*
2. **Brunello di Montalcino 1999** Gorelli Le Potazzine, Montalcino (€16) *From one of the most interesting estates in Montalcino,*

this is a Brunello combining the best of traditional knowledge with modern technology and technique.

3 **Chianti Classico 2002** Rocca di Montegrossi, Chianti Classico (€8.50) *The 2002 vintage in central Tuscany saw a lot of moaning over vintage-time rains following a cool summer, and a good bit of jiggery-pokery, mainly by way of excessive Merlot or Cabernet in the Chianti Classico. A few extremely rigorous, honest, and conscientious growers were at work, however, as this impeccable example from Marco Ricasoli's excellent estate demonstrates.*

4 **Salento Rosso Carminio 2003** Cantine Carrozzo, Puglia (€7) *This is a recent arrival among the hordes of producers trying to cash in on the international fame of Salice Salentino. Negroamaro in purezza, the wine displays all the plummy fruitiness and smooth structure that has made Salice Salentino famous.*

5 **Chianti Classico 2002** Isole e Olena, Chianti Classico (€12) *This wine was twice refused the denomination for being "untypical." With 85 percent Sangiovese, 10 percent Canaiolo, and 5 percent Syrah (20 percent would be permissible, many went well beyond), it admirably reflects what actually happened in that difficult vintage by being light but intense, aromatic, and of tenuous body.*

6 **Vernaccia di San Gimignano Fiore 2004** Montenidoli, Tuscany (€9.50) *Given the boring nature of most wines that go by this prestigious name, this one, entirely from free-run juice, surprises by its elegance, personality, and complexity.*

7 **Falanghina di Bonea 2003** Masseria Frattasi, Campania (€5) *Campania is full of fascinating grape varieties, and Falanghina is one of the best. Good Falanghina will have the accent on fruit flavors rather than oak, will be of pale color but intense aroma, and have a palate of some viscosity with a vein of acidity that leaves the mouth really fresh.*

8 **Rosso di Montalcino 2003** Argiano, Montalcino (€8) *The essence of what Rosso di Montalcino ought to be: not weighty and serious like its famous older brother Brunello, but lively and fruity, with notes, too, of pepper, flowers, and fresh earth; with, at the back, a good bite of tannin overlaid by a sweet-fruit finish.*

9 **Rosso del Soprano 2001** Palari, Sicily (€14) *Until this wine's senior partner, Faro DOC Palari, emerged a few years ago, most people were writing off Sicily's Nerello Mascalese and Nerello Cappuccio as wishy-washy and not worth growing. This wine introduces two more native Sicilian black varieties: Calabrese (a.k.a. Nero d'Avola) and Nocera. The result is a wine of great intrigue and elegance with notes of raspberry, rose, dark chocolate, and tobacco, not entirely unlike Nebbiolo and Pinot Nero.*

10 **Shardana 2000** Cantina di Santadi, Sardinia (€15) *This wine was made to measure for the US market and combines the local Carignano grape, in which the Cantina di Santadi famously specializes, with a small percentage of Syrah. It's international, yes, but individual—and it invites one to think that Sardinian Syrah could be a real success.*

Spain

John Radford

The two most encouraging features of the past year in Spain have been a growing awareness of the need for value for money in wine production and the increasing profile of emergent regions.

JOHN RADFORD

I spent a good part of the year visiting small producers in obscure parts of Spain (especially in the south, as the lists at the end illustrate). I conducted a dozen interviews with exporters, large and small, for an article in a trade magazine and was heartened to see that nearly all of them saw value for money as their prime target to get into export markets—a concept virtually unknown as recently as 20 years ago.

Given the advances in winemaking and the increasing involvement of universities in research and development, there is really no reason why any bad wine should be made at all, but alas, you can still find it if you look hard enough. Last summer I spent a few days in Toledo with my wife, and we ordered the house red at a sidewalk café. "I would never have dared do that, even five years ago," I told her, "but La Mancha is so reliable now, you can order with confidence!" Unfortunately, the wine proved to be thick, boiled to death in the fermentation vat, hopelessly overoaked, and oxidized. One interesting development has been in

JOHN RADFORD is a writer and broadcaster with more than 30 years' experience of the culture, landscapes, architecture, food, and wine of Spain. He is the author of *The New Spain* (Mitchell Beazley), which has won four international awards, a new edition of which was published in September 2004, and *The Wines of Rioja* (Mitchell Beazley Classic Wine Series), which was published in November 2004 and won the Livre Gourmand Best European Wine Book award at Versailles in 2005. He was awarded the Premio Especial Alimentos de España 2006 by the Spanish government. He is also the Chairman of the Spanish panel at the *Decanter* World Wine Awards.

exports of white wine from Spain, and not just the "big two" DOs of Rías Baixas and Rueda—indeed, one of my most exciting wine finds of the year is a white from Contraviesa-Alpujarra. Incredibly, according to the Federación Español del Vino, white wines are up 95 percent year on year, and following the big two are Godello wines from Ribeiro and Garnacha Blanca from Rioja and Priorat/Montsant.

Emerging regions: wines with a difference

Emergent regions are one of the most exciting areas for research. There has always been a popular supposition that anything south of Madrid and everything south of La Mancha was roasted rubbish, shriveled on the vine by the merciless sun, etc. What people forget is that eastern Andalucía is the most mountainous part of Spain (including Spain's highest peak, Mulhacén, at 11,424 ft [3,482 m]) and has the second-highest vineyards in Europe (see the Eastern & Southeastern Europe report for the highest). The combination of merciless sun all day and a massive temperature drop at night allows *bodegas* to make wines of quite astonishing quality. The Alpujarra mountains are a particularly high-quality area, split between Contraviesa-Alpujarra in the province of Granada and Laujar-Alpujarra in the province of Almería, with vineyards up to 4,488 ft (1,368 m; Barranco Oscuro—see lists) making nearly mile-high wines of an extraordinary complexity, especially whites from the Vigiriega grape (extinct everywhere else on the mainland) and reds from Tempranillo, Garnacha, and Cabernet Sauvignon. The soil is schist, and there are no insect pests and almost no cryptogams at these altitudes. Lower down the mountains in the province of Málaga, the wonderful old sweet stickies are still being made, but they are being overtaken by two new developments: sweet wines under DO Málaga and mainstream wines under DO Sierras de Málaga, most (but not all) of whose *bodegas* are in and around the city of Ronda (altitude 2,461 ft [750 m]). Unfortified sweet wines made from Pedro Ximénez and/or Moscatel are beginning to make their mark (see Bentomiz, DO Málaga, below), but mainstream wines offer

Grapevine

• **Sherry giant González Byass** is expanding its interests in Andalucía. The company already owns Beronia in Rioja and Castell Vilarnau in Cava/Penedès but is branching out with a range called La Moncloa under the VdlT Cadiz in Arcos de la Frontera. This is not one of the high crags of the south—the city is the highest point in the area at only 614 ft (187 m) altitude—but the early wines are showing well. The 2004 is a Cabernet Sauvignon/Syrah, which is to be launched in 2007, and there's a 2005 Syrah whose future has yet to be decided.

an exciting new world of quality and value. As an example, Descalzos Viejos (DO Sierras de Málaga—see lists) is producing a stunning wine from a former monastic vineyard in its own sheltered *conca*. They grow Garnacha, Syrah, and Cabernet Sauvignon; and around these parts, the Merlot and—especially—Petit Verdot are making wonderful wines. I confess that I'd be happier if there were more indigenous varieties and fewer "internationals," but when you taste the wines you can't fault the quality. Just north of Almería in the province of Murcia, the very obscure region of Campo de Cartagena is wriggling out from under a reputation of making sub-Valenciano sweet wines. Bodegas Serrano is the only significant producer, but it's making waves with barrel-fermented Syrah and Cabernet Sauvignon/Syrah wines that have great potential (if they can persuade themselves not to use plastic corks). Mallorca is starting to show real class, with the other Balearic Islands not far behind. Miquel Gelabert and Miquel Oliver are two of the superstar producers of the island (DO Pla i Llevant de Mallorca), and they have been joined by Castell Miquel, which makes wines under the VdlT Serra de Tramuntana-Costa Nord and VdlT Illes Balears. Once again they're growing Cabernet Sauvignon and Syrah (here labeled "Shiraz"), rather than the local Manto Negro and Callet, but the wines do speak for themselves.

All in all, the past year has been one of increasing diversity and exciting "finds" in the more obscure corners of Spain—and very encouraging indeed.

Grapevine

• **The year's biggest business news** has been the takeover of Allied Domecq by Pernod Ricard in 2005. Since Allied took over Bodegas y Bebidas in 2002, this makes Pernod Ricard one of the biggest wine producers in Spain, with *bodegas* in 10 DO zones, including Jerez. There are, however, rumors that original members of the group Bodegas Domecq in Jerez will be demerged, with some sherry brands going to Allied's bidding partner Fortune Brands of Lincolnshire, Illinois.

• **Cava should be promoted** to DOCa (or DOQ in Catalan) before the end of 2006. The foundations were put in place under the new wine law of 2003, but the sector had certain bureaucratic hoops to jump through before the final details could be sorted out.

• **The next "pastry-cutter" DO** was formed in summer 2005. Like Ribera del Júcar (2003), Uclés is currently part of DO La Mancha and will have the choice of making wines under either DO, according to quality. Again as with Ribera del Júcar, wines under the DO Uclés will have to be made with grapes traceable to mature vineyards in specific parts of the DO. All other wines must be badged as DO La Mancha. There's a parallel here with DO Cava, whose grapes must be traceable to particular vineyards, which may be surrounded by other vineyards belonging to DO Penedès.

BACK FROM THE DEAD

In *Wine Report 2006*, I mentioned that some CRDOs (regulating councils) were so desperate for investment that they'd probably welcome any new projects with open arms. So it appears to have been with the DO Condado de Huelva, which has been in the doldrums for so long that nobody remembers when the good times were. The fortified Pálido and Generoso wines (cheekily—and illegally—labeled "Fino" and "Oloroso") are still tootling along but are really only of local interest, although I tasted an excellent 15-year-old "Oloroso" that retails for just €3.50. However, the *jóvenes* made from Zalema, Huelva's indigenous white grape variety, have improved beyond measure—no longer dull, neutral, squeaky clean, and tasting of almost nothing at all, they have some decent herby fruit and freshness—at very low prices. The best have an admixture of Malvasía to give the fruit a bit of "musk." They're also growing Colombard (see Mioro in the lists) and, for reds, Tempranillo and Syrah—yes, I know, more "internationals," but at least the region is starting to turn out some decent wines at last.

NEW VDLT AREAS

Perhaps the most notable new VdlT area is Ribera del Queiles, a cross-border area between Navarra and Aragón. The name was coined by Bodegas Guelbenzu when it seceded from DO Navarra in 2002 because it wanted to source grapes from its properties in both *autonomías*. This was completely unofficial but has now been recognized. Interestingly, there have been campaigns for more than 10 years to establish a group

VdlT under the name Alto Ebro to include Rioja, Navarra, and Aragón, which was always scuppered by Rioja's lack of enthusiasm for the idea. Ricardo Guelbenzu seems to have succeeded (in part) where others have failed. Another new VdlT zone in western Andalucía is Sierra Norte de Sevilla, an area that once made sub-sherry fortified wines. New developments are largely in Cabernet, Merlot, *et al.*, with some Tempranillo, but the quality is excellent. Andalucía now has 17 VdlT areas, more than any other *autonomía* in Spain.

FIRST VCIG WINES ON THE SHELVES

The first of the new VCIG wines, introduced in the new Spanish wine law of 2003, have arrived on the market. All so far are from Castilla y León: the former designation was "Vino de la Tierra de …", and the new designation is "VCPRD …". They are Arribes (11 *bodegas*), Tierras de León (32), Zamora (6), Arlanza (9), and Benavente (still counting). Currently wines from these areas may carry old or new back labels according to when they were bottled. Encouragingly, most are growing indigenous grapes such as Mencía, Prieto Picudo, Juan-García, and Rufete, as well as Tempranillo, Garnacha, and, inevitably, Cabernet Sauvignon. The elevation of Arribes to this level effectively terminated the court case (see *Wine Report 2005*) in which the DO Ribera del Duero was rather unsportingly trying to prevent Arribes from using its old name (Arribes del Duero, established some years before the DO Ribera del Duero), because it was too similar. They do say that the best revenge is to succeed.

Opinion:
Olympic bid goes sour

There has been an upset between Catalunya and the rest of Spain. Catalunya is the richest region of Spain, and separatist factions have always been angry that the taxes they pay to Madrid are spent in the poorest areas of Spain. In the bid to stage the 2012 Olympic games—which London eventually won—Madrid had been one of the contenders, and it called for solidarity from all Spaniards. This was not forthcoming from Barcelona, and some separatist groups called for Catalans to campaign against the bid. The result led to calls for a boycott by other Spanish regions of all Catalan goods and particularly Catalan Cava, which is a mega-seller at Christmas. Sales fell by about 25 percent in Spain, though export markets were not affected. A knock-on effect was a reduction in the price offered to contract growers for grapes for the following harvest, which caused a great deal of anger, some of it culminating in vandalism of vineyards. You get the impression that some people, probably politically motivated, just can't see when they're on to a good thing. Cava is the world's biggest-selling sparkling wine; anybody who tampers with a market that size must be very stupid indeed.

Cut back irrigation

On a technical note, there still seems to be too much irrigation. It was permitted "on a case-by-case basis" under the 2003 wine law, but these days it's hard to find a vineyard without perforated hoses running along the rows. If we really want to make wine that is truly expressive of its place and time of origin, will pumping last winter's rainwater—or, even worse, bleached city water or local river water—over it improve the end product?

Unique grapes, unique opportunities

Headlines in the Spanish press on the announcement of the new wine law of 2003 focused on the fact that taxpayers' money would be used to promote wine (but not other alcoholic drinks) as part of the Mediterranean diet. If money is available for promotion, maybe the Spanish government could think about subsidizing plantings of and research into the country's indigenous grape varieties. They are there in profusion, and a few brave souls—most notably Miguel Torres with a range of old Catalan varieties and Juan-Carlos Sancha at Viña Ijalba in Rioja with the Maturana, but others too—have proved it can be done. Portugal and Greece have demonstrated what can be achieved when you have a grape that doesn't grow anywhere else.

Vintage Report

Advance report on the latest harvest

2005

This year was characterized by low rainfall in the early part of the year and then oppressive heat, with drought in many places during the ripening season and, paradoxically, outbreaks of hail in June, especially in Aragón. Late rains in the north interrupted the harvest, and, with a few exceptions, yield is down on 2004 between 20 and 40 percent, but only 14 percent overall because of high yields in developing areas—Rías Baixas had its second-biggest vintage ever. The resulting grapes were, however, dry and healthy, and the summer heat had reduced the risk of cryptogams. Northern regions (Rioja, Navarra, Aragón, Catalunya) are reporting good to very good quality. The south had a very cold start to the year, with Valdepeñas suffering 57 instances of frost between January and March, the most severe (13°F [−10.8°C]) in January, but summer heat made for a good and dry ripening season and an early harvest with yields down but quality very promising.

Updates on the previous five vintages

2004

Vintage rating: *Red—Rioja: 90, others: 80; White: 90*
This was an 'isometric' split, with the northwest and central south doing well and the north-central and northeast having a fair amount of dull and cloudy weather; although the latter part of the ripening season was warm and sunny in most areas, giving yields slightly up on 2003. The best reds are still in cask, and samples are showing rather better than expected. Rioja, particularly, came through with its second *excelente* year of the century.

2003

Vintage rating: *Red: 90, White: 90*
High levels of summer heat all across Spain brought the harvest forward by anything up to 10 days. Parts of Rioja suffered very badly, and vineyards with irrigation survived the best. Penedès harvested excellent reds with the exception of Syrah, which had suffered from the heat, and quantity was down almost everywhere.

2002

Vintage rating: *Northeast—Red: 60, White: 60;
Southwest—Red: 80, White: 70*

The 2002 vintage in Spain divided roughly into a southwest/northeast
divide, with the former having the better time of it. Damp conditions in
Catalunya extended to rain during the harvest with resultant rot, while in
the south, La Mancha picked very healthy fruit in excellent conditions.

2001

Vintage rating: *Red: 90, White: 90*

Excellent quality throughout Spain, with Rioja and Ribera del Duero
showing particularly well, and the south (La Mancha, Valdepeñas, etc)
making what may become some very long-lived wines. These wines are
starting to drink very well indeed. Good whites, too, particularly in Rías
Baixas and Rueda, for early drinking.

2000

Vintage rating: *Generally—Red: 60, White: 70;
better estates and Penedès—Red: 70–80, White: 80*

Better in the south than the north. Rioja produced a vast, dilute, and
unattractive vintage. Those *bodegas* that green-harvested and hand-selected
made some good wines: they have stood the test of time and are showing
very well. Some of the single estates and Penedès fared better than most.

Grapevine

• **The runaway success** of Vinaigre
de Jerez is having a knock-on effect.
Throughout the doldrum years, the
sherry business was kept alive by
large-scale sales of Brandy de Jerez
throughout Spain. With the decline of
the brown-spirits sector, Vinaigre de
Jerez came to the rescue, thanks to
TV chefs in many European countries
discovering its culinary properties.
Neighboring Condado de Huelva and
Montilla-Moriles quickly cottoned
on to the opportunities offered,
and both now have a DO, for
Vinaigre del Condado and Vinaigre
de Montilla respectively.

• **Unsuspected champions** discovered
during the year (see Top 10 lists)
included Divo from Ricardo Benito
in the DO Vinos de Madrid—not
widely known for world-class wines. It's
made with grapes from 60-year-old
Tempranillo vines, is aged for 14
months in new Alliers oak, and is quite
sublime (as is the price). The other is
Bruñal from Bodegas Ribera de Pelazas
in Arribes. This is a grape unknown
anywhere else in the world (and, no,
it's not the Brunello/Sangiovese—
they've checked) and exists in only
two small plots of 150-year-old vines
in the village of Ribera de la Pereña. It
crops at only 3.3 lb (1.5 kg) per vine
and the berry is very small. Production
is limited, but the price isn't: another
real superstar.

GREATEST WINE PRODUCERS

1. Alejandro Fernández (Ribera del Duero, Toro, La Mancha)
2. Alvaro Palacios (Priorat, Bierzo, Rioja)
3. Mariano García (Ribera del Duero, Toro, Rioja, Castilla y León)
4. Peter Sisseck (Ribera del Duero)
5. Xavier Ausás, Vega Sicilia (Ribera del Duero, Toro)
6. Carlos Falcó, Pagos de Familia (Dominio de Valdepusa)
7. Miguel Torres (Penedès/Catalunya)
8. Marcos Eguren (Rioja, Toro)
9. Telmo Rodríguez (ubique)
10. Benjamín Romeo (Rioja)

FASTEST-IMPROVING PRODUCERS

1. Ricardo Benito (Vinos de Madrid)
2. Masía Duch (Priorat)
3. Capçances (Montsant)
4. Finca Luzón (Jumilla)
5. San Alejandro Co-op (Calatayud)
6. San Gregorio (Calatayud)
7. La Setera (Arribes)
8. Borsao (Campo de Borja)
9. Verde Marte (Cariñena)
10. La Purísima (Yecla)

NEW UP-AND-COMING PRODUCERS

1. Pago del Vicario (Castilla)
2. Barranco Oscuro (Contraviesa-Alpujarra)
3. Parxet (Ribera del Duero)
4. Rauda (Ribera del Duero)
5. Buenavista (Contraviesa-Alpujarra)
6. Montreaga (Castilla)
7. Lomablanca (Cariñena)
8. Jesús Díaz (Vinos de Madrid)
9. Bentomiz (Málaga)
10. Castell Miquel (Illes Balears)

BEST-VALUE PRODUCERS

1. San Alejandro Co-op (Calatayud)
2. San Gregorio Co-op (Calatayud)
3. Descalzos Viejos (Sierras de Málaga)
4. Virgen de la Sierra (Calatayud)
5. Dominio Lasierpe (Navarra)
6. González Byass (La Mancha)
7. Félix Solís (Valdepeñas, Ribera del Duero)
8. Los Llanos (Valdepeñas)
9. Vinícola de Castilla (La Mancha)
10. Viña Bajoz Co-op (Toro)

GREATEST-QUALITY WINES

1. **Vinos de Madrid Divo 2000** Ricardo Benito (€141)
2. **Bruñal 2003** Ribera de Pelazas (€89)
3. **Priorat L'Ermita 2002** Alvaro Palacios (€390)
4. **Ribera del Duero Malleolus de Valderramiro 2002** Emilio Moro (€79)
5. **Rioja Culmen de Lan 2001** Lan (€79)
6. **Ribera del Duero Unico 1994** Vega Sicilia (€156)
7. **Toro 2001** Pintia (€24)
8. **Rioja Calvario 2001** Finca Allende (€56)
9. **Ribera del Duero Pingus 2001** Dominio de Pingus (€580)
10. **Rioja Cirsión 2001** Roda (€125)

BEST BARGAINS

1. **Sierras de Málaga 2003** Descalzos Viejos (€9)
2. **Ribera del Duero Flores Silvestres 2004** Rauda (€4)
3. **Arribes Viña Borbón 2004** Virgen de la Bandera Co-op (€2)
4. **Arribes Abadengo 2003** Ribera de Pelazas (€6)
5. **Ribera del Arlanza Viña Valdable 2004** Máximo Ortíz (€2.50)

6 **Castilla Isola Tempranillo/Syrah 2005** Montreaga (€3.50)

7 **Calatayud Castillo de Maluenda 2003** Jalón (€2.70)

8 **Utiel Requena Hoya de Cadenas Reserva 1999** Vicente Gandía (€4.25)

9 **Valdepeñas Viña Albali Gran Reserva 1996** Félix Solís (€5.60)

10 **Bierzo Tilenus 2004** Estefanía (€4.50)

MOST EXCITING OR UNUSUAL FINDS

1 **Contraviesa-Alpujarra Blancas Nobles 2004** Barranco Oscuro (€10) *This is made mainly from the Vigiriega, a grape that has died out elsewhere on the peninsula, though it still grows in the Canary Islands. It flourishes only at high altitudes (over 3,300 ft [1,000 m]) and is one of the most individual white wines I've ever tasted in Spain.*

2 **Ariyanas Dulce 2004** Bentomiz (€12 per half-bottle) *One of the "new-wave" wines from this ancient region, made from Moscatel harvested from mountain outcrops of vines and unfortified, with three months in new Alliers. Delicate and delicious.*

3 **Tinto 7 Meses Barrica Arribes del Douro Crianza 2003** La Setera (€9) *I listed this bodega last year as "up and coming," and it's kept its promise. The Crianza is made from the Juan García, which grows only in this corner of Castilla y León. Bright, delicious fruit coming through.*

4 **Serra de Tramuntana-Costa Nord Shiraz Stairway to Heaven 2003** Castell Miquel (€15) *This takes its name from an old stone stairway in the mountains of the north of Mallorca: cutting-edge winemaking and a wine of spice, structure, and power.*

5 **Ibiza/Eivissa Lausos 2003** Can Rich (€25) *Arguably the best winery on the island, and this is its flagship wine, made from organically grown Cabernet Sauvignon: perfumed, herby, musky, and delicious. Their other wines are equally good.*

6 **Condado de Huelva Mioro Privilegio del Condado '1955' Colombard 2004** Vinicola del Condado (€9) *A 50th-anniversary wine (hence the name) from this old-established bodega, barrel-fermented Colombard in French oak: lovely, warm, ripe, almost chocolaty fruit.*

7 **Sierra Norte de Sevilla Roble 2003** Colonias de Galeón (€10) *This is a Merlot, Syrah, Cabernet Franc, and Tempranillo mix with eight months in French oak: an "herby" start on the nose but good structure and weight in the mouth.*

8 **Laujar-Alpujarra Ben-Zuaique 2004** Vinos de Fondón (€4) *A Tempranillo/Cabernet mix with four months in French oak, and quite simply a steal at the price: big, soft Cabernet perfume on the nose, lovely rich Tempranillo fruit, and a gentle finish—delicious.*

9 **Zamora Gavión Reserva 2001** Viña Escuderos (€14) *Made with grapes from 100-year-old Tempranillo vines with 27 months in American oak, this has lovely, silky fruit with oaky notes and an elegant structure.*

10 **Sierras de Málaga Soleón 2003** Conrad Soleón (€14) *This is a brand-new bodega growing Cabernet Sauvignon, Syrah, Tempranillo, and Merlot, all of which go into Soleón, which then gets 14 months in oak. The final cupaje is different every vintage, but the 2003 shows magnificent fruit with deliciously spicy oak, in perfect balance.*

Sherry

Julian Jeffs QC

There have been so many false dawns that one no longer believes the occasional optimist who says that the traditional market for sherry is coming back.

JULIAN JEFFS QC

But does it matter? The *bodegas* in Sanlúcar sound happy: manzanilla sales are good, especially in Spain, where people are at last realizing how good it is; and the fino styles in general are doing well. What matters more is the steadily expanding connoisseur market. At long last, wine drinkers are realizing that sherry really is one of the world's great wines and the market for age-dated wines is steadily, if slowly, growing. VOS and VORS wines are increasingly found on merchants' lists. When it is presented at tastings, people tend to say, "I had no idea sherry could be like this," and its tiresome image of a wine for aunts to serve to vicars is at last going away. Not that there will ever be a mass market for such wines, any more than there will be for First Growth clarets. There are not enough of them and they cost too much. At first, they were practically the preserve of boutique *bodegas*; now, happily, everyone is selling them, recognizing a market that is here to stay.

JULIAN JEFFS QC became a Gray's Inn barrister in 1958, attained Queen's Counsel in 1975, and retired from practice in 1991, although he continued as a Deputy High Court Judge until 1996. His love of sherry began in 1956, when he was a sherry shipper's assistant in Spain, and this led to a passion for writing when his book *Sherry* (Faber & Faber) was published in 1961. He began a two-year stint as editor of *Wine and Food* in 1965, and in 1971 he created Faber & Faber's radically new Wine Series. Over the next 40-odd years he commissioned many of the most respected, long-lasting, and definitive works on wine. He held this position until 2002, when Faber & Faber sold the Wine Series to Mitchell Beazley. Julian has been chairman (1970–72), vice president (1975–91), and president (1992–96) of the Circle of Wine Writers, winning the Glenfiddich Wine Writer award in 1974 and 1978. His books include *The Wines of Europe* (Faber & Faber, 1971), *The Little Dictionary of Drink* (Pelham, 1973), and *The Wines of Spain* (Faber & Faber, 1999).

Mixed blessings

After four abundant harvests of good quality, 2005 produced a very limited quantity of truly superb quality. This has brought mixed reactions. For the big shippers with large vineyard holdings, it has been a blessing, but their vineyards account for only 31 percent of the whole. They have enough top-quality wines for their needs and no surplus to cope with. For the growers who are not shippers, including a large number of small ones, the story is very different. They have much less than usual to sell, and the price is fixed under a four-year stabilization plan, resulting in many unhappy faces.

Age no barrier to sales

According to the latest statistics, the only age-dated category not making headway is VOS amontillado, sales of which are down by 48 percent, but Pedro Ximénez sales are up 91 percent, and olorosos have soared by no less than 1,017 percent.

Overall production of VOS wines has increased by 239 percent— from 12,965 liters to 43,986—while the total production of VORS wines increased just 29 percent—from 94,965 liters to 122,725.

Younger age-certified sherries showed similar impressive increases, the 12-year-old category increasing 184 percent—from 7,210 to 20,500 liters—while the 15-year-old increased 69.5 percent—from 21,065 to 35,700 liters.

Compared with total sales of 62.8 million liters, these figures are very small, but one must bear in mind that manzanillas and finos, which account for 39 percent of the sales, fall outside these categories altogether, while the VOS and VORS wines represent a high proportion of the most expensive sherries, and the 12- and 15-year-old wines have only recently come on the market. The best wines are clearly making progress.

Grapevine

• **Two of the greatest men in sherry country** died in 2005: Antonio (Toto) Barbadillo, the leading light in Sanlúcar; and Alvaro Domecq, formerly of Domecq. When that was taken over, he bought Pilar Aranda. They will be greatly missed. It remains to be seen whether their *bodegas* continue as before. They probably will.

New VOS and VORS wines

A full list of VOS and VORS wines was included in *Wine Report 2006*. Since then there have been some additions.

Shipper	Style	Classification	Name
Bodegas Pilar Aranda	Oloroso	VORS	AD
Dios Baco	Palo Cortado	VORS	Baco Imperial
Pilar Plá Pechovierto	Amontillado	VORS	1830
	Oloroso	VORS	1/14
	Oloroso	VORS	1/7

Certified 12- and 15-year-old wines

There is now an official list of *Vinos de Jerez con Indicacion de Edad*—wines certified as 12 or 15 years old.

Shipper	Style	Classification	Name
Paternina	Amontillado	12 years	Bertola
	Pedro Ximénez	12 years	Bertola
	Oloroso	12 years	Bertola
Emilio Lustau	Amontillado	12 years	Sainsbury's
	Oloroso	12 years	Sainsbury's
Intermonte (Valdivia)	Amontillado	12 years	Sacromonte
	Oloroso	12 years	Sacromonte
	Pedro Ximénez	12 years	Sacromonte
	Palo Cortado	12 years	Sacromonte
Pilar Plá Pechovierto	Amontillado	12 years	Viuda Antonio Borrego
	Oloroso	12 years	Viuda Antonio Borrego
Hidalgo-La Gitana	Pedro Ximénez	15 years	Viejo Napoléon
Williams & Humbert	Oloroso	15 years	Dry Sack

Ruiz-Mateos looking to buy?

Ever since RuMaSa was disposed of by the state in 1983, the Ruiz-Mateos family (which does not appear to be strapped for cash) has been intent on making a comeback. It began by acquiring de Soto, then added Garvey, and most recently took over the production for Sandeman (see *Wine Report 2006*). In November 2005, it astonished the sherry world by announcing to the local paper that it was making a bid for González Byass. But it had not told González Byass, which sounded rather nonplussed and flatly denied it was for sale. It is said that the family has its eyes on other big names.

Opinion:
Classify mature fino

Age-dated sherries clearly have a great future, albeit on a small scale. Hitherto there have been very few of the youngest category: 12–15 years old, but now these are beginning to emerge. Lustau has two on Sainsbury's shelves in the UK, and soon there will be others. This is an area that could and should expand further. But what of finos? By the time they are that age, nearly all will have become amontillados, so an age classification is inappropriate. Still, the fact remains that some are much more mature than others. The three-year minimum is all right for cheaper and lighter wines, but some of the more mature finos deserve a category of their own. Of course, "you get what you pay for," and the more mature finos command premium prices, but it would help to have an indication of what they are on the label. This would give a fillip to top-quality wines, though the assessment would not be easy. Such a change would be difficult to monitor, but there seem to have been few difficulties with VOS and VORS wines, and surely there must be some move in that direction?

Grapevine

• **Two would-be VOS sherries** were turned down by the *consejo regulador* in 2005 on the basis of C14 testing (radiocarbon dating). It is good to know the authorities are being vigilant, that the age of all the age-dated wines on the market has been verified, and that the wines deserve their classifications.

• **A new boutique *bodega*,** Bodegas Valdivia, has been set up in Jerez *bodega* buildings built by Ruiz-Mateos and then taken over by Williams & Humbert. Run by Rafael Veas, formerly production director of Osborne, its first offerings of a 15-year-old amontillado and a 15-year-old oloroso are very promising. It intends to specialize in age-dated wines.

• **Torre Dama,** a small *bodega* in El Puerto de Santa María, which used to sell excellent wines under the Gomez brand, is no longer shipping.

• **Bodegas Tradición** has expanded its premises and its wine stocks. Selling only age-dated sherries of the highest quality, it has now started selling in the UK market.

Vintage Report

For sherry, vintage assessments *per se* are not particularly relevant because very little sherry is sold with a vintage year (*añada* sherry) and then it is not released for 20 years or more and is carefully selected, butt by butt. However, sherry lovers should be interested to know how much must was available for topping up the *soleras* and whether the quality of the wines has been good or bad. After a series of rather disappointing years, sherry has enjoyed four abundant ones in a row. Note that the maximum yield allowed is 80 hl/ha in the best vineyard area (Zono Superior) and 100 hl/ha in the rest.

Advance report on the latest harvest

2005

Vintage rating: *98*

A remarkably tactful vintage, producing a very small yield of top-quality must. Since recent vintages have been rather too abundant, this was good news for the shippers but less good news for the growers. The rainfall was very low. After a hot July punctuated by Levante winds, which dry the grapes, the vintage started early, on August 14, producing very small but exceedingly ripe and healthy grapes, their health demonstrated by the low gluconic acid content. The average *Baumé* was 11.93 degrees. Production was 66 hl/ha, and a total of 97,000 butts qualified for the DO. So why not a rating of 100? It very nearly justified it, but, owing to the small size of the grapes, there was not a lot of free-run juice for finos.

Updates on the previous five vintages

2004

Vintage rating: *90*

At 29 in (740 mm), rainfall was well above average (23.6–24.4 in [600–620 mm]) but was well distributed throughout the year. A damp spring caused mildew in some vineyards around Sanlúcar and Trebujena, but July and August were very mild with no Levante winds, which usually dry the grapes out, reducing yield, so they were harvested in excellent condition. Total production was 81.62 hl/ha, with 66.6 granted the DO, giving 138,244 butts. In the end, the maturity was excellent and the quality very good, with an alcoholic strength of 11.3 percent.

2003

Vintage rating: *95*

A yield of 64 hl/ha provided 138,000 butts of new wine for all the sherry *bodegas*. Rainfall was above average at 30 in (760 mm) but happened at the right times. Quality: after a hot summer, maturity was good (though overripe in a few vineyards), with an alcoholic strength of 12 percent.

2002

Vintage rating: *95*

A yield of 64 hl/ha provided a total of 137,888 butts of new wine for all the sherry *bodegas*. Rainfall: 23 in (594 mm). Quality: excellent—good maturity with an alcoholic strength of 11 percent.

2001

Vintage rating: *95*

A yield of 72 hl/ha provided a total of 152,102 butts of new wine. An early vintage. Rainfall: 18½ in (474 mm). Quality: exceptional—the grapes had a perfect level of maturation.

2000

Vintage rating: *90*

A yield of 65 hl/ha provided 135,542 butts of new wine. Rainfall: 25 in (639 mm). Quality: excellent.

Grapevine

• **After various takeovers,** the position of the important Domecq, John Harvey, and Terry brands seems to be somewhat confused. Terry and Harvey are now owned by Fortune Brands, together with the sherry and brandy *soleras*, and it markets the important brandy brands of Fundador and Tres Cepas. But the Domecq sherry brands and Carlos I belong to Pernod Ricard. When things have settled down, the position will no doubt become clearer.

• **Sanlúcar** *bodega* Infantes Orleans-Borbon, which used to be associated with Barbadillo, has severed the connection and gone independent.

GREATEST WINE PRODUCERS

1. González Byass (including Croft and Wisdom & Warter)
2. Domecq (including Harvey)
3. Osborne
4. Emilio Lustau/Luis Caballero
5. Ruiz-Mateos (Sandeman, Garvey, and José de Soto)
6. José Estévez (Valdespino and Real Tesoro)
7. Barbadillo
8. Hidalgo-La Gitana
9. Williams & Humbert
10. Sánchez Romate

FASTEST-IMPROVING PRODUCERS

1. José Estévez
2. Delgado Zuleta
3. Dios Baco
4. Pilar Plá Pechovierto
5. Emilio Hidalgo
6. M Gil Luque
7. Pedro Romero
8. Hijos de Rainera Pérez Marín

NEW UP-AND-COMING PRODUCERS

1. Pilar Aranda
2. Tradición
3. Rey Fernando de Castilla
4. Pilar Plá Pechovierto (El Maestro Sierra)
5. Juan Carlos Gutiérrez Colosia
6. Ferris
7. Dios Baco
8. M Gil Luque
9. Valdivia

BEST-VALUE PRODUCERS

1. González Byass/Wisdom & Warter
2. Domecq
3. Williams & Humbert
4. Emilio Lustau
5. José Estévez
6. Bodegas 501 del Puerto
7. Gutiérrez Colosia

GREATEST-QUALITY WINES

This selection has been hard to make since there are now so many top-quality wines, but it aims at including wines of every style, which are listed in order of price, bearing in mind that a good VOS or VORS must necessarily be more expensive than a good fino.

1. **San León Manzanilla**
   Herederos de Argüeso (€4.55)
2. **Tio Pepe Fino**
   González Byass (€5.90)
3. **Coquinero Fino**
   Amontillado Osborne (€6.61)
4. **Pastrana Manzanilla Pasada**
   Hidalgo-La Gitana (€7.42)
5. **VORS Amontillado del Duque**
   González Byass (€32)
6. **Viejo Hidalgo VORS Oloroso**
   Hidalgo-La Gitana (€34.05)
7. **Amontillado 51-1ª**
   Pedro Domecq (€48)
8. **Tradición VORS Palo Cortado**
   Tradición (€50)
9. **Victoria Regina VORS Oloroso**
   Paterrina (€72)
10. **Solera 1842 Oloroso Dulce**
    Valdespino (€70)

BEST BARGAINS

Again, in order of price.

1 **Las Medallas Manzanilla**
Herederos de Argüeso (€3.45)

2 **Fino San Patricio** Garvey (€3.99)

3 **Tio Diego Amontillado**
Valdespino (€10)

4 **Botaina Amontillado**
Pedro Domecq (€12)

5 **Palo Dos Cortados VOS**
Williams & Humbert (€33)

6 **Obispo Gascon VORS Palo
Cortado** Barbadillo (€14.48)

7 **Royal Esmeralda VOS
Amontillado** Sandeman (€19.25)

8 **Royal Corregedor VOS Oloroso**
Sandeman (€30)

9 **Matusalém VORS Oloroso
Dulce** González Byass (€36)

10 **Noé VORS Pedro Ximénez**
González Byass (€36)

MOST EXCITING OR UNUSUAL FINDS

1 **De Añada 1979 Oloroso**
González Byass (€125) *There
should be more vintage wines.
They are not very commercial,
but the high price makes up for
it, and they represent mature
sherry at its very best.*

2 **Fino Imperial VORS
Amontillado** Paternina (€72)
*Just occasionally a fino does not
turn into an amontillado with age
but retains its fino character, and
this is one of them, from the only
solera of its kind left in Jerez,
ex Diez Hermanos, of blessed
memory. Because there is no VORS*

*category for finos, it caused the
authorities a headache, so they
classified it as an amontillado.*

3 **Coliseo Amontillado** Valdespino
(€150) *When an amontillado
gets very old indeed it develops
a remarkable bouquet, but the
flavor is so intense that it is not
at all easy to drink. This is such
a one. You have to feel strong to
tackle it, but the rewards are
remarkable.*

4 **Victoria Regina VORS Oloroso**
Paternina (€72) *Another wine from
the soleras of Diez Hermanos,
this old, very complex oloroso is
certainly one of the finest of them
all, with an aftertaste that lingers
in the mouth impressively for a
very long time indeed.*

5 **VORS Amontillado del Duque**
González Byass (€32) *A classic
amontillado that is at once
approachable and affordable. It
is beautifully smooth, enormously
impressive, and available in
commercial quantities.*

6 **Antique Sherry Pedro Ximénez**
Fernando de Castilla (€31.25) *Age
gives it a dry, almost bitter finish.
It is beautifully balanced, complex,
and, unlike most, not a bit cloying.*

7 **Dry Sack Aged 15 Years**
Williams & Humbert (€26.50) *It
could be said that this is just the
right age: young enough to drink
easily but old enough to have real
depth. The oloroso is sweetened
with Pedro Ximénez, making it a
perfect wine on a cold day.*

Portugal

Richard Mayson

Portugal suffered the most severe drought in living memory in 2005. No one can remember anything quite like it.

RICHARD MAYSON

Almost no rain fell during the winter in mainland Portugal, and by mid-March 2005 88 percent of the country was classified as suffering from "severe" or "extreme" drought. As springs dried up and reservoirs were drained, entire communities were left without water. The situation was most severe inland and in the south of the country, parts of which began to experience near-dust-bowl conditions. The drought led to a diplomatic incident, with Portugal accusing Spain of drawing too much water from the Douro (Duero) River. Portugal is calling for compensation of €6 million after water levels fell below agreed limits.

As a result of the drought, proceeds from the hard-pressed agricultural sector are estimated to be 19.8 percent lower than in 2004. The cork harvest also suffered, with the total yield some 1 million *arrobas* below what was expected (1 *arroba* = 33 lb [15 kg]). Vines were better able to withstand the drought than most other crops or livestock, but young

RICHARD MAYSON writes and lectures on wine, dividing his time between London, Portugal, and a family business in England's Peak District. He speaks fluent Portuguese, having been brought up in Portugal, and is regarded as one of the most respected authorities on port, sherry, madeira, and the wines of Spain and Portugal. His interest in the subject goes back to his university days, when he wrote a thesis on the microclimates of the vineyards of the Douro Valley. His books include *Portugal's Wines and Wine Makers* (Ebury Press, 1992), *Port and the Douro* (Faber & Faber, 1999), and *The Wines and Vineyards of Portugal* (Mitchell Beazley), which won the André Simon award for the best drinks book published in 2003. A second, fully revised edition of *Port and the Douro* was published by Mitchell Beazley in 2004, and Richard is currently preparing a book on the wines of Madeira and a third edition of *Portugal's Wines and Wine Makers*.

vineyards suffered extreme stress, and yields fell as a result. In some parts of the country, yields were 30 percent below average and the total crop was the smallest since 1998 (see Vintage Report). Vineyard irrigation, now widespread in the Alentejo and much of southern Portugal, was authorized for the first time in the Douro, but it costs around €9,500 per hectare to install irrigation here, about three times more than in the Alentejo. Although substantial rain fell in November 2005, it is still too little to replenish reserves, and the drought of 2005 will probably have an impact on future growing seasons. Global warming is currently a hot topic among Portuguese growers.

Colares boosted by Macau investment

The historic Colares region, the only wine region in Europe to survive the 19th-century phylloxera epidemic unscathed, has been given a new lease on life by two foundations linked to the former Portuguese colony of Macau. The region has just 16 ha of vineyard remaining, and the Lisbon-based Fundação Oriente has taken over the management of 8.5 ha of abandoned vineyard planted in the 1980s by the now-defunct Allied Domecq. The wine, bottled under the name MJ Colares, is made entirely from ungrafted Ramico vines, the traditional grape variety in Colares. Elsewhere in Colares, the Fundação Stanley Ho has begun producing a varietal Aragonez (a grape new to the region) under the brand name Stanley. Stanley Ho (the "king of gambling"), one of Asia's richest men, held the Portuguese-government-granted gambling monopoly in Macau for more than 35 years.

R&D for five key markets

ViniPortugal, the all-embracing interprofessional body charged with promoting Portuguese wine at home and abroad, has established an agency named Investigação & Desenvolvimento (I&D), aimed at promoting innovation, and focusing on research, development, and communication. In 2006, ViniPortugal set a budget of €4.55 million to promote Portuguese wine in the key markets of Germany, Scandinavia, Portugal, the United States, and the UK.

Winegrowers unite

Five leading producers in the north of Portugal have formed the Independent Wine Growers Association. Led by Bairrada producer Luís Pato, the quality-focused group will coordinate promotion opportunities, including visits by journalists and tastings abroad.

Opinion:
Portuguese ad misses target

If you live in Portugal, Brazil, the UK, or the US and have an interest in wine, chances are that you will have seen the full-page advertisements for ViniPortugal. The adverts feature different cartoon figures, supposedly sophisticated consumers, cherishing a wine glass. In one ad a cherubic-looking young man with a quiff and perma-tan exclaims, "If someone asks what you are drinking, say it's a secret potion." In another, an alarmingly orange woman in a strappy black cocktail dress advises us: "Don't tell your friends," before revealing the secrets of Portugal's unique black grapes, concluding that "discovering the new generation of Portuguese reds is an amazing experience that you'll want to keep for yourself." The strapline reads: "Wines of Portugal. The best kept secret in Europe."

This is the response to Professor Michael Porter's Business Monitor report on the Portuguese wine industry, which recommended a thorough reappraisal of the promotion of Portuguese wines (see *Wine Report 2005* and *2006*). Porter identified the US and the UK as the countries "most suited to Portuguese export needs," hence the €2-million spend on advertising in these countries during 2005. But ViniPortugal does not seem to have done its homework. As one leading UK trade magazine said, "the campaign will not be rubbing shoulders with [leading UK ad agencies] Trevor Beattie or Charles Saatchi in this year's Advertising Effectiveness Awards."

Grapevine

• **The Vitis program** set up in 2000 to help growers replant vineyards with improved grape varieties has been given a budget of €35 million for 2005/06, which will be applied to around 4,500 ha of vines. Since 2000 the Vitis program has awarded €165 million and 20,000 ha of vineyard have been replanted.

• **Mateus Rosé** has been joined by Mateus Tempranillo, a new *rosé* from Valencia in southern Spain. This is the first extension to the famous brand of Portuguese *rosé* in its 60-year history. The launch was accompanied by an advertising campaign costing €1.8 million. Mateus has also launched its Portuguese *rosé* in a 25-cl "pocket-size" bottle.

• **Bairrada-based wine producer** Caves Aliança was voted among the top 20 firms in the world for the quality/price and diversity of its wines by the US magazine *Wine Spectator*.

• **JP Vinhos** (formerly João Pires) has been renamed Bacalhôa Vinhos de Portugal after Quinta de Bacalhôa, the company's flagship property at Azeitão on the Setúbal Peninsula.

Portugal has always been a proud nation, but it is also a small and isolated nation. The Portuguese continue to apply their own solutions to their own problems and, sadly, more often than not these are completely out of tune with their target markets. Portugal continues to miss small but vital marketing opportunities. For example, at a trade delegation dinner in China with senior Portuguese wine producers accompanying the president of the Portuguese Republic, the wine served was … Chilean! And I was dumbfounded when, at the opening of the London Serpentine Pavilion, designed by acclaimed Portuguese architects Alvaro Siza Vieira and Eduardo Souto Moura, Argentine wine was served.

Just as I was contemplating the ineffectiveness of the ViniPortugal campaign, a press release arrived, announcing that Wines of Argentina is setting up an office in the UK. It will be led by a man who spent 14 years promoting some of the world's top global brands, including Carrefour, Coca-Cola, and Ralph Lauren. Why can't the Portuguese learn from their competitors? With a limited budget, carefully targeted promotion is far more effective than blanket advertising. According to the minister of agriculture, Jaime Silva, "the wine sector is a priority for the government," yet the department's budget was cut by 8.3 percent in 2006.

One good thing to come from this, however, is a fundamental review of the numerous public institutions that govern the wine sector in Portugal, with a promise to "develop with the market and reduce the amount of intervention." Cutting bureaucracy at home is one thing, but Portugal desperately needs a targeted promotional campaign if it is to make any headway in key markets.

Grapevine

• **Caves de Raposeira,** the largest sparkling-wine producer in Portugal, is to open a *museu do espumante* (sparkling-wine museum) in 2008. Raposeira was famous during World War II as a supplier of sparkling wine to Germans unable to buy champagne.

• **Eight Portuguese cooperatives** in the Douro, Dão, and Alentejo have been coordinating the first exports of wine to China, worth €30 million a year.

• **Bright Brothers** has launched Bright Pink, a fruity *rosé* packaged in a "fast-chilling" 100 percent aluminum 75-cl bottle designed for pubs, clubs, bars, and picnics. The bottle is 66 percent lighter than a standard glass bottle.

• **Two Portuguese *rosés*,** Redoma from Niepoort and Quinta do Portal, won *Decanter* five-star awards in a comprehensive blind tasting of £5-plus *rosés* from around the world—proof that there is much more to Portuguese *rosé* than Mateus!

• **Quinta da Insua,** one of the oldest wine producers in the Dão region under the name Casa da Insua, is to be transformed into a luxury hotel run by the company Visabeira.

Vintage Report

Advance report on the latest harvest
2005

The winter of 2004/05 was the driest on record, with almost no rain falling from November to March (see above). Flowering and fruit set were successful throughout the country, but, lacking ground water in the soil, berries and bunches remained small. Hail cut a swath through vineyards on the northern margins of the Douro in June. Without any of the great bursts of heat experienced in 2003, the summer months (especially July) were warmer than average. By early August, many growers were predicting catastrophe, with vines losing their leaves and grapes drying up on the vine. However, a little light rain at the end of the month and more rainfall again on September 6 and 9 helped swell the grapes, especially in the north of the country.

For the Alentejo and the south, this was too little, too late, as the harvest (one of the earliest ever) was already well under way. Cool, clear weather continued into October. But with production down by as much as 30 percent, some concentrated but often fiercely alcoholic and unbalanced wines have been made. Farther north and toward the coast, the fall in yield was less marked (Dão actually registered an increase of 5 percent), and some excellent wines have been made by quality-conscious producers in Dão, Bairrada, and the Douro. At 5.7 million hl, overall production is expected to be the lowest since 1998.

Updates on the previous five vintages
2004

Vintage rating: 88

In the north, the wettest August for over a century resulted in generally slow but even maturation. Rain continued into early September and there were sporadic outbreaks of rot. As the harvest was about to get underway, the weather took a significant turn for the better. The late burst of summer heat was a godsend for the coastal regions, particularly Alenquer in Estremadura, where sugar readings had been very low. Some fantastic wines have been made. In Dão and the Douro, Touriga Nacional has performed especially well, producing fine, fragrant reds without the jamminess that could be found in 2003. Overall, 2004 has produced some wonderfully well-balanced reds with alcohol, intensity, and acidity, which should hold them in good stead for years.

2003

Vintage rating: *85*

The winter of 2002/03 was abnormally wet, which replenished the water table. At the end of July, the entire country sustained nearly three weeks of extreme heat. Photosynthesis slowed and the maturation process came to a standstill. By the start of September, the harvest was under way throughout much of southern Portugal, but sugar readings remained unusually low. However, as the warm weather continued, *Baumés* suddenly rose. Timing was everything, and those who got it wrong made unbalanced wines with high pH and surprisingly low alcohol.

The weather remained fine well into October, and growers in the north of the country managed to complete the harvest under clear skies. The Alentejo, Dão, and parts of the Douro suffered the most heat damage, whereas Bairrada enjoyed its best and most trouble-free vintage for a decade. The best wines will tend to be those from late-ripening varieties. With the exception of reds from Bairrada and parts of the Douro, wines from 2003 are likely to be forward and early maturing.

2002

Vintage rating: *65*

By early September, the grapes were generally in good condition, but it rained for five full days in the middle of the month. The unsettled weather continued into October, spelling disaster for Bairrada and Vinho Verde, where many growers watched their grapes rotting on the vine. Some excellent wines were made in the Douro by those who harvested early (see Port Vintage Report), and there are small quantities of good wine from the south. But, for most producers, 2002 is a vintage they would rather forget. The overall size of the harvest is about average at 6.6 million hl.

2001

Vintage rating: *85*

The 2001 harvest produced a hefty crop, although the north had an unusually cool and variable August, which led to some uneven ripening. Warm weather in early September saved the day, and some high sugar readings were recorded. Torrential September rain in the Alentejo brought *Baumés* down but, nonetheless, Moreto (usually an insipid grape) was harvested at 14 degrees *Baumé*. In the Dão and Alentejo, the harvest dragged on into late October. However, with total production at 7.6 million hl, 2001 seems to have matched quantity with quality.

2000

Vintage rating: *95*

Much of the flowering took place under adverse conditions, and by late May it looked as though 2000 would be the third small harvest in a row. But, unlike the two previous years, warm summer weather continued into October, allowing the harvest to take place throughout the country in near-perfect conditions. Bairrada, the Douro, and Dão produced some exceptional wines. Although yields were down dramatically in places, overall production was about average at around 6.7 million hl.

GREATEST WINE PRODUCERS

1. Niepoort (Douro)
2. Quinta do Crasto (Douro)
3. Quinta do Vale Meão (Douro)
4. Prats & Symington (Douro)
5. Sogrape (Douro, Dão, Alentejo)
6. Esporão (Alentejo)
7. Caves Aliança (Bairrada, Douro, Dao, Alentejo)
8. Luís Pato (Bairrada)
9. Quinta dos Roques (Dão)
10. Herdade do Mouchão (Alentejo)

FASTEST-IMPROVING PRODUCERS

1. Quinta do Vallado (Douro)
2. Caves Aliança (Bairrada, Douro, Dão, Alentejo)
3. Quinta do Passadouro (Douro)
4. Quinta de la Rosa (Douro)
5. Casa Cadaval (Ribatejo)
6. Quinta da Covela (Minho)
7. Real Companhia Velha (Douro)
8. DFJ Vinhos (Estremadura, Ribatejo)
9. Quinta do Portal (Douro)
10. Casa da Alorna (Ribatejo)

NEW UP-AND-COMING PRODUCERS

1. Cazes & Roquette (Douro)
2. Malhadinha Nova (Alentejo)
3. Quinta do Perdigão (Dão)
4. Manuel dos Santos Campolargo (Bairrada)
5. Lavradores de Feitoria (Douro)

6. Quinta dos Cozinheiros (Beiras)
7. Churchill Estates (Douro)
8. Herdade dos Grous (Alentejo)
9. Terras de Alter (Alentejo)
10. Muxagat Vinhos (Douro)

BEST-VALUE PRODUCERS

1. Adega Co-operativa de Pegões (Setúbal Peninsula)
2. Falua (Ribatejo)
3. DFJ Vinhos (Estremadura, Ribatejo)
4. Sogrape (Douro, Dão, Alentejo)
5. Dão Sul (Dão)
6. Casa Santos Lima (Estremadura)
7. Casa Ermelinda Freitas (Setúbal Peninsula)
8. Real Companhia Velha (Douro)
9. Bacalhôa Vinhos (Setúbal Peninsula, Alentejo)
10. Quinta dos Grilos (Dão)

GREATEST-QUALITY WINES

1. **Douro Pintas 2003** Wine & Soul (€38)
2. **Douro Batuta 2003** Niepoort (€80)
3. **Douro Vinha Maria Teresa 2003** Quinta do Crasto (€60)
4. **Alentejo Tonel 3-4 1996** Mouchão (€100)
5. **Barca Velha 1995** Ferreira (€100)
6. **Douro Reserva 2003** Duas Quintas (€25)
7. **Douro Reserva 2003** Quinta do Passadouro (€30)

8 **Douro 2003** Quinta do Vale Meão (€50)

9 **Alentejo Garrafeira Private Selection 2001** Esporão (€30)

10 **Alentejo 2003** Malhadinha Nova (€30)

BEST BARGAINS

1 **Dão Duque de Viseu Tinto 2003** Sogrape (€4)

2 **Alentejano Tagus Creek Shiraz Trincadeira 2005** Falua (€4)

3 **Douro 2003** Altano (€3)

4 **Vinha Grande 2001** Ferreira (€10)

5 **Estremadura 2004** Cortello (€3)

6 **Alentejo 2003** Monte da Ravasqueira (€8)

7 **Alentejo Chaminé 2003** Cortes de Cima (€6)

8 **Fontenario de Pegões Tinto 2003** Adega Co-operativa de Pegões (€2.50)

9 **Dão Colheita Seleccionada 2003** Quinta de Cabriz (€3)

10 **Alentejo Tinto da Anfora Grande Escolha 2001** Bacalhôa Vinhos (€15)

MOST EXCITING OR UNUSUAL FINDS

1 **Ribatejo Marquesa de Cadaval 2003** Casa Cadaval (€30) *A stunning blend of 70 percent Touriga Nacional and 30 percent Trincadeira from 70-year-old vines. The first really good wine I have tasted from the Ribatejo; sets the standard for the future of this underrated region.*

2 **Alentejo Verdelho 2004** Esporão (€7) *Wonderfully fragrant dry white made in the Alentejo from this famous Madeiran grape. Made by Australian David Baverstock, so it's probably not surprising that it is similar in style to the dry but fruity Verdelhos being made in South Australia.*

3 **Alentejo 2003** Malhadinha Nova (€30) *A massive, impressive, full-bodied red from a newcomer in the deep south of the Alentejo.*

4 **Escolha Tinto 2003** Quinta da Covela (€11.50) *An eclectic, vibrant, unoaked blend of Touriga Nacional, Cabernet Franc, and Merlot, from a quality-oriented estate in "no man's land" on the Douro River but outside the demarcated region.*

5 **Douro Sousão 2003** Quinta do Vallado (€14) *A varietal, the first as far as I am aware, from the Sousão grape, a variety that forms the backbone of Noval's famous Nacional port. Black, as you would expect from this tintureiro grape, but quite soft, round, and already good to drink.*

6 **Estremadura Reserve 2003** Chocapalha (€15) *A fine, fragrant, ripe, fleshy blend of Touriga Nacional, Tinta Roriz, and Alicante Bouschet. Proof that this underrated region north of Lisbon is capable of very great things.*

7 **Alentejo Touriga Nacional 2003** Cortes de Cima (€20) *Very expressive floral fruit, typical of Touriga Nacional, with weight, natural sweetness, and the concentration of a warm summer in the Alentejo.*

8 **Douro Redoma Rosé 2004** Niepoort (€12) *Serious rosé: raspberry, strawberry, rhubarb, with a touch of oak. Full-bodied and well balanced, this is a wine that will develop in bottle for five years. Decanter tasting five-star winner.*

9 **Alentejano Tagus Creek Shiraz Trincadeira 2005** Falua (€4) *Lovely spicy fruit with some grip— and good value, too.*

10 **Beiras Vinha da Costa 2003** Campolargo (€20) *Merlot, Tinta Roriz, and Syrah in a ripe, supple, surprisingly Bordelais red.*

Port & Madeira

Richard Mayson

While the abnormally hot temperatures of 2003 proved problematic for winemakers in Bordeaux and Burgundy, producers in Portugal's Douro Valley welcomed the weather, knowing that their vines could stand the heat.

RICHARD MAYSON

In the spring and early summer of 2005, 2003 made news by becoming the second declared port vintage of the 21st century and, for most of the major shippers, only the 25th declaration since 1900. The 2003 declaration was unanimous.

Coming from such a hot year, with yields as low as 17.6 oz (500 g) per vine, the 2003s are rich, powerful, and highly concentrated. A few wines express the heat of the vintage through their rather coarse, jammy fruit, and there are others that have a rather hard green edge from grapes picked before they were fully ripe. Tannin is the hallmark of the finest wines, making the best of the 2003s quite impenetrable and difficult to appreciate when first declared. The wines are certainly more challenging to taste at this stage than the atypical but super-ripe 1994s or the voluptuous but concentrated 2000s.

RICHARD MAYSON writes and lectures on wine, dividing his time between London, Portugal, and a family business in England's Peak District. He speaks fluent Portuguese, having been brought up in Portugal, and is regarded as one of the most respected authorities on port, sherry, madeira, and the wines of Spain and Portugal. His interest in the subject goes back to his university days, when he wrote a thesis on the microclimates of the vineyards of the Douro Valley. His books include *Portugal's Wines and Wine Makers* (Ebury Press, 1992), *Port and the Douro* (Faber & Faber, 1999), and *The Wines and Vineyards of Portugal* (Mitchell Beazley), which won the André Simon award for the best drinks book published in 2003. A second, fully revised edition of *Port and the Douro* was published by Mitchell Beazley in 2004, and Richard is currently preparing a book on the wines of Madeira and a third edition of *Portugal's Wines and Wine Makers*.

At the end of 2005, the port shippers reported a generally successful campaign, with the wines very well received by consumers. Prices were up by 3–4 percent on the hugely successful 2000s, but the quantity available was down by as much as 30 percent, due to strict selection and lower yields. Despite this, the shippers have been left with wine on their hands, since the wine trade does not seem particularly enthusiastic.

Under new management

The recent consolidation of the port trade that began in 2001 with the sale of Croft and Delaforce to the Fladgate Partnership and Sandeman to Sogrape continued in 2005. Port shippers JW Burmester and Gilberts, both family-owned until 1999, have been sold by cork producer Amorim to Sogevinus, the Spanish company that owns Cálem. The Fladgate Partnership has acquired the stocks and wine lodges belonging to the Spanish company Osborne, which has decided to concentrate on its core sherry and brandy business in Jerez. Castelinho, which filed for bankruptcy in 2004, has been sold to Stephan Christie, who owns Vasconcellos, a big BOB operator in France and Belgium. And Cockburn, the only major port shipper still in multinational hands, has been taken over by Fortune Brands in the break-up of Allied Domecq following its takeover by Pernod Ricard.

Wine tourism gains ground

With September 10, 2006 marking the 250th anniversary of the demarcation of the Douro, wine-related tourism continues to grow in the region. During 2005, the region received around 200,000 visitors, mostly on the 47 boats that now regularly ply the river during the summer. Lodging continues to increase, with both Amorim and Quinta do Portal opening hotels in their own vineyards during the year. Quinta de Romaniera, a large run-down estate upstream from Pinhão, is to be turned into an upmarket hotel by a French consortium led by Christian Seely, MD of Quinta do Noval since 1993 and of AXA Millésimes since 2001. The Spanish and Portuguese are proposing a joint branding of the Duero and Douro to promote tourism worldwide. In 2008, the historic buildings in the center of Régua will be home to the new Museum of the Douro.

Grapevine

• **The Douro and Port Wine Institute** (IVDP) has conducted its first domestic market research. The core Portuguese port consumer is male, 35–49, and buys between four and six bottles of port a year, mostly from supermarkets. Portugal is the third-largest market for port in the world, but much of this is accounted for by tourist purchases.

Opinion:
Undermining the premium image

The port industry continues to consolidate in the face of greater competition at the commodity end of the business. Four more shippers have changed hands in 2005, and rumor has it that at least three other independent shippers are up for sale. Over the past decade more than half the port companies have either been sold, merged, or closed their doors.

With production costs rising, a negative cycle is forming as some companies steadily lower prices to maintain cash flow, which undermines the overall pricing power of the commodity category. The high reliance on BOB for standard styles of port (ruby and basic tawny) means that shippers without strong brands of their own are not well placed to survive the continuing fall in prices. Although the volume of shipments was up by 1 percent in 2005, there was a decrease of 0.4 percent in value, chiefly due to France, the leading volume market, which registered a fall of 1.1 percent in volume and 2.6 percent in value.

The premium end of the market is showing solid growth. Even France is showing signs of increased demand for premium ports in quality restaurants, and the US is taking to aged tawny port. A number of shippers have met this with the launch of new reserve tawnies—wines that are aged in cask for a minimum of seven years but that do not qualify for the 10-, 20-, 30-, or 40-year indication of age.

The UK continues to be a battleground, with supermarket chains creating loss leaders for the pre-Christmas period. This means increased sales, but is the image of premium brands being damaged in the process?

Casa do Douro: new crisis

The insolvent Casa do Douro was once again a major cause for concern when the Banco Português de Negócios (BPN) threatened to seize the headquarters, lodges, and 17,000 pipes (9.3 million liters) of a total of 40,000 pipes of surplus port in August 2005. The threat of this destabilization of the market brought a number of shippers together, offering to buy up the wine. In the event, perhaps under political pressure, the BPN retreated. So the Casa do Douro, brought to its knees following the purchase of 40 percent of Royal Oporto in 1990, lives on, weakened still further, to face its next crisis. No government has yet had the courage to tackle this problem, but the majority Socialist administration has promised a root-and-branch study of port, the Douro, and its institutions in 2006.

Vintage Report

Advance report on the latest harvest

2005

Port—The harvest was one of the earliest on record after the driest and warmest growing season in living memory. Just 7.8 in (197 mm) of rain fell at Pinhão in the heart of the Cima Corgo from November to July (inclusive)—a reduction of 64 percent on the average. Upstream in the Douro Superior, even less rain fell, and there was no significant rainfall at all between November 2004 and August, when three days of rain delayed a particularly early harvest. By this time, several villages were without water and younger vines were showing signs of extreme stress. Flowering and fruit set in April were successful, but lack of water during the summer produced small berries and limited leaf cover. With mean July temperatures at Pinhão a degree or so above average, there was a high incidence of raisinization.

Picking began in the Douro Superior on August 22, followed by the Cima Corgo on September 5 and the westernmost Baixo Corgo on September 12—a good 10 days earlier than normal. Rain fell again on September 6 and 9. Sugar levels, already high, dipped for a few days before rising again to very satisfactory levels. The rain was followed by cool, clear skies, making it perfect harvest weather. Yields were down significantly in some parts of the region. Despite the challenging conditions, some very fine, concentrated wines have been made from older vineyards.

The *benefício* (the annual authorization of the quantity of grape must that may be fortified to make port) was 120,000 pipes (66 million liters)—10 percent below the expected total sales for the year.

Madeira—The island enjoyed an outstanding harvest. There was no shortage of high-quality grapes, with sugar readings as high as 14 degrees *Baumé* for Verdelho and Bual from the south side. The shippers are already setting aside their best *lotes* for colheitas and vintage madeiras. Readings of 12 degrees *Baumé* were not uncommon for Tinta Negra Mole, the island's principal variety, which, with heavy cropping, often struggles to reach 10 degrees *Baumé*.

Updates on the previous five vintages

2004

Vintage rating: *Port: 87, Madeira: 88*

Port—After rain in early and mid-September, the sunshine returned in the nick of time. Sugar levels rose suddenly and continued to rise as temperatures exceeded 86°F (30°C). With yields down slightly on the previous year, the overriding feature of 2004 is the balance of the musts. Some fine single-*quinta* wines will undoubtedly be declared following the universal declaration of 2003 (see main story).

Madeira—Some fine wines were made on all parts of the island. This was another dry year with the hottest temperatures for nearly 30 years at the end of July. Vineyards on the north side suffered from excess humidity in August but well-ventilated sites on the south side yielded the best grapes. Bual (of which there was no shortage) proved to be outstanding.

2003

Vintage rating: *Port: 94, Madeira: 90*

Port—An abnormally hot growing season produced some very promising wines. Yields were above average, and ports of a very high standard were made throughout the Douro region. One leading shipper has described it as a "textbook year." A vintage was unanimously declared in the spring and summer of 2005.

Madeira—An exceptional year, with a large production of healthy, generally disease-free grapes. This was an excellent year for Tinta Negra Mole and Verdelho, both of which registered good levels of ripeness. For Verdelho it was the best harvest for 10 years. Both Sercial and Bual produced some good wines, but for Malvasia it was a year with low production and some localized disease problems.

2002

Vintage rating: *Port: 70, Madeira: 85*

Port—Those who managed to pick before the rain set in have small quantities of good, possibly outstanding, wine. Although it is still too early to be certain, some producers in the Cima Corgo and Douro Superior should have sufficient quantities of high-quality wine to make a single-*quinta* declaration early in 2004.

Madeira—This vintage saw a large production and particularly good-quality Tinta Negra Mole on the south side and excellent quality with large volumes of Bual from Calheta at the extreme west. Bual and Tinta Negra

Mole in the Campanário district in the southwest suffered from a difficult vintage due to persistent fog in the last four weeks or so before the vintage. Malmsey and Sercial were inconsistent. Verdelho was excellent but limited in volume.

2001

Vintage rating: *Port: 85, Madeira: 75*

Port—With flowering taking place under optimum conditions and ground-water supplies thoroughly replenished, there was a large crop. Temperatures were uneven during August, but rain at the end of the month helped swell the grapes. Yields were up by 30 percent on 2000 in the A/B-grade vineyards. Overall, 2001 proved to be a useful year in which a number of single *quintas* have produced some fine vintage ports for drinking over the medium term. Madeira—There was a big production of Tinta Negra Mole, but the volume of Malmsey suffered due to *coulure* at flowering. Sercial and Verdelho from the northern vineyards suffered from particularly bad weather during flowering, which resulted in a greatly reduced vintage for these two varieties. Bual did not suffer as much, and volumes were normal.

2000

Vintage rating: *Port: 95, Madeira: 85*

Port—Low yields helped make some wonderfully concentrated wines—perhaps not as overtly rich as the 1994s, but with more poise and harmony than the 1997s. A fine vintage combined with some truly excellent wines made for a universal declaration in the spring/summer of 2002. Madeira—Good-quality Bual and Tinta Negra Mole from the south and west, and a very small crop of excellent-quality Verdelho from Camara de Lobos on the south side.

GREATEST WINE PRODUCERS

1. Graham
2. Fonseca
3. Quinta do Noval
4. Taylor
5. Barbeito (madeira)
6. Dow
7. Blandy (madeira)
8. Niepoort
9. Warre
10. Henriques & Henriques (madeira)

FASTEST-IMPROVING PRODUCERS

1. Croft
2. Delaforce
3. Poças
4. Porto Heredias
5. São Pedro das Aguías
6. Quinta do Portal
7. Quinta do Infantado
8. Cálem
9. Vista Alegre
10. Rozes

NEW UP-AND-COMING PRODUCERS

1. Quinta de Roriz
2. Quinta do Ventozello
3. Quinta Vale Dona Maria
4. Quinta do Tedo
5. Quinta do Silval
6. Porto Heredias
7. Quinta do Portal
8. José Maria da Fonseca and Van Zeller
9. Wine & Soul
10. Vista Alegre

BEST-VALUE PRODUCERS

1. Smith Woodhouse
2. Martinez
3. Gould Campbell
4. Sandeman
5. Justino Henriques (madeira)

GREATEST-QUALITY WINES

1. **Quinta do Noval Nacional Vintage Port 2003** (€750)
2. **Fonseca Vintage Port 2003** (€80)
3. **Graham's Vintage Port 2003** (€80)
4. **Blandy's Bual Madeira 1964** (€76)
5. **Graham's 20 Year Old Tawny Port** (€35)
6. **Quinta do Vesúvio Vintage Port 2000** (€60)
7. **Ramos Pinto Quinta do Bom Retiro 20 Year Old Tawny Port** (€45)
8. **Barbeito 20 Year Old Malvasia Lote 4122 Madeira** (€40)
9. **Graham's Malvedos Vintage Port 1996** (€35)
10. **Graham's Vintage Port 1985** (€85)

BEST BARGAINS

1. **Quinta do Vallado 10 Year Old Tawny Port** (€13)
2. **Quinta do Crasto LBV Port 1998** (€10)
3. **Blandy's Alvada 5 Year Old Rich Madeira** (€15)
4. **Warre's Bottle Matured LBV Port 1995** (€18)
5. **Fonseca Bin 27 Port** (€10)
6. **Graham's Malvedos Vintage Port 1996** (€35)
7. **Warre's Warrior Special Reserve Port** (€15)
8. **Noval Silval Vintage Port 2003** (€30)
9. **Poças Vintage Port 2003** (€30)
10. **Dow's Crusted Port** (€18)

MOST EXCITING OR UNUSUAL FINDS

1. **Cossart Gordon Verdelho Madeira 1934** (€240) *Kerosene and wood-smoke aromas, fantastically complex, vibrant flavors; unusually rich for a Verdelho, with wonderful concentration. Amazing wine.*
2. **Graham's Vintage Port 1983** (€75) *Powerful, concentrated wine, with great purity of fruit, from a vintage often overlooked even by the most serious of port enthusiasts. Still a long way to go. Good for another 25 years at least.*
3. **Croft Vintage Port 2003** (€40) *Croft is making fine vintage port again after spending three decades in the wilderness. Foot-trodden for the first time since 1963, this wine is voluptuous, with great purity of fruit. Not the biggest of the 2003s, but one of the most attractive.*

④ **Quinta de Roriz Vintage Port 2003** (€60) *Having supplied a number of different shippers in the past, this fine estate is making a name for itself in a joint venture between the owners and the Symington family. The 2003 Roriz is one of the best wines of the vintage: solid, ripe, and complete. Huge potential here.*

⑤ **Cossart Gordon Verdelho Colheita Madeira 1995** (€16.50) *A wonderfully expressive wine with much of the character and panache of a "vintage" or frasqueira madeira—proof that the relatively new colheita category, representing "early bottled vintage," is the means to drink fine madeira at a reasonable price.*

⑥ **Delaforce Curious and Ancient 20 Year Old Tawny Port** (€30) *The name itself is unusual, but the wine lives up to it: round, nutty, with a hint of tobacco—mature and long. An old brand currently being relaunched under new management.*

⑦ **Graham's Malvedos Vintage Port 1996** (€35) *There was a huge volume of generally rather attenuated ports in 1996, but this is robust yet voluptuous with plenty to go at for a decade or more. Lovely.*

⑧ **Vista Alegre White Port 1985** (€20) *A white port with a vintage is unusual in itself, but this wine is rich and spicy with wonderful woody complexity—a world away from the usual bland dry white port.*

⑨ **Quinta do Portal Vintage Port 2003** (€30) *A relatively new venture, Portal produced a lovely, sweet, floral 2003. Not a keeper but an attractive, fine, fruity port for the mid-term and something of a revelation.*

⑩ **Graham's The Tawny Port** (€14) *A genuine tawny port bottled without any indication of age blended from wines aged in cask for between seven and nine years. This wine fills a big gap in the growing market for tawny port.*

Grapevine

- **Fonseca's Quinta do Panascal** has won the Best of Wine Tourism Award from the General Assembly of Wine Capitals Network, a group of wine capitals that includes Rioja, Bordeaux, Cape Town, Florence, Melbourne, San Francisco, and Oporto. Cálem won the Best of Wine Tourism architecture award for its newly restored lodges in Vila Nova de Gaia.

- **Croft is targeting** the female market with a new reserve port called Indulgence.

- **The** *entreposto*, **or** *entrepôt*, of port lodges in Vila Nova de Gaia is being proposed for UNESCO World Heritage status.

Great Britain

Stephen Skelton MW

The *Champenois* really are coming! Over the past 18 months, rumors have been circulating about a champagne house planting a vineyard in England.

STEPHEN SKELTON MW

There was a report that Frazer Thompson, MD of Chapel Down, had been seen lunching *à deux* with Carol Duval-Leroy. Then I received a call from a farmer who had been approached by Duval-Leroy with an offer to buy his land, but the project foundered because the Brits would give them only a 75-year lease.

Happening upon Oz Clarke at a tasting, I asked him whether he'd heard anything. "Oh, yes," he said, "they are called Champagne Pierson Whitaker, and they are friends of my dentist." I visited Didier Pierson and his English wife Imogen Whitaker in Avize on the Côte des Blancs. The extended Pierson family farms 50 ha in the area, while Didier himself is winemaker to both the family and a big cooperative in the neighboring village of Grauves. With land at $440,000 a hectare in Champagne, expansion is next to impossible, so, knowing that English sparkling wine was gaining something of a reputation, why not look a little farther from home? Didier and Imogen studied the climatic and geological data and found

STEPHEN SKELTON MW established the award-winning Tenterden Vineyards in 1977 and made wine there for 22 years. His wines have won the Gore-Browne Trophy for the Best UK Wine on three occasions. He is currently a consultant to a number of UK vineyards and wineries. Stephen was a director of the United Kingdom Vineyards Association (UKVA) between 1982 and 1998 and chairman from 1998 until 2003. Having written on wine, winemaking, and viticulture since 1986, he published *The Vineyards of England* in 1989 and rewrote and updated this work under the new title of *The Wines of Britain and Ireland* (Faber & Faber, 2001). This book won the André Simon Award in 2002. Stephen became a Master of Wine in 2003, also winning the Mondavi prize, which is awarded to the candidate gaining the highest score in the written part of the examination.

10 acres on the Hampshire downs at Meonstoke, near Droxford. The land is owned by Sydney Chaplin, who, rather than sell the Pierson Whitakers the land, has gone into partnership with them.

In April and May 2005, Didier planted around 22,000 vines, all on 41B, the highest-rated rootstock for chalky soil, using the same clones of Chardonnay and Pinot Noir he has in Champagne. All were planted in rows 4 ft (1.2 m) wide with the vines spaced at 4 ft (1.2 m), which is just above the minimum density permitted in Champagne. Didier plans to complete the planting in 2006 with a further 0.5 ha of Pinot Meunier. He has been a regular visitor to Meonstoke, ferrying equipment and materials to look after his vines, doing the cultivating between the rows, the weed control beneath them, and keeping the young plants free from mildew with regular sprays of fungicide. Trellising and training the vines will be tasks for 2006. He intends to import a straddle tractor to cope with the ultra-narrow rows and will manage the vineyard himself. A building on the farm will be converted into a winery, and a Vaslin 2000 press has been ordered. The first crop is not expected until 2008.

Luckily for Didier, the harvest in Hampshire will be two to three weeks later than in Champagne, so he will be able to do both vintages. For now, Didier Pierson is the sole representative of Champagne to take the plunge and plant in the UK.

Grapevine

- **An infestation** of *Cochlicella acuta*, very small conical snails, has all but destroyed 1.25 ha of newly planted vines at Breaky Bottom vineyard near Lewes in East Sussex. During the dry months, these small snails have been finding moisture inside the plastic tree guards used to protect vines. I could not believe the extent of the damage until I saw it for myself and marveled at the large clusters of these tiny snails, perhaps 200–300 in a group, which had climbed to the tops of the bamboo stakes used to support the vines. Mollusk experts cannot decide how to rid the vineyard of these pests, and until this happens, replanting cannot take place.

- **Plumpton College in East Sussex** has opened a brand-new winery as part of its $1.75-million expansion scheme. The college now offers two-year full-time foundation degrees, one in wine production and the other in wine business, and a three-year full-time BSc honors degree in viticulture and oenology. It also offers a range of part-time and day-release courses on both vinegrowing and winemaking. Plumpton has some 6 ha of vines, both on site and at leased local vineyards, and its range of wines is starting to find favor with customers, sales having doubled in 2005, mainly due to the introduction of two new sparkling wines. My only gripe with Plumpton is that very few (if any) wines have been granted Regional or Quality wine status. Now it has a new winery, let's hope that it will start putting them into the scheme.

AIMING FOR POLE POSITION

Former Formula 1 world champion Jody Scheckter planted the first two of 10 intended acres of Chardonnay, Pinot Noir, and Pinot Meunier exclusively for sparkling wine at Laverstoke Park in 2006. With 2,500 acres of fully organic land (currently converting to biodynamic) and some of the oldest breeds of cattle, water buffalo, pigs, wild boar, sheep, and poultry, Laverstoke Park describes itself as "the biggest small-holding [homestead] in the world." Scheckter had originally considered buying a small champagne house to sell under the Laverstoke Park label, but when he realized that the best English wines fetch higher prices than lesser-known champagne brands, he looked closer to home. Scheckter aims to produce the UK's first super-premium sparkling wine, and with his competitive streak and Michel Salgues (who established Roederer Estate in California's Anderson Valley) as consultant, he stands a very good chance of success.

HMG SHOWCASES UK WINE

During 2005, when Britain held the EU presidency and hosted the G8 summit meetings at Gleneagles, English and Welsh wines featured quite heavily on menus. After many years of lobbying and cajoling, Government Hospitality, as the department is called, finally got the message and placed several large orders with Chapel Down, Breaky Bottom, Camel Valley, Sharpham, Biddenden, Llanerch, Heart of England, RidgeView Winery, and Three Choirs. Anthony Hanson MW (wine merchant, wine writer, and consultant to Christie's), who is on the committee that selects wines for HMG's use, was instrumental in persuading the committee to consider the wines.

Llanerch also sold five cases of its Cariad Celtic Dry for the British High Commissioner to South Africa, Lord (Paul) Boateng, to use in South Africa; and Wickham Vineyard in Hampshire supplied wine to the EU Commission.

CHAMPAGNE VARIETIES GAIN GROUND

The march of champagne varieties—Chardonnay, Pinot Noir, and Pinot Meunier—appears unstoppable. After 2003, everyone is assuming that the climate is changing for the better, and new plantings are set to exceed 150 ha by the end of 2006, bringing the total of these three varieties up to around 240 ha or one-third of the area under vine. Is this increase sustainable? Sales of UK sparkling wine are fairly limited, mainly because the good ones are in short supply and

Grapevine

- **Karin and Ross Hay** have left their jobs to take over Highdown Vineyard, a run-down property near Worthing in West Sussex. The 2.25-ha vineyard now boasts a new visitor center. Work is under way to restore the vineyard to full cropping, and their 2005 harvest came to just over 9,000 bottles. An additional 1,000 Chardonnay vines have been planted, and the vineyard will almost double in size by the end of 2006.

at the upper limit of what customers are willing to pay. Whether the market can be expanded by this type of increase in supply is open to question. One good thing is that sparkling wines improve as they keep and can be sold over a much longer period than still wines.

ENGLISH SPARKLING WINE: BEST IN THE WORLD—OFFICIAL!

RidgeView Wine Estate crowned a fantastic year by winning the IWSC's Yarden Trophy for the best sparkling wine with its Bloomsbury 2002. This is the second time in the last eight years that an English wine has won the trophy, 1993 Nyetimber Classic Cuvée having won it in 1998.

In 2005, RidgeView planted a further 4 ha on a neighboring farm, which will be managed by its team, and 2006 will see the expansion of Domaine RidgeView by further plantings. In total, the area under vine will amount to 12 ha. RidgeView aims to increase production from today's output of around 50,000 bottles to 100,000 bottles. An $85,000 government processing and marketing grant has been awarded and will be used primarily to extend pressing and labeling facilities, together with a doubling of the number of gyropalettes for automatic riddling.

JILLY TURNS A SOD

Camel Valley Vineyard owner Bob Lindo invited TV personality Jilly Goolden to plant the first vine in his latest vineyard of 5,000 Seyval Blanc and 3,000 Bacchus vines. Camel reports a great year, with one 6,000-bottle order on its way to Japan. A new sparkling-wine labeler, costing around $40,000, will help streamline the operation. Camel also won the only gold medal awarded to an English wine in the International Wine Challenge for its 2001 Cornwall Sparkling Brut, as well as a bronze for its 2004 Bacchus and a Seal of Approval for the 2004 Seyval Blanc.

BIRDS FLYING BACK?

My first vintage in the UK in 1978 was all but taken by birds, and for the next 10 years netting the entire crop was essential. Around the mid-1980s, the birds started to disappear and could be kept at bay by the usual bird-scaring devices—gas guns, firework-like "bird bangers," recordings of distress calls, stringing "humming tape" across the rows. The birds' disappearance was put down to a number of factors. Farmers got bad press for taking out hedges and using too many sprays, which either killed the birds' food or reduced weed levels in crops, which meant fewer weed seeds. I blamed cats—millions of them UK-wide—which together must eat tons of birds every day.

In 2005, however, several vineyard owners have reported increased bird damage, especially from pigeons. According to one avian specialist, the moisture in the grapes is what the birds actually want, and therefore the very dry September and October could account for the increased damage. In New Zealand, approximately 75 percent of the entire crop is netted at vast cost. Let's hope that widespread netting does not become necessary in UK vineyards.

Opinion:
Quality, quality, quality

Once again, I find the subject of quality (or the lack of quality) uppermost in my mind when I write my report. Why? Because there are just too many substandard English and Welsh wines still on the market. Although the labeling changes have made a difference, with many more wines now going through the Quality and Regional wine schemes (which apply only to still wines, not sparkling), the standard required to achieve a pass—and therefore to be able to put the name of the vineyard, the grape variety, and the vintage on the label, together with the words "England/English" or "Wales/Welsh" (depending on provenance)—is still lamentably low and, in reality, is a "no fault" hurdle over which wines entered must jump.

Most English and Welsh still wines are too expensive for their quality. There are far better wines available from overseas for the same money. This of course is not a UK phenomenon, as growers in areas such as Bordeaux, Burgundy, and Muscadet have discovered to their cost. Wines coming from countries where growing conditions are easier (more sunshine, cheaper land, and cheaper labor) and where yields are higher and can be bolstered by irrigation are bound to be cheaper. But the UK is different. Growers sell almost 100 percent of their wine in the UK, and therefore all wines, good or bad, find their way into a glass sooner or later. We do not have a sink of cheap wine or the ability to send wine for distillation that other countries enjoy. It is therefore even more important that every English or Welsh wine put on the market should be above average.

The tasting panels who judge the Quality and Regional wine programs must be composed of tasters who are experienced in tasting wines commercially available in the UK so that they can put the wines they taste into perspective. Tasters should be allowed to submit their scores without having to shout them out for all the other tasters to hear, because I am convinced that peer pressure is a brake on objectivity.

English and Welsh winegrowers should learn from the experiences of others who have struggled to break into the UK market. Quality—real, identifiable quality in the glass—is the only way to build a reputation and a lasting, profitable market. It would also be good if all UK-grown wines, still and sparkling, could be submitted to a tasting panel. Although there are not many, there are a few sparkling wines that are really below par and ought not to be able to fly the flag. Sparkling wine is the future; and the sooner that it, too, comes under objective scrutiny, the better.

Vintage Report

Advance report on the latest harvest

2005

Yet another strange year for UK growers. Despite what felt like a cool, somewhat damp summer with on/off sun and rain, September and October turned into very good months, and sugar levels ended up even better than those achieved in 2003, the hottest year on record! A few vineyards got caught by a hard mid-May frost—one lost 80 percent of its crop in one night—but in general, yields were above average, very clean, and certainly better-than-average quality. Sugar/acid balances seem to be perfect. This is the fifth year in a row that sugar levels have been above average, and one has to admit that global warming really is starting to bite. With the now very large area planted to Chardonnay and Pinots (both generally reckoned to be hard-to-ripen varieties in our climate), it is to be hoped that this situation continues.

Updates on the previous five vintages

2004

Vintage rating: *Red: 85, White: 89*

Despite the large yields, many of the 2004s have turned into really typical UK-grown wines with a good balance of fruit and acidity. A high proportion of the silver medals awarded in the 2005 UKVA Wine of the Year Competition went to 2004s. The best wines made from the Bacchus grape variety have good flavor with sufficient length for their style and have the typical freshness and fragrance this variety brings.

2003

Vintage rating: *Red: 92, White: 90*

An amazing year for UK winemakers. A trouble-free spring was followed by great summer weather, with temperatures hitting the high 90s (35°C), but the fall was the clincher. September and October were very warm, sunny, and almost completely dry. Grapes were harvested at unheard-of sugar levels, with potential alcohol levels of 11–13 percent in many vineyards. All competent growers appear to have made extremely good wines, with reds and sparklings from traditional varieties (that is, traditional champagne varieties) the stars. It was certainly the best year for red varieties that anyone can remember. In general, the 2003s are very good, with some in the "excellent" category.

2002

Vintage rating: *Red: 82, White: 85*

The overall crop was smaller than average, but an Indian summer resulted in exceptional quality, especially with the harder-to-ripen varieties, such as Chardonnay, and the successful red varieties: Pinot Noir, Rondo, Regent, and Dornfelder. Natural sugar levels, which usually languish around 7–9 percent, were well up into double figures in many cases. Several wine-makers made completely natural wines—that is, without chaptalization.

2001

Vintage rating: *Red: 75, White: 82*

This was a very fair year. No spring frosts and a good flowering combined to produce a larger-than-average crop. Temperatures were higher in 2001 than for centuries, and this was reflected in an early harvest of clean, ripe grapes. Reds had more color than usual, and the generally tough-to-ripen varieties, such as Riesling and Pinot Blanc, did well. Chardonnay and Pinot Noir for sparkling wine put in a good performance, and this should be reflected in the wines.

2000

Vintage rating: *Red: 70, White: 75*

This was a cooler-than-average year with a very wet harvest. Whites fared better than reds, and sparkling wines should be good. The best will keep, but the majority should have been drunk.

GREATEST WINE PRODUCERS

1. Nyetimber Vineyard
2. English Wines Group (Chapel Down)
3. RidgeView
4. Denbies Wine Estate
5. Camel Valley
6. Three Choirs
7. Sharpham
8. Stanlake Park (formerly Valley Vineyards)
9. Astley
10. Nutbourne

FASTEST-IMPROVING PRODUCERS

1. Yearlstone
2. Astley
3. Sandhurst Vineyards
4. Heart of England
5. Barnsole
6. Chilford Hall
7. Bookers
8. Glyndwr
9. Warden Abbey
10. Wyken

NEW UP-AND-COMING PRODUCERS

1. Bow-in-the-Cloud
2. a'Beckett's
3. Wroxeter Roman
4. Hoopers
5. Thelnetham

BEST-VALUE PRODUCERS

1. English Wines Group (Chapel Down)
2. Denbies Wine Estate
3. Three Choirs
4. RidgeView
5. Camel Valley
6. Stanlake Park (formerly Valley Vineyards)

GREATEST-QUALITY WINES

1. **Classic Cuvée 1999** Nyetimber Vineyard (£19.99)
2. **Pinot Noir 2003** Sandhurst Vineyards (£10.99)
3. **Pinot Noir 2003** Chapel Down (£12.99)
4. **Merret Bloomsbury 2003** RidgeView (£15.95)
5. **Fitzrovia Rosé 2002** RidgeView (£18.75)
6. **Bacchus Dry 2004** Camel Valley (£9.50)
7. **Hillside Chardonnay 2003** Denbies Wine Estate (£11.99)
8. **Blanc de Blancs 1999** Nyetimber Vineyard (£19.99)
9. **Dart Valley Reserve 2004** Sharpham (£7.50)
10. **Siegerrebe 2004** Three Choirs (£7.80)

BEST BARGAINS

1. **Flint Valley 2002** Denbies Wine Estate (£5.49)
2. **Brut NV** Chapel Down (£11.99)
3. **Coopers Brook 2003** Denbies Wine Estate (£5.99)
4. **Pinot Noir 2003** Sandhurst Vineyards (£10.99)
5. **Bacchus 2004** Chapel Down (£7.49)
6. **Dart Valley Reserve 2004** Sharpham (£7.50)
7. **Siegerrebe 2004** Three Choirs (£7.80)

MOST EXCITING OR UNUSUAL FINDS

1. **Pinot Noir 2003** Sandhurst Vineyards (£10.99) *England! You must be joking. Pinot fresh berry nose, with succulent, silky fruit and balanced oak on the palate.*
2. **Hillside Chardonnay 2003** Denbies Wine Estate (£11.99) *Beautiful balanced wine with attractive, mouthwatering citric notes and sensitive use of oak. A truly representative cool-climate Chardonnay.*
3. **Classic Cuvée 1998** Nyetimber Vineyard (£27.50) *This is possibly the best wine Nyetimber has ever produced and—if they don't sell it too quickly—will be around winning prizes for the next few years. Still quite crisp with a pronounced yet balanced acidity, the flavor of this wine is beyond compare. Champagne should watch its back!*

Belgium, Netherlands & Scandinavia

Fiona Morrison MW & Ronald de Groot

Things are looking ever better: three new appellations in Belgium, more Dutch farmers turning to wine production, and another increase in Danish wineries.

FIONA MORRISON MW   RONALD DE GROOT

BELGIUM

Belgium's desire to classify its vineyards seems to be reaching a conclusion. Three new appellations were created in 2005 in the Dutch-speaking part of the country, and two more in Walloon. In Flanders, a new zone, Heuveland, alongside Haspengouw and Hageland, has VQPRD status and is organized along the same lines as other European appellation wines. The other two designations are for Flemish table wine and Flemish sparkling wine, the latter category proving a popular choice among Belgian wine consumers.

In Walloon, two new sparkling-wine appellations are currently being created: one is for a VMQPRD for the region of Walloon, and one is for *crémant* produced from a specific region in Walloon. These five new designations are expected to be the last in Belgium, and the authorities hope that all wine producers in Belgium will adhere to one of these classifications.

FIONA MORRISON MW has spent more than 20 years in the wine trade around the world and speaks several languages. She became a Master of Wine in 1994 and is now a freelance wine journalist and lecturer. She is married to Jacques Thienpont, a wine *négociant* and owner of Le Pin in Pomerol, and together they divide their time between Bordeaux and Belgium, making, tasting, and promoting wine.
RONALD DE GROOT is owner and editor of the leading Dutch wine magazine *Perswijn*. Since 2003 he has been responsible for the Dutch edition of the French restaurant guide *GaultMillau* and is a freelance contributor to other media. As a wine consultant, he is a member of the KLM Royal Dutch Airlines tasting panel. He is also a member of one of Europe's leading tasting panels, the Grand Jury Européen.

Production in Belgium reached approximately 160,000 liters with the successful 2005 harvest, a 15,000-liter increase over the previous year. The goal for Belgian wine production is to reach 200,000 liters by 2010.

Although Belgian wine production is still dominated by the Dutch-speaking population, there are a handful of producers in Walloon who are sparking an interest in winemaking in the southern part of the country. Philippe Grafé, a well-known Belgian wine merchant, has built an ambitious winery at Domaine du Chenoy in Emines-La Bruyère, and the Biercée Distillery in Thuin, a picturesque village that attracts many tourists, has launched its Clos des Zoauves, which showed well in recent tastings. The star of the Belgian wine industry is undoubtedly Peter Colemont, whose tiny Clos d'Opleeuw in Limburg is an inspiration for other Belgian winemakers. His Chardonnay graces the list of the nation's top restaurants, and he shares his knowledge generously, giving weekly courses in oenology to aspiring winemakers.

Although hybrids make up the majority of plantings in Belgium, it was the Chardonnays from Genoels-Elderen and Clos d'Opleeuw that shone in tastings this year. Another surprise was the improved quality of the red wines, which are beginning to show true fruit character and personality—helped by the successful 2003 and 2004 vintages.

Belgian winemakers are in a positive mood, with sales going well. Many of the top producers sell out of their new vintages very quickly. Wine tourism has become popular with producers such as Genoels-Elderen and Meerdael, who make impressive efforts to welcome the public and explain winemaking to them.

THE NETHERLANDS

In addition to rising temperatures due to global warming, more Dutch farmers are considering becoming professional wine producers because of dwindling profits in other areas. The total number of vineyards of more than 1 ha has risen to 30, and an increase in the number of vineyards of 3 ha or more is also expected. By 2010, the number of professional producers should reach about 100. Agritourism is becoming a popular leisure activity in the Netherlands, so an important part of these small producers' revenue will come from tastings and guided tours.

Hybrids spur plantings

Hybrids have had an even more important role than global warming in the development of northerly and eastern vineyards in the Netherlands. Until 1996, no professional vineyards were found outside Limburg and Brabant, the southernmost provinces. Now, however, there are about

20 growers with more than 1 ha of vineyard in other parts of the Netherlands, an increase that is strongly related to the introduction of new mildew-resistant hybrids such as Regent and Rondo (black) and Johanniter, Merzling, and Solaris (white). As well as hybrids, mildew-resistant and faster-ripening crossings of grapes such as Cabernet Sauvignon will give a further impetus to planting countrywide.

DENMARK & SWEDEN

In **Denmark**, only a handful of growers make wine commercially, but the area under vine grows, albeit slowly, each year. The number of registered wineries has increased from two in 2001 to six in 2002, seven in 2003, and eight in 2004.

The best-known winemakers are Nordlund, Domaine Aalsgaard (Sjælland), and Skærsøgaard Vin in Jutland. Other members of the Danish Organization of Winegrowers are Vinperlen, Frederiksborg Vin, Solbjerggaard, and Degnemosegaard (all at Sjælland) and Lille Gadegaard (on the isle of Bornholm). The number of registered wineries is set to rise, since more vineyards have been planted recently. As in Sweden and the Netherlands, most new plantings are hybrids.

Despite the fact that the climate in **Sweden** seems less than appropriate for good winemaking, some farmers have started to grow vines. Lauri Pappinen founded Gutevin, a commercial vineyard on the island of Gotland, in 2000. With 7.5 ha, this is by far the biggest commercial vineyard in Scandinavia. He aged his red wine in new barrels for the first time in 2004, and his long-term aim is to produce 20,000 bottles per year from Rondo, Regent, Orion, Phoenix, Reichensteiner, and Madeleine Angevine 7672.

In mainland Sweden, Blaxsta Vingård, 75 miles (120 km) south of Stockholm, is making a Vidal icewine that has earned a good reputation—not so surprising, perhaps, given the success of Canadian Vidal icewine. Further plantings of hybrids in Sweden should lead to more wine production over the next few years.

Grapevine

• **Wijnhoeve De Colonjes** Regent Barrique 2003 failed to get a gold medal by only one point in the October 2005 Netherlands wine contest, showing the potential of this hybrid. The competition is run according to OIV guidelines, and it was a compliment to Wijnhoeve De Colonjes that it won a silver medal with a score of 87 points, the first red wine from the Netherlands to achieve such a result.

Opinion:
Improvements in Belgium

Winemaking is steadily improving in Belgium, and the enthusiasm of wine growers is encouraging. Hygiene is beginning to improve, and the wines are more stable than in the past. However, fewer than half of the wines tasted over the past year were deemed commercially acceptable by Ronald de Groot and myself, which makes the Belgian wine-drinking public somewhat forgiving about the quality of many of the wines.

Belgian wine production will always be a domestic industry, making very few waves on the international market, but, as it matures, growers seem to be concentrating on producing easy-to-drink, quaffable wines at reasonable prices.

It has been encouraging to see the growth of both sparkling-wine production and rosé wines, which find ready markets during the summer months. All in all, it has been an encouraging year for Belgian viticulture, with a couple of decent harvests and good sales to give growers confidence to continue.

Netherlands needs more professionalism

With increasing numbers of professional producers in the Netherlands, better wines are being made. But a lot of wines are still mediocre, due to inadequate winemaking skills, lack of good-quality grapes, or both. The producer is the determining factor here. Some professional producers do not produce decent wine, despite the fact that they have several hectares of vines and make wine every year. They survive by selling wine as a curiosity from the vineyard. Some amateur winemakers, on the other hand, do make good wine, but quantities are limited.

The quality of the best white wines is undisputed. Apostelhoeve whites can be found on many restaurant wine lists, and other good white wines are sold nationally. For reds and rosés it's a different story. Red wines, which are made from hybrids, often have a "foxy" flavor and lack finesse. Regent wines, for example, tend to be quite tannic and difficult, with a dry finish. Skilled producers, however, who pick the grapes as late as possible, have low yields, and use barrel maturation, can make acceptable wines, so there should be an improvement in red wines in the near future as producers become more experienced. Some decent rosé is made as well, which is a logical move, given the surge in its popularity in the Netherlands over the past few years.

Vintage Report

Advance report on the latest harvest

2005

Belgium—A wonderful spring resulted in an exceptional flowering. The summer, however, was disappointing: between July 15 and the end of August, the weather was wet and cloudy with relatively little sunshine. Luckily, the end of August and all of September were excellent and turned the harvest from an average one, to one of very good potential. By the end of September the natural alcohol levels in the grapes were higher than 10 percent. Compared to the small crop produced in 2004, both the quantity and the quality of the 2005 harvest were very good.

Netherlands—A slightly cooler summer forced producers to harvest a bit later than normal, but the grapes were generally ripe. Sugar and acidity were well balanced, producing quite powerful wines. Spring frosts and rain during flowering reduced the harvest by 20 percent. In general, it was quite a good vintage for Dutch growers.

Updates on the previous five vintages

2004

Vintage rating: *Belgium—Red: 87, White: 83;*
Netherlands—Red: 80, White: 82

Belgium—A mild winter and an unsettled spring, but good weather during flowering. The summer was disappointing, with dull weather and quite a lot of rain. However, the Indian summer in September and October brought optimism to the growers, and the crop was fairly abundant and of decent quality.

Netherlands—The season was cool, making it difficult for the grapes to ripen in the summer. In September and October, the grapes caught up to some extent, but rain disturbed the harvest. The wet weather contributed to a larger harvest than normal. Wines are more elegant in character and more "nervous," with higher acidity, but they are quite acceptable in quality. This is a vintage for lovers of a fresher style.

2003

Vintage rating: *Belgium—Red: 81, White: 85;*
Netherlands—Red: 83, White: 86

Belgium—A wonderful vintage on paper because of the high amount of sunshine during summer and fall. However, northern grape varieties are used to dealing with excess water and some vineyards suffered from hydric stress; the wines are not as concentrated and rich as the summer heat might have suggested, but there are some very good wines.

Netherlands—This was a very good vintage with a few exceptions. The wonderful summer and fall brought powerful wines, with some excellent examples with real complexity and more alcohol than usual. Vines on sandy soils suffered from drought, which stressed the vines, so there were some mixed results here. In general, as in other countries, there is less acidity, so wines are ripening faster.

2002

Vintage rating: *Belgium—Red: 79, White: 81;*
Netherlands—Red: 82, White: 84

Belgium—Another vintage saved by the sunny late-summer weather after mixed weather during a long growing season. Some attractive wines made people start to sit up and take notice of Belgian wines.

Netherlands—Quite a good vintage, with well-balanced wines, good acidity, and nice power. Saved by good fall weather.

2001

Vintage rating: *Belgium—Red: 68, White: 69;*
Netherlands—Red: 69, White: 68

Belgium—The reverse of recent vintages: the cool, wet weather during harvest created problems after a better-than-usual summer. Wines lacked concentration, and many were not very clean.

Netherlands—Quality was not very good because of bad weather during summer and fall. It rained nearly every day in September. Wines tend to be unbalanced, less concentrated, lean, and thin.

2000

Vintage rating: *Belgium—Red: 72, White: 73;*
Netherlands—Red: 77, White: 78

Belgium—Cool growing season and, compared to southern Europe, a dull and rather wet summer. Average wines.

Netherlands—Rather wet in midsummer, but better in September and October, when the weather was dry and sunny. Quite good wines, but lacking real ripeness. Many reds have a touch too much acidity.

GREATEST WINE PRODUCERS

1. Peter Colemont, Clos d'Opleeuw (Gors-Opleeuw, Belgium)
2. Apostelhoeve (Maastricht, Netherlands)
3. Genoels-Elderen (Riemst, Belgium)
4. Kluisberg (Bekkenvoort, Belgium)
5. Boschberg (Scherpenheuvel, Belgium)
6. Thorn (Limburg, Netherlands)
7. Meerdael (Oud-Heverlee, Belgium)
8. Wijnhoeve De Colonjes (Groesbeek, Netherlands)
9. Karthuizerhof (Kortessem, Belgium)
10. Hof Van Twente (Bentelo, Netherlands)

FASTEST-IMPROVING PRODUCERS

1. Peter Colemont, Clos d'Opleeuw (Gors-Opleeuw, Belgium)
2. Jos Beckx, Boschberg (Scherpenheuvel, Belgium)
3. Jos Vanlaer, Kluisberg (Bekkenvoort, Belgium)
4. H Vorselen, Thorn (Limburg, Netherlands)
5. Philippe Grafé, Domaine du Chenoy (Emines-La Bruyère, Belgium)
6. Freek & Anne Verhoeven, Wijnhoeve De Colonjes (Groesbeek, Netherlands)
7. Roelof & Ilse Visscher, Hof Van Twente (Bentelo, Netherlands)
8. Paul & Anne Vleminckx, Meerdael (Oud-Heverlee, Belgium)
9. John & Wilma Huisman, De Reestlandhoeve (Balkbrug, Netherlands)
10. Marc Henderix, Karthuizerhof (Kortessem, Belgium)

NEW UP-AND-COMING PRODUCERS

1. Peter Colemont, Clos d'Opleeuw (Gors-Opleeuw, Belgium)
2. Jos Beckx, Boschberg (Scherpenheuvel, Belgium)
3. Philippe Grafé, Domaine du Chenoy (Emines-La Bruyère, Belgium)
4. H Vorselen, Wijngoed Thorn (Limburg, Netherlands)
5. Paul & Anne Vleminckx, Meerdael (Oud-Heverlee, Belgium)
6. Freek & Anne Verhoeven, Wijnhoeve De Colonjes (Groesbeek, Netherlands)
7. Jos Vanlaer, Kluisberg (Bekkenvoort, Belgium)
8. Roelof & Ilse Visscher, Hof Van Twente (Bentelo, Netherlands)
9. Philippe Dumont, Clos des Zouaves (Thuin, Belgium)
10. Bollen Family, Hoeve Nekum (Maastricht, Netherlands)

BEST-VALUE PRODUCERS

1. Boschberg (Scherpenheuvel, Belgium)
2. Kluisberg (Bekkenvoort, Belgium)
3. Meerdael (Oud-Heverlee, Belgium)

④ Hof Van Twente (Bentelo, Netherlands)

⑤ Wijnhoeve De Colonjes (Groesbeek, Netherlands)

⑥ Elzenbosch (Assent, Belgium)

⑦ Thorn (Limburg, Netherlands)

⑧ De Reestlandhoeve (Balkbrug, Netherlands)

⑨ Tempelberg (Lubeek-Linden, Belgium)

⑩ Domaine du Chenoy (Emines-La Bruyère, Belgium)

GREATEST-QUALITY WINES

① **Chardonnay 2003**
Clos d'Opleeuw, Belgium (€20)

② **Chardonnay Blauw 2003**
Genoels-Elderen, Belgium (€11)

③ **Chardonnay Goud 2001**
Genoels-Elderen, Belgium (€22.50)

④ **Chardonnay Méthode Traditionnelle Sparkling Wine NV** Boschberg, Belgium (€12)

⑤ **Pinot Noir 2003**
Genoels-Elderen, Belgium (€21)

⑥ **Pinot Blanc 2004**
Kluisberg, Belgium (€10)

⑦ **Müller-Thurgau 2004**
Apostelhoeve, Netherlands (€9)

⑧ **Rosé 2004** De Reestlandhoeve, Netherlands (€7.90)

⑨ **Dornfelder 2004**
Karthuizerhof, Belgium (€7.50)

⑩ **Regent Barrique 2004**
Wijnhoeve De Colonjes, Netherlands (€10.50)

BEST BARGAINS

① **Auxerrois 2004**
Apostelhoeve, Netherlands (€9)

② **Pinot Auxerrois 2004**
Thorn, Netherlands (€8)

③ **Chardonnay Sparkling Wine NV**
Boschberg, Belgium (€12)

④ **Chardonnay MT Sparkling Wine NV** Meerdael, Belgium (€14)

⑤ **Dornfelder 2004** Karthuizerhof, Belgium (€7.50)

⑥ **Rosé 2004** De Reestlandhoeve, Netherlands (€7.90)

⑦ **Optima 2003**
Elzenbosch, Belgium (€9)

⑧ **Müller-Thurgau 2004**
Apostelhoeve, Netherlands (€9)

⑨ **Regent Barrique 2004**
Wijnhoeve De Colonjes, Netherlands (€10.50)

⑩ **Pinot Blanc 2004**
Kluisberg, Belgium (€11)

MOST EXCITING OR UNUSUAL FINDS

① **Pinot Noir 2003** Genoels-Elderen, Belgium (€21) *This may seem a little pricey for a Belgian wine, but, like the Clos d'Opleeuw Chardonnay, this wine rivals burgundy for its pure fruit, sweet, ripe strawberry flavors, and well-balanced fresh tannins.*

② **Chardonnay 2003** Clos d'Opleeuw, Belgium (€20) *This wine gets better and better each vintage. To temper the heat of the 2003 vintage, Peter Colemont added a smidgen of Gewurztraminer to keep freshness in the wine. Good spicy flavors, with an undercurrent of minerally acidity and a round mouth-feel.*

③ **Rosé 2004** De Reestlandhoeve, Netherlands (€7.90) *It is unusual to find a clean, fruity, and flavorful rosé made from hybrid grapes, but this one hits the mark with strawberry and plum aromas, good acidity, and attractive fresh flavors.*

④ **Chardonnay Sparkling Wine NV** Boschberg, Belgium (€12) *Fine acidity and clear, small bubbles, with light and spicy Chardonnay flavors, a touch of sweetness on the palate, and a clean, fruity, long flavor.*

⑤ **Optima 2003** Elzenbosch, Belgium (€9) *This hybrid grape does well in the northern climate and gives an aromatic wine with notes of lychees and mangoes. A touch on the sweet side, but its clean fruit flavors make this a popular wine.*

⑥ **Regent Barrique 2004** Wijnhoeve De Colonjes, Netherlands (€10.50) *Using hybrid grapes, Wijnhoeve De Colonjes makes the best red wine in the Netherlands. A serious wine with a dark, intense color, plums and spice, and a good core of acidity.*

⑦ **Chardonnay Goud 2000** Genoels-Elderen, Belgium (€20) *Genoels-Elderen has been the leading producer in Belgium for years. This 2000 shows how its barrel-aged Chardonnays can age well. Light and spicy, with flavors of apricots and cinnamon.*

⑧ **Pinot Auxerrois 2004** Thorn, Netherlands (€8) *An attractive wine, beautifully packaged, from a well-reputed producer. Good character with melon and crushed white-pepper aromas.*

⑨ **Riesling 2004** Apostelhoeve, Netherlands (€9) *This is one of the few successful Rieslings grown here, and not surprisingly it is made by the Netherlands' top producer. Good acidity and decent fruit flavors.*

⑩ **Regent 2004** Hof Van Twente, Netherlands (€10) *Good intensity with a plummy, peppery nose, some sweetness and ripeness, and a round, warm mouth-feel—an attractive, interesting wine.*

Grapevine

• **Wageningen University** has been running well-attended courses to help farmers become professional winegrowers. Areas in the Netherlands that have seen the biggest increase in new wineries are Gelderland, Overijssel, Flevoland, and the Beemster.

• **Philippe Grafé,** whose winery was destroyed by fire, has built a new underground cellar at Domaine du Chenoy near Naumur, Belgium. The first wines were released last year.

• **Marc de Brouwer** has an experimental vineyard in Uccle (on the outskirts of Brussels) with more than 30 different grape varieties. He has established a learning center where amateur winemakers can learn how to grow hybrids organically.

• **Belgian winegrowers** now have an excellent website and forum in the shape of www.vignes.be from Marc de Brouwer. He gives advice about resistant and precocious grape varieties suited to the northern climate, pruning and winegrowing techniques, and useful addresses of nurseries and other winemakers.

• **Sparkling wine** is set to take off with the introduction of the new appellations. One notable success is the Boschberg Chardonnay Sparkling Wine, an excellent value-for-money Belgian wine that can hold its head high against other sparklers.

• **The Scandinavian Wine Fair** in Paris in February 2006 was a platform for Scandinavian wines abroad. Consumers tasted wines and spirits made by Scandinavians, mainly those working in traditional wine-producing countries, but also some wines made in Scandinavia itself. Three Swedish wine producers were present at this well-attended fair.

Luxembourg

David Furer

The Clos des Rochers and Thill estates of Bernard-Massard have been awarded ISO 14001 certification by the European Society for Certification of Management Systems.

DAVID FURER

They are the first Luxembourg estates to win certification for rationalized winegrowing and winemaking that minimizes harmful effects on the environment.

Luxembourg has healthy sales of certified organic wines from France and Germany, but only Sunnen-Hoffman has exploited the opportunity to sell home-grown organic wines, although Bernard-Massard may well follow its lead in the future. In an effort to promote organics, Serge Fischer of the IVV has begun to circulate organic growing methods in his monthly technical briefs to growers.

In cooperation with the Ministry of Agriculture, Sunnen-Hoffman has launched a program to bring schoolchildren ages 8–12 on educational visits to learn about organic winegrowing and production, a first for viticulture and a noble effort from this organic and biodynamic pioneer.

DAVID FURER is the author of *Wine Places* (Mitchell Beazley, 2005), a contributing editor to the *Which? Wine Guide* and *Santé* magazine, and a contributor to *Hugh Johnson's Pocket Wine Book*. He also writes for *Wine Business Monthly*, *Food Arts*, *Virtual Gourmet Newsletter*, *Harpers Wine and Spirit Weekly*, *Decanter*, Australia's *Wine Business Magazine*, and Merrick's Media travel titles. He has led wine classes and guest lectured at Chicago, Oxford, and Cambridge universities, the Professional Culinary Institute, and Volkshochschulen in Germany. David is also a consultant for generic wine-trade organizations from Spain, Germany, and France, as well as for restaurants in London. He is a Certified Wine Educator, an Advanced Sommelier, and a Certified Sherry Educator.

Vineyard improvements

Jean-Louis Modert of Vinsmoselle has joined the chorus of quality-conscious *négociants* and private winemakers criticizing the prevalence of mismatches between grape varieties and soil types in Luxembourg, where vines are often planted in sites inappropriate to the variety. He remains hopeful, however, that research and experiments undertaken by the IVV will improve the situation, provided growers implement the recommended measures.

An experiment with "half-bunch" green pruning of rot-susceptible Pinot Gris, initiated by IVV agronomist Serge Fischer, has been applied by Guy Krier and Yves Sunnen. Fischer's own experiments with leaf-pulling Pinot Gris and Riesling vines, allowing improved air circulation, have resulted in a 20 percent drop in yield and a 10 percent sugar increase, with a longer hang time giving the wines better aromatic development.

Pinot stable

After a rapid five-year climb, Pinot Noir plantings have stabilized at 88 ha, or about 7 percent of total plantings, from zero in 1984. Rivaner, better known as Müller-Thurgau, remains a value product for the all-important Belgian market. Some growers are following the lead of Germany's Rheinland-Pfalz region, by making Rivaner in drier forms.

Pricing logic

There was an odd anomaly in ex-cellar prices for Luxembourg wines in 2005. Many growers who were shy in 2004 about raising prices in the face of a short but very popular 2003 crop have been pushed by economic reality into increasing prices for the average-to-good-quality but larger 2004. The notable exception is quality leader and oenologist Abi Duhr, who has lowered prices for his 2004 wines, stating simply, "While I'm happy with my 2004 wines, they just aren't as good as some other vintages."

Grapevine

• **Luxembourg** snagged six of the 222 gold medals at the 2005 Paris Vinalies wine competition, with two going to the relatively small Kohll-Leuck estate for its Crémant and the 2003 Pinot Gris from its home vineyard of Ehnen Kelterberg. *Guide Hachette*'s 2006 edition handed an impressive three Coup de Coeurs to Clos des Rochers and Schumacher-Knepper for its Rieslings and to Vinsmoselle for its Poll-Fabaire Crémant.

• **The Concours des Crémants** de France et de Luxembourg was hosted in Luxembourg in June 2005. Judges were drawn fairly from wine principals of the host country and the other participating regions: Alsace, Bordeaux, Burgundy, Die, Jura, Limoux, and Loire. The results confirmed Luxembourg's earlier fine performances with its Crémants, winning no fewer than 19 of the 72 golds awarded.

Opinion:
Crémant searches for an identity

The 15th anniversary of Crémants Poll-Fabaire, Vinsmoselle's visionary kick-start to what is now Luxembourg's best-known style of wine, took place in 2006. According to its marketing director Jean-Louis Modert, "The Poll-Fabaire line has enjoyed a growth of nearly 10 percent, to 1.08 million bottles sold in 2004." Modert projects growth of 6–8 percent for 2005 and 2006. His comments were echoed by Marc Gales, who projects 8 percent growth for his Crémants in 2005, especially in the traditional export markets of Germany and Belgium. With positive figures also projected by the remaining significant Crémant player, Bernard-Massard, Luxembourg's sparkling wines are poised to become known to a greater number of export markets.

The lack of a clear identity continues to hold back the Moselle's wines. A concerted effort on the part of exporting wineries and the IVV marketing arm to create a Crémant brand awareness in the minds of drinkers in northern Europe, North America, and the emerging Asian wine markets would go a long way toward establishing Luxembourg as the "must-have, mid-price" bubbly.

Breaking the quality barrier

Luxembourg has a seemingly immutable Top 10 list of producers, with others hovering just beneath—most notably Krier-Welbes, Claude Bentz, Desom, and Cep d'Or. The majority of Luxembourg's wineries make delicate and correct wines, staying in the safe middle ground, but spiraling housing prices and salaries for office jobs, increased competition from the New World, and a lack of inspiration or willingness to take chances could undermine their position. A little extra effort—better vineyard management, lower yields, and less reliance on added yeasts, cold fermentation, and stainless steel—could ensure a healthy future for these wineries.

Grapevine

• **The second Fête des Vins et Crémants,** at Luxembourg City's Place Guillaume, was an improvement on the first. Higher attendance was coupled with a much more sensible floor plan. As in 2004, many foreign visitors and residents from the US, Canada, Russia, Italy, and elsewhere mixed with the locals and their hounds, giving hope for Luxembourg as a wine exporter beyond its neighbors' borders.

Vintage Report

Advance report on the latest harvest

2005

Spring frosts damaged some vines in the northern villages, especially late-blooming Riesling. Hail later in the season left damaged berries, again in the north around the towns of Ahn and Grevenmacher, lowering yields to as little as 40 percent of the average. A wet July was followed by a cool and cloudy August. Except for the occasional light sprinkle, a perfect harvest began on September 19, three weeks earlier than in 2004, due to warmer temperatures in May, June, and September. Mildew did not pose major problems, and the majority of growers used the biological method of sexual confusion against moth infestation, limiting the need for insecticides. Musty notes from the mold esca will crop up in a few wines that haven't been selected well. The cool, damp ground led to some botrytis in the Pinots Blanc and Gris. Nearly all whites are showing well, and the Pinot Noirs will be an improvement over 2004, though not quite at the level of 2003. Expect good to great Crémants. Icewines of considerable quality are expected.

Grapevine

• The multivillage cooperative **Vinsmoselle** established a drinks distribution company, Disbolux, in late 2004 under the broad remit of "the production and distribution of alcoholic and nonalcoholic drinks" and other related activities. The current range and reach of its lines are tiny, but with time it may be poised to take on the diversified *négocians* such as Bernard-Massard.

• **Vinsmoselle,** ever on the move, opened a wine shop in Luxembourg City's old town in spring 2006. With an increase of 35 ha of vineyard from 830 ha in 2003, opening new sales avenues seems a rational solution to a domestic market becoming increasingly sensitive to outside competition.

• Former restaurateur Jean-Paul **Hoffmann** has joined his wife Marie Paule Mathes in running her father's winery and *négociant* business since the elder Mathes's retirement in June 2005. Great potential rests here with some of Wormeldange's best-situated Riesling vineyards, but key changes will be necessary to help this venerable winery regain its former status.

• **Management v. ownership conflict** brought the departure of the dynamic Jos Raguso from quality leader Alice Hartmann. Raguso's replacement, sommelier André Klein, has large shoes to fill. With talented German winemaker Hans-Jörg Befort remaining, the small Wormeldange estate continues to turn out some of Luxembourg's finest wines.

Updates on the previous five vintages

2004

Vintage rating: *Red (Pinot Noir): 85, White: 88*

Overall, a good year both for quantity and quality, comparable to the excellent 1998. IVV reported above-average health for grapes. A dry fall with cool nights and warm days followed a fairly dry summer, ensuring a classic vintage. Bad weather during blooming caused *coulure* in many Riesling vineyards, lowering yields. Pinots were less affected, though fall hail and late frost caused damage in scattered vineyards, mostly in the north. The grape harvest began on October 4 for Crémant base wines. Chilly nights supported retention of acidity and aromatic complexity. The high levels of malic versus tartaric acid in many whites may ensure a reasonably long life, though with an excessively sour character. Those who left Riesling on the vine to mature fully have been rewarded with great wines. Gewürztraminers are very good across the board, the best since 2001. Pinot Noirs range from average to good quality.

2003

Vintage rating: *Red (Pinot Noir): 90, White: 85*

As throughout the rest of Europe, a very long, hot, and dry summer made for very ripe grapes with low natural acidity, particularly for those who did not take care in the vineyard. This was the first year Luxembourg was allowed to acidify, so several inexperienced winemakers are finding disharmony in their wines. Auxerrois was completely harvested by the end of September, which allowed for some acid retention. There are a few difficult Pinot Blancs and many difficult Pinot Gris due to excessive residual sugar coupled with high alcohol, but most will offer pleasure for the near to mid-term. The relatively late-picked varieties Riesling and Pinot Noir can be excellent. They have maintained their regional character despite the intense summer heat. Rieslings often possess a bit of residual sugar, but those with enough balancing acidity should age well. There are many expressive *vendanges tardives* and *vins de paille*, and some terrific icewines from Riesling and Auxerrois for near- to mid-term consumption. This is the vintage that will put Luxembourg Pinot Noir on the map, if you can find any. With their atypically heavy fruit nose and palate, especially from those made with a large percentage of Riesling or Pinot Gris, Crémants made from this vintage are best avoided.

2002

Vintage rating: *Red (Pinot Noir): 83, White: 92*

Although the grapes were ripe, the high acidity levels of many 2002s meant longer fermentation periods for grapes from the more northerly, limestone-influenced soils. Since nearly all work in Luxembourg is done in steel tank, this translates to what are now very reduced wines. The best dry wines will take several years to open. Pinot Blanc, Riesling, Auxerrois, Gewürztraminer, and Chardonnay are all interesting to great, with many Pinot Blancs now beginning to open. Most Pinot Gris and Pinot Noirs rank as only okay, as they tend toward leanness. Good icewines were harvested in early January. Many fine Crémants are now available.

2001

Vintage rating: *Red (Pinot Noir): 80, White: 89*

Alternating hot and cold summer periods with much rain through September devastated quality hopes for early ripeners like Auxerrois. The best wines are classic, exhibiting crisp freshness and intriguing fruit; they will need years to open. Pinot Blanc and Gewürztraminer are good, as are the icewines harvested in December. Simple, but pleasant, Pinot Noirs are drinking well now. Several good to excellent Crémants were made, but most are now sold.

2000

Vintage rating: *White: 75*

Wines throughout the region are marked by an intense, darkish color and high minerality. Hopes for a classic, though short, harvest were dashed when rains hammered the region for three weeks, beginning in mid-September. The result was gray rot for those who did not spray and for many who did. Most wines are showing plenty of dilution or are going over, although a few pleasant surprises can be found, especially among dry and off-dry Rieslings where growers conducted strict selections. Icewines were generally unsuccessful due to rot problems.

Grapevine

• **A cross-border Schengen appellation,** proposed by Vinsmoselle, is being considered by the IVV before being formally proposed to neighbors France and Germany. Winegrowing municipalities from all three countries would benefit, with the dominant Vinsmoselle standing to benefit most.

IVV wine controller Marc Kuhn is in favor of the proposal, although he thinks that "it is a marketing-generated idea that will have a difficult time being realized," since Luxembourg vineyards are "A" level while its neighbors enjoy "B"-level status. Cross-border harmonization could also prove tricky.

GREATEST WINE PRODUCERS

1. Mme Aly Duhr & Fils
2. Alice Hartmann
3. Gales
4. Clos des Rochers
5. Krier Frères
6. Mathis Bastian
7. Duhr Frères
8. A Gloden & Fils
9. Thill Frères
10. Charles Decker

FASTEST-IMPROVING PRODUCERS

1. Schumacher-Knepper
2. Sunnen-Hoffmann
3. A Gloden & Fils
4. Cep d'Or
5. Mesenburg-Sadler
6. Vinsmoselle
7. Häremillen
8. Kohll-Leuck
9. Krier Frères
10. Linden-Heinisch

NEW UP-AND-COMING PRODUCERS

1. Cep d'Or
2. Schumacher-Knepper
3. Krier-Welbes
4. Mesenburg-Sadler
5. Henri Ruppert
6. Kohll-Reuland
7. Häremillen
8. Kohll-Leuck
9. Paul Legill
10. Desom

BEST-VALUE PRODUCERS

1. Gales
2. Mme Aly Duhr & Fils
3. Cep d'Or
4. Mathis Bastian
5. Vinsmoselle
6. A Gloden & Fils
7. Leuck-Thull
8. Krier-Welbes
9. Kohll-Leuck
10. Linden-Heinisch

GREATEST-QUALITY WINES

1. **Riesling Domaine & Tradition 2004** Mme Aly Duhr & Fils (€7)
2. **Riesling Puits d'Or Vin de Glace 2004** Mme Aly Duhr & Fils (€35 per half-bottle)
3. **Riesling Selection 2004** A Gloden & Fils (€9)
4. **Riesling Domaine & Tradition 2004** Gales (€8)
5. **Riesling Wintrange Fels 2004** Schumacher-Knepper (€7)
6. **Pinot Gris Domaine & Tradition 2004** Duhr Frères (€10)
7. **Riesling Supreme Remerschen-Jongeberg 2004** Krier Frères (€9)
8. **Riesling *** Wormeldange Koeppchen 2002** Alice Hartmann (€12)
9. **Pinot Gris Domaine & Tradition 2004** Clos des Rochers (€9)
10. **Pinot Noir Barrique Selection 2003** Mme Aly Duhr & Fils (€20)

Grapevine

• **Luxembourg has some** new black grape varieties. Nic Ries's Regent was launched in 2005 and Kohll-Reuland's St Laurent was premiered in 2006. Regent may be Luxembourg's answer to Germany's Dornfelder as a color enhancer, while St Laurent's character lends itself easily as a blending component to Pinot Noir. Can Merlot or Zweigelt be far behind?

BEST BARGAINS

1 **Gewürztraminer Ahn Hohfels 2004** Mme Aly Duhr & Fils (€5)

2 **Auxerrois Wintrange Fels 2004** Schumacher-Knepper (€5)

3 **Pinot Blanc Wintrange Fels 2001** Schumacher-Knepper (€4)

4 **Auxerrois Ehnen Kelterberg 2004** Kohll-Reuland (€5)

5 **Pinot Noir Coteaux d'Ehnen 2004** Kohll-Reuland (€8)

6 **Riesling Wintrange Fels 2004** Schumacher-Knepper (€7)

7 **Riesling Domaine & Tradition 2004** Mme Aly Duhr & Fils (€7)

8 **Pinot Noir Wormeldange Wäinbour 2004** Mesenburg-Sadler (€8)

9 **Riesling Remich Primerberg 2004** Gales (€7)

10 **Riesling Grevenmacher Fels 2004** Mme Aly Duhr & Fils (€6)

MOST EXCITING OR UNUSUAL FINDS

1 **Pinot Gris Sélection Rosé 2004** Vinsmoselle (€7) *Light pink color with a forward, dried-strawberry nose. Off-dry. First effort.*

2 **Crémant de Luxembourg Riesling Brut 2003** Linden-Heinisch (€9) *Low-intensity nose and very dry, balanced, medium-bodied, and surprisingly correct on the palate considering the vintage. Good length with a hint of minerality.*

3 **Riesling Äiswäin 2002** Linden-Heinisch (€26 per half-bottle) *Jean Linden-Heinisch used no added sulfur in this relatively dark, mature, petrolly, lanolin-scented, and minerally beauty, which was harvested on December 8. Bizarre, but drinks well.*

4 **Pinot Blanc Vendange Tardive Greiveldange 2004** Stronck-Pinnel (€12 per half-bottle) *Medium-sweet and medium intensity, with much vanilla from the new barrels, this* bruiser clocks in at a whopping 16 percent alcohol.

5 **Gewürztraminer Vin de Paille ** 2004** Schmit-Fohl (€40 per half-bottle) *Harvested in October but left to dry and pressed in February. Big, sweet nose of dried fruits and marmalade. Toasty, viscous, with a pleasant hint of oxidation. Warm and spicy finish.*

6 **Pinot Blanc Wintrange Fels 2001** Schumacher-Knepper (€4) *What a joy to find a mature wine at such a low price! Raisin, quince, and fig aromas lead to a palate of fleshy dried fruits with medium-high acidity and a pleasant finish.*

7 **Gris de Pinot Gris 2004** Kox (€6) *The grapes are destemmed and heated to 158°F (70°C) before being cooled for one day to 75.2°F (24°C), then pressed and fermented. Bone dry and slightly tannic with a "partridge eye" color.*

8 **Crémant de Luxembourg Hartmann Brut 2003** Alice Hartmann (€14) *In more normal vintages this ranks among the top wines in Luxembourg but, with the 2003 vintage, the barrique-enclosed malolactic fermentation and the icewine liqueur d'expédition make this an unwieldy beast of a bubbly.*

9 **Riesling *** Wormeldange Koeppchen 2002** Alice Hartmann (€12) *I'm very surprised that one of the Top 10 wines listed in Wine Report 2005 is still available. Comparable to the best dry Rieslings from South Australia.*

10 **Pinot Noir Barrique Selection 2003** Mme Aly Duhr & Fils (€20) *Without question, the finest red wine ever produced in Luxembourg of quality not likely to be seen again soon. This could be (and was) mistaken blind for a top Volnay. Made from a parcel of 777C clones planted in the early 90s.*

Switzerland

Chandra Kurt

The popularity of Chasselas among growers continues on its downward trend.

CHANDRA KURT

In the past five years, 22,000 Valais wine growers have invested more than SF 100 million ($70 million) in replanting their Chasselas vineyards. The Swiss government is subsidizing the replanting scheme, and growers will receive SF 5.7 million ($3.9 million) at the end of 2006. Chasselas is being replaced mainly by Petite Arvine, Cornalin, Amigne, and Humagne Rouge. Since 1991, the total area planted to Chasselas has decreased by 28.6 percent; it now covers only 26 percent of the Valais vineyards. Gamay, too, has fallen from favor, declining by 16.4 percent since 1991 to 15.9 percent of the total area. The main grape now is Pinot Noir, stable at 34 percent. The biggest cooperative, Provin, is promoting the replacement of Chasselas. Wine growers who are willing to replant their land with more popular varieties are offered help with financing and manpower.

Agrarpolitik 2011

The new agricultural policy, Agrarpolitik 2011, was sent to parliament for debate at the end of 2005. Three parts are relevant to wine: descriptions such as AOC, Vin de Pays (LW/Landwein), and Table Wine (TW/Tafelwein) will become obligatory; AOC wine has to be differentiated from other wines by clear labeling; and control will be centralized in one regulatory authority.

CHANDRA KURT is the author of several wine books, including the bestseller *Weinseller*, which she has been publishing for eight years. She is a freelance wine writer and contributes on a regular basis to leading public newspapers such as *Cash*, *al dente*, and *Schweizer Familie*, as well as leading wine publications such as *Hugh Johnson's Pocket Wine Book*. In 2004, her first fiction book, *Wine Tales* (Orell Füssli), was published; it was translated into Italian in 2005. She works for Swiss International Airlines and several Swiss retail institutions as a wine consultant. Chandra's website is www.chandrakurt.com.

Champagne hit hard

Wine growers of the Swiss-French village Champagne have been suffering since the court decision to bar them from calling their wine "Champagne." The new name, Libre-Champ, has turned out to be a total failure, with no one buying the wine. The growers' complaint to the European Court in Luxembourg is still active, however, so there may yet be hope.

Grapevine

• **Swiss wines** picked up 16 gold medals, 45 silver medals, and one of the eight trophies at the 2005 Vinalies in Paris.

• **Retail chain PickPay** has been bought by the discounter Denner, leading to more concentration in the wine market. PickPay sold more than 300 different wines, but the rumor is that Denner will take over only 10 percent of these, leading to the disappearance of a lot of brands. Denner continues its crusade to be the number-one wine retailer.

• **Switzerland now produces** more red wine than white. In 2005, 6,527 ha were planted with white varieties and only 8,392 ha with black. Since 2002, 438 ha of white varieties have disappeared, and 343 ha of black have been planted.

• **Swiss wine magazine** *Vinum* has bought the German wine magazine *Alles über Wein*, becoming one of the strongest wine publications in the German-speaking Swiss market.

• **Wine consumption has fallen** since the permitted blood alcohol level for drivers was reduced. In 2005, the Swiss drank around 10 liters per head less than they did in 1984, when they consumed 49.9 liters of wine per head per year.

• **Cornalin, the oldest Swiss grape,** grows in the city of Leuk in the Valais. The federal research station of Wädenswil has established that the vine has been growing there since 1798. In an ambitious project,

growers in the region grafted young Cornalin vines from a parcel of ancient "mother" plants and have produced Cornalin Vitis Antiqua 2004 (see www.vitisantiqua1798.ch).

• **Pure Cornalin is being produced** by more and more wine growers in the Valais. This dark-colored, spicy red wine is the new star of the region. Producers to watch for are Jean-René Germanier, Provins, and André Fontannaz.

• **Old Swiss grape varieties** come under the spotlight in Marcel Aeberhard's new book *Geschichte alter Traubensorten* ("History of Old Grape Varieties"; ISBN 3-908579-04-X), which looks at the older common Swiss grapes such as Chasselas, Completer, Räuschling, and Elbling.

• **The director** of the newly founded government institution Swiss Wine Communication quit his job at the end of 2005, leaving a financial hole of almost a million Swiss francs (about $700,000).

• **In 2005,** 1.5 million liters of Swiss wine were exported (958,340 liters of white and about 570,000 liters of red), an increase of 42 percent. The majority, 82.4 percent, went to Germany.

• **You can drink** between 250 and 400 different Swiss wines at any one of the Swisswinebar outlets that have recently opened in Bern, Lausanne, Geneva, and Brussels. For directions, go to www.swisswine.ch and click on the Swisswinebar box.

Opinion:
More wine-market concentration

Fewer companies own more and more shops, and more and more brands have disappeared. Around 70 percent of wine is sold by supermarkets and discounters, and the war between them intensifies each month, with promotions, advertising, and special offers. This is a good situation for consumers, who are taking advantage of bargain prices to trade up. The average spend is around SF 7.25 ($5.00) a bottle.

New World wines continue to suffer, and sales are falling drastically. Bulk red-wine imports from the US, Argentina, South Africa, and Chile have fallen. France, surprisingly, had the greatest loss of market share in bottled wines, but Chile came second. In 2004, 1,640,888 liters of bottled Chilean wine were imported; in 2005, the figure had fallen to 775,676.

What's in the bottle?

Suspicion about the "synthetic quality" of New World wines is growing. Wine magazines and wine journalists are paying more attention to what each bottle actually contains and are taking an interest in the differences between small and big wine companies. Health issues are becoming much more important: not only do consumers want to know exactly what they are drinking, but they have also changed their behavior. It is rare now to see anyone drinking wine with lunch; it is reserved for dinner and weekends. Reflecting this interest in wine-quality issues, the government is considering adopting EU regulations on labeling.

All this change opens the way for higher-quality wines from the region and from neighboring countries. Swiss wines are becoming more appreciated at home, and the government's vine-planting program, which is helping growers to improve quality with more interesting varieties than Chasselas, has come at just the right time. The fear that, with the appearance of the German discounter Aldi, Swiss supermarkets would lose wine customers has so far proved groundless, but, if Aldi were to decide to improve the quality of its wines, this could change. Selling wine does not get easier. Wine retailers need to be specialized, have a specific clientele, or be easily reachable. One sector that is gaining market share, however, is Internet sales—for both wine growers and supermarkets.

Vintage Report

Advance report on the latest harvest

2005

Prospects were gloomy until fall—lots of rain, little sun, and a rather cool summer. But luckily, September and October were blessed with unusually warm temperatures and a lot of sunshine. Overall, it was a year of low quantity but high quality. The total harvest was 990,000 hl (640,000 hl red), the smallest for 25 years. The harvest in the Valais was dominated by very good acidity and ripeness, and producers reported outstanding quality. The average *Oechsle* of Chasselas and Johannisberg, 79.1° and 96° respectively, outshone the hot year of 2003. Pinot Noir had an average of 94.5° *Oechsle* and Gamay 91.6°.

In the Vaud, a hailstorm on July 18 reduced the harvest drastically: in one night, a potential 34,900 hl of wine were lost, but the grapes that survived were of excellent quality. In total, 204,500 hl of white and 78,300 hl of red wine were harvested. Geneva reports a modest harvest of 0.63 liters per sq m, but excellent quality. Wines to watch out for will come from the Grisons, where Pinot Noir reached an average of 100° *Oechsle*, with an average harvest of 745 g per sq m. Müller-Thurgau showed 81° *Oechsle*. In all, 18,900 hl of red and 4,100 hl of white wine were harvested. Although quantity in the Ticino was 11.4 percent lower than in 2004, the *Oechsle* of the Merlot, at 87°, was higher.

Updates on the previous five vintages

2004

Vintage rating: *Red: 90, White: 90*

Most producers were happy that 2004 was not as hot as 2003. Though similar in quantity to 1998 and 2001, quality was far better than those years, and wines were more balanced than the extreme 2003s. In the Valais, red wines should have very good structure and balance. In the Vaud, the Chasselas had a lively, fruity freshness. Red wines in Geneva appear to have the edge on quality: the Pinot Noirs of the Drei-Seen-Region reached 90° *Oechsle*, while Chasselas was lower at 72°. The wines from Bündner Herrschaft had higher sugar levels due to the Föhn, the region's warm fall wind: 98° *Oechsle* for Pinot Noir and 73–78° for Müller-Thurgau. In general, reds and whites are harmonious and balanced. In the Ticino, Merlot reached an average of 86.6° *Oechsle*.

2003

Vintage rating: *Red: 91, White: 88*

Although many of the 2003 results are outstanding in quality and aroma, cellar work needed flexibility and skill. On the other hand, there was no problem selling better-quality wines, partly because the Swiss press wrote more about local wines than foreign ones for once. Wine quality is extraordinary. Pinot Noir reached an average 106° *Oechsle*, Müller-Thurgau 83°. In general, most of the varieties had *Oechsles* over 100, a quality level not seen since 1947. It was also a very early harvest—a month earlier than usual in the Grisons. Most Swiss vineyards finished their harvest by the end of August, and all the grapes were in by the end of September. Due to a difficult, very hot summer, there are two types of quality. Wine growers with more experience knew how to manage the high sugar levels, but a lot of the smaller growers produced overalcoholic wines with an overcooked taste. When buying wine, you have to know who did a good job in the cellar.

2002

Vintage rating: *Red: 90, White: 85*

Quality varies from good to excellent, with wines that are more elegant than full-bodied. In some regions, quantity dropped by as much as 30 percent over 2001, showing that growers reduced quantity to increase quality.

2001

Vintage rating: *Red: 89, White: 85*

A climatically difficult year produced a small crop of variable quality. In the Valais, the quality was very good indeed, while it was just average for the rest of the Romandie. It was excellent in Schaffhausen and the Grisons.

2000

Vintage rating: *Red: 93, White: 93*

A large harvest of exceptional quality all over Switzerland. Those who called 1997 the vintage of the century revised their judgment, because 2000 was even better! The very best came from the Grisons and the Romandie.

GREATEST WINE PRODUCERS

1. Daniel & Martha Gantenbein (Fläsch)
2. Jean-René Germanier (Bon Père, Germanier SA, Vétroz)
3. Hans-Ulrich Kesselring (Schlossgut Bachtobel)
4. Fromm Weingut (Malans)
5. Luigi Zanini (Besazio)
6. Werner Stucky (Rivera)
7. Daniel Huber (Monteggio)
8. Christian Zündel (Beride)
9. Charles & Jean-Michel Novelle (Satigny)
10. Marie-Thérèse Chappaz (Fully)

FASTEST-IMPROVING PRODUCERS

1. Daniel Marugg (Fläsch)
2. Simon Maye & Fils (St Pierre-de-Clages)
3. Thomas & Barbara Studach (Malans)
4. Cave des Cailles, Cédric Flaction (Sion)
5. Peter Wegelin (Malans)
6. Ruedi Baumann (Baumann Weingut, Oberhallau)
7. Stéphane Reynard & Dany Varone (Domaine Cornulus, Sierre)
8. Anna Barbara von der Crone (Castel S Pietro)
9. Jacques Tatasciore (Domaine de la Rochette, Cressier)
10. Clos (Domaines & Châteaux, Rolle)

NEW UP-AND-COMING PRODUCERS

1. Weingut Bisang (Dagmersellen)
2. Weingut Reblaube (Uetikon am See)
3. Nicolas Bonnet (Domaine de la Comtesse Eldegarde, Satigny)
4. Didier Joris (Chamoson)
5. Philippe Dariely (Martigny)
6. Sergio Monti (Cademario)
7. Jean-Claude Zurflüh (Grand, Buchs)
8. Meinrad Perler (Tenimento dell'Ör, Arzo)
9. Domaine du Centaure (Dardagny)
10. Jacques Tatasciore (Domaine de la Rochette, Cressier)

BEST-VALUE PRODUCERS

1. Provins (Sion)
2. Weinkellereien Volg (Winterthur)
3. Familie Zahner (Truttikon)
4. Domaine des Curiades (P Dupraz & Fils, Lully)
5. Vins Rouvinez (Sierre)
6. Domaine Les Hutins (Dardagny)
7. Philippoz Frères (Leytron)
8. Weinkellerei Rahm (Hallau)
9. Weingut Davaz (Fläsch)
10. Jean-René Germanier (Bon Père, Germanier SA, Vétroz)

GREATEST-QUALITY WINES

1. **Cornalin 2003** Jean-René Germanier (SF 33)
2. **Cayas 2003** Jean-René Germanier (SF 33)
3. **Hémine de Saint-Benoît Brut Prestige 2001** Provins (SF 24.90)
4. **Yvorne Grand Cru 2004** Château Maison Blanche (SF 18.50)
5. **Pinot Noir 2003** Daniel & Martha Gantenbein (SF 46)
6. **Castello Luigi Bianco del Ticino 2003** Luigi Zanini (SF 95)
7. **Ermitage Grain Noble 2002** Marie-Thérèse Chappaz (SF 44 per 500-ml bottle)
8. **Sauvignon 1er Cru 2004** Château du Crest (SF 16)
9. **Montagna Magica 2003** Daniel Huber (SF 51)
10. **Clos Corbassière Assemblage de Nobles Cépages 2001** Provins (SF 49)

BEST BARGAINS

1. **Maispracher Riesling x Sylvaner 2004** Buess (SF 12.70)
2. **Müller-Thurgau 2004** Schlossgut Bachtobel (SF 14)
3. **Aligoté 2004** Domaine des Curiades (SF 10)
4. **Chasselas 1er Cru La Feuillée 2004** Cave de Genève (SF 9)
5. **Pinot Noir 2004** Denis Mercier (SF 15.50)
6. **Garanoir de Satigny 2004** Domaine du Paradis (SF 11)
7. **Truttiker Weiss Riesling x Sylvaner 2004** Familie Zahner (SF 10)
8. **Pinot Noir 2004** Caves Fernand Cina Salgesch (SF 14)
9. **Gamay de Vétroz 2004** Cave de la Madeleine (SF 11.50)
10. **Fragolino Rosso Brut NV** Delea Losone (SF 9.50)

MOST EXCITING OR UNUSUAL FINDS

1. **Eyholzer Roter 2004** Chanton (SF 18) *Produced from the rare variety Hibou. Fruity, slightly spicy specialty from the Valais, with an intense raspberry note. If you love elegant Pinot Noir, this wine could be an interesting alternative.*
2. **Cabernet Sauvignon 2003** Domaine du Centaure (SF 19) *A very complex Cabernet Sauvignon from Geneva that smells like a New World wine and tastes like a Cabernet from Penedès. Good structure and aging potential.*
3. **Heida Maître de Chais 2004** Provins (SF 23.50) *Another specialty from the Valais. New release of a pure Heida (also called Païen or Gletscherwein). Very fresh and crisp on the palate, with good acidity.*
4. **Grand Pinot Noir 2003** Buchs (SF 25) *A new wine from the Sarganserland. Three friends, all Pinot Noir lovers, decided to create a wine to suit their own taste. The result is beautiful and will give a lot of pleasure to Pinot Noir lovers everywhere.*
5. **Completer Barrique 2004** Peter & Rosi Hermann (SF 25) *A traditional wine from the Grisons. Because of its high acidity, it might not suit everyone. Keeps for ages.*
6. **Fläscher Schiller 2004** Weingut Davaz (SF 16) *Rare wine from the mountain area of the Grisons. Usually sells out very quickly. A rosé made from Pinot Noir, Pinot Blanc, and Pinot Gris.*
7. **Sion Vin Mi-doux 2004** Cave des Cailles, Cédric Flaction (SF 29) *A sweet wine made from 100 per cent Chasselas. Rare and special, a first for a Chasselas in this style. Oily in structure, with lots of sweet fruity notes.*
8. **Cuvée Brut Z 2003** Weinkellerei Zweifel (SF 25) *Blend of Pinot Noir, Räuschling, and Riesling x Sylvaner (Müller-Thurgau). A festive sparkling wine with good acidity and structure with grapes from Lake Zurich.*
9. **Dagmerseller Schaumwein 2004** Weingut Bisang (SF 23) *New sparkling wine (traditional method) with grapes from the Lucerne region (60 percent Pinot Noir and 40 percent Riesling x Sylvaner [Müller-Thurgau]). Very elegant and fresh.*
10. **Arvine 2001** Jean-René Germanier (SF 33) *Dry white wine with a complex body and lots of structure. Some mineral notes, yet an almost buttery taste. The wine was fermented in barriques and is one of the best Valais Arvines.*

Austria

Philipp Blom

After a decade of rapid expansion, a more reflective mood is making itself felt.

PHILIPP BLOM

The great landmarks have been reached—top ratings, top restaurants, and top markets (more or less) secured. As exports of bottled wines rise more slowly than before and bulk exports are currently static, many producers enter a period of consolidation and continuing refinement, rethinking their styles and methods.

Two very positive trends are gathering force in response to this: more emphasis on regional styles and varieties, and a renewed interest in sustainable, organic, and biodynamic viticulture. It is a step, small but significant, to pull out of the global fashion for interchangeable wine styles and move further toward defining and realizing a uniquely Austrian wine style, which is already a reality for most whites, but not yet to the same extent for reds.

The hot 2003 vintage was, it seems, the end of the fashion for overblown power wines. Since other countries around the world can make gigantic Cabernets more reliably than Austria, avant-garde producers in the Burgenland are now putting more emphasis on uniqueness and *terroir*, mainly by basing their top reds on indigenous varieties such as Blaufränkisch, Zweigelt, and, at times, Sank Laurent, with Cabernet and Merlot excluded altogether, or used in a *cuvée* as junior partners. This is not entirely new, since outstanding wines using indigenous grapes have existed for a decade or more, but there is renewed enthusiasm behind the search for Austria's red-wine *terroir*.

PHILIPP BLOM is a writer and journalist (*Wine & Spirits Magazine*, *Revue du Vin de France*). His book *The Wines of Austria* was published by Faber & Faber in 2000 and appeared in a revised and extended edition in 2006. Among his other books are: *To Have and to Hold* (London, 2002), a history of collecting and collectors, *Encyclopédie—The Triumph of Reason in an Unreasonable Age* (London, 2004), and *Luxor* (Cologne, 2006), a novel. He lives in Paris.

A more sophisticated use of oak is another important part of this renaissance of much more subtle regional reds.

The move toward *terroir* identity is mirrored by an increased interest in the *terroir* itself, the soils, and their use. Having already done much to create a more sustainable agriculture in Austria through the EU co-financed OPUL program, Austrian winegrowers are taking this idea one step further. There are already considerable numbers of organic or even biodynamic winegrowers in the drier regions, such as the Kamptal and around Lake Neusiedl, while pest control without chemicals has left other growers, especially in Styria, more sceptical. In the Kamptal and the northern Burgenland, however, two independent collective initiatives by well-known growers are considering going biodynamic, "without being silly or sectarian about it," as one grower put it.

No half-measures at Halbturn

After a period of renovation and considerable investment, Schloß Halbturn is proving to be one of the most dynamic, and best, producers in the Burgenland. The man behind this transformation from the unexciting to the extraordinary is German winemaker Karl-Heinz "Carlo" Wolff, who has taken the reins and has surrounded himself with an enthusiastic international team.

Testing times

From the 1950s to the 1980s, when producers were oriented more toward production than quality, sugar levels were the one and only determining factor of ripeness and harvest date. Now, after much animated discussion many growers have abandoned this approach and are relying on tasting grapes and testing consistency over the use of the refractometer. Many wines testify to this more subtle and nuanced approach.

Back to the future

In line with the "return to the soil" of much of Austrian viticulture and its emphasis on local over international grapes, several old favorites are now beginning to make a comeback. There is a new generation of fine dry white wines made from Neuburger and Furmint, while among the red varieties, Sank Laurent is now being made quite differently by some producers, who are treating it less like Pinot Noir and more like Syrah—often with exhilarating results.

Opinion:
The lure of "green" practices

The trend toward organic and biodynamic viticulture among several outstanding Austrian growers looks like much more than a fashion: together with Burgundy, Alsace, and New Zealand, Austria is showing courage in finding new ways. As viticulture is the most polluting form of agriculture, this must be a good thing. Austria already has the least polluting wine production in the EU, as well as more organic and biodynamic growers per hectare than any other European country. Some of them, such as Nikolaihof in the Wachau, can look back on decades of experience.

Of course, not all "green" producers follow good practice. Some simply pollute differently (for example, with copper sulfate instead of other pesticides) or merely claim to be green while refusing to be controlled, but in Austria there is a great sense of purpose about this. Reputable growers such as Prager in the Wachau and a large group of top growers advised by the Californian Andrew C Lorand (including Hannes Hirsch and Fred Loimer in the Kamptal, Philipp Zull and Peter Veyder-Malberg of Graf Hardegg in the Weinviertel, most of the Pannobile group, and Uwe Schiefer in the South Burgenland) are planning to switch to biodynamic production.

Grapevine

• **After a bad spell in recent years,** accompanied by a loss of both clients and reputation, the 800-grower cooperative Freie Weingärtner Wachau has engaged a new, young team to restore quality and confidence. Led by the competent duo of director Roman Howarth and oenologist Heinz Frischengruber, FWW is beginning to make up lost ground.

• **The Tscheppe brothers,** heirs to an established 40-ha estate in South Styria, having already had to sell the estate to the Polz brothers, have finally decided to give up winemaking. The vineyards are likely to continue being operated by Polz, but the brand name is as yet unknown.

• **Vinea Wachau,** the all-powerful growers' association in the Wachau, looks set to abandon its insistence on natural cork for Smaragd wines, the highest wine category. This is long overdue, since, despite great efforts, some of these wines have been consistently plagued by cork problems.

Vintage Report

2005

It may be true that there is no longer any excuse for a bad wine, but quality comes at a cost. After an endlessly rainy fall, top growers paid the price in yields, which were down by as much as two-thirds in many regions for those who were determined to harvest late, and harvest only perfectly healthy material.

A cool spring led to irregular and protracted blossoming throughout Austria. The summer continued equally unsettled, with significant rainfall in August and a cool September with episodes of rain and fog. The grapes had developed healthily, and the weather finally changed on October 3 with a stretch of warm, dry, sunny weather that lasted into early November, after which conditions became more changeable. Those with the patience to wait harvested in November under near-ideal conditions, even if the persistent rain had caused a good deal of rot. Overall losses are around 30 percent, making this probably the smallest harvest since 1985. More ambitious producers who chose to harvest late, picking only the best material, lost a proportionately larger share of the harvest—up to 70 percent in some cases.

Early indications are that, in quality terms, 2005 is a good, though not outstanding, vintage, with elegant wines the main charm of which may be their varietal purity, similar to 2002. As in that vintage, top growers also made top wines. This will be a year with a large quality difference between elite producers and less conscientious ones, or those without the financial resources to afford losing most of a harvest. Expect pure fruit, elegant acidity, and good ripeness for white wines in Lower Austria. Early-ripening red wines here are likely to have done well, too. In Styria, vineyards may have suffered from Mediterranean low-pressure systems more than the rest of Austria, but with equivalent quantitative losses, producers were able to achieve full ripeness and good fruit for their wines. It is certainly a vintage to emphasize *terroir* over sheer fruit extract.

For once, early ripeness was not an advantage in the Burgenland, where growers had to deal with substantial botrytis infection. This is good news for sweet wines, and there will be outstanding TBAs this year, though in very small quantities. Many of the red-wine *barriques* also remained empty, since a small harvest was vinified, resulting in wines with fine varietal fruit, much leaner than in the two preceding years, and relatively low in tannins, likely to become charming, well-rounded wines for early drinking.

Updates on the previous five vintages

2004

Vintage rating: *Red: 88, White: 93, Sweet: 87*

This is one of those years bound to be misrepresented by any simple score, since the quality of wines depended on producers' care in the vineyard, and results vary widely. The climate was far from ideal, even if a beautiful August and early September rescued much of what had already been written off. If there are some great wines in the making, it shows that the producers are masters of their craft. Only the grapes of those producers relying on low yields from the start could achieve full physiological ripeness, and these will produce beautiful, clean, and strongly varietal wines with pronounced acidity. This is a vintage that may turn out to be particularly elegant for Grüner Veltliner and Riesling, very probably also for Chardonnay and Sauvignon Blanc. Quantities, however, were small.

Among the red wines, early ripeners such as Zweigelt had a clear advantage this year, and show dense, fine tannins indicative of considerable potential. Varieties such as Blaufränkisch often benefit from good, elegant acidity, while other, hotter grapes, such as Cabernet Sauvignon and Syrah, are likely to be fully ripe only in exceptional circumstances.

2003

Vintage rating: *Red: 94, White: 92, Sweet: 85*

Marked by two heat waves, in May and in late summer, this was an exceptional year. The harvest began in August, the earliest recorded date, and under ideal conditions, though younger vines especially suffered from drought. Growers who dealt well with the excessive heat (by leaving leaf canopies, for example) brought in a dream harvest.

This is a perfect year for red wines, and while conditions would have allowed another charge of blockbusters, many producers opted for denser, more structured wines. Growers who protected their grapes from sun stress also harvested white wines of astonishing freshness with beautiful acidity and great aging potential.

2002

Vintage rating: *Red: 90, White: 93, Sweet: 97*

In Lower Austria, 2002 will be remembered for the fall rains and floods that made many terraced vineyards collapse. Red wines are well balanced with ripe tannins, and the prevalent botrytis was good news for nobly sweet wines.

Styrian growers made expressive Sauvignon Blancs and Chardonnays, and in Lower Austria this difficult vintage proved to possess the seeds of true greatness for producers who practiced rigorous grape selection and who harvested late. Wonderfully balanced Rieslings and, to a lesser extent, Grüner Veltliners, especially in the Wachau and the Kamptal, show great elegance, depth, and enormous potential. In the best cases, this is a classic vintage.

2001

Vintage rating: *Red: 90, White: 89, Sweet: 85*

After a hot summer, September came with never-ending rain. The weather finally changed in October. These difficult conditions also brought with them a very work-intensive harvest, since healthy grapes had to be sorted. Two frosty periods in December, finally, allowed an icewine harvest. This was a real year to demonstrate conscientious vineyard work and good vinification; in general, it is marked by clarity and balance, with the reds less powerful than 2000 but possessing more charm. A good crop of botrytis wines was harvested, too. Will evolve quite quickly.

2000

Vintage rating: *Red: 88, White: 92, Sweet: 88*

A long, hot summer was ideal for late-maturing varieties. A November with low precipitation and above-average temperatures created perfect conditions for late-harvest wines. This was an extraordinary vintage, especially for red wines, with record must weights and dark colors. With its punch and body, this has been declared a great red-wine vintage— though I think too many of the wines are too high in alcohol and often overextracted, which is why I rate it below 2001, despite the ideal conditions. For white wines, this was an almost perfect year, with big Grüner Veltliners and Rieslings in Lower Austria, as well as Chardonnays in the Burgenland that were ideally suited for *barrique* treatment. Styrian growers, too, harvested wines of great concentration and harmony.

GREATEST WINE PRODUCERS

1. Alzinger (Wachau)
2. Bründlmayer (Kamptal)
3. Gross (South Styria)
4. Hirtzberger (Wachau)
5. Kollwentz (Neusiedlersee-Hügelland)
6. Knoll (Wachau)
7. Kracher (Neusiedlersee)
8. FX Pichler (Wachau)
9. Prager (Wachau)
10. Tement (South Styria)

FASTEST-IMPROVING PRODUCERS

1. Josef Gritsch (Wachau)
2. Karl Lagler (Wachau)
3. Undhof Salomon (Kremstal)
4. Hans 'John' Nittnaus (Neusiedlersee)
5. Weingut der Stadt Krems (Kremstal)
6. Söllner (Donauland)
7. Vorspannhof Mayr (Kremstal)
8. Birgit Eichinger (Kamptal)
9. Schloß Halbturn (Neusiedlersee)
10. Freie Weingärtner Wachau (Wachau)

NEW UP-AND-COMING PRODUCERS

1. Kurt Angerer (Kamptal)
2. Josef Bauer (Donauland)
3. Günter Brandl (Kamptal)
4. Johann Donabaum (Wachau)
5. Toni Drimmel (Thermenregion)
6. Kloster am Spitz (Neusiedlersee-Hügelland)
7. Gabi Mariell (Neusiedlersee-Hügelland)
8. Sepp Muster (South Styria)
9. Claus Preisinger (Neusiedlersee)
10. Rainer Wess (Wachau)

BEST-VALUE PRODUCERS

1. Günter Brandl (Kamptal)
2. Willi Bründlmayer (Kamptal)
3. Buchegger (Kamptal)
4. Emmerich Knoll (Wachau)
5. Schloß Gobelsburg (Kamptal)
6. Roman Pfaffl (Weinviertel)
7. Peter Schandl (Neusiedlersee-Hügelland)
8. Heidi Schröck (Neusiedlersee-Hügelland)
9. Ludwig Hiedler (Kamptal)
10. Alois Gross (South Styria)

GREATEST-QUALITY WINES

1. **Grüner Veltliner Smaragd Kellerberg 2004** FX Pichler, Wachau (€30)
2. **Riesling Smaragd Steinertal 2003** Alzinger, Wachau (€15.50)
3. **Sauvignon Blanc Zieregg 2003** Tement, South Styria (€28)
4. **Cuvée Comondor 2003** Hans 'John' Nittnaus, Neusiedlersee (€30)
5. **Blaufränkisch Dürrau 2002** Weninger, Mittelburgenland (€35)
6. **Nouvelle Vague Chardonnay TBA Nr 8 2002** Kracher, Neusiedlersee (€48)
7. **Riesling Heiligenstein Lyra 2002** Bründlmayer, Kamptal (€25)
8. **Riesling Smaragd Singerriedel 2002** Hirtzberger, Wachau (€45)
9. **Riesling Smaragd Wachstum Bodenstein 2002** Prager, Wachau (€30)
10. **Cuvée Salzberg 2000** Heinrich, Neusiedlersee (€45)

BEST BARGAINS

① **Grüner Veltliner Pichl Point Federspiel 2004** Schmelz, Wachau (€7)

② **Grüner Veltliner Novemberlese 2004** Günter Brandl, Kamptal (€11)

③ **Grüner Veltliner Loiser Weg 2004** Vorspannhof Mayr, Kremstal (€8)

④ **Gelber Muskateller 2004** Nigl, Kremstal (€8)

⑤ **Blaufränkisch Weinberg 2003** Kopfensteiner, Middle Burgenland (€9)

⑥ **Zweigelt Olivin 2002** Winkler-Hermaden, Southeast Styria (€15)

⑦ **Morillon Morafeitl 2002** Neumeister, South Styria (€16)

⑧ **Riesling Ried Bruck Smaragd 2004** Gritsch, Wachau (€12)

⑨ **Riesling Pfaffenberg 2004** Hagen, Kremstal (€9)

⑩ **Riesling Heiligenstein 2004** Birgit Eichinger, Kamptal (€12)

MOST EXCITING OR UNUSUAL FINDS

① **Pinot Noir 2002** Claus Preisinger, Neusiedlersee (€33) *With its sophisticated herbaceous nose and generous spiced fruit on the palate, this is one of a new generation of Austrian Pinots. Very exciting.*

② **St Laurent 2002** Hannes Schuster, Neusiedlersee-Hügelland (€22) *Fantastically deep and inky, with succulent, tarry, and mulberry aromas, and beautifully assertive structure. An astonishing success from a young winemaker.*

③ **Furmint Pepa 2002** Heidi Schröck, Neusiedlersee-Hügelland (€10) *Ripe mandarin notes, Christmas spice, Auslese character, fine wood notes— beautiful. Great, wooded length, playful. An old, marginal grape revived.*

④ **Pinot Noir 2003** Schloß Halbturn, Neusiedlersee (€30) *Austrian Pinot Noir is on the up. This one was love at first sight—it has fruit, refinement, class.*

⑤ **Riesling Achleiten 2004** Prager, Wachau (€25) *Appears for sheer beauty and aromatic purity. Complex interplay of aromas: fresh almonds, peach, and clarity. Intense, sweet fruit on the length.*

⑥ **Grüner Veltliner Tradition 2003** Schloß Gobelsburg, Kamptal (€19) *This wine was made using the methods of the early 1900s. Wonderful complexity and floral notes; there's simply nothing like it.*

⑦ **Riesling Steiner Hund Reserve 2003** Nikolaihof, Wachau (€23) *A biodynamic wine with phenomenal persistence. Slightly metallic nose, intense Riesling tones, pears and stone fruit. Remarkable.*

⑧ **Sgaminegg 2003** Sepp Muster, South Styria (€23) *A wine to defy all categories. Elegance and minerality at 15 percent alcohol. Made biodynamically, it perfectly reflects a powerful, exceptional vintage.*

⑨ **Riesling Dürnsteiner Freiheit Smaragd 2004** Schmelz, Wachau (€18) *Wonderful clarity, purity, and length from a producer who is now emerging as one of the Wachau's stars.*

⑩ **Grüner Veltliner Spitzer Point Smaragd 2004** Johann Donabaum, Wachau (€16) *Clear mineral tone, lovely varietal character, citrus fruit and light tobacco leaf, long and deep, with a beautiful, clear length.*

Eastern & Southeastern Europe

Dr. Caroline Gilby MW

EU membership continues to cast its influence across the region. Bulgaria and Romania are due to join on January 1, 2007 and are benefiting from considerable EU funds through the SAPARD program.

DR. CAROLINE GILBY MW

This is driving huge investment into (largely) Italian stainless steel, as well as vines and vineyards. As one producer put it, "It's a kind of massive BOGOF [buy one, get one free], since the EU refunds 51 percent of any investment."

Both countries have drawn up revised appellation schemes and have agreed new names for wines of specified geographical origin. Bulgaria is racing to prove its entitlement to the 153,000 ha agreed with the EU by registering growers (24,000 with 50,000 ha registered to December 2005), but since the estimated productive area under wine grapes is only 85,500 ha, this seems optimistic.

Looking farther ahead, Croatia is now in formal accession negotiations. Government strategy is to plant vineyards ahead of membership, and 7,000 ha of cleared forest have just been allocated to vineyards.

Macedonia became a candidate country in December 2005, with the aim of joining in 2010. EU funds are already flowing to pay for a vineyard

DR. CAROLINE GILBY MW is a freelance writer specializing in Eastern Europe and viticulture. She contributed to *Wines of the World* (Dorling Kindersley, 2004) and has been published in *Decanter*, *Harpers Wine and Spirit Weekly*, *Off Licence News*, and *New Scientist*. She is on the editorial board of the *Journal of Wine Research*. She has a PhD in plant sciences but left science to become senior wine buyer for a major UK retail chain. Caroline lectures for the WSET Diploma on tasting technique, vinification, and wine handling, as well as judging at international wine shows and working as a consultant to the wine trade.

register, due by the end of 2006. The industry has a long-term strategy to ensure that EU standards are met, as well as developing vineyards to meet international demand, recognizing that Vranec and Smederevka (currently 80 percent of production) have limited global appeal.

In Cyprus, the after-effects of joining the EU have been dramatic. The EU bans direct subsidies, which has brought cheap (heavily subsidized) bulk exports to a halt and forced a complete restructuring of the industry.

Vineyard restructuring—essential for progress

Across Eastern and Southeastern Europe, the issues of control over fruit costs and quality in the vineyard are fundamental. There are increasing signs that the problems of fragmented landholdings and lack of professional viticulture, which have been holding back wine production, are being addressed.

In **Bulgaria**, a lot of investment (including €55 million from the EU) is going into vineyards—both planting and renovation—as well as into winery equipment. Tracking down absentee landowners to buy land continues to be a challenge, but one that the major wineries have developed strategies to tackle. For instance, Stork Nest Estates has two teams, each with its own lawyer, driving around the country in battered cars seeking land. They are currently purchasing around 260 ha and aim for 1,000 ha by 2010. There is a land-swap program allowing fragmented plots to be exchanged for larger, consolidated areas belonging to the state. Wine producers increasingly understand the need to control fruit quality and supply, highlighted by the challenging vintage conditions in 2005. The recently published government strategy for 2005–25 recognizes that improving wine will require control over fruit quality and its origin. Encouragingly, there is a developing concept of *terroir* wines, such as Enira from Bessa Valley, Chateau de Val, Maxxima's Sensum, Villa Liubimetz, and others—an approach that is relatively new for Bulgaria.

Restructuring in **Hungary** seems set to follow a course of land falling out of cultivation. Currently there are 87,000 ha under vine, but some observers think this may fall as low as 50,000–60,000 ha. Growers appear to be hanging on for EU grants for grubbing up (Hungary is due to receive €9 million from the EU for restructuring). Grubbing up will particularly hit growers on the Great Plain, where agriculture is the major livelihood, but also where the need to remove poor-quality vines is greatest. Producers who survive should be more professional and should be able to carry out canopy management properly, a practice that is vital on Hungary's vigorous soils. Hungarian producers have a dilemma.

Exports are falling and the domestic market takes just 3 million hl of 4.8 million hl total production in 2004. This overproduction keeps prices as low as €0.20 per kg. At that price, producers need to compromise on quality and pick at 15 tons/ha to break even.

The need for restructuring in **Romania** is vast. The vineyard area is still falling, but until the vineyard register (required for EU membership) is complete, the true picture will remain unclear. Around half of Romania's 173,000 ha of wine grapes are still hybrids, which must be grubbed up, and Romania has negotiated replanting rights for just 30,000 ha. The national strategy is to concentrate on native varieties, and shift emphasis away from whites (currently 70 percent of production) toward reds, and to increase quality wine production. The larger commercial wineries are driving improvements in wine quality and, while they are increasingly investing in land of their own, only 7 percent of Romanian vineyards are over 5 ha. Small plots remain a major hindrance to economies of scale and professional full-time viticulture.

The industry in **Cyprus** is at a turning point. Until recently, the island produced more than 150,000 tons, most shipped in bulk for vermouth, *Glühwein*, and sangria. Grape growing here is small-scale and fragmented, with 20,000 growers farming just 17,000 ha, mostly part time. It's expensive mountain viticulture, requiring refrigerated trucks at harvest for decent quality, so without subsidies, ends don't meet. Growers' protests last year forced a new strategy, which focuses on abandoning vineyards and replanting better varieties at higher altitude, so far costing around €40 million. Nearly 2,000 ha were removed in 2004/05, bringing the 2005 harvest down to 60,000 tons.

Sodap has switched entirely from bulk to bottled wines; its new Kamanterena winery crushed just 8,200 tons this year, compared to 24,000 last harvest. The other big three (Loel, Etko, and Keo) have made similar moves away from bulk. Growers have not actually protested this year, though they are still unhappy with low grape prices.

Cyprus also wants to concentrate on its local grape varieties to create a sense of identity, but the most promising reds, such as Maratheftiko and Lefkada, are rare and usually interplanted with poor-quality Mavro. One winery reports paying CYP 1 per kilo to get individual Maratheftiko vines picked late. Land is expensive in Cyprus, and growers like to hang on to their little plots, so wineries will find it difficult to put together significant vineyards. However, they do need to establish long-term contracts, to work with growers to supply fruit of the right quality, and to move away from the current practice of relying on the spot market.

Opinion:
The supermarkets have arrived

Last year's *Wine Report* warned about the rise of western supermarket chains across Eastern Europe and the potential for damage to cozy domestic markets. It is already clear that supermarket chains are pushing aggressively into most of these markets and wine producers are being squeezed. Supermarket sales in Romania are booming, with Metro, Carrefour, Billa, and Cora opening new stores in 2005.

Up-front listing fees of €5,000–6,000 per product per store, plus another €3,000–5,000 for promotional positioning and featured offers, are being demanded. Currently wineries are responding by factoring discounts into their price list and developing new supermarket sales divisions. However, once Romania joins the EU and imports become easier, there will be serious competition.

In Hungary, market share of supermarkets is now up to 55 percent and growing. Tesco (number 1 in Hungary) is reported to demand listing fees of HUF 30,000 per varietal per store. Since it has more than 50 outlets, this costs up to HUF 1.5 million per label, plus logistics payments and extended credit terms. However, larger producers feel they have no choice but to pay up to keep their wines on the shelf. They are well aware of the situation in Lidl, where Hungarian wines have been delisted in favor of own-labels from Germany.

In Cyprus, locally owned supermarkets dominate wine sales already, and Carrefour has just bought the second-biggest chain, with Lidl due to open around 25 stores next year. Imported wines are already significant in Cyprus, and several New World brands are being promoted aggressively.

Getting the house in order

All these countries must take a hard look at their home markets, and build wine knowledge and pride in the local product while they still have some loyalty, or they risk being overwhelmed by aggressive global brands.

Romania has announced plans for a new generic wine agency, to be funded jointly by producer levy and the state. It is vital for Romania to educate its own consumers first while the market still has some protection (exports are under 10 percent) and while domestic wine consumption is creeping up toward 25 liters per head.

Croatia has become so successful as a tourist honeypot that East Germans and Hungarians, who would have gone to Lake Balaton in the past, are heading south over the border, creating problems for Balaton wineries that used to rely on these customers. However, tourism (especially from France, Italy, and Austria) is helping the wine industry in Croatia, where growers have switched from selling to co-ops for plonk to supplying for small-scale, high-quality wines from around 450 registered producers. It's not just tourist-driven, however; wine awareness has skyrocketed in Croatia, with wine clubs and wine magazines appearing, as well as specialist stores.

Slovenia's problem is that its internationally recognized superstars tend to go their own way, but they have to be persuaded to work in partnership with the bigger wineries, which can provide volume presence.

Cyprus has the lowest consumption per capita of any producer nation in Europe at 14 liters, even with 2.5 million tourists. Focus on cheap bulk exports and a lack of wine culture have allowed imports to reach at least 20 percent. Rather late in the day, producers are improving quality. Cyprus cannot afford to have two different producer organizations and must get Bacchus (regional wineries association) and the Cyprus Wine

Grapevine

• **The new Bessa Valley Winery** near Pazardjik, Bulgaria, opened in May 2005. The €6.5-million investment by Stephan von Niepperg (owner of Château La Mondotte and others) and Karl Hauptmann includes 135 ha of newly planted vineyards on land abandoned in the 1980s, bought from 800 owners. French winemaker Marc Dworkin is the manager. The first commercial vintage of Enira has been released with a Reserve to follow this year (2006).

• **Crljenak, the original Zinfandel,** is being replanted by Vina Grgic in Croatia on a 100-year-old vineyard site. The variety was down to just four vines but has been rescued and propagated.

• **Stork Nest Estates** is investing a further €5 million in winery and vineyard development across Bulgaria. In the south, 260 ha are being purchased, and the winery

plans to own 1,000 ha by 2010. The first crop of new varieties such as Malbec, Shiraz, Gamay, and Viognier was picked in 2005 from the company's own vineyards near Svishtov.

• **Belvedere Group** received an investment of €9 million from EBRD to use for planting vineyards, notably over 200 ha at Domaine Katerina and 40 ha at Oriahovitza in southern Bulgaria. It will also invest in a new winery near the Turkish border and a micro-vinification site at Domaine Sakar.

• **Cyprus wine history** has been traced back to 3500 BC, the oldest evidence in Europe. In May 2005, Italian archaeologists tested some pottery fragments that had been originally dug up near Limassol in 1933, and found traces of tartaric acid, showing that the jars had been used for wine.

Exporters Association (representing the four big wineries) together to jointly promote Cyprus as a wine country.

Hungary desperately needs its new wine promotion office—officially in existence since early 2005, but as a shell only. Parliament finally agreed funding in December 2005; producers will pay a sales tax of HUF 8 per liter—equivalent to the excise duty that has been removed. Sixty percent of funds are intended for wine marketing, with the remainder going to quality control. Hungary's major export success is Italian lookalike Pinot Grigio—not exactly communicating the message that Hungary has a wine identity in its own right.

In Bulgaria, local spirit *rakia* is commonly the drink of choice (about 80 million liters compared to 28 million liters of wine), or low-quality, home-made wine, which is still tax-free. There is a growing professional class in Sofia and Plovdiv that is becoming interested in wine, with several wine guides and magazines springing up, but there is a major opportunity in converting *rakia* drinkers to commercial wine in bottle. Promoting the image of Bulgaria has been written into government strategy, but not until around 2019, which may be far too late.

Grapevine

• **Egri Bikavér (Bull's Blood)** has protected status from the 2004 vintage, released in November 2005. There are two quality levels, with specified maximum yields and a minimum mix of varieties. Leading growers (originally led by the late Tibor Gál) aim to encourage inclusion of Kékfrankos in the blend, though this is not obligatory, and wines will have to pass a blind tasting.

• **Slovenia has adopted new wine laws,** bringing the number of regions down from 14 to eight, which should allow wineries more flexibility in sourcing grapes. Slovenia has applied to register Točaj as a trademark, now that Tokaj is permitted only in Hungary and Slovakia.

• **Possibly the highest winery in Europe** was opened in Cyprus in March 2005. At up to 4,855 ft (1,480 m), Kyperounda Winery has the highest vineyards in Europe; and at 3,609 ft (1,100 m), its state-of-the-

art winery is almost as high as the once-highest vineyards in Europe at Visp in Switzerland. Kyperounda is owned jointly by the Boutari family from Greece and Cyprus drinks distributor PhotosPhotiades. Minas Mina, who trained in Glasgow and Greece, is in charge of winemaking.

• **Winemaking standards** for Slovak Tokaji have been agreed, though Hungarian producers are still not happy with the quality levels of most Slovak Tokaji. The 2-*puttonyos* style currently produced in Slovakia will no longer be permitted from September 2005.

• **Starlings have been a major vineyard hazard** this year. An early harvest in Austria, due to disease pressure, left the birds with nothing to eat, so they moved on to Hungary. Weninger in Sopron reports losing half its Cabernet crop in spite of hiring two workers with guns. Szepsy in Tokaj also suffered heavy losses to starlings.

Vintage Report

Advance report on the latest harvest

2005

A variable year across the region, with producers in most countries reporting a late and difficult year.

The vintage in Romania was two to three weeks late and one of the smallest ever, at an estimated 433,000 tons (55 percent below 2004), giving an average yield of just 2.4 tons/ha. May was warm, but the heavy rains and hailstorms that followed caused damage at flowering and encouraged mildew. More heavy rains in late August caused gray rot, particularly in Dealul Mare and Vrancea. Overall quality is disappointing, with low sugars and high acid. Best results are around Recaş and Cotnari, where there was less rain.

In Bulgaria, harvest volumes are down by 30 percent, to 220,000 tons, and quality is below that of 2004. The cool summer and frequent rain meant more disease treatment than normal was required and ripening was delayed. Some vineyards around Plovdiv were damaged by flooding. Small growers suffered most, due to inadequate spraying; but where wineries own vineyards, they report some nicely balanced wines, with lower alcohol. In contrast, vineyards in the south (Sakar, Liubimetz) and southwest (Strouma Valley) had adequate early-season rains and a warm summer, giving good results.

Over the border in Turkey, quality is not good this year, due both to downy mildew and to the "war" between wineries fighting for supplies, resulting in grapes being picked too soon.

Hungarian conditions were challenging due to a rainy August bringing disease pressure, especially to thin-skinned whites. Wineries able to spray professionally and select fruit at harvest have generally achieved satisfactory quality. In the south, Villány had higher rainfall than normal, which affected early-ripening varieties. Warmer weather in late September into October meant later varieties were better, giving slow-maturing but potentially long-lived reds. Szekszárd also reports late but good-quality reds, though with only 55 percent of the normal crop. In Sopron, a small and very late, but high-quality, crop was severely damaged by starlings. In Tokaj, 2005 started badly, with heavy rains and flooding in May. Much of the summer was cold and damp, though a few warm weeks in August allowed sugars to be assimilated. Finally, a warm fall rescued a poor season and allowed botrytis development. Picking continued into December for some producers. *Aszú* berries are clean and with good acidity levels, so some producers, particularly in the north of the region, are very optimistic about the quality for *aszú* wines. Yields are below average, due to both weather and bird damage.

In contrast, Macedonia reports a good growing season, without any extreme weather. Good fruit set was followed by a warm July, but with cool nights. A brief rainy period in September affected Vranec quality, but later-ripening varieties were all picked in good condition.

Moldova also bucked the trend of its neighbors, with a much better season than 2004. June brought some rain, heavy in the north, but July, August, and September were warm and dry. Clean, healthy fruit, with good natural sugar, flavor development, and acidity, similar to 2003, is reported.

The damp summer in both the Czech Republic and Slovakia was rescued by a warm fall, giving good sugars and plenty of aromatics. Yields were down due to disease and starling damage.

Cyprus has produced a small harvest, but with fresh aromatic whites and promising reds.

Budding was 10 days early in Georgia, and the weather was extremely good until heavy rain and isolated but devastating hailstorms in late August, dashing hopes of an excellent vintage. Careful fruit selection was necessary, but overall quality is promising, especially for Saperavi, which is showing excellent varietal character.

Western Slovenia saw a harvest similar to 2004, though rain in July and August meant selection was vital. Warmer weather in late September gave better-than-expected quality in the reds, and whites are ripe but fresh. Eastern Slovenia was about a month behind, giving problems with achieving full ripeness.

Croatia had rains mid-harvest, so wines will be mediocre overall, especially whites, though Plavac Mali should have good structure.

Updates on the previous five vintages
2004

Vintage rating: *Red: 75, White: 80, Sweet: 80*

This vintage was at least two weeks later than normal and professional vine management paid off, since fungal disease pressures were high. Low yields were crucial to achieving full ripeness in many areas. The cool, damp spring replenished soil moisture after the dry 2003 season but delayed budbreak.

Romanian reds are lighter than 2003, but the whites are fresh with good aromatics.

The Bulgarian harvest was smaller than 2003, and reds are less ripe, though it is notable for fresh whites.

This was possibly the latest Hungarian harvest on record, though most growers are satisfied with the results. Whites and *rosés* are showing good fruit levels and crisp acidity, though reds around Lake Balaton ripened well only on favored sites. In the south, conditions were difficult, with decent results only with ultra-low yields and meticulous selection. In Tokaj, harvesting lasted into December, requiring several *tris*. Levels of botrytis are good but without great concentration, so wines are elegant and fruity in style, but mainly at lower *puttonyos* levels.

In the west of Slovenia, whites are fruity and fresh, while reds have good color and fruit—except for Cabernet, which showed green tannins. In the east, grapes were low in sugar with high acid, except where yields were severely reduced.

Continental Croatia reported a slightly better-than-average vintage, with some botrytis development for sweet wines. Coastal growers reported better-than-expected results, though yields are higher and wines less tannic than normal.

There were good aromatics in the Czech Republic and Slovakia, especially where growers picked late and botrytis development in November enabled production of sweet wines.

Georgia reported a very good vintage: expressive and well-balanced whites, and reds with fine, well-matured tannins due to the extended ripening period. It was a difficult year in both Moldova and Russia. Disease pressures were high and Moldovan whites are very high in acid.

2003

Vintage rating: *Red: 95 (except Ukraine & southeast Romania: 75), White: 90, Sweet: 90*

The hot, dry summer across Europe meant that most countries reported particularly good results for reds and a very early start to the harvest.

In Bulgaria, quality was very good, with high levels of sugar and polyphenols at harvest, but with unusually high acidity levels.

Western areas of Romania reported a warm, dry summer, and quality was very good. Dealul Mare was badly hit by drought at flowering, causing very poor fruit set, while Murfatlar had a disastrous rainy period just before harvest, as did neighboring Ukraine.

The 2003 harvest in Moldova was generous and of high quality, the best vintage in the previous five years.

Slovenia had a very early vintage with extremely high-quality reds (the best ever for some producers), though some whites suffered from low acidity.

Tokaj in Hungary saw drought affecting vines on free-draining soils. It was a long picking season, with a lower *aszú* yield than expected. Generally it was regarded as a good to very good year, but without the balancing acidity of 1999 and not as rich in sugar as 2000. Very good to outstanding results for dry and late-harvest wines. The rest of Hungary reported excellent reds and intense fruit flavors in whites, though low acidity in some varieties.

In Croatia, 2003 was a year with lots of extract, alcohol, and excellent quality. Cyprus also reported one of the best vintages in recent years and good quantities.

Riesling was not picked until October in Slovakia, but the results were excellent.

2002

Vintage rating: *Red: 80, White: 75, Sweet: 75*

A mixed year, ranging from outstanding in Transylvania to below average in areas such as northern Bulgaria and southeastern Romania, which were hit by heavy rains.

Hungarian wines were very concentrated. Reds, especially from the south, continue to show well. In Tokaj, hopes for a great *aszú* vintage were dashed by some rain in October, but wines are nicely balanced, especially for fruit harvested early.

Most areas in Romania showed very good quality but heavily reduced yields due to drought at flowering, though Murfatlar suffered rot. It was not a successful year for either Bulgaria or Macedonia. In Cyprus, quality was good, though low in quantity. Unusually, Turkey was hit by rain around harvest, resulting in more botrytis and weather damage than normal. Slovenian production was down 20–30 percent, but overall quality was high in both reds and whites.

2001

Vintage rating: *Red: 75 (Hungary & Slovenia: 89), White: 80, Sweet: 85*

A rain-soaked September caused mold development and poor flavors for some Tokaji producers, though some decent *aszú* wines have been made with ultra-careful selection. Elsewhere in Hungary, budding was early, with no late frosts, and summer was warm and dry. Early whites picked before the September rain were above average, and reds picked late were sound, too.

It was a good, ripe year in Romania, but small berry size due to the dry summer meant yields were slightly lower than 2000. Bulgaria suffered from a second year of drought, reducing crops by as much as 50 percent due to shriveling. Some producers reported good wines, but vines in poor condition shut down and failed to ripen.

2000

Vintage rating: *Red: 90, White: 80, Sweet: 95*

In Tokaj, this was an excellent vintage from a very long, hot, dry summer. The harvest lasted from August to the end of October, giving huge sugar levels and great flavors. A very good vintage across Hungary, with fully ripe fruit and high alcohol levels; the wines are maturing quickly, however, due to low acidity levels.

One of the finest recent vintages in Romania, showing ripe, healthy fruit, balanced acidity, and good keeping potential. A very good year in Bulgaria: disease-free fruit and high sugars, but dependent on vineyard management.

Grapevine

• **Atila Gere in Villány,** Hungary, has planted new vineyards of Syrah, Barbera, and, in partnership with Weninger, Pinot Noir and Tempranillo, adding to plantings of rare Transylvanian varieties such as Bakator, Balafánt, Csókaszőlő, Kékbajor, and Purcsin. The winery's first Syrah was bottled this year.

• **Carl Reh of Romania** planted a further 50 ha in 2005, bringing its total to 150 ha, of which 96 ha have been certified organic from 2005. Israeli experts have been advising on a new irrigation project.

• **Halewood Wine Cellars** will have a new winemaking team from the 2006 harvest. A new winery is being constructed at Tohani, and 75 ha of new vineyards have been planted in Transylvania, Dealul Mare, and Murfatlar.

• **Three new wineries were established** in Macedonia in 2005, bringing the total up to 31 commercial wineries, for a vineyard area of 22,400 ha. USAID has sponsored wine consultants from Napa to visit Macedonia to help wineries improve winemaking and establish an export organization.

• **Dionysos Mereni** has released Moldova's first icewine, a 2003 Riesling, reflecting wines made in Moldova for private consumption before 1940. Moldova is developing its first premium *garage* wines, including Chateau Vartely, which released its first wines in 2005, and Hotar Valley in Purcari.

• **Agricola Ştirbey in Drăgăşani,** Romania, is reviving ancient indigenous grape varieties. The first bottlings of Novac and Negru de Drăgăşani were released in 2006.

• **Moldova plans to develop** a "Wine City," costing around US$30 million, to be completed in time for a wine festival in fall 2006. Wineries are expected to fund 90 percent of the development, which should include wine cellars and restaurants.

• **Russia was the top** export destination for Moldovan wine in 2005, taking 85 percent of the country's production. From March 27, 2006, Russia banned all shipments of both Moldovan and Georgian wine, citing contamination with pesticides and heavy metals. Russia has been unable to produce analytical evidence to support this claim, and it is widely believed to be a political move to punish these countries for closer links with the EU. Wine is Moldova's biggest export earner, and the industry is devastated by this move.

GREATEST WINE PRODUCERS

1. Szepsy (Hungary)
2. Királyudvar (Hungary)
3. Domaine de Disznókő (Hungary)
4. Chateau Dereszla (Hungary)
5. Malatinszky Kúria (Hungary)
6. Gere Atila (Hungary)
7. Weninger (Hungary)
8. (Marjan) Simčič (Slovenia)
9. Edi Simčič (Slovenia)
10. Château Belá (Slovakia)

FASTEST-IMPROVING PRODUCERS

1. Recaş Winery (Romania)
2. Carl Reh Winery (Romania)
3. Szekszárd Winery (previously Liszt Winery) (Hungary)
4. Garamvári Szőlőbirtok (Hungary)
5. Csányi Winery (Hungary)
6. Damianitza (Bulgaria)
7. Belvedere Group (Domaine Menada, Domaine Sakar, Oriachovitza) (Bulgaria)
8. AurVin (Firebird) (Moldova)
9. Stork Nest Estates (Bulgaria)
10. Sodap (Kamanterena Winery) (Cyprus)

NEW UP-AND-COMING PRODUCERS

1. Bessa Valley Winery (Bulgaria)
2. Konyári (Hungary)
3. Grof Buttler (Hungary)
4. Chateau de Val (Bulgaria)
5. Pannonhalmi Apátsági Pincészet (Hungary)
6. Prince Ştirbey (Romania)
7. Kyperounda Winery (Cyprus)
8. Santa Sarah (Bulgaria)
9. Villa Liubimetz (Bulgaria)
10. Cekorov (Macedonia)

BEST-VALUE PRODUCERS

1. Recaş Winery (Romania)
2. Carl Reh Winery (Romania)
3. Pannonhalmi Apátsági Pincészet (Hungary)
4. Chateau Vincent (Hungary)
5. Nyakas Winery (Budai) (Hungary)
6. Nagyréde Winery (Hungary)
7. Törley Wine Cellars (Hungary)
8. Stork Nest Estates (Bulgaria)
9. Hilltop Neszmély Winery (whites) (Hungary)
10. Maxxima (Bulgaria)

GREATEST-QUALITY WINES

1. **Tokaji Aszú 6 Puttonyos 2000** Szepsy, Hungary (HUF 21,000)
2. **Tokaji Aszú Esszencia 2000** Château Dereszla, Hungary (HUF 16,000)
3. **Tokaji Aszú 6 Puttonyos 2000** Királyudvar, Hungary (HUF 14,600)
4. **Tokaji Aszú 6 Puttonyos Kapi 1999** Domaine de Disznókő, Hungary (HUF 15,000)
5. **Villány Cabernet Franc 2003** Malatinszky Kúria, Hungary (HUF 10,000)
6. **Solus Merlot 2003** Gere Atila, Hungary (HUF 12,500)
7. **Teodor Rdece Reserve 2000** (Marjan) Simčič, Slovenia (SIT 4,620)
8. **Duet Riserva 2002** Edi Simčič, Slovenia (SIT 9,000)
9. **Syrah 2003** Bock Pince, Hungary (HUF 14,000)
10. **Kékfrankos Selection 2003** Weninger, Hungary (HUF 5,300)

BEST BARGAINS

1. **Tramini 2005** Pannonhalmi Apátsági Pincészet, Hungary (HUF 1,400)
2. **La Cetate Merlot 2003** Carl Reh Winery, Romania (RON 22)
3. **Crystal Dry 2000** Chateau Vincent, Hungary (HUF 2,100)
4. **Budai Sauvignon Blanc 2005** Nyakas Winery, Hungary (HUF 1,400)

⑤ **Noblesse Sauvignon Blanc 2004** Haloze, Slovenia (SIT 900)

⑥ **Quercus Pinot Gris 2004** Vinska Klet Goriška Brda, Slovenia (SIT 938)

⑦ **Andante 2003** Degenfeld, Hungary (HUF 3,200)

⑧ **Oak-fermented Cabernet Sauvignon 2004** Vinprom Yambol, Bulgaria (BGN 5)

⑨ **Riesling 2005** Recaş Winery, Romania (RON 13)

⑩ **Albastrele Sauvignon Blanc 2005** Acorex, Moldova (MDL 60)

MOST EXCITING OR UNUSUAL FINDS

① **Enira 2004** Bessa Valley Winery, Bulgaria (BGN 24) *The first commercial release from the Bessa Valley investment by Stephan von Niepperg of Château Canon-La-Gaffelière. A single-estate wine, which is a rare thing for Bulgaria, and already showing great promise.*

② **Pinot Noir Réserve 2003** (Marjan) Simčič, Slovenia (SIT 4,320) *Marjan Simčič's reds show lovely elegance and subtlety compared to his hugely concentrated whites. This is just his second release of Pinot Noir.*

③ **Viognier 2003** Tibor Gál, Hungary (HUF 4,500) *Hungary's only Viognier, planted by the late Tibor Gál. Eger may be most famous for its "Bull's Blood," but this fine mineral Viognier shows the potential for whites in this northerly region, with its long, mild fall.*

④ **Pinot Blanc 2003** Grof Buttler, Hungary (HUF 3,200) *A new producer with 40 ha in Eger, already making an impression with its first releases from 2003. There's a plummy, concentrated Egri Bikavér and this rich "peaches and cream" Pinot Blanc.*

⑤ **Claret 2003** Chateau de Val, Bulgaria (BGN 15) *A ripe, rounded wine with a real sense of place, made from a mix of varieties (including Saperavi, Gamza, and Pamid) grown in a 100-year-old family vineyard. The EU may not take well to the name, but Bulgaria needs its new terroir producers to rescue its image from cheap varietal wines.*

⑥ **Sessio 2003** Konyári, Hungary (HUF 6,400) *The southern shore of Lake Balaton is not usually known for high quality, but this recently established boutique winery is setting new standards for the region with this finely crafted Merlot.*

⑦ **Crâmpoşie Selecţionată Sec 2004** Prince Ştirbey, Romania (RON 21) *A promising revival of an ancient variety from Drăgăşani, believed to be at least 3,000 years old. Fresh and fragrant on the nose with plenty of fruit weight, mineral notes, and good acidity—a white variety with some real character.*

⑧ **Petritis 2004** Kyperounda Winery, Cyprus (CYP 2.90) *From possibly the highest winery in Europe, with vineyards up to 4,855 ft (1,480 m). Xynisteri is usually vinified as a simple wine for drinking immediately. This is Xynisteri with a difference: part barrel-fermented to give much more weight and texture. It develops nicely for at least a couple of years, too.*

⑨ **Sensum 2003** Maxxima, Bulgaria (BGN 18) *Cabernet picked around Vidin in the far northwest, aiming to establish a reputation for quality in this part of Bulgaria. An elegant wine, with fine damson fruit, subtle oak, and violet overtones.*

⑩ **Privat 2004** Santa Sarah, Bulgaria (BGN 30) *The addition of some "knockout" Mavrud to the Cabernet Sauvignon gives this powerful wine a unique Bulgarian personality.*

Greece

Nico Manessis

The most alarming turn of events over the last year has been the sharp downturn of exports, from 15 percent of annual production to an estimated 12 percent.

NICO MANESSIS

Despite strong reviews and more than respectable showings in international competitions, with silver and gold medals awarded, especially to smaller producers, figures in some markets are plummeting.

Unsurprisingly, the biggest drop comes in the largest—and, historically, oldest (now 40-year-old)—German market. Traditionally composed of Greek importers selling to some 4,500 Greek restaurateurs, this market has had its day, its demise accelerated by Germany's current economic woes. It is going to be a tough landing, especially for the larger-volume *négociants* squeezed by the slow German economy and price-point pressure from New World powerhouses such as Australia, Chile, and tomorrow's giant, Argentina. On a more positive note, some specialist wine shops are importing mid-price wines directly and a number of sommeliers and consultants are listing Greek wines.

There are bright spots in the changing market. For the first time ever, thanks in part to the privately funded promotional work of All About

NICO MANESSIS is the author of *The Illustrated Greek Wine Book* (Olive Press, 2000) and the three editions of *The Greek Wine Guide* (Olive Press, 1994, 1995, 1996). He is currently working on a new book. He lectures on Greece in a variety of forums, such as the Université du Vin in France, the Ecole du Vin de Changins in Switzerland, and the Le Monde Institute in Greece. He has been writing articles on the wines of his native Greece in the international press for more than 12 years. Nico is a contributor to *Hugh Johnson's Pocket Wine Book* and is the wine critic for Athens' *Insider* magazine. Nico often judges in wine competitions in England, France, Spain, Switzerland, Germany, Cyprus, and Greece. He is chairman of the Greek panel at the *Decanter* World Wine Awards. Nico is based in Geneva, where he is a member of the Académie Internationale du Vin.

Greek Wine (see *Wine Report 2005*), the vast US market is embracing Greek wine with real verve. Greek restaurants have gone from ethnic to trendy (see below). Respected US commentators, such as Mary Ewing-Mulligan, Ed McCarthy, Doug Frost, and Michael Weiss, have discovered the new wines of Greece, and are lauding Greece's indigenous varieties, praising their difference and subtlety.

There are plenty of opportunities in new wine markets, such as Poland, Russia, the Indian continent, and China, which is hosting the 2008 Olympic Games. Since Athens is relaying the Olympic flame to Beijing, perhaps some wine from a country now ranking 14th in the top 20 largest wine producers could end up on the tables of the newly prosperous Chinese middle classes. This opportunity is too good to miss.

Rolland in Drama

The ubiquitous Michel Rolland is now consulting for all red wines made at the Kosta Lazaridi estate in Drama. The 2004 harvest was supervised by Rolland's associate, Canadian Steve Blais. Rolland himself came prior to the 2005 harvest and walked extensively among the 120 ha of red grapes.

So far, Rolland has asked for grapes to be picked riper, at a potential 14+ percent ABV, with the highest reaching 15 percent ABV. At this stage, he wants to see what the vineyard offers. He has not, so far, advocated micro-oxygenation, which is not practiced at Kosta Lazaridi, though it is known and used by other top estates elsewhere in Greece on both indigenous and international grape varieties.

The most exciting of the 2005 wines tasted by your contributor were tank samples of the estate's Merlots (prior to blending). Rich-tasting, with a spicy Greek spin, they were neither overextracted nor blowzy.

TV boost for Alpha Estate

Bernard Pivot, presenter of the famous French TV book show *L'Apostrophe*, is also known for his love of wine and his vineyard in Beaujolais. Pivot, who had not visited Greece for 20 years, took a TV5 crew to Alpha Estate, where they shot footage in the vineyard and interviewed Angelos Iatridis, oenologist and partner.

Though a Bordeaux graduate, Iatridis had no idea of Pivot's star status in French-speaking countries and was relaxed throughout filming. Pivot had nothing but positive comments on the progress of Greek wine, and was genuinely impressed with the concentration and freshness of Alpha Estate's wines, saying, "Wines like this make a mockery of the prevailing wisdom that Greece is too hot to produce fine wines." The Greek TV channel ERT has secured broadcasting rights for the home market.

Opinion:
Decentralization is vital

The public sector must move with the times and modernize archaic legislation first put in place in 1971. The modern Greek wine industry has to free itself from legislation tangled up in the slow-grinding cogs and politics of the ministry of agriculture in Athens. Decentralization is urgently needed—more than ever. It is imperative that appellation issues be moved to a local level, where requests for change can be dealt with by a local administration that can react quickly and initiate the necessary amendments appropriate to the region's specific requirements.

The best-educated generation of winemakers Greece has ever known should be in the vineyards and cellars, not spending precious time and energy lobbying for overdue changes to move Greek wine legislation into the 21st century.

Update: foreigners arrive

Further to *Wine Report 2004*'s "Foreigners wanted," we (almost) have some foreign investment in the northwest of Macedonia. Dutch couple Laurens and Annete Hartman have put their faith and money in the cooler-climate plateau (2,133 ft/650 m) of Amyndeo. Situated on a property close to the village of Vegoras, Karanikas Wines has moved from the Hatzis winery on the outskirts of Amyndeo to a three-story, gravity-flow, all-new winery. In addition to the existing 15-year-old Xinomavro vineyards, the Hartmans are planting Assyrtiko and Sauvignon Blanc. According to Laurens, future plantings will include "Riesling (my great white love), if possible. However, my ambition is to create the best red Xinomavro ever made. I first have to make small batches from low yields to learn the *terroir* and can then blend the desired red wine: an aromatic, complex, subtle, not massive, wine suitable for aging." Local boy Makis Mavridis, partner at Alpha Estate, the region's leading name, welcomes the incomers.

Grapevine

• **Argatia is leading** ampelographer-oenologist and author Haroula Spinthiropoulou's new winery, where she will put to use her experience with clonal selection. Located in Rodochori, Naoussa, Argatia is a partnership with her husband Panayiotis Georgiades. The clones in the vineyard near Yiannakochori are the aromatic white Malagousia with a little Assyrtiko and Athiri. The reds are Xinomavro and Negoska. There will be two types of red: a fresh, fruity young wine and a cask-aged reserve.

Vintage Report

Advance report on the latest harvest
2005

After the abundance of the two previous vintages, nature corrected itself with a yield drop of up to 15 percent. Summer had no extreme weather, and sunny days with cool nights produced ripe, healthy grapes. Berries were smaller in size and rich in flavor and color. Harvest dates were in a near-perfect time frame, and conditions during picking were textbook, with the exception of Nemea, which experienced heavy rain toward the end of harvesting. The northern vineyards of Naoussa, Amyndeo, Epanomi, Kavala, and Drama did particularly well in reds and whites. In the Peloponnese Patra, Mantinia did best. The dessert Muscats of Rio Patra are among the most fragrant and balanced in recent years. In the upper part of Nemea, wines harvested prior to the rain have deep color, with more body than the more delicate 2004s. Santorini made super-concentrated, bone-dry whites. Cretan dry whites, especially those made with central Crete's spicy Vilana grape, are astonishing for their levels of ripeness and freshness. Samos Muscats are perfumed and have real backbone, and they should age magnificently.

Updates on the previous five vintages
2004

Vintage rating: *Red: 88, White: 92*

Harvest started a week later than average for whites, and two or three weeks later for reds. White grapes ripened fully. International grape varieties were of a rarely seen homogeneous quality. Delicate indigenous whites are more concentrated, with natural high acidity. It is a rare and outstanding vintage for all white wines, including the sweet specialties. A dry and sunny October saved the red-wine harvest. Reds have good color and elegant tannins, and they are very fragrant. Across the board there is a more northern-latitude climatic imprint, not unlike the 1997 vintage, though with far more complete and distinctive wines.

2003

Vintage rating: *Red: 90, White: 88*

Unhurried ripening benefited from a moderate summer with no heat waves. In all but two regions—Naoussa and Goumenissa—both international and indigenous grape varieties produced exceptionally healthy, ripe, and balanced grapes, with some appellations producing wines the likes of which have rarely been seen. The island vineyards of Santorini and Cephalonia are the best. Reduced grape yields in central Crete produced whites and reds showing the unrealized potential of Greece's southernmost island. Muscats from Limnos and Samos are terrific. Eastern Macedonia produced outstanding wines, especially from imported varieties. The finicky, late-ripening Xinomavro, affected by yields that were far too high, struggled to ripen fully in Naoussa and Goumenissa. Reenergized Amynteo experienced the finest vintage since 1994. Nemea, in the Peloponnese, produced deep-colored, fruity wines from the lower-altitude valley subregions. The quality from the hillside vineyards is exceptional. The delicate and aromatic light whites of Patras show uniform consistency and *terroir* expression.

2002

Vintage rating: *Red: 75, White: 85*

Drama, Kavala, and Epanomi wines are all very good, vibrant, and fruity. Elsewhere, a contrast of extremes was the case. Santorini harvested a fraction of its usual tonnage. Naoussa was a washout, with unripeness and widespread rot. Nemea was a disaster, although a couple of higher-elevation vineyards produced healthy grapes, albeit in small amounts and with less color and body than usual. The unprecedented shortfall resulted in strong domestic demand for red wine, pushing up prices. Mantinia had little rot, good aroma, and satisfactory, if lower, levels of ripeness. Rhodes, which has the easternmost island vineyards, experienced the best vintage in years.

2001

Vintage rating: *Red: 90, White: 89*

Another very good vintage. Lower yields and higher acidities encouraged wines of notable quality in both colors. Crete, Cephalonia, and Santorini produced superb, crisp, dry whites. Following the previous year's heat wave, which had stressed Savatiano vines to their limits, Attica vineyards equipped with drip irrigation excelled. Mantinia had one of its finest harvests, with a quantity and quality not seen since 1998. Standout reds are to be found everywhere. Naoussa wines are delicious, without the overripe, jammy fruit found in the previous vintage. Those of Goumenissa are a little less ripe, though delicate. Nemea produced atypical wines, the best of them characterized by an inspired combination of class and ethereal edge. Balanced Samos Muscats are a delight.

2000

Vintage rating: *Red: 93, White: 88*

A superlative vintage for red wines, with healthy grapes in all regions. Some whites were at the limit of low acidity, but most were concentrated. Vineyards in Mantinia were generally stressed, causing loss of aroma and fruit. Santorini came up with superb, *terroir*-driven, bone-dry whites, and Crete upped its white-wine profile significantly. In Drama, Merlots were somewhat over the top; elsewhere, they are keepers. Without a doubt, it was one of the greatest Naoussa and Nemea harvests on record, the like not seen since 1994 and 1990. Some Naoussa single vineyards went for broke and harvested overripe grapes, losing the character of their *terroir*. Phenolic maturity in Nemea was perfect. The wines are packed with fruit, and the more structured top-notch labels will age up to 12 years. Amber Samos Muscats are a shade darker and duller on the palate, due to high temperatures and arid summer conditions.

Grapevine

• **Third-generation Domaine Papayanakos** has built the first energy-efficient winery in Greece, designed by leading architect Elena Stavropoulou. Located in the 2,000-ha Attiko Parko, a nature reserve, the area has been farmed since classical times. Surrounding the winery are old-vine Savatiano vineyards and small farms producing prize pistachios and figs, which are mostly exported. The winery now offers an outdoor café, catering for functions, and horseback riding through the vineyards. This reenergized region, with its picturesque countryside dotted with ruins of ancient temples and Byzantine chapels, has one of the most suitable climates for (almost) year-round wine tourism.

• **Over the last 10 years,** top Greek chefs have emerged in Brussels and London, offering Greek wine a much-needed platform. But nowhere has the healthy Greek diet been embraced more enthusiastically than Manhattan, where more than 15 Greek restaurants have emerged. Most of the pioneers, such as Periyali, Molyvos, and Mylos, were founded and are still owned or managed by Greek Americans. The Greek theme has now attracted non-Greek restaurateurs, who have upped the ante by sourcing and securing labels made in limited quantities. This poses a problem for the home market, since there is not enough to go around, and boutique estates and *négociants* are more than happy to sell abroad.

GREATEST WINE PRODUCERS

1. Ktima Gerovassiliou
2. Gaia Wines
3. Alpha Estate
4. Biblia Chora
5. Tselepos
6. Ktima Mercouri
7. Parparoussis
8. Sigalas
9. Oenoforos
10. Samos Cooperative

FASTEST-IMPROVING PRODUCERS

1. Hatzidakis
2. Mountrihas
3. Papayanakos
4. Thimiopoulos
5. Douloufakis
6. Wine Art Estate
7. Tsantalis (reds)
8. Palivos
9. Tetramythos
10. Ampelones Sakelaridou

NEW UP-AND-COMING PRODUCERS

1. Semeli Nemea
2. Dryopi
3. Karipidis
4. Kokkalis
5. Simeonidis
6. Manolesakis
7. Sokos
8. Manousakis
9. Economou
10. Argatia

BEST-VALUE PRODUCERS

1. Semeli Nemea
2. Samos Cooperative
3. Oenoforos
4. Creta Olympias
5. Ktima Mountriha
6. Ktima Mercouri

7. Katoghi-Strofilia
8. Skouras
9. Parparoussis
10. Boutaris

GREATEST-QUALITY WINES

1. **Gerontoklima Rematias Vertzami/Cabernet Franc 2000** Antonopoulos (€19)
2. **Nemea 2004** Mitravela Estate (€15)
3. **Alpha Syrah 2005** Alpha Estate (€23)
4. **Ktima Voyatzis Red 2001** Yiannis Voyatzis (€10)
5. **Nectar Muscat 2001** Samos Cooperative (€9)
6. **Avlotopi 2003** Tselepos (€23)
7. **Nemea Epilegmenos 2003** Parparoussis (€19)
8. **Syrah 2004** Ktima Mountriha (€12)
9. **Naoussa Xinomavro 2003** Katoghi-Strofilia (€10)
10. **Nemea Grande Cuvée 2003** Skouras (€13)

BEST BARGAINS

1. **Savatiano 2005** Papayanakos (€5)
2. **Kokkino se Mavro 2005** Mitravela (€6)
3. **Sauvignon Blanc 2005** Aidarinis (€6.50)
4. **Mantinia 2005** Antonopoulos (€6.50)
5. **Xerolithia 2005** Creta Olympias (€6.80)
6. **Drossalis Patra 2005** Parparoussis (€7)
7. **Samos Grand Cru 2005** Samos Cooperative (€7)
8. **Santorini 2005** Hatzidakis (€9)
9. **Biblia Chora White 2005** Biblia Chora (€9)
10. **Robola 2005** Gentilini (€10)

MOST EXCITING OR UNUSUAL FINDS

1 Ghi ke Uranos 2004 Thimiopoulos (€16) *A finely chiseled, ripe Xinomavro. Made from a mixture of rediscovered clones and the lowest yields in the region, this is the next big thing to emerge from an inertia-ridden appellation that has not yet realized the full potential of making long-lived crus.*

2 Mavrodaphne 1944 Karelas (€100) *A once-in-a-lifetime opportunity, probably never to be repeated. The finest and most balanced of all old Mavrodaphnes ever tasted, including other rarities such as the 1898 and 1873 vintages. Cheap for such a history-filled bottle. Ethereal.*

3 Alpha 1 2003 Alpha Estate (€48) *Alpha Estate's latest and top wine: in this vintage (the blend varies according to the vintage), an off-beat blend of 60 percent Tannat and 40 percent Montepulciano. Unfiltered essence made for very long keeping. Astonishing.*

4 Goumenissa Grande Réserve 2003 Tatsis Brothers (€16) *Great vintages are rare in this underrated, rain-plagued, mountainous region. Organically grown 65 percent Xinomavro and 35 percent Negoska. This GR goes all out to prove the standards that can be achieved. A lesser-known, affordable gem.*

5 Primitivo 2004 Karipidis (€10) *What a surprise! Redolent of black pepper, a spicy, savory example from the usually hot-climate southeastern fringes of the Thessaly plain.*

6 Tempranillo 2004 Ktima Pavlidis (€18) *A first. This relatively recent newcomer to Drama is diversifying the estate's grape mix in an area swamped with me-too Cabernets and Merlots.*

7 CV 2004 Creta Olympias (€11) *After years of research, the potential of red Cretan wine is now being tapped. Unusual, all-Mediterranean blend of Syrah, Malvasia Nera, and Kotsifali. Vibrantly fruity nose, herby, picked perfectly ripe for soft tannins. Strikingly different.*

8 Roussanne 2004 Manousakis (€21.50) *An inspired choice, matching this Rhône specialty to the sunny, windswept, limestone-schistous hills near Chania, on western Crete. Rounded apricot flavors, richly oaked, nutty.*

9 Anatolikos 2000 Gaia Wines (€20 per 50-cl bottle) *This trend-setting cellar has revived the long-dormant sweet Nemea appellation. Made from sun-dried Aghiorghitiko grapes, this is exotically perfumed and showcases how mannerly this indigenous star grape can be.*

10 Muscat 2004 Palivos (€26 per 50-cl bottle) *From the Rio Patras appellation, now shrinking due to urban development. Sun-dried and unoaked. Scintillating grapey freshness, satin-textured.*

Lebanon

Michael Karam

Lebanon is still getting to grips with its new-found independence from Syrian rule.

MICHAEL KARAM

While the regional financial markets are going crazy for all types of Lebanese stocks and bonds, investors monitoring the real sectors are waiting to see whether political stability and national consensus will prevail over sectarian schisms and external attempts to destabilize the country. Only then will a clear picture emerge of the level of foreign direct investment in real estate, tourism, retail, and agro-industry, including wine. The Bekaa Valley is now empty of Syrian soldiers and no longer viewed as Damascus's back garden. Landowners, long aware of the potential rewards of wine-grape cultivation, are reconsidering their options. At the beginning of 2005, there were 16 producers, compared to five in 1995. By the end of 2006, that number will have risen to 20, and others are poised to follow.

The mood wasn't always so bullish. The $28-million Lebanese wine industry anticipated the worst in the wake of the February 2005 assassination of former prime minister Rafik Hariri, but the subsequent Cedar Revolution and the telegenic images of flag-draped, doe-eyed Lebanese girls beamed around the world thrust Lebanon into the world's consciousness. The image of "war-torn" Lebanon has been replaced by "plucky" Lebanon, and this, they figured, was good news for wine.

MICHAEL KARAM has lived in Lebanon since 1992. He is a business journalist and wine writer. He is a contributor to Jancis Robinson's *Oxford Companion to Wine* and the author of *Wines of Lebanon* (Saqi Books, 2005), which won the 2005 Gourmand Award for the Best New World Wine Book. He has just finished writing the official history of Chateau Ksara. Michael's next book, *Arak and Mezze: The Taste of Lebanon*, will be published in 2007.

Enotria deal for Kefraya

In 2005, Enotria agreed to represent Château Kefraya in the UK. The impact was immediate, as Kefraya moved out of the lucrative but limited Lebanese restaurant sector and into the mainstream. Within months, Enotria had taken the label into the Lanesborough Hotel, the Michelin-starred Greenhouse restaurant in Mayfair, and the casinos of London Clubs International; overall sales in the UK improved by 20 percent.

Kefraya's hand was no doubt forced by the relatively healthy performance of rival Chateau Ksara and the smaller Massaya in the UK, represented by Halgarten and Thorman Hunt respectively. Chateau Ksara, with an average 25 percent year-on-year growth in the UK, is confident that it will be the first Lebanese producer to achieve a supermarket presence in the UK, while Massaya, a Franco-Lebanese collaboration, claims more than 60 percent year-on-year growth in 2005.

UVL reinvigorated?

Lebanon's Union Vinicole du Liban (UVL) elected a new committee in July, one that gave representation to all producers for the first time, although many of the smaller wineries remain unconvinced that UVL has their best interests at heart. President and owner of Chateau Musar Serge Hochar took serious flak for not fighting the OIV's decision to cancel the June 2005 Beirut congress, but was vindicated in his decision after the spate of bomb attacks that summer. Hochar is upbeat about what he calls the "new spirit" in the UVL now that there is wider representation among members, as well as plans for an association website.

However, his insistence that the UVL was never meant to be responsible for the marketing of Lebanese wine is sending unsettling signals. Hochar argues that the UVL cannot afford a full-on marketing initiative and that such a scheme would have to be funded by the public sector, perhaps via the future national wine institute. But members contend that this situation suits Lebanon's big three—Chateaux Musar, Ksara, and Kefraya—who, they claim, are in no hurry to implement a campaign that might see smaller producers make gains at their expense.

Grapevine

• **Serge Hochar** of Chateau Musar has been complaining for a while that his wines are ridiculously cheap: his 1998 Chateau Musar white sells in Beirut for LL 18,000 (roughly $13.00) and his 1997 red for LL 25,000 (about $18). Recently, his grumbles have become louder, so there might be a dramatic price hike. One source of Hochar's exasperation may be that he has been planting 60 ha in the Western Bekaa and has just splurged on a bottling plant in Ghazir. Or he may believe his wines are worth more.

EU REGULATION INSTIGATES ACTION

The advent of VI1, the new but not yet mandatory EU export regulation, has fast-tracked the establishment of the much-needed national wine institute. Intended to be responsible for all areas of grape growing and wine production, as well as the eventual creation of a system similar to the French *appellation d'origine contrôlée*, the institute would protect the name and quality of Lebanese wine.

LEBANESE BRAND NEEDS PROTECTION

Serge Hochar has voiced worries about the export of Lebanese grapes to Egypt, Jordan, and Syria. His concern is that wine will be passed off as Lebanese, which would harm the genuine article. The establishment of a national wine institute cannot come soon enough, since it could negotiate with the countries concerned to protect the Lebanon brand. In the meantime, the UVL is working with the EU to implement the widely used Geographic Indication (GI) system as a guarantee of the quality and the specific character of wine (and other agricultural products), while protecting product names from misuse and imitation.

ALL CHANGE

It has been a merry-go-round year for Lebanon's oenologists. Labib Kallas, who divided his time between a full-time job at Clos St Thomas, consultancies at Château Fakra, the Karam Winery, and the winemaking monks at Hamatoura, left Lebanon to begin a new challenge as the head winemaker for the Egybev winery in El Gouna, on Egypt's Red Sea Riviera. Kallas reports that he has been busy planting and is confident that he will be harvesting 2,000 tons by 2007.

Domaine Wardy's oenologist Diana Salemeh was headhunted by the new Château Ka. She was replaced by Frenchman David Ciry, who started in late 2005. Finally, Massaya has confirmed that its winemaking responsibilities have been taken on by co-owner Ramzi Ghosn, in order, he says, to ensure continuity of philosophy and quality.

Grapevine

• **Chateau Ksara,** which will turn 150 in 2007, is in the midst of a $7.5-million expansion program that includes 75 ha of vineyards, a new tasting room, and new equipment. The ambition is to increase production by 700,000 bottles per year, taking annual production to 2.7 million bottles. To celebrate its landmark birthday, the winery has produced a limited-edition birthday wine made from Cabernet Sauvignon and Arinarnoa. At the time of writing, the name had not been announced, but "Tsar" seems to be the favorite.

• **Cave Kouroum** seems to have emerged from its legal battle with neighboring Château Kefraya and established itself as one of Lebanon's most adventurous producers. At Vinexpo, the winery won seven awards, including two golds. Rumors that consultant Yves Morard, the colorful winemaker who put Château Kefraya on the map, and his son Cyril may have parted company with Cave Kouroum have been denied, and the dynamic duo is expected back for the 2007 harvest.

Opinion:
Buy Lebanese!

Ultimately, promoting Lebanese wine promotes Lebanon. Chile, Argentina, and South Africa, once beyond the pale, now invoke images of rolling vineyards, summer dining, and beautiful people. Wine can wash away a lot of bad memories and this sentiment has never been timelier for a Lebanon that is still riding the wave created by the popular demonstrations in 2005. Ideally, now is the time to launch an international generic campaign; however, with no one to finance such a venture, it probably remains a pipe dream. More viable would be a national marketing campaign emphasizing the quality of Lebanese wine, educating consumers on the health benefits of drinking wine over, say, whiskey or arak, and stressing the economic importance of buying Lebanese. It should also target tourists. Posters for Lebanese or Bekaa wine should be among the first images visitors see when they arrive at Beirut airport.

A national strategy

The quality of Lebanese wine has improved dramatically since the mid-1990s. Producers have responded to the lessons learned, working with a wider range of grapes, including "noble" varieties, but they know there is still work to be done. They have discovered that the Bekaa's flat vineyards generally give grapes with low alcohol, low polyphenolic maturation, and high acidity, whereas the slopes tend to produce grapes with high alcohol, a high level of polyphenolic maturation, but low acidity. To help producers grow grapes that can reach full polyphenolic maturation with lower alcohol and higher acidity, there should be a UVL/government-sponsored program of strategic planting of clones and rootstocks, selected according to the needs of the Bekaa's individual *terroirs*. Irrigation (until recently a dirty word in Lebanon) should also be provided where necessary. An extension of such a program to a comprehensive study of all Lebanon's *terroirs* would paint a more detailed picture of Lebanon's viticultural potential and produce better results in the bottle.

Bekaa Valley initiative

As far back as 1998, European experts pinpointed wine (along with olive oil and honey) as the most lucratively viable agro-industry. New grape plantations have changed the lives of many of the Bekaa Valley's struggling farmers. The landscape of many towns is changing as the demand for good *terroir* increases. However, the long-awaited national wine institute must, as in France, control the level of planting according to demand. Unchecked expansion will affect the price and quality of grapes and threaten the quality of future vintages.

A different strategy

Since 9/11, the number of non-Arab tourists to Lebanon has dropped by 90 percent. With a little imagination and vision, Lebanon could kick-start its stalled wine-tourism initiative. During the summer, when Lebanon hosts its celebrated international music festivals, a mixed itinerary of music and wine, arranged by the festival organizers and the UVL, could promote Lebanon, its wine, and its festivals to a wider international audience.

Presenting well

Low volume is not necessarily a handicap. Lebanon can compete if positioned correctly, but the wines have to look the part. Lebanese producers must be prepared to work (and to spend) to create the right image and raise their profile. There are some stunning Lebanese label designs that would give the Californians and Australians a run for their money, but in some instances, good wine is let down by poor labels. Lebanese wine is not cheap, and, if Lebanese producers are to venture out of the restaurant sector and charge more than $18 a bottle in the UK retail market, they will have to improve their packaging. It is up to the UVL to encourage this.

Grapevine

• **Domaine des Tourelles** is finally shaking off its postwar hangover. New winemaker Gerard D'Hautville has produced Marquis des Beys, the winery's first premium-quality red made from Cabernet Sauvignon, Syrah, and Merlot. Domaine des Tourelles makes Le Brun, arguably Lebanon's finest arak, and aims to produce a red of similar class in Marquis des Beys. Partner Nayla Issa el-Khoury has hinted that, if the wine performs as expected, the winery might eventually focus solely on Le Brun and Marquis des Beys, news that will disappoint fans of its hugely popular *rosé*.

• **Raymond Khoury,** like Cave Kouroum's Rahal family and Château Kefraya's Michel de Bustros, is a grape supplier turned wine producer. Chateau Khoury has planted 13 ha with a wide range of varieties (including difficult but potentially thrilling Pinot Noir). The estate, in the hills above Zahleh, will also have a tasting center and hotel. Khoury's son Jean-Pierre has finished his winemaking studies in France and is now responsible for production. Khoury's initial production level in 2006 was around 30,000 bottles, but he is confident that production will increase to 100,000 in the next decade.

Vintage Report

Advance report on the latest harvest

2005

Simply put, 2005 was a tough year, the most humid in nearly half a
century, especially in July and August, and results are expected to
equal 2004. The winter was long and wet, which impacted negatively
on the lower-lying areas of the Bekaa, where the grapes took longer
to ripen. In other areas, the grapes raced to maturity—the first picking
took place on August 18 and the last (Cinsault) on October 24. The time
span was phenomenal and reflected the performance of the various *terroirs*
on the Bekaa plateau. However, any interesting results of this freakish
summer were negated by excessive mildew, which affected the black
grapes especially. In contrast, it is a good year for whites, which showed
good acidity and pleasant floral aromas. The reds had a mixed year. The
traditional early ripeners—Cabernet Sauvignon, Merlot, and Syrah—all
ripened well but were hit by mildew, while Cinsault and Grenache were
helped by a cooler September that allowed them to compensate for the
humidity. Indeed, they may prove to be the better grapes. That said, the
wines may yet surprise.

Updates on the previous five vintages

2004

Vintage rating: *Red: 90, White: 85*

At the beginning of the harvest, the grapes had low sugar content and
medium acidity levels, but a sudden heat wave, two weeks later, changed
everything, producing grapes with higher sugar but still maintaining
medium acidity. It was as though there were two harvests in the same
year, and fermentation was affected accordingly. Generally, grapes picked
in the first two weeks of the harvest were fruity, round, and mellow, with
floral aromas, although Cabernet Sauvignon, one of the Bekaa staples,
was different: it was powerful, intense, concentrated, and leathery, with
red fruits. "Second-phase" grapes, especially Carignan and Cinsault,
developed more of a red-fruit character in smell and taste, while
smooth tannins became more obvious and the palate more velvety.

2003

Vintage rating: *Red: 91, White: 85*

A unique harvest came on the back of the wettest winter in 15 years and a 10-day heat wave in May, both of which contributed to a marvelous balance between acidity and sugar content and an exceptional concentration of phenol compounds due to dry weather in September. The whites were aromatic with high acidity, producing vivid gunflint notes, finishing with a pleasant, mild, and unctuous taste, while the reds produced intense color. They were more tannic than former vintages, but with balanced, mellow tannins, supple, and not astringent. All the different varieties were exceptionally fragrant, producing full-bodied and powerful wines.

2002

Vintage rating: *Red: 91, White: 85*

After four successive years of drought, there was a long, cold, rainy winter, followed by a mild July and a hot August. The vines took longer to ripen their grapes and had high levels of sugar, acidity, and tannin. Grape maturity levels varied from vineyard to vineyard, forcing growers to be selective. Fermentation went perfectly but, against all the odds, was very slow—therefore much longer—and the wines have turned out to be much bigger, riper, and fuller than expected.

2001

Vintage rating: *Red: 80, White: 70*

The crop was good, albeit 15 percent down, with ripe fruit but without much tannin or acidity. Fermentation progressed well, and the malolactic fermentation followed easily and naturally. The wines were easy and fruity, with good alcohol levels.

2000

Vintage rating: *Red: 80, White: 70*

The crop was healthy, although 15 percent down, with grapes that were sweet yet tannic, and with good acidity. Alcohol levels were higher than usual—almost the same as 1999. It was an easy harvest, and fermentation proceeded with hardly any problems. Malolactic fermentation followed its normal course. The wines were very well balanced, tannic, concentrated, and powerful.

GREATEST WINE PRODUCERS

1. Chateau Musar
2. Chateau Ksara
3. Massaya
4. Clos St Thomas
5. Château Kefraya
6. Domaine Wardy
7. Domaine des Tourelles
8. Vin Nakad

FASTEST-IMPROVING PRODUCERS

1. Massaya
2. Chateau Ksara
3. Clos St Thomas
4. Domaine des Tourelles
5. Cave Kouroum
6. Domaine Wardy
7. Château Kefraya
8. Château Belle-Vue
9. Karam Winery
10. Vin Nakad

NEW UP-AND-COMING PRODUCERS

1. Chateau Khoury
2. Château Ka
3. Château Belle-Vue
4. Cave Kouroum
5. Nabise Mont Liban
6. Karam Winery
7. Kfifane Winery
8. Clos de Cana

BEST-VALUE PRODUCERS

1. Chateau Ksara
2. Château Kefraya
3. Massaya
4. Domaine Wardy
5. Clos St Thomas
6. Château Fakra
7. Heritage
8. Domaines des Tourelles
9. Nabise Mont Liban

GREATEST-QUALITY WINES

1. **Chateau Musar 1988** (LL 80,000)
2. **Chateau Musar 1991** (LL 57,000)
3. **Comte de M 2001** Château Kefraya (LL 43,000)
4. **Cuvée du Troisième Millénaire 2002** Chateau Ksara (LL 30,000)
5. **Château St Thomas 2001** Clos St Thomas (LL 28,000)
6. **Silver Selection 2003** Massaya (LL 13,000)
7. **Chateau Musar White 1998** (LL 16,000)
8. **Réserve 2003** Massaya (LL 25,000)
9. **Chateau Ksara 2001** (LL 20,000)
10. **Private Selection 2003** Domaine Wardy (LL 30,000)

BEST BARGAINS

1. **Réserve du Couvent 2004** Chateau Ksara (LL 10,000)
2. **Cuvée Réserve 2002** Chateau Musar (LL 10,000)
3. **Rosé 2004** Domaine des Tourelles (LL 7,000)
4. **Cuvée de Printemps 2004** Chateau Ksara (LL 7,000)
5. **Le Fleuron 2004** Heritage (LL 5,000)
6. **Rosé du Printemps 2004** Domaine Wardy (LL 8,000)
7. **Les Gourmets 2003** Clos St Thomas (LL 8,000)
8. **Blanc de Blancs 2003** Heritage (LL 11,000)
9. **Blanc de Blancs 2004** Château Kefraya (LL 12,000)
10. **Cloud 9 2004** Karam Winery (LL 15,000)

MOST EXCITING OR UNUSUAL FINDS

① **Syrah de Nicolas 2004** Karam Winery (LL 30,000) *Only 5,000 bottles of this sumptuous wine were produced, demonstrating that South Lebanon has the terroir to compete with the Bekaa.*

② **Marquis des Beys 2003** Domaine des Tourelles (LL 18,000) *The renaissance of Domaine des Tourelles should be complete with this full-on and elegant Cabernet Sauvignon/Merlot/Syrah blend from new winemaker Gerard D'Hautville.*

③ **Private Selection White 2003** Domaine Wardy (LL 23,000) *Selim Wardy's flagship white made from Viognier and Muscat. Excellent acidity and a terrific fruity nose.*

④ **Les Emirs 2001** Clos St Thomas (LL 13,000) *Typically full-bodied Lebanese red made from Cabernet Sauvignon and Grenache.*

⑤ **La Renaissance 2003** Château Belle-Vue (LL 30,000) *A blend of Cabernet and Merlot that is full-bodied, fruity, and mouth-filling; a good wine to age.*

⑥ **St Michael 2005** St Michael Winery (LL 6,000) *One hundred percent Grenache and 100 percent delightful summer quaffing from this tiny winery in Masser el Chouf. Superb homemade organic wine—soft and supple.*

⑦ **Chardonnay 2004** Clos St Thomas (LL 15,000) *Better than the excellent 2003: as I wrote last year, a wine that defies the global ennui surrounding Chardonnay. Still perfumed and flinty, still fabulous.*

⑧ **Rosé du Printemps 2004** Domaine Wardy (LL 8,000) *Lebanon produces impressive rosé. This is one of the very best and up there with Domaine des Tourelles.*

⑨ **Cuvée Réserve White 2004** Chateau Musar (LL 9,000) *Made with indigenous grape Obeideh, this is the more accessible cousin of the Chateau white. Maybe not to all tastes, it has acidity and notes of fruits and nuts. A wine with true Lebanese character.*

⑩ **Syrah/Cabernet Sauvignon 2003** Cave Kouroum (LL 26,000) *A suave Syrah-dominated blend, weighing in at a whopping 14.5 percent alcohol. Lovely tannins and structure, awash with strawberry, chocolate, pepper, and tobacco.*

Grapevine

• **Selim Wardy,** owner of Domaine Wardy, has done it again. Undeterred by the poaching of his winemaker and by being beaten out by a rival producer over a consignment of grapes, the man who introduced single-varietal wines into the Lebanese market has captured the country's newly reclaimed independent spirit by bringing us Cuvée du Liban 2004, a patriotic blend of Cabernet Sauvignon, Cabernet Franc, and Merlot. Wardy has produced a limited quantity of 10,452 bottles, a celebration of Lebanon's surface area in square kilometers.

• **Château Belle-Vue,** the micro-winery in Bhamdoun owned by former Merrill Lynch investment banker Naji Boutros and his wife Jill, has finally released its first batch of wines: 6,000 bottles of La Renaissance 2003. In true micro-winery spirit, the wines will initially be available only from the winery.

Israel

Daniel Rogov

Carmel, the largest winery in the country, is going through a period of instability.

DANIEL ROGOV

Since the ousting of CEO David Ziv in May 2005, an almost entirely new management team has taken over, and it seems that recent policies, along with the accomplishments of recent years, are in danger of being reversed, casting a shadow on the future direction and viability of the winery.

In recent years, Carmel has risen from being a large producer of primarily mediocre wines to being a winery capable of producing truly excellent wines. These days, however, although embarking on an advertising campaign entitled "New Beginnings" and committing itself to following through on quality upgrades, it seems that many of the changes are being undertaken largely to improve the winery's financial standing. First, several talented winemakers have been released from their contracts. Second, the Handcrafted Wines of Israel project, which was designed to promote the wines of Carmel and a dozen boutique wineries outside Israel, has been abandoned. Carmel's third backward step—which goes against the industry direction of promoting Israeli wines as quality Mediterranean wines of interest to a sophisticated wine-drinking audience abroad—is to focus its export efforts almost entirely on kosher wine consumers. Equally important, although the winery has promised to continue releasing wines in its high-quality single-vineyard and regional series, it seems that far more attention is being directed at producing and promoting lower-priced and, to date, far lower-quality wines, such as Vino and Selected (labeled as Vineyards outside Israel).

DANIEL ROGOV is the wine and restaurant critic for the Israeli daily newspaper *Haaretz* as well as for the Israeli version of the *International Herald Tribune*. He is the author of *Rogov's Guide to Israeli Wines* and is a regular contributor to *Hugh Johnson's Pocket Wine Book*. Rogov also publishes wine and gastronomic reviews and articles on his website, Rogov's Ramblings (www.stratsplace.com/rogov/home.html).

Of the moves deemed as positive, it appears that Carmel is planning to close its winery in Rishon Le Tzion, which is too far away from the country's better vineyards, and to shift part of its operations to its second winery in Zichron Ya'akov in the center of the country and to the newly constructed winery in Ramat Dalton in the Upper Galilee. Another positive move is the decision to stop production of spirits, liqueurs, olive oil, and wine vinegar. In the meantime, Carmel continues to negotiate with several concerns wishing to buy a controlling share of the winery, perhaps the most influential of those being UDV, the Israeli arm of the Coca-Cola Bottling Company.

Israeli wines go abroad

After many years of inactivity, the Ministry of Agriculture and the Ministry of Trade and Industry have decided to promote Israeli wines abroad. Approximately US$1.3 million will go largely to a newly formed California-based group, headed by Doron Rand, the former CEO of Recanati Wineries, which will publicize, import, and distribute wines in the United States.

Stolen wines recovered

In November 2005, thieves broke into Dalton Winery and made off with more than 20,000 bottles. The Israeli police located the culprit and set up a sting operation. The suspect was given "good faith" money by the police and, after several days of negotiation, the wines showed up in a parking lot near a large Jerusalem pub. Although some of the bottles had been roughly handled, most of the cases had not been opened, and tastings held at the winery verified that the wines were neither tampered with nor stored badly while they were missing. The wines are back on the market.

Coca-Cola still on the lookout

The word in the trade these days is that "Coca-Cola isn't finished buying yet." Two years ago, in its attempt to become an all-beverage distributor, UDV, the Israeli branch of Coca-Cola, bought a junior partnership in Tabor Winery, a medium-sized winery producing about 300,000 bottles annually. In October 2005, Coca-Cola increased its holding to 51 percent, giving it full control and raising questions about the future plans of the winery. If the company does not succeed in buying out the far larger Carmel winery, speculators suggest that its plan is to increase production of Tabor to between 2 million and 3 million bottles annually.

Opinion:
Proper regulatory controls required

Since the country currently has no proper regulatory body and no valid appellation control system, labeling and bottling procedures at some wineries are done in an unprofessional, even haphazard, manner. Wines continue to be bottled in batches—sometimes over a period of several months, sometimes over a period of a year or more—and there is no guarantee that the same blend is used from batch to batch. In some cases it is difficult to tell precisely what is in the bottle at all. A bottle labeled as Cabernet Sauvignon may at times have aromas and flavors remarkably similar to those found in wines containing large amounts of Carignan or Argaman grapes.

Cut the red tape

The Israeli Wine Institute remains moribund and unproductive, and there is an increasing amount of overlap in the role of that organization, the Grape and Wine Board, and the Israeli Export Institute. What continues to be needed is a central body that will ensure orderly growth and increased sales, both locally and abroad. Perhaps the most important step would be to replace these obsolete and ineffective organizations with a new institute that could function via full-fledged and enforceable new regulations. Such a body should also have a public-relations function: publishing and distributing educational, promotional, and statistical materials; marketing and promoting Israeli wines abroad; and exhibiting at wine fairs and seminars. The new institute should conduct serious research on determining which grapes are best suited to different subregions within the country and should also encourage cooperation between local wineries.

Appellation system needed

It is increasingly clear that the country needs a proper appellation system. Although the land area of Israel is a mere 7,992 sq miles (20,698 sq km; 5 percent of the land area of California), like many winegrowing regions with a long north–south axis, the country has a large variety of microclimates. In the north, snow falls in winter and conditions are comparable to those of Bordeaux and the northern Rhône Valley, yet within a few hours' drive, one arrives at the Negev Desert, where the climate is similar to that of North Africa. The country is currently divided into five vine-growing regions (Galilee, Shomron, Samson, Judean Hills, and the Negev), but these regions are so badly defined that it is virtually impossible to know where one ends and another begins. Clear-cut rules for appellations should also be extended to labeling regulations.

Suit the grapes to the climate

Many wineries have engaged in overplanting an increasing number of grape varieties during the last decade, and some of these are not appropriate for the Israeli climate. This must be stopped, and there should be a major effort to focus on grapes that will give high-quality wines that can reflect the Mediterranean nature of the country. To complicate matters, several boutique wineries have been releasing 15 or more varietal wines and blends, though their production is below 100,000 bottles annually, which thoroughly confuses the public.

Grapevine

• **Despite structural and financial problems,** Carmel and Barkan continue to produce wines that consistently get rave reviews. Two other large wineries, Binyamina and Efrat, have now joined the ranks of wineries on the way up. Both wineries, now with well-trained winemakers, are in the process of modernizing their equipment, gaining better control over their vineyards, and producing wines that are capturing the attention of sophisticated wine drinkers.

• **"New Beginnings,"** Carmel's new advertising campaign, is perplexing more than a few people. It is certainly true that the winery has taken greater control over its vineyards throughout the country, that it is modernizing in major ways, that young, well-trained winemakers have been brought aboard, and that it has two new series, the Single Vineyard wines of enviably high quality and the Regional Series, which contains several very good to excellent wines. The problem with the campaign is that it implies that the new management initiated these processes, while in fact all these changes were instigated under former CEO David Ziv. Many cannot help but wonder precisely why, if the company is so proud of these accomplishments, they unceremoniously dumped the man who started them.

• **Despite the ever-increasing number** of small and medium-sized wineries appearing on the local scene, Ministry of Trade and Industry figures reveal that the eight largest wineries in the country—Carmel, Barkan, Binyamina, The Golan Heights Winery, Efrat, Recanati, Galil Mountain, and Tishbi—continue to control 95 percent of the market.

• **The battle for control** of Recanati Wineries was finally settled after nearly three years in the courts, with senior partner Lenny Recanati gaining full control over the winery that bears his family name.

• **The Golan Heights Winery,** currently owned by a consortium of *kibbutzim* and agricultural communes, continues to show annual profits, but it is rumored that the winery is seeking an outside investor or, alternatively, considering the option of turning to the stock market to finance further development.

Vintage Report

Advance report on the latest harvest

2005

One of the most promising years in the last decade, with a prolonged harvest of overall high quality, exceptionally good in many parts of the country for reds and whites alike. Barrel tastings reveal wines of excellent balance, structure, and aging potential.

Updates on the previous five vintages

2004

Vintage rating: *Red: 89, White: 91*

A short and hectic harvest, but an excellent crop. Barrel tastings and early releases show greatest strength for whites but good concentration and intensity for reds. Best wines will be elegant and cellar-worthy.

2003

Vintage rating: *Red: 90, White: 90*

An excellent vintage year for both reds and whites, with advance tastings revealing many intense and concentrated but elegant and age-worthy reds. Whites released are drinking nicely now and will cellar comfortably until 2008 or longer.

2002

Vintage rating: *Red: 84, White: 80*

Prolonged heat spells made this a problematic year, both quality- and quantity-wise. Some good and even very good reds and whites, but nearly all are destined for early drinking.

2001

Vintage rating: *Red: 87, White: 85*

This was one of the earliest harvest years in recent history. Overall, a better year for reds than whites, with the whites now fully mature or beyond their peak and the better reds drinking very well now and promising to cellar for four to five years longer.

2000

Vintage rating: *Red: 89, White: 89*

Whites and reds fared equally well during this good vintage. Better reds are just now approaching their peak, and better whites are still drinking well but are not meant for further cellaring.

GREATEST WINE PRODUCERS

1. Golan Heights Winery
   (Katzrin, Yarden, Gamla, Golan)
2. Castel
3. Flam
4. Margalit
5. Yatir
6. Galil Mountain
7. Saslove
8. Amphorae
9. Recanati
10. Carmel

FASTEST-IMPROVING PRODUCERS

1. Carmel
2. Barkan (including Segal)
3. Tabor
4. Dalton
5. Zauberman
6. Vitkin
7. Gush Etzion
8. La Terra Promessa
9. Binyamina
10. Efrat

NEW UP-AND-COMING PRODUCERS

1. Clos de Gat
2. Chateau Golan
3. Ella Valley
4. Sea Horse
5. Bravdo
6. Alexander
7. Gustavo & Jo
8. Bazelet ha Golan
9. Orna Chillag
10. La Terra Promessa

BEST-VALUE PRODUCERS

1. Galil Mountain
2. Golan Heights Winery
3. Dalton
4. Flam
5. Tabor
6. Amphorae
7. Recanati
8. Orna Chillag
9. Saslove
10. Tishbi

GREATEST-QUALITY WINES

1. **Cabernet Sauvignon Special Reserve 2003** Margalit (NIS 160)
2. **Cabernet Sauvignon Reserve 2003** Flam (NIS 155)
3. **Cabernet Sauvignon Kayoumi 2003** Carmel (NIS 135)
4. **Cabernet Sauvignon Yarden 2002** Golan Heights Winery (NIS 135)
5. **Yatir Forest 2003** Yatir (NIS 150)
6. **Elul 2003** Sea Horse (NIS 130)
7. **Special Reserve 2003** Recanati (NIS 135)
8. **Merlot Har Bracha 2002** Carmel (NIS 135)
9. **Cabernet Sauvignon Meron Vineyard 2004** Dalton (NIS 120)
10. **Cabernet Sauvignon Vineyards Choice 2003** Ella Valley (NIS 155)

BEST BARGAINS

1. **Cabernet Sauvignon 2004** Dalton (NIS 45)
2. **Chardonnay Unoaked 2005** Dalton (NIS 35)
3. **Classico 2004** Flam (NIS 65)
4. **Cabernet Sauvignon 2004** Galil Mountain (NIS 55)
5. **Merlot 2004** Galil Mountain (NIS 55)
6. **Merlot Gamla 2003** Golan Heights Winery (NIS 60)
7. **Cabernet Sauvignon 2004** La Terra Promessa (NIS 65)
8. **Shiraz 2003** Recanati (NIS 60)
9. **Chardonnay Bazelet 2004** Tabor (NIS 45)
10. **Pinot Noir Vitkin 2004** (NIS 55)

MOST EXCITING OR UNUSUAL FINDS

1. **Enigma 2004** Margalit (NIS 160) *From one of the very best boutique producers, a Bordeaux blend with a distinct Mediterranean flavor.*
2. **Cabernet Franc 2003** Margalit (NIS 160) *A relatively new grape on the Israeli scene. A remarkably full-bodied and well-balanced varietal wine with distinct aging potential.*
3. **Cabernet Franc 2003** Ella Valley (NIS 135) *Almost impenetrably dark and intense, with surprising but delicious tobacco, coffee, and herbal hints, complementing generous black fruits.*
4. **Viognier Yarden 2004** Golan Heights Winery (NIS 55) *The first successful Viognier wine released in Israel is a round, ripe, and harmonious wine, with classic spicy lychee and lime aromas and flavors.*
5. **Rosé de Merlot 2005** Amphorae (NIS 55) *The first rosé release from this boutique producer is surprisingly complex—perhaps the best rosé wine ever from Israel.*
6. **Noble Semillon Yarden 2004** Golan Heights Winery (NIS 80) *Best release to date of this wine, with generous botrytis influence and finely tuned balance between natural acidity and honeyed sweetness. Round, soft, and creamy, with good cellaring potential.*
7. **Heightswine Yarden 2004** Golan Heights Winery (NIS 85) *Made by cryoextraction in the winery, this year surprising even more than usual with its elegance and richness of honeyed apricot and peach aromas and flavors.*
8. **Chardonnay Reserve Negev Project 2003** Barkan (NIS 55) *Made from grapes grown in the Negev Desert, this medium-bodied unoaked white shows a stony dryness reminiscent at one moment of unoaked Chablis and at the next of a Loire Valley Sauvignon Blanc. Features white peaches, green apples, and citrus fruits on a herbaceous background.*
9. **Barbera 2003** Recanati (NIS 55) *This first Israeli varietal Barbera shows medium body and light tannins, allowing the cherry and berry flavors to come through nicely.*
10. **Zinfandel 2003** Sea Horse (NIS 120) *A complex, medium- to full-bodied, well-balanced wine with ripe and juicy flavors of wild berries, cherries, spices, and a hint of Mediterranean herbs.*

South Africa

Cathy van Zyl MW & Tim James

There's a growing commitment in the Cape to understanding wine as a unique product of soil, climate, and landscape.

CATHY VAN ZYL MW and TIM JAMES

Of course, it is partly a matter of marketing—seeking that "unique selling point" through invoking the natural beauty of the Cape vineyard setting and its biodiversity, while also taking advantage of an internationally expanding interest in the precise, differentiating origins of wines. Recognizing the concept of *terroir* has been part of South Africa's Wine of Origin system since its promulgation in 1973. The dissatisfaction that was felt with many aspects of the old regulatory regime led to too little credit being given to perhaps the oldest and least rudimentary appellation system (of regions, districts, and wards) in the New World.

It is a system that continues to develop and be refined. After decades in which official protection of the "estate" system precluded any label mention of vineyard origins, 2005 saw the first open mention on labels of "single-vineyard" wines. Such vineyards can be no bigger than 5 ha and must be officially registered—making the category rather more meaningful in South Africa than it often is elsewhere.

A further development of *terroir*-defined and registered vineyard sites will follow when it is decided what might be named "Terroir Specific

CATHY VAN ZYL MW and TIM JAMES work together on the quixotic and rigorously independent Grape wine-journalism project, which they founded as a magazine in 1999 but has transmuted into the website www.grape.co.za, for which Tim takes major editorial responsibility. Both also taste for the *John Platter Wine Guide*, and Cathy particularly is in increasing demand as a competition judge. She is also involved in wine education, and in 2005 she became South Africa's first Master of Wine to have qualified while remaining in the country. In addition to Grape, Tim James has written for numerous publications, including *The World of Fine Wine*.

Wine" (TSW) following the results of a multidisciplinary program at the ARC Infruitec-Nietvoorbij Institute of Viticulture and Oenology in conjunction with the University of Stellenbosch. Begun 10 years ago to identify what constitutes *terroir* and its effect on grape quality and style, this program has already had a significant impact on better matching between varieties and locations in the Cape winelands, as well as on current viticultural practices such as canopy management and trellising, and unlocking the potential of new winegrowing areas.

TSWs, says the report of a Wine & Spirit Board working group, will be wines with specific, identifiable, and constant differences, caused by factors such as soil types, local climate, and exposure. Areas for production of TSWs will be demarcated using environmental characteristics, as well as the "renown" of wine produced in those areas.

Grapevine

• **The wines of Klein Constantia,** one of the Cape's most historic properties, are now in the throes of a major workover, following the departure in 2003 of veteran winemaker Ross Gower and the arrival of young Adam Mason. Reds have not been strong for some time, and post-2001 vintages are in abeyance for a few years while they are being rethought. There is unlikely to be a 2003 release of the usually first-class Vin de Constance.

On the other hand, there's a promising new flagship white blend, Mme Marlbrook, a single-vineyard Sauvignon, Perdeblokke, and an emerging "earlier-drinking" KC range, including fruit from the Stellenbosch property Anwilka, which Lowell Jooste owns together with Bordeaux luminaries Bruno Prats and Hubert de Boüard de Laforest (its maiden 2005 released to much acclaim).

• **The number of "declassified"**—or missing—prestigious labels in 2002, notably reds based on bordeaux varieties, might surprise those who doubt the relevance of vintage in warmer climates. Look in vain on the shelves for Morgenster, Vergelegen Cabernet Sauvignon and Merlot, De Trafford Elevation 393, Neil Ellis Vineyard Selection Cabernet, Overgaauw Tria Corda, Cederberg V Generations, and Webersburg.

Meerlust downgraded near-iconic Rubicon to a mere "Red 2002" (as it has on two previous occasions), although owner Hannes Myburgh, like some others, would have preferred to retain the label and lower the price. But price fluctuations reflecting vintage quality are not widely accepted in South Africa.

• **Wines tainted** with *Brettanomyces* (Brett) seem increasingly common—or are they just more noticed as tasters and critics learn to recognize the character? Useful debate continues over just how problematic it all is, but there were discontented rumblings at, for example, some 2005 Veritas high-medalist wines being allegedly affected. Some cellars are going through radical cleanup treatments—hopefully out of the public eye. Ultra-premium Ernie Els, with at least one vintage publicly fingered as Brett-tainted, is now made in its own brand-new cellar, following Jean Engelbrecht's (the golfer owner's partner-in-wine) move from his family home of Rust-en-Vrede.

WINES GO FOR WARDS

Producer interest in defining the subregional origins of their wines is indicated by the growth in the number of wards, the smallest units of the WO system—defined only after expert examination of their plausibility. There are now well over 50, though certainly many do not find their way on to labels.

Nor, admittedly, are they of relevance to most consumers, particularly foreign ones, few of whom are going to be much interested in the tussle over the number and boundaries of wards into which the district of Walker Bay should be divided. And many importers and marketers were sourly disapproving of the aggregation of producers into regional blocks at the 2005 London Mega Tasting of South African wine, arguing that such concepts are irrelevant to their marketing.

Although an unarguable point in the short term, many applaud the stress that Wines of South Africa (WOSA) is putting on origin, and the devotion of many ambitious producers to seeking to establish and express the nature of their *terroirs*.

BIODIVERSITY RULES, OKAY?

A vital and ambitious part of WOSA's strategy is to link Cape wine, via the concept of *terroir* (though the word tends to be downplayed), to the immense richness of the Cape winelands' natural diversity: "Variety is in our nature" runs the main catch phrase. The fourth biennial Cape Wine trade show (held in Cape Town in April 2006) hosted a Wine Diversity Conference, looking at different aspects of the subject, from ecology to marketing to social diversity.

Making the concept relevant, even to many who are dubious about *terroir* claims for Cape wine, is the Biodiversity and Wine Initiative (BWI), an eminently practical partnership between the Botanical Society of South Africa and the South African Wine and Brandy Company, which is actively promoted by WOSA (www.bwi.co.za). The wine industry is starting to do its bit to help save the Cape Floral Kingdom. An ironic thought, perhaps, when one thinks of monocultural landscapes, where all life other than vines is destroyed with the expensive help of agro-chemicals. What chance does the variety of life have when industry starts muscling in?

In fact, increasing numbers of wine producers are joining the BWI as members and committing themselves to the project through specific undertakings to preserve natural vegetation on parts of their estates. BWI project director Tony Hansen is hopeful: "If 50 percent of the wine industry's 5,000 farmers and cellars sign up with the BWI, over one million hectares of natural vegetation could be preserved."

Biodiversity guidelines have also been incorporated into the Integrated Production of Wine guidelines, certification of which provides assurance to wine buyers of sustainable farming practices.

BWI members are also encouraged to showcase their natural environment as well as their wines by incorporating ecotourism activities such as hiking trails or bird hides on their farms. The world's first biodiversity wine route, the Green Mountain Eco Route, has recently been launched in the Overberg region of Elgin, Bot River, and Villiersdorp.

THE HUNT FOR NEW TERROIR

Some believe South Africa's best *terroirs* are still to be discovered and have begun planting vineyards far from traditional production areas. A wine "geographical unit" has been proclaimed covering KwaZulu-Natal, but it is, to say the least, uncertain whether we can expect wines of much interest from this largely tropical zone.

More promisingly, there's Bamboesbaai (Bamboo Bay), providing grapes for the Fryer's Cove label; Sedgefield on the east coast, which has yet to have its first harvest; and Land's End and First Sighting from Cape Agulhas. Agulhas Wines, which owns the First Sighting brand, claims its Uintjieskuil vineyard (named for a local plant) is the most southerly in the country.

The *terroir* pioneers are mainly small independents; industry giant Distell joined the excursion only recently with a joint venture called Lomond Wines. Two Sauvignon Blancs are on the shelves: Sugarbush and Pincushion, also named after indigenous plants. They are from neighboring vineyard blocks to demonstrate the diversity of the *terroir*.

REACHING OUT WITH PLEASURE

The Soweto Wine Festival, the first such event in a "black township," marked an important stage in broadening South Africa's wine culture to include the black majority as informed consumers. While cynics point to the industry's need to develop the local market at a time when exports are challenged, Vukile Mafilika of the Black Vintners' Alliance spoke of hoping to convince new consumers of the pleasures of wine: "Come sample our wines. But don't come because we are black; come because they are good-quality wines." Attendance at the three-day festival was good and enthusiastic, and there are plans to make it an annual event.

TACKLING FOETAL ALCOHOL SYNDROME

Long after the decline of the "dop" system, whereby Cape winery workers were paid partly in liquor and plied with it through the day, the social consequences remain, with alcoholism-ravaged and impoverished communities and a terrible level of fetal alcohol syndrome (FAS). While there remains little in the way of concerted social and industry response to the situation, Beyers Truter of Beyerskloof and formerly of Kanonkop headed the launch of a new initiative: the Fetal Alcoholism and Interrelated Treatment Help Fund (Faith). Fronted by some prominent wineland personalities, Faith (at www.faithfund.co.za) will raise money and awareness, assisting projects such as the recently formed Pebbles Project (www.pebblesproject.co.za).

NOUVELLE IS NEW

Local wine lovers are learning to be blasé about new variety names appearing on labels. One of the latest is home-grown: Nouvelle, created decades ago by oenologist Chris Orffer through crossing Semillon and Crouchen Blanc, but planted commercially only in 1997. Packed with pyrazines, Nouvelle can offer the fashionable green-pepper and grass character and green tropical-fruit flavors sometimes previously achieved with (illegal) additives. Boland Kelder was first to market with a well-accepted single varietal, but Nouvelle's future will probably be mainly in blends.

CHANGE SLOW BUT STEADY

There has been much frustration at delays in producing a solid, long-term —and sustainable—black economic empowerment initiative for the wine industry within the framework of the Economic Empowerment Act. But individual deals continue to be announced, and most of the country's largest players—including KWV, Distell, and Dominion Wine Company—and a small yet growing number of family-owned concerns now share ownership of equity and management positions with black partners. These deals are characterized as "direct empowerment"; there is also an increasing trend of so-called "indirect empowerment." This can be achieved through mentorships and contracting or procurement of consumables and services from black-owned and black-empowered businesses, such as Boland Vineyards International using a partly black-owned marketing company.

FIRST WINES FROM BLACK WINEMAKERS

It's a few years since we saw the first trickle of black winemakers since the demise of apartheid. Two have now realized a dream of making wines under their own labels. Mzo Mvemve, winemaker for the Cape Classics Indaba range, launched Sagila with the blessing of his employers, Gary and André Shearer. And Tseliso Rangaka offers three new wines from his family's Stellenbosch farm, M'hudi (Setswana for "harvester").

Grapevine

• **White blends are on the rise.** Who would have thought, five years back, that they would have taken two of the niggardly 11 five-star ratings in the prestigious *John Platter Wine Guide 2006*? They also occupy the top places in our own Top 10 list and neatly exemplify the two main styles: Vergelegen blending Sauvignon and Semillon; Palladius with Viognier, Chenin, Chardonnay, and Grenache Blanc. Prestige wines were usually red—bar an occasional Chardonnay or Sauvignon. Now there are more and more flagship white blends, and this might well be the Cape's most exciting category—even above the much-vaunted Shiraz.

Opinion:
Riesling's name still taken in vain

In response to producer and critical agitation, a working group was set up by the Wine & Spirit Board to look again into the situation where the name Riesling in South Africa is, scandalously, reserved for the lackluster grape now known to be Crouchen Blanc, while the real thing must be encumbered by Weisser or Rhine as a prefix for local sale. Not altogether surprisingly, giant producer Distell was victorious with its objections to change, protecting big-selling Nederburg Riesling and Theuniskraal Riesling (both made from Crouchen). As a result of the board's short-sighted and irresponsible weakness, the Cape's (real) Riesling plantings decline apace, though a few fine wines continue to be made.

You can't eat equity

Given the high capital costs associated with vineyards and cellars, it must be asked whether the focus of black economic empowerment (BEE) on black economic equity rather than social upliftment and poverty reduction is not misguided. It is unlikely that many of the employee trusts result in meaningful dividends after tax, interest, and loan repayments. Greater investment in housing, schooling, health care, job creation, and equity opportunities in allied industries with far lower barriers to entry could have a greater impact (equity deals will logically follow). Or does owning a percentage of something amount to "usefully empowered," even when something is next to nothing?

Conflicts of interest

It's not something unique to South Africa, of course, but too many journalists are also consultants to wineries, or own wine shows, or provide professional public-relations services to parts of the industry.

Buying your way onto wine lists

Increasingly irritating to smaller producers is the cozy (and corrupt, some would say) relationship between some restaurants and a few of the very biggest wine producers. It goes far beyond supplying logo-bearing umbrellas or ice buckets: a producer can pay large sums to have a major influence on a wine list; and a few restaurants now try to extort substantial payment from even small producers (the famous ones generally excepted, of course).

Vintage Report

Advance report on the latest harvest
2006

Vintage generalizations are risky, especially for diverse areas; 2006 seems likely to require particularly careful selection. Much threatened: winds hampered shoot growth and caused uneven set; ripening months saw heat stressing vines and auguring sky-high sugars; runaway fires burned or smoke-contaminated vineyards, especially in Franschhoek. Less naturally, for a crucial few harvest weeks, a series of power cuts brought major problems to cellars without generators. But most winemakers in all areas seem enthusiastic about quality. Drought meant small, concentrated berries. Combinations of factors that are not always fully understood gave many pHs that were lower than usual, and satisfactory ripeness at lower sugar levels, with alcohols down a welcome degree or two—though not everywhere (not the Overberg, for example). Sauvignon, Chenin, and Pinotage seem to be among the best performers; Shiraz notably less so. Volumes should be much the same as the modest 2005s.

Updates on the previous five vintages
2005

Vintage rating: *Red: 85, White: 85*

A tricky, short harvest in general; early-season rain promoted mildew and excessive vigor, then heat announced shorter hang times than usual, as sugar levels soared. Some growers, particularly inland, had to contend with unseasonal mid-harvest rains. The total yield just topped 1.2 million tons, about 12 percent less than 2004. Reds all around are concentrated, if alcoholic; full, firmly structured wines came from the coastal regions. There are exceptions, but whites are mostly average.

2004

Vintage rating: *Red: 88, White: 88*

Long and mainly healthy harvest, with one of the largest-ever crops. Cool conditions during flowering prompted uneven berry set; many of the best growers did a green harvest to promote even ripening. Shiraz and Merlot are particularly fine, as are early-picked Chardonnay and Sauvignon Blanc.

2003

Vintage rating: *Red: 95, White: 90*

Across the board, yields were up some 12 percent on 2002. Quality-wise, the vintage stands well above many in the past 25 years, with well-structured, generous reds and fine whites.

2002

Vintage rating: *Red: 75, White: 80*

Prolonged winter rains led to downy mildew and excessive botrytis; an intense February heat wave accelerated ripening, and many had to accommodate late-maturing whites/early-ripening reds simultaneously. Shiraz emerged relatively unscathed.

2001

Vintage rating: *Red: 88, White: 88*

A hot, dry, largely disease-free vintage, yielding highly concentrated, tannic reds. Whites picked between the heat waves were full of flavor but alcoholic.

Grapevine

• **Hamilton Russell Vineyards** celebrated its 25th vintage of Pinot Noir in 2006, while former HRV winemaker Kevin Grant, who left after 10 successful vintages to do his own thing in 2004, added a Chardonnay and a Cabernet/Merlot to the Sauvignon Blanc appearing under the Ataraxia label. Grant's own Pinot Noir vineyards in the Hemelen-Arde ("Heaven and Earth") Valley made vinously famous by HRV come on-stream only in 2010.

• **Following earlier maiden launches** from Bon Cap Winery (the Cape's first organically grown Viognier, the first organic-certified port-style wine), vintage 2006 saw this dynamic Robertson outfit making the first Méthode Cap Classique wine from organically grown Chardonnay.

• **Embossed bottles** are becoming more common. First off the mark were the collegial vintners of the prime Constantia region, stressing their architectural heritage with a stylized Cape Dutch gable and the words "1685 Constantia South Africa" molded in glass. The Worcester Winelands Association followed with an apparent world first: there have been many labels with Braille script, but here the claret bottle itself is embossed with "100% Worcester, South Africa." The town of Worcester is as well known for its institutions for the blind and the deaf as it is for its substantial wines.

• **Lanzerac Rosé,** a former iconic wine in a skittle-shaped bottle, has come back to the shelves with much fanfare. When businessman Christo Wiese acquired the Lanzerac property and brand, the previous owners (now merged into Distell) retained rights to the most famous couplings: Lanzerac Pinotage and Lanzerac Rosé. By agreement, the former label reverted to Wiese a few years ago, but he got his hands on the Rosé rights only in 2006.

GREATEST WINE PRODUCERS

1. Vergelegen
2. Sadie Family
3. Boekenhoutskloof
4. Kanonkop
5. Thelema
6. Hamilton Russell Vineyards
7. Rustenberg
8. Steenberg
9. Charles Back (Fairview, Spice Route, etc)
10. Jordan

NEW UP-AND-COMING PRODUCERS

1. Capaia
2. Vilafonté
3. Tokara
4. The Foundry
5. Tulbagh Mountain Vineyards
6. Solms-Delta
7. Fryer's Cove
8. Saronsberg Cellar
9. Katbakkies
10. Tierhoek

FASTEST-IMPROVING PRODUCERS

1. Rijk's
2. Lammershoek
3. Constantia Uitsig
4. The Winery
5. Groot Constantia
6. Paul Cluver
7. Kleine Zalze
8. Scali
9. Robertson Winery
10. Bein Wine

BEST-VALUE PRODUCERS

1. Perdeberg Cooperative
2. Buitenverwachting
3. Eikendal Vineyards
4. Alto Estate
5. Du Toitskloof
6. Van Loveren
7. Villiera Wines
8. Welgemeend Estate
9. Paul Cluver
10. Porcupine Ridge (Boekenhoutskloof)

Grapevine

• **Inner-city winemaking** is not a new concept for Jean-Vincent Ridon of Signal Hill. The resident Frenchman has a vineyard in the Cape Town residential suburb of Oranjezicht, and he was invited by the mayor of Paris to work on the 2001 vintage of Clos Montmartre. In another coup, in 2005 he secured the prestigious contract for a winery at a vast redevelopment in the central business district, Mandela Rhodes Place (maiden vintage in 2006).

• **Despite Viognier's apparent ubiquity,** it still occupies less than 1 percent of the national vineyard (up from nonexistence a decade ago). In line with the rest of the world, its popularity among growers—and, they hope, among drinkers—seems to increase daily, as does the number of varietal bottlings. Viognier also appears, à la Côte Rôtie, as an adjunct to many a Shiraz or even with other reds (including co-fermented with Pinotage from the ever-innovative Charles Back of Fairview).

• **Wineries are upping** the culture option, with art appreciation and acquisition the latest "must do" activity on the Cape's wine routes. Numerous cellars now give artists an opportunity to show their work. Some galleries are as casual and informal as that at Zorgvliet, while others are as grand as Tokara's. Now the Hess Group's Donald Hess—art collector, wine producer, and new owner of Glen Carlou—has added exhibition space at the Paarl winery to build on his success with the Hess Collection Winery in Napa.

GREATEST-QUALITY WINES

1. **Vergelegen White 2004**
Vergelegen (R226)
2. **Palladius 2004**
Sadie Family (R237)
3. **Vin de Constance 2000**
Klein Constantia (R275)
4. **Columella 2003**
Sadie Family (R390)
5. **Merlot Reserve 2003**
Thelema (R257)
6. **Schaapenberg Reserve 2003**
Vergelegen (R245)
7. **Crescendo 2003** Cordoba (R170)
8. **Christine 2001**
Buitenverwachting (R160)
9. **Semillon 2005** Steenberg (R130)
10. **Syrah 2003**
Boekenhoutskloof (R245)

BEST BARGAINS

1. **Chardonnay 2004**
Vergelegen (R69)
2. **Cabernet Sauvignon 2001**
Buitenverwachting (R85)
3. **The Summer House 2002**
Morgenster (R55)
4. **Sauvignon Blanc Reserve 2004**
Cape Chamonix (R43)
5. **Petit Chenin 2005**
Ken Forrester (R30)
6. **Roulette 2003**
Lammershoek (R105)
7. **Sauvignon Blanc 2005**
Durbanville Hills (R39)
8. **Chenin Blanc 2005** Perdeberg
Cooperative (R16—farm only)
9. **Goats do Roam White 2004**
Charles Back (R36)
10. **Colombard 2005** McGregor (R25)

MOST EXCITING OR UNUSUAL FINDS

1. **Pinotage/Syrah 2004**
The Observatory (R100) *Perhaps the most elegantly exuberant Pinotage-based wine around, from a biodynamically farmed Perdeberg vineyard. Recalls winemaker Tom Lubbe's other base in Roussillon.*
2. **Black Rock Red 2004** The Winery (R93) *Enchanting southern-Rhône-inspired blend. Unlike many peers, this trades on elegance rather than power.*
3. **Gewurztraminer 2004** Paul Cluver (R59) *The aromatic joys of growing this variety in cool Elgin.*
4. **Roussanne 2004** Rustenberg (R115) *Peachy, unoaked, and rounded rarity from a respected and regal producer with the Cape's first 2.5 ha of the variety.*
5. **La Siesta Grenache Blanc 2005** Signal Hill (R39) *Exuberantly and zippily rings the changes for local palates bored with Chardonnay and the other, better-known Blancs. South Africa's first varietal bottling.*
6. **Syrah/Carignan 2003** The Observatory (R189) *Defiantly against the prevailing ultra-ripe blockbuster grain: early picked (12.5 percent alcohol), mostly older oak. Intellectual, soulful stuff.*
7. **Enthopio 2003** Vriesenhof (R60) *Muscular yet supple Pinotage-dominated blend from Pinotagephile and ex-rugby international Jan Coetzee.*
8. **Lekkerwijn 2004** Solms-Delta (R56) *The Cape's best yet example in the increasingly interesting category of rosé; from Mourvèdre, Grenache, and Viognier.*
9. **Green on Green 2004** Jack & Knox Winecraft (R66) *Oak wraps itself gently around this silky, lemon-fresh Semillon from Bruce Jack and Graham Knox—seekers-out of special vineyards.*
10. **Agostinelli Barbera 2004** Fairview (R78) *Part of an experimental range of young-vine wines from the Italian part of the Swartland.*

California

Dan Berger

In the middle of the first decade of the 21st century, California's wine production was growing in volume due to greater consumer demand and large harvests.

DAN BERGER

At the same time, the industry was sinking in terms of number of owners, as multinational corporations took over more and more brands. But instead of shelf space accommodating the existing brands, many of the larger wineries began to create even more brands.

The trend of a single company pushing a dozen brands on the market was first seen as a viable strategy a decade earlier by Fred Franzia of Bronco Wine Co. in Ceres, in California's central San Joaquin Valley. Franzia, related by marriage to Ernest Gallo, acquired wine brands like a stamp collection and soon had companions to his own Forest Glen and Forest Ville brands such as Hacienda, Rutherford Vintners, Napa Ridge, Estrella, Grand Cru, Crane Lake, and the hugely successful Charles Shaw, the $2 wine dubbed "Two-Buck Chuck."

Virtually every wine in the Franzia portfolio sold for less than $10 a bottle, and the multiple brands filled shelves that otherwise might have held competing wines. Part of the Bronco strategy was to make use of the company's 33,000 acres of vineyard land, almost all of it in the hot, interior San Joaquin Valley.

The multiple-brand idea was so successful that many others began to fill the under-$10 niche. The major player was the world's largest

DAN BERGER contributes a nationally distributed wine column weekly to Creators Syndicate; publishes his own weekly newsletter on wine, *Berger's Vintage Experiences*; and writes trade-magazine articles for US magazines *Cheers*, *Beverage Dynamics*, and *Wines and Vines*, as well as *Off Licence News* and *Decanter* in London. He is a speaker at major wine symposiums around the world and is a judge at numerous wine competitions in the United States and abroad. He also coordinates the Riverside International and Long Beach wine competitions in southern California.

wine company, New York-based Constellation Brands, with its upscale Simi, Ravenswood, Columbia, Estancia, Mount Veeder, Robert Mondavi, and Franciscan labels. Adding to its lower-priced Dunnewood and Blackstone names, in late 2005 the company acquired the fast-rising HRM Rex Goliath brand from Nicholas Hahn, giving Constellation more power in the $10 niche.

In reaction, many upmarket brands looked to their regional marketing arms for assistance in getting the word out that a wine bearing a label with a subappellation was worth paying more to acquire. Gallo was already using nearly a dozen different brands, Kendall-Jackson added a handful (including two smaller boxed wines), and Foster's Group also added new brands.

At the same time, growers and wineries in both Mendocino and Sonoma counties began to discuss the impact that a self-funded marketing initiative would have on their members. It coincided with the 15th anniversary of a hugely successful merger of growers and wineries in the Lodi-Woodbridge winegrowing district.

Percentage of truth

The federal government approved a proposal by California's Wine Institute that lowers the minimum amount of wine from a vintage from 95 percent to 85 percent in wines with a state or county designation. This plan gives winemakers more flexibility in blending, allowing them to even out quality from one year to the next. The rule applies only to wines with an American Viticultural Appellation, such as Napa Valley or Sonoma Mountain.

Dubious additives

Numerous California wineries are using wine additives called Mega Purple or Mega Red to their red wines, notably those wines that sell for $20 and under. The additives, which are legal because they are by-products of grapes, add color to wines, as well as weight and texture, since they contain a high percentage of sugar and have an aroma that might charitably be called "Central Valley Red."

Grapevine

- **Consolidation of the US wine market** continued with the acquisition of Allied Domecq's wine assets by Fortune Brands, the parent company of Geyser Peak and Wild Horse Winery. After the $14.2-billion deal, Fortune gained control of huge Clos du Bois, as well as Carneros-based Buena Vista.

Opinion:
Misleading label terms

Consumers are increasingly questioning whether some wines are worth their exalted pricing, and this is leading many winemakers to reconsider how they have escalated prices in the last decade.

Part of the strategy that led to higher pricing was the use of terms on labels that indicated a higher quality—terms such as Reserve, Old Vines, Special Selection, Estate, Barrel Select, and so forth. But most of these terms have no meaning. There is no legal definition for them.

For example, a number of wineries have used the term "estate" to imply grapes grown on a small farm, when in fact the wines are made in the hundreds of thousands of cases and are anything but estate wines.

Seeking to display their quality, many wineries focused on their appellations and on telling the consumer all the benefits of each of them. Despite the fact that many of these wines do not have any regional distinctiveness, that is the message we are getting.

Since wines are being made from riper and riper grapes, the regional character is being compromised, which makes it harder to justify some of the "appellation character" statements that we see in press releases and on back-label copy.

Some wines seem immune from consumer concern over their prices. In particular, the so-called cult Cabernets of the Napa Valley remain a hot commodity with the wealthy. Many have risen in price in the last year with no discernible decline in sales. Phelps's Insignia, rated as one of the greatest red wines in the world year after year, rose $15 a bottle to $145 with the 2002 vintage, even though some earlier wines were far more impressive.

Higher alcohol levels in many California wines have also had a negative impact on some savvy retailers and restaurant wine buyers. In the last year, many of the gatekeepers have been avoiding the brutish beasts, claiming that they and their patrons want to consume wine with food and the massively constituted red wines especially may be fine for the tasting table, but not the dinner table.

It's true that the "hot" brands remain the major quest of the wealthy, but better-balanced red wines are the primary goal of many retailers and restaurateurs.

Vintage Report

Advance report on the latest harvest

2005

Spring was one of the coolest on record in California's north coast, with rains hammering at the vines late. A June 9/10 rain left more than 1 in (25 mm) of water, and measurable amounts were recorded as late as June 16. This left the area with severe mildew problems, necessitating drastic measures in some areas to prevent botrytis from developing. Cool weather in late spring and summer exacerbated the problems, and the harvest was a curious one, with some black grapes (such as Pinot Noir) being picked before whites. Most areas of the state reported a bumper crop, and the harvest was one of the largest on record. But in portions of coastal strips, such as along the Sonoma Coast and in Russian River and Green Valley, Pinot Noir tonnage was down to a fraction of normal. However, the cool weather provided excellent acid levels, and overall quality was rated to be exceptional.

Updates on the previous five vintages

2004

Vintage rating: *96*

A warm spring got vines off to a fast start. But two months of cooler weather followed, then two weeks of summer heat. That made for one of the earliest harvests in decades, running three to four weeks ahead of normal. The first grapes, for sparkling wine, were picked on July 23. Quality was rated as excellent. Tonnage declines of about 5 percent were reported in most Napa and Sonoma regions. The decrease followed nearly a decade of overproduction and low prices, both of which prompted growers to reduce acreage and slow new plantings.

2003

Vintage rating: *93*

Early rains and late heat spikes contributed to lower overall yields. The result was a vintage of high quality, good color concentration, and intensity of flavor. Heat in March led to shatter, reducing crop size. Then a cold May left the crop a month behind schedule. Dramatic heat spikes in September moved the harvest forward a bit after many felt it would be a late year. There was a rush to get everything harvested, and much came in at the same time. Reds had high acid, high sugar, and low pH, making for wines that were hard to judge early on, but winemakers were pleased with the balance they got.

2002

Vintage rating: *90*

No prolonged summer heat, just many short heat spells late in the season, resulting in excessively high sugars in many varieties. The heat spells occurred after a relatively cool summer, so sugars rose quickly. Some awkward reds; whites survived better, since the slightly cooler summer left Chardonnay, Sauvignon Blanc, and Pinot Gris with good acids.

2001

Vintage rating: *93*

A warm summer followed by a cooling trend in September brought acids back up. Some fruit was harvested early, leading to better acidity structure. An excellent vintage with great potential for reds that will be aged.

2000

Vintage rating: *89*

An El Niño vintage. Flavors for most grapes were satisfactory, but many reds lacked body and richness unless harvested late, although the later flavors were a little contrived. Many reds appear to be aging reasonably well. Choose carefully.

Grapevine

• **Supermarkets are watching you,** as many chains ask major wine companies to adopt radio frequency identification (RFID) technology for their wine bottles. The idea is that the tiny RFID attachments will allow markets to track wine sales more closely. They are also useful for inventory control. Another use of RFID technology may well be to target sales to buyers in certain demographic groups.

• **Organic viticulture** is spreading, albeit without much fanfare. Numerous smaller California wineries are moving toward organic farming, with some adopting the even more radical biodynamic approach. Although the methods are more time-consuming, and thus a bit more costly, adherents argue that organic and biodynamic grapes make better wines.

• **White wines with lower alcohol,** unabashedly targeting women, are hitting US store shelves. White Lie from Beringer has only 9.8 percent alcohol.

GREATEST WINE PRODUCERS

1. Joseph Phelps
2. Stag's Leap Wine Cellars
3. Navarro
4. Au Bon Climat
5. Gloria Ferrer
6. Freemark Abbey
7. Gary Farrell
8. Robert Sinskey
9. Gundlach Bundschu
10. Dutton Goldfield

FASTEST-IMPROVING PRODUCERS

1. Trentadue
2. Firestone/Curtis
3. Beckmen
4. Ortman
5. Morgan
6. Mahoney
7. Clos du Bois
8. Dry Creek
9. Castoro
10. Charles Krug

NEW UP-AND-COMING PRODUCERS

1. Sonoma Coast Vineyards
2. Campion
3. Robert Hall
4. Foley
5. Shannon Ridge
6. Katherine Hall
7. Holdredge
8. Sesquipedalian
9. Copeland Creek
10. Rusack

BEST-VALUE PRODUCERS

1. Fetzer
2. Sutter Home
3. Kendall-Jackson
4. Bogle
5. Dancing Bull
6. McManis
7. Canyon Road
8. Toad Hollow
9. Jewell
10. Mirassou

GREATEST-QUALITY WINES

1. **Insignia Cabernet Sauvignon 2002** Joseph Phelps, Napa Valley ($145)
2. **Gewurztraminer 2004** Navarro, Anderson Valley ($16)
3. **Pinot Noir 2003** Dutton Goldfield, Russian River Valley, Sanchietti Vineyard ($52)
4. **Pinot Noir 2003** Morgan, Santa Lucia Highlands, Gary's Vineyard ($45)
5. **Cabernet Sauvignon 2000** Corison, Napa Valley, Kronos Vineyard ($75)
6. **Syrah 2003** Dutton Goldfield, Russian River Valley, Cherry Ridge ($35)
7. **Zinfandel 2002** Gary Farrell, Russian River Valley, Maple Vineyard, Tina's Block ($36)
8. **Zinfandel 2003** Dutton Goldfield, Russian River Valley, Morrelli Lane ($35)
9. **Cabernet Sauvignon 2001** Beringer, St. Helena, Chabot Vineyard ($90)
10. **Toreador Zinfandel 2004** Rancho Zabaco, Sonoma Valley, Monte Rosso Vineyard ($50)

Grapevine

• **The Alcohol and Tobacco Tax and Trade Bureau,** which regulates wine in the United States, says it is looking at developing a technique to determine the varietal makeup of bottled wine. It also said that it is investigating whether wine bottles should have larger and more detailed warning labels, including a listing of "ingredients."

BEST BARGAINS

1. **Reds 2003** Laurel Glen Vineyards, Lodi ($8)
2. **Sauvignon Blanc 2004** Canyon Road, California ($7)
3. **Syrah 2003** Bishop's Peak, Edna Valley ($16)
4. **Edelzwicker 2004** Navarro, Mendocino ($11)
5. **Pacific Rim Riesling [2004]** Bonny Doon, America ($9)
6. **Stone Cellars Zinfandel 2003** Beringer, California ($8)
7. **Petite Sirah 2003** Bogle, California ($10)
8. **Cabernet Sauvignon 2003** Stephen Vincent, California ($9)
9. **Chenin Blanc 2005** Dry Creek, Clarksburg ($13)
10. **Cabernet Franc 2004** Hahn Estate, Santa Lucia Highlands ($14)

MOST EXCITING OR UNUSUAL FINDS

1. **Chasselas Doré 2004** Berthoud, Sonoma Valley ($15) *Pineapple, white plums, and pears, and a hint of sake! Dry but still succulent.*
2. **Chenin Blanc 2004** Milat, Napa Valley ($18) *Melon, ripe peach, and fresh tarragon. Relatively sweet, but perfect balance.*
3. **Grignolino 2001** Heitz, Napa Valley ($14.25) *Distinctive black and red pepper, herbal notes, a trace of spice, and a faint hint of orange peel.*
4. **Sonoma Coast Chardonnay 2002** Hawk Hill Vineyard, Sonoma Coast ($55) *Dramatic floral and complex notes of shallots and hazelnuts; bone dry, no malolactic. A long-lived, racy wine for food.*
5. **Grenache Rosé 2004** Beckmen, Santa Ynez Valley, Purisima Mountain ($15) *Maraschino cherry, strawberry, cranberry, and a hint of watermelon. Dry but succulent.*
6. **Abraxas 2004** Robert Sinskey, Carneros ($28) *Dramatic blend of Pinot Blanc, Pinot Gris, and Gewurztraminer, with a dash of Riesling. Exotic spicy aroma, succulent, but dry. No malolactic or oak.*
7. **Cabernet Sauvignon 1999** Mayacamas, Napa Valley ($65) *An Old World style of Cabernet with classic herbal nuances and a long future ahead.*
8. **Barbera 2003** Shannon Ridge, Lake County ($19) *A first-ever release from a new winery and a near-perfect expression of the variety, with bright cherry fruit and a load of acidity for pairing with food.*
9. **Sauvignon Blanc 2004** Nalle, Dry Creek Valley ($20) *A cross between the Loire and Graves: 60 percent malolactic, but no oak; lime-scented and bracing acidity. Needs five more years.*
10. **Cluster Select Late Harvest Riesling 2003** Navarro, Anderson Valley ($29 per half-bottle) *Stunning Riesling florality with hints of peach, apricot, and honey. Perfect acid to balance 22 percent residual sugar.*

Grapevine

• **Interstate shipping,** which became a near-reality after a May 2005 ruling by the US Supreme Court, now allows greater consumer access to the nation's boutique wines. Sensational Rieslings from Michigan and New York are being shipped around the country, and some of California's tiny (and underfunded) wineries now have outlets in far-flung states. At the end of 2005, some wineries reported that Internet sales had jumped by 20–30 percent following the ruling.

Pacific Northwest

Paul Gregutt

The 2005 federal Supreme Court ruling on interstate wine-shipping laws basically tossed that hot potato right back at each state.

PAUL GREGUTT

The high court ruled that shipping laws had to be applied equally to both in-state and out-of-state wineries. In Washington, whose wine industry is second only to California in terms of US production, that has led to a hardening of positions on all sides, and there is no resolution in sight.

Since Prohibition ended, Washington has had a state-run liquor control board and a three-tier distribution system for wine and spirits. But in-state wineries may bypass the three-tier system and ship directly to consumers in-state. They may also ship wines directly to any reciprocal state whose laws allow their wineries to ship to Washington.

The Washington Wine Institute, hoping to open up shipping across the nation, is lobbying for a change in the law to allow any winery in any state to ship wine directly to Washington customers. This change would mean that Washington wineries could ship to nonreciprocal states, such as New York.

Another complication is the ongoing lawsuit filed by Costco Wholesale Corporation against the Washington State Liquor Control Board (WSLCB). In February 2004, Costco, the nation's largest wine retailer, headquartered in Seattle, Washington, charged the WSLCB with "establishing and supporting monopoly power, imposing a trust, fixing prices, limiting production, regulating transportation, conferring privileges and immunities, lending state credit, and discriminating against out-of-state wineries and brewers."

PAUL GREGUTT lives in Seattle and is the wine columnist for *The Seattle Times*, *Yakima Herald-Republic*, and *Walla Walla Union-Bulletin*. He is a contributing editor to *Wine Enthusiast* magazine and the author of *Northwest Wines* (Sasquatch Books, 1996). His next book (to be published mid-2007) is *Insider's Guide to Washington Wines* (University of California Press).

In broad terms, the suit seeks to overturn restrictions that prevent the Seattle-based chain from purchasing wine directly from producers, receiving volume discounts, and engaging in the type of discount pricing that it applies to virtually every other type of consumer product in its 470+ stores.

The WSLCB has been supported by the strangest of bedfellows— the Washington Beer & Wine Wholesalers Association (WBWWA), which ordinarily finds itself at odds with the state over its dual role of both regulating and selling wine and spirits. But in this instance the wholesalers argue that allowing unimpeded direct shipping of wines would put small independent wineries and breweries out of business, hurt distributors, and ultimately reduce product choice for the consumer.

As the suit moved ponderously toward a hearing in the spring of 2006, Costco chief executive Jim Sinegal called that argument "nonsense" and noted that less regulated states have a better selection and lower prices. Which seems true: as the laws now stand, Washington's complex liquor regulations add significantly to the cost of a bottle of wine purchased in-state; so much so that even wines produced in Washington may frequently be purchased at lower prices in California and elsewhere.

Anticipating a Costco victory, the Liquor Control Board filed a brief threatening to eliminate all direct shipment of wine and beer. This lit a fire under the Washington Wine Institute, which lobbies for the state's wine industry. They too filed a brief decrying any such proposal as "crippling" for the hundreds of small (under 2,500 cases) producers who comprise the vast majority of the state's wineries.

Meanwhile, the WSLCB has initiated a comprehensive task-force study to evaluate a potential overhaul to the entire antiquated system. Long overdue!

Red Mountain poised for development

Washington's Red Mountain AVA, home to the state's priciest grapes (Klipsun), its most experimental vineyard (Ciel du Cheval), and its newest joint-venture winery (Col Solare), seems to be ripe for further development. After all, although it includes 4,000 acres within its boundaries, barely 700 have been planted. The reason? Lack of water.

Now it appears that the dam preventing new development, so to speak, is giving way. The state Department of Natural Resources, which owns hundreds of raw acres of Red Mountain land and controls the region's water rights, has accepted bids for long-term leases of four parcels. Some 86 acres have been leased for new vineyards and wineries. The new leases set into motion the first stage of an ambitious plan, backed by most of the wineries and vineyards currently located within the AVA, to expand tourism in the region.

A similar concept is being explored in Walla Walla, where Norm Mckibben (Pepper Bridge), Chris and Gary Figgins (Leonetti Cellar), and Marty and Megan Clubb (L'Ecole No 41) have purchased 1,700 acres of high-elevation (900–1,500 ft [274–457 m]) land surrounding the existing Seven Hills vineyard. Two deep basalt wells have found ample water, and the group is now working with the county for permission to divide the 1,000 plantable acres into 20- or 40-acre parcels. These will be sold as estate vineyard sites once the partners have selected their own vineyard blocks. Before further development can begin, the partners are completing work on the infrastructure of pumps, ponds, power, and roads. A long waiting list of interested parties is already in place.

New Horse Heaven Hills AVA

Washington State gained its seventh appellation with the certification of Horse Heaven Hills in August 2005. The Horse Heaven Hills AVA stretches along south-facing slopes above the Columbia river on the Washington/ Oregon border. It currently includes four wineries with 6,040 acres of wine grapes planted—roughly one-fifth of the state's total acreage. According to the Washington Wine Commission, as much as two-thirds of the region—570,000 acres—could one day produce quality grapes.

Horse Heaven Hills' 20 vineyards already provide grapes for many of the region's premier wineries. Major grape varieties for which it is known are Chardonnay, Riesling, Semillon, Syrah, Merlot, and Cabernet Sauvignon. The first vineyard to be planted was the Mercer Ranch, in 1972. Now called Champoux vineyard, it is home to some of the oldest Cabernet vines in the country.

The state's largest winery, Columbia Crest, is headquartered in the heart of the AVA, and Ste. Michelle's red wines are made at its Canoe Ridge Estate facility a few miles down the road. The region is protected from the bitter freezes that can strike eastern Washington by its proximity to the warming influence of the Columbia River. Another defining factor is its relentless wind, which keeps canopies dry and helps control disease, while moderating temperatures throughout the growing season.

Why the name? Legend has it that a rancher, camping in the hills 150 years ago, followed his horses up a mountainside to an upland meadow where they were happily chewing on bunch grass. "Surely this is horse heaven," he was heard to remark.

Opinion:
Overhaul of the Liquor Control Board

Washington State Governor Christine Gregoire has asked the Washington State Liquor Control Board for an independent review of projected revenue growth, the impact of increased sales on public safety, operational and policy efficiencies, and possible organizational restructuring.

The laws governing the purchase, sale, and distribution of beer, wine, and spirits in Washington date back more than 70 years. They are hopelessly out of date. The state is caught in the untenable position of having to both regulate and sell these products, opening it up to charges of being a state-run monopoly. It also finds itself trying to manage its thousands of stores profitably, while not appearing to promote the use of alcohol.

It has a burgeoning, multibillion-dollar wine industry under its supervision (one of the few agricultural success stories in a state where the apple, asparagus, and wheat industries are on life support), yet state liquor stores cannot hold wine tastings, distribute educational materials, or even sell corkscrews!

There are more than 800 wineries in the Pacific Northwest, double that number in California, and hundreds more scattered across the rest of the country. Almost none of them is benefiting from laws that make their products extremely difficult to market, distribute, ship, and sell.

Online shopping is here to stay. The current regulations are confusing, haphazardly applied, and often irrelevant. A complete and thorough overhaul of how to redesign the system to manage all these issues is a daunting task, to be sure, but the current situation is clogging up the courts and making criminals of consumers who just want a glass of wine with their dinner.

Fewer single-vineyard Pinots, more affordable bottles

Spurred on by the movie *Sideways*, consumers are becoming enamoured of the charms of Pinot Noir, and the big wine companies are taking notice. Suddenly, in splashy new lineups such as Twin Fin (Constellation Brands), Pinot is the star of the show. The good news is that, for the first time in a long time, consumers have a wide array of under-$10 Pinot Noirs to choose from, at least from California.

Oregon vintners have not stood up so well to the competition. The newfound consumer enthusiasm for Pinot Noir should serve them notice that most people are not looking for a $60 single-vineyard bottling. They want soft, fruity, and light Pinot Noir costing $8. California now owns the category. Oregon, which used to be "Da Man" for Pinot outside Burgundy, had better watch its back.

Oregon's best Pinot producers have been making single-vineyard wines for the past two decades, but in recent vintages a dribble has become a flood. These single-vineyard Pinots are virtually always more expensive than the blends, and prices have crept steadily up from the mid-$30s to $60 and up. Most of the time, a winery's reserve-level blended Pinots are cheaper and just as good, if not better, than its single-vineyard wines. Producers should make more blends at reasonable price points and limit the single-vineyard releases to those that truly warrant them.

Quick shots across the bow (and barrel)

Let's get serious about defining and/or limiting the use of the term "Reserve" on wine labels. There is no more abused, misleading, and frequently worthless adjective on a wine label than "Reserve"—unless you know and trust the reputation of the producer. The Washington Wine Quality Alliance (WWQA), a voluntary organization of wineries and grape growers, has set out guidelines for its members. Among them: reserve wines must be among the higher-priced wines produced by the winery and can apply only to the greater of 3,000 cases or 10 percent of the winery's production of the given varietal or blend. A good start—and one that California, with industrial wineries churning out hundreds of thousands of cases of reserve this and that, might wish to emulate.

There are too many awards, medals, and ratings competitions concocted by small magazines that use them to flatter wineries and sell ads. Advice to wineries: if you want medals, awards, and scores to mean something, investigate the person or publication awarding them. Of course you are delighted when the editors of *Tongue Monthly* give your wine a Triple Platinum Salubrious Cork of the Year award. But what does that really mean? How independent are their voices? One quick measure of an award's merit: is the publication that bestowed it ever truly critical of a wine or winery? If the lowest rating they ever publish is good, then what's bad?

Lose the plastic corks! Is there anything more ugly and off-putting than some lime-green, lemon-yellow, or hot-pink piece of plastic in your wine bottle, even if it is designed to match the lime-green lizard, lemon-yellow truck, or hot-pink babe on the label? These plastic monstrosities are not just ugly, they're almost impossible to remove. And good luck trying to force one back in once you've pried it loose! Dump the plastic and switch to screwcaps, or try one of the new processed-cork products on the market if you are worried about TCA.

Haven't we had enough of these absurd critter wines? Kangaroos and lizards, penguins and salmon—all manner of birds and beasts have been showing up lately, as if a bright color and a cute story can compensate for the lousy wine. I finally snapped when I got the press release for a lineup called Three Blind Moose. Good grief, don't you marketing people have real work to do? These corporate entities should spend more on the wine and worry less about "youth-oriented" labels and new lines of dull wines with stupid stories and animal names. The press, the trade, and, yes, even those young consumers will be happy to support good-quality wines offered at a reasonable price. That's the real marketing opportunity, not more animals. Three Blind Moose indeed! What's next—Four Deaf Dachshunds?

Stop shipping wines in polystyrene. There are plenty of recyclable alternatives. Polystyrene is clogging up our oceans and consuming more and more landfill.

Grapevine

• **For the second time** in six months, the Washington Wine Commission has hired a new executive director. Jane Baxter Lynn abruptly resigned in January 2005, barely six months after being hired. Her successor, Robin Pollard, has a diverse background in state government, tourism, and agriculture. She will continue the initiatives set in place last year to brand the Washington wine category and will concentrate on legislative issues facing the Washington industry. Successful programs such as Taste Washington, Washington Wine Month, and the Auction of Washington Wines are expected to continue unchanged.

• **The state's most successful** regional wine-marketing program, the Walla Walla Valley Wine Alliance, announced the hiring of a new executive director, Elizabeth Martin-Calder. Martin-Calder has previously worked in marketing and communications for the Portland Art Museum and in the travel industry. The Walla Walla Valley is now home to more than 70 wineries and 35 growers and is on a fast track to becoming the Napa of the Northwest.

• **Col Solare,** the joint venture between Chateau Ste. Michelle and Piero Antinori, reached a milestone in 2005 as Antinori and CEO Ted Baseler broke ground atop Red Mountain for a dedicated Col Solare winery and vineyard. "Red Mountain's reputation for producing superb red varietals such as Cabernet Sauvignon and Merlot led us to choose this site," said Baseler. "We hope to open in time for harvest in 2006."

Vintage Report

Advance report on the latest harvest

2005

Washington—An unusually long harvest lasted from Labor Day (September 5) through Halloween, as Washington winemakers dodged raindrops and waited out cool October for late-ripening reds. Moderate temperatures throughout the summer ensured that there were no heat spikes; even on Red Mountain the grapes never shut down. Walla Walla bounced back from almost no crop in freeze-struck 2004. Warm sites (Wahluke Slope, Red Mountain) fared especially well. Whites are plump, juicy, and balanced. The early take on reds is extremely upbeat: yields are down, flavor concentration way up. "The best vintage since 1999" is the consensus viewpoint.

Oregon—Western Oregon vineyards experienced a late, cool, rather wet vintage. Finished wines will have less alcohol than in recent hot years, with plenty of natural acidity and fewer jammy flavors. Pinot Noir producers are calling 2005 a return to finesse and elegance. Yields were lower than average across the state, though up slightly from 2004. Eastern Oregon sites in the Columbia Gorge and Walla Walla Valley AVAs had an exceptional vintage in line with Washington's.

Updates on the previous five vintages

2004

Vintage rating: *Washington—Red: 84, White: 78; Oregon—Red: 90, White: 84*

Washington—A severe January freeze wiped out most of the 2004 Walla Walla harvest. Elsewhere, a very hot summer turned cool and wet at harvest, causing rot problems and turning what began as a very early vintage into one of the latest on record. Attentive vineyard management and careful selection made some excellent, concentrated red wines, especially Merlot, Syrah, and Cabernet, but more generic bottlings may be patchy. White-wine grapes were more prone to rot and quality will be variable.

Oregon—A wet spring, poor set, vine disease, significant bird damage, and mildew dramatically reduced yields across the state. Blistering July heat in the Willamette Valley was followed by 2 in (50 mm) of rain in late

August/early September. For some vintners, patience was rewarded as sunny fall weather ripened the fruit. The best Pinots will show deep color, bright raspberry and mulberry fruit, and complex, long, fruit-driven flavors.

2003

Vintage rating: *Washington—Red: 90, White: 88; Oregon—Red: 90, White: 86*

Washington—A dry, scorching-hot summer cooled off during harvest. White wines are ripe and fruity, with forward, precocious flavors and lower acid levels. Merlot shows superb color, complexity, and balance. Cabernet Sauvignons are dark and concentrated; Syrahs are packed with juicy fruit.
Oregon—A cold, wet spring; a brutal July heat wave; cold, wet weather at harvest; and finally a late-season heat wave! Overall the Pinots from top producers outshone the overhyped 2002s, with deep, ripe, and sweet flavors.

2002

Vintage rating: *Washington—Red: 88, White: 90; Oregon—Red: 76, White: 86*

Washington—A record crop with high sugars, high acidity, and high extract. The white wines were juicy and crisp; the reds immediately accessible and loaded with bright, fresh fruit flavors. A little less concentration than the 2001s or 2003s.
Oregon—A cold, wet spring in the northern Willamette Valley, then heavy rains as harvest was beginning. Too many of the Pinots are ungenerous and unyielding, with strong scents of tomato leaf and beets, and earthy, hard tannins.

2001

Vintage rating: *Washington—Red: 92, White: 90; Oregon—Red: 89, White: 87*

Washington—Picking extended well into November, and the red wines are structured to age well over the medium term; they are stylistically midway between the classic, austere 1999s and the broadly fruity 2000s. Syrahs look to be the best of the reds, while the white wines are unusually ripe and tropical.
Oregon—Those who did the extensive green-harvesting and sorting at crush made wines with clean fruit and great elegance. For average

wineries, the 2001s are soft, forward, and simple. For the reserve and single-vineyard Pinots, some brilliant successes can be found.

2000

Vintage rating: *Washington—Red: 87, White: 86; Oregon—Red: 91, White: 91*

Washington—A few Merlots and Cabernets from favored sites are standouts, but the reds, though ripe enough, lack the structured concentration of the 1999s and 2001s. Most whites (except Rieslings) should be consumed by now.

Oregon—A magic vintage for Oregon. The Pinots show loads of fruit, with lovely blackberry and cherry notes, as well as smooth, sweet tannins.

GREATEST WINE PRODUCERS

1. Quilceda Creek (Washington)
2. Leonetti Cellar (Washington)
3. Andrew Will (Washington)
4. Sineann (Oregon, Washington)
5. DeLille Cellars (Washington)
6. Betz Family (Washington)
7. Ken Wright Cellars (Oregon)
8. Cayuse (Washington)
9. Spring Valley Vineyard (Washington)
10. Domaine Drouhin (Oregon)

FASTEST-IMPROVING PRODUCERS

1. J Bookwalter (Washington)
2. K Vintners (Washington)
3. Raptor Ridge (Oregon)
4. Covey Run (Washington)
5. Dunham Cellars (Washington)
6. Matthews Cellars (Washington)
7. Cristom (Oregon)
8. Buty (Washington)
9. Pepper Bridge (Washington)
10. Chateau Ste Michelle (Washington)

NEW UP-AND-COMING PRODUCERS

1. Beresan (Washington)
2. Fielding Hills (Washington)
3. Januik (Washington)
4. Cadence (Washington)
5. Syncline Cellars (Washington)
6. Rulo (Washington)
7. Mark Ryan (Washington)
8. Robert Karl Cellars (Washington)
9. Harlequin Wine Cellars (Washington)
10. Gamache Vintners (Washington)

BEST-VALUE PRODUCERS

1. Covey Run (Washington)
2. Columbia Crest (Washington)
3. Barnard Griffin (Washington)
4. Snoqualmie (Washington)
5. Firesteed (Oregon)
6. Waterbrook (Washington)
7. Columbia Winery (Washington)
8. Erath (Oregon)
9. L'Ecole No 41 (Washington)
10. Pine & Post (Washington)

GREATEST-QUALITY WINES

1. **Cabernet Sauvignon 2002** Quilceda Creek, Washington ($80)
2. **Reserve 2002** Leonetti Cellar, Washington ($95)
3. **Ciel du Cheval Vineyard Red Wine 2003** Andrew Will, Washington ($45)
4. **Stone River Red Wine 2003** Beresan, Washington ($28)
5. **Cailloux Vineyard Syrah 2003** Cayuse, Washington ($45)
6. **Merlot 2003** Fielding Hills, Washington ($28)
7. **Ciel du Cheval Vineyard Red Wine 2003** Cadence, Washington ($38)
8. **Ethos Chardonnay 2003** Chateau Ste Michelle, Washington ($30)
9. **La Cote Rousse Syrah 2003** Betz Family, Washington ($44)
10. **Semillon/Sauvignon Blanc 2004** Buty, Washington ($21)

BEST BARGAINS

1. **Riesling 2004** Townshend, Washington ($10)
2. **Gewurztraminer 2004** Covey Run, Washington ($7)
3. **Johannisberg Riesling 2004** Latah Creek, Washington ($7)
4. **Gewürztraminer 2004** Columbia Winery, Washington ($9)
5. **Pinot Grigio 2004** Covey Run, Washington ($7)
6. **Fumé Blanc 2004** Barnard Griffin, Washington ($9)
7. **Sauvignon Blanc 2003** Arbor Crest, Washington ($8)
8. **Pinot Gris 2003** Firesteed, Oregon ($10)
9. **Merlot 2004** Pine & Post, Washington ($5)
10. **Two Vines Shiraz 2003** Columbia Crest, Washington ($8)

MOST EXCITING OR UNUSUAL FINDS

1. **Merlot 2003** Fielding Hills, Washington ($28) *Exciting because Merlot is so rarely exciting from anywhere in the United States. This is enhanced with 17 percent Cabernet, 5 percent Syrah, and 2 percent Cab Franc; vibrant fruit is polished to a fine luster, with perfectly applied oak "seasoning."*
2. **Cailloux Vineyard Syrah 2003** Cayuse, Washington ($45) *This is biodynamic and planted on an ancient river bed, rock-strewn and more like Châteauneuf-du-Pape than Walla Walla. Cranberry, pomegranate, and cherry meet rock and gravel and pepper.*
3. **Stone River Red Wine 2003** Beresan, Washington ($28) *Once again Beresan has created a Syrah/bordeaux blend of grace and elegant power. Along with a few spots on Red Mountain, Beresan and a few other rock-strewn Walla Walla vineyards show more distinctive terroir than anywhere in Washington.*
4. **Abbott Claim Pinot Noir 2004** Ken Wright Cellars, Oregon ($50) *Strikingly original Pinot Noir, this does not clobber you with jam. Rather, it is layered with subtle flavors of citrus, juniper, pine needles, dried herbs, and mint.*
5. **Champoux Vineyard Cabernet Franc 2004** Sineann, Oregon and Washington ($42) *Many winemakers in the Northwest think Cabernet Franc is the most exciting red-wine grape to hit the region since Syrah. Peter Rosback brings rich, ripe, luscious cherry fruit that deepens into black-cherry liqueur through a long, lush finish.*

6 Estate Pinot Gris 2004 Cristom, Oregon ($17) *In Oregon they make a dense, fruit-laden style of Pinot Grigio and call it Pinot Gris. Cristom's is at the top of the heap, from high-density plantings, select clones, and native yeasts.*

7 Bésoleil Grenache 2003 Betz Family, Washington ($35) *Grenache was one of the original vinifera plantings in Washington, used for simple sweet rosé, then abandoned. But it's slowly coming back, and here's why it should.*

8 Carmenère 2002 Reininger, Washington ($35) *One of a handful of varietal Carmenères made in Washington, this is a chewy, tart, racy wine with strong herbal elements and lots of black pepper.*

9 Cuvée Forté Brut NV Mountain Dome, Washington ($30) *A reserve cuvée—half Pinot and half Chardonnay—and just the second such release in the winery's two-decade history. Though NV, it is based on the very ripe 1998 vintage.*

10 Arneis 2004 Ponzi, Oregon ($20) *I know of no other Arneis in the Northwest, and it's too bad—this is delicious. Penetrating scents and flavors show pineapple, citrus, peach, and tropical fruits; and the piercing aromatics blossom on the tongue into a long, seductive marmalade of a wine.*

Grapevine

• **Chateau Ste. Michelle Wine Estates,** parent company to Ste. Michelle, Columbia Crest, Snoqualmie, Col Solare, and Northstar, among others, has struck a purchase agreement with Dean and Shari Derby, the owners of Walla Walla's Spring Valley Vineyards. Its estate-grown Merlot, Cabernet, and Syrah have received outstanding reviews since their first vintage in 1999. Under the terms of the agreement, the Derbys, fourth-generation wheat farmers, keep their land. Ste. Michelle gets the Spring Valley brand and a 10-year lease on the 40-acre vineyard. The winery plans to continue to make and market the wines as before.

• **Chateau Ste Michelle** named Joshua Maloney as its new red-wine maker, reporting to head winemaker Bob Bertheau. Maloney will work at the company's Canoe Ridge Estate winery near Paterson, Washington. Most recently, Maloney was assistant winemaker at Estancia Estates in charge of the Merlot program.

• **The Port of Walla Walla** is planning to build a winery village at its airport property. The proposed cluster of buildings will serve as an incubator for startup microwineries in the region. Many of the most successful, such as Reininger and Dunham, began life in bare-bones warehouse spaces leased from the port. The new village will include four or five new 2,000-sq-ft (186-sq-m) buildings offered on six-year leases.

• **Rex Hill Vineyards** has filed suit against Supreme Corq of Washington, alleging that the company's synthetic corks failed to seal properly, spoiling thousands of bottles of Pinot Gris, Sauvignon Blanc, and Chardonnay. Rex Hill claims that more than 30,000 cases of wine were ruined and had to be pulled from the international market, damaging its reputation. The winery, which has switched to screwcaps beginning with 2004 white wines, is reportedly seeking $1.4 million in damages.

Atlantic Northeast

Sandra Silfven

The New York wine industry has been the slumbering giant for years: third in production behind California and Washington, but last place for national recognition or much goodwill from the state legislature.

SANDRA SILFVEN

Well, the giant is napping no more, and lawmakers, looking for one bright spot in agriculture to brag about, are even kissing up.

Following a US Supreme Court ruling, the state swiftly dismantled the ban on direct wine shipping, which could beef up sales by 25 percent for wineries with significant visitor mailing lists. Thanks to major backing from beer, wine, and spirits giant Constellation Brands, a $6-million visitors' center called the New York Wine & Culinary Center should be open in Canandaigua by the time you read this (scheduled for summer 2006). As New York's answer to Napa's COPIA, but more consumer-interactive, the center will serve as a gateway to wine and agriculture throughout New York State and is expected to draw 76,000 visitors annually.

Other signs of confidence are Long Island's Wolffer selling futures for its $125 Premier Cru Merlot; Heron Hill charging a little less for a split of icewine; Susan Wine and Robert Ransom opening an all-New York wine bar next to their all-New York tasting room in SoHo; Senator Hillary Clinton's New York Farm Day, featuring New York wines and foods for the most popular reception on Capitol Hill; and a doubling of the growth rate in new wineries, with 63 in the first half of the present decade.

A new four-year Bachelor of Science programme geared to all aspects of growing and making wine, with emphasis on cold-climate issues, has

SANDRA SILFVEN lives in Dearborn, Michigan, and has worked at *The Detroit News* for more than 30 years in reporting and editing positions. She has written about wine for most of her career, and she produces the Michigan Wine Report for Detroit News Online (www.detnews.com/wine).

started at Cornell University in Ithaca, New York; and to top it all off, Napa Valley winemaker Scott Harvey gave his blessing to New York Riesling by purchasing more than 10 tons of it from Anthony Road Wine Company in Penn Yan to make an "American" Riesling.

Numbers impress the bean counters, and Jim Trezise, president of the New York Wine and Grape Foundation, went looking for them and parlayed them into headlines. One survey by the New York Agricultural Statistics Service found that wineries are the state's fastest-growing sector in agriculture and tourism, drawing 10 times as many visitors as they did two decades ago; another, conducted by Napa-Valley-based MKF Research, found that New York wineries generate more than $3 billion annually for the state's economy.

"For years, the wine industry has been the fastest-growing part of New York's two largest economic sectors, agriculture and tourism. Now we have solid data on the enormous economic benefits we generate," Trezise said.

Grapevine

• **Hybrids and labruscas** are still significant and win their share of fame: Goose Watch (New York) Diamond was best white wine at a Riverside International Wine Competition; Casa Larga's Fiori delle Stelle (Vidal) icewine won the New York Governor's Cup; a late-harvest James River Cellars Dolce Vino (Chardonel) won the Governor's Cup in Virginia. At a recent Best of the East banquet in Lancaster, Pennsylvania, the first six of the Top Ten most-awarded wines in the East were hybrids and labruscas.

• **Christian Butzke,** former staff oenologist at UC Davis and winemaker at Sakonnet Vineyards in Rhode Island, joined Purdue University in Indiana to replace retired oenology professor and wine icon Dr. Richard P. Vine. He will work closely with state vintners and explore the concept of an "IQ"—Indiana Quality alliance—to elevate the quality and reputation of the state's wines.

• **Virginia winemaker/consultant** Michael Shaps and his wife Christie are partners with vintners David and Ellen King (King Family Vineyards) in VaVino, a new wine bar, retail shop, and education center in Charlottesville, devoted to Virginia wines. Shaps is also making wine for the new DelFosse Winery in the Monticello appellation and has joined with long-time friend Michel Roucher-Sarrazin (formerly of Chartron et Trebuchet) of Burgundy to start Shaps & Roucher-Sarrazin, which will import wines into the US.

• **Dr. Konstantin Frank Vinifera Wine Cellars** in New York promoted Mark Veraguth to senior winemaker to replace Morton Halgren, who left to devote time to his own winery, Ravines Wine Cellars, on the east side of Keuka Lake.

• **Larry Mawby of Michigan's L. Mawby Vineyards** sought help from retired Roederer Estate winemaker Michel Salgues, who changed the way Mawby handles fresh-pressed juice. The result is a cleaner, purer, more delicate expression of fruit. Mawby also began a three-year planting program of Pinot Noir clones recommended by Salgues to expand production by 50 percent.

SHIPPING CONTROVERSY RAGES ON

With alcohol laws being rewritten nationwide following the US Supreme Court ruling requiring equal shipping rights for in-state and out-of-state wineries, the borders are slowly opening up. New York, Connecticut, and Michigan passed limited direct-shipping bills, with measures to regulate sales and collect taxes and to allow wineries to retain their long-held right to self-distribute to restaurants and shops. Peter Saltonstall at King Ferry/Trealeaven (New York), John Martini of Anthony Road (New York), Gary Crump of Priam (Connecticut), and Don Coe of Winery at Black Star Farms (Michigan) worked tirelessly on behalf of vintners. At the time of writing, the shipping and self-distribution issues were still undecided in many states.

NATURAL CALAMITIES

Sourcing grapes has become an issue, especially in challenged growing areas and at times of natural disasters. New York now lets farm wineries source grapes from out of state when agriculture officials determine there is a shortage of 40 percent or more. Pennsylvania's new law lets vintners source 25 percent within a 350-mile (560-km) radius of the winery, but only fruit or juice, not bulk wine. Connecticut changed its law to cut the amount of estate-grown grapes required to 25 percent. The rest can come from Connecticut or elsewhere in the US. However, the origin of mixed-origin wines must be reflected in their appellation or designation.

Grapevine

• **Paul Lukacs,** long-time wine writer and chair of the English Department at Loyola College in Maryland, singled out 40 American wines to celebrate in *Great Wines of America* (WW Norton, 2005). Only four were not on the West Coast: Bedell Cellars Reserve Merlot (New York), L. Mawby Vineyards Talisman (Michigan), Horton Viognier (Virginia), and Dr. Konstantin Frank Dry Riesling (New York).

• **New Jersey** lost pioneering vintner and scientist Michael Fisher of Amwell Valley Vineyard, who established the winery in 1978 with the help of Philip Wagner of Boordy Vineyards in Maryland. He was instrumental in passing the state's Farm Winery Act in 1981. The Northeast also lost Barbara Adams, director of the Seneca Lake Wine Trail, and Joanne Smart, cofounder of Chateau de Leelanau in Michigan.

• **Bryan Ulbrich** of Michigan's Peninsula Cellars, whose wines have dominated the Michigan Wine & Spirits Competition for the past five years, launched Left Foot Charley, a sideline venture with wife Jennifer, featuring a dry and a sweet Riesling, a Pinot Grigio, and a Gewurztraminer. Ulbrich has fun with the name because, as a kid, he was always falling down due to an inward-pointing left foot. Corrective shoes fixed the problem. (He takes the wine seriously.)

• **The new Acorn Hill Vineyards** in Virginia, on a 300-acre farm north of Charlottesville, is owned by horse breeders Jess and Sharon Sweely. With 20 of a planned 50 acres planted, production began in 2006 with Frantz Ventre, formerly of Jefferson Winery, as winemaker, and Oliver Asberger from Keswick managing the vineyards.

Opinion:
Building steam

I still taste wines—especially reds—that are too green, too hard, too oaked, and occasionally flawed, but far less frequently than before. The best growers today choose not to imitate the great wine regions of the world but to focus on what they can do best, cultivating their own regional style. In a blind tasting, it's getting so you can pick out a Long Island Merlot, a Virginia Cabernet Franc, a Finger Lakes Riesling, and a Michigan Riesling.

On the other hand, Chardonnays across the region are so much better that it's hard to tell where they come from! Many of the best vintners have given up on all-barrel fermentation. The fruit just isn't ripe enough to integrate with the oak. The best ones incorporate a mix of barrel and steel fermentation, so the pure fruit character can be lifted up by the spice of the wood, not buried under it. Some leave wood out altogether. Michigan applauded when Bryan Ulbrich of Peninsula Cellars made a Chardonnay in 2004 the way he makes his world-class Gewurztraminers and Pinot Blancs: fermented in steel. Also, adequate bottle-age is a must for the best reds. Bordeaux-style blends from the Finger Lakes and Long Island Merlots need a good four years in bottle to knit flavors and soften tannins. Eric Fry at Lenz holds his Merlots five years or more, and they drink like satin. About the time California is releasing its 2001 Cabs, Fry is just releasing his 2000 Merlot.

Labeling and packaging have also caught up with modern marketing standards. Vintners etch their fervor on to the glass itself or print it on the label—few more passionately than Eric Miller of Chaddsford in Pennsylvania, and David Braganini of Braganini Reserve in Michigan. Clearly, parts of the Northeast have the quality to build a world-class reputation, but another "Judgment of Paris" is needed.

Grapevine

- **Virginia consulting winemaker** Doug Fabbioli of Wyndham Winery has established his own line, Bella Luna Vineyards in Louden County.

- **Sakonnet Vineyards** in Rhode Island elevated long-time assistant winemaker Elaine Bernier to winemaker, replacing Christian Butzka.

- **Prince Michel in Virginia,** producing exciting wines with single-vineyard designations, was sold to Virginia real-estate developer and grape grower Terry Holzman and his wife Kristin. Sister wineries Rapidan River and Madison were rolled into Prince Michel.

Vintage Report

Advance report on the latest harvest

2005

The New York Finger Lakes were still recovering from vine loss in a freeze the previous year, but crops in most states were average to above average, and quality in most states is expected to be high. Some areas experienced drought, while others had rain at just the right time. Virginia battled Japanese beetles and European red mites. Week-long rains in mid-October ruined a significant number of late-ripening reds on Long Island.

Updates on the previous five vintages

2004

Vintage rating: *Red: 85, White: 89*

In a smaller-than-average vintage with challenges from the weather, the whites are exciting, with bracing acidity and enough fruit to carry the day. Reds are on the lighter side and still need more time to determine their outcome.

2003

Vintage rating: *Red: 74, White: 88*

It was a small vintage that yielded some stunning crisp whites, but reds had low sugars, diluted acids, and light tannins. Many were declassified.

2002

Vintage rating: *Red: 90, White: 94*

Most states, with the exception of Virginia and New York's Finger Lakes, were thrilled with the quality of all of the whites and, almost uniformly in the Northeast, the reds. Flavors are rich and intense for whites, concentrated with balanced acids for reds.

2001

Vintage rating: *Red: 92, White: 94*

Except for New Jersey, which was deluged with rain at harvest, this was an excellent vintage for both reds and whites. Fruit, tannins, and wood are integrating nicely in the premium Cabs and Merlots.

2000

Vintage rating: *Red: 72, White: 84*

Except for New York, this was a difficult vintage for most states, with cool weather, rains, and hurricanes. Jim Law of Linden Vineyards in Virginia called it "awful." Long Island Merlots are outstanding.

GREATEST WINE PRODUCERS

1. Dr. Konstantin Frank (New York)
2. Wolffer (New York)
3. Bedell (New York)
4. L. Mawby (Michigan)
5. Paumanok (New York)
6. Lenz (New York)
7. Linden (Virginia)
8. Peninsula Cellars (Michigan)
9. Chaddsford (Pennsylvania)
10. Sakonnet (Rhode Island)

FASTEST-IMPROVING PRODUCERS

1. Bel Lago (Michigan)
2. Kinkead Ridge (Ohio)
3. Sheldrake Point (New York)
4. St. Julian (Michigan)
5. Mon Ami (Ohio)
6. Clover Hill (Pennsylvania)
7. Adams County (Pennsylvania)
8. Priam Vineyards (Connecticut)
9. Domaine Berrien Cellars (Michigan)
10. Jewell Towne Vineyards (New Hampshire)

NEW UP-AND-COMING PRODUCERS

1. Bellview (New Jersey)
2. Keswick (Virginia)
3. Comtesse Therese (New York)
4. Brys Estate (Michigan)
5. DelFosse (Virginia)
6. Ravines (New York)
7. Gill's Pier (Michigan)
8. Blenheim Vineyards (Virginia)
9. Bellhurst (New York)
10. Maple Ridge (Ohio)

BEST-VALUE PRODUCERS

1. Lakewood (New York)
2. Fox Run (New York)
3. Horton (Virginia)
4. Firelands (Ohio)
5. Debonne (Ohio)
6. Swedish Hill (New York)
7. Fenn Valley (Michigan)
8. Oliver (Indiana)
9. Ferrante (Ohio)
10. Mount Nittany (Pennsylvania)

GREATEST-QUALITY WINES

1. **Estate Selection Merlot 2000** Lenz, New York ($23)
2. **Estate Selection Merlot 2001** Wolffer, New York ($37)
3. **Rkatsiteli 2004** Dr. Konstantin Frank, New York ($24)
4. **Chardonnay Unwooded 2004** Peninsula Cellars, Michigan ($14)
5. **Blanc de Blanc NV** L. Mawby, Michigan ($18)
6. **Chardonnay Hard Scrabble 2002** Linden, Virginia ($22)
7. **Red Assemblage 2001** Paumanok, New York ($36)
8. **Cabernet Sauvignon Owner's Reserve 2001** Chateau LaFayette Reneau, New York ($50)
9. **Merlot Reserve 2002** Bedell, New York ($30)
10. **Merican 2001** Chaddsford, Pennsylvania ($40)

BEST BARGAINS

1. **Meritage 2002** Salmon Run, New York ($13)
2. **Dolce Vino 2004** James River Cellars, Virginia ($13)
3. **Pinot Grigio 2004** Firelands, Ohio ($10)
4. **Vignoles 2004** Mount Nittany, Pennsylvania ($14)
5. **Long Stem White 2004** Lakewood, New York ($7)
6. **Riesling 2004** Oliver, Indiana ($10)
7. **Main Road Red NV** Bedell, New York ($12)
8. **Blue Heron NV** St. Julian, Michigan ($7)
9. **Red Seraph NV** Sharpe Hill, Connecticut ($12)
10. **Diamond NV** Goose Watch, New York ($8)

MOST EXCITING OR UNUSUAL FINDS

1. **Merlot Premier Cru 2002** Wolffer, New York ($125) *Wolffer has the confidence—and vines— to pull off a super-premium Merlot with abundant, tight-knit, high-octane fruit to easily shoulder all the 100 percent new French oak.*
2. **Cabernet Sauvignon 2003** Kinkead Ridge, Ohio ($18) *From Ripley, Ohio? Goes to show what a meticulous Oregon grape grower can bring to the limestone ridges overlooking the Ohio river.*
3. **Norton 2004** Keswick, Virginia ($18) *Norton is a native American grape thought to be the only one worthy of making a dry table wine. Young Nortons are usually big and clumsy. This one is big and lush.*
4. **Traditional Merlot 2002** Comtesse Therese, New York ($18) *A well-knit powerhouse, and only the second vintage for tax lawyer/ vintner Therese K. Dilworth.*
5. **Dry Riesling 2004** Winery at Black Star Farms, Michigan ($14) *Racy acidity, vibrant fruit—good enough to make the menu at Shaw's Crab House in Chicago.*
6. **Chardonnay Reserve 2003** Fox Run, New York ($15) *Great tropical flavors and oak integration.*
7. **Due Rossi 2004** Chaddsford, Pennsylvania ($25) *As rustic as Barbera can be, this "two-red" blend of Sangiovese and Barbera shows a suave side of the beast.*
8. **Chambourcin 2004** Tomasello, New Jersey ($18) *The 2001 vintage was the one that converted vinifera drinkers to this beloved red hybrid in the Northeast. Now, the 2004 is going for a repeat.*
9. **Blaufrankisch 2004** Channing Daughters, New York ($22) *Lemberger gets a blast of energy in the Hamptons. So nimble, so fresh, so perfect in fruit and acid balance.*
10. **Traminette 2004** Fenn Valley, Michigan ($14) *This cold-climate hybrid substitute for Gewurztraminer is often timid and boring. This one has zing!*

Grapevine

- **Pennsylvania's Clover Hill** completed a 15,000-sq-ft (1,394-sq-m) addition to its production facility for a new tasting room and hospitality areas.

- **Ohio Grigios** are catching on. Pinot Grigios by Firelands and its sister winery, Mon Ami, took Best Wine honors two years in a row in the Ohio Wine Competition.

- **Lakewood Vineyards** in New York has started a barrel program, air-curing New York wood, and tried it out with the 2005 vintage.

Other US States

Doug Frost MW

The 2005 US Supreme Court decision striking down certain aspects of the bans on wine shipping ought to allow for sought-after wines to flow into the center of the country. It ought to, but will it happen?

DOUG FROST MW

Wine is flowing into the center of the country already, along with grapes and juice. The rise in the number of wineries has outstripped the states' ability to provide grapes. Nearly every large winery surveyed expressed the need for more grapes within their borders, for better vineyards, and for more appropriate varieties. Nearly all of them were shopping outside their states' borders for grapes, juice, and wine, most finding what they sought in California, Washington State, New York State, and Pennsylvania.

The newest wineries are increasingly located near their customers and far away from the vineyards. In Colorado, for instance, they are popping up on the Front Ranges, closer to Denver and the moneyed skiing tourists, but the best vineyards are in the West. The wineries have to bear the burden of shipping grapes and/or wine across a vast and mountainous state. They have to travel to the vineyards to monitor required viticulture. And it's more difficult to convince farmers that far-away wineries and invisible customers will be avid buyers for new vineyards.

This scenario also transpires in other non-coastal states. If the growth of each state's fledgling wine industry is the goal, an appropriate and orderly increase in local vineyards, as well as an understanding of those vineyards, must accompany the growth in wineries. Instead, chaos prevails. Wineries continue to ship from the coasts and are even more likely to follow fad grapes blindly. It seems that nearly every US winery is preparing to release

DOUG FROST MW is the author of two wine books, including *On Wine* (Rizzoli International Publications, 2001). He is one of only three people in the world to hold the titles of both Master Sommelier and Master of Wine.

a Syrah, most of which were grown on the West Coast. The viticultural experience required of good winemaking is not going to develop when the grapes are drawn from large vats thousands of miles away.

In the long term, increasing competition for local grapes will attract local farmers. In a haphazard manner, this local growth is starting to happen. Riesling in Colorado costs more than top-flight Riesling from California. Chardonel from Missouri can cost the same as Napa Valley Chardonnay.

We're from the government and we're here to help

Murli Dharmadhikari, who was instrumental in the development of high-quality Missouri wine in the 1980s and 1990s, is now the extension oenologist for the Department of Food, Science, and Human Nutrition at Iowa State University. Sorkel Kadir, assistant professor of Horticulture at Kansas State University, is offering detailed expertise to all prospective vineyard owners. Colorado's Wine Industry Development Board has brought Oregon winemaker Bill Musgnung in as winemaking consultant.

In Kentucky, Kaan Kurtural has begun employment as the state viticulturist, and at the University of Kentucky, Tom Cottrell, formerly of Sonoma's Chalk Hill Winery, has a role as the extension winemaking specialist. Similar positions have been filled by luminaries such as Christian Butzke at Purdue University in Indiana. Perhaps the beacon in all this is the University of Minnesota, where Peter Hemstad, among others, has been integral in the development of new grapes, new techniques, and vineyards—not just in Minnesota but throughout the area. Hemstad, senior grape breeder at the University of Minnesota, has contributed to successes in Canada as well as in the upper United States.

Why this new-found government love and support for wine? Most states have recognized that significant revenues can be earned through the sales tax and tourist dollars generated by wineries. They are beginning to realize that providing academic support to their fledgling industry is the only investment required to support these (mostly small) businesses.

Grapevine

• **Another delicious icewine** was made by Wisconsin's Wollersheim Winery in 2005. It was picked on December 9 at 15°F (–9°C), with sugars at 38.6° Brix.

• **A lawsuit filed** by Indiana winery Huber Estates is still pending, but it claims that Kentucky's regulations allowing in-state wineries to ship wine while out-of-state wineries are prohibited is unconstitutional. Sound familiar? The outcome this time might go against the local wineries. There seems to be a strong movement in the Kentucky legislature to respond by banning all wine shipping.

BLACKSTOCK TO BECOME WINEMAKERS

Blackstock Vineyards has been the fruit source for many of the most notable wines the state of Georgia has created in the last decade. Some wineries seem nearly dependent on the northern Georgian vineyard for their best wines. Viognier from Blackstock Vineyards has become among the most sought-after fruit in the southeastern US. "Five out of the last six vintages of our Viognier have won a gold medal at a good competition somewhere," points out Blackstock Vineyards owner David Harris.

Harris is deeply respected in the viticultural community, but he is candid about the shortcomings he sees in the area's vineyards. "Every single canopy I've seen in the southeastern US is out of balance," he notes. He complains that too many vineyard managers try to create balance through canopy hedging and repeated dropping of fruit.

He has also been the source of some very interesting Touriga Nacional for wineries such as Silver Coast. And he believes in his vineyard's ability to ripen Sangiovese and Mourvèdre. But Harris is most bullish on Viognier and Merlot: "I'm confident in Georgia's ability to ripen Merlot, [though] Viognier is a heart-breaker."

David and his wife Trish broke ground on a winery in early 2005. A storage room was pressed into service as a fermentation room for the 2005 harvest, when several thousand cases were produced. The winery will reach its goal of 5,000 cases within the next two years, it is hoped.

DEATH OF ROBERT WOLLERSHEIM

Robert Wollersheim, who pioneered modern viticulture in Wisconsin and built one of the most successful winemaking enterprises in the Midwest, passed away on December 11, 2005. His estate, Wollersheim Winery, was first planted in the 19th century by the famous Agoston Haraszthy, who is considered the source of many of California's important grapes.

Wollersheim, who learned winemaking from his German grandmother, bought the land and buildings that would become Wollersheim Winery in 1972 and purchased Cedar Creek Winery, Wisconsin's best-known winery, in 1990.

He began his career as an engineering manager at the University of Wisconsin–Madison Space Science Center but described his early passion for vineyards as a "70s thing … back to the land." He struggled to find the right grapes but by the mid-1980s had built a strong and thriving business.

Cedar Creek and Wollersheim Winery have grown even more successful in recent years, and 2005 saw production reach 1 million bottles. His daughter Julie and son-in-law Philippe Coquard, who is also the winemaker, have followed ably in Bob Wollersheim's large footsteps.

Opinion:
Mixed signals from the middle

Only in America could you ask for a doctor, and a lawyer shows up instead. The maladies that afflict the wine industry are not going to be cured by recent legal decisions; in fact, the lawyers will benefit more than wine consumers.

The 2005 Supreme Court decisions are cause for good cheer if you live in Michigan or New York. For the rest of us, the overly optimistic hope that wine shipping will spread like wildfire across America is premature at best. The US wine industry remains a hodgepodge of rules and regulations, and states that have prohibited shipping of all wines up to now are not going to change their tune just because others have.

Rather, the likely scenario is closer to the back and forth that played out in New York and Michigan, in which state legislatures and governors' offices were tossed between the powerful wholesalers and the little local wineries. Certainly, the anti-shipping forces are losing the PR battle; the press routinely painted a picture of a small and beleaguered winery, a few angry and vocal wine lovers cheated of their favorite cult vintage, and a faceless spokesperson for the wholesaler industry prophesying doom if the shipping bans are overturned. The card played by the wholesalers and their legislature protectors is that only the wholesalers can prevent consumption of $100 bottles of Napa Valley Cabernet by masses of unprotected children. Any fair-minded journalist is quick to point out that the Federal Trade Commission concluded in 2003 that shipping bans have no measurable effect on under-age alcohol consumption.

In Pennsylvania, the sad tale of the little wineries cheated of their Christmas 2005 business by the Grinch called the Pennsylvania Liquor Control Board (PLCB) was too tempting for the media. The PLCB quickly backed down when public opinion turned against protectionism.

Wineries in states where the wine industry is still nascent, however, remain at a distinct disadvantage. Most importantly, unless these states already allow shipping within their borders, they now have a strong incentive to continue their total prohibition on shipping. States such as Alabama, Kansas, Kentucky, Oklahoma, Tennessee, Utah, and Florida appear ready to fight for as long as necessary. The states of Utah, Kentucky, and Tennessee still classify wine shipping as a felony offense, akin to larceny and robbery.

Happy developments

In Washington State, the goliath retailer Costco is suing to be allowed to buy wine directly from wineries. The preliminary rulings have been in favor of Costco, but the case is not yet settled and will probably wend its way to the US Supreme Court by the end of 2006. But the opportunities for massive change are apparent. If retailers can seek the best price for a wine from anyone selling that wine, the dominoes protecting the wholesale industry will fall. Many observers believe that Costco will prevail. Then retailers, and indeed restaurateurs, will find it possible to sue on similar grounds, and true cross-border wine shipping might begin.

The other ballyhoo is the Gallup poll showing that Americans, for the first time in history, prefer wine to other alcoholic beverages. The 20–30-year-old set is more accepting of wine than beer. At a minimum, these developments have encouraged countless would-be winery owners, and the dramatic growth in wineries in the middle states will continue. The presence of these wineries in farming communities cannot be overstated. New York State saw front-door visits increase 10 times over between 1985 and 2003. New wineries in other states will also have an impact on US consumers' perception of wine; that it is normal, or, at the least, local.

Grapevine

• **Winery growth** in non-coastal states has been nothing short of phenomenal. Kentucky has seen a 30 percent increase in wineries since 2003; Illinois now has more than 50 wineries, a tenfold increase since 1990. And the wineries are finding new customers: Texas wine sales were up 16 percent in 2005, and Missouri now accounts for more than 8 percent of wine sales in the state.

• **Two new grapes** are showing great promise in the northern climes of the upper Midwest. A new red called Marquette is drawing raves from growers. And LeCrescent, an aromatic white, is producing succulent, balanced, and flavorful wines.

• **North Carolina,** preparing for its own potential court cases regarding shipping, has ruled that both in-state and out-of-state wineries must get a permit. Fred Gregory, chief deputy counsel for the North Carolina

Alcohol Beverage Control Commission, says it is now less expensive for out-of-state wineries to ship to North Carolina than it is for in-state wineries, so the Supreme Court's decision will have little or no short-term effect in that state either.

• **Florida Bill SB 1114,** signed into law by Governor Jeb Bush, allows restaurant patrons to take home unfinished wine bottles—a pretty reasonable stance if the government wants to encourage responsible drink-and-drive policies. But most states prohibit it. Just when the Illinois state legislature looked set to ban all wine shipping in the state, the little wine industry in the southern portion of the state is fighting back and may yet retain its ability to ship wine. In New Mexico, a state-mandated server training program, created by the anti-alcohol zealots at the Robert Wood Johnson Foundation, equates alcohol with heroin. How helpful.

Vintage Report

Advance report on the latest harvest

2005

Georgia and the Carolinas saw a cooperative harvest. In Missouri, Kansas, and Illinois, early whites such as Vignoles and some Chardonel suffered from rot because of rain in August. Later whites and reds did well because of a lot of sunshine and limited rainfall during September through late October. Wisconsin saw a good crop, but inclement weather contributed to a lack of intensity. In Texas, things look very promising. The Hill Country experienced a damaging spring hailstorm, reducing the crop, and fungal pressure close to harvest further reduced crop size. The High Plains had one of the finest vintages in a decade. Arizona and New Mexico both saw some bumper crops, while the growers on Colorado's Western Range are elated by the quality of their crop. Idaho's vintage started out with 26 in (660 mm) of rain in June and July alone, but the season turned out far better than feared, with very good ripeness to the tannins.

Updates on the previous five vintages

2004

Rain was the main story of the vintage, whether it was the trio of hurricanes to hit the southeastern US in rapid succession or the torrents that struck Texas, with rains of a remarkable 60 in (1,520 mm) in over the summer. Missouri experienced many of the moisture and mildew problems of other regions in the south and southeast. Colorado's vineyards saw significant losses due to the spring frost, and the same cold spell created problems in Nebraska. Idaho growers, however, were delighted with the vintage, and Wisconsin growers were reasonably happy.

2003

The theme in most areas was spring damage. In central Texas, eastern Wisconsin, and Missouri, freeze and frost damage created very small crops, in some cases one-third the normal size. The wines, however, are often good. Missouri's whites are in short supply, but the reds are very good.

Wisconsin's whites are excellent. Texas lost a lot of crop, both reds and whites, but Colorado saw a very big, high-quality crop. Idaho's wines were big and perhaps a bit too hard.

2002

Idaho's reds were slightly high in alcohol, but the whites show nearly ideal balance. Missouri's white grapes were all very clean coming in, with some pretty Chardonels. The reds are intense and concentrated. In New Mexico, this was yet again a drought year, with forest fires not far away. The wines show good concentration as a result. Georgia was a victim of the excessive rains that the rest of the Atlantic Coast also saw, including the Carolinas. All vineyards were cooler than normal, and the wines are a mixed bag. Texas experienced cooler temperatures and higher precipitation than normal.

2001

In Idaho, even ripening and a warm, quick year resulted in good quality in whites and reds. White wines are even crisper than usual, and the reds show balance and length. Some lovely white wines were made in Missouri, though the Vignoles was difficult. Some reds are a bit stingy, but some Nortons are delightful. For New Mexico, this was year four of the drought, and forest fires raged throughout much of the area.

2000

Idaho had a warm, ripe vintage with very good acidity, resulting in wines of some longevity. Wines in Missouri are as well balanced as any in the last four years, and some Nortons are tops. It was another good year in New Mexico.

GREATEST WINE PRODUCERS

1. Stone Hill Winery (Missouri)
2. Gruet Winery (New Mexico)
3. Augusta Winery (Missouri)
4. Callaghan Winery (Arizona)
5. Montelle Winery (Missouri)
6. Galena Cellars (Illinois)
7. Flat Creek Estate (Texas)
8. Alto Vineyards (Illinois)
9. Pend d'Oreille (Idaho)
10. Koenig Winery (Idaho)

FASTEST-IMPROVING PRODUCERS

1. Crown Valley Vineyards (Missouri)
2. Holy-Field Vineyard (Kansas)
3. Adam Puchta Winery (Missouri)
4. Llano Estacado (Texas)
5. Tiger Mountain Vineyards (Georgia)
6. Mount Pleasant Winery (Missouri)
7. Milagro Vineyards (New Mexico)
8. Carlson Vineyards (Colorado)
9. Cuthills Vineyards (Nebraska)
10. Fredericksburg Winery (Texas)

NEW UP-AND-COMING PRODUCERS

1. Sutcliffe Vineyards (Colorado)
2. Sister Creek Vineyards (Texas)
3. Quivis (Texas)
4. Rockhouse Vineyards (North Carolina)
5. Kiepersol Estate (Texas)
6. Somerset Ridge (Kansas)
7. Crown Valley Vineyards (Missouri)
8. Childress Vineyards (North Carolina)
9. Dry Comal Creek (Texas)
10. Williamson Cellars (Idaho)

BEST-VALUE PRODUCERS

1. Bookcliff Vineyards (Colorado)
2. St James Winery (Missouri)
3. Les Bourgeois Winery (Missouri)
4. Augustina Backpacker (Colorado)
5. Cedar Creek Winery (Wisconsin)
6. Cuthill Vineyards (Nebraska)
7. Wollersheim Winery (Wisconsin)
8. Biltmore Estate (North Carolina)
9. Garfield Estates (Colorado)
10. Milagro Vineyards (New Mexico)

GREATEST-QUALITY WINES

1. **Brut Rosé NV** Gruet Winery, New Mexico ($13)
2. **Vignoles Late Harvest 2004** Holy-Field Vineyards, Kansas ($14)
3. **Cream Sherry NV** Stone Hill Winery, Missouri ($15)
4. **Padre's (red blend) 2004** Callaghan Winery, Arizona ($28)
5. **Travis Peak Select Moscato d'Arancia 2004** Flat Creek, Texas ($16)
6. **Norton Estate 2002** Adam Puchta Winery, Missouri ($24)
7. **Seyval Blanc 2004** Augusta Winery, Missouri ($8)
8. **Norton Port 2004** Stone Hill Winery, Missouri ($20)
9. **Riesling Ice Wine NV** Windridge Vineyard, Koenig Winery, Idaho ($20)
10. **Sangiovese 2003** Flat Creek Parker, Texas ($35)

BEST BARGAINS

1. **Cynthiana 2003** Holy-Field Vineyard, Kansas ($18)
2. **Cream Sherry NV** Stone Hill Winery, Missouri ($15)
3. **Ensemble (Vidal Blanc) 2004** Chrisman Mill Vineyards, Kentucky ($14)
4. **Sauvignon Blanc/Colombard NV** Crown Valley Vineyards, Missouri ($14)
5. **Signature Rhone 2004** Llano Estacado, Texas ($11)
6. **Viognier 2003** Bookcliff Vineyards, Colorado ($13)
7. **75th Anniversary Estate (white blend) NV** Biltmore Estate, North Carolina ($16)
8. **Vidal Blanc 2004** Cedar Creek Winery, Wisconsin ($8)
9. **Rocko Red 2004** Alto Vineyards, Illinois ($10)
10. **Dry Vignoles 2004** Montelle Winery, Missouri ($11)

MOST EXCITING OR UNUSUAL FINDS

1. **Petit Manseng 2004** Tiger Mountain Winery, Georgia ($25) *A bone-dry version with tang in place of flesh, but it's a lot of fun.*
2. **Bacio del Sole (port-style) 2004** Prairie State Winery, Illinois ($18) *Simple and round, this is a very easy drinker for its alcoholic weight and, while short in finish, it has some depth.*
3. **Touriga Nacional Cape Fear Blood Wine 2004** Silver Coast Winery, North Carolina ($14) *The Portuguese have decided that this port grape makes very good table wines, and apparently it can do well in other climes, too. This version is wisely more fun than serious, more fruit than wood.*
4. **Traminette 2004** Alto Vineyards, Illinois ($10) *As with one of its parents, Gewurztraminer, this*

grape can be too perfumed and commonly lacks elegance. Alto Vineyards has created something of happier balance.

⑤ Petit Verdot Reserve 2004 Fredericksburg Winery, Texas ($25) *As tannic as many Texas wines are, it's perhaps surprising that Petit Verdot (always tannic as well) handles the Texas climate well.*

⑥ Viognier 2004 Bookcliff Vineyards, Colorado ($13) *A soft, light, gentle version of the grape.*

⑦ Very Late Harvest (icewine) 2005 Wollersheim Winery, Wisconsin ($22) *Made from the St. Pepin, an Elmer Swenson hybrid, this augurs well for the icewine style in the northern plains and Great Lakes areas.*

⑧ Cabernet Sauvignon 2003 Milagro, New Mexico ($18) *Warm, peppery, leafy, and probably Italianate according to someone's scale, though it's not the elegant side of the family. Not that it has to be consumed with food, but it sure is helpful.*

⑨ Signature Rhone 2004 Llano Estacado, Texas ($11) *Another rough-and-tumble wine from Texas, but this blend of Carignan, Syrah, Grenache, Mourvèdre, and Viognier has plenty of fleshiness and fruit.*

⑩ deChaunac 2004 Cuthills Vineyards, Nebraska ($20) *Raspberry flavors and aromas, with some notes of black cherry and black pepper.*

Grapevine

• **On May 5, 2005,** Texas governor Rick Perry signed SB 877, which opened Texas to wine shipping by declaring the entire state "wet" for wine shipments. Texas lawmakers overwhelmingly approved the bill, which allows out-of-state wineries to ship wine directly to Texas consumers, including those who live in dry areas. Winemakers in California and elsewhere are no longer required to sell through Texas retailers.

• **Gruet Winery** released a rich and juicy Syrah in February 2006. The quantities of this first vintage are very light, fewer than 3,500 cases, which is a small amount for a winery as successful as Gruet. The results are encouraging in the vineyard with clone 697 (also called the Shiraz clone), and the results in the winery are just as positive.

• **Minnesota's first AVA** is the Alexandria Lakes Viticultural Area. Minnesota's first federally recognized wine region has only one winery—Carlos Creek, which has 40 acres of grapevines around Alexandria. It also brings in grapes from outside Minnesota. Such AVAs are likely to remain a curiosity at best. The West Elks AVA is only now beginning to show up on Colorado bottles. North Carolina's Yadkin Valley AVA has had better acceptance; numerous wineries are using the AVA on their labels.

• **Waiting for approval** is a vast, new, and meaningless AVA called Upper Mississippi River, which encompasses southeastern Minnesota and parts of Wisconsin, Iowa, and Illinois.

• **Richard Childress,** North Carolina's former moonshiner and NASCAR racing star, has opened an eponymous winery. His rapid success has traded on the image of NASCAR fans as anything but the quiche and Chardonnay set. Nonetheless, the winery has produced solid wines in a short period of time, courtesy of winemaker Mark Friszolowski. It has also released a new wine called Fine Swine Wine, blended to go with barbecues.

Canada

Tony Aspler

According to the Wine Council of Ontario, the 2005 crop shortfall will result in the loss of C$100 million to the province's 100 wineries.

TONY ASPLER

To maintain their shelf space on Liquor Control Board of Ontario shelves, the wineries will be allowed to blend up to 99 percent of offshore wines with locally grown wines and label them "Cellared in Ontario." The current legislation for "Cellared in Ontario" wines allows the wineries to blend up to 70 percent imported wines. The joke doing the Internet rounds shows an Ontario wine label in a red circle. The caption reads: "Caution: This bottle may contain traces of Ontario wine." However, legislation permitting the use of offshore wines will not affect Ontario wines that bear the VQA seal (Vintners Quality Alliance, Canada's appellation system), which must be produced from 100 per cent of grapes grown in designated viticultural areas.

TONY ASPLER is the most widely read wine writer in Canada. He was the wine columnist for *The Toronto Star* for 21 years and has authored 11 books on wine and food, including *Vintage Canada*, *The Wine Lover's Companion*, *The Wine Lover Cooks*, and *Travels with my Corkscrew*. His latest book is *Canadian Wine for Dummies*. Tony is a member of the North American advisory board for the Masters of Wine, creator of the annual Ontario Wine Awards competition, and a director of the Independent Wine & Spirit Trust. He is also a director of the Canadian Wine Library and serves on Air Canada's wine-selection committee. At the Niagara Grape & Wine Festival 2000, Tony was presented with the Royal Bank Business Citizen of the Year award. Tony also writes fiction, including a collection of wine murder mysteries featuring the itinerant wine writer-cum-detective Ezra Brant: *Blood is Thicker than Beaujolais*, *The Beast of Barbaresco*, and *Death on the Douro*. His latest book is *The Wine Atlas of Canada* (Random House, 2006). Tony is the co-founder of the charitable foundation Grapes for Humanity (www.grapesforhumanity.com). His website can be found at www.tonyaspler.com.

The ongoing problem is what happens to these offshore wines blended with token amounts of Ontario wine when they end up in Ontario's government-run liquor stores? The consumer reaches for a familiar label only to find that the wine does not taste the way he or she remembered it. I would like to see a warning stripe across labels of wines that have been blended with offshore material so that they are instantly recognizable to the consumer. Looking for the VQA symbol on the capsule or reading the fine print on the back label is not enough to maintain the integrity of the local industry.

Last to move west

Until this year, Peller Estates (Andrés Wines, Canada's second-largest winery conglomerate) was the only major Canadian wine-producing company not to have established an estate wine presence in British Columbia. The situation changed dramatically in 2005 with the purchase of Cascadia Brands, which included Calona Vineyards and its vineyard holdings in the southern Okanagan, and later Red Rooster Estate Winery, near Penticton, with its vineyards. Prior to the purchases, Peller Estates owned only a partnered vineyard interest in Rocky Ridge Vineyards, in the Similkameen Valley. The Andrés winery facility in Port Moody, established in 1961, has been closed, and Peller Estates and Calona Vineyards operations are being consolidated at the Calona winery complex in Kelowna. Andrés also operates a red-wine fermentation facility at Inkameep Vineyards in Oliver.

Grapevine

• **Paul Bosc,** the founder and owner of Château des Charmes in Niagara-on-the-Lake, Ontario, was presented with the Order of Canada, the country's highest honor, in 2005. Bosc was cited for his outstanding contribution to the Canadian wine industry. He is only the third vintner to receive the honor. The other two were the late George Hostetter of Brights Wines and Donald Ziraldo of Inniskillin. Paul Bosc is a fifth-generation winegrower with family roots in Alsace. He holds a viticulture and oenology degree from the University of Burgundy, France.

• **Ontario legalized BYOB** by passing legislation to allow diners to take their own wine into restaurants that opt into the BYOB program. Corkage charges are left to the discretion of each restaurant. In practice, these range from zero to C$60 per bottle. Restaurants must obtain a special license to be part of the program. The legislation also permits patrons to take home unfinished bottles of wine that have been securely recorked.

2005 BC CROP SHORTAGE

Five years ago, some winery operators in British Columbia were asking who was going to be able to use all the grapes that were being planted. This year, however, with a crop 20 percent smaller than normal, the question was "Where are all the grapes going to come from?" There has been a lot of development: winery openings; new winery licenses; and a lineup of additional winery applications. In the fall of 2005, there were reports of extravagant sight-unseen offers for grapes as wineries sought to replenish sold-out wine stocks under the combined pressure of a smaller crop and additional wineries chasing tonnage.

WINE AUTHORITY FOR BC

Out of sight of most BC wine consumers has been the less-than-unified relationship between larger wineries, responsible for most of the production volume in British Columbia, and many of the smaller operations, which account for the majority of licensed wineries. Former agriculture minister John van Dongen sought to unify the industry with a new BC Wine Authority, which would be at arm's length from the industry and govern all aspects of wine standards, while the BC Wine Institute would be relieved of overseeing wine standards and instead would focus primarily on sales and marketing, as well as advocacy issues with the government. In the summer of 2005, van Dongen was succeeded as minister by Pat Bell, who reaffirmed the main objectives of his predecessor and named an interim board for the Wine Authority with representation from all sectors of the industry. Their blueprint for the future will have to be approved by a double majority system covering both the large and small winery groups.

VINCOR SOLD TO CONSTELLATION

Vincor International, Canada's largest wine company and the eighth-largest in the world, having initially beaten off a hostile takeover bid from the world's largest wine conglomerate, Constellation Brands, finally succumbed on April 3, 2006. After three months, the New York State–based giant pulled the plug on their C\$1.48-billion offer for Vincor, only to return with a sweetened offer that included over C\$7 million for Vincor chairman Don Triggs' Delaine Vineyard brand and its 95-acre vineyard. The question now is: will the ultra-contemporary winery Frank Ghery designed for Vincor's La Clos Jordanne ever be built? From its origins as Château-Gai and Brights Wines, Vincor is now better known through its individual winery labels: Inniskillin, Sawmill Creek, Braeburn Cellars, Ancient Coast, L'Ambiance, and Jackson-Triggs in Ontario; and Sumac Ridge, Hawthorne Mountain Vineyards, Inniskillin Okanagan, Jackson-Triggs, and Osoyoos Larose in British Columbia. Vincor also owns wineries in Quebec, New Brunswick, California (RH Phillips), Washington State (Hogue Cellars), Western Australia (Goundrey, Amberley), New Zealand (Kim Crawford), and Western Wines in the UK. Vincor operates a chain of retail wine stores called Wine Rack.

Opinion:
Are you a wine fascist?

Recently a wine writer colleague (who will remain nameless to preserve his marriage) offered the following confession: "When my in-laws come over for dinner I open my best red wines … because they only drink white." I nodded in the way you do when you are horrified by such candor while at the same time realizing that you are guilty of the same kind of oenological fascism. Own up. When was the last time you wondered if your guests were worthy of the wine?

Richard Nixon may or may not have been a crook, but he was one of my brethren when it comes to cellar control. Nixon, apparently, had a passion for red bordeaux, particularly Château Margaux. In *All the President's Men*, Woodward and Bernstein's book about the Watergate cover-up, the *Washington Post* reporters refer to Nixon's practice of serving wine aboard the presidential yacht, USS *Sequoia*. At one dinner for senators from the South, he instructed his staff in how the wine was to be poured. Since the senators' predilection was for bourbon, which they drank liberally before dinner, Nixon had the waiters pour Mouton Cadet during the meal, since the senators' palates were already anesthetized. He had a bottle of Margaux 1966 wrapped in a towel served only to him. Bravo, says I.

There is no greater torture for a wine lover than to see great wine being guzzled by those who (a) don't know what they're drinking, and (b) would rather have something else if they were offered a choice. During a visit to Moët & Chandon, the Comtesse de Maigret told me of an occasion when her late husband found himself host to Nikita Khrushchev and his entourage. In 1960, the Russian leader was on a state visit to France, and his wife and other ladies of the party were taken on a tour of Paris. Part of the itinerary was a visit to the film set of *Can-Can*. Mrs. Khrushchev was so offended by the sight of chorus girls kicking up their legs and showing their bloomers that she had to be escorted out of the film studio. To avoid a diplomatic incident, a visit to Moët & Chandon was hastily arranged, and the Comte de Maigret's graceful salon, L'Orangerie de Trianon, was descended upon by a hundred Russians. Champenois hospitality is legendary, and the Comte ordered his cellar master to disgorge sufficient quantities of champagne from the Russian leader's birth year (1894) to slake the thirst of the KGB agents. And he watched sadly as they knocked back the rare vintage champagne as if it were vodka.

Secret agents are not the only culprits. Stories of teenagers who get into their parents' wine cellars and carry off bottles of First Growth bordeaux and domaine-bottled burgundy to parties have become urban legends. To avoid the problem, the canny collector will set aside one shelf in the cellar that is available to anyone in the household of drinking age.

Another aspect of the oenological fascism syndrome is the "conjuror host." He can make a bottle disappear before your very eyes. You are invited to a dinner party and you would like to bring along a bottle of wine that you have been saving but have never quite found the right occasion to open. You know that your host has a good cellar, so he and his guests will appreciate the wine. When you hand the bottle to him, he looks at the label; his eyes widen and he smiles. He thanks you profusely and immediately disappears with it down to his cellar as if the ambient temperature in the hallway might affect its health. And that is the last you will ever see of it.

Grapevine

- **Canadian golfer Mike Weir** is following Australia's Greg Norman and South Africa's Ernie Els into the wine vats. The left-handed Masters winner released his own label, Mike Weir Estate Winery. Two wines were offered initially: Chardonnay 2001 and Cabernet/Merlot 2002, both 100 per cent Ontario-grown fruit. The wines were made at Creekside Estate in Ontario's Jordan Station, a short drive from Niagara Falls. Proceeds from the sale of these wines will go to the Mike Weir Foundation, a charity for children. Weir introduced his wines to fellow golfers at the Nissan Open and will formally invite them to join him at the Bell Canadian Open this summer. Three hundred cases of the Chardonnay and 1,100 cases of the Cabernet/Merlot were produced.

- **Dan Aykroyd,** star of the movie *Ghostbusters* and TV's *Saturday Night Live,* has invested C$1 million in Niagara Cellars Inc., the holding company that owns four Ontario wineries—Lakeview Estates, Birchwood Estates, Thomas & Vaughan, and EastDell Estates— as well as the importing agency Diamond Estates Wines & Spirits. Aykroyd, whose company Alloy Brands launched Patron Tequila in Canada in summer 2005, wants to play a proactive role in promoting Canadian wines globally through his House of Blues venues. House of Blues Entertainment Inc., in which Aykroyd is a co-founding investor, has 10 night clubs in North America and is the third-largest purveyor of live music on the continent. The company plans to expand the network to 20 club venues in the US, Canada, and Europe over the next 10 years.

Vintage Report

Advance report on the latest harvest

2005

Ontario—For the Ontario wine industry it has been the best of times and the worst of times. The 2005 harvest, thanks to the hottest, driest growing season on record, has produced the best fruit the wineries have ever seen, particularly for bordeaux varieties. But because of the horrendously cold winter and early spring that preceded it, killing off buds and splitting vines, quantities are down drastically. A normal Ontario harvest will produce an average of 50,000 tons of grapes. This year the growers will be lucky if that figure reaches 20,000 tons. Not only was it the earliest harvest on record for table wines, but it was the earliest harvest in the province's history for icewine. Henry of Pelham picked on November 24.

British Columbia—The growing year differed from the hot growing seasons experienced from 2002 to 2004, highlighted by a long, warm, and sunny summer without extreme high temperatures. A clement fall with some sun and a few brief rain showers allowed the grapes to reach full maturity over a period that extended to early November for the latest varieties. The spread-out harvest period allowed for longer hang times, which resulted in intense flavor characteristics shown by early wine samples. Another contributing factor to the favorable flavor profiles was a smaller crop, down anywhere from 10 to 30 percent, depending on location and variety. This is believed to be mainly due to rainy conditions during the blossom period, which resulted in generally smaller berries and cluster weights, lowering the crop size. Early wine tastings and winemaker comments indicate a vintage of well-balanced wines with fewer of the 15 and 16 percent alcohol readings that popped up here and there in recent vintages. An excellent though slightly smaller vintage is the prospect.

Grapevine

- **In keeping with their "lotus land"** mentality, British Columbia vintners have begun to choose nontraditional names for their wineries. Forget about such mundane topographical descriptors as Ridge, Valley, Mountain, Creek, or Hill. How about Dirty Laundry, Laughing Stock, Therapy, and Blasted Church? And, yes, in BC there is a Lotusland Vineyards.

Updates on the previous five vintages

2004

Vintage rating: *Ontario—Red: 85, White: 92;*
British Columbia—Red: 91, White: 92

Ontario—A cool, elongated growing season began with so much rain that winemakers gloomily predicted another 1992. But Nature smiled in the fall, and throughout September into the first week of October the sun shone and rescued the harvest. Tonnage was about normal after the previous year's disastrously low grape production. The earlier-ripening varieties—Pinot Noir, Chardonnay, Pinot Gris, and Gewurztraminer— showed better than the bordeaux varieties. This year is better for whites, with lively acidity.

British Columbia—Summer weather was very good until a dramatic shift to cool, moist conditions began in August and continued for a month. Grapes were slowed in ripening, but the cooler weather gave the vines the time they needed to pack the fruit with flavor and intensity without generating excess sugar and low acid, and some outstanding white wines resulted. On the downside, the cool, moist conditions caused some scattered fungus problems, resulting in up to 20 percent crop loss in some cases. The return of warm, sunny conditions in the third week of September continued through into November, allowing red wines to complete the ripening process and produce good-quality wines.

2003

Vintage rating: *Ontario—Red: 85, White: 90;*
British Columbia—Red: 94, White: 91

Ontario—The Indian summer encouraged maximum ripeness, but it also woke up the ladybugs. The horrendously cold winter reduced the tonnage of grapes to below 50 percent of normal yields. Some varieties, such as Sauvignon Blanc and Merlot, were down to 25 percent of the 2002 harvest, but the quality of the fruit was good because of Nature's Draconian thinning.

British Columbia—A record grape crop following the hottest and sunniest year ever. The 2003 red wines are potentially even better than the highly lauded 2002s. Bill Dyer at Burrowing Owl used extended maceration on his Cabernet Sauvignon for the first time.

2002

Vintage rating: *Ontario—Red: 86, White: 85;*
British Columbia—Red: 94, White: 94

Ontario—Yields were slightly down from predicted levels, but the quality and concentration of fruit were excellent. Winemakers are predicting that 2002 will be one of the best vintages on record, particularly for red wines.
British Columbia—It is now likely that 2002 will go on record as being the best vintage yet, surpassing 1998 by having more moderate heat for further flavor development and allowing white wines to retain natural acid balance.

2001

Vintage rating: *Ontario—Red: 88, White: 83;*
British Columbia—Red: 89, White: 94

Ontario—A vintage compromised by the presence of ladybugs, which affected the flavor of some wines. Some Sauvignon Blanc was harvested almost two weeks earlier than usual. Rains in late September and October slowed down some of the mid-season harvesting, which helped the reds.
British Columbia—A high-end vintage for most whites. Red wines also did well, with excellent fruit ripeness and a softer-than-average tannin structure in all but the latest-ripening varieties.

2000

Vintage rating: *Ontario—Red: 80, White: 84;*
British Columbia—Red: 85, White: 89

Ontario—One of the worst years since 1987, but those who gambled and left fruit on the vine were rewarded with a late burst of sunny weather in October. Chardonnay and Riesling performed surprisingly well.
British Columbia—A cool early September opened up into a warm, sunny fall, allowing crops to ripen fully, with higher sugar levels than 1999.

GREATEST WINE PRODUCERS

1. Jackson-Triggs Vintners (British Columbia)
2. Sumac Ridge (British Columbia)
3. Blue Mountain Vineyards (British Columbia)
4. Henry of Pelham Family Estate (Ontario)
5. Black Hills (British Columbia)
6. Quails' Gate (British Columbia)
7. Stratus (Ontario)
8. Malivoire (Ontario)
9. Pillitteri Estates (Ontario)
10. Inniskillin (Ontario)

FASTEST-IMPROVING PRODUCERS

1. CedarCreek Estate (British Columbia)
2. Fielding Estate (Ontario)
3. Summerhill Estate (British Columbia)
4. Golden Mile Cellars (British Columbia)
5. Tawse Winery (Ontario)
6. Recline Ridge (British Columbia)
7. Lang Vineyards (British Columbia)
8. Coyote's Run (Ontario)
9. Sandhill Small Lots (British Columbia)
10. Vineland Estates (Ontario)

NEW UP-AND-COMING PRODUCERS

1. Le Clos Jordanne (Ontario)
2. Laughing Stock Vineyards (British Columbia)
3. Orofino Vineyards (British Columbia)
4. Glenterra Vineyards (British Columbia)
5. Flat Rock Cellars (Ontario)
6. Legends Estate (Ontario)
7. Huff Estate (Ontario)
8. Arrowleaf Cellars (British Columbia)
9. Silver Sage Winery (British Columbia)
10. Norman Hardie Winery (Ontario)

BEST-VALUE PRODUCERS

1. Colio Wines (Ontario)
2. Calona Wines (British Columbia)
3. Jackson-Triggs Vintners (Ontario)
4. Lakeview Cellars (Ontario)
5. Gehringer Bros Estate (British Columbia)
6. Jackson-Triggs Vintners (British Columbia)
7. Greata Ranch (British Columbia)
8. Sumac Ridge Estate Winery (British Columbia)
9. Magnotta Wines (Ontario)
10. Hernder Estate (Ontario)

GREATEST-QUALITY WINES

1. **Black Sage Vineyard White Meritage 2004** Sumac Ridge, British Columbia (C$19.99)
2. **Carlo Negri Signature Merlot 2002** Colio Wines, Ontario (C$59.95)
3. **Black Sage Vineyard Cabernet Franc 2003** Sumac Ridge, British Columbia (C$16.99)
4. **Nadja's Vineyard Riesling 2004** Flat Rock Cellars, Ontario (C$19.95)
5. **Platinum Reserve Meritage 2002** CedarCreek Estate, British Columbia (C$39.99)
6. **Robyn's Block Chardonnay 2002** Tawse Winery, Ontario (C$48)
7. **Phantom Creek Syrah 2003** Sandhill Small Lots, British Columbia (C$29.99)
8. **Mystic River Gewurztraminer 2004** Wild Goose, British Columbia (C$18.95)
9. **Vintners Private Reserve Chardonnay 2003** Peninsula Ridge, Ontario (C$42)
10. **Proprietors Grand Reserve Riesling Icewine 2002** Jackson-Triggs, British Columbia (C$60)

BEST BARGAINS

1. **Chardonnay 2004** Hawthorne Mountain Vineyards, British Columbia (C$12.39)
2. **Pinot Blanc 2003** Sumac Ridge, British Columbia (C$11.29)
3. **Cabernet/Merlot 2002** Creekside Estate, Ontario (C$12.95)
4. **Riesling 2003** Château des Charmes, Ontario (C$10.95)
5. **Chardonnay 2004** Stoney Ridge Bench, Ontario (C$11.95)
6. **Semillon 2003** Mount Boucherie, British Columbia (C$11.90)
7. **Heritage House Vidal 2003** Legends Estate, Ontario (C$12)
8. **Trius Riesling 2003** Hillebrand, Ontario (C$13.95)
9. **Rotberger 2004** Gray Monk, British Columbia (C$13.49)
10. **Okanagan Reserve Cabernet Sauvignon 2002** Inniskillin, British Columbia (C$15.99)

MOST EXCITING OR UNUSUAL FINDS

1. **Barrel Fermented Chardonnay 2002** Niagara College Teaching Winery, Ontario (C$18.95) *A big, strapping, buttery, toasty wine made by oenology students under Jim Warren.*
2. **Sandstone Gamay Reserve 2002** 13th Street, Ontario (C$25) *More Oregon Pinot Noir than Beaujolais in style; rich and concentrated black-cherry flavor.*
3. **Zweigelt Icewine 2004** Summerhill Estate, British Columbia (C$150) *Perfectly captures the "cherries and chocolate" of the St Laurent parent rather than the leathery berry character of its Lemberger side.*
4. **Rock Oven Red 2003** Kettle Valley, British Columbia (C$35) *Unusual blend of Shiraz and Cabernet Sauvignon. Like other Kettle Valley reds, this is a big wine—the most recent release, big, jammy, and plummy, with velvet tannins.*
5. **Okanagan Zinfandel 2003** Inniskillin, British Columbia (C$29.99) *Canada's only domestic Zinfandel. Big, robust, distinctive varietal aromas and flavors set against smooth, mellow tannins.*
6. **Black Muscat 2003** Blue Grouse, British Columbia (C$15.90) *Complex bouquet of everything from cassis to lychee from this unique blend of three Muscat varieties.*
7. **Vidal 2004** Ancient Coast, Ontario (C$8.45) *Usually reserved for icewine, this off-dry Vidal has a floral nose and tropical fruit flavors.*
8. **Riesling Semi-Dry 2004** Fielding Estate, Ontario (C$12.95) *Ontario Wine Awards gold medallist. Semi-dry, tropical fruit, lime, and honey, with a hint of petrol.*
9. **Vivace 2004** Glenterra Vineyards, British Columbia (C$15) *A blend of exotic vinifera and hybrid white varieties grown on Vancouver Island. Crisp, fruity, with a smooth flavor profile.*
10. **Framboise NV** Southbrook Farm & Winery, Ontario (C$14.95) *Yes, it's a fruit wine but good enough to have been sold at Harrods. Like liquid raspberry jam, but with good balancing acidity.*

Chile

Peter Richards

Chile's economy is booming, and wine sales continue to grow—so why the insistent rumble of discontent from the country's wine industry in 2006?

PETER RICHARDS

In a word: money. The Chilean wine business had it particularly tough in 2005 due to a dollar in free fall and a strong peso—a situation caused in large part by the strength of its economy and record copper sales. Because Chile has the highest export rate of any wine-producing country (75 percent of production) and invoices mainly in dollars, this currency imbalance has hit profits hard. Industry observers estimate profits may be down by as much as 20–30 percent in 2005.

Viñas de Chile president Aníbal Artiztía believes that, when the figures come in, the balance sheets for 2005 will show the worst comparative results in 15 years. The industry has repeatedly called on the government to intervene, but their pleas have fallen on deaf ears.

The impact of this situation is already being felt across Chile. Grape prices for the 2006 harvest have plummeted as wineries pass on the cost of falling margins to grape producers. Bulk wine shipments have slowed as maintaining competitive prices becomes unsustainable. Belt-tightening is taking place within the industry and further consolidation is expected.

There is a silver lining to this cloud, however. First, the situation is forcing producers to adopt realistic and long-term measures toward covering themselves when such events occur in the future. In addition, the faltering domestic market—until recently scorned by many producers—has rapidly gained in allure and may experience something of a

PETER RICHARDS is a freelance wine writer. His first book was *Wineries with Style* (Mitchell Beazley, 2004). Chile is a specialist focus for Peter, who has lived and worked there and now travels regularly to the country. He covers Chile for many wine publications, and his next book is *The Wines of Chile* (Mitchell Beazley, 2006).

renaissance as wineries court the Chilean public in order to boost profits in pesos. What is more, falling bulk exports and rising average prices may mean headaches for some producers, but they are music to the ears of those in the industry who believe Chile should be targeting a more premium market.

Acquisition fever

A flurry of acquisition activity marked 2005, and more is expected in 2006 as consolidation becomes an increasingly attractive option in the face of falling margins and ever-growing international competition.

In March 2005, Chile's largest producer, Concha y Toro, bought ailing Limarí cooperative Francisco de Aguirre for US$17 million. The move was significant not just for the way in which it underlined Limarí's emergence as a wine region of undoubted promise. It also marked a new phase of consolidation and expansion in the Chilean wine industry, within which increasing control over owned vineyards was seen as an attractive policy in the face of high grape prices.

Shortly afterward, it was announced that the Southern Sun Wine Group—owners of Tarapacá, among other wineries—had acquired a new member in mid-size Maipo winery Casa Rivas. At the same time, Santa Rita, which had lost out to Concha y Toro in the bid for Francisco de Aguirre, made an ambitious play for control of fellow Maipo stalwart Undurraga. The move was ultimately unsuccessful, but sources suggest that Santa Rita's owner, the Claro group, remains on the lookout for further acquisitions. Chile's other major player, San Pedro, is also reportedly eyeing acquisition options.

Grapevine

• **Measures to protect** Chile's native forest may end up hindering its wine industry. Legislation under consideration in the Chilean senate could mean restrictions on new vineyard plantings. The law looks set to redefine the boundaries of Chile's native forests and will also impose restrictions on developing slopes with an incline greater than 45 degrees. Wine-industry officials are lobbying to prevent the law from being passed in its present form.

• **While most of Chile** was engaged in hearty back-slapping after sealing its free-trade agreement with China in late 2005, the Chinese began to size up their new business partner's assets, wine included. Industry sources have indicated that at least two deals are being negotiated between Chinese investors and Chilean wineries.

EXPERTS EXPECT EXPONENTIAL EXPORTS

By 2014, Chile will be exporting more than 10 million hl of wine at a value of over $1.8 billion, according to a study published in 2005.

In order to supply such projected growth, a minimum of 67,000 ha will need to be added to the country's vineyard, which as of 2004 was 112,056 ha. Annual production will be 12.9 million hl.

At least, that's the optimistic forecast, according to ODEPA, the Chilean government agricultural research department that carried out the report, entitled Chilean Agriculture 2014. The figures represent a so-called high hypothesis, based on an annual growth rate of 8 percent in both volume and value. The "low hypothesis," calculated on a yearly increase of 5 percent, would see an annual production by 2014 of 10.5 million hl and exports of 7.6 million hl at $1.36 billion.

Either scenario would represent startling growth for a country whose production was in decline until 1995, when output hit a nadir of 3.1 million hl, and whose exports in 1986 amounted to 100,000 hl at a value of $12.6 million. By contrast, in 2004 Chile was exporting 4.7 million hl of wine at a value of US$835 million, while total production stood at 6.3 million hl.

TERROIR RESEARCH BREAKS NEW GROUND

Terroir has become the hot topic on the lips of progressive Chilean winemakers. The phenomenon is not merely talk: many initiatives are now under way, examining Chile's soils, climate, viticultural practices, clones, and rootstocks, all aimed at delivering workable results to growers.

The most high-profile of these is Casa Silva's three-year study taking place across Colchagua. An initial report delivered in early 2006 showed that significant results had already been collated with regard to Syrah, Carmenère, and Cabernet in different sites in the valley. De Martino has continued its ongoing detailed study of *terroir* across Chile; its team also conducted a comparative tour of French regions in 2005. Matetic, Concha y Toro, Montes, and Lapostolle are all actively engaged in similar research and development.

The trend is not restricted to individual producers. Studies are also being undertaken on a regional level, with Cachapoal, Maule, Maipo, and even Itata working to unravel the secrets of their respective *terroirs*. In mid-2006, Colchagua began a three-year process to map its geological, climatic, and viticultural conditions. Viticultural consultants have never been in such high demand.

Grapevine

- **Burgundian producer** Louis-Michel Liger-Belair could provide the next high-profile foreign venture in Chile. The Vosne-Romanée winemaker is looking to establish a small project for Pinot Noir and Chardonnay production. All Liger-Belair will say about where he intends to grow the grapes is that it will be "an area that gives long maturation."

Opinion:
Expand the local market

Chile would do well to get its own house in order before taking on the world. In the past decade, the country's wine producers have been transfixed by export markets, to the extent that Chile now sends a massive 75 percent of its production abroad. But more time and energy should be spent developing the market in their own back yard.

The truth is that real wine culture is thin on the ground in Chile. Much of the wine sold locally is low-grade stuff in cartons. Annual per capita consumption is stuck in a rut at around 16 liters. Beer is far more popular. Winemakers drink Coke with their meals. Social polarization doesn't help: in Chile, the top 20 percent of the population earns 60 percent of the income, and the bottom 20 percent earns just 3.3 percent. Waiters are almost universally inept when wine is at hand, and most restaurants have worrisomely dull lists. As a result, producers have been reluctant to fight what they see as a tough battle to convince Chileans to turn on to wine and trade up.

This is a short-sighted and potentially damaging strategy. In the first place, a strong local market makes sense in terms of a ready-made customer base. It would also help counteract adverse currency fluctuations such as the current one. But, more important, developing a sound wine culture (and the notion of gastronomy that this necessarily entails) would be enormously beneficial in helping to convince others around the world that Chile is a country worth getting to know, worth exploring, and worth buying into.

Chilean wine producers need to ply their home turf. Generic body Wines of Chile needs a brief and resources to convince the nation to drink more (and better) wine. More wines need to be made available to the domestic market, and glaring price disparities, which still exist, should be remedied. Sommeliers have to raise standards across the board in restaurants. Only by doing this can Chile become a proud, well-balanced wine nation.

Grapevine

• **Glassy-winged sharpshooters,** insects that are vectors for Pierce's disease, have devastated crops on Easter Island, raising fears about a possible influx into Chile. The source of the infestation is thought to have been an ornamental plant brought from California via Tahiti in 2005. Agricultural authorities in Chile have been put on alert.

Vintage Report

Advance report on the latest harvest

2006

Caution and concern were evident among winemakers as the 2006 vintage began. The general early consensus was that this was shaping up to be a sound but unexceptional vintage, albeit a difficult year to call at the outset. Spring and summer conditions were mixed after heavy winter rains had boosted groundwater levels, which later led to excess of vigor in many sites. In early September, a particularly severe and widespread spring frost hit not just the usual areas (Casablanca, Curicó), but also regions like Colchagua, which were largely unprepared. Early-budding varieties were most affected, such as Chardonnay in Casablanca (with losses of up to 50 percent in some vineyards) and Merlot in warmer areas. A January heat wave was followed by a cool start to February. Some dilution and lack of ripeness are expected, and many producers are predicting late-season rains. After the optimism surrounding the 2005 vintage, the initial reaction to 2006 is notably more guarded.

Updates on the previous five vintages

2005

Vintage rating: *Red: 96, White: 93*

Chile's most hyped vintages in recent times have been the odd years: 1999, 2001, and 2003. While 2005 is no exception to this rule, it is different to its predecessors in character—this was not simply a hot, dry year but a long, moderate season that led to a late harvest and wines with notable freshness, complexity, and natural balance. Reds fared the best and offer good to outstanding quality; whites are good to very good. Overall, this was an excellent vintage for Chile.

2004

Vintage rating: *Red: 89, White: 86*

An uneven vintage that gave good, if variable, results. A hot summer and rainy fall meant that this was something of a pressurized harvest in which good vineyard management was crucial. Alcohol levels tend to be quite high and, while the wines generally show good concentration and often notably ripe character, this has resulted in some imbalance, especially in whites from coastal appellations like Casablanca and San Antonio. One to drink sooner rather than later.

2003

Vintage rating: *Red: 93, White: 92*

Generally a very successful vintage, with concentrated, ripe reds and characterful whites. This was a warm year with a long, dry fall, and the wines tend to reflect this in their maturity and intensity. A classic warm Chilean vintage that gave consistent quality and good to excellent wines across the board.

2002

Vintage rating: *Red: 79, White: 84*

It pays to be circumspect with the 2002 vintage because this was a patchy year in which some parts of the country performed well and others (mainly Colchagua to the south) struggled due to particularly damaging late-season rains. Some dilution and lack of proper maturity are evident, especially in the reds, particularly as they age; whites are generally more successful but also benefit from early drinking. Choose your producer, and region, with care.

2001

Vintage rating: *Red: 94, White: 93*

A very successful vintage that gave wines with good levels of ripeness and concentration, but also a fine natural balance. The best 2001 wines continue to age gracefully and improve in the bottle.

Grapevine

• **Chile's viticultural horizons** continue to expand. Errázuriz has just planted an ambitious new vineyard in Chilhué, just 8 miles (13 km) from the coast in Aconcagua. Ventisquero is looking to plant in Huasco (to the north of Elqui, in Atacama territory) as well as coastal Maipo. This would be near Concha y Toro's new vineyard in Navidad, 7.5 miles (12 km) from the shoreline in what is effectively coastal Cachapoal. Torres's pioneering site in coastal Maule is starting to produce fruit, and to the north, several wineries have embarked on trials in maritime conditions in far western Colchagua. Meanwhile, high in the Andes, new projects are under way in both Elqui and Curicó.

GREATEST WINE PRODUCERS

1. Concha y Toro
2. Montes
3. Errázuriz
4. Cono Sur
5. Almaviva
6. Viñedos Orgánicos Emiliana
7. Casa Lapostolle
8. Santa Rita
9. De Martino
10. Los Vascos

BEST-VALUE PRODUCERS

1. Concha y Toro
2. Misiones de Rengo
3. Cono Sur
4. San Pedro
5. Viñedos Orgánicos Emiliana
6. Ventisquero
7. La Rosa
8. Santa Rita
9. Viñedos Emiliana
10. Valdivieso

FASTEST-IMPROVING PRODUCERS

1. Altaïr
2. Matetic
3. Casa Marín
4. Tabalí
5. Garcés Silva (Amayna)
6. Pérez Cruz
7. Calina
8. Haras de Pirque
9. Viña Leyda
10. Casa Silva

GREATEST-QUALITY WINES

1. **EQ Syrah 2004** Matetic, San Antonio (CLP 22,000)
2. **Sideral 2003** Altaïr, Rapel (CLP 20,000)
3. **Almaviva 2001** Almaviva, Maipo (CLP 59,900)
4. **20 Barrels Chardonnay 2004** Cono Sur, Casablanca (CLP 12,000)
5. **Coyam 2003** Viñedos Orgánicos Emiliana, Central Valley (CLP 10,000)
6. **Lot 5 Chardonnay Wild Yeasts 2004** Viña Leyda, San Antonio (CLP 12,500)
7. **Purple Angel 2003** Montes, Colchagua (CLP 29,000)
8. **Clos Apalta 2003** Casa Lapostolle, Colchagua (CLP 59,000)
9. **Amayna Sauvignon Blanc 2005** Garcés Silva, San Antonio (CLP 7,800)
10. **Single Vineyard Carmenère 2003** De Martino, Maipo (CLP 8,900)

NEW UP-AND-COMING PRODUCERS

1. Kingston
2. La Reserva de Caliboro (Erasmo)
3. Gillmore
4. Neyen
5. Quintay
6. Polkura
7. Antiyal
8. Los Maquis
9. Odfjell
10. Falernia

Grapevine

• **New converts** to the biodynamic cause in Chile include La Reserva de Caliboro in Maule and Seña in Aconcagua. The latter was converted to biodynamics in 2005 following the split between Errázuriz and Mondavi.

• **Production figures** for the 2005 vintage show that total output was 7.89 million hl, up 25 percent on 2004.

BEST BARGAINS

1 **Adobe Syrah 2004** Viñedos Orgánicos Emiliana, Colchagua (CLP 4,250)

2 **Pinot Noir 2005** Cono Sur, Colchagua (CLP 4,000)

3 **Reserva Cabernet Sauvignon/Syrah 2004** Misiones de Rengo, Rapel (CLP 4,000)

4 **Limited Edition Cabernet Sauvignon/Carmenère 2004** Montes, Colchagua (CLP 5,300)

5 **Viognier 2005** Cono Sur, Colchagua (CLP 4,000)

6 **Casillero del Diablo Cabernet Sauvignon 2004** Concha y Toro, Central Valley (CLP 3,500)

7 **Gato Negro Shiraz 2004** San Pedro, Central Valley (CLP 1,350)

8 **Sauvignon Blanc 2005** Los Vascos, Casablanca (CLP 3,500)

9 **Marqués de Casa Concha Syrah 2004** Concha y Toro, Cachapoal (CLP 6,990)

10 **Barrel Select Carmenère 2003** Santa Ema, Maipo (CLP 4,980)

MOST EXCITING OR UNUSUAL FINDS

1 **Erasmo 2001** La Reserva de Caliboro, Maule (CLP 15,000) *Ambitious but exciting debut vintage: a bordeaux blend made by an Italian in the backwater territory of Maule.*

2 **Amayna Barrel Fermented Sauvignon Blanc 2004** Garcés Silva, San Antonio (CLP 7,800) *Chile's most successful attempt at barrel-aged Sauvignon to date.*

3 **Bayo Oscuro Syrah 2003** Kingston, Casablanca (CLP 23,000) *Cool-climate Syrah is all the rage in Chile, and this highly promising new producer is already producing one of the country's finest.*

4 **Vendimia Tardía Riesling 2003** Torres, Curicó (CLP 9,850) *It's not often you find a balanced, botrytis-affected sweet wine from Chile, but this is one.*

5 **Legado Syrah 2004** De Martino, Choapa (CLP 5,990) *This spicy red is opening up uncharted territory: Choapa is between Aconcagua and Limarí.*

6 **The Blend 2003** Errázuriz, Aconcagua (CLP 16,990) *Cabernet, Syrah, Sangiovese, and Carmenère— it's full-on stuff, but it works.*

7 **Neyen 2003** Neyen, Colchagua (CLP 32,000) *Impressive debut vintage made from old vines in Apalta.*

8 **Visión Riesling 2004** Cono Sur, Bío-Bío (CLP 8,300) *Chile's far south continues to delight and surprise with its potential, and this wine is one of its best advocates.*

9 **Unusual Cabernet Sauvignon/Shiraz/Zinfandel 2004** Terramater, Maipo (CLP 18,000) *A strange combination of varieties for Chile adds up to make an almost Italianate wine.*

10 **Ilusión Reserva Lo Mejor Chardonnay 2003** Gracia, Bío-Bío (CLP 11,900) *Understated but elegantly constructed Chardonnay from a new venture in Chile's far south.*

Grapevine

• **Flashy new wineries** are all the rage in Chile. Take Apalta, which was only just recovering from the party to open Montes's impressive new feng shui winery when, in January 2006, Casa Lapostolle unveiled its stunning new construction just around the corner amid much pomp and ceremony. Both projects are reported to have cost in excess of US$6 million. It would appear that investor confidence has not been overly troubled by the recent exchange-rate niggles.

Argentina

Tim Atkin MW

Improved quality and the continuing weakness of the peso have enabled Argentina's exports to grow at a faster rate than any other wine-producing country over the past three years.

TIM ATKIN MW

The latest figures from Wines of Argentina show that exports to the end of 2005 stood at just over 12 million cases, up from 4.68 million in 2002. The only dark cloud on the horizon is that the average case price has actually fallen during this period, although 2005's figure was slightly higher than 2004's.

The United States remains the most important export market for Argentina and has a significantly higher per-case price than the UK, Argentina's second-biggest export market. The US has 19.63 percent of the market by volume and 23.62 percent by value, compared with the UK's 18.24 percent and 14.55 percent, respectively. This confirms that Argentina is still regarded as a source of inexpensive rather than premium wines in the UK. The current levels of promotion-led competition between the major retailers have meant that an estimated 80 percent of all Argentine wine is sold on promotion in the UK. This partly explained the decision to open a generic office in 2006 (see below).

After the US and the UK, Argentina's major markets are Brazil, Canada, the Netherlands, Denmark, Germany, Finland, Mexico, and (perhaps surprisingly) France.

TIM ATKIN MW is the wine correspondent of *The Observer* and wine editor at large of *OLN* and *Class* magazines. He has won more than a dozen major awards for his wine writing, including five Glenfiddichs and four Lanson Wine Writer of the Year honors. He first visited Argentina in 1994, since when he has returned to the country on eight occasions to taste its wines, dance the tango badly, and eat copious amounts of protein. Tim judges wines all over the world and is co-chairman of the International Wine Challenge, the world's biggest blind-tasting competition.

Exports continue to be dominated by a handful of companies, with La Riojana (19.56 percent), Peñaflor (15.49 percent), and Bodegas Esmeralda (10.34 percent) accounting for more than 45 percent of sales overseas. The next seven largest importers in order are La Agricola, Norton, Trivento, Graffigna, Finca Flichman, Fantelli Jesus, and Finca La Celia.

Vineyards increase

Argentina's vineyard area has begun to grow again after the wholesale uprooting of the 1980s. The total area under vines now stands at 212,659 ha, according to the Instituto Nacional de Vitivinicultura. Since 2000, Argentina's vineyard area has increased by 11,546 ha (5.74 percent), although it is still way below the 300,000 ha plus of the late 1970s.

Mendoza remains the most important wine region by far, accounting for 69.89 percent of plantings, followed by San Juan (22.13 percent) and La Rioja (3.85 percent), Río Negro (1.35 percent), and Catamarca (1.11 percent). The rest of the country's wine regions, including Salta and Neuquén, have less than 1 percent of the total area under vine.

The age of Argentina's vineyards remains a comparative plus. A total of 51.35 percent of the total area is planted with vines that are 25 years old or more. By comparison, 15.89 percent has been planted since 2000, most of it with international varieties.

The most planted varieties are now Malbec (21,183 ha), Bonarda (17,224), Cabernet Sauvignon (16,184), Syrah (10,846), Torrontés (7,957), Merlot (7,095), and Chardonnay (4,771). Black plantings are increasing at a much faster rate than whites. Since 2000, the former have grown by 25.82 percent, while the latter have fallen by 5.08 percent.

Grapevine

• **Michel Rolland's love affair** with Argentina shows no sign of abating. As well as being involved with three projects of his own, Val de Flores, Yacochuya, and Clos de los Siete (co-owned with a group of friends from Bordeaux), he also consults, among others, for Norton, Salentein, Finca Sophenia, Bodega Los Angeles, and Etchart. The world's most famous oenologist even has his own consulting laboratory in Mendoza, called EnoRolland, run by Gabriela Celeste. His association with Argentina can only be good for its prestige.

• **Argentina is not best known** for its sparkling wines, but the sector was highlighted at a tasting in London recently. No fewer than 10 companies showed their fizzes, the quality of which varied from the distinctly ordinary to the highly promising. The stars of the tasting were the Don Cristobal 1492 Brut Blanc de Blanc, Luigi Bosca's Boheme, a blend of 60 percent Pinot Noir/Pinot Meunier and 40 percent Chardonnay, and Rosell Boher's Traditional Method Brut. Sparkling wine.

LONDON BASE FOR WINES OF ARGENTINA

Argentina plans to open its first-ever generic office in the UK in 2006, using the threefold increase in funding generated by COVIAR (the Corporación Vitivinícola Argentina). The decision was made at a meeting in Mendoza during a seminar co-organized by Wines of Argentina and COVIAR in December 2005 to determine the country's wine-export strategy. Details were unclear as this book was going to press, but Wines of Argentina intends to appoint a UK director in the first half of the year. In all probability, the office will operate from the Argentinian embassy in London. This follows the earlier appointment of Fernando Farré as the Buenos Aires-based managing director of Wines of Argentina. Wines of Argentina is made up of 90 different wineries covering the country's main wine-producing regions and is self-funded.

Grapevine

• **Top producer Nicolás Catena** has announced that, from the 2003 vintage, he will offer two wines under his signature label, Nicolás Catena Zapata. The wine has previously been released solely as a blend of Cabernet Sauvignon and Malbec (with a 52/48 split in 2001). Catena says that the quality of the company's high-altitude Malbecs from 2003, 2004, and 2005, as well as increasing global interest in non-Cabernet varieties such as Shiraz/Syrah, Tempranillo, and Grenache, has convinced him to release a pure Malbec under the Nicolás Catena Zapata label. "I am beginning to think that Malbec does not need Cabernet Sauvignon to make a great wine."

• **Mendoza has been elected** as one of the world's eight wine capitals, joining Melbourne, Bordeaux, San Francisco, Oporto, Bilbao, Florence, and Cape Town (see www.greatwine capitals.com). The network aims to encourage international tourism, as well as economic, academic, and cultural exchanges between cities.

• **Trapiche,** Argentina's largest wine producer, has launched three single-vineyard Malbecs to highlight "the extraordinary potential of Argentina's terroirs." The three wines, all from the 2003 vintage, are from growers José Blanco (in Ugarteche), Felipe Villafañe (La Consulta), and Pedro Gonzalez (El Cepillo). The idea in future will be to choose the three best Malbecs from the company's top 100 growers.

• **Norton has changed** the name of its top wine, Norton Privada, to Privado in Brazil after it was pointed out that *privada* was Portuguese for "toilet."

• **Finca Flichman,** which has been owned by the Portuguese company Sogrape since 1998, is to launch a new international wine brand called Misterio, aimed at the entry-point sector of the market. The range will consist of Chardonnay, Malbec, Shiraz, and Cabernet Sauvignon.

• **Trapiche has announced** a US$10-million investment plan for the next five years to support its sales drive on the export and domestic markets. Most of the money will be spent on planting new vineyards, installing two new grape reception lines, improving the air-conditioning system in the barrel cellar, and increasing stainless-steel storage capacity by 2 million liters.

Opinion:
Don't bet exclusively on Malbec

Over the past five years, Argentina has proved beyond doubt that Malbec is a world-class grape. For tasters who had grown up on the greener flavors and harder tannins of Cahors, there was always a doubt about Malbec's pedigree. It was valued as a blending grape in Bordeaux, but could it perform as a solo varietal? Argentina has proved that it can. Even comparative skeptics, such as Nicolás Catena, who believed that Cabernet Sauvignon was the country's best bet to strut upon the world stage, has conceded that the Malbecs from the 2003, 2004, and 2005 vintages deserve to be bottled solus under his top label.

Most of Argentina's best reds are produced from Malbec, from Noemía to Cobos, Val de Flores to A Crux. As these wines garner ever-higher scores from journalists and command increasingly high prices in Argentina and the US (if not necessarily the UK), I fear that more and more producers will be tempted to concentrate on Malbec to the exclusion of other grape varieties.

Understandably, Malbec is the most planted grape variety in Argentina, with 21,183 ha of the country's 212,659 ha of vineyards, according to the Instituto Nacional de Vitivinicultura. The figure has increased by 29.57 percent since 2000, and grew by 56.35 percent between 1990 and 2000. This is as it should be, given the variety's quality, but there is a real danger that, in its rush to promote Malbec, Argentina will lose sight of what makes it unique in the New World: its diverse viticultural heritage.

No country in the world, Old or New, can match Argentina's lineup of grapes. Just consider a few of the varieties Argentine winemakers have at their disposal: Cabernet Sauvignon, Merlot, Syrah, Tannat, Petit Verdot, Barbera, Pinot Noir, Cabernet Franc, Grenache, Bonarda, Sangiovese, Tempranillo, Chardonnay, Viognier, Sauvignon Blanc, Pinot Gris, Riesling, Verdelho, and Torrontés.

It would be a shame if some of these varieties were overlooked in favor of Malbec. Argentina is an old winemaking country in some respects, but modern viticulture and winemaking are little more than 20 years old. Some of the best cooler-climate growing areas are even more recent than that, and we don't yet know how different varieties will perform in, say, the higher-altitude vineyards of San Juan, Salta, or Mendoza or the depths of Patagonia. On a recent visit, the quality of wines I tasted from little-planted varieties such as Tannat, Petit Verdot, and Caladoc suggests that, now more than ever, Argentina should prize its viticultural diversity.

Vintage Report

Advance report on the latest harvest

2006

The 2006 vintage is already being hailed as one of the finest ever in Argentina, producing red wines with deep color, soft tannins, and intense flavors. The whites are also very good, especially from higher-altitude vineyards in areas such as the Uco Valley. In Mendoza, the season was marked by a cool, snowy winter followed by warmer-than-average temperatures in spring and summer. Higher-than-normal levels of humidity meant that the vines did not suffer from heat stress. Partly because of the increased humidity, there was pronounced diurnal temperature variation, which promoted slow grape maturation and well-balanced wines. In January, temperatures in Mendoza varied between 50°F (10°C) and 90°F (32°C). On the minus side, Mendoza suffered from a large hailstorm on December 27, 2005, which hit the subregions of Perdriel and Vistalba. There was a second, less damaging storm in the first week of March, which affected the areas of Medrano and the central eastern region. Yields are up on 2005, with some wineries talking about an increase of 20 percent. Reacting to a potentially large crop, many leading producers used fruit thinning in December and January to reduce yields by up to 50 percent.

Updates on the previous five vintages

2005

Vintage rating: *Red: 93, White: 92*

A cooler ripening season and a late harvest produced elegant, full-colored wines with intense fruit flavors and a slightly lower degree of alcohol than usual. The lower-altitude vineyards suffered from a heavy frost in October and November 2004, with Cabernet Sauvignon and Merlot particularly badly hit. January and February were cool. There were fears that rains in January might pose problems, but good work in the vineyards avoided this. Much more serious, at least in Perdriel, were the hailstorm and heavy rains that fell on February 14. March was somewhat warmer, bringing on complete ripeness of the grapes, which were harvested in good condition and with no sign of dehydration. In San Juan, several producers rated 2005 as one of the best-ever vintages, with Syrah vines showing particularly well. The best Malbecs and Chardonnays are most impressive in 2005, especially from high-altitude vineyards, where late fall was dry and sunny, yet comparatively cool.

2004

Vintage rating: *Red: 94, White: 90*

The summer was hot and dry, with temperatures remaining high during the nights. Some rain fell at the end of January, leading to a rapid spurt in growth. In February, temperatures fell and there was a little more rain. In order to minimize the effects of botrytis, the picking of white grapes began on February 8. For the black grapes, however, picking was later than usual due to delays in achieving optimal phenolic ripeness. The white wines are full of flavor, with crisp acidity, while the best reds are outstanding, with deep color, full tannins, good aging potential thanks to thicker skins, and intense varietal character.

2003

Vintage rating: *Red: 97, White: 94*

Each year, a group of experts meets in Mendoza to evaluate the vintage. For the 2003 vintage, the official position is that the white wines are "very good" and the reds "outstanding." Spring was cool and dry, but the summer was the hottest on record, with rainfall well below average. Some vineyards suffered from heat stress, which called for carefully managed irrigation. The fall was cooler, and grapes were picked in ideal conditions. Opinions are divided as to whether the wines are as good as those from the excellent 2002 vintage, but some vineyard managers, such as Alejandro Sejanovich at Catena Zapata, think that in some vineyards 2003 outperformed 2002. Cabernet Sauvignon was the star variety in 2003, although some of the high-altitude Malbecs are outstanding, too.

2002

Vintage rating: *Red: 98, White: 94*

Considered in Mendoza to be the best vintage for 10 years or more, with plentiful water for irrigation and close to ideal conditions. The ripening period was long, with cool, dry weather. This gave wines with concentrated fruit flavors. In Salta, in the north, the vintage took place 10 days earlier than usual. There are many outstanding wines from this vintage, with the best reds showing fruit concentration, deep color, ripe tannins, and marked aging potential. The top reds are still drinking very well and will continue to improve for five to eight years or more.

2001

Vintage rating: *Red: 89, White: 91*

Generally considered a good vintage, though the wines lack the concentration of flavors of the 2002s. Chardonnays are most successful.

GREATEST WINE PRODUCERS

1. Norton
2. Catena Zapata
3. O Fournier
4. Terrazas
5. Val de Flores
6. Fabre Montmayou
7. Viña Cobos
8. Pulenta Estate
9. Yacochuya
10. Noemía

FASTEST-IMPROVING PRODUCERS

1. Trapiche
2. Navarro Correas
3. O Fournier
4. Familia Zuccardi
5. Pascual Toso
6. Finca Flichman
7. Lagarde
8. Dominio del Plata
9. Salentein
10. Altas Cumbres

NEW UP-AND-COMING PRODUCERS

1. Carlos Pulenta
2. Cristobal 1492
3. Finca Sophenia
4. Malma
5. Saurus
6. Finca de Altura
7. Finca La Florencia
8. Callia
9. Bodega del Fin del Mundo
10. Alma 4

BEST-VALUE PRODUCERS

1. Callia
2. Familia Zuccardi
3. Pascual Toso
4. Doña Paula
5. Trivento
6. La Riojana
7. Norton
8. Clos de los Siete
9. Finca La Celia
10. Lurton

GREATEST-QUALITY WINES

1. **Cobos Malbec 2003** Paul Hobbs, Luján de Cuyo (AP 250)
2. **Nicolás Catena Zapata 2001** Catena Zapata, Mendoza (AP 280)
3. **Felipe Villafañe La Consulta Single Vineyard Malbec 2003** Trapiche, Mendoza (AP 180)
4. **Terrazas 2002** Cheval des Andes, Mendoza (AP 280)
5. **Privada 2003** Norton, Luján de Cuyo (AP 210)
6. **Malbec 2003** Val de Flores, Valle de Uco (AP 150)
7. **Gran Corte 2003** Pulenta Estate, Agrelo (AP 94)
8. **A Crux Malbec 2003** O Fournier, Valle de Uco (AP 110)
9. **Lindaflor Malbec 2003** Monteviejo, Valle de Uco (AP 142)
10. **Malbec 2003** Noemía, Patagonia (AP 250)

BEST BARGAINS

1. **Pinot Noir Oak Cask 2004** Trapiche (AP 25)
2. **Sauvignon Blanc 2005** Doña Paula (AP 12)
3. **Shiraz/Malbec Reserve 2004** Trivento (AP 10)
4. **Pinot Grigio 2005** Finca La Celia (AP 20)
5. **Chardonnay 2004** Finca La Florencia, Familia Cassone (AP 12)
6. **Malbec 2005** Norton (AP 12)
7. **Bonarda 2005** Alamos (AP 20)
8. **Syrah 2004** Pascual Toso (AP 12)
9. **Malbec Colección Privada 2004** Navarro Correas (AP 15)
10. **Viognier La Linda 2005** Luigi Bosca (AP 15)

MOST EXCITING OR UNUSUAL FINDS

1. **Tannat/Malbec 2004** Doña Paula (AP 45) *A 65/35 blend of Tannat and Malbec aged in French oak for 18 months from Luján de Cuyo. The acidity of the Tannat really lifts the rich fruit of the Malbec.*
2. **Tomero Petit Verdot 2004** Carlos Pulenta (AP 60) *Like his brother Eduardo at Pulenta Estate, Carlos Pulenta is doing fantastic things with this underrated variety. As you'd expect, the perfume is delightful.*
3. **Verdelho 2005** Cristobal 1492 (AP 20) *To my knowledge, this is the only Verdelho in Argentina. It's grapey and exotic, with crisp acidity and plenty of perfume.*
4. **Chardonnay/Semillon 2005** Infinitus (AP 12) *A notably good buy, this herbal, unoaked Patagonian blend is remarkably stylish at the price.*
5. **Corbec Appassimento 2002** Masi (AP 55) *A blend of Valpolicella's Corvina with Malbec, this rich, super-concentrated wine was made using the* appassimento *technique of the Veneto.*
6. **Caladoc Textual 2004** Santa Julia (AP 35) *Made from a crossing of Malbec and Grenache, this oak-aged first release from Santa Julia is a revelation. The first of many in Argentina?*
7. **Gala 3 2005** Luigi Bosca (AP 75) *A highly unusual, partially barrel-fermented blend of Viognier, Chardonnay, and a little Riesling, from a company whose white wines are some of Argentina's best.*
8. **Syrah/Tannat 2005** Callia (AP 12) *Confirmation of the potential of these two varieties in the warm conditions of San Juan, this juicy, deeply colored red deserves to clean up on export markets.*
9. **Mora Negra 2003** Finca Las Moras (AP 50) *Combining two grapes that work well together (30 percent Bonarda and 70 percent Malbec), this top-end blend from San Juan is full of personality.*
10. **Malamado Malbec 2003** Santa Julia (AP 50) *A fortified Malbec with a portlike 19.5 percent alcohol, this is one of several brilliantly off-the-wall wines from Santa Julia. There's a fortified Viognier, too.*

Grapevine

• **Argento,** Argentina's leading wine brand worldwide, is now handled by the Argento Wine Company, a three-way partnership between Bodegas Esmeralda (producer of Argento), current distributors Bibendum, and the Adelaide-based International Wine Fund. Launched in 1999 by Nicolás Catena, Argento currently sells a total of 500,000 cases in 32 different markets. Argento is strong in Norway, Denmark, Belgium, Switzerland, Sweden, and Brazil, as well as the UK.

Australia

Huon Hooke

Aussie jokes about the European wine lake are looking a bit lame, since Australia went into the 2006 vintage with around 2.5 billion liters of wine, largely from the record 2005 harvest, still lying in tanks unsold.

HUON HOOKE

That is a record quantity of stock, and, barring Nature's intervention, the 2006 harvest will be another bumper one. Contracts are being abandoned all over the country. The big risk going into vintage was that growers may be encouraged to make their own wine rather than leave the crop on the vines. This is likely to dig them into a deeper hole. They might believe that this will be adding further value to the grapes, but it is a value they will never be able to recoup, since it will be next to impossible to sell a new brand in such a crowded market.

The grape surplus is impacting on the entire wine market, as brands proliferate (more than 100 new producers open their doors each year) and "cleanskins"—no-frills bottles with either a minimal label or no label at all, sometimes distressed sales, vintage ends, or unsaleable wines—nibble away at sales of branded wines. At the same time, it is becoming

HUON HOOKE is coauthor of *The Penguin Good Australian Wine Guide*, the country's most respected buyer's guide. He is a wine-marketing and production graduate of Roseworthy Agricultural College and has been a weekly columnist for the John Fairfax Group of newspapers since 1983. Huon writes columns in the Good Living section of the *Sydney Morning Herald* and the *Good Weekend* magazine of the *Herald* and *Melbourne's Age*. He is also contributing editor of Australian *Gourmet Traveller Wine* magazine and writes for various other publications, such as *Decanter* and *Slow Wine*. He has been judging in wine competitions since 1987 and judges eight to 10 shows a year in Australia and abroad. Huon has judged in New Zealand, South Africa, Chile, Belgium, Slovenia, Canada, and the US. He currently chairs several Australian competitions and is a senior judge at Adelaide and Sydney.

ever harder for new and small producers to get their wines into retail stores, especially the major chains, Coles Myer and Woolworths. In December 2005, Vintage Cellars (Coles's premium line of more than 100 stores) admitted it was pruning its product lines from 7,500 to 2,500.

Yellow Tail goes upmarket

Yellow Tail is the latest export success story, especially in the United States. But the Yellow Tail name stood for A$10 wines—until now. In late 2005, Yellow Tail owner Casella Wines released, with a fanfare, two premium reds under a new Yellow Tail Premium label. Both from the 2003 vintage, they're a McLaren Vale Shiraz, winner of the trophy for the best previous-vintage red at the Brisbane Wine Show, and a Wrattonbully Cabernet Sauvignon, winner of the equivalent trophy at the Melbourne Wine Show. That double is a rare achievement in itself. And the price? Wait for it … A$50 each. They are both very good wines in the high-alcohol, high-glycerol, super-ripe, sweetly opulent, fruity/oaky style. Yellow Tail is the number-one imported wine brand in the US; its total global sales up to November 2005 were 23 million cases.

Heritage liquidated

The liquidation of Heritage Fine Wines, one of two wine-investment companies that went broke in early 2005, is slowly grinding on. Heritage owed A$2.8 million, and the other company, WineOrb, A$1 million. According to its liquidator, Peter Ngan, WineOrb was so badly managed that most of the A$15 million worth of wine it held on behalf of clients would have to be sold to pay costs and secured creditors. This is being contested in the courts.

The collapse of Heritage meant that hundreds of investors have had 1.3 million bottles of wine tied up for nearly a year while a stocktake (costing more than A$3.9 million) was carried out. This wine, valued at A$70–80 million, was held in five cellarage facilities on behalf of investors. Liquidator Nick Crouch has levied fees to pay his costs: A$3 per bottle and rising. Several wineries lost substantial sums: Gilbert's Siding lost A$600,000, Balnaves A$130,000, and Wirra Wirra a smaller amount. Heritage was founded on an ambitious plan to ship fashionable blockbuster Australian red wines to wealthy US collectors, a market that fell apart in 2003–04. Shortly before WineOrb collapsed, auctioneer Langton's had warned its clients about wine-investment companies making extravagant promises of overly optimistic returns. See www.cellarit.com.au for more details.

Opinion:

Bigger but not better

One of the biggest stories of 2005 was Foster's acquisition of Southcorp. This created Foster's Wine Estates—at time of writing, the world's biggest wine company. Before long, Foster's started retrenching people and putting wineries on the market—usual procedure following a takeover. With the much-expanded Wynns winery in Coonawarra, Foster's no longer needed Jamiesons Run, while its modern Rosemount winery in the Hunter meant that The Rothbury Estate was expendable, too. At time of writing, neither had been sold. If you list all the wineries that have been sold or closed to winemaking by Foster's/Beringer Blass and its precursor Mildara Blass in recent years, it is quite a long one; it includes, among others, Knappstein (Clare); Saltram and Krondorf (Barossa); Ingoldby and Andrew Garrett (McLaren Vale); Yellowglen, Yarra Ridge, St. Huberts, and Balgownie (all in Victoria); and Briar Ridge and The Rothbury Estate (Hunter Valley). This is how the modern corporate side of the wine business works. Massive wineries like Wolf Blass Bilyara and Penfolds Nuriootpa are unquestionably state of the art, and the winemakers know their onions, but one cannot escape the feeling that the attention to detail and handmade care that are possible with small-lot winemaking must be compromised.

Melbourne bans unfinished whites

The Royal Melbourne Wine Show has at last taken some steps toward eradicating the practice of judging and awarding unfinished wines. At the 2005 judging, no unfinished white wines were allowed. Not only did this make the judges' job a lot easier at one of the nation's biggest wine competitions (with 4,389 entries in 2005), it restored some credibility to what should be one of Australia's most important competitions. Regrettably, Melbourne still judges and awards unfinished reds, which means the Jimmy Watson Trophy is still being awarded to a barrel sample of red wine about 17 months old that has yet to be finally blended and bottled. However, the show has a new wine committee, and more changes are possible. Brisbane's Royal Queensland Wine Show is the other dinosaur, still judging and awarding unfinished whites and reds.

Brett strikes Mount Langi

Brettanomyces phobia claimed its first big scalp when Mount Langi Ghiran decided not to release its A$56 flagship Langi Shiraz 2002. The wine had been tasted and rated very highly by critics prior to release, but tests showed unacceptable levels of Brett-associated compounds, which were thought to be increasing as the wine aged. The 2002 was rated one of the best ever Langi Shirazes—a once-in-a-decade vintage, according to winemaker Trevor Mast. But did the company overreact? Was it scared of criticism from a small number of "Brett Nazis" among fellow winemakers, the media, and the wine trade? What is clear is that the new owners, the Rathbone family of Yering Station and Parker Coonawarra Estate, intend to cast Langi Shiraz as a top-level wine, and they will go to great lengths to uphold its reputation. Brettanomyces has become the latest obsession of wine tasters. There is a suspicion that some people invoke Brett to damn any wine they don't like, while scientists say all red wines have some Brett.

Predators prowl

Pernod Ricard, which owns the Orlando Wyndham Group in Australia, has swallowed Allied Domecq, owner of New Zealand's Montana, creating yet another leviathan drinks company. This follows the amalgamation of Beringer Blass and Southcorp, which follows the incorporation of Hardys into Constellation, and so the mega-takeovers continue. The seemingly pointless process of big fish being gobbled up by even bigger fish could continue until there are just a couple of big global liquor conglomerates left, circling each other like the last two crazed gladiators left standing at the end of a Roman bloodbath. It seems to have a lot to do with wealth, quite a bit to do with ego, and precious little to do with quality.

Grapevine

- **Bannockburn** looks to be back on track, following the resignation of founding winemaker Gary Farr after 26 years. Giaconda's Rick Kinzbrunner offered to help out during the 2005 vintage, and later in the year former Moorilla Estate winemaker Michael Glover was appointed. Glover is making all the right sounds about the great *terroir* of the property and the vineyard being more important than the "cult of the winemaker."

- **New Zealand wine imports** rose by 16 percent in September 2005 compared to the previous year. Sauvignon Blanc was largely responsible, which was no surprise to anyone setting foot in a Sydney or Melbourne bottle shop. Australians have gone ape about Kiwi Savvy: 55 percent of the Sauvignon Blanc drunk by Australians is from New Zealand. We are also drinking more Semillon/Sauvignon blends, but less Chardonnay.

- **Petit Verdot** from Murray Valley is enjoying success as a varietal red wine. This hot, irrigated region is the source of much inexpensive Aussie wine. "PV" is often an unwooded "fruit bomb," marketed young, and inexpensive— around A$10–15. Kingston Estate's Bill Moularadellis predicts that Petit Verdot will eventually be the preferred black grape in the warmer regions because it's so well suited to the climate.

Vintage Report

Advance report on the latest harvest
2006

Early indications are that most of Australia has had a good to very good season, with a very early start in the southern regions from Coonawarra to the Yarra Valley and Mornington Peninsula, and down to Tasmania. Harvest was three weeks early in the Yarra—and abbreviated, with most varieties ripening closer together than usual. Sound grapes were the norm with no disease pressure. The main issues in all southern areas are likely to be overripeness and higher-than-desired alcohols. Western Australia's experience was almost the mirror opposite: an extremely cool summer caused very late ripening, with high expectations for white wines but worries about getting reds fully ripe. South Australia in general had a mild season with very good results, especially in the Murray Valley (Riverland) and Clare, which looks to be as good as 2005, with high natural acids— of particular benefit to Riesling. With record volumes of wine still lying in tanks from the 2005 vintage, the wine industry was relieved that early forecasts were for a slightly smaller harvest.

Updates on the previous five vintages
2005

Vintage rating: *Red: 95, White: 96*

This is an outstanding vintage—the best since 2002 and possibly 1998. It gave benchmark wines of all the classics: Rieslings in the Clare and Eden valleys, Semillons in the Hunter Valley, Shiraz in the Barossa, Cabernet in Coonawarra, and Pinot Noir in Tasmania and the Yarra Valley. The whites are tops, but there are standout reds throughout South Australia, Victoria, New South Wales, and Tasmania. Western Australia is the only glitch: mid-vintage rain upset the pattern. Production equaled the 2004 record, although high yields in the high-quality regions were not a problem as in 2004. A second successive year of big tonnage meant the pressures of oversupply and low prices were intensified.

2004

Vintage rating: *Red: 92, White: 86*

Though not as massive as originally estimated, the crop was a record. The southern parts of Victoria had high yields and avoided temperature extremes. Yarra Valley quality is good despite a wet end to the vintage: whites are very good, but lower yields would have made it a top red year, too. Coonawarra had big yields and, while quality is mostly good, overcropped vineyards struggled to ripen. Clare had a good vintage despite suffering in the February heat, and the Rieslings are good but forward. McLaren Vale and the Barossa made excellent Shiraz, and the Adelaide Hills had a decent vintage overall. The Hunter made very good Semillon and Chardonnay, but reds are light.

2003

Vintage rating: *Red: 88, White: 84*

Universally, 2003 was a year of reduced yields caused by general drought, with small bunches of small berries. Rain close to harvest resulted in berry split, further cutting yields in several regions, from Tasmania to central Victoria to McLaren Vale; smoke taint from disastrous January bushfires in the alpine valleys of northeast Victoria added insult to injury. Some noted "big red" regions, such as Heathcote, Barossa, and McLaren Vale, struggled to attain flavor ripeness despite very high alcohols, because a hot summer abruptly turned into a cool late summer and fall. There are some reds with unripe tannins. The best wines are Shiraz and Chardonnay, with patches of excitement created by Clare and Eden Valley Riesling, Adelaide Hills Sauvignon Blanc, Coonawarra Cabernet and Merlot, and Yarra Valley Pinot Noir. Southern Victoria had a very good vintage. Late rain spoiled the Tasmanian vintage and, to a lesser degree, the Great Southern in Western Australia. Margaret River was just fair, and quite variable.

Grapevine

- **Arch-traditionalist Bob Roberts**— who for 35 years refused to follow fashion and instead made consistently delicious, ageworthy red wines with underplayed oak and moderate alcohol—has sold Mudgee's icon winery Huntington Estate. But all's well: the buyers are next-door neighbors Tim and Connie Stevens of Abercorn, another quality winery. Bob and Wendy Roberts established Huntington in 1969 and breathed new life into the Mudgee region. They established the celebrated Huntington Music Festival, which will continue.

2002

Vintage rating: *Red: 94, White: 95*

Record cool temperatures during the summer brought South Australia an outstanding vintage, especially for white wines in Clare and the Barossa—and even McLaren Vale, not noted for fine dry whites. The Riverland had a great year with some fine whites and reds showing superb color and varietal flavor. There is a slight question mark over flavor ripeness for reds in cooler areas like Eden Valley. The Hunter Valley, Mudgee, Orange, Hilltops, and Riverina all had an excellent vintage, while southerly regions like Tasmania and southern Victoria were able to ripen their grapes fully. Southern yields were miserly, especially in cool regions such as Tasmania, Yarra, Mornington, and Geelong. Western Australia was less favoured, but whites are good.

2001

Vintage rating: *Red: 90, White: 80*

This was one of the hottest summers on record in South Australia, bringing an early harvest of good, rich, ultraripe reds. The whites were also remarkably decent, because the heat wave preceded *véraison*. A good Hunter Semillon year, although it was a wet harvest for the Hunter, Mudgee, Cowra, and Orange; and a very good year for southern Victoria and Tasmania—especially for Pinot Noir. It was a special year for Western Australia reds, especially Margaret River Cabernets. Other highlights are in Eden Valley, the Adelaide Hills, and—for big reds—the Pyrenees.

GREATEST WINE PRODUCERS

The brands that qualify the umbrella company for inclusion are listed after the parentheses.

1 Foster's Wine Estates (national)
   Penfolds, Seppelt, Wynns, Rosemount, Coldstream Hills, Devil's Lair
2 Hardys (national)
   Hardys, Houghton, Yarra Burn, Brookland Valley
3 Lion Nathan (national)
   Petaluma, Knappstein, Stonier, St. Hallett, Mitchelton
4 Cullen (Margaret River)
5 Grosset (Clare Valley)
6 Shaw & Smith (Adelaide Hills)
7 Moss Wood (Margaret River)
8 Cape Mentelle (Margaret River)
9 Henschke (Eden Valley)
10 Brokenwood (Hunter Valley)

FASTEST-IMPROVING PRODUCERS

1 Woodlands (Margaret River)
2 Sandalford (Margaret River)
3 De Bortoli (Yarra Valley)
4 Capercaillie (Hunter Valley)
5 Juniper Estate (Margaret River)
6 Kaesler (Barossa Valley)
7 Millbrook (Perth Hills)
8 Meerea Park (Hunter Valley)
9 Wise Wines (Margaret River)
10 Casella (Riverina)

NEW UP-AND-COMING PRODUCERS

1 Castagna (Beechworth)
2 Tomboy Hill (Ballarat)
3 Toolangi (Yarra Valley)
4 Chalice Bridge (Margaret River)
5 Philip Shaw (Orange)
6 Pirie (Tasmania)
7 Michael Unwin (Grampians)
8 McHenry Hohnen (Margaret River)
9 Heathcote Estate (Heathcote)
10 Faber (Swan Valley)

BEST-VALUE PRODUCERS

The brands that qualify the umbrella company for inclusion are listed after the parentheses.

1 De Bortoli (Riverina)
   Windy Peak, Gulf Station, Black Creek, Deen De Bortoli, Sacred Hill
2 Hardys (South Australia)
   Stepping Stone, Leasingham, Bastion, Banrock Station, Oomoo
3 Peter Lehmann (Barossa Valley)
4 Cheviot Bridge/Long Flat Wine Company (national)
5 Taylors (Clare Valley)
   Wakefield Estate in Europe
6 Mitchelton (Goulburn Valley) Preece
7 Westend (Riverina)
   Three Bridges, Richland
8 Nugan Estate (Riverina)
   Cookoothama, Talinga Park
9 Orlando Wyndham (national)
   Jacob's Creek, Jacob's Creek Reserve, Richmond Grove, Wyndham Estate
10 Foster's Wine Estates (national)
   Seppelt, Leo Buring, Saltram, Annie's Lane, Ingoldby, Rosemount, Wynns, Wolf Blass

GREATEST-QUALITY WINES

1 **Reserve Bin 03A Chardonnay 2003** Penfolds, Adelaide Hills (A$85)
2 **Warner Vineyard Shiraz 2002** Giaconda, Beechworth (A$60)
3 **Vat 1 Semillon 1998** Tyrrells, Hunter Valley (A$48)
4 **Gladstones Cabernet Sauvignon 2003** Houghton, Margaret River (A$64)
5 **Prendiville Cabernet Sauvignon 2002** Sandalford (A$95)
6 **Reserve Shiraz/Viognier 2003** Yering Station (A$58)
7 **Hanlin Hill Riesling 2005** Petaluma, Clare Valley (A$28)
8 **Watervale Riesling 2005** Grosset, Clare Valley (A$33)
9 **Riesling 2005** Howard Park, Great Southern (A$25)
10 **Wallcliffe Sauvignon Blanc/ Semillon 2002** Cape Mentelle, Margaret River (A$35)

BEST BARGAINS

1 **Gramp's Five Generations Cabernet/Merlot 2002** Orlando Wyndham, South Australia (A$16)
2 **Cabernet Sauvignon 2003** Water Wheel, Bendigo (A$18)
3 **Watervale Riesling 2004** Richmond Grove, Clare Valley (A$19)
4 **Oomoo Shiraz 2004** Hardys, McLaren Vale (A$15)
5 **Semillon 2005** Peter Lehmann, Barossa Valley (A$10)
6 **Padthaway Viognier 2004** Stonehaven, Limestone Coast (A$17)
7 **Hand Picked Riesling 2005** Wirra Wirra, Adelaide Hills (A$18)
8 **Bin 65 Chardonnay 2005** Lindemans, Southeast Australia (A$10)
9 **Sacred Hill Cabernet/Merlot 2005** De Bortoli, Riverina (A$6)
10 **Talinga Park Cabernet/Merlot 2004** Nugan Estate, Riverina (A$10)

MOST EXCITING OR UNUSUAL FINDS

1 Aeolia Roussanne 2004 Giaconda, Beechworth (A$85) *Like nothing else in Australia (where Roussanne is rare), this has been compared to Beaucastel Blanc. Concentrated fruit, barrel-fermented, malo'd, and aged on lees, it's a bright-yellow-colored, spiced-honey-scented wine of great richness and mouth-filling generosity.*

2 Tappa Pass Vineyard Selection Shiraz 2002 Henschke, Barossa (A$57) *An exciting new wine, based on a quality grape grower called Fechner. The fruit used to go into the Keyneton Estate red. This is classic, spicy, meaty, cool-year Shiraz with the extra layer of complexity conferred by a great year. Charcoal, spice, blackberry, and cedar; deliciously succulent.*

3 Georgia's Paddock Nebbiolo 2004 Jasper Hill, Heathcote (A$53) *Nebbiolo adds an exciting new string to this famous Shiraz-maker's bow. Heathcote is otherwise untested for Nebbiolo, and this early effort is extremely promising.*

4 TGV Tempranillo Grenache Viognier 2004 Yalumba (A$35) *Yalumba is Australia's most experienced grower and maker of Viognier, and this eyebrow-raising blend is more than a novelty. Viognier seems to add a similar soft, velvety succulence as it does to Shiraz.*

5 Baillieu Myer Family Reserve Viognier 2004 Elgee Park, Mornington Peninsula (A$40) *A few Viognier growers are starting to achieve balance and subtlety*
along with the distinctive character of the grape that has proven so elusive. Elgee Park is one.*

6 Pinot Grigio 2004 Miceli Iolanda, Mornington Peninsula (A$20) *Australia's most exotic-tasting PG, with delicious mineral, honey, and spice flavors and a fine texture. Anthony Miceli isn't afraid of a little botrytis, nor of solids in the fermenting juice.*

7 Pemberton Reserve Chardonnay 2003 Wise Wines, Pemberton (A$35) *Pemberton is a small, emerging region in southwest Western Australia, cooler than Margaret River and well suited to Chardonnay. This is one of the best yet made there.*

8 Kevin Cabernet Sauvignon 2001 Woodlands, Margaret River (A$78) *Woodlands is one of the oldest Margaret River vineyards, recently revived after a hiatus when the grapes were sold off and the label vanished. The 2001, a great Cabernet from one of the best vintages in recent times, is an exciting portent.*

9 Prestige Viognier 2004 Haan, Barossa Valley (A$35) *Haan makes two Viogniers: one from the shaded grapes inside the canopy; the other from exposed fruit on the outside. This is the former: a more subtle, refined wine.*

10 Marsanne 2004 Ravensworth, Canberra (A$18) *Ravensworth is the new brand from Bryan Martin, who works at Canberra icon winery Clonakilla. Marsanne is rare in the district, and this is a complex style with a lot of winemaker input, resulting in delicious, honeyed, nutty nuances.*

New Zealand

Bob Campbell MW

I estimate that 70–80 percent of New Zealand's wine is made by companies with overseas ownership.

BOB CAMPBELL MW

France became the biggest stakeholder in New Zealand's wine industry in 2005 when Pernod Ricard purchased Allied Domecq (NZ) (formerly Montana Wines, the country's largest winemaker). Only two of New Zealand's six largest wineries—the Villa Maria group and Delegat's—can boast local ownership.

While there are many benefits of global ownership, the loss of local control is unsettling. Large international companies such as Pernod Ricard, Constellation Brands, LVMH, and Foster's can offer the sort of marketing prowess and distribution access that locally owned wineries can only dream about. They can provide investment and, in some instances, technical assistance to make better and more sophisticated wines. Certainly, New Zealand's burgeoning export sales would be leaner without offshore ownership.

My concern lies with the rather different philosophies that drive locally owned and offshore-owned wineries. Villa Maria's owner, George Fistonich, for example, is motivated as much by a desire to make great wine as he is to make a profit. He has an emotional as well as a financial investment in winemaking. His business decisions are influenced by a sense of pride in what he has achieved and what he has yet to achieve.

A different set of dynamics applies to decision-makers in large multinational companies, where the expectations are to optimize profits and increase investment value. The wine industry needs to be profitable to survive, but it needs to have soul to retain its individuality and character.

BOB CAMPBELL MW lives in Auckland, where he is group wine editor for ACP Media and wine editor for five magazines within that publishing company. He writes for publications, including *Wine Spectator*, in seven countries, and has judged at wine competitions in seven countries. Bob established his own wine school in 1986, and 18,000 people have graduated from his wine diploma course.

"FAMILY OF TWELVE" FORMS ELITE GROUP

In a move that has evoked cries of "elitism" from some wineries not in the club, 12 prestigious family-owned wineries have formed an alliance to promote their wines worldwide. They have christened their group the Family of 12. They are: Kumeu River and Villa Maria (Auckland); Millton Vineyard (Gisborne); Craggy Range (Hawke's Bay); Palliser and Ata Rangi (Martinborough); Fromm, Nautilus, and Lawson's Dry Hills (Marlborough); Neudorf (Nelson); Pegasus Bay (Waipara); and Felton Road (Central Otago).

REPORT WARNS OF TOUGH TIMES

New Zealand's Ministry of Agriculture and Forestry (MAF) has released a review of Marlborough's grape-growing industry. The report looked at 18 grape growers and found that falling grape prices and the pressure to increase quality had reduced confidence that profits would grow, at least in the short term. There is increasing pressure for smaller, less efficient growers to merge with others or to quit the industry. Bulk varieties are no longer financially viable, but replacing vines with premium varieties is costly, involving capital expense and loss of income until full production is regained.

Cowboy operators out to make a quick profit are seen as a threat, since their activities could result in a loss of quality and the eventual commodity status of wines that presently command a premium price. There is also a fear of oversupply. The large 2004 vintage was a wakeup call for many growers who had grown used to supplying grapes in a seller's market for many years.

In the long term, growers feel that the trend toward winery-owned vineyards could make them obsolete. Some smaller growers were considering leaving the industry while land prices were high. The high cost of frost protection, water shortages, vineyard diseases, and the shortage of labor were all cited as areas of major concern.

Grapevine

• **Villa Maria Estate** has purchased the small Marlborough-based wine producer Thornbury—an active exporter, with 90 percent of its wine going offshore. It is many years since Villa Maria owner George Fistonich bought the Hawke's Bay wineries Esk Valley and Vidal. He has successfully maintained independent marketing and production status for both wineries and can be expected to adopt a similar arm's-length strategy with Thornbury.

• **Winemaker Mike Weersing** was found to be over the legal breath-alcohol limit while driving home from a wine tasting. Weersing admitted drinking one bottle of beer after the tasting—an almost compulsory practice at such events. The judge accepted that Weersing had "unintentionally absorbed" alcohol during the wine tasting and did not suspend his driver's license, although he did have to pay a small fine.

KIWI CAPS OFFER A NEW TWIST

With an estimated 85 percent share of the market, screwcaps have made a near-total takeover of New Zealand's wine-closure market. Most screwcaps are imported from France (Stelvin) and Australia (Auscap).

Despite the obvious appeal (to me, at least) of "Kiwicap," Stephan Jelicich, managing director of Esvin Wine Resources, has christened his new screwcaps "Alvis," although it has little to do with venerable British motor cars or Memphis, Tennessee.

Advantages for local winemakers include branding on smaller batches and a shorter delivery time: weeks instead of four or five months. The new caps carry a 10-month warranty, the longest for any screwcap supplier, according to Jelicich.

"We estimate that 95 percent of New Zealand wine will soon carry a screwcap, although there will always be a handful of small producers in areas such as Hawke's Bay and Martinborough that stick to corks," added Jelicich.

DELEGAT'S WINS THE BATTLE OF OYSTER BAY

In a battle that captivated the wine industry and investors, Delegat's successfully repelled a takeover for Oyster Bay Marlborough Vineyards (OBMV) from Marlborough grape grower Peter Yealands.

OBMV represents a substantial investment in land and vineyards. Delegat's established the publicly funded vineyard and takes the entire crop of grapes at an independently calculated price. After a fierce battle that began with an opening offer to shareholders by Yealands of NZ$3.10, the price seesawed to NZ$4 with a temporary victory to Delegat's.

Yealands successfully complained to the NZ Stock Exchange that information had been withheld and the bidding reopened. Delegat's finally sealed a win at $6 a share, enough to guarantee a controlling, if expensive, ownership.

Grapevine

- **Pinot Noir 2007** will be staged in Wellington between January 31 and February 3, 2007. It will adopt a theme similar to the two previous Pinot Noir conferences in New Zealand's capital city in 2001 and 2004. Speakers and panelists include Matthew Jukes (UK), Claude Bourguignon (France), Pierre-Henri Gagey (France), Ch'ng Poh Tiong (Singapore), Michel Bettane (France), and Dr. Peter Dry (Australia).

- **New Zealand's first kosher-certified wines** were made by Nelson's Tasman Bay winery in the 2005 vintage. A Sauvignon Blanc and a Pinot Noir were made by Norman Lever, a kosher winemaker and observant Jew who traveled from Melbourne for the vintage. The wines will be distributed by the world's biggest kosher-wine distributor, the Royal Wines Company of New York.

Opinion:
Kiwi on French label causes furore

Cries of righteous indignation filled the air when Nelson winemaker Greg Day was prevented from selling his slightly tacky Kiwi White label in Sweden by a French winery that had registered the brand "Kiwi" in the European market. The cries got louder when it was revealed that an English company owned the European rights to "Aotearoa" (the Maori name for New Zealand). But wait … haven't New Zealand winemakers been ripping off French terms since they first learned how to ferment grapes? While most have dropped terms like champagne, burgundy, and claret, French words still abound on back labels.

Winery websites wanting

Perhaps it's a universal problem, but I am constantly irritated by out-of-date information on winery websites. Wineries that pride themselves on their attractive cellar-door sales areas neglect their websites despite the fact that they attract far more traffic and have the ability to promote, or demote, the winery's image. My favorite websites include Craggy Range, Villa Maria, and Pernod Ricard NZ.

Unoaked and unpalatable

Unoaked Chardonnay should be more popular than it is at a time when wine drinkers are seeking wines with greater fruit focus. Instead of using top-quality Chardonnay grapes to elevate the status of the unoaked category, winemakers have produced a second-class sipper by downgrading quality and price. There are one or two exceptions, such as the excellent Felton Road Chardonnay, but in general, unoaked Chardonnay has a deserved reputation of being a pretty lackluster wine. It's too late to resurrect the style. Perhaps it's time to introduce a new breed of "lees-aged Chardonnay," using premium grapes and adding extra complexity with exposure to the yeast lees during maturation in tank or old barrels. It just might fly.

Grapevine

• **Ager Sectus,** owner of the Crossroads, Southbank, and Braided River brands, has purchased the Marlborough winery and vineyards of The Crossings. The purchase gives Ager Sectus wineries and vineyards in Marlborough and Hawke's Bay.

Vintage Report

Advance report on the latest harvest

2006

Flowering and fruit set occurred very early throughout the country. Early flowering increased the risk of damage by late winter frost, but there were no reports of frost damage. The weather after flowering was nearly perfect in every region until late in March, when most regions experienced heavy rain, the fallout of tropical cyclone Wati, which dissipated before reaching New Zealand. By that time, most white grape varieties had been harvested from Hawke's Bay and farther north. Winemakers in those regions then had to decide whether to harvest their first black grapes under pressure or wait in the hope of a return to fine weather. Marlborough and most other South Island regions, particularly Central Otago, had an exceptionally early harvest. Marlborough's Sauvignon Blanc crop was mostly harvested before the rains fell. When this report was filed, the weather outlook appeared to be fairly stable. Most winemakers appeared confident that a warm, dry fall would result in the balance of the crop being harvested in good condition. If they're correct, it will be a generally excellent vintage.

The indications are that quantity may be down slightly, but the increased vineyard acreage will result in a record harvest of around 165,000 tons.

Updates on the previous five vintages

2005

Vintage rating: *North Island—Red: 86, White: 80; South Island—Red: 79, White: 87*

The vintage yielded 139,400 tons of grapes, down on 2004 due to wet, cold weather during flowering. A long, dry Indian summer brought Auckland/Northland its best-ever harvest in quality terms. The Hawke's Bay vintage was dogged by rain, particularly in the early stages. Winemakers are impressed and even surprised by the deep colors and good flavors in red wines, but most admit that whites were less successful. Martinborough suffered from rain, but the wines generally, and Sauvignon Blanc in particular, are very good indeed, although some suffer from slightly elevated alcohol levels. Some Canterbury producers were affected by frost at the beginning of October and generally poor flowering. Quality is average to good. A below-average year for Central Otago Pinot Noir with a few obvious exceptions.

2004

Vintage rating: *North Island—Red: 80, White: 78;*
South Island—Red: 72, White: 78 (except Sauvignon Blanc: 70)

New Zealand's largest-ever vintage was more than double the frost-affected 2003 vintage. It was a generally cool vintage with heavy February rain. Central Otago was hit by frost at the beginning and the end of the season. Sauvignon Blanc was 88 percent higher than the previous record vintage in 2002. Marlborough Sauvignon Blanc is variable, with many dilute and high-acid wines. Warm, dry weather at the end of the vintage helped compensate for difficulties early in the season. Hawke's Bay has produced some excellent reds, although Cabernet Sauvignon struggled to ripen fully in some districts.

2003

Vintage rating: *North Island—Red: 60, White: 65;*
South Island—Red: 75, White: 80

All regions except Central Otago and Nelson suffered frost damage, ranging from minor in Auckland to severe in Hawke's Bay. The North Island suffered from generally wet conditions, while the South Island was relatively dry, with drought in some areas. Many grape growers in frost-affected areas tried to recover some production by harvesting later-ripening grapes from "second set," but this often resulted in unsatisfactory wines with varying ripeness levels. The crop of Marlborough Sauvignon Blanc was significantly reduced by frost, although quality was good, with some outstanding wines made.

2002

Vintage rating: *North Island—Red: 83, White: 85;*
South Island—Red: 88, White: 88

A long, hot, dry spell of fall weather resulted in many outstanding wines. Gisborne enjoyed a vintage that several winemakers called the best ever. Hawke's Bay produced many good whites and reds. A high crop of Sauvignon Blanc in Marlborough led to some variation in quality, but the best wines were exceptional. Canterbury had a cool, late vintage with average to above-average wines; Central Otago boasted some of the region's best-ever reds.

2001

Vintage rating: *North Island—Red: 65, White: 70;*
South Island—Red: 83, White: 88

Almost every malady imaginable seemed to afflict this vintage. It is officially described as a "typical New Zealand vintage [with] a lot of regional variation," although the wines of the South Island are significantly superior, while an Indian summer favored later-ripening varieties in the North Island.

GREATEST WINE PRODUCERS

1. Villa Maria
2. Dry River
3. Felton Road
4. Craggy Range
5. Neudorf
6. Ata Rangi
7. Cloudy Bay
8. Te Mata
9. Fromm
10. Kumeu River

FASTEST-IMPROVING PRODUCERS

1. Saint Clair
2. Mount Riley
3. Olssen's
4. Sacred Hill
5. Allan Scott
6. Tohu Wines
7. No 1 Family Estate
8. Astrolabe
9. Kaituna Valley
10. Amisfield

NEW UP-AND-COMING PRODUCERS

1. Escarpment
2. Kawarua Estate
3. TerraVin
4. Muddy Water
5. Rockburn
6. Camshorn
7. Kusuda
8. Johner Estate
9. Woollaston Estates
10. Kathy Lynskey Wines

BEST-VALUE PRODUCERS

1. Spy Valley
2. Montana
3. Villa Maria Estate
4. Morton Estate
5. Drylands
6. Coopers Creek
7. Mission Estate Winery

8. Seifried Estate
9. Mount Riley
10. Babich

GREATEST-QUALITY WINES

1. **Block 5 Pinot Noir 2004** Felton Road (NZ$67)
2. **Chardonnay 2004** Dry River (NZ$48)
3. **La Strada Chardonnay 2004** Fromm (NZ$40)
4. **Reserve Pinot Noir 2004** Villa Maria (NZ$49.85)
5. **Mate's Vineyard Chardonnay 2004** Kumeu River (NZ$47)
6. **Encore Riesling 2004** Pegasus Bay (NZ$35 per half-bottle)
7. **Seddon Vineyard Pinot Gris 2005** Villa Maria (NZ$31)
8. **Sauvignon Blanc 2005** Cloudy Bay (NZ$29)
9. **Ormond Nurseries Gewürztraminer 2003** Waipara Hills (NZ$35)
10. **Blanc de Blancs 2000** Deutz (NZ$37)

BEST BARGAINS

1. **Marlborough Chardonnay 2004** Framingham (NZ$22)
2. **Aspire Chardonnay 2004** Matariki (NZ$20)
3. **Chardonnay 2004** Mount Riley (NZ$19)
4. **Gewurztraminer 2005** Spy Valley (NZ$20)
5. **Riesling 2005** Palliser (NZ$18)
6. **Gravel Pit Red Merlot/Malbec 2004** Red Rock (NZ$20)
7. **Special Reserve Blanc de Blancs Méthode Traditionnelle NV** Lindauer (NZ$18)
8. **Pinot Gris 2005** Spy Valley (NZ$20)
9. **Sauvignon Blanc 2005** Saints (NZ$17)
10. **Sauvignon Blanc 2005** Shingle Peak (NZ$19)

MOST EXCITING OR UNUSUAL FINDS

① Moutere Chardonnay 2004
Neudorf (NZ$52) *Ideal vintage conditions, vine age, and experience have produced what is arguably New Zealand's best-ever Chardonnay. It's a remarkable Puligny-Montrachet lookalike: taut and complex, with appealing hazelnut, whole-wheat, and mineral-salts influences.*

② Kupe Pinot Noir 2003
Escarpment (NZ$60) *Larry McKenna is New Zealand's Pinot Noir guru, so expectations were high when he developed his own Martinborough vineyard. His first Pinot Noir made entirely from home-grown fruit delivers even more than the most optimistic McKenna fan expected.*

③ Pioneer Block 1 Sauvignon Blanc 2005 Saint Clair (NZ$30)
Terroir rules! Saint Clair is New Zealand's supreme Sauvignon Blanc maker. With the release of four Pioneer Block single-vineyard wines they've reached a new level of quality—at least with Block 1, from a coolish site in the upper Wairau Valley.

④ Bullnose Syrah 2004 Te Mata (NZ$44) *This elegant, understated wine bucks the trend of big, full-flavored Syrah and is all the better for it. It's a great example of a subtle wine with surprising power and complexity.*

⑤ Reserve Pinot Noir 2004
Kawarau Estate (NZ$40) *This organic producer beat all comers in Central Otago's difficult 2004 vintage. Complex wine with a perfect balance of plump black-fruit flavors and firm, ripe tannins.*

⑥ Old Vine Gewurztraminer 2004
Stonecroft (NZ$30) *"Old Vine" in this instance means around 20 years, positively decrepit for New Zealand. The strong Turkish-delight and lychee flavors in this concentrated wine offer an encouraging glimpse of the benefits that vine maturity might offer the country's winemakers in the years ahead.*

⑦ Select Riesling 2004
Framingham (NZ$35) *An Auslese-style (hence "Select") Riesling with low alcohol (8.1 percent) plus lots of residual sugar and racy acidity. Vibrant wine with incredible purity. A top example of an emerging New Zealand style that believers hope will lead a Riesling renaissance.*

⑧ Gimblett Gravels Vineyard Chardonnay 2004 Craggy Range (NZ$26.50) *Although the vineyard site inevitably makes a contribution to the quality and character of this very appealing wine, I believe clever winemaking is a greater factor. It's a tantalizing mix of citrus, oak, yeast lees, and sizzled butter flavors, with a seductively silken texture.*

⑨ The Terraces Malbec/Merlot/CF 2002 Esk Valley (NZ$120) *NZ's most famous wine, made from a steep hillside vineyard. It's always a massive wine, but this is the most massive, with over 15 percent alcohol and very dense flavors—a true fruit bomb! A wine waiting to be discovered by Robert Parker Jr.*

⑩ J Cabernet Merlot/Malbec 2003 TerraVin (NZ$42)
Marlborough is generally regarded as unsuitable for Cabernet Sauvignon and marginal, at best, for Merlot and Malbec. TerraVin has beaten the odds with this remarkable wine, thanks to its steep, north-facing vineyard.

Asia

Denis Gastin

Both the number of operational wineries and the number of countries in which wine is made continue to expand as the Asian wine revolution gathers traction.

DENIS GASTIN

Some of the concoctions appropriating the name "wine" in Asia will continue to astound those with a conventional, "Western" view of wine. But there are now at least 700 wineries in 12 countries principally or exclusively producing grape wine, many at the higher end of quality expectations.

More than half of them are in China, in 26 provinces, and a quarter in Japan, concentrated principally in Yamanashi and Nagano. China provides the bulk of the industry in Asia: the OIV now ranks it as the world's sixth-largest wine producer. Japan has forged most of the region's quality benchmarks thus far, on a boutique scale. But now there are new contenders: India and, perhaps even more surprisingly, Thailand, where progress in recent years has been stunning, in terms of the level of activity in the industry, strides made in the pursuit of quality styles, and the substance of the new players. Other countries in which there is an established winemaking tradition are Korea, Vietnam, and Indonesia. Fledgling operations can be found in Taiwan, Sri Lanka, and Bhutan. In *Wine Report 2006*, we introduced the latest addition, Myanmar (Burma)…

DENIS GASTIN is a feature writer and Australian correspondent for Japan's liquor-industry newspaper, *The Shuhan News*, and a regular columnist for *Wine Review* in Korea. He contributes to various other journals and to wine reference books, including *The Oxford Companion to Wine*, *The World Atlas of Wine*, and Hugh Johnson's *Wine Companion* and *Pocket Wine Book*. His particular interests are the more unusual aspects of winemaking, the more remote and least understood regions of the wine world, and the groundbreaking work that some of the industry champions have been doing with exotic grape varieties and new wine styles.

… and now we can add Cambodia!

Frustrated by disappointing returns from vines initially planted for table grapes, grower Chan Thai Chhoeung invested US$10,000 to buy rudimentary winemaking equipment and has produced Cambodia's first grape wine. From 2 ha of vines at Phnom Banorn, about 20 minutes' drive from Cambodia's second-largest city, Battambang, a rosé and a red wine are produced from Kyoho, Black Queen, and some Shiraz grapes. Early plantings of Chenin Blanc were not successful and were abandoned. The initial vines were brought in from neighboring Thailand.

Grapevine

• **Korea's Green Agriculture Association,** consisting of 50 grape growers on tiny Daebu Island (in the Yellow Sea, off Gyeonggi province), has made an excellent start with a range of three wines under the Grand Coteau label produced from the American hybrid Campbell Early. There is a white, a "pink," and a red. The pink is particularly good and looks to be the ideal expression of this unlikely wine variety. Grapes were first planted after the Korean War and now total around 600 ha. Wine, however, is a very recent destination for the grapes and currently consumes the minor proportion of the crop.

• **China's COFCO Wines,** having successfully completed the management integration of the three operational centers of its Great Wall Group and having deposed its arch-rival Changyu as the leading seller of grape wine in China, has embarked on a fourth wine venture focused on the booming luxury-wine market segment. Based at Yantai, in Shandong, it will be a joint venture with Shandong Longhua Company (45 percent share) and will trade as COFCO Nava Valley Jundung Co.

• **Château Mercian's** new Kiiroka Koshu has made an impressive debut. The 2004 vintage, released in the spring of 2005, sold out in weeks, so production was tripled for the 2005 vintage. It has even more complex aromas and flavors, reflecting further advances in the ongoing research and development Mercian is carrying out in collaboration with Bordeaux University's Professor Denis Dubourdieu and Dr. Takatoshi Tominaga. The compound grapevine 3-mercaptohexanol (3-MH) has been isolated as the source of Koshu's distinctive aromas—described variously as resembling green pear, grapefruit, passion fruit, or even white flowers—and the objective of the work is to maximize this varietal characteristic.

• **Bali's Hatten Wines** is undergoing a rethink of grape varieties and viticultural practices on the back of growing export-market recognition. Shiraz and Chambourcin are being trialed, with the help of Barossa vigneron/winemaker Steve Schubert, and are doing well in the intensely tropical climate—the Shiraz, due to its general toughness, and the Chambourcin because of its natural resistance to fungal diseases. Different trellising and vine-management practices are also being introduced in longer-established vineyards to allow more air and sunlight on to the grapes to improve disease resistance and allow better skin development. But the best hope for a Hatten Red, to complement the increasingly popular rosé, lies with the newly introduced varieties. Time will tell.

INCENTIVES SPUR FURTHER EXPANSION IN INDIA

A further measure of the firming official support for the fledgling wine industry in India is the decision in December 2005 by the government of Maharashtra State, where two-thirds of the Indian industry is concentrated, to double the excise tax on imported wine from Rp 100 to Rp 200 per litre. This applies on top of the basic national import duty of 100 percent and an additional duty of 75 percent, putting the total duty/tax imposition on imported wine effectively at around 400 percent for sales in Maharashtra. When very good local wines retail at Rp 300–600, that is a heavy load for the imported wines to carry. It comes on top of an earlier incentive deal that includes a 100 percent exemption from excise duty for 10 years for new wine ventures, simplified licensing provisions, and sales tax relief. It's not surprising that the state's new Grape Wine Parks are bursting at the seams: at least 36 new wine-producing ventures have started in Maharashtra since the first incentive package was launched in 2001.

FOREIGN AFFAIRS WITH CHINESE WINE

Foreign involvement in China's wine industry kicked up sharply in 2005 with major equity restructuring in three of the top four wineries. Changyu sold a 33 percent stake to Italy's Illva Saronno Group, complementing its longer-standing collaborative arrangements with France's Castel Group. The World Bank–affiliated International Finance Corporation also took a 10 percent stake. Dynasty, in which Rémy Cointreau has long held a minority holding, made a spectacular debut on the Hong Kong Stock Exchange with a float of 300 million shares that were quickly snapped up by global investors. Tonghua sold a 29 percent stake to Hong Kong-based Macro-Link Holdings.

Some other impressive new foreign ventures are in the process of getting their first wine to market. Outstanding among them is Bodega Langes, the love child of Austrian crystal magnate Gernot Langes-Swarowski, who owns 100 percent of this grand new venture avowedly focused on producing "world-class" wines at its elaborate "château" at Changli, Hebei province. Another is the Sino-French Château, a collaborative experimental and demonstration project sponsored by the Chinese and French governments in Hebei, also focused on the premium end of the market.

NEW VARIETIES IN THAILAND

Varietal experimentation gathers pace in Thailand, with some striking outcomes in this intensely tropical environment. While Shiraz (Syrah) and Chenin Blanc continue to cement their place as the cornerstones of the Thai wine industry, PB Khao Yai winery has released an impressive Tempranillo (Pirom Reserve label) from the 2004 vintage. GranMonte Vineyards is another winery in the Khao Yai region experimenting with this variety, as is

Shala One in northern Thailand, but neither has yet released a Tempranillo wine. Siam Winery has released Thailand's first Colombard (Monsoon Valley label), a zesty debut for this variety, which has previously been used only in small quantities by some wineries to blend into Chenin Banc to reinforce its structure. PB Khao Yai has a small planting of Pinot Noir but with no conclusive results thus far.

... AND ALSO IN INDIA

Meanwhile, in India, Sula Vineyards has extended its pioneering efforts with the release of a full-bodied, powerfully colored and flavored 2005 Zinfandel, following on from an earlier release of a Zinfandel Blush Rosé. Based on market reaction to these wines, plantings of Zinfandel in the Nasik region are expanding and are expected to stand at around 100 ha in 2007. Sula also has plantings of Merlot, Grenache, and Viognier but has not, as yet, released them as single-variety wines. Grover Vineyards, though, has released a Viognier/Clairette blend from vines planted in the Nandi Hills on the outskirts of Bangalore at an altitude of 3,215 ft (980 m). This is also a first for India.

FARM GATE OPENS FOR WINERIES IN JAPAN

Agricultural land ownership regulations that have prohibited corporate entities from owning or even operating farming land have been a constant source of frustration for Japanese wine companies trying to forge new quality benchmarks or to expand their winemaking activities—forcing them to rely almost exclusively on small-scale (generally micro-scale) farmers to grow their grapes. But, with an aging population, the number of farmers in Japan is now almost half the level of 25 years ago—and plunging. Early steps to facilitate an agribusiness sector were taken in 2003 with the introduction of regulations permitting companies to rent farmland in specially declared zones. From September 2005, the law has been extended to allow corporate rental of land anywhere in the nation. Ownership provisions cannot be far away. Suntory was one of the first wineries to take advantage of the regulation changes. Others are sure to follow as the big corporate players in the Japanese wine industry increasingly commit to quality domestic wine outcomes.

Grapevine

• **India's Sula Wines** continues to set a cracking pace of expansion. In *Wine Report 2006*, we reported that production was forecast to reach 500,000 bottles in 2005: well, in hindsight, you can make that one million! Sula is now working on its third winery, and that will double capacity again: 5,000 hl will be added for the 2006 crush and another 5,000 hl for 2007. Sula has also taken over the management of ND Wines, the second-largest winery in Nashik, and will market ND wines from 2006.

Opinion:
Action needed on integrity

Label integrity and formal industry winemaking standards are the compelling issues of the moment in Asia. Although progressives understand that international standards must be met, much of the traditional end of the industry still seems motivated by the convenience afforded by ambiguous production and labeling codes. Government remains very much in the background.

A basic issue is origin. Some efforts are being made to reduce the scope for ambiguity by introducing regional AOC systems—for example, in China and Japan. But a bigger issue is country of origin: labeling practices condone the use of imported bulk wine, imported grape must, and imported grapes in "local" wine.

Grape varieties are increasingly stated on labels, but most countries have no rules governing this—or vintage declarations. Alcohol-content levels stated on labels are unreliable.

Undoubtedly, there are producers who still value the flexibility that lax labeling laws present, but the practices of the few are damaging the status of the increasing number who are deadly serious. Change is on the way, though.

China's official decision to ban a local concoction known as "half juice wine" from hijacking the name "wine" is commendable—especially since government action was urged by the industry itself.

In Thailand, the grape-wine industry has come together to establish a Thai Wine Charter that will set it apart from the more informal fruit-wine industry. In Myanmar, the newest wine country in Asia, there is a determined effort to get it right at the outset. An industry charter has already been written in collaboration with the relevant local ministry.

Back to the vineyard

Another big constraint on producing good wine in Asia is the slow emergence of a genuinely wine-focused viticultural tradition. Most traditional grape growers are not yet confident enough to commit to the different viticultural practices required for good wine, and wineries are limited (by land ownership laws, among other things) in the extent to which they can do this themselves. With heavy investment in modern winery equipment now behind them, the next challenge for most Asian winemakers lies in the vineyards, with yield management and ripeness the priority targets.

Vintage Report

Advance report on the latest harvest
2006

India—A monsoon of record severity and duration caused heavy leaching of nutrients in rocky vineyards in Maharashtra, while some clay vineyards were waterlogged. The long tail to the monsoon delayed pruning until early October. Yields will be lower than usual, with low bunch weights widespread. In early February, Sauvignon Blanc was generally coming off in good condition and reds were holding well in the Nasik vineyards, but in the warm region of Solapur in southern Maharashtra, higher-than-normal heat was causing desiccation of some black grapes before reaching optimal ripeness. Farther south, in Bangalore, conditions were generally more favorable, with lower temperatures permitting slower bunch maturation, promising stronger aromas in the whites and good concentration in the reds.

Thailand—Heavy rains in November and December caused some early fungal disease that reduced yields, and strong, cool easterly winds from November through to early January caused canopy damage, particularly in Khao Yai, which led to slow and uneven ripening in some vineyards. Radical canopy and bunch management was helping most vineyards to ultimately bring in good-quality grapes, but with dramatically reduced yields.

Updates on the previous five vintages
2005

China—For the second year running, Shandong province had heavy summer rains that caused widespread fungal disease and great difficulty reaching acceptable ripening. Combined with early frosts, yields were well down, forcing the larger wineries based in Shandong to look to other regions, especially the western regions, for fruit. This drove prices up. Hebei province fared much better, since it was spared the worst of the rains and enjoyed higher temperatures; most black grape varieties achieved satisfactory sugar levels.

Japan—Overall it was a difficult vintage, due principally to a shortage of sunshine days and generally lower temperatures, making it difficult to ripen fruit. Rain was less of a problem than usual late in the vintage, so some patchy recoveries were made and fungal damage was generally contained. In Yamanashi, Koshu didn't ripen well, but some producers report excellent results with Muscat Bailey A. Conditions were little better in Nagano: quality in Merlot varies among producers and Chardonnay was good rather than excellent.

India—Late monsoon rains affected early-pruned vineyards, causing lower yields, especially for Sauvignon Blanc. Later-pruned vineyards were unaffected and benefited from a cooler-than-normal ripening period.

Thailand—In Khao Yai, rain finished early after pruning in September, resulting in good fruit set and no disease. Mild weather throughout the vintage produced very good results in both early- and later-ripening varieties. It was an exceptional vintage in the Chao Phraya Delta region: very little rain, no disease, and cool weather from November through to harvest in February. Volume was low, but sugar levels were higher than previous years. At Loei, in the north, Chenin Blanc was the best in 10 years, and Shiraz came in well, too.

2004

China—Heavy rains in July and August caused widespread mildew outbreaks throughout the north and northeast, especially in Shandong and Hebei provinces, and much fruit was picked far too soon. Huailai was generally affected less by summer rains than other parts of Hebei. Conditions in Shanxi were much better, with good sugar and acid levels and few losses to disease. The northwest was, as usual, dry throughout, but yields were lower.

Japan—The year began well with prolonged warm, dry weather after *véraison*, which saw good early fruit development. But a blitz of typhoons late in the season caused many wineries to take fruit early. For others, fungal disease caused losses in quality and volume. As usual, the valleys fared worst and the more elevated and inland locations did best.

India—It was a very good year for whites in Maharashtra and quite good for reds. The cool period extended until mid-February, longer than usual, resulting in slower ripening and more complex flavors. Conditions were very favorable around Bangalore, adding to the region's growing reputation for consistency.

2003

China—Very wet conditions in the eastern provinces (Hebei and Shandong) produced big berries with low sugar and acid levels in most white varieties, though late-maturing reds were generally of good quality. Fungal disease was a problem in most regions and was particularly devastating in parts of Shanxi province. Even in the west, where conditions are generally more amenable, colder and wetter weather than usual impacted adversely on quality. Overall, 2003 was not a good year.

Japan—Extensive summer rainfall severely dented yields and kept sugar levels low in all the major regions. A few of the later-picked varieties saw some recovery when rains eased late in the harvest in some locations—in Yamanashi and the Komoro district of Nagano, for example. But, overall, it was a poor year and the wines generally suffer from suppressed natural flavors and colors.

India—Vintage was over early in Maharashtra. Warmer weather throughout the ripening period and a weaker monsoon season saw fruit ripening early, relatively free of disease. Sauvignon Blanc and more aromatic wines are not as intense as in some years, but the reds have lots of flavor and color. In Bangalore, conditions were close to ideal.

2002

China—Grapes were very late to ripen in Hebei province, but wineries that could delay picking produced wines with good flavor and color. Grape growers in Shandong province made even better use of the cooler and drier conditions, achieving desired sugar levels and robust coloring, with very little rot.

Japan—Conditions were very good in Japan's main regions, Yamanashi and Nagano. There were a few typhoons in the early summer but no damage to vines or fruit. With sustained sunshine and little rain late in the season, the vineyards enjoyed much lower levels of rot, encouraging growers to wait for optimal ripeness before picking.

Grapevine

• **Kenneth Kim's Comfe Winery** at Anseong, about 80 km (50 miles) from Seoul, seeks to resurrect the winemaking tradition brought to Korea in 1901 by Catholic missionary Father Antonio Combert. The original vines were Muscat, and it is this variety that provides the base for the new venture. The local product is currently being supplemented with wine (principally Syrah and Cabernet) made from juice he imports from his California operation. But he aims to quickly replace that with classic vinifera varieties now being planted, with his encouragement, by local farmers.

India—A weaker-than-usual monsoon season delivered drier-than-normal conditions, which favored even ripening patterns and made rot more manageable. The white varieties came off well in Bangalore, as did most of the reds. In Maharashtra, it was an excellent year overall.

2001

China—Conditions were generally very good. Extended dry spells during a late ripening period in Hebei saw good sugar levels and color, although some vineyards sustained hail damage. Parts of Shandong suffered both late spring frosts and summer hailstorms, so yields were reduced and fungal disease was brought on by late rains.

Japan—Both Yamanashi and Nagano had an excellent vintage. The wines are generally softer and more fully flavored than usual, reflecting unusually good ripening conditions.

India—A very good year, with slow, even ripening conditions and a relatively dry harvest.

GREATEST WINE PRODUCERS

1. Château Mercian (Japan)
2. Dragon Seal (China)
3. Suntory (Japan)
4. Grace Winery (Japan)
5. Sapporo (Japan)
6. Great Wall (China)
7. Manns Wine (Japan)
8. Changyu (China)
9. Dynasty (China)
10. Indage (India)

NEW UP-AND-COMING PRODUCERS

1. Vini Suntime (China)
2. Sula Vineyards (India)
3. Domaine Sogga (Japan)
4. Tsuno Winery (Japan)
5. Shanxi Grace (China)
6. GranMonte (Thailand)
7. Yamazaki (Japan)
8. PB Valley Khao Yai (Thailand)
9. Asahi Yoshu (Japan)
10. Shidax Château TS (Japan)

FASTEST-IMPROVING PRODUCERS

1. Katsunuma Winery (Japan)
2. Grover Vineyards (India)
3. Coco Farm (Japan)
4. Honbo Shuzo (Japan)
5. Okuizumo (Japan)
6. Siam Winery (Thailand)
7. Hayashi Noen (Japan)
8. Kuzumaki Winery (Japan)
9. Takahata (Japan)
10. Château de Loei (Thailand)

BEST-VALUE PRODUCERS

1. Dragon Seal (China)
2. Château Mercian (Japan)
3. Sula (India)
4. Grace Winery (Japan)
5. Grover Vineyards (India)
6. Sapporo (Japan)
7. Izutsu (Japan)
8. Tsuno Wines (Japan)
9. Siam Winery (Thailand)
10. Dynasty (China)

GREATEST-QUALITY WINES

❶ Kikyogahara Signature Merlot 2001 Château Mercian, Japan (¥20,000)

❷ Cabernet/Shiraz 2005 Sula Vineyards, India (Rp 375)

❸ Cabernet Sauvignon 2005 Dragon Seal, China (Rmb 120)

❹ Kirimaya Syrah 2004 GranMonte, Thailand (THB 551)

❺ Dindori Reserve Shiraz 2003 Sula Vineyards, India (Rp 550)

❻ Chairman's Reserve 2002 Shanxi Grace, China (Rmb 388)

❼ Solaris Komoro Chardonnay 2002 Manns Wine, Japan (¥5,000)

❽ Hokushin Chardonnay 2004 Château Mercian, Japan (¥6,300)

❾ Primavera Chenin Blanc 2003 GranMonte, Thailand (THB 897)

❿ La Reserve Cabernet Sauvignon/Shiraz 2003 Grover Vineyards, India (Rp 565)

BEST BARGAINS

❶ Kiiroka Koshu 2005 Château Mercian, Japan (¥2,300)

❷ Cabernet/Shiraz NV Grover Vineyards, India (Rp 360)

❸ Huailai Merlot 2005 Dragon Seal, China (Rmb 70)

❹ Rubaiyat Koshu Sur Lie 2004 Marufuji Winery, Japan (¥1,500)

❺ Kayagatake Rouge 2004 Grace Winery, Japan (¥1,680)

❻ Campbell Early Rosé 2005 Tsuno Winery, Japan (¥1,220)

❼ Cabernet Franc/Cabernet Sauvignon/Merlot Rosé 2003 Shanxi Grace Vineyard, China (Rmb 68)

❽ Unwooded Chardonnay 2004 Tsuno Wines, Japan (¥2,200)

❾ Reserve Chenin Blanc 2003 PB Khao Yai Winery, Thailand (THB 420)

❿ Village Thai Shiraz 2003 Wang Nam Keow Winery, Thailand (THB 590)

MOST EXCITING OR UNUSUAL FINDS

❶ Sparkling Campbell Early Rosé NV Tsuno Winery, Japan (¥1,600)
Probably the world's only sparkling Campbell Early, a quality low-alcohol (10 percent) vivid-pink sparkling wine from a grape traditionally more comfortable on the table than in a glass, from this innovative winery on Japan's southern Kyushu Island.

❷ Pirom Khao Yai Reserve Tempranillo 2004 Khao Yai Winery, Thailand (THB 825)
The first commercial release of Tempranillo in Asia, setting a very high benchmark.

Grapevine

• **Coco Farm Winery,** in Japan's Tochigi prefecture, continues to turn new ground in viticulture and winemaking. In May 2006, it released its very first wine from pioneering plantings of Madiran's black-grape staple, Tannat, in tiny quantities. Another fruitful endeavor has been with the American labrusca variety Norton: the first wine from this variety will be released in early 2007, in larger quantities. Coco Farm's first release, in 2006, of a wine from the local wild mountain-grape hybrid Shokoshi is an outstanding wine that will encourage others persevering in the quest for unique Japanese wine styles. Winemaker Bruce Gutlove is also experimenting with barrels made of oak from 125-year-old forests on Japan's northern island, Hokkaido.

3 **Empery Cupid Wild Grape Wine 2002** East of Eden, South Korea (Won 25,000) *Previously ranked here, and ranked again because it retains interest, and is improved with lower alcohol and residual sugar levels. From wild amurensis mountain grapes, virtually organic.*

4 **Monsoon Valley Colombard 2005** Siam Winery, Thailand (THB 400) *The first commercial release of Colombard in Asia. Not a classic variety, but producing here a very drinkable version from vines in the Pak Chong Hills, northeast of Bangkok.*

5 **J-Fine Koshu/Chardonnay Le Primeur 2005** Château Mercian, Japan (¥1,585) *Blend of 70 percent Koshu with 30 percent Chardonnay, which does not overpower the delicate Koshu varietal character but adds pleasing substance to the wine. Released each year in November and sells quickly.*

6 **Domaine Rubaiyat 2002** Marufuji Winery, Japan (¥4,500) *Cabernet-based blend with 34 percent Petit Verdot imparting the very firm structure and 22 percent Merlot a softening sweet fruit overlay.*

7 **Koshu Dry 2004** Grace Winery, Japan (¥2,100) *A style experiment (with input from Bordeaux University) that effectively highlights the delicate lychee/musk/pear characteristics of this variety—at just 10 percent alcohol.*

8 **Zinfandel 2005** Sula Vineyards, India (Rp 350) *The first release in Asia of a full-on Zinfandel, following a rosé version in the previous vintage. Impresses with its potential in an unlikely location, in the right hands.*

9 **Forêt Wine Grand Rosé** Kuzumaki Winery, Japan (¥1,500) *Not a conventional rosé style, and from an extremely rare native hybrid variety (from a crossing of a Japanese and a Russian strain of the wild mountain grape and Seibel 13053)—the only example commercially available, in fact. An exotically appealing drink.*

10 **Maki no Sho Aka Shokoshi 2005** Sawanobori Family Wines, Japan (¥5,500) *An impressive red wine made by pioneering Katsunuma winery Katsunuma Jozo for the family that created the Shokoshi variety (through extensive crossing of Japanese, Russian, and Himalayan strains of the wild mountain grape) and grew these grapes. It achieves the rich color, texture, and natural sweetness that elude most mountain-grape wines.*

Grapevine

• **Results at Japan's** third National Wine Show confirm the substantial upgrade in local wine standards in recent years. The panel of local and international judges awarded 13 gold, 66 silver, and 122 bronze medals. This compares with 4 gold, 14 silver, and 123 bronze in 2004, and 2 gold, 21 silver, and 103 bronze at the inaugural 2003 show. Again, the classic *Vitis vinifera* varieties dominated: of the 13 gold medals awarded, six went to straight Merlots, one to a Cabernet/Merlot blend, and two to Chardonnays. But it was encouraging that the local Koshu variety took gold for the first time (two medals), plus 24 silver medals. Among the silver and bronze medal winners, Muscat Bailey A fared particularly well, and wines from the wild mountain grape Yamabudo and hybrids of this vine appeared in the medal count for the first time.

Organic & Biodynamic Wines

Monty Waldin

The announcement in late 2005 by Eduardo Chadwick of Errázuriz that its Seña vineyard is being converted to biodynamic practices was hugely significant for Chile and the organic wine movement.

MONTY WALDIN

From an organic perspective, Seña's arrival, via the Mondavi-Errázuriz joint venture, was unwelcome. Seña was twice the price, yet less generously flavored, than Errázuriz's flagship red, Don Maximiano, even though both brands shared some vineyards; and creating Seña's own flagship Aconcagua vineyard merely indicated what we already knew: that cutting down trees to make way for vines, especially conventionally farmed ones, often creates not just ugly wines, but ugly, erosion-prone vineyards, too.

The Seña vines were planted across the slopes to make them easier to manage, rather than up and down the slopes, which, though slower to work and more expensive in the short term, is less environmentally damaging from an erosion standpoint. Weedkillers were used under the

MONTY WALDIN While working on a conventionally farmed Bordeaux château as a teenager, Monty Waldin realized that the more chemicals were applied to a vineyard, the more corrective treatments became necessary in the winery. When the opportunity arose to write about wines for both trade and consumer magazines, he specialized in green issues. His first book, *The Organic Wine Guide* (Thorsons, 1999), has now been joined by *Biodynamic Wines* (Mitchell Beazley, 2004). This is the first guide dedicated to the world's biodynamic wine producers. Monty's interest in biodynamism was stimulated in 1999 by six months working on the Fetzer family's biodynamic Home Ranch vineyard in California's Mendocino County, where livestock husbandry and vegetable growing were integral to the vineyard. Previous winemaking experience in Chile and Bordeaux contributed to his *Wines of South America* (Mitchell Beazley, 2003) and *Discovering Wine Country: Bordeaux* (Mitchell Beazley, 2005) books. Monty moved to Tuscany to learn Italian while preparing his latest book, *Discovering Wine Country: Tuscany* (Mitchell Beazley, 2006).

young vines, removing the ground cover that would bind soil clods and stop erosion. Negating Chile's trump card of phylloxera-free soils by planting vines on phylloxera-tolerant rootstocks also limits Seña's icon brand's *terroir* credentials. The argument was that rootstocks were an insurance against nematodes. But if you encourage your vines to produce only shallow roots by drip-feeding chemical fertilizers through the irrigation lines, you must accept that topsoil-loving nematodes will want to feed on your vine roots.

After acquiring the Mondavi stake in Seña, the Errázuriz chairman Eduardo Chadwick embarked on a trip to the 2004 Australian Biodynamic Wine Forum (see *Wine Report 2006*) and promptly hired California's best-known biodynamic consultant, Alan York, for Seña. Horns for the biodynamic horn manure 500 spray were buried in the vineyard while a throng of snap-happy journalists looked on, putting the biodynamic cart well and truly in front of the media horse.

In spite of its claim to be a vine paradise, Chile is becoming a graveyard for failed organic projects. Some high-profile organic conversions have run aground, because Chilean wineries have discovered that running organic and non-organic systems in what is known as "parallel production" confuses vineyard workers, is a vineyard manager's nightmare in terms of invoicing, and puts marketing gurus fearful of the organic cuckoo in the conventional nest in a tail-spin.

Marketing departments have yet to devise a believable riposte to the question, "If organic is so good, why aren't all your wines green?" MontGras's MD Patricio Middleton claims that taking its flagship Ninquén Hill vineyard out of organic certification for "marketing reasons," leaving this project, in his words, as "almost organic," reinforces the suspicion that conventional wineries have yet to grasp what real organic farming is all about. The message here is: we can market organic wine from Chile's viticultural paradise, but we are not up to growing it ourselves.

From a practical standpoint, MontGras's decision to fulfill the organic marketing niche by buying in organic grapes makes sense; and if you're going to go 100 percent organic it also makes sense, says Alan York, to plan organic or biodynamic vineyards from scratch, like Matetic/EQ has done. This makes a successful conversion more likely than having to "retrofit," in York's words, a poorly (from a biodynamic perspective) designed vineyard like Seña's or VOE's.

Should Seña's biodynamic project fail, the implications will reverberate not just in Chile and California, but elsewhere, too. Skeptics will argue, somewhat justifiably, that if biodynamics can't work in Chile, it can't work anywhere. They will also say that the biodynamic wine movement has become a marketing tool for premium brands in need of a relaunch.

This is why you could be forgiven for thinking that the real story coming out of Chile in 2005 is not Seña's Damascene conversion, but Alvaro and Marina Espinoza's decision to build a biodynamic winery in the Maipo Valley for their premium Antiyal brand using "green construction" techniques.

It's a small operation. The winery will process grapes from less than 10 ha (in total): half a hectare of Cabernet Sauvignon near Buín, 2 ha of Carmenère and Cabernet from the Maipo plain; and 7 ha of newly planted vineyards at El Escorial, site of the "green" winery. The El Escorial vineyard is several hundred yards higher up the Andean foothills than the Buín vineyard, so ripening is slower and potentially more complex. The first full vintage for El Escorial's vineyard will be 2006.

Grapevine

- **The world's highest** certified organic vineyard, Cabernet de los Andes in the Fiambala Valley, Catamarca Province, Argentina, is fermenting red wine from 8 ha of biodynamically managed vines (50 ha in total) in 600-liter ceramic pots made by local artisans that are placed outdoors in the vineyard. The wine, to be known as Full Moon Cellars, is then transferred to the winery for malolactic.

- **UC Davis PhD student** Alfredo Koch's Finca Koch will be the first Argentine winery with a biodynamic vineyard. Its 5-ha Finca El Lucas in Agrelo is in transition to Demeter-certified biodynamic status.

- **Former LA screenwriter** Adam Morganstern launched a website dedicated to organic and biodynamic wine called The Organic Wine Journal (www.organicwinejournal.com), inspired by Morganstern's visits to Sonoma winemaker Tony Coturri. "We don't care about official organic or biodynamic certification if we know the vineyard practices are sound," says Morganstern.

- **Casa Lapostolle's** organic hectarage jumped from one-fifth to nearly one-third of its 330-ha vineyard between 2004 and 2005,

with organic Syrah being developed at the relatively cool Las Kuras vineyard in Requinoa, Chile.

- **Luis Felipe Edwards** produced its first (as yet unnamed) organic wine in 2005, a 4,000-case red (95 percent Cabernet/5 percent Carmenère), taken from an 8-ha certified organic plot of its 130-ha San José de Puquillay vineyard in Colchagua, Chile.

- **Chevelswarde,** the UK's oldest certified organic vineyard, dating from 1975, is now back on stream after a total replant of its Vitis vinifera vines in favor of hybrids, with Regent and Rondo now contributing to Chevelswarde's first red wines. Roy Cook recorded his highest-ever sugar levels from the white hybrid Solaris at Sedlescombe Vineyard in 2005 and has planted more of the red hybrid Regent to keep up with consumer demand.

- **Will Davenport's** eponymous English winery doubled in size in 2005 to take account of demand for its bottle-fermented sparkling wines, as gyropalettes were installed for automated remuage. Davenport lost what would have been his first crop of Pinot Noir to pheasants in 2005 and rebranded his still white and sparkling wines under the Limney label.

BOUCHET DEATH

The death of François Bouchet in December 2005 after a long illness sees the loss of France's best-known biodynamic wine consultant at a critical time. Bouchet, a former inspector for the official biodynamic body Demeter France and winegrower at Château Gaillard in Touraine, oversaw a number of vineyard conversions at prestigious French domaines such as Leroy, Leflaive, and d'Auvenay in Burgundy, Huet in the Loire, M Chapoutier in the Rhône, and Deiss, Ostertag, and Zind Humbrecht in Alsace.

Bouchet preferred his clients to adopt a classic biodynamic strategy, learning over a three-year period how to make and apply biodynamic spray preparations, after which the vineyard owner would be biodynamically self-sufficient. Bouchet abhorred what he described as "short-cut biodynamics," in which the compost preparations (502–506) are combined with horn manure (500) in a spray unofficially known as prepared horn manure or 500P.

Imported from Australia, the prepared horn manure spray negates the laborious process of making compost and appeals to farmers with large holdings or steep sites where compost-spreading is problematic. Bouchet described prepared horn manure as "an abomination. It was never outlined by Rudolf Steiner [creator of the biodynamic method in 1924] and for good reason. Combining horn manure and the compost preparations causes an imbalance in the soil. It creates an opposition between horn manure, which helps build matter, like thicker vine roots, and compost, which helps break down matter in the soil. Prepared horn manure is fine if you want your vines to grow like vegetables, with all the roots in the topsoil, where no *terroir* flavors are found." It will be fascinating to see whether Bouchet's traditional views, now carried (among others) by Bouchet's one-time associate Jacques Mell of Biodynamie Conseil in Reims, can counter the "abomination" of prepared horn manure counseled by Burgundy-based Pierre Masson.

AUSTRALIAN CONFERENCE

The 8th International Conference on Organic Viticulture was hosted by the world organic umbrella body (IFOAM) during the 15th IFOAM Organic World Congress in Adelaide, Australia, in September 2005. Among those presenting papers was Prof. Dr. Randolf Kauer, Professor of Organic Viticulture at the University of Applied Sciences Wiesbaden, Geisenheim, Germany. Kauer is researching the reduction of copper use in organic viticulture. His paper argued that phosphonic acid can help plant resistance to cryptogams with no environmental toxicity. Kauer's initial results show that limited use of phosphonic acid between budburst and flowering will not create residues in the wine. A drawback for organic producers is that phosphonic acid is not naturally occurring, unlike, for example, recognized organic treatments copper and sulfur.

CURRENT STATUS OF CERTIFIED ORGANIC VINEYARDS

Country or region	Hectares certified organic	Percentage of vineyards	Year	Comments
Europe	<82,000	<2.2	2005	*Around half of Europe's organic vineyards are found in Italy, a reflection partly of the subsidy-hungry nature of Italian farmers, who were paid handsomely to convert to organics; but also of Italy's polycultural or extensively farmed vineyards, a legacy of postwar sharecropping. Such vineyards, although becoming less prevalent, are inherently suited to organic farming. It is also easier for Italian farmers to commercialize a range of crops from a smallholding (wine grapes, olives, fruit, nuts, vegetables) via a powerful and well-organized cooperative movement.*
Argentina	2,000	1.8	2006	*Argentina's organic vineyards are found in Mendoza (75%), La Rioja (20%), Salta province (3%), and Patagonia (2%).*
Australia	<2,200	<1.5	2006	*A rapid recent rise in organic vineyard conversions raises doubts about the thoroughness of inspections. A number of long-standing organic growers suggest that rule-breaking is occurring, since inspections can be too infrequent. Attempts by independent third parties to investigate spray regimens are hampered by Australia's business privacy laws, which make the national organic accreditation body a lame duck. Statistical data on Australia's organic and biodynamic wine sector are thin, but a review of current data-reporting protocols should see a more accurate picture emerge by the end of 2007.*
Austria	<1,250	<2	2006	*While Austria's organic vineyard increases remain steady at around 15% year on year, Demeter Austria reports a doubling of biodynamic vineyards (albeit from a low base), from four (44 ha) in 2004, to eight (77 ha) in 2005, with nine more in conversion (109 ha).*
Canada	<160	1.5	2006	*Only two of Canada's wine-producing provinces have organic vineyards: British Columbia (<60 ha) and Ontario (<100 ha). There is one Demeter-certified biodynamic vineyard, Feast of Fields, in Ontario.*
Chile	<2,000	<1.9	2006	*Chile's organic vineyards are concentrated in Maipo Valley (33%), Colchagua Valley (20%), and the emerging Maule Valley (15%).*
England	<20	<0.5	2006	*The UK's half-dozen certified organic vineyards are confined to England, but only Chevelswarde, Davenport, and Sedlescombe ferment and bottle their own wines.*
France	17,900	<2	2006	*France is maintaining a 10% year-on-year growth increase for organic vineyards, which are most concentrated where the risk of fungal disease is lowest, hence Languedoc-Roussillon (30%), Provence (25%), and Alsace (12%) lead the way.*
Germany	2,015	2.0	2005	*The main regions for organic vineyards are Baden-Württemberg (652 ha) and Rheinland-Pfalz (1,222 ha, mainly Rheinhessen rather than Pfalz).*
Greece	<1,200	5.5	2005	*Greece's organic vineyards account for more than 10% of its organic farm area, the highest in the EU.*

Country or region	Hectares certified organic	Percentage of vineyards	Year	Comments
Italy	40,500	5.1	2005	*The main areas for organic vineyards are the Veneto and the southern Italian regions of Apulia and Sicily. Biodynamic vineyards are far less significant in Italy than in France: fewer than 20 wine-grape vineyards held the official biodynamic Demeter certification in 2005.*
New Zealand	<200	<1.5	2006	*New Zealand's biodynamic certifier, the Bio Dynamic Farming and Gardening Association in New Zealand, is reviewing its Demeter (biodynamic) standard to create wine-specific protocols to tempt more vineyards into biodynamic certification. For the first time, the keynote speaker at the BDFGANZ's 2005 conference was a wine producer, James Millton of The Millton Vineyard.*
Portugal	<1,100	<0.5	2005	*Portugal's organic statistics also include a proportion of non-wine grapes. Portugal has around 100 organic wine-grape growers, but less than a dozen make wine commercially.*
Slovenia	<100	<0.2	2005	*Slovenia's organic standards conformed to EU norms even before the country's accession to the EU in 2004. The biggest challenge here is not the paperwork, but wine quality.*
South Africa	<350	<0.35	2006	*South Africa is (finally) drawing up its own national organic legislation, which should follow the European model in recognizing the term "wine from organically grown grapes" but not unsulfited or "organic wine."*
Spain	16,500	1.4	2004	*These figures do not differentiate between growers in first-year, second-year, or full organic conversion. La Mancha, Rioja, and Penedès are driving Spain's organic wine scene, which, like Spain's organic food sector, is mainly geared to exports.*
Switzerland	<250	<2.0	2005	*Over 10% of Swiss farmland is certified organic, compared to just 1.7% of Swiss vineyards.*
Uruguay	27	<0.2	2006	*The organic wine movement lacks inspiration here, since Uruguay's first and only certified organic wine producer, Vinos de La Cruz, produces lackluster wines from a 27-ha portion of its 65-ha vineyard.*
US: California	<3,500	<1.7	2006	*While California's organic hectarage stagnates due to poor premiums for certified grapes, biodynamic conversions keep rising. Demeter USA certifies more than 330 ha biodynamic, mainly in Mendocino County, with ex-Bonterra supremo Paul Dolan's Dark Horse (28 ha) and Patti Burke-Fetzer's Patianna Vineyards (29 ha) joining Bonterra's McNab and Butler Ranches (90 ha), Jimmy Fetzer's Ceago del Lago (80 ha), and Benziger (40 ha).*
US: Oregon	<600	<10.0	2006	*Oregon's leading organic certification body, Oregon Tilth Certified Organic (OTCO), certifies around 600 ha of wine-grape vineyards, with King Estate (90 ha) taking over from Cooper Mountain (48 ha, biodynamic) as Oregon's biggest organic vineyard, followed by Sokol Blosser (32 ha), Croft (18 ha), and Cattrall (9 ha).*

Opinion:
Time to recognize some hybrids

Wines made from fungal-resistant hybrid crossings with the same "unfoxy" quality characteristics as *Vitis vinifera*, such as those developed in Germany, should be officially recognized across the EU as being eligible for quality-wine status. So far, only the Bundesortenamt (Federal Plant Patent Office) in Germany has given Regent, Solaris, and Johanniter such status. Over a dozen hybrids are accepted as *Vitis vinifera* equivalents in Germany, while in the UK, Orion, Phoenix, Regent, and Rondo are recognized as being of quality-wine status. These vines offer one solution to the use of copper in the vineyard, for which no effective alternative acceptable to organic rule-makers has been found.

Global standards required

A globally recognized organic grape-growing standard is desirable for those who believe there are too many contradictions in the way certification bodies operate—for instance, tolerance of parallel production (when only part of a vineyard is farmed organically) and the use of organic raw materials in compost (manure from animals fed only on organic material rather than on "organic materials where available").

Grapevine

• **The number of organic Beaujolais** producers will nearly double between 2005 and 2007, from nine to 17, as Denis Longefay (Brouilly), Domaine de la Fully (Brouilly), Domaine de la Bonne Tonne (Morgon), Domaine du Mont-Calme (Morgon), Domaine de l'Eglantine (Morgon), Claude & Bernard Roux (Régnié), Domaine des Barronières (Beaujolais), and the biodynamic Michel Guignier (Fleurie and Moulin à Vent) complete the three-year organic conversion process.

• **Champagne,** with fewer than 20 certified producers, remains France's black hole for organics. Producers in conversion include Thierry Demarne (Aube), Benoît Lahaye (Bouzy), Pierre Larmandier (Vertus), and Leclerc-Briant (Epernay), all of whom are biodynamic. Perhaps Champagne's 30,000 other growers are waiting for the CIVC-sponsored research into comparisons between IPM, organic, and biodynamic grape growing.

• **Loire conversions:** the 40-ha Domaine Vacheron in Sancerre began a three-year biodynamic reconversion here from pruning in 2005. Thierry Germain's 100,000-bottle biodynamic Domaine des Roches completed organic reconversion of its Saumur Blanc and Saumur-Champigny vineyards in 2005. Louis-Jean Sylvoz's Château de la Roche, which ploughs its 6.5 ha of Touraine Azay le Rideau vineyards by horse, gained full organic certification from the 2005 vintage.

Swiss certification bodies such as IMO (Institut für Marktökologie, which certifies Antiyal and Viñedos Orgánicos Emiliana in Chile, for example) are much stricter over the issue of parallel production than other European certification bodies, setting wider "buffer zones" between organic and conventionally farmed parcels.

Sadly, a world organic grape-growing standard is unlikely to appear while growers in European countries continue to argue over, for example, exactly how many kilograms of copper per hectare per year may be used to counter downy mildew.

A global winemaking standard seems even farther away, especially in the EU, where no organic winemaking standard exists, meaning that wines must be described as "made from organically grown grapes" and not as "organic wines." Perhaps the EU could adopt the winemaking rules featured in the United States' National Organic Program, which do permit use of the term "organic wine" if, for example, no sulfur dioxide is used during winemaking.

Transparent labeling

The listing of aids, agents, and additives on labels would expose some of the spuriously marketed "natural" wines made by conventional producers. It would also indirectly promote the work of the best organic growers, who bottle without fining or filtering wines, which remain stable in bottle until consumed.

Grapevine

• **Michel Chapoutier's Domaine de Bila-Haut** in Latour de France (Roussillon) forfeited its organic certification in 2005 when it sprayed a nonauthorized product to counter grapeworm on part of its 75-ha vineyard. Chapoutier considered placing the affected vines under a separate administrative structure from the organic ones (known as 'parallel production') to preserve Bila-Haut's organic status, but ultimately decided the best approach was "all or nothing" as far as certification was concerned.

• **Pfalz producer Bürklin-Wolf,** Germany's largest privately owned estate, is converting its 90 ha of vineyards to certified biodynamic methods. Its most famous *Einzellage*, the Forster Kirchenstück, is now plowed by horse, with all organic and biodynamic spraying done by hand rather than by tractor. Pfalz winemaker Stefan Dorst, who also consults to the organic Laibach estate in Stellenbosch, is supervising winemaking.

• **The VDP,** Germany's association of leading producers, now has 15 members with certified organic vineyards, including Prinz zu Salm-Dalberg (Nahe), Georg Siben Erben (Pfalz), Freiherr Heyl zu Herrnsheim and Wittmann (Rheinhessen), and Graf von Kanitz (Rheingau).

GREATEST WINE PRODUCERS

1. Domaine Leroy (Burgundy, France)
2. Domaine Marcel Deiss (Alsace, France)
3. Domaine Zind Humbrecht (Alsace, France)
4. Ferme de la Sansonnière/Marc Angeli (Loire, France)
5. Domaine Huet (Loire, France)
6. Nikolaihof (Wachau, Austria)
7. Domaine Leflaive (Burgundy, France)
8. Domaine Pierre Morey (Burgundy, France)
9. Domaine des Epeneaux/Comte Armand (Burgundy, France)
10. Viñedos Orgánicos Emiliana (Central Valley, Chile)

FASTEST-IMPROVING PRODUCERS

1. Bodega Noemía (Patagonia, Argentina)
2. Seresin (Marlborough, New Zealand)
3. Domaine Le Ciste/Eric Laguerre (Roussillon, France)
4. Domaine Rossignol-Trapet (Burgundy, France)
5. Château Moulin du Cadet (Bordeaux, France)
6. Davenport Vineyards (East Sussex, England)
7. Aguatierra (Limarí Valley, Chile)
8. Salicutti (Tuscany, Italy)
9. Leclerc-Briant (Champagne, France)
10. Cullen (Western Australia)

NEW UP-AND-COMING PRODUCERS

1. Cullen (Western Australia)
2. Bürklin-Wolf (Pfalz, Germany)
3. Dark Horse (Mendocino County, California)
4. Leclerc-Briant (Champagne, France)
5. Veteris Conventus (Mendoza, Argentina)
6. Château Moulin du Cadet (Bordeaux, France)

7. Domaine du Clos du Rouge Gorge (Roussillon, France)
8. Luis Felipe Edwards (Colchagua Valley, Chile)
9. Domaine Vacheron (Loire, France)
10. Chevelswarde (Leicestershire, England)

BEST-VALUE PRODUCERS

1. Domaine Huet (Loire, France)
2. Viñedos Orgánicos Emiliana (Central Valley, Chile)
3. La Riojana Cooperative (La Rioja, Argentina)
4. Domaine de la Grande Bellane (Rhône, France)
5. Domaine Le Ciste/Eric Laguerre (Roussillon, France)
6. Domaine Zusslin (Alsace, France)
7. Stellar Organics (South Africa)
8. Perlage (Veneto, Italy)
9. Casal dos Jordões (Douro, Portugal)
10. Cave Coopérative La Chablisienne (Chablis, France)

GREATEST-QUALITY WINES

1. **Clos de Vougeot 2001** Domaine Leroy, Burgundy, France (€330)
2. **Altenberg de Bergheim 2000** Domaine Marcel Deiss, Alsace, France (€61)
3. **Gewurztraminer Grand Cru Hengst 2003** Domaine Zind Humbrecht, Alsace, France (€45)
4. **Vouvray Clos du Bourg Demi-Sec 1996** Domaine Huet, Loire, France (€22)
5. **Steiner Hund Riesling Reserve 2001** Nikolaihof, Wachau, Austria (€40)
6. **Anjou Blanc La Lune 2001** Domaine de la Sansonnière, Loire, France (€21)
7. **Chevalier-Montrachet 2003** Domaine Leflaive, Burgundy (€250)
8. **Meursault 2002** Domaine des Comtes Lafon, Burgundy (€120)

⑨ **St Emilion Grand Cru Classé 2003** Château Moulin du Cadet, St Emilion, Bordeaux, France (€32)

⑩ **Coyam Red 2003** Viñedos Orgánicos Emiliana, Colchagua Valley, Chile (CLP 9,900)

BEST BARGAINS

① **A Lisa Río Negro Tinto 2004** Bodega Noemía, Patagonia, Argentina (AP 48)

② **Adobe Chardonnay 2005** Viñedos Orgánicos Emiliana, Central Valley, Chile (CLP 4,300)

③ **Vouvray Le Mont Sec 2004** Domaine Huet, Loire, France (€15)

④ **The Ladybird Red 2004** Laibach Estate, Stellenbosch, South Africa (R95)

⑤ **Aidani-Assyrtico 2005** Hatzidakis, Santorini, Greece (€9.45)

⑥ **Bonterra Chardonnay 2004** Bonterra Vineyards, California (US$14)

⑦ **Genolí Rioja Blanco 2004** Viña Ijalba, Spain (€3.95)

⑧ **Le Ciste Rouge 2004** Vin de Pays des Côtes Catalanes, Domaine Le Ciste/Eric Laguerre, Roussillon, France (€12)

⑨ **Prosecco Spumante NV** Perlage, Veneto, Italy (€5.70)

⑩ **La Source Chablis 2003** Cave Coopérative La Chablisienne, Chablis, France (€12)

MOST EXCITING OR UNUSUAL FINDS

① **Gamay Noir 2004** Brick House Vineyards, Willamette Valley, Oregon (US$21) *Traditionally fermented rather than carbonically macerated Gamay, smelling of red fruit rather than of bananas and bubble gum.*

② **Rosso di Montalcino 2003** Salicutti, Tuscany, Italy (€18) *Energetic red showing how deep-rooting Sangiovese remained unstressed in a pressure-cooker vintage.*

③ **Poggio a'Venti IGT Toscana Rosso 2004** MassaVecchia, Tuscany (€29.50) *Mouth-filling, earth-laden, old-vine Sangiovese, fermented in open-topped wooden tanks.*

④ **Oberdiebacher Fürstenberg Riesling Spätlese 2004** Weingut Kauer, Mittelrhein, Germany (€9.80) *Old-vine Riesling (planted 1956), whose inherently fine structure is enhanced, rather than drowned by, 60 g/l of unfermented sugar.*

⑤ **Le Poiré Fiefs Vendéens VDQS Rouge 2003** Domaine St Nicolas (Michon), Loire, France (€17) *Southwest France's tannic Négrette gets an outing on the Loire's Atlantic coast.*

⑥ **Xarel-lo Classic 2004** Albet I Noya, Penedès, Spain (€4.35) *Cava staple, the Xarel-lo grape, shows its still white-wine pedigree.*

⑦ **Monastrell 2004** Casa Mon Frare, Valencia, Spain (€3.05) *Moody French Mourvèdre metamorphoses into "more, please" mainstream Monastrell on Spain's Mediterranean coast.*

⑧ **Iced Riesling 2003** Frogmore Creek Vineyard, Tasmania, Australia (A$23) *Lush Riesling with a crisp backbone showing Tasmanian terroir character.*

⑨ **Limney Horsmonden Dry 2005** Davenport Vineyards, East Sussex, UK (£6.80) *Un-Germanic-tasting white organic blend of the über-Germanic Ortega, Bacchus, Faber, Huxelrebe, and Siegerrebe grapes.*

⑩ **Regent Oak Matured Red 2004** Sedlescombe Organic Vineyard, East Sussex, UK (£12.95) *A juicy, English oaked red that, unlike some of its conventional peers, is not grown in a polytunnel.*

Wine & Health

Beverley Blanning MW

Is it time to change the message on wine and health? An increasingly complex picture is emerging. If you are looking for good news, this is not the place: this year's report is somewhat gloomy.

BEVERLEY BLANNING MW

The good news is that there is still consistency in the large body of research about the positive effects of moderate wine consumption for a range of conditions, but especially for the Western world's number one killer, cardiovascular disease. This is now well established (and noted in previous editions of *Wine Report*). The more disturbing news is that important exceptions are now being highlighted: for women, for the young, and for different ethnic and genetic groups. Numerous studies now suggest that even moderate consumption of alcohol has potentially negative health consequences for many people. Much of this research requires further validation. For example, one limitation on our understanding of wine is the continued lack of specific information about wine compared to other drinks. It is likely that results may differ significantly by beverage. And understanding patterns of consumption is likely to be particularly relevant to predicted health outcomes.

Younger drinkers may be at risk

More research into the effects of alcohol on younger people is needed. Most studies focus on the benefits of alcohol to middle-aged men and

BEVERLEY BLANNING MW is a wine writer based in London. She writes for a number of publications and tastes and travels widely. She also lectures, judges at international wine competitions, and organizes tasting events. Beverley became a Master of Wine in 2001, specializing for her dissertation on the effects of wine on cardiovascular health.

post-menopausal women, who are at greater risk of cardiovascular and other diseases. Now, several pieces of work on younger adults suggest that there may be no discernible benefits of alcohol consumption for younger age groups.

The benefits of the U-shaped curve may not apply to the young. In the U- or J-shaped model, the risk of mortality is lowest for moderate consumers (the lowest point of the U or J), greater among abstainers (the left-hand side), and much greater still for heavy drinkers (on the right).

One such piece of research is an epidemiological study of men working in the construction industry in Germany. The results showed the familiar U-shaped (or J-shaped) association between alcohol consumption and all-cause mortality over a 10-year period. But when the data were analyzed by age group, it emerged that the U-shaped relationship existed for all ages except the under-35s. For this age group, mortality was shown to increase in a linear fashion with alcohol consumption. The study is limited by the small number of deaths in the 25–34 age group and the high risk of fatal accident in the construction industry (nearly a third of the under-35 deaths were due to accidents, compared to 6 percent in the 55–64 age group). The study suggests that further work is needed to understand the effects of alcohol on the under-35s.

Evidence supporting this finding comes from an earlier, UK-based study, which analyzed mortality from a number of causes (including various cancers, cardiovascular disease, cirrhosis, pancreatitis, and injuries) and modeled risks for men and women at different ages and different levels of alcohol consumption. The conclusions were similar to the German study: namely, that men under 35 minimized risk of death by abstaining from alcohol. For women, the results again showed a direct negative dose-response relationship to alcohol up to age 45. A very slight U-shape curve was apparent for women aged 45–54, but it was not until age 54 that women appeared to derive any significant benefit from light to moderate alcohol consumption. For men, the U-shaped curve is apparent from age 35, and the benefit is more pronounced than for women.

Neither of these studies shows the variances between different alcoholic drinks, so it is possible that wine's higher concentration of polyphenols and its healthier traditional consumption patterns (regularly, with food) may make a difference to these results. But what the studies do suggest is that alcohol—still considered the most important beneficial element of wine—has potentially detrimental effects on younger people, even at low levels of consumption. It also suggests that there is no accumulated benefit over time to be derived from drinking alcohol. Much of the recognized health risk of alcohol to young people relates to the immediate consequences of heavy drinking (such as accidents and violence), so it is appropriate to focus on these dangers. However, it seems that even "sensible" regular consumption may have negative health implications for younger people, especially women.

Coronary atherosclerosis: a study on under-45s in the United States attempted to establish the relationship between alcohol consumption and coronary atherosclerosis in young adults. The study measured coronary calcium (a strong predictor of future heart disease) over a 15-year period and compared this with alcohol consumption. The results showed that drinkers had more coronary calcification than abstainers. Even low levels of consumption were associated with increased coronary calcium. However, the breakdown of results by ethnic group showed that only black men showed a linear increase in coronary calcium with increasing consumption; for white men and for all women, 1–6 drinks per week were associated with a slight reduction of observed calcification levels, which subsequently rose at a level of 7 or more drinks per week. If the results are broken down further, it can be seen that participants who preferred wine to beer or liquor showed lower levels of calcification. This suggests that wine may confer compensating benefits, or may be consumed in a different pattern than beer and spirits, with more positive health outcomes. Coronary calcification increased in wine drinkers only at 14+ drinks per week, and to a lower level than that seen in those who preferred beer or liquor. For these groups, elevated levels were seen at 7+ drinks per week. As has been shown by many and various studies, binge drinking appeared to be the most harmful pattern of drinking.

Grapevine

• **A US analysis** of nine studies from the US, Britain, Sweden, and Italy showed that people who drank alcohol had a reduced chance of developing non-Hodgkins lymphoma. Compared to non-drinkers, the risk was 27 percent less. The reason for this apparent association is unclear, but since the observation held for all types of alcoholic drinks, this suggests it is the alcohol that is beneficial.

• **A group of US researchers** measured the relationship of alcohol consumption and kidney function in a large population of healthy men (the Physicians' Health Study, covering more than 11,000 doctors). The results suggest that moderate alcohol consumption may have a protective effect on renal function. The lowest risk of kidney dysfunction appeared to be among the group consuming at least seven drinks per week. Other studies have linked alcohol consumption with kidney damage, particularly at higher levels. The authors of this study point out that they did not look at the potentially harmful effects of alcohol.

THERE IS A GREAT NEED TO UNDERSTAND BINGE DRINKING

Binge drinking is associated with sensational headlines of drunkenness, loss of control, and antisocial behavior. But most "bingers" will never make news with their behavior and may, indeed, be unaware of the dangers of their drinking patterns. This is because the definition of a binge for health professionals is far lower than the layperson's usual understanding of falling-down drunk.

The UK government defines a binge as drinking twice the recommended limit in a single day (that's 6 units or 3–4 glasses of wine for a woman, 8 units for a man). UK health provider BUPA discovered in a recent survey that around a quarter of Britons (11 million people) drink at least double the daily limit on a night out, including almost half of 18–24-year-old men. Seventy percent do not consider themselves binge drinkers, and most are unconcerned about the amount they drink. The implications of this for long-term health are significant. Medical research consistently shows the dangers of binge drinking. While it is well known that people routinely underestimate their consumption when reporting behavior to researchers, it is noteworthy that the level of drinking likely to be harmful to health may be lower than most people think.

Bingeing harms the heart: Heart attacks are significantly more common on Mondays than on other days of the week, and it has been suggested that one of the causes might be weekend binge drinking. Dutch researchers attempted to show whether otherwise healthy individuals showed any potentially harmful cardiac changes in response to short-term heavy drinking. The researchers measured abnormalities in electrocardiograms (ECGs) of men and women aged 24 to 56. Three-quarters of the 20 participants showed ECG changes following a controlled episode of excess drinking. The results were similar for tests using red wine and those using Bacardi Breezers. This is a small-scale piece of research but still of interest, given the association between ECG cardiac abnormality and sudden death.

Bingers suffer abnormal brain-wave activity: A Dutch experiment measured electrical activity in the brains of 22–27-year-old male students consuming various amounts of alcohol per week. The students were defined as "heavy drinkers" (consuming more than 360 g [12.7 oz]) of alcohol per week, or 45 UK units, or "light drinkers" (consuming less than this amount). Participants abstained from alcohol in the 24 hours before the test. The researchers found that the heavy drinkers showed abnormalities in the synchronization of their brain waves, one of which is linked to defective memory. The light drinkers showed no such abnormalities.

Effects of binge drinking while pregnant: A study of the children of black women in the US attempted to establish whether drinking while pregnant affected their children's behavior or intelligence. A total of 500 seven-year-olds were assessed. The researchers found that there was no relationship between IQ scores and total consumption of alcohol by their pregnant mothers. However, children who had been exposed to binge drinking before birth (defined as five or more drinks at a time, at least once every two weeks) were 1.7 times more likely to be mentally retarded and 2.5 times more likely to show significant delinquent behavior. The researchers concluded that the amount of alcohol consumed per occasion may be more critical than the total amount consumed.

MORE FINDINGS ON BREAST CANCER

A German study has concluded that women carrying a particular gene involved in the breakdown of alcohol have a greater risk of contracting breast cancer. The researchers looked at the gene that produces the enzyme alcohol dehydrogenase, which is responsible for the breakdown of alcohol into acetaldehyde, a known carcinogen. It was found that women who were moderate drinkers and had breast cancer had a significantly greater frequency of the mutant gene than women who had alcohol-related diseases but did not have breast cancer. The authors concluded that women carrying the abnormal gene were 1.8 times more likely to develop breast cancer than those without this version of the gene. According to researcher Prof. Dr. H.K. Seitz, the prevalence of the gene in the general Caucasian population is around 20 percent, but there is currently no way for most people to find out whether they carry this

greater risk. This is undoubtedly an area of research that will continue to provide more precise information on the associations between alcohol and disease.

The same study also looked at the effect of drinking on blood concentration of estradiol, the major female sex hormone. A high level of this hormone is known to be associated with increased risk of breast cancer. The researchers found that estradiol levels increased even with low consumption of alcohol, especially at the midpoint of the menstrual cycle.

FRENCH PARADOX WORKS ON RATS

A study on rats has been shown to support the original French paradox, namely that regular consumption of red wine (rather than any alcohol) may counter the negative health effects of a high-cholesterol diet. Alcohol is known to improve the ratio of HDL ("good") cholesterol to LDL ("bad") cholesterol, but the additional impact of wine's polyphenols is less well documented. In this experiment, one group of rats was fed on a high-cholesterol diet, supplemented with alcohol-free red wine, while others were fed on a standard diet, with and without the red wine. It was found that the wine did not affect the rats' cholesterol levels, but it did reduce the tendency of the blood to clot. The authors note that the alcohol-free red-wine supplementation "almost completely reverted the prothrombotic effect of the cholesterol-rich diet."

GOUT MAY NOT BE CAUSED BY WINE

Gout is caused by the deposition of uric acid crystals in joints. Harvard researchers have found that different alcoholic drinks have differing impacts on blood levels of uric acid, which in turn could affect the likelihood of developing gout. There was no association for men or women between wine intake and uric acid levels. This was not the case for other drinks. Uric acid levels were highest for beer, followed by liquor.

ALCOHOL AND *HELICOBACTER PYLORI*

A large survey of over 6,500 people in Germany has provided further evidence that alcohol consumption helps eliminate *Helicobacter pylori* infection. This bacterium is present in approximately half the world's population, but it is not understood why some people develop peptic ulcers as a result, while others do not. The results of this survey showed that regular consumption of any alcoholic drink (25–50 g per day, or 4–6 UK units) reduced *H. pylori* infection.

ALCOHOL AND COGNITIVE IMPAIRMENT IN MIDDLE AGE

In a British study, adults born in the same week in 1946 were tested at age 43, and then 53, for signs of cognitive impairment. Test scores declined in all groups over the 10-year period. For men, light and moderate drinkers (1–2 or 2–4 drinks per day) showed less decline in cognitive scores than abstainers or heavy drinkers; for women, memory-test scores were higher for drinkers at all levels, but visual-search scores were worse for all drinkers compared to abstainers. The researchers note that the reasons for these observations are not yet understood.

NASAL SYMPTOMS LINKED TO ALCOHOL

Many people claim to suffer from an allergic-type reaction to certain types of wine, but a recent Swedish study has, for the first time, quantified the prevalence of this phenomenon. The results suggest that alcohol-induced nasal symptoms affect more than 3 percent of the general adult population. Sufferers are likely to be female, slightly older than those not suffering from the condition, and more likely also to suffer from asthma, chronic bronchitis, or chronic pulmonary disease. In the survey, subjects were asked a series of questions about symptoms experienced when they drink alcohol and asked to specify the beverage or beverages that led to the symptoms. The most frequently cited drink was red wine, followed by white wine, beer, and then spirits. Twice as many women as men reported symptoms, which included runny nose, sneezing, nasal obstruction, breathlessness, cough, and itching. The study did not look at subjects' drinking habits, but the authors say that their impression is that these are people who drink moderately, or even less than the average, due to their symptoms.

Opinion:
Current practices that should stop

- Sensationalist media reporting of issues relating to wine and health.
- Ban on ingredient labeling—of particular interest to vegetarians, buyers of organic food, and those with allergies.
- Misleading information on wine bottles relating to the health risks of wine.

Things that should be happening

- Clearer dissemination of information about the meaning of moderate drinking and, especially, binge drinking.
- Up-to-date and unbiased reporting of the benefits of moderate wine consumption and dangers of binge drinking.
- International standardization of the definitions of a unit of alcohol and moderate consumption. Both vary enormously from country to country, causing consumer confusion over safe or desirable consumption levels.
- Unit labeling on bottles to indicate number of units per bottle—of increasing importance with rising alcohol levels in wine.
- Greater focus on the effects of drinking on women's health, especially breast cancer.
- Greater focus on the effects of drinking on the young.
- More research distinguishing between wine and other drinks.
- More research on patterns of consumption. Specifically, given the focus on the dangers of binge drinking, there is a need to understand how wine is now consumed compared to its traditional patterns.
- Research on the benefits of red versus white wine.

Grapevine

- **Low levels of alcohol consumption** have traditionally been thought safe, or even beneficial, for breast-feeding women. But a study in the US on lactating women showed that alcohol interfered with the two key hormones that govern lactation. Oxytocin measured in the women's bloodstreams declined significantly following alcohol consumption and led to reduced milk production and ejection.

TOP WINE HEALTH BENEFITS

1. Increased longevity from regular, moderate consumption, especially for men over 45 and post-menopausal women.
2. Significant protection from cardiovascular diseases with moderate consumption.
3. Lowered risk among drinkers, especially wine drinkers, of many other diseases, including stress-related illnesses and the common cold.

TOP WINE HEALTH HYPES

1. Drinking is good for you—it always depends on individual circumstances.
2. The benefits of consumption are accrued equally by young and old—recent studies indicate that the elderly benefit the most.
3. Resveratrol is the most important beneficial agent in wine.
4. Wine is necessarily a better option than beer or spirits—much as we'd like to think so, a lot more research is needed to prove this. Lifestyle factors and a tendency toward moderate consumption may explain wine's apparent superiority over other drinks in some studies.
5. Red wine is significantly better than white in providing health-related benefits.
6. The idea that regular, moderate consumption of wine is an acceptable substitute for improving health outcome in place of changing diet and other lifestyle factors, such as regular exercise.

TOP WINE HEALTH DANGERS

1. Most dangers come from excessive consumption. Risks include:
   - alcoholism;
   - risk of accidents;
   - violent crime;
   - domestic violence;
   - child abuse;
   - suicide and depression;
   - severe damage to every system in the body and increased susceptibility to many different diseases;
   - fetal alcohol syndrome (FAS) in babies born to women who drink heavily during pregnancy.
2. Increased risk of breast cancer, even at low levels of consumption. This is of greatest significance to young women, who have less to gain from the protective effects of alcohol against cardiovascular disease.
3. Increased risk of health problems for women drinkers at relatively low consumption levels.
4. Ignorance of sensible drinking levels, especially underestimating the dangers of excessive drinking and what constitutes a binge.
5. Increasing levels of dangerous consumption among the young, who appear to have little, if anything, to gain in terms of health benefits and much to lose.

TOP WINE HEALTH MYTHS

1. Drinking is bad for you.
2. Drinking is good for you.
3. Drinking any alcohol while pregnant significantly increases the risk of FAS.

Grape Varieties

Dr. François Lefort

GM vines are on their way to European vineyards: the first open field trials of genetically modified grapevines have begun in France and Germany, despite skepticism from growers and consumers.

DR. FRANÇOIS LEFORT

Oidium (powdery mildew) and downy mildew have been problems for growers since the 19th century. The usual method of combating mildew is to spray with fungicides, but the fungi are becoming resistant to chemicals. Spraying also raises environmental issues and health-and-safety concerns. A more recent disorder is grapevine fan leaf virus, which is spread by nematodes (see below). Since it is a viral disease, there is no cure; however, chemicals are used against the nematode vector.

Grape breeders have been trying to develop fungus-resistant varieties since the end of the 19th century. These new varieties, mainly from France, Germany, and the US, were produced by "classical breeding"— a technique that creates totally new varieties. The process is a long one, taking at least 30 years from the initial crossing. In classical breeding, genes from other *Vitis* species are introduced into a *Vitis vinifera* variety, but the new variety is not, for instance, a Chardonnay with new resistance characteristics, because the breeding process loses a part of the Chardonnay genome. So modifying a given variety for a single desired character was—until recently—quite impossible.

Scientists searching for solutions to these problems looked to genetic transfer. This method modifies grapevines in a targeted way without

DR. FRANÇOIS LEFORT is a professor at the University of Applied Sciences of Western Switzerland in Geneva. He has been working on the diversity of grapevine varieties for many years. François is the creator of the Greek Vitis database and the coauthor of the Bulgarian Grapevine database. He is involved in building similar databases in Russia and Ukraine.

changing their essential character. First developed in the 1980s, genetic transfer inserts a very small number of genes into grapevines. The first research, by French scientists, was supported by Louis Vuitton Moët Hennessy, and the results, published in 1998, were very promising. As public concern about GMOs grew, LVMH stopped research in 2000. Genetic transfer research continued in Germany, Australia, Canada, and the US. The LVMH results and genetic material were given to INRA in France, which continued the research, albeit at a slower pace.

Germany: GM grapevines

German scientists of the German Federal Grapevine Research Center in Siebeldingen have been looking for quality and fungus-resistant characters transmittable to established grape varieties. Resistance characters transferred to grapevines are resistance to the main fungal disease agents of grapevines: *Plasmopara viticola* (downy mildew), *Uncinula necator* (oidium/powdery mildew), and *Botrytis cinerea* (gray rot). Fungus-resistant vines should reduce fungicide application and result in less environmental contamination and lower production costs. Field trials for three GM varieties—Dornfelder, Riesling, and Seyval Blanc—began in 2005 in Siebeldingen. Resistant genes have been successfully transferred from barley into grapevines, and the 130 transgenic vines will be tested for their fungus resistance.

These trials, which will include wine-quality assessment, will last for 10 years, although GM varieties are not expected to reach the market for 25 years. The foreign genes will not alter the wine quality of the transgenic

Grapevine

• **Wine Grape Growers Australia** and the Winemakers' Federation of Australia are proposing a "vine retirement scheme" to pull up thousands of hectares of less popular varieties, such as Cabernet Sauvignon, in 2006 in an attempt to curb overproduction in Australia. There are also state incentives to turn extra wine stocks into ethanol. What is surprising is that Cabernet Sauvignon is now seen as a less popular variety.

• **After several years of testing,** Bruce Reisch of NYS Agricultural Experiment Station, Cornell University at Geneva, New York, has recommended a list of "less risky" varieties to New York growers. All the varieties are interspecific grapevine hybrids: La Crescent, Ravat 34, NY76.0844.24, Vignoles, Traminette, NY62.0122.01, Cayuga White, and Vidal Blanc (white); Frontenac, GR 7, Maréchal Foch, St Croix, NY70.0809.10, Chambourcin, Chelois, and NY73.0136.17 (black). Some of the hybrids, such as Vidal Blanc, Maréchal Foch, and Chambourcin, are old French hybrids.

grapes or the wine quality of adjacent non-GM vines if cross-pollination occurs, since cross-pollination results in only the seeds carrying foreign genes and not the flesh of the berry.

France: GM rootstocks

Until work stopped in 2001 when 400 transgenic rootstocks were pulled up, French scientists had been researching resistance to diseases affecting the rootstock and not the grafted scion. This approach could be more acceptable to growers and consumers because the rootstock does not affect the grape berry itself, which is genetically determined by the genome of the grafted variety. Rootstocks are also prevented from producing leaves and flowers in the vineyard, to avoid any risk of gene transfer to wild grapes (almost extinct in Europe thanks to phylloxera) or to other grapes.

Work resumed in 2005 at INRA Colmar with the long-awaited authorization from the French Ministry for Agriculture for open field trials of transgenic rootstocks made resistant to grapevine fan leaf virus, a damaging disease with no cure. Grapevine fan leaf virus is a virus transmitted by soil nematodes that attack the vine's roots.

Rootstocks made resistant to the virus cannot be infected by nematodes. The fact that the foreign gene is only in the rootstock and not in the grafted scion or the grapes could make this strategy more acceptable to the public, since the wine will not be a GM wine. Once scientific assessment has been carried out, genetically modified rootstocks could be on the market quite quickly, offering a choice of the usual rootstocks but with resistance to fan leaf virus. There are, however, about 40 viruses that attack grapevines, so it will take a while to make GM vines resistant to them all.

Seventy transgenic rootstocks, surrounded by non-transgenic rootstocks and a Pinot Meunier vineyard, were planted in experimental open vineyards in September 2005. The trial is authorized to run for four years, and the vineyard will be destroyed on completion. The transgenic rootstocks will not be allowed to flower, and no wine will be produced.

INRA Montpellier, which is continuing with its classical breeding programs, has produced a hybrid rootstock that is partially resistant to grapevine fan leaf virus.

Opposition from the industry has been fiercer than expected. Terre et Vin du Monde, an association of 400 top world producers that includes Château Latour, Château Pichon-Longueville, Domaine de la Romanée-Conti, and Egon Müller, has declared its firm opposition to GM grapevines. The organization, which had originally asked for a GM moratorium, recently hardened its stance by totally opposing trials anywhere in the world. Its influence resulted in an INAO ban on GM grapevines, GM yeast, and GM bacteria in 2002, but it has not so far been authorized by the Minister of Agriculture.

South Africa: the total GM kit

South African researchers are working on GM grapevines, GM yeasts, and GM bacteria for winemaking in the Winetech Biotechnology Program (WTBP). South African grapevine gene transfer research aims to improve resistance to disease and adaptation to unfavorable environmental conditions. The genes transferred to grapevines to improve fungal resistance are a yeast chitinase, a yeast glucanase, an antifungal peptide, and grapevine polygalacturonase-inhibiting proteins (PGIPs). The first transgenic field trial is currently under development.

Researchers have produced various new GM yeast strains in efforts to improve wine clarification and juice yield, to generate new aroma profiles, or to produce antioxidants and other compounds with an impact on human health. These yeast strains are currently being further developed through SunBio, a biotechnology development company. South African GM yeasts have been accepted by the FDA and are now being used for winemaking in the United States.

The WTBP researchers are studying wine bacteria to explore the role of lactic acid bacteria involved in malolactic fermentation and in the production of antimicrobial agents called bacteriocins, which can inhibit the growth of spoilage organisms. The goal of gene-transfer technology is to develop lactic acid bacteria that can perform enhanced malolactic fermentation. Still in the preliminary stages, this research focuses on genomic sequences of commercially important lactic acid bacteria and the development of genetic tools and expression systems.

The South African wine industry gives generous financial support to GM grapevine research. Public concern or opposition does not seem to affect WTBP plans, although they do concede that their most important challenge is to "educate the consumer."

GM grapevine research is currently being carried out in several other countries, including the United States and Australia. Given the huge amounts being pumped into this research, it seems that GM grapevines, rootstocks, yeasts, and bacteria will soon be an important part of viticulture. Great changes are on the way. It will be interesting to see whether the consumer will be open to "education."

IS GRUBBING UP THE ONLY WAY?

To deal with overproduction, the French authorities decided to grub up 10,000 ha of vineyards over a three-year period. Despite subsidies of up to €15,000 per hectare in 2005 in Bordeaux, the program failed to attract enough participants, and only 1,800 ha were destroyed. While such subsidies help growers in the short term, they do not offer a sustainable framework for viticulture.

Instead of looking for other approaches, such as promoting organic viticulture and authorizing disease-resistant varieties in appellation areas, the sclerotic French wine system supervised by ONIVINS once again opts for the worst solution.

Anti-alcohol campaigns, state restrictions on advertisements, and loss of traditional market share are all among factors aggravating this crisis. Some specialists are calling for an urgent ban on chaptalization to prevent extreme measures such as pulling up vineyards, claiming that banning the use of 60,000 metric tons of sugar each year to increase the alcoholic content of wine would go a long way toward easing the situation.

WHITE IS THE MUTANT

A basic question about berry color was recently answered by molecular genetics. Red plant pigments called anthocyanins are responsible for the color of grape skins. Until now, it was thought that white varieties developed from black varieties by independent mutational events.

However, a Japanese team studying the anthocyanin synthesis pathway showed that the insertion of a retrotransposon, a kind of jumping gene, in one gene of this pathway suppressed the expression of anthocyanins in white varieties.

In some black grapes derived from white varieties by bud mutation and in vitro culture techniques—such as Ruby Okuyama (black skin) derived from Italia (white skin), and Flame Muscat (black skin) derived from Muscat of Alexandria (white skin)—the same team also detected the tracks of some sequence remains from this retrotransposon in the gene of interest. This proved that reversion from white-skinned varieties to black-skinned varieties occurred. Reversion happened when another mutation event deleted the inserted retrotransposon, leading back to a functional gene. The now-functioning gene meant that a black variety could be bred from a white parent.

The initial mutation event leading to the appearance of white varieties is certainly very ancient and happened long before grapevine domestication (around 6000 BC). This research explains why all white varieties harbor this mutation in the same gene of the anthocyanin synthesis pathway.

Most widely cultivated white grape varieties
Global, wine grapes only.

Grape variety	Acres in 2005*	Main countries
1. Airén	756,300	Spain
2. Chardonnay	458,900	US, France, Italy
3. Ugni Blanc	274,600	France, Italy, Argentina
4. Rkatsiteli	264,800	Ukraine, Georgia, Moldova
5. Sauvignon Blanc	199,900	France, Moldova, US
6. Riesling	135,400	Germany, Ukraine
7. Macabeo	125,400	Spain, France
8. Muscat of Alexandria	116,400	Spain, Chile, Algeria
9. Aligoté	109,200	Italy, Spain, Croatia
10. Catarratto Bianco Comune	107,200	Italy

*Estimated. Source: Patrick W. Fegan, Chicago Wine School, 2006.

Most widely cultivated black grape varieties
Global, wine grapes only.

Grape variety	Acres in 2005*	Main countries
1. Cabernet Sauvignon	701,300	France, Chile, US
2. Merlot	694,400	France, Italy, US
3. Grenache	518,500	Spain, France, Italy
4. Tempranillo	500,500	Spain, Argentina, Portugal
5. Syrah	357,700	France, Australia
6. Carignan	274,600	France, China, Tunisia
7. Bobal	219,800	Spain
8. Pinot Noir	215,500	France, US, Germany
9. Sangiovese	190,100	Italy, Argentina, US
10. Monastrell/Mourvèdre	184,100	Spain, France, Australia

*Estimated. Source: Patrick W. Fegan, Chicago Wine School, 2006.

Most widely cultivated gray/*rosé* grape varieties
Global, wine grapes only.

Grape variety	Acres in 2005*	Main countries
1. Pinot Gris	63,800	Italy, Germany, US
2. Criolla Grande	57,400	Argentina
3. Cereza	44,800	Argentina
4. Gewürztraminer	39,600	Moldova, France, Ukraine
5. Grenache Gris	5,900	France
6. Roditis	2,500	Greece
7. Catawba	2,400	US
8. Grolleau Gris	1,400	France

*Estimated. Source: Patrick W. Fegan, Chicago Wine School, 2006.

Fastest-growing white grape varieties

The greatest global increase in recent plantings of white (wine only) grape varieties.

Grape variety	Acres in 2004*	Acres in 2005*	% increase**
1. Ugni Blanc	338,400	374,600	10.7
2. Chardonnay	432,900	458,900	6
3. Sauvignon Blanc	193,100	199,900	3.5

*Estimated. **Some increases may reflect improved data collection rather than an actual increase in acreage. Source: Patrick W. Fegan, Chicago Wine School, 2006.

Fastest-growing black grape varieties

The greatest global increase in recent plantings of black (wine only) grape varieties.

Grape variety	Acres in 2004*	Acres in 2005*	% increase**
1. Cabernet Sauvignon	633,800	701,300	10.7
2. Merlot	647,800	694,300	7.2
3. Syrah	334,800	357,700	6.8
4. Grenache	513,400	516,500	0.6

*Estimated. **Some increases may reflect improved data collection rather than an actual increase in acreage. Source: Patrick W. Fegan, Chicago Wine School, 2006.

Fastest-growing grey/*rosé* grape varieties

The greatest global increase in recent plantings of grey/rosé (wine only) grape varieties.

Grape variety	Acres in 2004*	Acres in 2005*	% increase**
1. Gewürztraminer	36,700	39,600	7.9
2. Pinot Gris	60,800	63,800	4.9

*Estimated. **Some increases may reflect improved data collection rather than an actual increase in acreage. Source: Patrick W. Fegan, Chicago Wine School, 2006.

Grapevine

• **Marselan was authorized** for Vin de Pays d'Oc wines in December 2005. Marselan (Cabernet Sauvignon x Grenache Noir, INRA 1961), which was resurrected and registered as an official variety in 1990, promises to be very popular.

• **The number of Muscat varieties** has been clarified by genetic profiling. Out of 64 Muscats, there are only 20 genetically different varieties, with the remaining 44 being synonyms. Most of the synonyms were Muscat White or Muscat of Alexandria crossed with other varieties.

• **In Vietnam,** grapevines are mainly cultivated for table grapes and raisins, though a small amount of wine is made in northern regions. Evaluation of foreign (US, French, and German) and domestic varieties has been going on for 10 years. Three domestic vines, NH-02-04, NH-02-10, and NH-02-1, look promising as wine varieties.

BEST WINES FROM NEW VARIETIES OR NEW CLONES

This year experimental wines from the Federal Research Centre on Grapevines at Siebeldingen in Germany form an important part of the list. Although they are experimental, the wines are also available to buy, so it is possible to taste new varieties at a reasonable price. Making the wines available advertises the excellent work of the research center and spreads the word to growers, who can try new fungus-resistant varieties that require no chemical treatment.

1 **QmP Siebeldinger Mönchspfad Regent 2003** Institut für Rebenzüchtung, Germany (€8.50 per 50-cl bottle) *Experimental red dry wine from Regent [Gf 67-198-3: (Silvaner x Müller-Thurgau) x Chambourcin (= Joannes Seyve 26205); BAFZ Geilweilerhof] (14.5 percent). Bronze medal, Economic Chamber of Rheinland-Pfalz. Aged in oak. Regent is said to be one of the most fungus-resistant red varieties currently available.*

2 **QmP Siebeldinger Mönchspfad Reberger 2003** Institut für Rebenzüchtung, Germany (€7 per 50-cl bottle) *Experimental dry red wine from Reberger [Gf 86-2-60: Regent x Lemberger (= Blaufränkisch); BAFZ Geilweilerhof, 1986] (14 percent). Silver medal, Economic Chamber of Rheinland-Pfalz.*

3 **Gamarêve 2003** Domaine Le Vieux Clocher, Caves Leyvraz & Stevens, Switzerland (SF 15) *Red wine from Gamaret (= Gamay Noir x Reichensteiner, Agroscope Changins, 1970), matured in oak casks. Integrated production.*

4 **Kerner 2004** Domaine de la Côte d'Or, Switzerland (SF 13) *Dry white wine made from Kerner (= Riesling x Trollinger, Weinsberg/Württemberg State Wine Institute, Baden, Germany, 1969). Trollinger is the German synonym for the Italian variety Schiava Grossa. Late flowering provides frost resistance. It was the fourth most planted variety in the 1980s in Germany and currently covers 6,500 ha.*

5 **Siebeldinger Mönchspfad Villaris Kabinett 2004** Institut für Rebenzüchtung, Germany (€3.20) *Off-dry, 11.5 percent. White wine made from the fungus-resistant variety Villaris [Sirius (= Bacchus x Villard Blanc) x Villard Blanc (= Seyve-Villard 12-375); with Bacchus (= Müller-Thurgau x [Riesling x Sylvaner]); BAFZ Geilweilerhof, 1984].*

6 **QbA Siebeldinger Mönchspfad Phoenix 2004** Institut für Rebenzüchtung, Germany (€2.60 per 100-cl bottle) *Dry white wine (11.5 percent) made from the fungus-resistant variety Phoenix (= Bacchus x Villard Blanc; BAFZ Geilweilerhof). Has a slight Muscat aroma.*

7 **QmP Siebeldinger Mönchspfad Felicia Spätlese 2004** Institut für Rebenzüchtung, Germany (€3.80) *Off-dry white wine (11.5 percent) made from Felicia [= Sirius x Vidal Blanc (= Ugni Blanc x Rayon d'Or); BAFZ Geilweilerhof, 1984].*

8 **Finger Lakes Traminette 2001** Amberg Wine Cellars, US (US$9.99) *Off-dry white wine from Traminette (= Joannes Seyve 23.416 x Gewürztraminer; Barrett, Cornell Geneva University, 1965).*

⑨ **Melody 2004** Goose Watch
Winery, Finger Lakes, US (US$6.79)
*Dry white wine from Melody [=
Seyval Blanc x Geneva White 5 (=
Pinot Blanc x Ontario); Cornell
Geneva University, 1965].*

⑩ **Vin de Pays des Alpes de
Haute-Provence Marselan 2004**
Domaine de la Madeleine, France
(€3.97) *Pure red wine from
Marselan (= Cabernet Sauvignon
x Grenache Noir, INRA
Montpellier, France, 1961).*

BEST WINES FROM UNUSUAL, OBSCURE, OR REDISCOVERED GRAPE VARIETIES

① **Coteaux du Languedoc La
Méjanelle Cuvée 1811 2003**
Château des Mazes, France (€8.90)
*Red wine from a blend of
Grenache, Syrah, and old Carignan
vines. Matured for a year in
French oak. (The castle was
built in 1811.)*

② **Vin de Pays d'Oc Cuvée 1811
2004** Château des Mazes, France
(€8.90) *White wine from a blend
of Sauvignon and Viognier, vinified
and matured for 6–7 months in
new French oak.*

③ **Gaillac Vin d'Autan 2003**
Domaine des Très-Cantous, Bernard
& Robert Plageoles, France (€35 per
50-cl bottle) *Sweet white wine
(9.8 percent) made through
passerillage from Ondenc, which
originates in the Tarn region.
Ondenc is an old Gaillac variety
that has been revived thanks to
the efforts of Robert Plageoles. It
is now registered as a variety for
the appellation. Acreage is limited
to 6 ha in the Gaillac area.*

④ **Gaillac Ondenc 2004** Domaine
des Très-Cantous, Bernard & Robert
Plageoles, France (€9.50) *Dry white
wine from Ondenc.*

⑤ **Vin de Pays des Côtes du Tarn
Prunelard 2004** Domaine des
Très-Cantous, Bernard & Robert
Plageoles, France (€11.50) *Full-
bodied red wine from Prunelard—
another almost extinct traditional
Gaillac variety revived by Plageoles.
Acreage is limited to 6 ha in the
Gaillac area.*

⑥ **Vin de Pays des Côtes du Tarn
Mauzac Noir 2004** Domaine des
Très-Cantous, Bernard & Robert
Plageoles, France (€6.50) *Red wine.*

⑦ **Vin de Table Audace 2004**
Stéphane Tissot, France (€29.90 per
half-bottle) *Sweet red wine made
from Poulsard, an old variety of
Arbois wines in Jura. Biodynamic
production.*

⑧ **Vin de Pays de l'Ile de Beauté
Bianco Gentile 2004** Antoine
Arena, France (€19.50) *Organic
white wine from Bianco Gentile—
a traditional white variety from
Corsica that is almost extinct.*

⑨ **Bordeaux Cep d'Antan 2004**
Domaine de Bouillerot, France
(€6.80) *Red wine from a blend
of Carmenère, Petit Verdot, and
Malbec.*

⑩ **Bourgogne César 1999** Maison
Simonnet Febvre, France (€12.90)
*Red wine from César—an old
burgundy variety.*

Classic Wine Vintage Guide

Serena Sutcliffe MW

The burgeoning mystery of the fine-wine world is the unprecedented availability of great old wines ("trophy" wines) and their ability to taste increasingly young.

SERENA SUTCLIFFE MW

I am going to be brutal: most of these "miracles" seem to emanate from Europe, to our eternal shame, and most are then sold (and sold and sold) in America and Asia. However, they do appear in the UK—recently it was Cheval Blanc 1961 with the Catalan flag on the cork.

Thirty years ago, these wines had almost disappeared. Things like Mouton 1945, Cheval Blanc 1947, Lafleur 1947, Margaux 1900, Pétrus in a variety of vintages, Latour 1961, all frequently in large formats, Yquem 1921, and, from the previous century, 19th-century Lafite— the usual litany (plus Romanée-Conti and La Tâche in various sizes and years, plus more recent Henri Jayer burgundies)—were very rarely found, usually in old family cellars in the region of origin and in a few old country estates in Europe. Now, they are made to order and two a penny. One recorked trophy bottle becomes 100—cloning at its most efficient. They are generally bought by less experienced collectors who rightly wish to "experience" these mythical wines. They mostly taste quite good and are pronounced "amazingly youthful" (very accurate). Some are bought

SERENA SUTCLIFFE MW is the head of Sotheby's International Wine Department, with auctions in London and New York. Fluent in several major European languages, she became interested in wine while translating for the UN in France in the 1960s. In 1976 she became the second woman to qualify as a Master of Wine. Serena later served as chairman of the Institute of Masters of Wine. She is a regular lecturer and broadcaster in Europe, the United States, and Asia, the author of several books on wine, and she regularly writes for publications all over the world. Serena is married to fellow MW David Peppercorn.

to impress, or as an "investment," and then they are sold on and scattered even more widely.

Genuine old wines are not powerful, lusty, robust, and consistent. They are often light-textured, ephemeral, very inconsistent, and aging every day. For example, the fabulous old Montroses I tasted recently, direct from the château, showed more age than they did 10 years ago. Real old wines are often lingering, lacy, ethereal, magic; they are also often volatile, acid, and mushroomy. The surgically altered monsters out on the block are great brutes that never age. They have trout lips and scars under the hairline. I do not like them, nor those making fortunes trading in them. This is a blot on the wine trade I knew and loved.

PEAKING VINTAGES

BORDEAUX

1997 Provides lovely drinking from now.

1994 Peaking.

1993 Peaking.

1992 Peaked—pretty well a washout.

1991 Peaking, but hardly any made.

1987 Forget it.

1985 Approaching peak except for First Growths, top Seconds, and top Right Banks.

1984 Mostly unpleasant, as well as past their best.

1983 Mostly at their peak, except for gems like Margaux, Palmer, and Pichon-Lalande.

1982 Many have peaked, except for First Growths, Super-Seconds, top St-Emilions, and Pomerols. Gruaud-Larose excellent.

1981 Drink now for optimum pleasure.

1980 Mostly too old.

1979 Peak, but top wines are still drinking well. Try Haut-Brion!

1978 Peak, but top wines are still drinking well, *pace* Ausone, Lafite, Pichon-Lalande.

1977 Forget it.

1976 Peaked. Lafite and Ausone still looking good.

1975 Mostly peaked. Exceptions include Pétrus, Latour, La Mission Haut-Brion, Pichon-Lalande, Cheval Blanc.

1974, 1973, and 1972 Enough said.

1971 Peaked. Top Pomerols still glorious *viz* the heavenly, "roasted" Pétrus La Mission Haut-Brion is excellent

1970 Mostly peaked. Exceptions include Pétrus, Latour, La Mission Haut-Brion, Trotanoy, La Conseillante, Pichon-Lalande, Ducru-Beaucaillo Palmer, Giscours, Beychevelle.

1969 and 1968 Don't even think about

1967 Peaked a long time ago. Pétrus st good.

1966 Mostly peaked. Exceptions include Latour, Cheval Blanc, Pétrus, Haut Brion, La Mission Haut-Brion.

1964 Mostly peaked. Exceptions include Pétrus, Latour, Haut-Brion, La Mission Haut-Brion.

1962 Peaked, although the Firsts are st good.

1961 Most wines still wonderful. That small crop gave the vital concentration.

1959 The top wines are still magic.

RED BURGUNDY

1997 Delicious drinking now.

1994 Drink now, since that dry finish will intensify.

1992 Delicious now, but hurry.

1990 *Grands crus* have further to go.

1989 *Grands crus* have further to go, *premiers crus* lovely.

1988 The very top wines mostly have further to go.

1987 Should have been drunk.

1986 As above. Even Jayer is at its best.

1985 Mostly at, or over, its peak, except for top *grands crus* such as Drouhin's Bonnes Mares, La Tâche, and all DRC.

1984 Don't go there.

1983 A very few are hanging on.

1982 As above, for different reasons.

1981 Peaked.

1980 Past their peak and even those brilliant Jayers should be drunk. La Tâche still amazing.

1979 Peaked.

1978 There are still some wonders at the top. They have a signature gaminess. DRC splendid.

1977 Treat them as if they were never there.

1976 Peaked a long time ago, with the odd, rare exception.

1975 Should not be mentioned in polite society.

1974 Unpleasant and old.

1973 Peaked a long time ago.

1972 One or two survivors, *viz* de Vogüé's Musigny Vieilles Vignes.

1971 Stay with DRC or similar here.

1970 It is pretty well all over.

1969 Some survivors at *grand cru* level, with scent and finesse.

1966 A few still live gloriously on— Romanée-Conti is mind-blowing.

1964 A few terrific wines at *grand cru* level.

1962 A few top wines are still magnificent.

1961 As above.

1959 As above.

WHITE BURGUNDY

1999 You can start on the lesser wines.

1998 Many are ready.

1997 Very nice drinking now.

1996 Some greats, some looking flat.

1994 Mostly at their peak.

1993 As above.

1992 As above—they matured faster than many believed.

1991 Mostly at their peak.

1990 Some top wines still have a bit to go, others are glowing right now.

1989 As above.

1988 Mostly at their peak or over it.

1987 Peaked.

1986 Mostly peaked. Some *grands crus* are lovely right now.

1985 Many of the top wines are so fat and full they will stay around for ages, such as the Bâtards of Ramonet and Niellon. I prefer it to 1986.

1984 Peaked a very long time ago.

1983 Some tremendous wines at the top. They seemed alcoholic and heavy when young, but, boy, are they marvelous now. Some of the greatest white burgundies of my life come from this vintage, such as Corton-Charlemagne from Latour and Bonneau de Martray.

1982 Virtually all peaked a long time ago.

1981 Peaked a long time ago.

1980 As above.

1979 Virtually all peaked some time ago.

1978 As above, but some gems live on, such as Chablis Les Clos from Drouhin, which now looks like a Côte d'Or wine.

1976 Peaked, but there are some stunners still around at *grand cru* level.

1973 Peaked, with the odd surprise at *grand cru* level.

1971 Peaked, with some stunners left.

1970 As above.

1969 As above.

1967 It starts getting esoteric from here, but the odd surprise.

1966 Mostly history, but DRC's Montrachet makes history.

1964 Peaked a long time ago, with a few exceptions hanging on.

1962 Peaked, of course, with a few marvelous exceptions.

1961 As above.

RED RHONE

2002 Drink quickly, if from the south.

1997 Drink from now.

1994 In my view, start drinking up.

1993 Peak.

1992 Peak.

1991 Peaked for the south, fine for the north.

1990 Excellent, the best will keep.

1989 As above.

1988 As above.

1987 Peaked, so drink now.

1986 As above.

1985 At peak, although the best will keep.

1984 Peaked.

1983 Peaked for the south but the top wines from the north still have life in them.

1982 Peaked everywhere, although the north is better.

1981 Peaked for the north, a few good ones left in the south.

1980 Peaked.

1979 Peaked, but the best are still drinking well.

1978 At its peak, mostly, with some amazing wines at top level.

1976 Peaked some time ago, but Hermitage La Chapelle lives on to delight.

1972 As above.

1971 As above, but throw in Rayas, too, as well as Chave's glorious Hermitage.

1970 Peaked, but great Hermitage La Chapelle.

1969 Peaked, but glorious La Chapelle, with Chave and Rayas still in there.

1967 Peaked, but tremendous La Chapelle.

1966 As above.

1964 As above.

1962 As above.

1961 The top wines are still out of this world (La Chapelle *et al*).

1959 As above.

PORT

2000 Wonderful, but keep.

1997 Don't touch—too young.

1994 As above.

1992 As above.

1991 As above.

1985 Lovely drinking now, as evinced by Dow.

1983 As above.

1982 Drinking well now and over the next few years.

1980 As above.

1977 Drinking very well now but will obviously keep.

1975 Drink up fast.

1970 Fabulous vintage, glorious now but will stay that way for ages.

1966 Excellent wines right now, but will keep, of course. The fruit in them is quite beautiful. Taylor's is magnificent.

1963 Huge, powerful wines, for drinking or keeping.

1960 Beautiful now.

1958 Mostly peaked but don't say that to Noval Nacional! Extraordinary wine.

1955 Superb now and not about to fall off the perch.

1950 Drink up, but the Nacional is eternal.

1948 Great now.

1947 Drink now.

1945 Still there, after all these years. Mammoth. Graham is great.

GERMANY

2000 For early drinking.
1999 Drink up at the bottom end.
1996 Broach and enjoy.
1995 Broach and enjoy.
1994 Peak.
1993 Approaching peak but the best will mature in splendid fashion.
1992 Peak.
1991 Peak.
1990 Excellent, and the best will age beautifully.
1989 As above.
1988 As above.
1987 Peaked.
1986 Mostly peaked.
1985 Mostly at peak.
1984 Dreadful vintage.
1983 Mostly peaked but some wines beautifully present.
1982 Peaked a long time ago.
1981 As above.
1980 Forget it.
1979 A very few survivors.
1976 Tremendous, with a plethora of fantastic wines still vying for top honors.
1975 As above, especially for the Mosel.
1971 The tops and still magnificent in the upper echelons.
1967 Peaked some time ago but a few stunning survivors at TBA level.
1959 At peak—and glorious too.
1953 Peaked, with a few beauties left.

GREATEST-QUALITY AUCTION WINES

❶ Château Haut-Brion 1961
A magnum comparison between this and the La Mission 1961 at a wonderful dinner with friends in the country. This time the Haut-Brion was just so deliriously, heart-stoppingly beautiful that, for me, it swept the board against the powerful La Mission. One felt privileged to be the arbiter here.

❷ Château Ducru-Beaucaillou 1961 At a tremendous dinner at the château, amid a lineup of brilliance. A jewel to rival the Firsts from the start, and it remains so. Seductive and scented, opulent, sweet, and lacy—utter bliss.

❸ Château Montrose 1928 This came in a whisker ahead of the 1945 and 1947 at an amazing vertical of Montrose organized by the château and Bipin Desai, held at Taillevent. In the 1990s, the 1929 appeared more magical, but now it is the glorious coffee beans and berries depth and huge flavor of the 1928 that are staggering.

❹ Château Pichon-Lalande 1945 Another great vertical over lunch at Taillevent, organized by the château and the indefatigable Bipin Desai. It could have been the 1959 or the 1961, but this year I have 1945 "on my mind," and this was just so unbelievably intense, with huge concentration and a massive, meaty character—you almost wondered if American oak came into the equation! One looked into the very heart of a wine here.

❺ La Tâche 1985 A magnum to start a very long Saturday dinner in the country. It was absolutely ready, which somewhat surprised me, but it is just so mouthwateringly delicious that you have to have more … and more. Silky texture and all the red fruits.

❻ Romanée-Conti 2001 Yes, I know it is a crime to broach it, but this was a tasting and one has to reassess… This is a high-octane miracle with its scent of extreme purity and an amazing flavor of sugared wild strawberries that explodes on to the palate. Wine like no other.

❼ Malvasia 1880 (bottled 1956, shipped through Blandy's) At David Peppercorn's lunch to celebrate

50 years in the wine trade—and it was worth waiting for. Liquid walnuts, immense complexity, and with that battle between sweetness and acidity that is so drop-dead fascinating in great madeira.

8 Dom Pérignon Oenothèque 1973 An extraordinary tasting session presided over by Richard Geoffroy at the abbey of Hautvillers produced this ethereal beauty, the "personification" of Dom Pérignon, with a scent of summer evenings in fields, plus perfect poise and purity, the empty glass exuding marshmallow.

9 Sassicaia 1988 Shared with David at home. The unbelievable wild herbs, cassis, lavender, and blackberries bouquet was matched by the totally mouth-filling, black-currant, thick velvety taste. There is a touch of mint and a real dark-chocolate finish. Will go on for ever—I have always thought it superior to the 1985.

10 Perrier-Jouët Belle Epoque 1979 In magnum at a vertical chez P-J in Epernay. A fascinating nose of nuts, allspice, and coffee beans led into a stunning, toasty, orange zest and citrus taste, combining youth and power.

MOST EXCITING OR UNUSUAL AUCTION FINDS

1 Penfolds Grange 1979 Unusual, since you can scarcely find it now, and exciting—well, because it is! Some might say it was getting on a bit, but, served as a surprise at the end of a dinner with historic bordeaux and burgundy (and an ultra-generous host), it was heart-stoppingly sensational, lusty, and deep, and bursting with flavor and energy.

2 Château Filhot 1929 Filhot is usually passed over in the pantheon of top Sauternes, but this vintage is outstanding—so fruity and youthful it set the home dinner guests buzzing. I matched it with a terrine de foie gras (and the 1923).

3 Château Gruaud-Larose 1982 Not the most vaunted 1982, but it flew the flag with vigor at a tasting for Bath University Wine Club, after a run of more exalted names. It was full of fruit and body and in great form. Totally satisfying.

4 Forster Jesuitengarten Riesling Spätlese 1989 Bürklin-Wolf This is a glorious, fat, spicy, warm, and round wine, still with great freshness. Spiced apples. Just the thing at the end of a frantic day—and at 10 degrees of alcohol, a bottle between two (as an apéritif) is perfect.

5 Château Pavie-Macquin 1997 I defy anyone to guess this is 1997. It is a miracle of rich, deep chocolate and plums—heady and spicy, with a finish of cocoa. A humdinger of a wine: a simple supper bottle turning out to be marvelous.

6 Rùbico Lacrima di Morro d'Alba 2004 Marotti Campi I am not sure how I came by this one (records sometimes fail me!), but if you are after morello cherry and velvety bliss, look no further.

7 Cabernet 1985 Lake's Folly, Hunter Valley Dredged from our cellar—fascinatingly, it had no deposit. Ironlike, mint-leaf nose, with an inimitable strong iron tonic and cocoa taste. Amazingly youthful, with a finish of dark chocolate. And all this on 12.2 degrees of alcohol!

8 Puligny-Montrachet 1994
Etienne Sauzet *Sauzet is not always on song, but this straight village wine from a forgettable vintage had loads of limes and smoke, with a lovely lanolin texture, pure fruit, and balancing acidity—very beautiful. Wine is full of contradictions.*

9 Sonoma Cabernet Sauvignon Reserve 1987 Kalin Cellars *Another 12.2 degrees of alcohol comes good! The black-currants and wild-herbs nose of California, with the elegance of a top bordeaux—but no 1987 claret would ever taste like this. Sweet, soft, and pure.*

10 Dogaia Rosso del Ticino 2001
Guido Brivio *It took a Swiss friend with a perceptive palate to winnow this out. Made from Gamaret and Merlot, with malolactic in new barrels, it is just so super, spicy, and rich. This has to be from low yields and I suspect may find its way only into local auctions.*

BEST AUCTION BARGAINS *(hammer price)*

1 Coteaux du Layon Le 20 1998
Philippe Delesvaux; at the New York September 2005 sale (12 half-liters: US$175) *Brilliant winemaker, to-die-for wine—how can people ignore these mouthwatering miracles?*

2 Meursault 1er Cru Perrières 2000 Domaine Michelot; at the London July 2005 sale (12 bottles: £180) *Excellent producer, on top form, and a wonderful year for white burgundy—a win-win buy.*

3 Châteauneuf-du-Pape 1998
Domaine de Marcoux; at the London September 2005 sale (12 bottles: £220) *A domaine doing no wrong—well, it is run by two sisters. Their 1998s are fabulous, and this is a sheer gulp of the sun.*

4 Château Milens St-Emilion 1998; at the New York April 2005 sale (12 bottles: US$350) *Inside-track, superb, ripe, gummy stuff, made under the supervision of Jean-Luc Thunevin. Top Right Bank year, too.*

5 Château Pichon-Lalande 1989; at the London September 2005 sale (12 bottles: £480) *An aberration at this price, both classic and exotic at the same time. It just slipped through—it pays to be alert in the saleroom.*

6 Château Pontet-Canet 2000; at the London October 2005 sale (12 bottles: £240) *Not bad for impressive, classy Pauillac that could be another 1928 or 1929 for PC.*

7 Riesling Clos St-Théobald Rangen de Thann Sélection de Grains Nobles 1998 Domaine Schoffit; at the New York March 2005 sale (12 half-liters: US$375) *Nectar at a giveaway price—one of those occasions when I wish I could raise my hand!*

8 Vosne-Romanée 1er Cru Les Beaux Monts 1998 Emmanuel Rouget; at the New York September 2005 sale (12 bottles: US$475) *Rouget seems to come in under the radar, in spite of his credentials as nephew and disciple of Henri Jayer.*

9 Nuits-St-Georges 1er Cru Les Saint Georges 1996 Dominique Laurent; at the London October 2005 sale (12 bottles: £240) *Laurent wines really deliver the goods in terms of impact and flavor, but the English have not woken up to them.*

10 Darmagi Cabernet Sauvignon 1996 Gaja; at the New York December 2005 sale (6 magnums: US$650) *In a sale with virtually no bargains, up pops this one—it only goes to show…*

Wine Auctions & Investment

Anthony Rose

Despite the ongoing expansion of the fine-wine market beyond French borders, bordeaux continues its UK-saleroom domination, in 2005 taking 60–80 percent of business (Christie's and Liv-ex respectively).

ANTHONY ROSE

It's a different story in the US market, now the biggest in the world, where Sotheby's New York had 41 percent of its business in bordeaux (64 percent worldwide) and a substantial 38 percent in burgundy. Burgundy accounted for 21 percent worldwide at Sotheby's, a figure similar to Christie's 20 percent. Beyond the two French classic regions, Sotheby's figure of 8 percent in New York for sales of California wines was significantly higher than the Rhône (5 percent) and Italy (3 percent), although sales of California wines outside the US remain negligible.

For some time now, prices for the best younger bordeaux vintages have been outstripping older vintages, but 2000 bordeaux prices (and the few 2003s that appeared) came off the boil in 2005, except for Le Pin and Pétrus. This was partly due to the surge in prices for mature bordeaux in the fall of 2005 thanks to the British government's SIPPs program. With the prospect of being able to offset money paid for fine wine against pensions in 2006 (a prospect dashed by the Chancellor in the fall), prices rose some 15 percent toward the end of the year. The wine exchange, Liv-ex, reported a record month in September, with turnover up 60 percent. The so-called Parker effect is generally held responsible for high prices for

ANTHONY ROSE is the award-winning wine correspondent for *The Independent* and writes for a number of other publications, including *Wine & Spirit* magazine and *Harpers Wine and Spirit Weekly*. He specializes in the auction scene, writing a monthly column on the subject for *Decanter* and contributing to *The Oxford Companion to Wine* on auction and investment. Anthony is married to an Australian wine photographer and lives in London.

top young vintages, but there are other important factors: the trend toward drinking wines younger, the health of the US economy, and the strength of the dollar. There was further evidence that the Parker effect itself, while still powerful, was showing signs of waning. Apart from the fact that Parker has farmed out Germany, joining Burgundy, Alsace, and Italy as the province of other critics, a US poll indicated that fewer wine consumers were influenced by him as a more educated public has become aware that the Parker points system pushes up prices.

Top vintages of Pétrus performed strongly in 2005, along with 1998 Cheval Blanc, while the 1961 Latour à Pomerol reached a remarkable $94,800 (£51,200) and Lafleur $88,875 (£48,000). Yet, Le Pin aside, the demand for garage wines continued to wane at auction, with Valandraud and La Mondotte falling. Buyers were perhaps a little skeptical of the aging capabilities of the fruit-forward styles, although California icons such as Harlan, Screaming Eagle, and Bryant Family remained strong. In the Rhône, well-reviewed, new, so-called premium Châteauneuf-du-Pape was received with skepticism.

Bordeaux saw increasing demand in 2005 for the top 50-odd blue-chip trophy wines from the best older vintages, notably 1945, 1959, 1961, 1982, 1986, 1989, 1990, and, to an extent, 1996. According to Sotheby's New York, several factors explain the significant strengthening of the market, with prices rising more in 2005 than in any year since the boom of 1996/97: a shortage of mature wine on the market; condition starting to become less consistent; the strengthening of the dollar; big bonuses in London; a revitalized East Asian export market; and speculation about the perceived impact of SIPPs. The extent to which older vintages are drying up is hard to gauge. While higher prices suggest that consumption is fueling demand, some, such as Chris Munro at Christie's, think that quite a few people are still sitting on vintages as far back as 1982.

Nevertheless, the 1982 vintage reached new heights with $10,000 (£5,000+) per case for First Growths, Latour and Lafite especially, becoming a reality. The 1989 and 1990 vintages continued to provide relative value, except for 1990 Latour, Pétrus, and Cheval Blanc, which were very strong. The 1995s and 1996s finally crystallized, with First Growths moving back up over the £2,000 ($3,600) mark to achieve, Lafite especially, significant gains. In contrast, the great Millennium vintage, which started life from a high base, showed little or no upward movement. The 100-point 2001 Yquem had a good run, trading up to £2,800 ($5,100) after opening at £2,200 ($4,000) per case (Liv-ex) and large-format bottles were also back in favor, with half-bottles commanding substantial premiums. At the other end of the scale, 1997 bordeaux started to diminish in volume, and 1999 and 2001 bordeaux were waiting in the wings to replace it as "glugging claret" in 2006.

Driven by the US market, burgundy, DRC especially, had a strong year in 2005 with the fine and rare end of the market achieving stratospheric prices. Burgundy has increased as a percentage of lots in catalogs, although it is perhaps more polarized even than bordeaux, with substantial demand for relatively few names from great vintages. Among the most sought-after names, icons DRC and Henri Jayer apart, are Roumier, Dujac, Ponsot, Dugat, Leroy, and Lignier (reds), and Coche-Dury, Leflaive, Lafon, and Ramonet (whites). Top years like 1978, 1985, 1989, 1990, 1993, 1995, 1996, and 1999 achieved the best results.

The Rhône performed relatively well, with huge excitement over the 12-bottle case of 1961 Jaboulet Hermitage La Chapelle, which fetched £41,800 ($76,000). The arrival of the Guigal 1999s was met with considerable interest, while top vintages of Rayas achieved high prices with Beaucastel Hommage à Jacques Perrin, Chave Ermitage Cuvée Cathelin, and Bonneau Cuvée Spéciale remaining strong.

With the exception of Sassicaia, the market for Italian wines was static, as it was for vintage port, which was affected by large quantities of young vintages at high prices. The shortage of mature port suggests possible price rises for the 1980, the 1983, and the 1985. Mature champagne has also seen a leap, with Krug (a magnum of 1953 Krug Collection sold for $12,925 [£7,385]), Cristal (methuselahs of the 1990 Millennium Cuvée sold for $10,575 [£5,700]), and Dom Pérignon the principal objects of desire.

All prices have been converted at historic exchange rates.

Guest Comment: The Net

Guest writer Andrew Caillard MW of Langton's, which has teamed up with Christie's in a joint-venture online auction in Asia, writes:

The introduction of the silent-bid wine auction in the 1980s, followed by the deployment of Internet auction technology in the late 1990s, has changed the auction format irreversibly. The vibrant cut and thrust of the live auction room is gradually dwindling as Internet trading becomes part of our daily lives. While the auction process remains the same, the traditional expert wine auctioneer is increasingly becoming a market analyst and valuer, the electronic bidding system taking care of the sale process.

The electronic format, which attempts to replicate the live auction environment, differs in that all lots are sold at exactly the same moment. The excitement of an Internet auction sale occurs in the last 30 minutes before the auction closes. Catalogs for Internet auctions provide potential buyers with data on vintage conditions, regional information, and tasting notes, as well as the usual information on lots, estimated prices, and conditions of sale.

THE AUCTIONEERS

On the eve of its 240th anniversary and the 40th anniversary of its wine department, Christie's claimed pole position in 2005 for the fourth year in succession. Its 43 sales conducted across nine sale locations realized £22.4 million ($42 million), up 15 percent on 2004. In the UK and Europe, 33 Christie's sales totaled £14.1 million ($24.3 million).

With the top lot of the year the case of 1961 Hermitage La Chapelle, European highlights featured a new partnership with the Hospices de Beaune, whose 145th auction in November was organized by Christie's; a London sale of Pétrus and Latour sourced directly from the châteaux cellars; the auction of the late Alan Clark MP's wine cellar in September; and an auction return to Vinexpo. Christie's announced a major global expansion to its network, joining forces with Langton's, Australia's premier wine auction house, to build on a 15-year alliance and co-market an auction in Asia in early 2006. Langton's experienced 5 percent growth, with sales of £6.1 million (A$15.1 million) in 2005.

In America, NYWines/Christie's, finishing fifth in revenue ranking, held 10 sales totalling $15.6 million (£8.4 million), with the top lot, a 24-half-bottle case of 1947 Château Cheval Blanc, realizing $88,125 (£50,071). Conceding that the large majority of big cellars are in the US, Christie's Chris Munro said, "The figures can be skewed; competition is fierce, and if you're prepared not to make money, you will win. Zachys' turnover is great, but its margin is minimal to attract business. If you can sustain that business long-term, fine, but you can't. We want to maintain our global position but not at any cost."

In Zachys' third year in auctions, its eight New York and two (with Wally's) Los Angeles auctions expanded on 2004 to achieve a total turnover of $33.8 million (£18.3 million), with the percentage of lots sold rising to 96.78, up from 95.56 in 2004. Finishing third, Sotheby's 16 sales worldwide were up more than 40 percent, bringing £15.7 million ($29.1 million), a 40 percent increase on 2004. Six Aulden Cellars/Sotheby's auctions in the US totalled $18.6 million (£10 million), compared to $12.6 million (£6.8 million) in 2004, the high point being the November 5 auction of Finest Burgundy and Rhône from an Extraordinary Private Cellar realizing $4.7 million (£2.5 million). In the UK, 10 Sotheby's sales brought £5.7 million ($10.5 million), up £1.3 million ($2.4 million) on 2004.

Acker Merrall & Condit's 22 brick-and-mortar and online auctions grossed $20.9 million (£11.3 million), its best year, up from $18.7 million (£10.1 million) in 2004. The rising clout of Internet auctions was illustrated by California-based specialist WineBid.com, which reported a $20-million (£10.8-million) turnover, up from $16 million (£8.6 million) the previous year. Four sales by Hart Davis Hart, a new Chicago company, registered $9.5 million (£5.1 million) and in San Francisco, Bonhams & Butterfields' six auctions fetched $5.6 million (£3 million). Morrell & Company's four brick-and-mortar and online auctions brought $3.9 million (£2.1 million), marginally down on 2004. With four sales bringing in $1.6 million (£0.9 million), Edward Roberts International, a small Chicago house established in 2001, had its best year to date.

LANGTON'S

The news that Christie's was to team up with Langton's to strengthen a 15-year alliance and co-market an auction in Asia focused considerable interest on the premier Australian auction house, which in 2005 posted 5 percent growth with a total turnover of £6.1 million (A$15.1 million). As auctioneer Andrew Caillard MW reported, the other high point was the release of Langton's Classification of Australian Wine in July 2005. The top regions are Barossa Shiraz (including Eden Valley), Margaret River Cabernet and Chardonnay, Coonawarra Cabernet, and Hunter Semillon (McWilliam's and Tyrrell's).

Among the outstanding performances in 2005, McWilliam's Lovedale Vineyard Semillon was hot property, along with Giaconda Chardonnay, Best's Thompson's Reserve Shiraz, Clonakilla Shiraz/ Viognier, Noon Reserve Shiraz, and Yalumba Octavius. The critically maligned 2000 Grange defied predictions, outperforming the acclaimed 1986, 1991, 1996, and 1998 vintages, while the multi-trophy-winning 2002 Seppelt St Peter's Shiraz was also a strong performer. The 1998 Grange gained strength, adding around 20 percent in value over the year. Other price highlights per bottle include: 1998 Penfolds RWT magnum A$403 (£161), 1998 Rockford Basket

Press magnum A$403 (£161), 1998 Greenock Creek Roennfeldt Road Shiraz A$388 (£155), 1998 Henschke Hill of Grace A$375 (£150), and 1998 Mount Mary Quintet A$208 (£83).

Langton's top five bottle prices in 2005 were A$48,300 (£19,320) for a 1951 Grange; A$20,700 (£8,280) for a 1953 Grange; A$19,550 (£7,820) for a 1985 Grange imperial; A$14,950 (£5,980) for a 2000 Mouton imperial; and A$4,945 (£1,978) for a 1955 Grange.

Australian dollars have been converted to pounds sterling at 0.4.

ALAN CLARK'S CELLAR

At Christie's, the cellar of the late Alan Clark, former Tory MP, womanizer, automobile enthusiast, and diarist, fetched £56,000 ($102,000). The most important lot in the sale was 12 bottles of 1961 Château Palmer, which sold for £7,700 ($14,000). The highest-priced lot in the sale was £8,250 ($15,000) for a case of 24 half-bottles of 1967 Château d'Yquem, referred to by Clark in his *Diaries*: "I had put the chairs out on the lawn, but drizzle started. I got a bottle of Yquem 67 on ice—the first this year. We sat in the red library. The Yquem did its work on an empty stomach and I sparkled."

ZACHYS' SALE

Five cases of Henri Jayer Vosne-Romanée Cros Parantoux, spanning vintages from 1955 to 1999, fetched $88,500 (£47,790) in a record-breaking sale at which Zachys, a major northeastern merchant and auction house based in Scarsdale, NY, was offering more than 17,000 bottles worth $6–9 million (£3.2–4.8 million). The "largest single-owner American cellar" grossed $9.8 million (£5.3 million), making it the third-highest wine-auction total in modern history and the largest sum generated by a single-owner American cellar.

Two magnums of 1947 Château La Fleur made $53,100 (£28,670) and $44,840 (£24,200), while a jeroboam of 1990 Romanée-Conti fetched $44,840 (£24,200), the same price as a jeroboam of 1962 La Tâche, and a single magnum of 1947 Cheval Blanc sold for $42,480 (£22,940). Two single magnums of 1961 Jaboulet Hermitage La Chapelle went for $18,880 (£10,200) each, and two six-bottle lots of 1990 Guigal Côte Rôtie La Mouline sold for a total of $17,700 (£9,560), with a case of 1974 Heitz Martha's Vineyard Cabernet Sauvignon making $15,340 (£8,280). The world auction record was set by Sotheby's former partner Sherry-Lehmann in 1999 with the $14.4-million (£7.8-million) sale of 48,000 bottles owned by Christen Sveaas, a Norwegian businessman, in New York.

US dollars have been converted to pounds sterling at 0.54.

HOSPICES DE BEAUNE

At the 145th Hospices de Beaune, the annual charity auction made €5.08 million (£3.48 million), compared to €3.03 million (£2.08 million) in 2004. The majority of the take came from 647 barrels of red wine and 142 barrels of white wine, among the highlights of which were barrels of Bâtard-Montrachet, Cuvée de Flandres, which fetched €65,923 (£45,157) each, and Clos de la Roche, Cuvée Georges Kritter, which each sold for over €20,000 (£13,700). Although there was some grumbling that prices weren't higher for the excellent 2005 vintage, Anthony Hanson MW, senior consultant to Christie's International Wine Department, considered the Hospices sale a success, with turnover up 32 percent on the previous year. A new feature of the November weekend auction was that private individuals could participate for the first time. The Extraordinary Sale of Wine in Bottle from the Private Reserve of the Hospices totalled €212,582 (£145,619).

Euros have been converted to pounds sterling at 0.685.

THE LIV-EX INDEX

After two flat years for the fine-wine market, Liv-ex's three major indices all posted healthy double-digit gains in 2005.

Liv-ex indices and other asset classes in 2005:

Commodity/index	% return
Brent Crude	48.3
Nikkei 225	40.2
Liv-ex Claret Chip Index	22.7
Liv-ex 100 Fine Wine Index	18.7
Gold	17.7
FTSE 100	16.7
Liv-ex 500 Index	12.6
UK Gilts	6.4
Stanley Gibbons 100 (rare stamps)	6.4
FT House Price Index (England & Wales)	3.0
S&P 500	3.0

Exceptional growth 1999–2005

Position '06	'05	'04	'03	Vintage	Wine	1999	2002	2003	2004	2005	% growth[1]	% growth annualized[2]
1	7	7	5	1982	Pétrus	7,800	19,550	16,215	14,690	20,900	168	17.84
2	9	5	0	1982	Le Pin	11,550	15,950	27,495	18,380	26,600	130	14.9
3	2	4	0	1998	Le Pin	2,900	6,540	7,590	9,180	6,230	115	13.58
4	4	0	0	2000	Margaux[3]	N/A	2,400	3,910	4,570	3,400	113	13.37
5	10	8	9	1989	Pétrus	6,156	14,832	11,500	8,640	12,870	109	13.07
6	5	0	0	2000	Mouton[3]	N/A	1,850	2,990	4,370	3,110	94	11.7
7	1	1	0	1961	Latour	7,920	8,580	34,098	29,020	14,300	81	10.34
8	8	10	3	1982	Lafleur	5,532	15,756	9,825	10,260	9,340	69	9.11
–	3	2	1	1978	La Tâche	5,136	15,630	14,330	15,860	N/S	N/A	N/A
–	6	6	7	1978	Guigal Côte Rôtie La Landonne	2,736	6,744	6,000	5,440	N/S	N/A	N/A

Prices in GBP per case of 12 bottles (best hammer price achieved in year indicated).
Sources: Christie's, Sotheby's, and Morrell's.

1 Percentage growth between July 1, 1999 and June 30, 2005.
2 Annualized growth between July 1, 1999 and June 30, 2005.
3 £1,600 en primeur in 2001.

Blue-chip growth: 1998 vintage

Position '06	'05	'04	'03	Wine	1999[1]	2002[2]	2003[2]	2004[2]	2005[2]	% growth[3]	% growth annualized[4]
1	2	3	3	Pétrus	3,800	7,520	6,460	7,260	9,680	155	16.85
2	1	1	1	Le Pin	2,900	6,540	7,590	9,180	6,230	115	13.58
3	4	4	4	Cheval Blanc	1,150	2,110	1,840	1,725	2,420	110	13.19
4	3	2	2	Trotanoy	800	1,740	1,550	1,210	1,470	84	10.66
5	5	6	6	Haut-Brion	875	1,090	1,230	1,210	1,470	68	9.02
6	6	7	5	Lafite	800	1,150	1,035	1,060	1,245	56	7.64
7	7	9	8	Mouton	780	910	800	940	1,130	45	6.37
8	9	10	10	Latour	780	780	710	665	1,020	31	4.57
9	8	8	9	Margaux	780	830	860	750	1,010	30	4.4
10	10	5	7	Ausone	1,150	1,420	1,725	935	1,300	13	2.06

© A Rose 2006

Prices in GBP per case of 12 bottles.
Sources: En primeur prices (excluding VAT): Wine Society in bond.

1 En primeur price July 1, 1999.
2 Best auction price in year indicated.
3 Percentage growth over July 1, 1999 and June 30, 2005.
4 Annualized growth over July 1, 1999 and June 30, 2005.

Blue-chip growth: 1999 vintage

'06	'05	'04	Wine	2000[1]	2003[2]	2004[2]	2005[2]	% growth[3]	% growth annualized[4]
1	1	6	Latour	775	900	1,080	880	14	2.14
2	3=	5	Margaux	775	912	960	858	11	1.71
3	5	3	Pétrus	3,650	5,076	3,680	3,960	9	1.37
4	2	2	Lafite	775	1,092	1,040	825	7	1.05
5	3=	1	Haut-Brion	775	1,476	960	770	−1	−0.11
6	6	4	Mouton	775	936	780	748	−4	−0.59
7	8	7	Cheval Blanc	1,146	1,272	960	1,020	−11	−1.92
–	7	10	Le Pin	3,300	N/S	3,330	N/S	N/A	N/A
–	10	8	Ausone	1,146	1,044	N/S	N/S	N/A	N/A
–	9	9	Trotanoy	550	408	410	N/S	N/A	N/A

(Position columns headed: '06 | '05 | '04)

© A Rose 2006

Prices in GBP per case of 12 bottles. **Sources:** *En primeur* prices (excluding VAT): Wine Society in bond, Pétrus Corney & Barrow, Trotanoy and Le Pin Berry Bros & Rudd.

1 *En primeur* price July 1, 2000. **2** Best auction price in year indicated. **3** Percentage growth over July 1, 2000 to June 30, 2005. **4** Annualized growth over July 1, 2000 to June 30, 2005.

Blue-chip growth: 2000 vintage

'06	'05	Wine	2001[1]	2002[2]	2003[2]	2004[2]	2005[2]	% growth[3]	% growth annualized[4]
1	–	Le Pin	2,640	N/S	N/S	N/S	18,000	582	37.67
2	6	Pétrus	5,500	N/S	8,370	10,580	15,280	178	18.55
3	5	Latour	1,600	2,375	3,450	3,280	3,680	130	14.88
4	1	Margaux	1,600	2,400	3,910	4,570	3,400	113	13.37
5	2	Mouton	1,600	1,850	2,990	4,370	3,110	94	11.7
6	7	Haut-Brion	1,600	2,095	2,990	3,000	2,970	86	10.85
7	4	Las-Cases	780	N/S	1,640	1,680	1,430	83	10.62
8	3	Lafite	1,600	2,050	3,220	4,200	2,690	68	9.04
9	9	Cheval Blanc	2,500	N/S	5,290	3,900	3,820	53	7.32
10	8	Ausone	2,400	N/S	N/S	4,180	3,250	35	5.18

(Position columns headed: '06 | '05)

© A Rose 2006

Prices in GBP per case of 12 bottles. **Sources:** *En primeur* prices (excluding VAT): Wine Society in bond, Corney & Barrow, Berry Bros & Rudd.

1 *En primeur* price July 1, 2001. **2** Best auction price in year indicated. **3** Percentage growth over July 1, 2001 to June 30, 2005. **4** Annualized growth over July 1, 2001 to June 30, 2005.

Viticulture

Dr. Richard Smart & Dr. Caroline Gilby MW

Have appellations become meaningless? A meeting in Paris of the European Confederation of Independent Winemakers heard wine economist Patrick Aigrain claim the appellation system has become moribund.

DR. RICHARD SMART   DR. CAROLINE GILBY MW

He blames the proliferation of AOC wines (there are now 450!) for this situation, with 75 percent of French wine bearing geographic reference. He says that this confuses and turns off customers. A similar message was sent at the Royal Economic Society in Nottingham. A study by Olivier Gergaud from the University of Reims and Victor Ginsburgh of the Université Libre de Bruxelles argues that winemaking technologies, not *terroir*, determine wine quality.

DR. RICHARD SMART BSc Agr, MSc, PhD, DScAgr, termed by some "the flying vine-doctor," is an Australian vineyard consultant with clients in 24 countries. He is now resident in Tasmania, Australia, where Tamar Ridge Wines is his principal client. He began his career in viticulture research in Australia, spanning to Israel, the US, France, and New Zealand. Richard is the principal author of *Sunlight into Wine* (Winetitles, 1991) and is considered an authority on canopy management of grapevines. He has regular columns in *The Australian & New Zealand Wine Industry Journal* and California's *Practical Winery & Vineyard*, is published widely in scientific and other journals, and was viticulture editor for two volumes of *Jancis Robinson's Oxford Companion to Wine*.

DR. CAROLINE GILBY MW is a freelance writer specializing in Eastern Europe and viticulture. She contributed to *Wines of the World* (Dorling Kindersley, 2004) and has been published in *Decanter*, *Harpers Wine and Spirit Weekly*, *OLN*, and *New Scientist*. She is on the editorial board of the *Journal of Wine Research*. She has a PhD in plant sciences but left science to become senior wine buyer for a major UK retail chain. She lectures for the WSET Diploma on tasting technique, vinification, and wine handling, and judges at international wine shows, as well as working as a consultant to the wine trade.

The pair collected data on environmental conditions and winemaking techniques across the 100 vineyards of the Haut-Médoc in 1990, including First Growths Mouton Rothschild, Latour, Lafite-Rothschild, and Margaux. The data were compared with the prices that certain vintages fetched on the wine market and the scores they received from tasters, including Michael Broadbent MW and Robert Parker.

The results, the authors say, show that winemaking techniques completely overshadow the effect of *terroir*. "The French *terroir* legend obviously does not hold—at least in the Médoc region," they say.

Yet more hanging

Arguments continue about "hang time" in California; it was a hot topic at the Unified Symposium in Sacramento. Increasingly, questions are being asked (and not only in California) about the abilities of winemakers to taste grapes and predict wine styles. Their tendency is to call an "ideal" date of harvest, which, interestingly, is always in the future! So consumers the world over are being provided with table wines of increasing alcohol content, with more and more now seen at over 15 percent and even 16 percent alcohol. Some California commentators have suggested that wines of more than 14 percent alcohol deserve a new classification, since they are no longer suited to "table wine" categorization, not being suitable for consumption with food. The term "social wine" has been suggested but has not met with universal support.

But a backlash is beginning. Some wine journalists are protesting against the perceived American cult of "bigger is better." Manufacturers at the SITEVI grape growers' and winemakers' Expo at Montpellier featured machines to take sugar out of grape juice and alcohol out of wine. In other quarters, some winemakers are making a feature of their "normal," lower-alcohol table wines, of 13 percent alcohol or less, which are finding consumer acceptance. More importantly, many people are asking, "Where is the proof that delayed harvest (and higher alcohol) makes for better wine anyway?"

Grapevine

• **GM rootstocks in Alsace:** French research institution INRA has set up open-air field trials of 70 different genetically modified rootstocks in Colmar in Alsace. The rootstocks were planted in September 2005 and have been engineered to be resistant to the grapevine fan leaf virus, which causes *court-noué*, for which there is currently no effective treatment. A multidisciplinary team, including local citizens, was set up to address concerns about this trial. Very strict protocols have been agreed, including removal of all inflorescences, to prevent the escape of any GM material.

FRENCH WINE INTO BIOFUEL?

French wine sales lost to the New World and declining national consumption have led to widespread riots by French farmers. Disaffected farmers caused over €2 million worth of damage to the French railroad system in southern France in May. Police used tear gas against rampaging Burgundian winemakers protesting about government-imposed cuts on wine yields in September.

Will biofuel be the solution to surplus production? Grape-based alcohol (ethanol) is added to conventional fuel after distillation of wine. France is already the third-largest producer of ethanol in Europe, at the moment largely from sugar beet and cereals. So ONIVINS, the state-run wine body, is looking at the possibility of turning surplus wine into biofuel. For years, surplus wine from La Mancha in Spain has been distilled and sold to Brazil to support their biofuel program. Maybe France will follow suit. Put a little Cabernet in your tank? Or Chablis?

ARSENIC AND VINEYARD POSTS

Ever wondered about the green color of vineyard posts seen especially in New World vineyards? They are green because they are treated with copper, chromium, and arsenate to preserve them from rot. There were concerns in New Zealand's Marlborough region that chemicals leached from the posts might contaminate soils and ground water. While traces were found near the posts, the concentrations over the whole vineyard were very low. Similarly, there was no risk to ground-water quality or human safety.

ROOTS DETERMINE QUALITY

South African researchers have investigated why some vineyards responded positively to early-harvest rainfall in the dry, hot 2004 season and others did not. After detailed investigations of canopies and roots, they found that vineyards that were capable of ripening fruit properly had new lateral shoot growth and healthy young leaves. The vineyards showing ripening problems had only old, senescing, and poorly functioning leaves. The explanation for this was found below ground. Vines with extensive root systems with lots of fine roots supported new leaf growth. In a way, this result reinforces the *terroir* concept, in that soil conditions determine the nature of the root system.

SCIENTIST QUESTIONS GM VINES

Professor Carole Meredith, who spent 22 years at UC Davis and was instrumental in establishing the International Grape Genome Program, has questioned the value of GM vines, which have been proposed by many as the solution to catastrophic diseases like Pierce's disease. She says it is unlikely that we will ever see a disease or insect overcome by a single gene. Further, Meredith asks the important question, "Is it still Chardonnay if it is a genetically modified grape?" Some Californian grape-growing counties have adopted bans on GM crops, including grapes.

NEW FRENCH–ITALIAN GENOME PROJECT

The French and Italian governments announced a €6-million vine genome project in November 2005. The project chief, Enrico Pe, surprisingly stresses that the scheme does not involve genetically modified organisms, but it does include top biotechnology laboratories. Claims are made that vines will be produced with more resistance to pests and diseases, and that grapes will contain more molecules beneficial to wine quality. All of this sounds like genetic modification to the author [RES]. Pe claims that the study will enhance the scientific profile of Italy.

GLOBAL WARMING COULD SPREAD PATHOGENS

Climate change is causing concern about transmission of grapevine pathogens. Several economically significant diseases such as grapevine leaf roll and *flavescence dorée* have insect vectors whose spread is limited by climatic factors. Changes in temperature recorded at Bernkastel-Kues show that flowering occurs 13.4 days earlier compared to 1967, and average annual temperature is up by 3.2°F (1.78°C). As an example, it is expected that rising temperatures will allow mealy bug, currently found only in glasshouses in Germany, to escape and transmit grapevine leaf roll. The leafhopper that is the vector for *flavescence dorée* (or grapevine yellows) is limited by climatic factors: it requires sufficient summer temperatures to complete its life cycle. It appears to be extending its range farther north and has recently been found in Austria for the first time. This is potentially a severe threat to viticulture in countries like Germany, currently unaffected by *flavescence dorée*, that need to put in place regular monitoring to ensure that any infestations are quickly eradicated.

ETHYLENE REGULATES CHAMPAGNE

Champagne Mumm has been using ethylene in 50 ha of vineyards this year to regulate flowering, crop load, and ripening time, and it claims better results than using green-harvesting. It appears particularly useful for Pinot Noir and for young and high-yielding vines. Spraying with ethylene can bring flowering to an end after 10 days instead of the normal 15 or more days, giving more consistent ripening, as well as reducing the number of bunches and thus lowering yield. It can also open up bunches, which improves air circulation and reduces the risk of botrytis. Timing is crucial—too early and all the flowers may be destroyed; too late and there is no benefit. The mechanism appears to be through ethylene's role as a natural regulator of floral abscission.

PIERCE'S DISEASE: ALTERNATIVE APPROACHES

It appears that Pierce's disease, which is vectored by sharpshooters, has alternative hosts in the weed species commonly found around vineyards. In Californian vineyards, 27 out of 29 species tested were found to host the bacterium responsible for the disease,

Xylella fastidiosa. This highlights the need for weed control and removal around susceptible vines. Another approach may be through installation of high fences. Researchers have found that the glassy-winged sharpshooter cannot fly over high fences. The drawback is that these fences need to be at least 16 ft (5 m) high and made of a special UV protective cloth pulled tight against posts. The high cost of such protection means that it would be of use only for particularly high-value crops such as nurseries and super-premium vineyard sites.

OLD BEFORE THEIR TIME

Atypical aging (ATA), first detected in 1988, is now recognized as a viticultural issue, though research has yet to pin down the definitive mechanism responsible for the problem. Lack of nitrogen, lack of water, early harvest, competition from cover crops, and overcropping have all been implicated in causing ATA.

Research suggests that early harvest dates are a key cause, regardless of variety, and that nitrogen levels in berries are also implicated. Delaying harvest is correlated with increased nitrogen in the fruit and appears so far to be the best viticultural tool against ATA, in spite of increased risks of botrytis and disease with late picking in cool-climate regions.

TRIAL AND *TERROIR* IN VALPOLICELLA

Cantina Valpolicella Negrar, the biggest Amarone producer, has reported results from its *terroir* trials. Twelve plots of Corvina clone 48 are being compared, and results already show clearly that good vine management cannot compensate for a poor site. Several previously unregarded sites appear to have potential for very high-quality individual *crus*.

This year, the Cantina has planted trial vineyards looking specifically at pruning and training techniques such as Guyot, and also a vineyard with 48 different varieties (20 of them indigenous) to understand how each will do in the local climate and soils.

Grapevine

• **Researchers in France** are attempting to use a vine's own defense signals to reduce dependence on agrochemicals. Plants release chemicals when attacked by pathogens or predators that switch on defense mechanisms within the rest of the plant and even in neighboring plants; researchers would like to replicate this. In New Zealand, trials at Waipara are attempting to use the plant's chemical signals, hung in "tea bags" around the vines to attract beneficial insects to prey on grapevine pests.

• **More fungi** cause grapevine trunk diseases. Grapevine trunk diseases are responsible for significant losses to the wine industry worldwide (estimated at $260 million in California alone in 1999). It was originally thought that *Eutypa lata* was responsible for most vine-canker development and dieback in California, but other fungi are now implicated, including *Botryosphaeria* species, as well as several other members of the *Eutypa* family.

Opinion:
New World response to Old's *terroir*

Tamar Ridge Wines of Tasmania is on track to become one of the largest cool-climate premium wine producers in Australia. The winery and vineyard team uses "world-best technology" to manage the vineyards to improve wine quality. For the 2005 harvest, this involved using infrared images taken from a plane. These images are known to correlate with vine vigor.

It was observed in the cool 2004 ripening season that some vineyards had a majority of yellow leaves, leading to premature defoliation, and that these vineyards showed delayed maturity and produced wine of lesser quality. This was related to nitrogen deficiency and water stress.

The vineyard images were used for harvest planning. At Tamar Ridge there are two brands, Devil's Corner being the lower price point and Tamar Ridge the higher. It helps harvest planning to classify the vineyards pre-harvest, since different vinification methods may be used.

More variable blocks were allocated to Devil's Corner. Some variability could be overcome—for example, by adding more water or fertilizer. Other blocks offered the possibility of differential harvesting, where there were large and quite clear zones of different vigor, which were discrete. This turned out to be quite simple, using two tractors with bins that could be interchanged.

Sauvignon Blanc is becoming a flagship wine for Tamar Ridge. Block 8 is the source of the fruit, and it was found to have clear zones of high and low vigor. There was higher vigor on the deeper soil to the north, with green leaves and long shoots. Fruit on these vines showed typical Sauvignon taste characteristics near harvest despite good yields (10.2 tons/ha), yet the fruit on stressed, lower-vigor, and lower-yielding vines (6.1 tons/ha) had no such typicity. French studies have shown that water stress and nitrogen stress will reduce flavor compounds in Sauvignon Blanc. The fruit was differentially harvested, with that from high-vigor vines kept separate from low-vigor vines during fermentation. As expected, the higher-vigor fruit made clearly the best wine and was classified to Tamar Ridge, while the wine from low-vigor vines went to Devil's Corner. Similar results were found with Pinot Noir, suggesting that low-vigor vines, while lower-yielding, did not improve wine quality because of poor leaf health.

An aerial infrared image is as useful to a vineyard manager as an X-ray is to a doctor. Undoubtedly this vineyard "micro-management," or "zonal viticulture" (call it what you will), is the way of the future and offers vineyard managers even more opportunities to make better wine in the vineyard. Further, it will be invaluable in explaining *terroir* effects. And for cool-climate producers, there is an obvious need to pay more attention to leaf health and vine balance, and less to crop regulation.

Grapevine

• **Research reported** by Giovanni Martelli of the University of Bari shows that nearly 60 different viruses have been recorded in *Vitis* species—more than any other woody crop. The researchers suggest that *Vitis* may have a low level of natural resistance to virus infection. Research is being directed at developing resistance through both traditional breeding and using transgenic pathogen-derived techniques.

• **The EU has announced** a further round of funding for restructuring vineyards in Europe. Member states will receive €450 million, with France, Italy, and Spain accounting for around 75 percent of the funds. The program aims to adapt production to market demand by switching grape varieties, improving vine management, and relocating vineyards.

• **Most northerly vineyard?** In Flen, Sweden, just 560 miles (900 km) from the Arctic Circle, Goran Amnegard of Blaxta Wine is growing 2.5 ha of vineyard with plants he brought from Canada. He has converted a 17th-century barn into a winery, and he produces 25,000 bottles of grape and fruit wine a year. His task is made doubly hard by the choice of classic French varieties like Merlot and Cabernet Sauvignon, which have difficulty ripening in warmer climates in some years. Not unexpectedly, his Vidal icewine is a winner, with 30 percent exported to London.

• **Tutankhamun drank red wine.** Spanish scientists studied amphorae from the First Dynasty (around 3000 BC) and identified tartrate crystals, which are found only in wines based on grapes. Further, residues were found in the amphorae of Tutankhamun's tomb (dating from 1325 BC) of syringic acid, proving that the wine stored in the large jars was indeed red. The jars were labeled with product, year, source, and even the name of the vine grower, but with no mention of wine color.

• **Two Croatian yachts** set sail for southern Greece in June 2005 on an expedition to find the roots of the variety Malvasia. The voyages were the brainchild of winery proprietor Ivica Matosevic. The two Croatian scientists who used DNA profiling to solve the mystery of the origin of California's Zinfandel were on board. They tested indigenous varieties around the town of Monemvassia, whose name is thought to be the origin of the name Malvasia. This trip should resolve the question of whether Croatia's Malvazja Istarska variety has its origin on the Peloponnesian peninsula of Greece.

• **Hungary has seen an increase** in extreme weather events over the past decade, including freezing damage, summer drought, and unpredictable rainfall of 11–34 in (290–870 mm) per year. The research institute in Eger has been investigating the effect of irrigation and fertigation on the cold-hardiness of Chardonnay, pruned at different levels. Both these techniques delayed cane ripening by as much as a month, but did not appear to have an effect on the vines' freezing tolerance.

Wine Science

Dr. Ron Jackson

The replacement of cork and cork substitutes by screwcaps continues unabated.

DR RON JACKSON

Initially, screwcap use was largely restricted to white wines. The almost total elimination of oxygen seepage into the wine is one of its principal benefits. Many people in the wine industry thought that slow oxygen ingress through the cork was beneficial (if not essential) to the proper aging of red wines. This belief seems misplaced. Hart and Kleinig, with Southcorp, have shown that, even with premium red wines (Penfolds Bin 389 Cabernet Sauvignon/Shiraz), closure with screwcaps favors wine development.

Dimethyl sulfide: Dr. Jekyll or Mr. Hyde?

Dimethyl sulfide is one of a growing list of aromatic compounds that can be beneficial to a wine's aroma at low concentrations but becomes a fault at higher concentrations. It can generate cooked-cabbage or shrimp-like odors at above-threshold values, whereas it possesses asparagus-, corn-, and molasses-like aspects at barely detectable concentrations. Its presence in wine often increases during aging and is thought to contribute to the development of an aged bouquet. Segurel and co-workers have recently demonstrated that dimethyl sulfide significantly enhances the fruity attributes of Syrah and Grenache Noir wines, as well as providing truffle and black-olive flavors.

DR. RON JACKSON is the author of *Wine Science* (Academic Press, 2000), *Wine Tasting* (Academic Press, 2002), and *Conserve Water Drink Wine* (Haworth Press, 1997), and he has contributed several chapters to other texts and encyclopedias. Although retired, he maintains an association with the Cool Climate Oenology and Viticulture Institute of Brock University in Ontario, Canada, and has held professor and chair positions at the botany department of Brandon University in Manitoba, Canada.

Yeasts affect icewine flavor

Asked what makes one wine different from another, people probably will suggest *terroir*, variety, vintage, or winemaker. Unless you are a microbiologist, it is unlikely that the choice of yeast strain or how the yeast is activated would be the answer. Researchers at the CCOVI in Ontario have shown that one of the most influential factors affecting the flavor of icewines is how the yeasts are acclimatized prior to addition to the juice. Depending on these conditions, the flavor of the icewine can change dramatically, varying from raisiny, buttery, and spicy, to peach/terpene-like, to honey and orange, to pineapple/alcoholic.

"Memorableness"

Functional magnetic resonance imaging (fMRI) is a powerful tool in investigating how the brain processes information. In *Wine Report 2006*, I commented on how this instrument had been used to study the effect of marketing-induced bias on brain activity. This instrument has recently been used by Berns and co-workers to show that reward centers in the brain are more activated when the favorable stimulus is unanticipated. Is this the neurological origin of the experience most of us have had on unexpectedly drinking a superior wine? This is what Amerine of Davis called "memorableness."

My first experience of the "heavens opening" occurred when tasting an inexpensive (at that time) Spanish white wine—Marqués de Murrieta Ygay. Being relatively new to wine, I did not think the wine's goldish tint suggested anything abnormal. When I swirled the wine and raised the glass to my nose, I was dumbfounded. It was the best wine I had ever tried. I have tasted the wine many times since, still find it exquisite, but it no longer engenders the awe it did that first time. Subsequently, I have had similar experiences when the denouement was more than expected. This may be because, when anticipating greatness, the wine must surpass all expectations to fully stimulate the reward centers of the brain.

Grapevine

• **Castriota-Scanderbeg** and co-workers have provided physical evidence that training and experience affect brain data analysis during tasting. Sommeliers and novice tasters had an fMRI comparison while sampling wine. In sommeliers, brain activity shows many more neurons stimulated, principally in the orbitofrontal cortex, the area associated with high-level integration of sensory data. In contrast, only gustatory and emotional regions were activated in novice tasters. The evidence provides clear proof of what one would expect, that sommeliers' training permits them to detect a much wider range of sensations in the wine.

COLOR BIAS

Scientists are by training doubters, demanding multiple sources of evidence before having confidence in their beliefs. Recent data from Osterbauer and co-workers provide new support for the view that color has a marked influence on wine perception. Until now, the evidence has come solely from psychophysical experiments, noted in previous editions of *Wine Report*. Osterbauer has now supplied direct evidence from MRI (magnetic resonance imaging) studies. These have shown that color stimuli modulate odor responses in the brain. Although their study does not provide a precise neuronal explanation of how color affects flavor perception, it provides clear evidence of the effect color has on odor response.

PSYCHOLOGICAL INFLUENCES

It has long been known that information or comments made during a tasting can influence perception. Until recently, evidence for this phenomenon was primarily anecdotal, and its neurological mechanism unknown. In a series of experiments, Rolls and co-workers supplied subjects with a test odorant (valeric acid, possessing an unpleasant odor) combined with Cheddar-cheese flavor. When simultaneously shown the term "body odor," the subjects found the mixture much less pleasant than when it was described as "Cheddar cheese." A similar response occurred when the subjects were supplied with odorless air. Subsequent tests combined with fMRI showed that the orbitofrontal cortex (known to be the site of odor and taste integration) was more activated when the sample was marked "Cheddar cheese" than when labeled "body odor." This demonstrates how verbal expressions can directly influence the brain's interpretation of sensory inputs.

AUDITORY BIAS

Auditory stimuli, at least for sparkling wines, can be added to the list of factors that may affect wine perception. Zampini and Spence have shown that the high-frequency sounds emitted during bubble rupture increase the perception of effervescence. The visual aspect of the rising chain of bubbles has long been considered an important factor in assessing the quality of sparkling wine. To this, we can now add the sound produced by bursting bubbles.

WHAT'S IN THE FINISH?

For many experts, a long finish is the quintessential sign of wine quality. However, if asked to explain this phenomenon, experts are hard pressed to give an answer. Wine scientists are equally unable to provide a full explanation, but parts of the answer are starting to appear.

A long finish seems to be related to factors that delay the rapid escape of aromatic compounds from the wine. Ebeler at Davis has extended previous research by demonstrating that polyphenols (tannins) can interact weakly with aromatic compounds. By extending the duration over which aromatic compounds escape from the wine, the finish is prolonged. Other constituents, such as proteins, starches, and fats, have the same effect on food flavors. In most cases, the concentration of these latter constituents is too low to have significance on aromatic release in wines. Mannoproteins liberated from dead and dying yeast cells are the principal exception, notably in sparkling wines. They not only retard the release of aromatics, but also favorably influence bubble nucleation and development.

SKIN CONTACT

Prolonged skin contact (maceration) during fermentation is standard practice in the production of red wines. It was also widely used in the production of many white wines in the past. Current practice is to minimize contact between the juice and pomace (grape skins and seeds) after crushing. Although this may produce a "clean," fruity wine, such wines generally age poorly. More complex wines with greater aging potential are typically given several hours' maceration before separation from the pomace.

This practice has usually been considered beneficial due to the increased uptake of varietal flavorants, which tend to occur principally in grape skins. However, the better aging potential the procedure provides seems to come from the enhanced uptake of caffeic acid and acetyl-cysteine. Caffeic acid, long known as an important antioxidant in white wines, and acetyl-cysteine have been shown by Roussis and co-workers to effectively inhibit the oxidative loss of fruit-smelling esters, as well as important varietal aromatics such as

linalool. This is an important finding for varieties, such as Muscat, that depend primarily on terpenes for their varietal aroma. Wines from such varieties are well known to lose their varietal character within about two years.

OAK AND AROMA LOSS

It is a common belief that maturation in oak benefits only wines with distinctive varietal aromas. The argument is that oak masks more subtle fragrances. This may be partially true, but it is not the whole story. Young wines with little varietal aroma often depend for their fragrance on ethyl esters produced by yeasts during fermentation. Chassagne has shown that these fruity-smelling esters are effectively adsorbed into the staves of oak barrels, resulting in significant aroma loss. Also adsorbed are important varietal aromatic terpenes, such as linalool. Because of the involvement of terpenes in the varietal character of several premium white varieties, such as Riesling, this partially explains why such wines, if exposed to oak at all, are matured in large-volume cooperage, not new barrels, which have a high ratio of surface area to volume.

FOOD AND WINE

For years I have searched for perfect matches between food and wine. With the possible exception of salmon and champagne, my trials have generally been unsuccessful. Most food flavors seem unassociated with those characteristic of wines. In what wine does one find flavors similar to those found in meat, fish, vegetables, sauces, most spices, or condiments? It was with an element of relief that I read Nygren and co-workers' study of the interaction of cheese and wine.

Although the specific effects varied slightly, depending on the type of cheese-and-wine combination, a suppression of sensory attributes was a consistent finding. The more pronounced the wine flavor, the more significant was its suppression by the cheese, and vice versa. Heymann has confirmed and extended these findings. Attributes such as sweet pepper, oak flavor, and astringency were diminished after sampling cheese. In contrast, the perception of a buttery fragrance and bitterness increased with some, but not all, cheese selections. The enhancement of a wine's buttery flavor has also been noted by Hersleth and co-workers. The effect was more pronounced in a natural setting (reception room) than under laboratory conditions. As most people are aware, the tasting environment is almost as important to wine appreciation as is its sensory quality. Thus, the wonderful regional wine sampled while relaxing on vacation often loses its allure when tasted at home.

KEEP LABELS SIMPLE

Ever feel that you cannot find the flavors so lovingly described on the back label? You are not alone. Research conducted by Bastoan and co-workers indicates that consumers generally find these descriptions useless, if not discouraging. Professionals tend to use terminology that is considered more precise, describing the wine in terms of specific taste and flavor sensations: black currant, cherry, raspberry, apple for aroma; truffle, berry jam, leather for bouquet; and sour, astringent, peppery, tannic for taste. In contrast, consumers tend to use more abstract and holistic terms, such as smooth, subtle, balanced, rich, and flavorful.

For producers to communicate effectively with consumers, the terms used on wine labels need to change. Describing the aroma precisely is important to the professional but not to the consumer. Most consumers seldom consciously smell a wine before they drink it. They seem to want more general expressions with which they can empathize and use in selecting a wine they might like.

OAK FLAVOR INCREASES WITH AGING

One of the most pronounced flavor characteristics imparted during maturation in oak comes from the extraction of oak lactones. Depending on individual sensitivity to oak lactones, tasters' reactions to these compounds may differ, finding their presence either desirable or undesirable. Winemakers generally like oak flavors, while wine critics seemingly do not. A discovery in Australia may partially explain why they tend to differ. Wilkinson and co-workers found that compounds extracted from oak may be transformed into oak lactones following removal of the wine from oak. Thus, a winemaker may consider a wine's oak flavor perfectly balanced at bottling, but by the time it is sampled, the flavor may have become too intense for critics.

WINE SLEUTHS AT IT AGAIN

Two recent reports have extended our knowledge of ancient wine. One describes an investigation into the chemical nature of the most prized of ancient Egyptian drinks, *shedeh*. It was considered to bestow divine powers and was always served in the most valuable vessels. Of three amphorae found in the burial chamber of King Tutankhamun, one was labeled *shedeh*. Despite its frequent mention in ancient Egyptian texts, whether it was derived from grapes, pomegranates, dates, or a mixture was unknown. Guasch-Jané and co-workers have been able to establish that *shedeh* was made from black grapes. By testing a 2-mg sample of black residue from the bottom of the amphora, they were able to identify the presence of tartaric acid as well as syringic acid. Of fruit found in the Mediterranean and Near East, only grapes produce tartaric acid. Syringic acid is a marker breakdown product for malvidin, the most frequently found pigment in red grapes. Exactly how *shedeh* differs from *irep*, the standard term for wine in ancient Egyptian, is unknown. There is, however, some written evidence that has led scholars to consider that the wine was baked.

In a separate study, McGovern and co-workers report on the contents of sealed vessels recovered from two ancient sites in China. Sophisticated analysis has revealed that a fermented beverage derived from rice, honey, and fruit was being made in China some 9,000 years ago. This is some two centuries before the production of wine in the Middle East. The clear evidence of tartaric acid suggests the possible use of grapes, of which many species grow in China (about half of all grape species are native to China). However, hawthorn also grows indigenously in China. Because its fruit produces tartaric acid, it is not possible to determine whether the tartaric acid in the jar comes from grapes, hawthorns, or a mixture. In the same article, the authors also comment on the liquid contents of sealed bronze vessels (about 1250–1000 BC) found at a different site. The rice wine these vessels contained was reported to have still been fragrantly aromatic when opened.

Grapevine

• **Recent research** highlights the erosion of tooth enamel as a hazard for wine tasters. Wine's acidity, chiefly from tartaric acid (the salt of which is called "cream of tartar"), slowly but progressively erodes tooth enamel. Drinking wine with meals markedly reduces this action, since wine acids react with proteins in the food. The problem is principally associated with the protracted retention of wine in the mouth during critical assessment.

• **It seems that** researchers are finding new wine pigments almost monthly. The latest addition to the expanding list of compounds has been dubbed "oaklins." These brick-red substances form as a reaction product between catechins (tannin subunits) and aldehydes extracted from oak. The more we know about wine color, the more we realize how much more there may be to this increasingly complex topic.

Opinion:
To breathe or not to breathe

When I am asked whether wine should be opened before serving, I always say no, but I am quick to point out why my advice differs from "traditional" wisdom. Certainly the fragrance of a wine will slowly change as it sits in an open bottle. When opened, the equilibrium between aromatic compounds in the space above the wine ("head space") and those dissolved in the wine will change. As compounds disperse from the head space into the surrounding air, similar molecules will begin to escape from the wine. What is important is that each aromatic compound reacts differently, some being released slowly, others quickly. Aromatic compounds also differ in how quickly they diffuse into the surrounding air. The result is that there is the potential for the wine's fragrance to change continuously following opening.

I like to observe this dynamic change. It is like watching a blossom open. Some people appreciate only the mature bloom, others enjoy seeing the flower open. I am of the latter persuasion. Every transformation in fragrance and flavor is a joy to behold. Why limit oneself to some predefined optimum moment? Opening the bottle immediately before serving permits the maximum evolution of aroma and bouquet in the glass.

On a historical note, breathing originated with decanting. It was used to eliminate an all-too-frequent fault of wine during the 19th century: "bottle stink." The phrase probably refers to the combined presence of hydrogen sulfide and various mercaptans. These probably formed in the sediment that was common in wine before the development of adequate fining techniques. Pouring the wine into a decanter an hour or two before serving not only separated the wine from the sediment, but also allowed oxygen to inactivate the rotten-egg odor of hydrogen sulfide and favored the dissipation of the skunky odors of mercaptans. When the use of fining eliminated the accumulation of large amounts of sediment, the habit of decanting was discarded, but the practice of opening the wine in advance ("breathing") remained.

Wine aging

Chemical technology now seems poised to tackle the mysteries of wine aging. Why most wines do not age well is now partially understood. Slow oxidation destroys the aromatic compounds crucial to the fragrance of young wines. However, the chemicals that develop and generate a desirable aged bouquet in some wines are still unknown. Without knowing their chemical nature, providing the optimal conditions for their development is largely hit and miss. Keeping wine under cool conditions, away from light and oxygen, using specific varieties and careful vinification are all that is known after centuries of trial and error. Wonderful as it is, our present knowledge is inadequate to fill grocery shelves with high-quality, affordable wines for an ever-growing population of savvy consumers. This is a topic in dire need of dedicated investigation.

Wine language

One of the fascinating aspects of wine language is that it often tells more about the taster than the wine. Most florid descriptions poetically express the taster's emotional reaction to the wine. Such analogies can be justified if they focus attention on the central attributes of a wine. The cutest I have heard recently came from Andrea Immer, who described Pinot Noir as "lingerie for the tongue."

Descriptive terms also reflect your olfactory past. When you smell a wine, the brain attempts to match the sensory signals received with pre-existing odor memories. This explains why certain descriptive terms, such as truffles, violets, and irises, typify regions where these objects occur and from which the taster comes. Equally idiosyncratic are expressions such as cigar box, wet wool, leather, East Indian store, and mother's pumpkin pie.

Knowledge also markedly affects the terms used. The greater your wine experience, the more frequently aroma descriptors reflect the color of the wine. For example, red wines are typically considered to have flavors associated with red fruits (strawberry, raspberry, cherry, red currant), whereas white wines are thought to possess aromas resembling green or yellow fruit (peach, apricot, melon, Granny Smith apple) or flowers. With further experience, wine flavors are often simply related to the internal standards developed for particular wine styles or grape varieties.

Grapevine

• **When sparkling wine** is maturing in contact with dead yeast cells from the second fermentation, the yeast cells self-digest, releasing compounds that favor the stabilization of the bubbles that will form in the glass. In addition, nutrients are released that could promote the growth of bacteria. In a recent study by Castro and Rius in Spain, several common bacteria were isolated from sparkling wine during this in-bottle maturation period. The researchers suggest that some of these bacteria may be involved in generating the attributes typically associated with these wines. Although this is an interesting idea, they have not shown that the bacteria are metabolically active during the maturation period. Thus their role in the flavor and effervescence characteristics of sparkling wines is still unclear.

Wine on the Web

Tom Cannavan

Founded by Rowan Gormley under Richard Branson's watchful eye in 2000, Virginwines.co.uk is the sole UK survivor of several start-ups that attempted to sell high volumes of wine through purely online retailing.

TOM CANNAVAN

Virgin Wines certainly became a household name, but doubts continued about the company's profitability.

Now Direct Wines has taken over the majority shareholding in Virgin Wines from the Virgin Group. Better known to UK consumers under its trading arms such as Laithwaites and The *Sunday Times* Wine Club, Direct Wines has swept all before it to dominate the UK direct-selling market but has done so almost entirely through conventional direct mail and affiliate marketing deals, not the Web. So where does Virgin fit in its plans?

A spokesman for Direct Wines said: "Virgin Wines is being run completely separately by founder Rowan Gormley. Direct Wines has provided a great deal of expertise in many areas, but Rowan's understanding of the Internet-only model is second to none, and in this area Direct Wines has much to learn. It is Direct Wines' objective to help put Virgin Wines on a secure footing with a long-term future."

So it looks as if the Internet will still be an important route to market for Virgin Wines, and both parties could gain in this marriage.

TOM CANNAVAN, editor of consumer drinks magazine *Fine Expressions*, has published wine-pages.com since 1995, making it one of the world's longest-established online wine magazines, as well as one of the most popular. He also publishes beer-pages.com with beer writer Roger Protz. According to Jancis Robinson MW, "wine-pages.com should be of interest to any wine lover seeking independent advice" (*Financial Times*). In Richard Ehrlich's opinion, "if all sites were this good, we'd spend more time surfing than drinking" (*The Independent on Sunday*), and Robert Parker finds wine-pages.com a "superb site. All-inclusive, friendly, easily navigated, with plenty of bells and whistles" (*The Wine Buyer's Guide*).

Virtual wine tasting

Virtualwine.co.uk is an Internet-based business that held its first "virtual tasting" early in 2006. The idea is that Virtualwine stages regular tastings, hosted by figures from the wine world, and these are broadcast over the Internet. Anyone can join in from the comfort of their own home by powering up their PC.

I applaud this use of Internet broadcast technology within the wine arena, but to be honest, I have reservations about the way the concept is pitched. Virtualwine is presented as a "club," with photographs of happy groups of friends, glasses in hand, gathered around computer screens. This grates slightly, given that the cost of participation in each event is not just a £20 "tasting fee," but also the purchase of a mixed case of the wines to be tasted from Virtualwine. Virtualwine suggests a guideline total of around £120 for each event.

Don't get me wrong: the wines are not bad value, but it seems clear that selling wine is Virtualwine's underlying business plan, not running a tasting group. It is possible to participate for £20 without buying the wines, but why would you?

Boom boom

The normalization of online shopping continues. Just a few years ago, buying goods on the Web was seen as dangerous and difficult, but at Christmas 2005, 61 percent of us named the Web as our top shopping destination. The Interactive Media in Retail Group reported that UK Internet sales in November 2005 broke the £2 billion ($3.5 billion) barrier for the first time, with 24 million shoppers spending an average of £94 ($165) each online in a single month.

The reasons for the boom are pretty obvious: just a few years ago shopping on the Web was a deeply frustrating business. Slow dial-up connections meant a single purchase took ages, and frequent crashes meant a huge number of transactions were started but never finished. Now shopping by Internet is a breeze, and the time, effort, and shoe leather saved by buying online have many people hooked. There are also serious savings to be made online, particularly with books, DVDs, and electronics.

But will the Web capture more and more wine sales? Well, there is no doubt that convenience is one key attraction of buying wine online, but price will remain crucial. Tesco Online is a hit with "everyday" wine drinkers due to an endless stream of BOGOF and half-price case deals, but most wine retailers find it hard to compete head on with local stores. Warehousing, packaging, subsidized deliveries, and dealing with breakages negate any cost savings in retail premises and staff.

Opinion:
Fading print

Movement and consolidation were seen in the world of consumer wine magazines in 2006. *Wine International* was sold to specialist trade publisher William Reed, which immediately set about streamlining its portfolio. After 23 years in print, *Wine International* disappeared, to be replaced by a new hybrid magazine called *Wine & Spirit*, which has a wider drinks focus and a new editor. This magazine is pitched at both consumers and the drinks trade.

At the same time, a brand-new drinks magazine called *Fine Expressions* (www.fineexpressions.co.uk), of which I am the editor, hit the streets, but rather than focusing solely on wine, it covers Scotch whiskey, beer, and liquor, as well as associated "lifestyle" topics like food and travel.

While a number of niche wine magazines remain around the world, there is no doubt that the success of the Internet has stolen a sizable chunk of the print market dedicated to wine. The number and quality of online wine-information sites mean that many wine lovers now get all the advice, information, and news they need from the Web, and most of it is free.

Those researching just about any topic now consider the Web as their first port of call. The instant accessibility, searchability, and real-time updating of websites cannot be matched in print, nor can the sense of community engendered by forums, chat rooms, and the greater interactivity between the publication and its readers.

The strength of print magazines remains their better readability, the quality of photography and design, and the portability of the medium. Reading magazines on trains, boats, and planes, or sitting on the deck on a summer day are, for now, key advantages.

But as technology progresses (some airlines now have seat-back surfing and browsing capability) and the costs of print production remain high, how long can specialist magazines dedicated to such niche subjects resist the erosion of their market? The key to that is probably advertising; if the big advertisers switch their allegiances into online or more generalized lifestyle titles, the road for dedicated wine magazines could be steeply uphill.

Alexa ratings

Alexa.com is the nearest thing we have to an independent "circulation count" for websites. Partnered by Google, Alexa tracks the surfing behavior of 10 million people, building up a picture of which websites they visit. This allows Alexa to compile popularity rankings for hundreds of thousands of websites, broken down into categories. Instances of vote-rigging by unscrupulous webmasters occur (some of the entries in Alexa's published "Top 10 wine sites" are deeply suspicious), but the results remain useful.

Alexa's top 10 most visited wine websites:

1. www.winespectator.com
2. www.erobertparker.com
3. www.novusvinum.com
4. www.wine-pages.com
5. www.franklandestate.com.au
6. www.foodandwine.com
7. www.localwineevents.com
8. www.biltmore.com
9. www.decanter.com
10. www.wine-lovers-page.com

Best Internet wine sites

All sites in the first two "best" lists are free-to-access, English-language sites unless qualified by the following codes. These codes also apply to the Best Regional Wine Sites, although the primary language for many of these will be the appropriate native tongue.

[S] = paid subscription required for some/all content
[R] = no paid subscription, but registration required for some/all content
[E] = non-English-language site, but with English-language version

Editor's note: I asked Tom Cannavan not to include his own site, wine-pages.com, in any of the lists he compiled because, inevitably, he would either be accused of self-promotion or (more in line with his character) he would not rate his site highly enough. However, I would place wine-pages.com at number two under Best Wine Sites and number one under Best Wine Forums. Although I have a small corner at wine-pages.com, I receive no payment. TS

Grapevine

- **jancisrobinson.com** has had a makeover since *Wine Report 2006*, but it remains independent and free of advertising. An online version of the *Oxford Companion to Wine* is one of its killer applications. Subscription is £69 per annum ($119 or €99)—not cheap, but the quality is high.

- **Christopher Burr MW**, the force behind uvine.com, has launched secretsommelier.com. The site features podcasts of wine courses and tastings. (Podcasts are audio broadcasts that you can play on your PC or download to your mp3 player.) This site is a bit crassly commercial, festooned with advertising and entreaties to buy wines through affiliate partners, but there is some good material.

BEST WINE SITES

1. www.wine-searcher.com [S]
2. www.erobertparker.com [S]
3. www.winespectator.com [S]
4. www.bbr.com
5. www.jancisrobinson.com [S]
6. www.wineloverspage.com
7. www.wineanorak.com
8. www.decanter.com [R]
9. www.wine-journal.com
10. www.burgundy-report.com

BEST WINE FORUMS

1. www.ukwineforum.com
2. www.erobertparker.com [R]
3. www.wldg.com
4. www.auswine.com.au/forum
5. www.westcoastwine.net
6. http://groups.msn.com/bordeaux wineenthusiasts
7. www.enemyvessel.com/forum
8. forums.egullet.com [R]
9. www.superplonk.com/forum [R]
10. www.cellartasting.com

BEST WINE RETAILERS ON THE WEB

1. www.bbr.com (UK)
2. www.wine.com (US)
3. www.oddbins.com (UK)
4. www.majestic.co.uk (UK)
5. www.bevmo.com (US)
6. www.wineaccess.com (US)
7. www.auswine.com.au (Australia)
8. www.winecommune.com (US)
9. www.finewinelist.net (UK)
10. www.uvine.com (UK)

BEST SMALLER INDEPENDENTS SPECIALIZING IN REGIONS

1. www.yapp.co.uk (Rhône and Loire)
2. www.domainedirect.co.uk (Burgundy)
3. www.rogerharriswines.co.uk (Beaujolais)
4. www.nickdobsonwines.co.uk (Austria, Switzerland)
5. www.frenchandlogan.com (Germany)
6. www.lsfinewines.co.uk (South of France)
7. www.southafricawines.co.uk (South Africa)
8. www.australianwinesonline.co.uk (Australia)
9. www.englishwine.co.uk (England)
10. www.click4abottle.co.uk (Hungary)

BEST REGIONAL WINE SITES

Sites in national language.
Those with an English-language
version marked [E].
Argentina
www.winesofargentina.org [E]
Australia
www.wineaustralia.com
www.winestate.com.au
Austria
www.austrian.wine.co.at [E]
www.weinserver.at
Belgium
www.boschberg.be [E]

Grapevine

• **wine-searcher.com** remains the definitive service for finding and comparing prices of fine wines, but for everyday wines there are more generic price-comparison services that might be useful. Try typing "Banrock Station" (for example) into the search boxes of kelkoo.co.uk, shopping.com, pricedash.com, or checkprices.co.uk to see what comes up. The sites make their money by collecting referral fees from featured merchants if you buy, so don't expect them to be comprehensive.

Brazil
www.academiadovinho.com.br
Bulgaria
www.bulgarianwines.com [E]
Canada
www.canwine.com
www.winesofcanada.com
   British Columbia
   www.bcwine.com
   Ontario
   www.winesofontario.org
Chile
www.winesofchile.org [E]
China
www.winechina.com/en/ [E]
www.wineeducation.org/chinadet.html
Croatia
www.hr/wine [E]
Cyprus
www.cyprus-wine.com [E]
www.cosmosnet.net/azias/cyprus/
   wine1.html [E]
Czech Republic
www.znovin.cz [E]
www.czecot.cz/?id_tema=16 [E]
Denmark
www.vinavl.dk
www.vinbladet.dk/uk/ [E]
Estonia
www.veiniklubi.com
France
www.frenchwinesfood.com [E]
www.terroir-france.com [E]
www.abrege.com/lpv
   Alsace
   www.alsacewine.com [E]
   www.alsace-route-des-vins.com [E]
   Bordeaux
   www.bordeaux.com [E]
   www.wine-
   journal.com/bordeauxfirst.html
   www.medoc.org [E]
   www.sauternes.com
   Burgundy
   www.bivb.com [E]
   www.burghound.com
   www.burgundy-report.com
   Champagne
   www.champagne.fr [E]
   www.champagnemagic.com [E]

Corsica
www.corsicanwines.com [E]
Jura
www.jura-vins.com [E]
Languedoc-Roussillon
www.languedoc-wines.com [E]
www.coteaux-languedoc.com [E]
www.vinsduroussillon.com
Loire
www.interloire.com
www.loirevalleywine.com [E]
Provence
www.provenceweb.fr/e/mag/terroir/
vin [E]
Rhône
www.vins-rhone.com [E]
Southwest
www.vins-gaillac.com [E]
Georgia
www.gws.ge [E]
Germany
www.winepage.de [E]
www.germanwine.de/english [E]
   Macedonia
   www.macedonian-heritage.gr/Wine
   [E]
Hungary
www.winesofhungary.com [E]
Indonesia
www.hattenwines.com [E]
Israel
www.israelwines.co.il [E]
www.stratsplace.com/rogov/israel [E]
Italy
www.italianmade.com/wines/home.cfm
[E]
www.italianwineguide.com [E]
   Piedmont
   www.piedmontwines.net [E]
   Tuscany
   www.chianticlassico.com [E]
   www.wine-toscana.com [E]
Japan
www.kizan.co.jp/eng/japanwine_e.html
[E]
Latvia
www.doynabeer.com/wine [E]

Lebanon
www.chateaumusar.com.lb [E]
www.chateaukefraya.com [E]
Luxembourg
www.luxvin.lu [E]
Malta
www.marsovinwinery.com [E]
Mexico
mexicanwines.homestead.com [E]
Moldova
www.turism.md/eng/wine [E]
Morocco
www.lescelliersdemeknes.com [E]
New Zealand
www.nzwine.com
www.tizwine.com
Peru
www.virtualperu.net/peru_vino.html [E]
Portugal
www.portugal-info.net/wines/
general.htm [E]
www.vinhos.online.pt
   Madeira
   www.madeirawineguide.com [E]
   www.madeirawinecompany.com [E]
   Port
   www.ivp.pt [E]
   www.portwine.com [E]
Romania
www.aromawine.com/wines.htm [E]
Russia
www.russiawines.com [E]
www.massandra.crimea.com [E]
Slovenia
www.matkurja.com/projects/wine [E]
South Africa
www.wosa.co.za

www.wine.co.za
www.grape.co.za
Spain
www.filewine.es [E]
www.jrnet.com/vino [E]
www.verema.com [E]
   Ribera del Duero
   www.riberadelduero.es [E]
   Rioja
   www.riojawine.com [E]
   Sherry
   www.sherry.org [E]
Switzerland
www.wine.ch [E]
Tunisia
www.tourismtunisia.com/eatingout/
wines.html [E]
United Kingdom
www.englishwineproducers.com
www.english-wine.com
United States
www.allamericanwineries.com
   California
   www.napavintners.com
   www.wineinstitute.org
   New York
   www.fingerlakeswinecountry.com
   Oregon
   www.oregonwine.org
   Texas
   www.texaswinetrails.com
   Washington
   www.washingtonwine.org
   www.columbiavalleywine.com
Uruguay
www.travelenvoy.com/wine/uruguay.
htm [E]

Grapevine

• **Online wine sales** within the EU are possible, though the red tape and logistics mean that not many websites sell outside national borders. French big player wineandco.com does, as do an increasing number of specialists. English-language websites clapp.it/eng/index.html (Sicilian wines) and picwines.co.uk (Languedoc wines) are just two that are worth a look.

• **Christie's has set up** a full Internet auction facility in association with Australian auction house Langton's, which trades solely via the Internet (langtons.com.au). Christie's has historically concentrated on prestigious saleroom events, but David Elswood, head of Christie's International Wine Department, is well versed in online wine auctions.

BEST WINE-SITE LINKS

www.bboxbbs.ch/home/tbm
www.bluewine.com
www.grape-nutz.com/links.html

BEST VINTAGE-CHART SITES

www.erobertparker.com/info/vintage
chart1.asp

BEST TASTING-NOTES SITES

www.erobertparker.com [S]
www.finewinediary.com
www.winemega.com [E]
www.stratsplace.com/rogov
www.yakshaya.com
www.thewinedoctor.com
www.winenotes.co.uk
www.metawines.com
www.cellartracker.com

BEST WINE-EDUCATION SITES

www.wset.co.uk
www.wineeducation.org
www.wineeducators.com
wine.gurus.com
www.royagcol.ac.uk/postgrad_courses/
course_sheets/wine.htm

BEST VITICULTURE SITE

http://wineserver.ucdavis.edu

BEST OENOLOGY SITE

http://winemaking.jackkeller.net

BEST GRAPE-VARIETIES SITE

www.wine-lovers-
page.com/wineguest/wgg.html

BEST SITES FOR FOOD-AND-WINE PAIRING

www.foodandwinematching.co.uk
www.stratsplace.com/winefood.html

THE FAR SIDE OF WINE

www.valentinomonticello.com
www.rupissed.com
www.winespirit.org
www.winelabels.org
www.gmon.com/tech/stng.shtml
www.bonnydoonvineyard.com/
doontoons
www.howstuffworks.com/question603.
htm

Grapevine

• **While researching** Canadian wine after a recent visit there, I found a small treasure trove of information that is of minority interest, but is simply one of the nicest online multimedia wine resources I've come across. Go to the Canadian Broadcasting Corporation's archive at archives.cbc.ca and type "wine" into the search box. The story of "Canada's Wine Renaissance" is told via a wonderful timeline with hours of high-quality video clips.

• **"Splogs" and "zombies"** are two new words added to the Internet dictionary, both referring to worthless websites with no original content. These sites abuse a legitimate revenue-generating scheme run by Google called Adsense. Adsense displays sympathetic advertising links on subject-specific websites, with Google and the host site sharing revenue. Now various wine-related splogs and zombies have sprung up, containing no more than lists of wine-related words (to fool the search engines into finding them) and pages of money-spinning Adsense links. Beware these rogue traders cluttering up cyberspace.

The 100 Most Exciting Wine Finds

A number of these wines will be available on certain markets, but many are so new, restricted in production, or downright obscure that the only way to get hold of them would be to visit the producer-if he has not already sold out.

The entire *raison d'être* of this section is to bring to the attention of serious wine enthusiasts the different and most surprising wines being developed in classic areas, the best wines from emerging regions, and other cutting-edge stuff. The prices are retail per bottle in the local currency of the country of origin (see About This Guide, p.5). My tasting note follows the contributor's own note, for comparison or contrast, or simply a different take.

Touraine Gamay Cuvée d'Eos 2003 Domaine Jacky Marteau (Loire Valley, €9) *Fine, spicy fruit—the back label says blackberries (mûres) … I'd go with that. A hint of surmuri, almost overripe grapes on the nose. Palate and attack all soft fruit and fraîcheur—big, fat, and enticing allspice finish.* Charles Sydney
Very ripe, creamy-blackberry aromas: striking! A melange of creamy-blackberry and strawberry fruit on the palate, both individually distinct. Quite rare and extraordinary for a Loire red, and a totally ridiculous price! A brilliant selection, Charles; thank you. TS

Alpha Syrah 2003 Alpha Estate (Greece, €23) *Bright fruit with black pepper spice. Deftly fuses concentration with elegance. Finely oaked. Poised. Good aging potential; at its peak in 8–10 years. From the never-ceasing-to-surprise vineyard of Florina.* Nico Manessis

The most impressive wine (by far) from the most impressive estate (by far) I visited in Greece in early 2006. It has beautiful Syrah fruit of such elegance and is supported by tannins that are so silky and ripe that I suspect most bottles will be consumed years before this wine starts to show its true potential complexity. TS

Saumur-Champigny Lisagathe 2003 Philippe Vatan, Château du Hureau (Loire Valley, €15) *Huge mass of soft, sweet blackberry fruit—without even a hint of pepper, green or otherwise. Great concentration on the middle palate, and fine length. A wine that just pretends it's easy to drink but that will keep on getting softer and more complex.* Charles Sydney
Definitely, Charles. All chocolate and soft fruits, yet with nice grippy tannic acid on the aftertaste. Beautiful. TS

Rully Les Pucelles 2004 Domaine Henri and Paul Jacqueson (Burgundy,

€10) *Very lovely peachy fruit, excellent harmony, and lots of finesse.*
Clive Coates MW
Class, Clive, class. Beautifully restrained use of oak. This is what they called a "wow" wine in the old days. TS

Tappa Pass Vineyard Selection Shiraz 2002 Henschke, Barossa (Australia, A$57) *This is classic, spicy, meaty, cool-year Shiraz with the extra layer of complexity conferred by a great year. Charcoal, spice, blackberry, and cedar; deliciously succulent.*
Huon Hooke
Huge cassis aroma, very fine and complex in the mouth, with the potential to achieve vastly more complexity. Incredibly fresh, luscious, black-fruit flavors. My advice is to keep it as long as you can keep your hands off it. In my house, that won't be very long at all. TS

Croft Vintage Port 2003 (Port & Madeira, €40) *Lovely, perfumed fruit, open and expressive; rich and fleshy, quite soft initially, pure and focused. By no means the biggest wine of the vintage, but fine and sinewy, with rapier-like length. One for the medium term. The best Croft since 1970.*
Richard Mayson
Deep-colored for Croft, with neat, beautifully focused, bright fruit on the palate. All too easy to drink now, it will be a dream wine in 10 years. TS

Graham's Malvedos Vintage Port 1996 (Port & Madeira, €35) *Vibrant berry fruit, powerful, focused with great purity of flavor. Sleek and ready to drink now with sufficient depth and concentration to develop over the next 10 years.*
Richard Mayson
The fruit aromas are so perfumed, particularly on the palate, with a big smack of sweetness on the finish, making it a delight to drink now, but it really needs five of those 10 years for the layered fruit complexity to begin to unfold on the finish. TS

Delaforce Curious and Ancient 20 Year Old Tawny Port (Port & Madeira, €30) *The palest pink-amber-orange tawny, supremely delicate meld of dried fruits, and a hint of freshly roasted almonds on the nose; silky smooth with creamy concentration of flavor, like the finest white chocolate. Finishes with great poise and finesse. As near a perfect example of a 20-year-old as you will find.* Richard Mayson
I was looking forward to this, since 20-year-old is my favorite tawny (the best 30-year-old and over-40-years-old being too liquorous, and most 10-year-olds not really tawny enough for my liking), and I was not disappointed either. Your note says it all, so I'll just add "exquisite." TS

Côtes du Jura Chardonnay A la Percenette 2004 Domaine Pignier (Jura & Savoie, €9) *A pale greenish color, with a youthful appley and mineral nose, and oak emerging after a while. It is dry-with almost steely lemon acidity-stony, and mineral: almost reminiscent of a Chablis. The oak is noticeable but well balanced, and the finish is very fresh and mineral. A lovely lightness to it.* Wink Lorch
Truly a stunner, Wink, and I can't believe I'm saying that about a Chardonnay, but it has such intensity of acid-charged, oak-laced minerality of fruit that if it was Chablis, it would cost €39, not €9! TS

Pinot Noir 2003 Schloß Halbturn, Neusiedlersee (Austria, €30) *A summer lawn, leafy notes, complex; lovely fruit. Good tannic backbone. Nobility and refinement. Long.* Philipp Blom
A delightful Pinot Noir, full of grace and elegance. TS

Coteaux du Layon Rablay Le Vilain Canard 2003 Domaine des Sablonettes (Loire Valley, €25.60 per 50-cl bottle) *Vibrant amber-gold color with a lovely glacé mandarin nose leading straight to the same on the palate-a mass of fruit, fraîcheur, and*

concentration. Maybe the alcohol shows a touch, but with a balance of 13 percent to 200 g/l of sugar, this is pretty damn fine. Charles Sydney

All pineapples and cream—and as clean as a whistle, despite the deep color suggesting oxidation with high levels of VA, both of which are noticeable by their absence. Domaine des Sablonettes is the finest producer-and organic to boot. TS

Château Messile-Aubert Montagne-St-Emilion 2003 (Bordeaux, €13)

Lovely, highlighted fruit aromas on the nose; the palate is full of very luscious, sweet fruit with a freshness rare in 2003 on the Right Bank. Delicious early drinking, while the way the wine kept and improved on ullage also suggests aging potential. David Peppercorn MW

Dramatic fruit and restrained use of oak make this a very classy claret for the price. I'm certainly going to buy some! TS

Côtes du Roussillon Ciel Liquide 2003 Domaine Padié (Languedoc-Roussillon, €20)

Darkly transparent ruby in the glass; ripe southern 2003 fruit on the nose, moderated on the palate by soft tannins and a gentle touch of acidity. The flavor is almost northern in its classic elegance. Restrained and fine on the finish. Paul Strang

Absolutely gorgeous, Paul—just one glass and I'm in heaven! TS

Château Ducla Expérience XII Bordeaux Blanc 2004 (Bordeaux, €12)

A wine of pronounced character, very spicy, scented nose, creamy impression on the palate, full-flavored with an extra lift at the finish; the result of an unusual 52 percent Sauvignon Gris with 48 percent Sauvignon Blanc and cask fermentation with lees stirring. And it tastes even better on ullage! An experience worth having. David Peppercorn MW

There's not much Sauvignon Gris in Bordeaux these days, and it is a more subtle form of Sauvignon; thus it's no surprise that the Sauvignon Blanc bullies its way to the top of this cuvée. On initial taste, the minority Sauvignon Blanc in this wine was so distinctive and expressive that it fought with the oak, but I followed your lead, David, and tasted this on ullage the following day, and all I can say is wow! The varietal excesses were subdued, the Gris brought an orderly calm to the squabbling in this wine, and the oak became seamless. Beautiful. TS

Ariyanas Dulce 2004 Bentomiz (Spain, €12 per half-bottle)

Instantly recognizable but delicate Moscatel nose, with herby scents up front and a hint of honeyed sweetness in the background. Gentle sweetness on the palate but with clean, fresh acidity, this Málaga doesn't cloy, and it manages a crisp, mineral finish that is ultimately dry. John Radford

Beautifully perfumed Moscatel fruit that just swells and swells in the mouth, finishing with a bright, crisp finish that I find distinctly sweet, but so refreshing and—yes—a minerality that is atypical for both variety and origin. A brilliant find, John. TS

Amarone di Marchetto 2001 Trabucchi, Verona (Northern Italy, €30)

A superb wine of the eastern Valpolicella terroir: wonderful aromatic array, with clean-edged blackberry, licorice, dried plum, mint, and thyme; remarkably sapid with a distinctive minerality and earthiness-dense but also crisp and lively on the palate. An excellent expression of the year 2001 from a most estimable producer. Franco Ziliani

All those who, like me, are put off the Amarone style by its raisiny-oxidative character should check this wine out. A whole potpourri of floral elegance pervades this entire wine, with only a touch of breakfast tea on the finish to hint that it is indeed an Amarone. TS

Syrah/Cabernet Sauvignon 2003
Cave Kouroum (Lebanon, LL 26,000)
An award-winner at Vinexpo 2005, this is a real fistful of Syrah that will develop into a thoroughbred with time. It weighs in at a whopping 14.5 percent alcohol and may still be a little too playful for some wine drinkers, but it has lovely tannins and the structure to carry it along and allow the full spectrum of flavors— strawberry, chocolate, pepper, and tobacco—to develop into a very suave wine over time. Michael Karam
One of the best Lebanese wines I've ever tasted, and I've been tasting this country's wines since I met Serge Hochar at the Bristol World Wine Fair 30 years ago. The nose on this wine is all chocolaty-oak at the moment, but the fruit will dominate in a few years, and it is the cleanest, freshest, sweetest, non-VA-lifted fruit I've encountered in a Lebanese red wine. TS

Edelzwicker 2004
Navarro, Mendocino (California, US$11)
Stylish and aromatic white with Gewürztraminer and Riesling on the nose, dramatic spice note in the mid-palate, and a complex finish that's off-dry but balanced by good acidity.
Dan Berger
An Edelzwicker that boasts more Gewürztraminer spice on the nose and palate than most pure Gewürztraminers from the New World normally do. If this was sold as a Gewürztraminer, the acidity would be too high, but an Edelzwicker (now that's a wine name the French won't bother to defend!) is supposed to be blended with other more acidic varieties; thus the balance is fine. TS

Sangiovese 2003
Flat Creek Parker, Texas (Other US States, US$35)
Tannic and spicy, this is good wine only if you can overlook the rough astringency. But there is an interesting wine there... Doug Frost MW
I think you're doing it down, Doug.

Maybe it depends what side of the Atlantic you're on, but I don't find any "rough astringency." If only 95 percent of Italian Sangiovese were this good! It looks light in color compared to most other US reds, particularly those from California and Washington, but it has more elegance than weight, so is not lacking in fruit, flavor, or length. TS

Grüner Veltliner Tradition 2003
Schloß Gobelsburg, Kamptal (Austria, €19)
Oxidative softness and complexity and great depth, dried-flower aromas, and opulent but fine delicate hints of wood. Deeply individual and exhilarating. Philipp Blom
Although I know what you mean, it's not at all oxidative—just a softening effect from the micro-oxygenation effect of the barrels. The result is very classy indeed. TS

A Crux Malbec 2003
O Fournier, Valle de Uco (Argentina, AP 110)
Sourced from 85-year-old vines in the high-altitude Uco Valley, this is Argentine Malbec at its most richly expressive. The alcohol is on the high side at 14.5 percent, but this oaky, youthful, densely packed, ultra-ripe red has the concentration to age for a decade or more in bottle. Tim Atkin MW
A big but beautifully proportioned wine—thus not in the least bit heavy, due to its perfumed, ultra-ripe fruit having enjoyed a relatively slow véraison. Lovely depth and length, with tremendous potential complexity. TS

Riesling Dürnsteiner Freiheit Smaragd 2004
Schmelz, Wachau (Austria, €18)
Full, clear, typically fine Riesling aromas; delicate acidity, pure and long, great persistence. Philipp Blom
Beautiful peachy fruit, with floral retronasal aromas creating the finesse. TS

EQ Syrah 2004
Matetic, San Antonio (Chile, CLP 22,000)
Attractive, inviting aromas of grilled dark fruit, savory meat, herbs, and spice. The palate is

well integrated and complex, with sleek fruit, firm but round tannins, and a touch of warming alcohol. A stylish rendition of cooler-climate Chilean Syrah. Peter Richards

Definitely sleek and stylish. In its own style this is in the same quality league as Craggy Range Le Sol from New Zealand. TS

Jurançon Les Jardins de Babylone 2004 Didier Dagueneau (Southwest France, €40 per 50-cl bottle)

Dagueneau does not aim for ultimate sweetness in the sense that Cauhapé or Guirouilh do; elegance and restraint underlie this gentle extraction from Petit Manseng. *Moelleux* and not a vendange tardive wine, relatively pale, citrus fruits prominent on the nose; in the mouth, gentle, exotic flavors, with the acidity balancing perfectly the modest sugar levels. Long, subtle, and deeply satisfying. Paul Strang

Beautifully elegant, sweet, ripe citrus and pineapple fruit on the palate, with gentle notes of fresh oak on the finish. The level of VA is higher than I would have liked, but much less than that found on the average Canadian icewine, and the balance between fruit and acidity is so exquisite that I am willing to forgive this wine almost anything. TS

Antique Sherry Pedro Ximénez Fernando de Castilla (Sherry, €31.25)

I have long been a great admirer of the wines from this boutique bodega, which has fine old wines but does not get them certified as VOS or VORS. Although I am not a great fan of Pedro Ximénez, this one strikes me as exceptional. It is very sweet, but it is much less cloying than most, more complex in its flavor, and with excellent length. Julian Jeffs QC

It's an amazing wine to taste, but like all PX it has the consistency of engine oil! Top quality indeed, but I'm sure that you have it on ice cream, Julian, like most of the wine trade! There's a big

deposit in the bottle that requires strenuous shaking to dislodge from the sides. You should do this 24 hours before opening, and decant the wine. TS

Black Rock Red 2004 The Winery (South Africa, R93)

Harmonious marriage of predominantly Shiraz (76 percent) with Carignan/Grenache. Rich and pure; cranberry fruit infused with green tea, lavender, and the Cape's beloved savoriness. Young, but without the clumsiness and brashness of youth, this southern-Rhône-inspired blend demonstrates that elegance need not be sacrificed at the altar of power. Cathy van Zyl MW

Elegance and freshness dominate this wine, which shows how well-used oak works well with delicious, sappy fruit. TS

Buzet La Badinerie du Pech 2002 Domaine du Pech (Southwest France, €10)

Very dark (the black wine of Buzet?), with good, obstinate legs. A young curranty nose suggests the Cabernet Franc influence. A basketful of young fruits spills onto the palate, chased by licorice and prunes. The finish is still developing, and the wine should be at its peak in 2007. Immensely promising. Paul Strang

With intense flavors, and layers of fruit waiting to unfold, this is a serious red wine for the price. TS

Barolo Monprivato Riserva Cà d'Morissio 1997 Giuseppe Mascarello, Langhe (Northern Italy, €125)

A wine of consummate elegance, with an aromatic complexity rich in subtle tonalities. The tannins are plentiful yet velvety, the wine exhibiting sweetness of ripe fruit and a breadth of flavor allied with an enjoyment quite out of the ordinary. From a great if rather forward vintage, it is magnificent already but destined to live a long time. Franco Ziliani

Great Barolo, this wine is indeed rather forward due to the year, but it has the tannic structure to outlive me! TS

Viognier 2003 Tibor Gál, Hungary (Eastern & Southeastern Europe, HUF 4,500) *Hungary's only Viognier, showing a fine balance between apricot and spice aromas, followed by peachy fruit and mineral undertones, with plenty of weight and a lingering finish.* Dr. Caroline Gilby MW

Powerful but beautiful oak aromas overwhelm the varietal character, yet I found it very beguiling, with a lovely weight of fruit, as you point out, and excellent acidity and length. Despite the obviousness of the oak, it is one of the best Viogniers I have tasted. TS

Merret Bloomsbury 2003 RidgeView (Great Britain, £15.95) *Toasty, almost oaklike nose with great Pinot fruit. Balanced acidity and a succulent middle palate add up to a really drinkable, enjoyable sparkling wine.* Stephen Skelton MW

My sample was obviously disgorged much more recently than yours, Stephen, since there is no hint of toastiness, let alone "oaklike" aromas. This illustrates perfectly how difficult it is for critics to review sparkling wines when they are disgorged to order, as they so often are, and the wine the consumer buys bears no relation to the one the critic tasted! In its freshly disgorged mode, the nose on this wine shows great finesse, with elegant, yeast-complexed fruit on the palate. TS

Pinot Noir 2003 Sandhurst Vineyards (Great Britain, £10.99) *Huge Pinot character on the nose, together with some sensitively used oak notes. On the palate, the fruit is just so ripe and attractive that it belies its origin. This is a wine that shows what Pinot in a great year in a marginal climate can do.* Stephen Skelton MW

It's a miracle considering how difficult it is to get Pinot Noir right in the winery, even when the grapes arrive full of potential. This should be a peach of a wine if carefully cellared for 2–4 years, but it will be interesting to see what future hot years yield when winemakers have had a few Pinot Noir vintages under their belts. TS

Faugères 2003 Domaine du Météore (Languedoc-Roussillon, €4) *Garnet and clear, fairly translucent; initial burnt aromas give way to ripe brambly fruit; showing "hot" character of the year. Very southern, but a suitable partner for spicy food. Persistent flavor and finish; rather more than "simple."* Paul Strang

Your "initial burnt aromas" come across to me as hot stones, and you're absolutely right about the brambly fruit follow-through. What a find for €4-an absolute steal! TS

Silver Selection 2003 Massaya (Lebanon, LL 13,000) *Cinsault, Mourvèdre, Cabernet Sauvignon, and Grenache combine to produce one of Lebanon's most characteristic and affordable reds. Good use of Cinsault from a winery that is proud of how it uses this unfashionable grape. Deep cherry red, with a lovely nose of framboise that is a prelude to rich, cooked fruit and pepper in the mouth, yet supple and soft with decent length. This is where modern Lebanese wine should be going.* Michael Karam

A deliciously fresh and ridiculously easy-to-drink red wine that, because of its emphasis on Cinsault, is not predictably Cabernet or in the least bit international. You are right, Michael—this is where Lebanese wine should be going. TS

La Cote Rousse Syrah 2003 Betz Family, Washington (Pacific Northwest, US$44) *A dark, dense, tannic wine, tightly wound and vertically structured. Dark roasted scents suggest espresso and moist earth, along with classic Red Mountain minerality. Clean, silky, fully ripe, but sleekly styled cherry and plum fruit finishes with dense, chocolaty tannins. Definitely a wine to tuck away for a few years.* Paul Gregutt

Big, blowzy, toasty-roasted fruit aromas make it more cappuccino than

espresso for me, Paul. Rich, concentrated black fruits on the palate, which does indeed finish with chocolaty tannins. I love this wine, although I suspect the toasty-roasted aromas might put some people off. TS

Cabernet Sauvignon 2003

Water Wheel, Bendigo (Australia, A\$18) *Rich and concentrated blueberry, cassis, and blackberry fruit; very ripe, but the Cabernet identity shines through. Solid tannin grip to close. Its generosity of sweet, very ripe fruit is seldom seen at this price.* Huon Hooke Yes, I get that sweet blueberry aroma just before the richer, riper, more intense cassis fruit. It has such a lovely, creamy finish, leaving a tingly impression in the mouth that demands another sip—great value! TS

Traminer Concept No. 1 Trocken 2004 Winzerverein Sommerhausen, Franken (Germany, €8) *Gentle, spicy aromas and the fragrance of rose petals distinguish this wine from the generally more opulent Gewürz style of lychees and Turkish delight. Subtle and dry, it's equally suitable for drinking with or without food.* Michael Schmidt

Match this to Traminer in Alsace (the pathetic Klevener de Heiligenstein) and Jura (which is increasingly impressive, but totally non-aromatic), and your "gentle, subtle, less opulent" spice is really quite assertive! In fact, I think it is Gewürztraminer, not Traminer. It certainly has the correct low acidity, and rather than jazz this up, Sommerhausen has opted to leave a spritz of gas to liven up the finish. This works without ruining the spice— something that increased acidity does. Great with smoked-haddock mousse. TS

Chignin-Bergeron Saint Anthelme 2004 Denis & Didier Berthollier (Jura & Savoie, €9) *Denis Berthollier's first inspiration in white wine was Château de Beaucastel's white (as this, from 100 percent Roussanne). Pale yellow,*

it has an attractive honey and fruit-salad nose. It is dry (often not the case with Bergeron) with a crisp acidity lacking in 2003. It's fermented and matured in oak for nine months, and the oak shows through on the palate, balancing well with the fruit and building to the finish. It has a wonderful, soft texture. Wink Lorch

A serious wine with a difference, this Roussanne is far more minerally than anything from the Rhône or Australia, and unbelievably classy for the price. TS

Gimblett Gravels Vineyard Chardonnay 2004 Craggy Range (New Zealand, NZ\$26.50) *Very classy Chardonnay that earns a big check in every box. It has concentration, complexity, a great texture, and that indefinable X factor that raises it above the herd. I particularly like the wine's lovely wholemeal/hazelnut flavors and creamy texture.* Bob Campbell MW

Yes, it is oaky; and yes, I was almost flippant about this wine when tasting a number of Craggy Range wines with Steve Smith earlier in the year, but that's because I am invariably all Chardonnay'd out, and I think Craggy's other single-vineyard varietals are far more interesting. However, when tasted in the company of other Chardonnays, it does stand out, even when some of the others are pretty damn good. Ultimately, I have to say there is too much oak influence, but I agree totally with everything you say, Bob. TS

Sion Vin Mi-doux 2004 Cave des Cailles, Cédric Flaction (Switzerland, SF 29) *This sweet wine was made from 100 percent Chasselas and reached 127° Oechsle. The slightly buttery nose shows aromas of bananas and ripe apples. On the palate, there are lots of sweet cooked fruits and a charming sweetness. Acidity is not too strong. A new way of drinking Chasselas.* Chandra Kurt

A tremendously fresh and elegant

wine, with canned pears and Beauty of Bath apples on the palate, and a focused, clean, refreshing finish. TS

Vouvray Sec Clos de la Bretonnière 2004
Jacky Blot, Domaine de la Taille aux Loups (Loire Valley, €10) *Delightfully intense and concentrated dry Chenin (genuinely dry, none of that "9 g of residual sugar" rubbish here) with gras and minerality being held up by the oak fermentation and maturation. Brilliant now; brilliant in five years or more—if you've got any left. I won't!* Charles Sydney

Hey, Charles, ship this down to South Africa before they get the wrong idea about how Chenin Blanc should taste. Truly expressive from nose to finish. Brilliant! TS

Alentejano Tagus Creek Shiraz Trincadeira 2005
Falua (Portugal, €3.50) *Deep, youthful color, big, ripe, and forward from a warm vintage; supple, sweet cherry fruit from Trincadeira complemented by the spice and blackberry character of super-ripe Shiraz. Both these varieties are well matched in this inexpensive red.* Richard Mayson

So young, fresh, and vibrant. Really needs three years in bottle to show anything like its true potential. Obviously some whole-bunch fermentation going on here. Delicious. Can't believe the quality for the price! TS

Estremadura Reserve 2003
Chocapalha (Portugal, €15) *Fine, fragrant, floral black-currant fruit; full-flavored and fleshy, wrapped around a ripe tannic core. Judicious use of oak complements the unusual but exciting blend of fruit (Touriga Nacional, Tinta Roriz, and Alicante Bouschet).* Richard Mayson

Only modern Portugal could produce such an expressive, exciting, full, rich red such as this—clean, full of Touriga fruit, and lovely drying tannins on the finish. TS

Cossart Gordon Verdelho Colheita Madeira 1995
(Port & Madeira, €16.50) *Pure, expressive, redolent of tea leaves and dried flowers, slightly smoky, with fine, dry, cognaclike flavors. Lovely, accessible madeira with real character.* Richard Mayson

A brilliant, powerful, knockout finish for the price demonstrates the wisdom of allowing vintage-dated madeira to be bottled after just five years, as opposed to 20 years for so-called vintage madeira. TS

Privada 2003
Norton, Luján de Cuyo (Argentina, AP 210) *This outstanding blend of 40 percent Malbec, 30 percent Merlot, and 30 per cent Cabernet Sauvignon is one of Argentina's best reds but is priced some way below most of the country's icon wines. This is a soft, spicy, coffee-bean/chocolate-perfumed red showing excellent oak integration and fine-grained tannins.* Tim Atkin MW

Initially deceptively soft on the palate, but those finely grained tannins start to pucker the mouth once the wine has gone down, and the only way back to that deliciously soft, elegant fruit is to take another mouthful, and another, and another. TS

Marcillac Lo Sang del Païs 2004
Domaine du Cros (Southwest France, €4.50) *Brilliant ruby color shot with violet, a full bouquet of red- and black currants; blackberries, too, with spice. Carries through with more of the same on to the palate. The idiosyncratic character derives from a lot of iron and manganese in the soil. Ideal with charcuterie.* Paul Strang

A delightfully soft and easy-to-drink red wine that is fairly bursting with red and black fruits on the nose and palate. Not too alcoholic (turned out to be 12 percent): a relief in this age of high-octane headline grabbers. TS

Cabernet Sauvignon Kayoumi 2003
Carmel (Israel, NIS 135) *Luscious and elegant, this deep-garnet,*

full-bodied, softly tannic wine shows fine structure and balance. On the nose and palate, a generous array of black currants, blackberries, and spicy wood on first attack; these yielding nicely to hints of Oriental spices, chocolate, and tobacco. Enjoyable now, but don't hesitate to cellar this one until 2014. Daniel Rogov
A menthol edge without any herbaceous pyrazines upsetting the deliciously ripe, sweet blackberry fruit. TS

Barbera 2003 Shannon Ridge, Lake County (California, US$19)
Black-cherry fruit, but in a lighter style, with the same bright acidity that marks some of the best Barberas of Italy. More succulent, though, and truly delivers fruit. Dan Berger
Big cedary-oak fruit nose, with bright acidity to lift the fruit on the palate, making it very easy to drink. TS

Estate Selection Merlot 2000 Lenz, New York (Atlantic Northeast, US$23)
Coming off mostly 26–27-year-old vines and held five years before being released, this Merlot demonstrates how the big, complex flavors and tannic structure of Long Island (NY) reds can marry into something glorious if you give them time. Sandra Silfven
A lovely wine, Sandy. Mellowing on the nose, with beautiful fruit that's ready to drink now but has more than enough acidity to allow for at least another five years' aging in a good cellar. TS

Cuvée Forté Brut NV Mountain Dome, Washington (Pacific Northwest, US$30)
This is the winery's reserve cuvée, half Pinot and half Chardonnay, made from the best of the best grapes and vintages. (Just the second release in the winery's two-decade history.) Though NV, it is based on the very ripe 1998 vintage. Mountain Dome's most elegant sparkling wine, it has a fine, textured mouthfeel and nicely nuanced flavors of pear, apple, and light citrus. Paul Gregutt

A tad fat if I'm to be super-critical, but the palate is bursting with impressive yeast-complexed fruit that could take a few more years on yeast (which is one hell of a compliment). TS

Bruñal 2003 Ribera de Pelazas (Spain, €89)
Dark, spicy, subtle "woodsmoke" on the nose; big, almost toffee-richness on the palate, with warmth, spice, and myriad complex flavors capped by a long, mouth-filling finish full of autumnal fruit flavors. John Radford
This needs 10 years in bottle! TS

Marsala Vergine Riserva 1962 Carlo Pellegrino, Sicily (Central & Southern Italy, €45)
Brilliant amber/caramel color, luminous, slightly old-gold on the rim. A very complex bouquet recalling apricot, date, fig, dried fruit, tobacco, dried mushrooms, candied fruits, saffron, flint, and dark chocolate. Uppish alcohol (19 percent) but perfectly balanced with nothing aggressive. In the mouth, it is dry, clean, sapid, salty, and nervous, inviting one to drink; it leaves the palate perfectly clean. Franco Ziliani
The finish is vibrant and complex, with just a memory of sweetness on the never-ending finish. A forgotten classic. Stunning! TS

Chardonnay Unwooded 2004 Peninsula Cellars, Michigan (Atlantic Northeast, US$14)
The most exciting producer of white wine in Michigan, if not the whole Northeast, treated a great batch of Chardonnay juice the way it does Riesling, Pinot Blanc, and Gewurz-fermented in steel. Bryan Ulbrich gave up on barrel-fermented Chards in 2000 when he couldn't get the fruit–wood integration right. This wine has evolved over the months, tempering the herbaceous flavors and broadening the apple, pear, and tropical-fruit character. It's most unique for an American, let alone Michigan, vineyard to produce flavors this focused. Sandra Silfven

The sort of wine that builds in the glass over lunch. This is definitely the way to go for Michigan Chardonnay, but as good as it is in today's context of the state's wine evolution (and it does have finesse), I think we'll look back on it and wonder what all the fuss was about when Bryan is eventually happy with making this variety. In the meantime, I recommend the good folk of Michigan buy this in preference to any Chablis AOC and even some Chablis premiers crus. TS

Nadja's Vineyard Riesling 2004

Flat Rock Cellars, Ontario (Canada, C$19.95) *This wine won the Canadian Wine Awards top Riesling prize and it deserved it. Pale straw color; minerally floral nose; full on the palate, with tart lime and green-apple flavors; lovely mouthfeel with great length. Very Mosel Kabinett in style, but heftier on the palate.* Tony Aspler

With a bit of bottle age between your tasting and mine, the minerally floral nose has become very petroly. I see what you mean about Mosel Kabinett, but it has a bit too much alcohol, and is far too dry, to be convincing. However, it is tremendously expressive Riesling and well deserving of its top prize. TS

Chianti Classico 2002

Rocca di Montegrossi, Chianti Classico (Central & Southern Italy, €8.50) *From a modest year, this wine overcomes its disadvantages with a clean, mature nose recalling violets, earth, and gladioli. On the palate, it's rich and earthy, with a good but not exaggerated tannic backbone, full of flavor and highly drinkable.* Franco Ziliani

Brilliant, ready-drinking, truly expressive Chianti, with addictive, chocolaty-black-currant fruit. A true bargain. TS

Pioneer Block 1 Sauvignon Blanc 2005

Saint Clair (New Zealand, NZ $30) *Classic Marlborough style with plenty of passion-fruit flavors together with an underlying lemon-grass character and a sweaty/boxwood-hedge influence. Seductive wine with a gentle texture and lingering finish, from one of Marlborough's top Sauvignon Blanc producers.* Bob Campbell MW

Yes, Bob, all those things (bar the sweaty stuff: keep those dirty thoughts to yourself!), but especially the passion fruit and lemon grass. Super fresh. So intense, it's perhaps too much for some. TS

Costières de Nîmes Scamandre 2003

Domaine Renouard (Rhône Valley, €14) *This wine displays a deep ruby color. Nice red fruits on the nose and luxurious cedar flavors. Medium-bodied, this Costières de Nîmes offers intense aromas with a long, mineral finish.* Olivier Poels

Lovely toasted oak and roasted fruit aromas, with pleasingly dry fruit on the palate. Excellent food wine. TS

Robyn's Block Chardonnay 2002

Tawse Winery, Ontario (Canada, C$48) *Straw color, more restrained and elegant than this winery's Beamsville Bench Reserve; toasty, tangerine bouquet; full-bodied, mouth-filling, great balance, with buttery, melon, pineapple, and toast flavors that linger on the palate to a roasted hazelnut finish. Well-integrated oak.* Tony Aspler

I was trying to convince myself of the tangerine, Tony, and almost got there. I think it's the alcohol that is giving this impression. I find this wine more complete than complex, with plenty of well-integrated oak. Food detracts; best on its own, with friends. TS

Ribatejo Marquês de Cadaval 2003

Casa Cadaval (Portugal, €30) *Refined, elegant, floral-berry fruit, with some of the qualities of a fine Cabernet-based wine but made from Touriga Nacional and Trincadeira. Intense, bitter-sweet character and fine-grained tannins.* Richard Mayson

So Portuguese, so distinctive, and so beautiful. Now that's something you could not say about many reds from this country 10 years ago. TS

Black Sage Vineyard White Meritage 2004 Sumac Ridge, British Columbia (Canada, C$19.99) *Lush gooseberry and peach fruit bouquet with floral overtones leads to complex, mouth-filling flavors of orchard fruit, melon, and green mango. Great structure and balanced oak treatment with a long, tangy finish. A rich, beautifully crafted white wine with depth and complexity.* Tony Aspler
A very elegant, super-fresh melange of classic Bordelais varieties. Good food wine. TS

Corbec Appassimento 2002 Masi (Argentina, AP 55) *This is a bit of a curve ball, even by Argentine standards. It's an Italo-Argentine blend of the Veneto's Corvina with Malbec, made using the ripasso technique. The result is an Argentine wine with a marked Italian accent, with the acidity of the Corvina lifting the weight of the Malbec.* Tim Atkin MW
I suppose if any Italian producer in Argentina is going to employ the ripasso process, it would have to be Masi, but its use here is very understated and totally fresh, with absolutely no oxidative overtones, and the result on a Corvina-lifted Malbec is more than a little bit interesting. I'd love to see how this wine develops after a few years in bottle—not many, say 2–3 years. TS

Arneis 2004 Ponzi, Oregon (Pacific Northwest, US$20) *It's too bad Ponzi doesn't make more of this lovely wine, or inspire someone else in Oregon to plant Arneis. Penetrating scents and flavors show pineapple, citrus, peach, and tropical fruits, and the piercing aromatics blossom on the tongue into a long, seductive, marmalade of a wine. Unique and flavorful.* Paul Gregutt
Pungent, leaf-green aromas from nose to palate, where they mingle with intense passion-fruit flavors to produce something that is a million miles away from the overhyped, underwhelming examples of Arneis found in Piedmont. TS

Aeolia Roussanne 2004 Giaconda, Beechworth (Australia, A$85) *Concentrated fruit, barrel-fermented, malo'ed and aged on lees, it's a bright-yellow-colored, spiced-honey-scented wine of great richness and mouth-filling generosity.* Huon Hooke
Certainly has more finesse than most Australian Roussanne. TS

Roussanne 2004 Rustenberg (South Africa, R115) *A subtle nose of pear, ginger, and fynbos belies the weighty mouthfeel, emphasized by just a brush of tannin from the barrel-fermented smidgen, and enlivened by firm acidity. Long, with white peaches on the finish, this wine offers jaded local palates a refreshing—if somewhat expensive—alternative to retail shelves overflowing with Chardonnay, Chenin, and Sauvignon Blanc.* Cathy van Zyl MW
Thankfully not overoaked like most Australian Roussanne, this wine has lovely fresh notes and has obviously been immaculately handled in the cellar. But, to be super-critical, it does have a tad too much alcohol. I love it, nonetheless, and think it would be interesting to age two or three years, when it will deserve to be served with food. That's the third exceptional Roussanne in this year's tasting. TS

Chablis Vieilles Vignes 2004 Domaine Christophe & Fils (Burgundy, €7) *Clean, crisp, refreshing, yet with no lack of underlying concentration. It will last.* Clive Coates MW
A man after my own heart! This sort of wine would be bog-standard Chablis when we were lads, Clive, but in those days, bog-standard Chablis was something to write home about. Now any Chablis bearing such clean lines as this and with such wonderfully fresh, crisp, orchard fruits is rare indeed. TS

St-Chinian Lo Tabataïre 2002 Domaine du Tabatau (Languedoc-

Roussillon, €9) *Brilliant, limpid deep garnet in the glass, the nose of berry fruits taking time to develop (decanting recommended). Some natural vanilla, lightly crushed peppercorns, and spices burst on the palate, followed by prunes. Nicely balanced with good acidity and soft tannins. Elegant and fine, reflecting the lighter character of this vintage. Good long finish.* Paul Strang *We're singing from the same hymn sheet, Paul: elegant, indeed, and that burst of spice with underlying crushed white peppercorns augurs well for the future.* TS

Cabernet Sauvignon Reserve 2003

Flam (Israel, NIS 155) *Made from grapes harvested in Kerem Dishon and Kerem Ben Zimra in the Upper Galilee, this full-bodied, dark-garnet/deep-purple wine was oak aged for about 14 months. Generous black-currant and cherry fruits with mineral, herbal, and light earthy aromas and flavors all come together with a hint of oak that at one moment feels toasty and another spicy. Super-smooth tannins and a long finish. Approachable now but best 2007–12.* Daniel Rogov *Plenty of sappy, sweet spearmint fruit, with nicely judged tannins that would be quite dry and puckering but for the sweetness of fruit, and this all makes for a very long and clean finish.* TS

Château Lezongars L'Enclos Premières Côtes de Bordeaux 2001

(Bordeaux, €10) *This cuvée from the older vines in this Premières Côtes vineyard has a satisfying depth of fruit and richness of flavor and real harmony, which makes it my favorite ahead of their more aggressive Special Cuvée. A wine that really tastes well above its Premières Côtes station.* David Peppercorn MW *Smooth and satisfying, with nicely balanced, soft-tannin structure. A civilized wine for the table.* TS

Grenache Rosé 2004

Beckmen, Santa Ynez Valley, Purisima Mountain (California, US\$15) *Cranberry and black-cherry notes with bright fruit in the mid-palate (almost a light red!), with the weight to go with a wide array of barbecued foods.* Dan Berger *You're right, Dan: it does have the color of a light red, but it also has more of the weight and structure of a light red than a rosé. In a black glass and served at room temperature, it would be assumed by most tasters to be a red wine, and the touch of oak helps in that respect. Probably too good for a barbecue.* TS

Ethos Chardonnay 2003

Chateau Ste Michelle, Washington (Pacific Northwest, US\$30) *A brilliant effort, sophisticated and modern. Leesy, textured, long, and elegant, the winemaker's light touch balances hints of herb, yeast, and new oak against gorgeous fruit. No reliance on buttered-popcorn flavors or excessive new toasty oak.* Paul Gregutt *Seriously structured, nicely oaked Chardonnay, with deep flavor. A food wine. I'm surprised I can enthuse about an oaked Chardonnay these days, Paul, and not sure that I should thank you for it!* TS

Gramp's Five Generations Cabernet/Merlot 2002

Orlando, South Australia (Australia, A\$16) *Dark color; concentrated black currant and mint aromas; deep, firm, ripe fruit plus persuasive tannins; a gutsy, solid red that comprehensively transcends its modest price point.* Huon Hooke *There is something other than mint for me, and it makes the nose a bit rustic. But I'm totally convinced on the palate, with its rich, ripe fruit that threatens sweetness, yet never gets there because the balance of tannins has been calculated to perfection.* TS

Lemberger Junges Schwaben 2003

Wachtstetter, Württemberg (Germany, €20) *Gentle aromas of black currant, mint, and seaweed are supported by a prudent use of oak with scents of roasted coffee beans and chocolate.*

None of the elements is obtrusive; this is a finely crafted wine. Michael Schmidt
Bags of soft fruit overlaid by subtle aromas of coffee and chocolate oak. It is indeed a finely crafted wine, and well worth €20 in my estimation. TS

Côtes du Rhône Villages Kayyâm 2004 Mas de Libian (Rhône Valley, €7)
Perfect to drink now, full of fruit and spice flavors. This delicious value-for-money wine is a pure pleasure-sweet and refreshing. Olivier Poels
The rich, saturated fruit in this wine packs a lot of flavor per euro, although its hot, spicy finish would have benefited from half a degree less alcohol (15 percent on label), but that's nitpicking at this sort of price! TS

Auxerrois 2004 Apostelhoeve, Netherlands (Belgium, Netherlands & Scandinavia, €9)
The wine is open on the nose with a lot of white fruit-pear, apple, and citrus-and is lively and well balanced on the palate, with good length. Ronald de Groot
The freshness of this wine was such a relief after so many oaky Chardonnays, even if a couple were very good. You have to go to the most northerly villages of Alsace to find Auxerrois as fresh as this, and even then they lack the fruit that this delightful wine has. I reckon this wine is worth twice the price. TS

Cabernet Sauvignon Special Reserve 2003 Margalit (Israel, NIS 160)
Rich, ripe, and concentrated, with layer after layer of dark plum, currant, anise, mocha, black cherries, and sage. An oak-aged blend of Cabernet Sauvignon and Petite Sirah (87 percent and 13 percent respectively), this distinctly Old World wine has excellent balance between wood, lively acidity, and well-integrated tannins. Complex and long. Best 2008–13. Daniel Rogov
I know what you mean, Rogov: it's that dry, herbal oak that gives the fruit its Old World feel or, more accurately, its Old World feel c. 1970s—reminiscent of Cabernet blends before new oak became so fashionable. I like the sweet fruit in this wine and the drying tannins on its finish. One to serve from a decanter into large, fine-quality glasses at the table, to fox the wine geeks! TS

Tinto 7 Meses Barrica Arribes del Douro Crianza 2003 La Setera (Spain, €9)
Rich, dark plummy/damson fruit on the nose; big, warm fruit and strong but manageable tannins balance it off on the palate as it develops in the mouth. Lovely long finish; a wine with a great future. John Radford
After the covers came off, I noticed that this claimed to be 15 percent alcohol. If asked to guess blind, I doubt that I would have put it at much more than 13.5 percent. As it happened, this wine was tasted immediately after another 15 percent wine, and by comparison it seemed such a relief, alcoholically, and tasted so remarkably fresh. Pretty impressive for any producer who can achieve that sort of elegance at such a high strength, especially at such a cheap price. TS

Salento Rosso Carminio 2003 Cantine Carrozzo, Puglia (Central & Southern Italy, €7)
This pure Negroamaro has perfumes born of the sun. It's sweet, warm, suave, and tight, recalling plum, cherry, blackberry, and licorice with hints of chestnut and goût de terroir. In the mouth, it is ample, finely woven, rich of material, mature, pulpy, and finishing dry with firm but correct tannins, good length, and plenty of flavor. Franco Ziliani
An excellent-value, expressive Salento Rosso, full of lively fruit, with a mellow creaminess on the finish to balance the tannins. TS

Pinot Gris Domaine & Tradition 2004 Clos des Rochers (Luxembourg, €9)
Very fine and minerally, with flavors of red apple and peach and a long, warm, spicy finish. David Furer
Rich and satisfying in a fresh, elegant,

more-than-Pinot-Blanc-but-not-quite-Pinot-Gris way (although certainly more expressive than most Italian Pinot Grigio). TS

Alpha 1 2003 Alpha Estate (Greece, €48) *Bright fruit, strongly reminiscent of wild cherry and black figs. Dense with allspice and freshness on the very long finish. It has exemplary balance for such a concentrated wine and the structure for aging for up to 15 years.* Nico Manessis
Greek Tannat and Montepulciano! Decant at least five hours before serving. Quite extraordinary, but the wines from Alpha stepped up another level from the 2005 vintage (see Alpha Syrah on p.403), when its state-of-the-art winery came on-stream, whereas the first three vintages were made in rented premises. TS

Pinot Noir Barrique Selection 2003 Mme Aly Duhr & Fils (Luxembourg, €20) *Deep, dark red; brown spices, plum and dark cherry on the nose; a well-balanced, medium-bodied palate with subtle shadings of spices, red fruits, and chalk. Medium length. Better in a few years.* David Furer
Alcohol comes through a tad on the aftertaste, making it seem higher than the 12 percent claimed on the label, but the beautiful coffee-oaked fruit in this wine makes it an exceptional red for Luxembourg, thanks in part to the extraordinarily hot conditions enjoyed by this marginal viticultural region in 2003. TS

Eyholzer Roter 2004 Chanton (Switzerland, SF 18) *Pale red, with an expressive, fruity nose. Lots of raspberry and black-cherry notes. Crisp and elegant structure. A specialty from the Haut-Valais marked by freshness and liveliness. Some spiciness on the finish. Drink slightly chilled.* Chandra Kurt
Very spicy on the finish, but also on the nose, with a striking floral aroma

to the fruit on front and mid-palate: violets and rose petals. Very fresh, pure, and elegant, and so expressive of the style that I've come to know you like, Chandra. TS

Pirom Khao Yai Reserve Tempranillo 2004 Khao Yai Winery, Thailand (Asia, THB 825) *Appropriates a surprising amount of the traditional varietal characteristics despite its vastly different tropical growing environment—a deep reddish hue, ripe, smoky berry aromas, with a soft yet fulfilling palate structure and good length.* Denis Gastin
A Thai Tempranillo: only you could dig up such a wine, Denis! An obvious touch of VA-lift, and there is a distinct high-yield feel about the wine, but there is plenty of that smoky, sweet berry fruit you mention, and it's great to see how quickly Thai wines are developing. TS

Heida Maître de Chais 2004 Provins (Switzerland, SF 23.50) *Not for nothing is this grape also called "wine from the glacier" (Glestcherwein). Very pale and fresh, with lots of good acidity. This refreshing table wine is dominated by notes of citrus fruits. Good balance between fruit and acidity. The finish is complex and almost a little bit fat.* Chandra Kurt
You're right: soft, almost fat, yet crisp and refreshing, citrusy fruit. How weird. TS

Dão Duque de Viseu Tinto 2003 Sogrape (Portugal, €4) *Lovely savory, smoky, cask-aged aromas and flavors, somewhat akin to mature Rioja; soft and smooth initially, yet with just enough grip and backbone to cope with rich food. Well-ripened spicy fruit tempered by oak. Tastes like a wine worth twice the price!* Richard Mayson
Savory-coffee oak on the nose, with delicious, elegant fruit on the palate. It's remarkable just how good this large-volume brand of Dão has become. Serve it in large, fine, expensive glasses

at dinner, and no one would imagine that it's just a €4 wine. TS

Amayna Sauvignon Blanc 2005
Garcés Silva, San Antonio (Chile, CLP 7,800) *San Antonio is starting to create some very distinctive styles of Sauvignon that major on a broad palate structure and ripe aromas. Amayna's third release is full of roasted grapefruit, honey, and peach, with a spicy, full-on palate.* Peter Richards
A big, serious Sauvignon Blanc that leans more to Bordeaux than anywhere else, but with much higher alcohol and more complexity than varietal character. When the covers came off, I discovered that it boasted 14.5 percent ABV, which is big for a red wine and frankly far too whopping for a dry white. It is produced from clone 242 (French) and UCD1 (of Marlborough fame). Despite its high alcoholic strength, I really liked this wine, but I think it would be even better with a greater contribution from UCD1 and less alcohol. TS

Nemea 2004
Mitravela Estate (Greece, €15) *Black-cherry essence, textured sappy style. Spicy vanilla notes lifted by elegant, melt-in-the-mouth tannins. A Nemea made from 30+-year-old bush vines.* Nico Manessis
That spicy vanilla has more than a bit of bubble gum on the nose and palate, but it will be overwhelmed by the fruit if well cellared for 3–4 years. TS

Pinot Noir 2005
Cono Sur, Colchagua (Chile, CLP 4,000) *This is one for bargain lovers. In this line, Cono Sur has consistently produced what must be one of the world's best-value Pinots. Perfumed, fencerow fruit and a fresh, balanced, berry-fueled palate.* Peter Richards
Pure strawberry fruit. Ridiculously low price! TS

Hillside Chardonnay 2003
Denbies Wine Estate (Great Britain, £11.99) *The beauty of this wine is its great attractive acidity, which is a cross between lemons and limes, with enough alcohol and oak to temper the acid. This is what really good Chardonnay from a cool climate should taste like.* Stephen Skelton MW
Elegant, toasty Chardonnay, with a long, fresh, sweet-yet-crisp fruit finish, and toastiness coming back on the aftertaste. Probably the greatest English Chardonnay ever made, but if I'm to be super-critical, this standard has been achieved by a relatively simple elegance born of ripe fruit rather than an abundance of true finesse, which must be the next stage for English Chardonnay. TS

Ribera del Duero Flores Silvestres 2004
Rauda (Spain, €4) *This has lovely, delicate aromas, literally "flowers of the forest" in high summer, with delicious musky fruit on the palate and just enough tannin to throw it into relief. Long, warm finish. More bodegas in RdD should be making wines like this (and at this kind of price) with grapes from their young vines.* John Radford
Absolutely right about the floral aromas, John; this might not be a fine wine per se, but it is very fresh, soft, and suicidally easy to drink. If only all €4 wines from Spain were this good! TS

Riesling Domaine & Tradition 2004
Gales (Luxembourg, €8) *Harvested at September's end from the Gales' recently acquired Remich Primerberg vineyards, this exhibits the nose and palate of wet stones and a complex finish of citrus, peach, and apple. Medium intensity, tapered finish.* David Furer
Elegant plum and white-peach fruit on the palate. Keep three years for the terpenes to develop bottle aromas. TS

QmP Siebeldinger Mönchspfad Reberger 2003
Institut für Rebenzüchtung, Germany (Grape Varieties, €7 per 50-cl bottle)

Dark-red full-bodied wine, with a nose of forest fruits and discreet oak; rather like a southern French wine, with smooth tannins and good length. Dr. François Lefort

I have not had much experience of Reberger (Regent x Lemberger), but this example certainly has a more classic vinifera character than other hybrids that have been recently and uniquely permitted for wine production by EU authorities. Good length, with nice grippy tannins on the finish. TS

Pinot Noir Réserve 2003 (Marjan)
Simčič, Slovenia (Eastern & Southeastern Europe, SIT 4,320) *Not many Pinot Noirs are produced in Slovenia and certainly not at this level of quality and finesse. Simčič has a surprisingly fine touch with his reds—a young but graceful wine with notes of wild strawberry and cocoa, and an elegant structure.* Dr. Caroline Gilby MW

First bottle corked. Second bottle clean. A touch of VA-lift on the nose, but the palate is excellent, with fresh, sappy fruit and a nice grippy finish. TS

Minervois Les Aspres 2002
Domaine Cros (Languedoc-Roussillon, €18) *Almost a Guigal style of wine, pure Syrah, deep brooding color, peppery and spicy on the nose, with huge concentration; tannins just starting to soften, complexity on the finish starting to develop with age. Twenty months in new barrels have mercifully left the fruit more or less intact.* Paul Strang

The oak hits you immediately, and it returns pretty quickly after a brief appearance of the mid-palate fruit. While I appreciate this wine might develop more favorably, I still think that 10 months in new oak would have been more than enough. TS

Syrah 2004 Ziereisen, Baden
(Germany, €28) *Eighteen months in oak have not managed to subdue the pronounced morello-cherry aromas backed up by an abundance of*

pepper and spice. Will it improve with age? Not in my house, where I would not be able to keep my hands off it! Michael Schmidt

This has so much ground white pepper on the nose that I felt like sneezing, yet it is surprisingly soft in the mouth. Fascinating to find a German Syrah, but I'm sure it will be even more fascinating when the vines are older, and the grapes are riper, to provide the concentration and depth of fruit that is lacking and to replace the spadeful of ground white pepper with just a pinch of cracked black peppercorn for complexity. TS

Condrieu Côte de Vernon 2003
Georges Vernay (Rhône Valley, €45) *This is a fabulous combination of concentration and elegance. With rich aromas of exotic and tropical fruits, combined with a mineral touch, the wine has a steely finish.* Olivier Poels

Gosh, Olivier, where's the wine? It has so much oak that I'm still pulling splinters out of my teeth! TS

Pinot Noir 2003 Genoels-Elderen,
Belgium (Belgium, Netherlands & Scandinavia, €21) *The warm climate in 2003 helped red-wine production in Belgium, and Genoels-Elderen has shown the way forward with this quite sweet and well-made Pinot Noir. Aged for one year on fine lees in barrels and a further year in bottle, this is well balanced with honest Pinot Noir flavors, soft tannins, and decent depth for the northern climate.* Fiona Morrison MW

Belgium comes an honorable third behind Luxembourg and England in the 2003 stakes to produce the best red wine in a marginal viticultural region blessed by extraordinary climatic conditions. I think it would have been even better with a little acidification—not something I normally encourage. It would also have benefited from just two-thirds the time in barrel, but unlike winemakers in true red-wine regions, these guys had just one chance to get it right. This vintage in Belgium reminds me of the missed opportunities in England in 1976. TS

Sparkling Campbell Early Rosé NV

Tsuno Winery, Japan (Asia, ¥1,600) *Vivid pink color with luscious rosewater/fruit-candy aromas and flavors. Although on the bouquet it threatens to be sweet, it has a surprisingly fresh finish. A real mind-stretcher.* Denis Gastin
There is no mistaking the strawberry-jelly aroma in this medium-sweet sparkling wine, but the carbonic gas does the native American hybrid no favors, highlighting more "foxiness" than in the still version recommended in Wine Report 2004. TS

Vinos de Madrid Divo 2000

Ricardo Benito (Spain, €141) *A wonderful, rich, subtle perfume with ripe summer fruits, hints of oak, but dark, hidden fruits below the surface. On the palate, big but austere fruit, power, soft tannins… dark chocolate and damson? Plum? Rich mince-pie mincemeat, cinnamon, a hint of tar? Unbelievably complex.* John Radford
And high VA, John… although some of the best vintages of Australia's Grange also had high levels of VA, so at this price I suppose I will have to give it the benefit of doubt for the next 10 years or so. TS

Côtes du Jura Savagnin Cuvée Privilège 2003

Domaine Ganevat (Jura & Savoie, €13) *A very pale lemon-green; almost confit (crystallized) lemons on the nose, with a touch of creamy oak. These flavors are repeated on the palate, which shows good fresh acidity for a 2003 (it was not acidified) and excellent concentration. With two years on lees in demi-muids (600-litre casks) that have given it depth, it exemplifies Savagnin when made in a non-Jurassien way.* Wink Lorch
Mind-blowing, Wink, but it could have
been mind-altering had there been less oak influence: thank goodness they did not use small barriques! Savagnin requires a light touch.* TS

Empery Cupid Wild Grape Wine 2002

East of Eden, South Korea (Asia, Won 25,000) *A sweet red wine with intense Amarone-style fruit concentration. Dense purple color with exotic wild-berry and raisin aromas and flavors.* Denis Gastin
Unfortunately, I had this after the wonderful Amarone from Trabucchi, and Amarone-style it isn't! It has vastly more acetaldehyde than even the most oxidative Amarone, and without the fruit to back it up, the acetaldehyde is horribly spiky. I still wonder if it's the grape, as claimed, or crude production methods and conditions, as I suspect—but you've been there, Denis; I haven't. And you've got strong support from Huon Hooke, so I'll put it in the book-launch tasting to see if my wine-scribe colleagues think I'm being wholly ungenerous. TS

Cabernet/Shiraz 2005

Sula Vineyards, India (Asia, Rp 375) *This has all the boisterous richness of New World Shiraz but is cleverly tempered with 20 percent Cabernet Sauvignon—though the label on the domestic market indicates the varieties in reverse order! The Cabernet tones down the Shiraz marginally and firms up the structure. Good fruit concentration, very modern style—and a real bargain at this price.* Denis Gastin
In the UK it's labeled simply Shiraz. I'm probably being unfairly harsh on a wine from a country with so few wineries, and even less experience, but in terms of expectations on the international market, this wine is let down by aromas that are not so much reductive as indicative of the overuse of cheap inert gas. Having said that, I think the fruit underneath this wine shows potential, so I'll probably also show this at the launch. TS

Index